JOHN HEILPERN

John Osborne:
A Patriot for Us

VINTAGE BOOKS
London

Published by Vintage 2007

2 4 6 8 10 9 7 5 3 1

Copyright © John Heilpern 2006

John Heilpern has asserted his right under the Copyright, Designs
and Patents Act 1988 to be identified as the author of this work

First published in Great Britain in 2006 by
Chatto & Windus
Random House, 20 Vauxhall Bridge Road,
London SW1V 2SA

www.vintage-books.co.uk

Addresses for companies within The Random House Group Limited
can be found at: www.randomhouse.co.uk/offices.htm

The Random House Group Limited Reg. No. 954009

A CIP catalogue record for this book
is available from the British Library

ISBN 9780099275862

The Random House Group Limited makes every effort to ensure
that the papers used in its books are made from trees that have been
legally sourced from well-managed and credibly certified forests.
Our paper procurement policy can be found at:
www.randomhouse.co.uk/paper.htm

Typeset by Palimpsest Book Production Limited,
Grangemouth, Stirlingshire

Printed and bound in the UK by
CPI Cox & Wyman, Reading RG1 8EX

To Rachel and Sydney
in Memory of Sam and Ray

What aim do you wish to achieve, where are you going, what
is in your soul? In a word, who are you? What are you?

Turgenev, Fathers and Sons

Contents

List of Illustrations xi

Preface xiii
1 The Hurst 1
2 A Patriot for Us 13
3 Mother and Son 21
4 Every Day is Mother's Day to Me 31
5 Father and Son 42
6 The Naked Christ 53
7 Why Ozzy was Expelled from School 64
8 The First Father Figure 69
9 The Apprentice Actor in Search of a Home 78
10 What is Truth and What is Fable? 86
11 Aunt Edna's Knitting Needles 93
12 The Apprentice Playwright in Search of an Audience 103
13 First Love, First Marriage 113
14 First Divorce 123
15 A Subject of Scandal and Concern 133
16 The Father Reclaims the Son 151
17 Proceed to Texas 162
18 Critics 168
19 Context is All 174
20 Three Prize Victims 187
21 Success 196
22 A Typical Night on Montana Street 207
23 Take My Wife – Puhleeze! 213
24 Good, Brave Causes 228
25 Damn You, England 239
26 The Biggest Floperoo Ever 249

27 Runaway Lovers   255
28 Another Perfect House Party   262
29 The Case of Osborne's Son   270
30 Spiritual Longing   276
31 Third Marriage   283
32 Inadmissible Evidence   294
33 A Patriot For Me   303
34 The Death of George Devine   316
35 Breakdown   322
36 The Real Thing   334
37 My Dear Tony   346
38 Lost Illusions   352
39 The Chapter of Accidents   362
40 Watch It Come Down   378
41 A Better Class of Person   389
42 Country Matters   400
43 What Happened to Nolan   414
44 En Route to Shropshire   427
45 Strindberg's Man in England   437
46 Déjàvu   445
47 The End   460
Epilogue and The Search for Faith   475

Notes and Sources   486
Index   515
Acknowledgements   527

List of Illustrations

First section
1 John Osborne's family (Estate of John Osborne)
2 John Osborne's sister, Faith (Estate of John Osborne)
3 John Osborne, aged three (Estate of John Osborne)
4 John Osborne with his mother and cousin (Estate of John Osborne)
5 John Osborne in rep with Pamela Lane (Raymonds News Agency)
6 John Osborne on his houseboat, 1956 (Getty Images)
7 Scene from *Look Back in Anger*, 1956 (Hulton-Deutsch Collection/ CORBIS)
8 John Osborne and Kenneth Haigh, 1956 (Getty Images)
9 John Osborne and Mary Ure on their wedding day, 1957 (Hulton-Deutsch Collection/CORBIS)
10 John Osborne and Mary Ure, 1959 (Getty Images)
11 John Osborne and Mary Ure (Estate of John Osborne)
12 Francine Brandt (Estate of John Osborne)
13 Max Miller
14 Laurence Olivier in *The Entertainer*, 1957 (Hulton-Deutsch Collection/ CORBIS)
15 Albert Finney in *Luther*, 1961 (Hulton-Deutsch Collection/CORBIS)
16 John Osborne (Zoe Dominic)
17 John Osborne at home (Mark Gerson)

Second section

18 John Osborne with Joan Plowright and George Devine, 1959 (Time Life Pictures/Getty Images)

19 At a nuclear disarmament rally with Shelagh Delaney, Vanessa Redgrave and Doris Lessing, 1961 (Getty Images)

20 Nicol Williamson in *Inadmissible Evidence*, 1964 (Zoe Dominic)

21 Nicol Williamson in *Inadmissible Evidence*, 1978 (Donald Cooper)

22 Scene from *A Patriot for Me* (Zoe Dominic)

23 Richard Burton and Claire Bloom, filming *Look Back in Anger*, 1958 (Getty Images)

24 Tony Richardson and Albert Finney, on the set of *Tom Jones*, (Getty Images)

25 Jocelyn Rickards (Islay Lyons)

26 Penelope Gilliatt (Camera Press)

27 John Osborne with baby Nolan (Estate of John Osborne)

28 John Osborne with Jill Bennett, 1968 (Hulton-Deutsch Collection/CORBIS)

29 John Osborne with Jill Bennett, 1969 (Getty Images)

30 John Osborne with Helen, 1981 (Jane Bown, Camera Press)

31 John Osborne with Nolan (Jane Bown, Camera Press)

32 John Osborne at The Hurst (Jane Bown, Camera Press)

33 John Osborne with Helen and their dog (Estate of John Osborne)

34 Painting of John Osborne (Anthea Hadley)

35 *The Hotel in Amsterdam* at the Donmar Warehouse in 2003 (Robbie Jack/Corbis)

36 *Epitaph for George Dillon* at the Comedy Theatre in 2005 (Camera Press)

Preface

When I began work on Osborne's biography, hoping for the best, I asked his wife, Helen, "What does no one know about your husband?"

The absurdly speculative question also asked for her trust. For we might imagine a hundred things about this famous man and investigate a hundred more, but what – if anything – could none of us possibly know about him?

Her response was his private notebooks. Over twenty of them had survived sporadically from the late 1950s until his death. There were missing years. Some had most likely been lost in the various moves and marriages, noticeably during the marriage to his third wife Penelope Gilliatt in the early sixties. Much later ones contain hundreds of pages of notes for *Déjàvu*, his last play, with every line meticulously numbered like a vast laundry list. But the notebooks changed everything.

No outsider had read them before. In the closing pages of his 1981 autobiography, *A Better Class of Person*, he published random extracts from them that were mostly lists of aphorisms. ("She can have the top of my egg any day." "Don't be afraid of being emotional. You won't die from it." "The great English virtue, old age . . .") Similarly, the notorious, goading entry from his 1964 notebook, quoted in the final chapter of the second part of his autobiography, *Almost a Gentleman*: "Whatever else, I have been blessed with God's two greatest gifts: to be born English and heterosexual." But in no sense did any of this mischief prepare me for the revelations to come.

Whatever the circumstances of Osborne's life, in or out of fashion, successful or not, the central message of his notebooks reveals a life of darkest suffering. Fear is their mysterious centre, grief the outcome. The notebooks were written uncensored, spontaneously on the wing, when depression began to immobilize him and the confusion and pain of being alive proved too much. There are entire pages when he sounds like a desolate Beckett character astride the grave and there are merciful times when he found sanctuary in playful puns and lighter thoughts scribbled like graffiti to be polished later for a play. But in their streams of consciousness, the notebooks also reveal within Osborne's fragile melancholy a staggering self-loathing and guilt.

That is why I was shown them with an unusual warning. He most frequently wrote them – Helen Osborne warned me – during sleepless nights when severely depressed. He didn't record anything in them when he was content or happy. Nor were they diaries or journals in the traditional sense. I wasn't to expect entries such as, "Wonderful party at the Oliviers last night. Met Garbo." These interior monologues of self-purging thoughts and haphazard notes, of lists of betrayers and lists of the dead, reveal a man in mourning for his life from the earliest years to the last.

The notebooks aren't the whole story. They are a key to it and a window on his soul. What caused his depressions would send me in time on an obsessive search for the one explanation of Osborne's torment and fury that might account for everything – the "Rosebud Theory". And, after a great deal of luck, I believe that this piece of the tragic puzzle of his life was eventually found.

This is an "authorized" or "official" biography, though I prefer to avoid the weighty formality those forbidding terms can imply. I take seriously James Joyce's malign description of the biographer as "biografiend" (or blood-sucker). Lytton Strachey thought that "Discretion is not the better part of biography". Michael Holroyd's gentler description of the prying process as "intimacy with strangers" is, perhaps, preferable. But all biographers are peeping Toms, there being no choice. They might be neo-spiritualists or graverobbers, mystic companions or stalkers, eavesdroppers, invisible lovers, professional burglars, amateur shrinks, intrusive Zeligs, grand prosecutors or despairing older siblings. But they *peep*.

Until now, we have had only Osborne's word for his turbulent life. But he believed – and stated publicly – that his two volumes of autobiography were a creative act and ultimately a pre-emptive strike against his own obituaries. "One should approach it as if it were a novel," he wrote in June 1991, advising his old friend Tony Richardson, who was at work on his own autobiography. "It's *your* dream, no one else's. Facts are secondary. Feelings are real."

In that cavalier sense, Osborne resembled Frank Harris who, when asked by Max Beerbohm if he ever told the truth, was rumoured to have replied, "Occasionally. When invention flags."

It is my job to get at the truth behind the legend of Osborne and his self-invented myth. But how fictional were his autobiographies? Both his challenging persona and plays disturbed people precisely because he was a truth-teller. The man himself was incapable of hiding anything. Hence the scathing portrait of his loathed mother in A Better Class of Person. But that controversial and masterly memoir about his youth wasn't, I believe, a process of invention, but of interpretation. When I interviewed Osborne's cousin Tony Porter who grew up with him as a child, he told me that when he read the book in which he appears he was astonished by its accuracy and detail. Osborne possessed a photographic memory.

It wasn't the facts that cousin Tony disputed. It was the way Osborne interpreted them. "I didn't think his mother was that bad," he told me. But she was Osborne's mother – not his. The memory of growing up with her in poverty, feeling alone and unwanted, belonged uniquely to Osborne.

He was on shakier ground with his 1991 *Almost a Gentleman*, completed a decade after the first volume. Unusually for this fluent writer, he had great difficulty writing it. A paranoid Osborne saw betrayal everywhere at the best of the times, and his sketchy narrative paid off a number of old scores and dispatched ex-wives like unwanted footnotes. Osborne's bias was my opportunity. He also evaded the depths of his private suffering. His daughter, Nolan, abandoned by him when she was sixteen, was scarcely mentioned.

Almost a Gentlemen also ended almost thirty years before he died, so there was much about his life that had yet to be told. It isn't my intention, however, to prove or disprove the autobiographies. During interviews with people who knew him well, I occasionally read back to them what he had written about them and thus understood the nature of a stoic wince. But my hope is that this book about Osborne's life and times will exist in its own right, attempting to answer those questions that Turgenev posed: "What aim do you wish to achieve, where are you going, what is in your soul? In a word, who are you? What are you?"

Finally, it is my declared intention to reclaim the place of *Look Back in Anger* in British history from recent revisionists who would have us believe that its impact was somehow minor or even negligible. The aim in that unapologetic sense is to right a wrong. The hope is that the plays as a whole will be seen in a fresh light, and with them the significance today of Osborne, the unyielding advocate of individualism in conformist times, whom I came to see as a patriot for us.

John Heilpern, 2006

I

The Hurst

I may be a poor playwright, but I have the best view in England –
John Osborne at home in Shropshire

As I remember it now, when I first visited Osborne's house in Clun, deep
in the Shropshire hills, I was struck by its remoteness from what he called
the *kulcher* of London. Though a dramatist may write as well in the tweedy
shires as in literary Hampstead, it was as if he had fled all contact with the
theatre that had been his life. He moved to Shropshire for good with his
wife, Helen, in 1986 and the Clun valley with its surly sheep, close to the
Welsh border in Housman country, is about as far from the metropolis as
you can get without actually leaving England.

> Clunton and Clunbury; Clungunford and Clun
> Are the quietest places under the sun
> A.E. Housman, not at his best.

The famously urban dramatist was a countryman at heart who loved the
place as his own chunk of ancient England, unless, that is, he was the play-
acting *poseur* some took him for. He began as an actor, after all. What role,
then, was he playing? Former Angry Young Man now morphed into curmudgeonly country squire? The noncomformist clamped as brawling Tory blimp?
The ex-playwright? He had taken to signing his name "John Osborne, ex-
playwright" even as he continued struggling with new plays in the wreckage
of a life ruled by disorder and passion. Had he become that sentimental
relic or absurdist *thing*, an English Gentleman? But Osborne, everyone knew,
wasn't a gentleman.

He was almost a gentleman. Scholarly literary critics attributed the title
of his second volume of autobiography in 1991, *Almost a Gentleman*, to
Cardinal Newman. Osborne had quoted from Newman's *The Idea of a
University*, 1852, in a learned epigraph: "It is almost a definition of a

gentleman to say he is one who never inflicts pain." The problem with scholarly critics, however, is they don't know their Music Hall. He didn't owe the title to the exalted source of Newman, but more typically to the low comedy of one of Music Hall's great solo warriors in comic danger known as Billy "Almost a Gentleman" Bennett.

A rousing poetic monologuist – "Well, it rhymes!" – Bennett reached the height of his considerable fame in the 1920s and 30s. He was billed as "Almost a Gentleman". His signature tune, "She Was Poor, But She was Honest", was renowned:

> It's the same the whole world over,
> It's the poor what gets the blame.
> It's the rich what gets the pleasure,
> Isn't it a blooming shame?

Osborne was no intellectual and Billy Bennett's sunny vulgarity and pathos appealed to his taste. Bennett also created surreal acts entitled "Almost a Ballet Dancer" and "Almost Napoleon". But it was "Almost a Gentleman" that made his name as he nobly played his part in ill-fitting evening dress and army boots. Thus Osborne posed stagily for a Lord Snowdon portrait for the cover of his autobiography in full country gentleman regalia – tweed jacket, buttoned waistcoat, fob watch, umbrella – all topped off nicely with the prop of a flat cap, traditional emblem of the working man. But if we look closer at the Snowdon picture, this image of the sixty-year-old dramatist is too raffish to be gentlemanly. The tweed cap is at a jaunty angle, there's a dandy in the foppish, velvet bow tie, a showman in the long silk scarf draped over-casually round his shoulders. The opal signet ring he's wearing suggests an actor-manager of the old school or perhaps a refined antiques dealer of a certain age. The distinguished film and theatre director Lindsay Anderson, known to Osborne as "The Singing Nun", wondered if he was auditioning in the photograph for the role of Archie Rice's old Edwardian dad. But his chin is up, as Anderson shrewdly noted, his expression still defiant, promising combat outside the Queensberry rules.

I was visiting the Osborne home, The Hurst, three years after his death, and as the car nosed up the long driveway that winds through neighbouring farmland I was unprepared for the grandeur of the 1812 manor house on the hill. The Hurst with its twenty rooms is set in handsome, stony isolation on thirty acres with well-trodden garden paths through woodland and orchard, a clock tower, various outbuildings, and a village-size pond big enough for its own island and plentiful trout.

I had anticipated something much less impressive even by Osborne's standards – a cottage perhaps, or country pile overgrown with weeds. I'd heard that he had been in financial trouble for years, and was all but bankrupt when he died. In fact, local tradesmen had cut off his credit at one low point and he was left sleepless with anxiety that the house itself would be foreclosed on by the bank.

Two years before his death, three of his friends had grown so alarmed at the state of his finances, they organised a meeting to try to help him. There were various plans to sell the copyrights of his plays in return for a lump sum to settle debts. But one of the problems they hoped to solve was the fact that Osborne spent more than he earned. Playwright David Hare, theatre producer Robert Fox, and Robert McCrum, Osborne's editor at Faber & Faber, met him at the Cadogan Hotel in Belgravia where he stayed when visiting London. He nicknamed it "Oscar's Place" (Oscar Wilde was arrested there). But he was a proud man and the meeting with the three do-gooders went disastrously.

"You might try cutting back a bit on the champagne, John," one of them had the temerity to suggest.

It was like asking someone to breathe less oxygen. Osborne and champagne were as inseparable as Fortnum & Mason. He drank it from a silver tankard – "like white wine", as his third wife, Penelope Gilliatt, observed dryly. When in younger days he shared a flat with the director Tony Richardson, the only food they ever had in the place was a fridge full of Dom Perignon and oranges. When he was married to wife number four, Jill Bennett, they kept a fridge in the bedroom to save them the inconvenience of going downstairs to fetch the "shampoo".

On summer days at The Hurst, he greeted guests dressed in a boater and striped blazer like a rep actor in a touring production of *The Boy Friend* as he held up a bottle of champagne in welcome.

"And I can tell you this," he protested at the meeting, flooring them all. "I'm not getting rid of the horses!"

His two trusty hacks, as indestructible as tractors rusting in a barn, had been in the family for years, along with two donkeys and three dogs. But broke he was. "Hang onto the house, if you possibly can," he said to his wife during the last days.

"Welcome to Chateau Calamity," she said with a smile when I arrived, and offered me champagne.

It had come as a surprise when Helen Osborne telephoned me unexpectedly in New York, where I've lived for many years, and said with typical diffidence, "I don't suppose you would be interested in writing John's authorized biography?"

My first instinct was to run. "It's certainly an honour to be asked," I said, playing for time.

"Well, you don't *sound* very honoured," she replied, which was also typical.

I first knew her when she was Helen Dawson, the admired arts editor and sometime drama critic of the *Observer* in the heyday of David Astor's editorship during the 1960s. I joined the paper soon after her, and often sought out her company as she beavered away behind filing cabinets. Osborne famously dismissed critics as treacherous parasites, but he married two of them – Helen and film critic Penelope Gilliatt. Then again, he said of actresses that they made impossible mistresses and even worse wives, and he married three – his first wife, actress Pamela Lane, second wife Mary Ure, and fourth wife, Jill Bennett.

His fifth – or "Numero Cinque" as Osborne often called her – was the only one of his wives, it's widely believed, to make him happy. They were married on 2 June 1978, and lived together for eighteen years. They were apart for no more than a few days during all that time.

It was through my friendship with her at the *Observer* that I eventually got to know Osborne a little, though I had met him earlier when his 1968 play *The Hotel in Amsterdam* with Paul Scofield was playing in Brighton – Osborne's favourite place on earth, lost paradise of the dirty weekend. "Oh blimey – not *you* again!" the stage carpenter would greet him, whenever one of his plays opened at Brighton's Theatre Royal. He looked elegant and young when we met that day. He said hello in a slightly camp, relaxed drawl, and he clearly didn't give a damn. I remember envying him a bit. He was on top of the world, or so it seemed.

Soon afterwards, I met him again and he looked at me suspiciously. I was wearing Paul Scofield's suit from the play.

My first wife designed the costumes for two of Osborne's plays, and *The Hotel in Amsterdam* was one of them. Scofield's suit had been specially made for the production by Doug Hayward, the bespoke Savile Row tailor to the stars. Hayward was tailor to the dandyish John Osborne. The suit itself was an amazing hunter green with black brocade round the lapels. (This was the Sixties.) But Scofield didn't actually wear it in the play because it didn't suit him. It was therefore up for grabs.

Although it was a little tight on me, I was proudly wearing it, after a decent interval, when I bumped into Osborne at Don Luigi's restaurant in the King's Road.

"And how are *yew?*" he asked, still looking doubtfully at me in the treasured suit.

I subsequently met him socially on several occasions and each time he struck me as the very opposite of his combative image. I found him a gentle man, and almost excessively polite. He was gossipy and fun, and highly instinctive. And there were times when he seemed surprisingly vulnerable – as if camouflaging some sadness.

I saw him again when he and Helen were in New York during the Eighties. The city still enchanted him. He had first visited Manhattan in his meteoric twenties when two of his plays were running simultaneously on Broadway (*Look Back in Anger* and *The Entertainer*). One night, we were walking along Broadway back to the Algonquin Hotel on West 44th St, where he always stayed, when he began to lean forward peculiarly like a strange version of Groucho Marx in a strong headwind. He told me it was the best way to walk, particularly over long distances, and called it "The Countryman Tramp's Walk". It had been taught to him by his eccentric grandfather. And now he taught it to me. We tried it out together, doing the Countryman Tramp's Walk along the Great White Way, and even New Yorkers, who've seen everything, looked curious as we surged past them.

The last time I saw him was when he and Helen visited New York again in September 1984. He was then fifty-four and his plays were out of fashion. But they were a relaxed couple, enjoying each other's company – enjoying treats. He greeted me with an affectionate, whiskery kiss smack on the lips, which pleased us both, like sharing a secret.

That night, the three of us went to the Algonquin's Oak Room for a jolly supper and cabaret, and drank so much champagne I had to go to bed for two days afterwards. But as the resident pianist performed a Noel Coward medley while giving a pseudo-sophisticated impersonation of Coward, a sense of déjà vu descended on the table. Osborne began to grow morose.

When the cabaret finished, the pianist went to shake the hands of the audience, as entertainers in New York like to do, and Osborne looked suddenly embarrassed. "He won't remember me," he murmured disconsolately.

"Welcome back, Mr Osborne," the pianist greeted him, shaking his hand warmly.

"Well, thank you very much!" he replied, beaming.

The evening went swimmingly after that. We talked about the great Music Hall artists who had influenced him. He saw them as a warrior class of gods and heroes even in pitiful failure like Archie Rice in *The Entertainer*.

5

And when I told him that I'd seen the great Max Wall perform the same hilarious act six times, he was mightily impressed. He worshipped him, and had cast the legendary comic as Archie in his own production of *The Entertainer* during the Seventies. To his delight, he remembered that Max asked him in rehearsals if he could add just one line to the famous play. The intrigued, but wary, Osborne replied, "Of course, Max. But what's the line?"

It was, "Take my wife, *puh-leeze*!"

Osborne could scarcely stop laughing. (And the line went in the play.)

Now, over a decade later, I was visiting his widow for the first of several visits to begin work on his biography.

Two slobbering chocolate labradors flattened me against the front door of The Hurst in muddy confusion. "Down boys!" Helen Osborne ordered. But the boys, when up, seemed practically her size. At only five-foot-two, she was petite. (Her husband was tall and rangy, over six feet.)

Once inside this well-lit place, however, it was clear that, countryman or no, only a man of the theatre had once lived there. The hallway was crowded with framed posters of several of the plays. Leonard Rosoman paintings of the 1965 production of *A Patriot for Me* ascended the staircase. Surprisingly corny cushions spelt out embroidered messages from a bench: "You ARE leaving on Sunday, aren't you?" "It is difficult to soar like an eagle when you're surrounded by turkeys." "Eat Drink and Remarry!"

The Osborne family tree was prominently displayed in the hallway like a proud, sly joke on English heraldry. No blue blood there – but publicans on both sides of the family from the nineteenth century, with domestic servants, a dressmaker, a billiard-marker, brass polisher, timber merchant and several carpenters stretching back to the eighteenth. Osborne's Welsh roots go back to his great-great-grandfather – a carpenter who crossed the Bristol Channel from North Devon to live in Newport, Monmouthshire, in the early nineteenth century. "Osborne" is a popular Welsh surname stretching back to the thirteenth century.

An Elisabeth Frink sculpture of an alarming harbinger bird stood guard like a totem in the hallway outside the drawing room – the *best* room – with its grand floor-length windows looking out onto the landscape. The statuette of Osborne's 1963 Oscar for the screen adaptation of *Tom Jones* stood on a small corner table looking in its neutered, absurdly golden way as incongruous as the framed photograph next to it of George Devine in drag. Devine, whom Osborne worshipped, was the founding artistic director of the English Stage Company at the Royal Court Theatre and appeared

onstage as a fetching Queen Alexandra during the notorious drag ball scene
of *A Patriot for Me*. "You know," he said to Osborne one night in his dressing
room as he puffed on his pipe in his garter belt and high heels, "the price
of lipstick today really is *outrageous*."

A photograph of another Osborne hero, Max Miller, last of the Music
Hall greats – "a god, a saloon-bar Priapus", he described him – was displayed
nearby in a place of honour. "As soon as the orchestra played 'Mary from
the Dairy', I usually began to cry before he came on," Osborne wrote.
"And when he did appear, I went on doing so, crying and laughing, till
the end."

Among other possessions in the room were clues to a life: a Snowdon
photograph of John and Helen Osborne – both sunny, he in white suit, she
in pink stripes and straw hat – hosting one of their summer garden parties
when jazz bands played in tents and theatre grandees rolled around in the
flower beds. Osborne named them "Cranmer's Annual Summer Balls" in
celebration of Archbishop of Canterbury Thomas Cranmer, founder of the
Reformation, martyred 1556. The parties were held in the grounds of their
Edwardian house in Edenbridge, Kent, a commuter's distance from London.
"Horrible kiddies drowned in pool by request," the coveted invitations used
to say.

On another wall of the room: a quite famous 1956 photograph of Devine
and his Royal Court team sitting on top of an open-air London bus in
Sloane Square with Osborne and Tony Richardson, both in their twenties, transparently unable to take their eyes off the young, laughing blonde
with a hint of Monroe in the front row. She was Mary Ure, who became
Osborne's second wife. A Patrick Procktor painting of that great, ruined
actor Nicol Williamson – Osborne's "delinquent cherub" – reminded us
that he possessed such dangerous mastery of self-loathing and terror as
the lawyer Bill Maitland cracking up in *Inadmissible Evidence*, that no
other actor has yet been able to equal him in the role. And among much
else – a Rosoman painting of Maximilian Schell, who played the homosexual hero, Alfred Redl, in *A Patriot for Me*, a photograph of Osborne
with Olivier, and another of Trevor Howard as the crumbling, furious
Handel raging against the dying light in Osborne's film biography of the
composer.

Grief filled the empty rooms of The Hurst with his absence yet I half-
expected him to walk in at any moment wondering what I was doing there
nosing around. The atmosphere of the house remained an inviting, clubby
haven from a world in which the leading player was unavoidably absent.

Osborne's description of the kitchen setting in his 1992 *Déjàvu* – his last play and sequel to *Look Back in Anger* – is a replica of the kitchen in his own home:

> . . . THE PRESENT. SUNDAY MORNING.
> The large kitchen of a country house of the kind sometimes advertised as "a minor gentleman's residence" . . . It is possibly the oldest part of the house with the original stone flags from an earlier period gleaming, leading off to a large butler's pantry, rooms for hanging game and preparing other fruits of the countryside. A few ancient hooks hang down from the high ceiling and a huge Aga dominates one side of the stage.

I often talked with Helen there as she puffed habitually on cigarettes sending up smokescreens. During breakfast, she scanned a pile of news-papers, which encouraged ritual groans, or she studied the racing form. Her temperament was to back the underdog. She had a weakness for outsiders – betting cautiously against the odds for unlikely winners to romp home. "This is *the big one!*" she announced one day about a hot tip named Dr Spin she'd heard about through the grapevine. We tuned in to watch the race breathlessly on the telly. But Dr Spin barely made it round the course.

"There's one for the knacker's yard," she groaned when he limped home. "I'm never listening to *them* again. What a frightful flop! What a *swizz*."

She often used quaint "English-isms" like "swizz", "tosh" ("absolute tosh!"), "wet egg" ("I don't want to be a wet egg, *but* –").

Her husband used to study the racing form as if cramming for a crucial exam. His notion of sporting activity was a day at the races and an occa-sional game of snooker. It was the larkiness of her life with him, the jokes and mundane, intimate things between them that she missed the most, while missing everything – living now on a wing and a prayer to keep the house, as she put it, "against the odds of a socking mortgage and an abyss of back tax, dependent on the fragility of revivals, the availability of theatres, directors and the love lives of actors, the seating capacity of a playhouse in Tel Aviv or the state of the deutschmark".

She adored Osborne, everyone knew. Following the public wreckage of his murderous marriage to Jill Bennett when he was destroying himself, she was the one who gave him his life back. Now she could scarcely bring herself to speak about him in the past. "You see, he's still here in my heart and always will be," she said, and so it remained until she died.

She deflected the maudlin with good humour, however. Cheerful cards from her would be signed "The Widow of Oz". Or she might recount a conversation she had with Osborne at his graveside: "I don't know how to tell you this, John, but Andrew Lloyd Webber has been made a lord . . ."

There were times when the sadder she felt, the funnier she might become. The business of death has always possessed rich comic potential, particularly in the theatre, and she explained how Osborne's death on a Christmas Eve was typically inconvenient for all concerned. "The whole country was at a standstill over Christmas and I had to make the funeral arrangements, you see."

But, somewhere between the hospital and the mortuary, they lost the body.

As she told the farcical story I tried to keep a straight face. But she was laughing herself now. There had been a mortifying administrative error at the morgue due to a big influx over the holidays.

But first, there had been the ritual visit of the undertaker, known as "Ron the Box". "Ron the Box needed to know about the choice of graveyard plot," she explained. "Did I want a single or a double? Well, I thought I might as well book my own while I'm at it. So I said I'd like a double please. And he said, 'Do you want to be side by side, or on top of each other double-deep?'"

He cautioned that double-deep could present subsidence problems.

"Then we'll make it semi-detached rather than maisonette," she decided sensibly.

Ron the Box went away to make the necessary arrangements. "But he rang up to tell me they couldn't find John anywhere. 'That's funny,' I thought. Because I was sure he'd left the hospital. I got on the phone to check with the mortuary. But they said, 'Oh dear. He's not with us, I'm afraid.' There was a terrible to-do. He'd gone AWOL! John would have had such a good laugh at it all."

Helen Dawson was ten years younger than Osborne when they married in 1978. He was then forty-six. She was the only one of his wives to take his name. Yet little is known about her publicly. In contrast to the famous ex-wives, she always preferred to keep in the background. Her fierce protectiveness of Osborne was well known, however. Loving literary wives are the Medusas of marriage. In her admired biography entitled *Vera (Mrs Vladimir Nabokov)*, Stacy Schiff christened the prickly, over-dedicated wife of Vladimir Nabokov "international champion in the Wife of a Writer Competition". Vera served morbidly through six decades of marriage as Nabokov's editor, agent, typist, researcher, secretary, chauffeur, nursemaid, cook, housekeeper and shield. Helen Osborne undertook several of the

Nabokovian roles with the certain exception of companion butterfly-catcher. She was Osborne's proudly anti-feminist typist, editor, proof-reader, organizer, researcher, go-between and spouse. She supported him in every way. But there was always formidably more to her than the role of simpering, passive wife.

As well as "Numero Cinque", he called her "The Geordie Tyke" (she was born in Newcastle); "The Warrior Wife"; and "WOW" (Washout Wife). The first volume of his autobiography, A Better Class of Person, was dedicated "To Helen"; his second, Almost a Gentleman, "To Lucy" – which intrigued people sensing scandal. No one knew who Lucy was. But the fifth Mrs Osborne was also known jokily between them as the secretary "Lucy Climping" – named after the town of Climping near Bognor Regis.

Perhaps it's the last thing we might expect from a man who was compared to a misogynist Rottweiler that he took such pleasure in the whimsical. It first came to light in the much-maligned Bear–Squirrel games between Jimmy Porter and his abused wife, Alison. "Poor bears!" Porter cries, foreseeing the steel traps. "Oh, poor, poor bears!"

Osborne's nickname for his first wife, Pamela Lane, was "Squirrel", and hers for him was "Bear". Film star Mary Ure didn't have a nickname – a bad sign, as if one didn't suit this beautiful but commonsense Scots girl. His name for Penelope Gilliatt, his third wife, was "Banks", which she also called him, perhaps because he was rolling in money at the time. The nickname for his fourth wife, Jill Bennett, was "Gypsy", which he later amended to "Adolf". She also called him "Gypsy", or "God". "God can't come to the phone today . . ." His former mistress and subsequent lifelong friend from the 1960s, costume designer Jocelyn Rickards, was "Joybells" or more frequently "Dolly". Peculiarly, "Dolly" was also a family name for Osborne's hated mother.

He gave his wife Helen a nickname, too, which she blushed to tell me was "Twinkle". "Oh, dear," she said. "You're not going to put that in the book, are you?"

I could see how she must have spoilt Osborne a bit, as all writers need to be spoilt. "They need to be loved and cared for and given money," the writer-hero of Osborne's Hotel in Amsterdam announces emphatically to one and all.

"When in doubt have a good lunch," she advised me one day when I was worrying over something. "John always did."

She was wry and feisty and Osborne's kindred spirit. She loved the theatre but, like him, tended to dread going. She was fun, seeming to be unworldly, without guile, but she could be bolshie and guarded. You would not mess with her lightly. "I always knew you were a few sandwiches short of a picnic," she wrote to a blundering, future ex-friend. She was a fighter who was as spikily uncompromising in the embattled essentials as Osborne always was. Self-effacing about her own talent, she was exceptionally bright. Before she met Osborne, when she was the arts editor of the *Observer*, she coincidentally edited the drama reviews of the mighty Kenneth Tynan – Osborne's first champion – as well as the film reviews of his third wife Penelope Gilliatt.

"What was the difference between working with Tynan and Gilliatt?" I asked.

"Ego and agony," she replied without blinking.

It was early spring when I visited The Hurst that first time and one morning she picked daffodils from the garden to place on his grave. St George's churchyard bordering the village of Clun is only a few minutes' drive from the house, and she visited the graveside every week.

Osborne was buried in his purple Turnbull & Asser smoking jacket. It was Helen's opening-night gift for the revival of *Inadmissible Evidence* in 1978 and he was so delighted with it, he exclaimed: "I want to be buried in it!" With it, the opal ring she gave him that he always wore. He had taken to carrying a well-thumbed edition of *Hamlet* in a pocket of the smoking jacket like a talisman, so she slipped the copy into a pocket before the burial. Except for the role of Hamlet, he had crossed out every other part in the play.

This was less a case of *Hamlet* without the Prince, more the Prince without everyone else. The treasured pocket edition was his "whip through" acting edition from the early 1950s when he played his Hamlet at the Victoria Theatre on Hayling Island ("not an island but an isthmus", he wrote) which seated about 300 people in the rear end of a small hotel. He had become the company manager by default, and with little or no acting experience behind him in the great classical roles, he decided to close the season with his own two-hour version of *Hamlet*, playing the noble Prince himself.

But on opening night, a euphoric nervous high led him to the comfort of a few stiff drinks. "As a Hamlet, it was a passable impersonation of Claudius after a night's carousing," he later said of his own lurching performance, during which he made a grab for both Ophelia and Gertrude. There were never more than thirty people in the audience and one night one of them was his mother. She was reluctant to see *Hamlet* in the first place.

"I've seen it before," she remarked to her companion. "He dies in the end." During the scrambled curtain call, she sighed at the sight of her son, "Well, he certainly puts a lot into it, poor kid."

"Ah, there he is," Helen said in the deserted country churchyard as she quickened her step toward the graveside where someone else had left fresh flowers before her. The inscription on the headstone of Welsh slate reads:

JOHN JAMES OSBORNE
PLAYWRIGHT ACTOR AND FRIEND
1929–1994
"Let me know where you're working
tomorrow night – and I'll come and see YOU."

The quotation – that prideful threat of every deluded entertainer and actor who ever exposed himself to the whims of critical acclaim and cruel derision – is the parting shot of Archie Rice in *The Entertainer*. "You've been a good audience. Very good. A very *good* audience. Let me know where you're working tomorrow night – and I'll come and see *you*." Osborne wrote of Archie's last words, first spoken on stage by Laurence Olivier, "It was to be Olivier's face, but, I hoped, *my* voice – possibly my own epitaph." And now here his widow stood in silent tears.

2

A Patriot for Us

What's he angry about? Why does the sun turn?
Osborne notebook entry, 8 October 1981

His possessions – walking sticks in the hall, dandyish clothes in the wardrobe, spectacles and pens on his desk – were still in place at the house. "Not necolatry, but pleasant comfort," Helen Osborne explained. But that Regency desk facing the wall of his impressive library upstairs wasn't for the committed slog of writing. It was too small, too cramped for a tall man like him. He fired off postcards from there, sending smoke signals of friendship and war. He wrote his plays by hand in lined notebooks while sitting next to the desk in a deep, well-worn armchair, where I now sat making notes on him – his house, his secrets, his wives and lovers, everything.

Osborne's desk in the library tells us something about him: the priapic Aubrey Beardsley prints facing it on the wall, the pipes in the rack – he first smoked a pipe when he was fifteen hoping it would give him the foggy, contemplative air of a thinking man, like J.B. Priestley – the Swan matches, the *Spectator* Appointment Diary, a 1950s paperclip inscribed "Caramel Is The Best", a list of members of the Garrick Club, a wooden school ruler, the *Oxford Book of Quotations*, a plastic clock with a landscape of Shropshire, a miniature clay teddy bear in a top hat, and next to a pair of Chekhovian pince-nez, another teddy, quite big, protecting a cuddly smaller one.

It would be a rush to judgment to claim the teddies as Osborne's "Rosebud". True, he had a teddy bear as a child. It was his only personal possession, he claimed, in a joyless childhood. But there were too many of them around the house, like fey talismen warding off evil, to be the secret to anything except his surprising whimsy. In the guest room where I slept, for example, a teddy in a velvet clip-on bow tie was perched on a sofa facing the bed. I didn't notice him at first. He was *discreet*.

Whimsy, like irony, is a deeply English trait and Osborne was no stranger
to either. It was in 1998, after all, that the breast-beating Gwyneth
Dunwoody, Labour Member of Parliament, demanded the return from
American soil of Winnie-the-Pooh, as if the Donnell Library on West 53rd
Street in Manhattan had stolen the Elgin Marbles. Ms Dunwoody claimed
that Pooh and his furry friends – given by A.A. Milne to his American
publishers in the 1940s – were being held *against their will*. Whereupon
Mayor Rudolph W. Giuliani, ever the melting heart, personally visited
Pooh and family imprisoned in their bulletproof, climate- and light-
controlled display case, to announce to a concerned England:
"*Fuhgeddaboutit.*"

Whatever the merits of the case of Pooh's abduction, however, Osborne
liked to surprise house guests by waking them with tea and the morning
papers in his dressing gown with his favourite Paddington Bear scarf wrapped
around him like Dr Who.

DEATH OF AN ANGRY MAN
THE BRINGER OF BILE
LAST RAMBLINGS OF AN ANGRY OLD MAN
PRISONER OF DISSENT
ANGRY YOUNG MAN WHO GREW OLD DISGRACEFULLY
ANGRY WITH EVERYONE – ESPECIALLY WOMEN
THE DANDY WITH A MACHINE GUN

These were the headlines that greeted his death, as I leafed through the
bulging cuttings book in the library. But among the many obituaries and
tributes, a *Times* editorial caught my eye because it described him as a
"patriot". The reference was a riff on the title of Osborne's *A Patriot for Me*
whose outcast-hero ultimately celebrates the Self – the freedom of the individual even before country. Osborne's own nonconformism and passion, the
mischief and unyielding battle for individualism, made him a patriot for
himself, too. But *The Times* took a different emphasis. It described his anger
at England as the voice of a "true patriot, outraged by the blunderers ruining
his homeland".

A PATRIOT FOR US

. . . What distinguished him from many contemporary dramatists was a
love of his country, its customs, music, liturgy. Sometimes this love was
expressed in anger.

. . . Those who claim that Osborne underwent a character change
from angry young man to clubland reactionary underestimate him. He

was that rare thing, a persistent rebel. He revolted against the political correctness and nonsensical European bureaucracy of recent years
as vigorously as he had revolted against the stuffy postwar
Establishment. Behind his cynicism lurked the belief that intelligent
objection was worthwhile. "There aren't any good, brave causes left,"
rages Jimmy Porter, the anti-hero of *Look Back in Anger*. It is a tribute
to John Osborne's belief in the power of writing that he never quite
believed this.

He was an apparent paradox: a Cavalier *and* a Roundhead, a traditionalist in revolt, a radical who hated change, a protector of certain musty old
English values, a born dissenter who wasn't *nice*. He was a patriot for himself,
a patriot for England. But whose England?

Cyberspace had yet to reach The Hurst. Dot-com to Osborne would
have been as alien a force as a pan-sexual Holy Spirit. The *Word* – God's
English language – was not created to be *processed* on Earth. He had only
lately discovered the Walkman. He had taken to listening to marching
bands and Handel on his vigorous daily walks in the Shropshire hills with
the dogs yapping at his heels – but if he came across a stranger, he whipped
off the earphones and hid them as if they were a crime against nature.

Was this why I had heard that Osborne had gone mad toward the end?
"You do realize he was mad," I was informed more than once with an off-
hand air, like being offered nuts with a cocktail. Rumour had reached
London that Osborne had been seen howling in the hills like a deranged
Lear on the heath.

It was the Walkman. He sang along with the music, hooting to the sky.
He might not have realized how loudly, but he knew *Don Giovanni* by heart.
"The Dragoon Guards and the Highland Brigade get me up the slopes," he
wrote. "Handel may lift me up to the peak. On my way down, anything
from Elgar, Richard Strauss to Fats Waller."

One afternoon, I went for a walk in the grounds of The Hurst wearing
his boots. They were a good fit, which made me feel uncomfortable. It was
raining lightly outside and Helen Osborne, who wasn't precious about these
things, said, "You best wear these." Her husband had big feet. The dogs
followed me through the woods, wondering what was going on. They were
the two affectionate labradors, Barnum and Bailey, and the Springer spaniel
Offa, named after nearby Offa's Dyke. During the walk, I met a young man
named Andrew Williams, aged about thirty, who had looked after the place
since the Osbornes came to live there. He was the one who told me about
the singing walks.

"If you were working in the garden, he'd come out and say, 'It's hot out here, boys. I'll go and get you a drink,'" he explained when I asked what Osborne was like to work for. "He was quite charming. He'd bring you a great big tumbler of vodka or whisky, enough to put you on your back. And he'd go off singing with his dogs and his personal stereo on. You could hear this roar in the woods sometimes. That's how he sang. You'd hear it in the distance and you might wonder what was going to appear, and all of a sudden there's John waving his walking stick in the air with the dogs trundling along."

The music tapes on a library shelf, piled in a disorderly way as if played all the time, tell their own tale – from "Magic Moments with the Royal Scots Dragoon Guards" to "Boogie Woogie Hits"; Handel, Verdi, Vaughan Williams, Elgar, Puccini and Strauss, and more eclectically, Fats Waller, Vera Lynn, Dave Brubeck, Noel Coward, Russian Orthodox church music, and "The Best of Paul Robeson".

There was no telephone in the library – banished along with the use of postcodes. He disliked being interrupted when working, and if he had to take a call he said he felt like a sulky dog summoned from his dinner plate. He was superstitious about answering the phone anyway. He believed the ringing heralded bad news.

The library was serious, studious even. Osborne was a self-educated man who read widely from early childhood. "Always with his nose in a book," his mother sighed disapprovingly, wishing he could be like other boys. Essentially, it was a working reference library: with a solid English history section – the complete Gibbon and Pepys, Boswell's *Johnson*, several volumes of *The Boy's Own Annual* from his childhood; a comprehensive biography section; all the fat word dictionaries and reference books – from the *Dictionary of National Biography*, to *Birds of the British Isles*, two sets of *Encyclopaedia Britannica*; and four shelves of his plays in different editions and translations. Erudite books on the history of Music Hall were followed by an impressive poetry section, though Betjeman (a friend of Osborne's) and Larkin are about as modern as we get.

Shelves full of Holy Bibles (King James version only) are found in another section as musty as a monastery, along with volumes of Luther's *Works* and a selection of liturgical and spiritual titles, including the seventeenth century *Holy Living, Holy Dying* that he read every day towards the end of his life.

He was a Christian, and therefore a sinner. Scribbled shakily on a cigarette pack his wife found by his deathbed in hospital were the words "I have sinned" – the last words he wrote.

A lacerating sense of sin ran through the latter part of Osborne's life

A Patriot for Us

like infected blood. His Protestantism – which he returned to in crisis as he approached fifty – wasn't a pose or righteous countryman-style mocked by some as "Christian Blimp". He read the Lesson in church, usually attending at Evensong. But he went to church only when he felt cheerful! Not when he felt low.

"God's got enough problems without hearing mine," he explained.

Faith became central to Osborne and to how in his angst and self-contempt he viewed the wormy mess of life. Yet at a point when there was no evidence of churchgoing or God in his life, he made the remarkable choice of the ecstatic rebel Luther for the historical drama he wrote in 1961. The gutter candour and poetry of *Luther* – Tynan wrote admiringly – might have come from the pulpit oratory of Donne.

In a pivotal speech of the play, Luther says:

> This I know; reason is the devil's whore, born of one stinking goat called Aristotle, which believes that good works make a good man. But the truth is that the just shall live by faith alone. I need no more than my sweet redeeemer and mediator, Jesus Christ, and I shall praise Him as long as I have voice to sing; and if anyone doesn't care to sing with me, then he can howl on his own. If we are going to be deserted, let's follow the deserted Christ.

To paraphrase Osborne on that stinking goat Aristotle, good works don't necessarily make a good man. The turbulent artist lives and dies on his own shaky plateau somewhere between God's embrace and the envy of the patron saints of mediocrity. Yet society prefers to see the artist as a fine upstanding example of humanity blessed with the virtuous normality of a bank manager. The need still exists to believe that good art is created by good people. "How could Osborne be so cruel?" is the question frequently asked about him with indignant, reflexive piety. He abandoned his daughter via a cruelly abusive letter when she was sixteen – never to speak to her again. He reached for his poisoned pen to damn Jill Bennett in print when he learned of her suicide.

Do we still believe, in spite of all evidence to the contrary – Mozart's infantilism, Coleridge's morphine, Pound's fascism, Baudelaire's syphilis, O'Neill's alcoholism, Plath's suicide, Wagner's anti-Semitism, Hemingway's bullet, Van Gogh's *ear* – that good and great art can only be created by good and great and normal human beings?

"Thank God, I'm normal," goes Archie Rice's winking, ironic song in *The Entertainer*. But with Osborne, reverse logic applies. How could someone who wrote with such devastating candour and savagery seem so agreeable? When it came to his battles and his beliefs, I was to learn that he could be as uncompromising as Martin Luther nailing his principles to the door of the Castle Church in Wittenberg. But the disparity between Osborne's public reputation and the private man is striking.

"He was an affable, lovely champagne-drinking man," John Mortimer told me, while pausing a moment to add, "and an absolute shit, of course."

Mortimer, a convivial, Rumpoleish man, particularly over lunch, enjoyed Osborne's company on and off for many years. (Osborne's nickname for him was "Blake Wordsmith".) "Speak as you find," he amplified. "He was always very nice to me."

While the same was said by admirers of Stalin – "He was always very nice *to me*" – it was clear that Mortimer was genuinely fond of him. He believed that Osborne's achievement in theatre ranks higher than Harold Pinter's, and that his early model, against the rebellious grain, was Noel Coward. The way Osborne raised hackles and stirred the blood reminded him fondly of his own father, who would say almost anything to start an argument. "I can't imagine anyone actually *liking* music . . ."

Osborne could dominate company if the mood took him, stirring things up, raising the ante against boredom. The "lovely champagne-drinking man" wasn't predictable, and he wasn't always lovely. The civility could become silky, his geniality threatening with wolfish grins. He was a truth-teller who unsettled people, provoking extreme reactions for and against. (He still does.) He put the highest price on loyalty, leaving him wide open to betrayal. He feuded with friends and colleagues alike, causing nuclear fallouts over big and small things.

"Do you think you are a paranoid person?" he was asked in a 1968 *Observer* interview. "Oh yes," he replied blithely. "I see treachery everywhere. In my opinion, you should never forgive your enemies because they're probably the only thing you've got."

"Little" was a belittling word in his vocabulary. Not little vendettas, big ones; not little passions, big, unruly, bloody ones. His clamorous feuds were public and unforgiving. Yet his mildness dumbfounded strangers when they met him. Contrary to his confident, combative myth, he often seemed tentative and diffident. He struck many people I met as fastidiously *polite*, almost courtly. When asked out to dinner, he was known to present flowers to the hostess. He once said about himself that he couldn't understand how anyone could be offended by him – ever! The most common impression of him at his big annual summer parties, for example, is of a generous host looking on at the action like an amused guest – a benign outsider at his own party, sipping champagne from a silver tankard.

*

In or out of fashion, he remained famous all his life. Regularly interviewed by the fearless broads of Fleet Street, he reduced them to pussycats forgiving all the goading mad misogyny and anti-feminism, the knee-jerk homophobia, the *stuff*. "How cantankerous will he be? He is not known to suffer fools gladly, and when he eventually appears and starts pouring champagne, he seems courteous, even benign . . ." – Lynn Barber, *Independent on Sunday*. "I remember when I first went to interview him, how struck I was by his extraordinary good looks and palpable charm . . ." – Polly Devlin, *Vogue*. "He was prickly and truculent on the outside, but inside the sweetest and kindest of men . . ." – Lynda Lee-Potter, *Daily Mail*.

Osborne *sweet*? In the 1970s, he attended a party given by the actor Brian Cox and was astonished to find that Cox's gentrified Fulham house in Harbord Street was in the same street where his Grandma Grove – his mother's mother – had rented rooms for forty years at eight shillings a week. The house was also just around the corner from Osborne's first school, Finlay Road Infants, where he was casually beaten up in the playground on the first day.

"He was a sweet man," Cox told me. "People thought he wasn't, but he was. He loathed Fulham, too. It was where he spent his childhood." Cox, the straightforward working-class Scot, liked him. "John was very polite, he was gentle. And he always thought that no one remembered him." It coincides, incidentally, exactly with my own impression of Osborne when I met him in New York in the 1980s.

But even further back in time on 17 May 1961, we find Violet Bonham Carter writing in her diary:

> He couldn't have been more different from anything I expected. He was perfectly delightful – calm, robust, sensitive, natural & carrying his "success" as though he was unaware of it . . . I have never met anyone gentler, less "angry" than John Osborne . . . He is exactly Raymond's age – 31. [Raymond was her son.]

And in 1957 in a *Sunday Times* profile of the newly famous Osborne, we find the same consistent impression: "Mr John Osborne, gentle-voiced, courteous . . ."

What happened to him when midnight struck and he transformed into Dracula? The dramatist Willis Hall – who with Keith Waterhouse co-wrote *Billy Liar* and who also wrote *The Long and the Short and the Tall* – knew him for many years after they first met at the Royal Court in 1958. They used to have lunch together at Wheeler's in Soho and in later years saw each other occasionally at the Garrick Club. Hall, a generous, guarded Yorkshireman, was to give me one of the wittiest insights into him:

"I've always remembered his words of advice after *The Long and the Short and the Tall* became successful. 'Look, don't spend your life going to see the Polish productions and the Turkish productions. Stay at home and get on with the next play.' I liked him on sight. John for me was the gentlest person I've ever met in my life. I never recognized the image of him as the hard, angry man. I found him the complete opposite. He was a soft person. It was just that when you put a pen in his hand he changed completely."

Whereupon he asked, "Do you happen to know a film called *The Hands of Orlac*? What happens is that this fellow gets his hands chopped off in an accident and they stitch on a murderer's hands to replace them. The murderer's hands take over . . ."

I rushed to consult Halliwell's trusty *Film Guide* which confirmed that *The Hands of Orlac* (not to be confused with *The Beast with Five Fingers*) tells the story of a murderer's hands grafted onto a concert pianist who's lost both his hands at the wrist. The surgeon who performs the intricate operation is insane, though not always. And the pianist is forever overcome by strange, murderous urges. There have been three different versions – the last in 1961 with Mel Ferrer, Donald Wolfit and Christopher Lee, which is the one Willis Hall remembered.

And that's not all. Osborne played Orlac in the stage version. He played the demon with the murderous mitts in his youth when he was an unknown rep actor in Ilfracombe, Devon. The adaptation was by Mary Hayley Bell, the wife of John Mills, and re-titled *Duet for Two Hands*.

3

Mother and Son

At least a man who hates his mother has a standard of excellence in
mind.

'Osborne notebook entry, 1984'

Osborne was a man who was incapable of filtering his emotions or censoring
himself. Though he appeared outwardly reserved, taking life's measure
through a watchful, studious gaze, his instinct was animal. By temperament,
he proceeded uncensored from the gut and his unstoppable animosity toward
his mother was unyieldingly cruel, comic and devastating.

You are not supposed to hate your mum; you are supposed to love her.
If you happen not to care for her, it is widely considered good manners to
keep it to yourself. But Osborne kept few, if any, secrets, and dissembling
wasn't in his nature. He not only hated his mother, he hated her publicly.

His 1981 autobiography, *A Better Class of Person*, turned her into a
national character – "The Mother of John Osborne" – a cockney grotesque
out of Dickens, an exaggerated pantomime figure, a Wicked Witch or
Widow Twanky with her heavy face powder that "showered off in little
avalanches when she leant forward over her food". He described her clin-
ically like some test-tube specimen or corpse laid out for inspection on a
mortuary slab:

Her face was a floury dark mask, her eyes were an irritable brown, her
ears small like her father's ("He's got Satan's ears, he has"), her nose
surprisingly fine. Her remaining front teeth were large, yellow, and
strong. Her lips were a scarlet-black sliver covered in some sticky slime
named Tahiti or Tattoo, which she bought with all her other make-up
from Woolworth's. She wore it, or something like it, from the First
World War onwards. She had a cream base called Crème Simone, always
covered up with a face powder called Tokalin . . . This was all topped

off by a kind of knicker-bocker glory of rouge, which came in rather pretty blue and white boxes – again from Woolworth's – and looked like a mixture of blackcurrant juice and brick dust. The final coup was an overgenerous dab of California Poppy, known to schoolboys as "fleurs de dustbins".

His pathological feelings toward her remained unchanged all his life. When she died in 1983, aged eighty-seven, he began an article for the *Sunday Times* with the words, "A year in which my mother died can't be all bad." (The article was primly rejected.)

As I sifted through his notebooks, there were times when I came to believe that, from Osborne's jaundiced point of view, only a combined portrait of Lady Macbeth and Medea could do his mother justice. Yet his actions toward her were considerate and far beyond what might be expected of a dutiful son.

He supported her financially from his first success until she died, paying all bills. He was ashamed of her, yet she was with him on his opening nights. "Nemmind, eh?" she consoled him after reading the disappointing first reviews of *Look Back in Anger*. "Perhaps you'll be in the limelights the next time." He pilloried her in public, yet he took her with him on family vacations to New York, Los Angeles, Paris, Cannes, the Bahamas, and so on. He gleefully said that he heard her announce during a trip to Florence: "Well, a lot of thought's gone into it."

She embarrassed him, and yet he introduced her to everyone. "Oh, Mr Robinson," his mother said to Paul Robeson (who was in Stratford playing Othello to Mary Ure's Desdemona). "It's such an honour for us to meet you. Especially my son. You see, he's always been very sorry for you darkies." At which Osborne remembered, "a large, gentle smile spread over his face".

During the 1960s and 70s, he was close to John Betjeman, then Poet Laureate, and he took him along for evenings with his mother at her flat in Lupus Street, Pimlico. With them was Betjeman's long-time companion, Lady Elizabeth Cavendish, sister of the Duke of Devonshire. "Gosh, he'd done his mother *well*," Lady Elizabeth told me. "I remember seeing her flat. It was lovely. I met her lots of times and I felt she was very much part of his life. It sounds snobbish to say she had all the humour of a barmaid, but she did. She was fun to be with. We all used to sing Music Hall songs together round the piano. 'All the nice girls love a sailor!' Remember that one? Hettie King in a sailor's uniform. But I didn't sense any antagonism between John and his mother, and he had a low tolerance level. I was left with the impression that he was a good son. Why did he take us to meet her if he hated her? Why did he see her? My other friends who dislike their parents don't see *them*."

On the opening night of *Hedda Gabler*, starring his fourth wife Jill Bennett, Osborne and his mother were descending the narrow staircase backstage at the Royal Court after visiting Bennett in her dressing room. His mother went in front of him when, on a sudden impulse, he seemed to push her down the steep stairs. The murderous gesture was token, however. She stumbled, and nothing was said.

He recorded in his notebook that he longed for her to die. "Wrote to my mother – if you can call it that. Wish she'd die but, of course, she won't." He preferred the humiliating, neutered "*it*" for her, as if refusing to acknowledge even her parenthood.

He would refer to her as a piece of inherited comic kitsch, like flying ducks over the mantelpiece or Russian wolfhounds that held aloft lampshades in more affluent lower middle-class homes. He tried to palm her off onto reluctant friends, asking them to take her out for lunch or a day trip to Brighton. "Oh, go on," he pleaded with them. "You can have the chauffeur."

But she was by his side at fashionable restaurants; she was made welcome at his theatre parties. One of his favourite stories was about the disastrous day his mother met the Oliviers. She accompanied him and his third wife, Penelope Gilliatt, to a house-warming party given by Olivier and Joan Plowright to celebrate their new home in Royal Crescent, Brighton. There, a mortified Osborne watched his mother, who didn't like the look of oily caviar, try slyly to hide her portion of priceless beluga by grinding it slowly into the newly laid carpet with her shoe. Watching this, the house-proud Oliviers froze in wounded disbelief, and Osborne's mother looked down at the mess and blamed it all on Penelope's sister, Angela.

The Oliviers – Osborne wrote bitterly – would remind him of the incident for another decade.

There are no petty grievances in the open warfare between mother and son where all wounds are mortal. But the social humiliations he suffered at his mother's undoubtedly gnarled hands seem more like wickedly amusing stories he dined out on, compared to the description in his notebook of "the disease" that was his genetic curse. From his schooldays, he could never even bring himself to call her "mum" or "mother" to her face.

What on earth had she done to him?

Osborne was born in Fulham on 12 December 1929. "The boundaries of my earliest territory extended from Hammersmith Broadway with its clattering trams and drunken Irishmen to the Fulham Palace Road, a long road leading to Putney Bridge," he wrote in his autobiography. "On the left there is a huge cemetery (containing first my sister and then my father), a stonemason's scrapyard of broken tombstones and dead daffodils in milk bottles. It stretches as far as Fulham Broadway where my mother would walk past my sister's grave on her way to pay the bill at the Gas, Light and Coke Company and my father took me off to the old Granville Theatre or dropped in at Lyons for his favourite black coffee and brown bread and butter on the way to his regular visits to Brompton Hospital."

The darker side of his life was already mapped out for him there, in the mute despondency of those Fulham streets and in the rented rooms shrouded in lace curtains where he was weaned on reproach and failure. One night, when he had turned sixty, he was being taken to the trendy River Cafe near Hammersmith Bridge on the Thames, but the car got lost along the Fulham Palace Road. "I've spent a lifetime trying to escape this place," he said, peering out of the car window at the memory of his wretched childhood.

His father, Thomas Godfrey Osborne, was born in Newport, Monmouthshire, and he worked as an advertising copywriter and commercial artist on Fleet Street until his health collapsed with tuberculosis. He was an ailing and reticent figure, prematurely old with white hair in his twenties, a sympathetic man who enjoyed good books and pubs, and played the piano during family sing-songs. He was Osborne's one protector-figure in the family. "Leave the boy alone," he would say during the domestic rows.

Archie Rice says about his wife, Phoebe: "She's tired, and she's tired of me," and the same was true about Osborne's parents. They were tired, and tired of each other. Thomas Godfrey was often absent from home and Osborne described the marriage as a "blundering misalliance". His father died of TB in 1940 aged thirty-nine, and his son, then just ten years old, mourned the loss for the rest of his life.

Osborne wrote that his sister Faith, or Fay, died of TB when he was two and that she was spoken of "as if she were some exquisite prodigy". But he had scarcely any real image of her. "The remembrance was small. And later, as an adult, I often resented her wilful departure, leaving me alone to carry the burden of our mother." He said he wanted "an inseparable team" – an ally, a beautiful older sister.

His mother, Nellie Beatrice, née Grove, sometimes known as "Bobby" or "Dolly", was the daughter of publicans. She met her future husband when she worked behind a bar in the Strand and it was commonly believed by the Osbornes that he married beneath himself. She complained that the classier, eloquent Welsh side of the family "passed looks" of smirking condescension whenever she spoke. She sometimes marmaladed the language like Mrs Malaprop. Her parents had managed a succession of pubs in London until flamboyant Grandpa Grove lost everything. "*I'm* not a barmaid. I'm a victualler's assistant – *if* you please," she protested, for the refinements of the class system have always been entrenched both high and low.

When the upper middle-class Jill Bennett described Osborne as "a Welsh Fulham upstart", it was meant as an insult, but it was accurate. His mother left school when she was twelve, his father at fourteen, and Osborne himself at fifteen.

Nellie Beatrice's first job was scrubbing floors in an orphanage. She became a cashier at sixteen in Lyons Corner House in the Strand – not a lowly job for one so young – and then a barmaid on and off for the rest of her working life. According to Osborne she was a popular barmaid, bawling out her risqué wartime catchphrases to the noisy delight of the punters: "Oi! Get up them stairs!" "I know – don't *tell* me. Second thing he did was take his pack off!" Or, "One Yank and they're off!"

Even Osborne paid tribute to her genius that shone at the bar: "No one could draw a pint with a more perfect head on it," he wrote, "or pour out four glasses of beer at the same time, throwing bottles up in the air and catching them as she did so."

She was happiest at the pub – the mistress of her boozy, convivial kingdom, having a good laugh with the regulars and the GIs on leave until the ritual shout, "Time gentlemen, *puh-lease!*" Nellie Beatrice – a name that doesn't seem quite real, like some stage name for a saucy entertainer in Victorian Music Hall – had a touch of showbiz about her. The pub was her stage. When her son became a success and took care of her financially, she preferred to keep working.

In 1960, an enterprising *Empire News* reporter found her still at work behind the bar of a modest hotel in Ewell. The headline reads: ANGRY YOUNG MAN'S MOTHER PULLS PINTS. There's a photograph of her captioned, "I always knew John would be famous." The scoop begins: "The charming lady I found pulling pints at the Spring Hotel, Ewell, laughed and said: 'I don't work as a barmaid because I'm hard up. I like doing it. My son makes me a very generous allowance indeed.'"

"Mrs Nellie Beatrice ('Bobby') Osborne does not look her 66 years," the *Empire News* went on. "'I never did stand in John's way,' said Mrs Osborne. 'I allowed him to develop the way he wanted. He was not a strong boy – survived double pneumonia and double this and double that. I can remember the other children bringing him home from school because he had been sick. But look at him now!'"

Osborne tended to divide people who met his mother into two categories: those who found her a colourful "character", and the discerning few who didn't. The general impression I've gathered from a handful of people who met her is that she was "a harmless old trout who sent him up the wall just by *being there*"; "chalk and cheese to John"; "judgmental, like any mother"; "a pleasant enough woman who sat quietly at his parties terrified of saying the wrong word"; "a bit coarse, screaming with laughter after two gins"; "common"; "nice enough!"; and the back-handed "not nearly as bad as he painted her".

She enjoyed a drink and the jelly-eeled ambiance of weekends in Brighton. (So did her son.) She was never known to complain much to anyone, including doorstepping Fleet Street hacks wanting to know about his public caricature of her. She demurred that "It was just John." Both Penelope Gilliatt and Jill Bennett called her Mum (which irritated him). She tactfully claimed that she liked all his wives, pointing out each time that "this is the best one". When Osborne married Mary Ure, she remarked that she was luckier than his first wife because he was now a success. "Mary's got the cream," she said.

Sunny and placid in public, she was disconsolate in private. During the unending wars between mother and son, her tearful, semi-literate letters to him reveal the palpable emotional violence and hurt between them. In *A Better Class of Person*, he quoted from the following letters that she sent after explosive rows – quoting them without comment, as if none were necessary. He was telling us, in effect, "This is the cross I had to bear". But what he didn't see – or couldn't acknowledge – is that within his mother's muddle and guilt, she's pleading with him to be understood and accepted for who she is.

London SW1 (mid-1960s)

My dear John,
Now, first thank you both [he was married to Penelope Gilliatt] for my nice lunch and drinkie . . .

How right you were when you said I was wicked. I have known this for a long time, and selfish and self-pitying, you have only confirmed what my brother told me long ago. But I was too much of a coward to admit it this afternoon.

There is no crime in being any of these things. The dreadful thing is to know and be told of them by a son whom I have deep affection for.

However I do think you are kind and sweet, also brave to want to be friends with me. But my dear it's a responsibility you must risk as I am what I am.

It's beyond my control to adjust myself. I have tried – and it's failed, so please don't ask me to do the impossible . . .

The truth is I'm afraid: *really afraid*. I must face up to my own selfish stupidity and fight this out alone and so adjust myself somehow.

I ask for no forgiveness or make any excuse for my behaviour, and repeat I am what I am.

You John have come from a finer stock, the Osbornes, gentle, sweet and kind. Hold on to these. They are rare and which I greatly envy.

Please read this letter with the sincerity it is written. My love to you both and thank you again.

Mum

London sw1 (late 1960s)

Dear John,

I know how you feel toward me and you have reason to dislike me so. I have never been much of a Mother, and so only deserve to know how you have felt toward me for a long time now. I make no excuses, only ask you not to be bad friends . . .

This is the best I can do as I'm not a good writer or at anything come to that.

God bless you, always

Mother

London sw1 (1970s)

My dear,

How are you? I think of you so much . . . I beg of you to forgive me. I honestly don't know what to say or do. I'm nearly going out of my mind knowing that you have cut me out of your life. God, I dare not think you will never see me again. It does not bear thinking about. I wake up with such horrible guilt . . .

Please John I beg of you to help me in my great distress. I know it is unforgivable and a big thing to ask of you.

My love as always. Take care of yourself.

Mother

London SW1 (1970s)

My dear dearest John,
I've nearly gone mad thinking what for Godsake have I done to hurt you so much. I can't ask you to forgive me, it is too much for the cruel treatment I have given you. Moods are so hard and difficult to explain. I hardly know what to say to your kind and sad letter. I am now crying and so choked up. Oh dear God do understand and believe I did and do not mean to hurt you. It just boils down to the truth let's face it: I am and feel the most horrible creature alive cheap and low. Here I am living on luxury by your brains and in return you receive such cruel and unkind punishment. It sounds so damn stupid and does not make sense. Hughie Green [the TV entertainer] was on television last night. He was out in India and showed us the picture of a beautiful temple. He said it was the loveliest thing he had ever seen. I thought of you . . .
    Your loving
    Mother

When she wrote those letters begging for his forgiveness, she was elderly – about seventy years old – and Osborne was middle-aged. There was never to be any understanding or peace between them.

The Osborne home wasn't a welcoming one. If it had been, he wouldn't have spent all the time he could at the home of a childhood friend, Mickey Wall. He could recall no family gatherings in his own house, no school friends greeted warmly with hugs and welcoming teas. Nellie Beatrice, the star turn at the pub, resented the drudgery of domestic life and the burden of her sick husband. It left her anxious, biting her nails down to the quick. Tired from work behind the bar, she cleaned the house neurotically. Her obsessive preoccupation with germs and cleanliness even extended to washing the pennies in her son's moneybox in boiling water and Dettol. "Handing over the Hoover to my mother," Osborne wrote in a memorable aside, "was like distributing highly sophisticated nuclear weapons to an underdeveloped African nation."

Life had turned out hard and disappointing for her. Her ailing husband was often confined to sanatoriums in the remote hope of curing his TB. But there were frequent separations when he chose to leave home. "My parents saw little of each other. What happened between them I have no way of knowing," Osborne wrote. "My father, when he was not in Brompton Hospital or Colindale Sanatorium, seemed to stay in digs a long way from us in Harrow and Hounslow on his own, and my mother would occasionally deliver a clean shirt and socks to his landlady. He would come to see us when he was able and I have a vague remembrance of them hitting each other. They seldom took me out together."

In her bitterness, Nellie Beatrice told her son that his place in the world was never likely to differ from her own. She chain-smoked irritably in her curlers, ruling her spotless hoovered world with disapproving black looks. "I've had enough tragedy in my life," she repeated in mantras of discontent. "What's she ever done for you?" "I knew it wouldn't last." "Don't expect anything. Then you won't be disappointed." "Don't get above yourself."

Even a loving signature on her letters to him must have seemed like an echoing nightmare nag that could never be escaped. "Always in my thoughts. Mother."

In a blistering polemic entitled "Wrath", he described her cruelly as "an inordinately selfish ingrate as ever gorged her gums with Meals on Wheels." "The grabbing, uncaring crone of my childhood," he recorded in his note-book, and waited for her to die. But longevity ran in the family. Nellie Beatrice lasted until she was eighty-seven. Great-grandmother Ell lived to be about a hundred. Grandma Grove, who worked as an office cleaner at Woolworth's, lived to be 103 and receive a telegram from the Queen. "She is a tough, sly old Cockney," he wrote of Grannie Grove, "with a harsh, often cruel wit, who knows how to beat the bailiffs and the money-lenders which my grandfather managed to bring on her. Almost every day of her working life, she has got up at 5 o'clock to go out to work, to walk down what has always seemed to me to be the most hideous and coldest street in London. Sometimes when I have walked with her, all young bones and shiver, she has grinned at me, her face blue with what I thought was cold. 'I never mind the cold – I like the wind in my face.' She'd put her head down, hold onto her hat and *push*."

As a boy, Osborne sought out the company of people like his grandma and all the great-uncles and great-aunts. He found them interesting (and he was a good listener). "There was no cachet in youth at that time," he noted. "One was merely a failed adult."

His mother's family, the rowdy Groves, were known somewhat contemp-tuously as "the Tottenham crowd". "Even if they did get drunk and fight, they were responding; they were not defeated," a defensive Osborne wrote in 1957 about the fractious family gatherings he relished as a child.

There was Uncle Lod, an undertaker with a reputation for getting wildly drunk at weekends. The mysteriously discontented and taciturn Uncle Henry, married to the ill-used beauty Auntie Rose, was a well-known musician in Tottenham who threw himself under a train. Auntie Winnie was an affectionate spinster with little hair who worked all her life in a north London hospital. He described Aunt Min as "a very gloomy woman who appeared to spend much of her time collecting milk bottles, putting out milk bottles and complaining about the milkmen".

Aunt Queenie Phoebe Adelina Rowena Grove – his mother's despondent sister – was married to poor, sexually repressed Uncle Sid, a clerk in a firm of ribbon-makers who was furtively in love with a dashing aircraftsman. Then there was roguish three-times married Uncle Jack, who claimed he lost his right arm during the war, though the loss was the outcome of having been run over by his own ice cream van in Southend.

Grandpa Grove was a raffish personality who used to run a pub frequented by theatrical folk, including Marie Lloyd. According to family folklore, Marie Lloyd was chucked out of the bar by Grandma Grove – then pregnant with Osborne's mother – for being drunk and disorderly. Whereupon the beloved star of the Edwardian stage screamed back at her up the stairs, "Don't you fucking well talk to me! I've just left your old man after a weekend in Brighton!"

It was Osborne's only family link to the theatre.

Grandpa Grove, with his Edwardian's champagne taste for tarts and oysters, was an early influence. Billy Rice, the father of Archie in *The Entertainer*, is a part-portrait of him and symbol of a vanished era of England. Osborne described Billy carefully in the stage directions to the play: "When he speaks it is with a dignified Edwardian diction – a kind of repudiation of both Oxford and Cockney that still rhymes 'cross' with 'force', and yet manages to avoid being exactly upper-class or effete. Indeed, it is not an accent of class but of period. One does not hear it often now."

Grandpa Grove's flamboyance also appealed, as well as a certain bohemian style, including his taste for Abdulla Egyptian cigarettes (the brand Osborne smoked later in life). Grandpa pretended that he held an important job working for Lord Beaverbrook. "One of the finest men in England, laddy," he announced to the young Osborne. "Be like him." He also prophesied ambitiously that he would live to see the day when two things happened to his grandson – that he would either be Prime Minister of England or the next George Bernard Shaw.

4

Every Day is Mother's Day to Me

I'll say this for him – he's never been ashamed of me.
Nellie Beatrice on her son

When Osborne was seven, the family moved out of London to the suburban housing estates of Stoneleigh in commutable Surrey. He called it a "Byzantium of pre-war mediocrity". His mother worked there throughout the war and for many years later at a mock Tudor pub in an early mall known as the "Shopping Parades". His happiest moment during the Blitz, and possibly in his entire life, came when a bomb fell close to their home and blew her off the lavatory. "I looked on at the funniest, most enjoyable sight I had ever seen," he remembered gleefully.

They would move house many times because of her restless, surly complaint, "I'm fed up with this dead-and-alive hole." Beyond her life at the pub, she had no friends, it seems. "Dear John, I never see or speak to a soul and no one comes to see me," she wrote to him in later years.

During childhood, he spent much of his time in other people's homes – fleeing his own. When he was nine, his only friend for a few forlorn months was twelve-year-old Joan Buffen who came from a middle-class local family with superior vowel sounds. She was a stuck-up little thing according to Nellie Beatrice, but his first crush. They played doctor together and "The Adventures of Robin Hood" in the park. She bossily played Robin Hood rather than the traditional casting of Maid Marian. Osborne cast himself as the aristocratic Sir Guy, describing his role as "contemptuous, feared and solitary". He was her lapdog.

"What do you think a girl like that could see in you?" his mother sneered. "You'll see. They're all the same. Time you learnt it now before you're *really* unhappy."

His one true friend was the dashingly self-assured Mickey Wall – or M. Geoffrey Wall, as he preferred to be addressed. Mimicking his style,

Osborne signed his school books using his middle name thus: "J. James Osborne".

When he began writing poetry and short stories at school, he re-named himself "James Osborne" for a while. (He thought "John Osborne" too commonplace.) Devil-may-care Mickey Wall eased the purgatory of Ewell Day School. He showed fretful Osborne the way.

Mickey's friendship aside, schools were places of dread and bullying humiliation for Osborne. When the lonely Nellie Beatrice routinely kept him home for company, he connived in the truancy. She would explain to the Schools Inspector, a looming presence in their lives, that he was "over-sensitive" and "delicate". Osborne was often ill as a child, and was strangely fearful of crowds and noise. Boisterous children's parties upset him, even Punch & Judy shows and circus clowns filled him with queasy premonitions. Later, during the Blitz, he was content to sit in a damp Anderson air-raid shelter studying war maps of Europe with his gas mask by his side, alone and unobserved, as if in hiding from a hostile world.

The Walls' welcoming, messy house was a second home for him with its generous open-house in contrast to his own immaculately scrubbed, germ-free digs and the sullen company of his mother. He vividly remembered that his shared enthusiasms with Mickey began with comics like *Hotspur*, *Wizard* and *Dandy*. The two school friends became early archivists of the first issues of *Magnet* and *Gem.*, later devouring and skipping through books like *Gulliver's Travels*, *Tale of a Tub*, *Rape of the Lock*, even histories of the world by Wells, and various chapters of Everyman Editions of Tacitus and Suetonius. Then it was on to *The Scarlet Letter*, *Alice in Wonderland*, Kipling, Stevenson, Dumas, Hugo, Edgar Allan Poe – despising on principle boys' bestsellers of the day, like the adventures of Biggles.

Mickey declared at thirteen that he might become a philologist. (He ended up a clerk in the Transport Department of County Hall.) But thanks to Mickey's flighty curiosity in socialism, Osborne also received a solemn early training, as he described it, in "indelibly dull books about people like George Lansbury and J.B. Thomas, books about the General Strike, the Jarrow March and, of course, every available word of Orwell. We bought Strachey's *The Theory and Practice of Socialism*, *The Road to Wigan Pier*, *Guilty Men* and many other Gollancz orange-covered editions." Existentialism – "the macrobiotic food of the day" – along with the "impenetrable brown rice of Heidegger, Kierkegaard, Jaspers, and of course, Sartre" defeated the impossibly precocious schoolboys. But a delight in books was the foundation of Osborne's entire education.

Inseparable as a comedy team, Osborne and Wall remained best friends for five years, junior outlaws in spirit. They formed the Viper Gang Club which struck anonymously against anyone who displeased them. They sent out postcards warning malevolent teachers: "The Viper Gang Is Watching You." The Gang was the prototype of Osborne's more renowned Playwrights Mafia, formed in the 1970s to hit back at evil drama critics by any means necessary.

He concluded nostalgically about Mickey Wall: "When he was about fourteen, a pedantic socialist and professed democrat, he enjoyed quoting Horace about the common herd of men and holding them at bay. *Odi profanum vulgus et arceo*. 'I loathe the uncouth, vulgar throng.'"

Hatred, Osborne also noted, would never rush that cool head.

The only photograph I've found among Osborne's possessions of mother and son together is a 1946 holiday snapshot without any sense of holiday or fun. Three figures are pictured on the edge of a beach, which might be Brighton (Osborne's favourite resort) or Margate (his father's favourite). In the centre is Nellie Beatrice, a sourpuss with a perm, it seems, elegantly dressed for the seaside in her pristine coat with her handbag tucked under her arm. She looks prim, even grim, staring into the camera. On her left is Osborne's cousin Peter Grove, aged about sixteen, in jacket and tie, and on her right is the gangly, adolescent John Osborne, also aged about sixteen, looking self-consciously sharp in his white shoes and dark suit with a white open-necked shirt. There's a studied casualness about his cool pose. All three have a cigarette in their hand, the better to soak up the sea air.

Say cheese! Only relaxed cousin Peter obliges, grinning broadly. Nellie Beatrice manages a reluctant half-smile. The teenage Osborne seems to raise a little smirk. His left arm is round her shoulder, but mother and son barely connect.

The faded photo is evidence of one of their "outings". Flush with generous tips from GIs at the pub, his mother would take them both for slap-up teas and cream cakes "Up West" to the Regent Palace Hotel in London's West End. Gin and tonic was her tipple. There would be fish and chips at the French-speaking Trocadero, the swankier version of Lyons Corner House, where the fifteen-year-old Osborne grandly smoked a cigar like a toff, while pretending he wasn't with his mother who coyly chose the cigar from the box as if they were out on a date. "That looks a nice one, dear."

There was the warm, womb-like escapism of an afternoon "at the pictures" – the double feature, the newsreel, the dutiful short about the Cornish potteries. Osborne went two or three times a week to the movies – whenever he could. The fantastic luxury of the Art Deco cinemas was always preferable to "a cold room with a mantleshelf lined with unpaid bills from doctors, coalmen and the Gas, Light and Coke Company". He could recite the dialogue of *The Four Feathers* and *The Prisoner of Zenda* by heart. He lapped up the louche glamour of the American B-movies of small-time gangsters and low-cut society dames.

He was raised on movies and stagestruck early by Music Hall, the Ivor Novello shows and chorus girls at the Hippodrome with their inviting, plumdumptious, unblemished thighs. "I was about thirteen when I saw a revival of an old Twenties musical comedy, *The Lilac Domino*," he remembered. "I was overwhelmed by the beauty of the girls in it, longing to be on stage with them and take every one of them in turn to dinner at the Trocadero."

Both parents took him to the theatre. It was a Saturday night treat when his father collected him and took him to the music hall. At other times, mother and son spent all day together forlornly treading the plush carpets of the superior department stores in Kensington High Street – his "Appian Way to the West End" – the morose mother dragging the bored, bratty son behind her, and no money to buy anything, until they trudged back home on the District Line with Nellie Beatrice complaining about her aching feet.

He was his mother's reluctant companion. They were each other's burden. When he began work in the theatre and was living happily in salty Brighton with an actress ten years older than him, he was still visiting his mother dutifully on "Black Mondays" – her day off work. They still had their obligatory teas together, followed by the usual aimless traipse round the stores, or a film or a show where they needn't speak to each other.

The adult Osborne believed that he would be lucky to outlive his father and reach the age of forty and the superstition was a legacy from wretched childhood.

At twelve he was bedridden for almost a year with rheumatic fever. He spent the lonely months listening to music and variety shows on BBC radio while reading an entire set of 1919 children's encyclopaedias lent to him by the lady who lived next door. "In the evenings," he remembered, "I used to hear her throwing plates at her husband."

After nine months or so, his mother took him out in a wheelchair. His description of himself is nightmarish: "I felt like a discarded litter basket or an old pramful of coal, waiting for her to stop chattering in the warmth inside the shops."

He was following in the footsteps of his sick father, taking regular check-ups at Brompton Hospital, waiting with anxious Nellie Beatrice on benches for hours to be summoned for an X-ray and indifferent treatment. He was monitored regularly for TB. The rheumatic fever had left him with a heart murmur. He was sent for a "cure" to a hated convalescent home for sick or dying boys.

Then, like the curse of Job, came acne, boils and blisters, a twisted appendix, and life-threatening peritonitis made more agonizing by his mother's accidental treatment of him with castor oil. ("They said it was the worst thing I could have given him," she sighed.) A mastoid operation left him with a shaved head, and he disguised the baldness with a black beret that singled him out like a spindly bohemian curiosity.

He was a medical mess of a boy whose phenomenal litany of problems also included recurring migraines, bedwetting and fainting. He suffered from migraine on and off throughout his life, turning in middle-age to homoeopathic medicines for help. His bedwetting in childhood was mocked by his mother who threatened him with the degradation of exposure; his protective father rescued him, taking him to see a doctor who diagnosed anxiety. His "blooming fainting fits", as Nellie Beatrice called them, could happen during distressing film sequences like Olivia de Havilland's birth-pangs or the amputation of a Confederate soldier's leg without anaesthetic in *Gone With the Wind*.

He commented wryly that the fainting invariably took place in public where it could cause the maximum irritation and embarrassment for his mother.

Nellie Beatrice kept their lives afloat, but she was incurious about him. According to Osborne, the only play of his that she told him she liked was *A Taste of Honey*, which was written by Shelagh Delaney.

In fact, she did take pride in his work (and told him so). But she couldn't express what his accomplishment meant. When he became famous, she referred to him with honeyed deference. "He's a great *artiste*, you know," she said slyly during his Beau Brummel phase in the 1970s. Mockery was her belittling way with him in his childhood, and when she worked at the pub it became a social style. Her guilt-ridden letters plead with him to forgive her behaviour and accept her, while other letters to him read more like a cosy chat over the garden wall:

"English weather is always pulling down the blind on beauty. Treated myself to a pair of curtains. Cost nearly £2, gosh everything is a price, you could get the same ones for 10 shillings a few years back, but it will brighten things up a bit. Had a damn depressing letter from Queenie, so sent her a pound to cheer her up." She rambled on to him contentedly: "This is me after two large gins – sorry dear."

"I am looking forward to seeing my dearest Mother bless her. In her last letter she said, 'What do you think of all the Royal babies? Isn't it wonderful.' I answered: 'What's so wonderful?' I could not care less. Each one has 5 doctors for one baby. Good God said I. They ought to give birth to gold mines."

She expressed relief that he indulged her "bad English". "It's so strange John I love beautiful English, nice words and quite frankly you would be surprised what a lot I *do* know – but the sad thing is I don't know where to put them – and I'm afraid I should land them in the wrong places, furthermore I can't spell them. So no nice words. No go!"

Other letters were effusive: "John Osborne my dear son. Loyal. Kind. Sweet and understanding."

When he sent her flowers on her birthday, she wrote back: "Thank you with all my heart. John – the kindest son in the world." When he took a fall while riding with Jill Bennett (an accomplished horsewoman), she sent over a consoling bottle of wine with the note: "How I have cried and thought of you. Poor dear it was rotten luck. Please be careful when riding again. God bless you."

As well as the habitual confessions of guilt there were spiky letters of peculiar self-regard: "Well, as my Dad always told me, I turned out to be a real gem. Although at times I had a bitter tongue which was not always my fault." There was sympathy about his work: "My special thoughts are of you and I feel rather concerned about you having trouble and upsets over your play. [The Lord Chamberlain's censorship of A *Patriot for Me*] Honestly, with all the money you have made it certainly has not come easy for you."

Her righteous telegram the day after the critics savaged A *Bond Honoured*, his one-act adaptation of a Lope de Vega play produced at the National Theatre in 1966, reveals a fervent, maternal protectiveness:

7 June 1966

MY DEAR SON HOW DARE THESE CRITICS PULL TO PIECES SUCH FINE WORK. FOR TEN YEARS THEY HAVE INSULTED YOUR WORK IN THE THEATRE. TO ME THEY JUST SMELL. I HATE THEM. KEEP UP YOUR COURAGE AND GUTS AND DON'T LET THEM HURT YOU.

But the hurt had been caused long before, locked in what he called her "loveless embrace". "I can read John like a book," Nellie Beatrice would announce to all at the pub. His private notebooks describe how she goaded and humiliated him publicly throughout his childhood and in the years when he was a failed actor – mocking his puny body, his ambition, virtually everything about him.

Two or three of her catchphrases were cheerfully anti-Semitic. ("There's no separating a Jew from his cashbox!" she would announce from behind the bar to raucous laughter.) One of her more bizarre sayings, "Only a Jew", was a reference to a beloved old Music Hall sketch entitled "Humanity" – a little moral fable about a virtuous Jew who becomes best friends with a Gentile, who sleeps with his wife. The sketch was performed by the popular entertainer John Lawson. "He's like John Lawson's son!" Nellie Beatrice would shout at the pub, pointing to her cringing son as she added for an easy laugh: "Only a Jew."

An entry in his notebook of November 1955 has the title of "My Mother" as if settling down to the sentiment of a lovingly prosaic school essay. The entry is both a helpless expression of enduring hurt and a private confessional of contempt:

So much malice directed at apparently innocent objects. Those eyes which missed nothing, and understood nothing. There is a particular kind of Cockney cruelty which she had inherited, and which she always exploited to the full. Often it would start good-naturedly – but soon the real spleen and envy behind it would begin to show themselves to the gallery . . . She would hold up my pennilessness, my bony frame and long face, my accent, my clothes, my manners, and yell with laughter. When she began to sense my inner rage about to spill over, the shouting would subside to, "But he's a good kid, though. He thinks I don't know what he's thinking, but I can read John like a book." After this outrage perhaps she would make a show of paying homage to my unseen talents. How "intellectual" I was. "I'll say this for him – he's never been *ashamed* of me. He's always let me meet his friends – and they're all theatrical people, a good class all of them, they speak nicely."

Then he added witheringly:

I was ashamed of her all right. I was ashamed of her as part of myself, because she seemed to represent the conflict in myself, because she was a disease from which I was suffering, and would go on suffering until one of us died. I was ashamed because when I was with her I was never whole . . . introducing her to others was inviting them into my sick room to watch my agony.

Later in the same 1955 notebook, he wrote down the sugary lyrics of a popular Music Hall song as if throwing up all over them:

> Every day is mother's day to me
> Since I was a baby on her knee
> For what can take the place
> Of that careworn smiling face . . .

Osborne was then aged twenty-six and living on an old Rhine barge on the Thames with the actor Anthony Creighton. Three months previously, *Look Back in Anger* had been accepted for production at the Royal Court Theatre. Life had never held out such hope and promise for him. Yet his mother was the object of his tortured private thoughts – the "disease" within him to be viewed in his sickroom as a specimen of his torment. "A disease that's in my flesh," as Lear says of Goneril. "Which I must needs call mine . . ."

The hatred never abated. Fifteen years later in 1971 when his marriage to Jill Bennett was souring, he wrote:

Saw my mother on Monday for lunch . . . She was more self-involved, detached and full of her old greed. I've never liked her. No, I've loathed her. But, watching her, not listening to her, I felt, as always, dislike for myself. But, this time as if it were distaste and a verdict on myself. A caricature, an embarrassment. Nothing to listen to, no ear. Not just old age. She's always been like that. The grabbing, uncaring crone of my childhood. I, a middle-aged man, feeling older and older than ever, both wishing the other far away. I sit with my wife, my mother, my daughter, the rest. With nothing to say to one another. Only emptiness and desperate twitchings of flight.

In 1985 – two years after Nellie Beatrice died – Osborne's screenplay of *A Better Class of Person*, the autobiography of his early years, was televised with Eileen Atkins playing his mother. Atkins, the admired and intelligent actress whose beady eyes could wither an albatross at a glance, had a personal insight into the world of Nellie Beatrice. She had been good friends with Helen Osborne for many years, and she and her husband, a film producer, spent weekends with the Osbornes at their home in Kent. By coincidence, she also had a troubled relationship with her own working-class mother, who toiled in London as a seamstress during the day and a barmaid at night. Her father was an electric meter reader and eccentric who was arrested during the war for reading a meter in Hackney while disguised as Adolf Hitler. He was known locally as "Mr Funnyman".

Osborne unnerved Eileen Atkins and she was wary of him, although there were fun times. "We felt a common bond because of our backgrounds," she told me. "I was ashamed of my mother, as John was of Nellie Beatrice. It's a myth that parents always love their children, and we talked about it and we would laugh together. But you have someone who wants to crawl out of the working-class, which is what my mother was trying to do, and what his mother was trying to do. And what's so funny about that? Why punish someone for the 'wrong' accent? What's the *right* one? My poor mother used to talk about 'the lav', and when I got to grammar school I said to her, 'It's not the lav, it's the toilet.' So she learned the word toilet. And when I got to drama school, I said to her, 'It's not the toilet, it's the *loo*.' And I can remember her crying out in frustration, 'I don't know what I'm supposed to say anymore.' Before she died, I came to understand her better and I stopped blaming her for everything. Whereas John never could see anything positive in his mother. He wanted to be the victim, and he wanted her to be the monster."

The "mistake" she made in portraying Nellie Beatrice in the TV film was in sympathizing with her. "I thought this poor woman worked day and night, had a husband sick with TB, and there she is slaving away for both the father and the sulky son. And both of them loathed her. She may have been a monster, but my God, she must have been tired. She must have been exhausted. But John never saw any redeeming factors. He just didn't want there to be any excuses for her at all."

The film of *A Better Class of Person* was well received, but Osborne never spoke to Eileen Atkins again.

Nellie Beatrice died aged eighty-seven on 23 January 1983. Osborne, then fifty-four years old, didn't attend the funeral. Mother and son hadn't seen or spoken to each other for seven years.

Eight years before she died, and no longer in good health, she had agreed to move into a Retirement Home carefully recommended by Mrs Gould's Residential Advisory Centre for the Elderly. At the last minute, she refused to go. Osborne continued his financial support after seeing her for the last time. His own doctor saw her regularly, social workers visited her. It would be sentimental of us to expect him to show much emotion at her death, and he didn't. He received the news quietly and debated whether he should attend the funeral.

According to Helen Osborne, he had stopped seeing Nellie Beatrice when he returned home angrily after visiting her in her Pimlico flat. She'd spent the entire evening ignoring him as she watched television. "That's the last bloody time," he complained in utter exasperation. "She just watches the telly." Her apologetic letters to him in the 1970s were probably the outcome of blistering rows caused by her turning her back on him to watch TV with her cats in her lap during his reluctant, dutiful visits. She preferred the company of Bruce ("I'm in Charge") Forsyth and particularly of Hughie Green on *Opportunity Knocks*, describing them both needlingly to him as "her gods".

Helen Osborne never met her. She cleared the Pimlico flat of its few possessions and found a few scrapbooks with reviews of Osborne's early plays and some faded newspaper articles about him. There was a dog-eared "Memory Lane" photo album of 1960s holiday snaps, and pictures of Osborne with his baby daughter, Nolan, her only grandchild from his marriage to Penelope Gilliatt. There were inscribed copies of his published plays. But she was most surprised and intrigued to find several elaborately beaded evening gowns hanging in her closet still carefully wrapped – but never worn. They looked quite recently bought. There were as many as ten of these gowns.

When she told Osborne about them, he was amazed. He had no memory of seeing her in them at all, and could scarcely believe it. Her clothes were carefully planned "rig-outs", as she called them. He remembered them mockingly for their matching tan period. Nor would she have worn formal beaded gowns at the informal Royal Court. But the mystery isn't too difficult to solve.

Nellie Beatrice dreamed of living a glamorous, carefree life. She wanted to be the belle of the ball.

Soon after her death, Osborne wrote this last obsessive notebook entry about her:

> Nellie Beatrice: Two things. She didn't show affection but that she feigned it. Gratitude also. It was her lying that was so offensive. Her underestimation of my intelligence and sensibility. Also, of course, she discouraged ambition. She even denigrated me, especially physically, making me feel an ugly mess. My spots: she was indifferent and unthoughtful.

It's as if the successful, middle-aged man were still the bewildered, insecure adolescent. But there the final, depressing entry about her trails off like a weary prizefight that has punched itself out, and ends with him noting one of her echoing put-downs: "Oh dear. You don't seem to be very lucky, do you?"

The scars of Nellie Beatrice marked Osborne's life – from his sense of self ("I was ashamed because when I was with her I was never whole"), to his defensiveness and self-abasement, his emotional needs and his volatile relationships with various wives lost in his "deserted battlefields of marriage beds". "Blood-sucking vampires," as Jimmy Porter in foul mood described women in general. When Osborne looked back on his life, he quoted E.M. Forster: "As each of us looks back into his or her past, doors open upon darkness."

The more I looked into the darkness of his past, the more the unhealed wounds of his childhood festered throughout his life. "I've nearly gone mad thinking what for Godsake have I done to hurt you so much," his mother had written to him, pleading in her confusion for understanding. But whatever the cause of the furies between them, I would come to learn that the key to Osborne's hatred of her was provoked by the unending sense of devastation and loss caused by the death of his father.

5

Father and Son

> For twelve months I watched my father dying when I was ten years
> old . . . You see, I learnt at an early age what it was to be angry –
> angry and helpless. And I can never forget it.
>
> Jimmy Porter, *Look Back in Anger*

Osborne lamented the loss of his father all his life, and this sense of abandonment haunted him and made him desolate. "I was born with a sense of
loss, a feeling of things withheld and banished," he wrote in his 1985 notebook when he was fifty-six. "This initial deprivation of inheritance, this
original theft abided and was confirmed in failed love, marriage, begetting
of children and the love of an eternal."

The date of that bleak note – written on 11 November when he was
severely depressed – is significant. As each New Year approached or passed,
the memory of his father's death consumed him with loss. Shortly before
Christmas 1939, he learned that his tubercular father had perhaps six weeks
to live. Thomas Godfrey died on 27 January 1940. Osborne had just turned
ten.

Many years later, into middle age and beyond, he would sometimes write
in a notebook on the anniversary of his father's death the single entry: "My
father died today." Depression gripped him at other times, but invariably
around the anniversary – approaching the end of the year and the beginning of the new – he was brought to a state of such immense despair that
he could scarcely function.

Few people knew of Osborne's descents into the abyss. He would sometimes refer to them in a deliberately offhand way, as if he were suffering
from little more than a bad case of lingering flu. But he was incapable of
seeing anyone when he was deeply depressed and he never wrote publicly
about it.

The depressions lasted on average from three to six weeks. But the worst lasted for four months. He wasn't what is generally known as a "manic depressive". There were no euphoric highs. His zest for life went on as usual until he was consumed by despondency and lay in his darkened bedroom.

30.10.66

I'm putting the date. I don't quite know why – not for my record. But I feel such despair, what words, desolation, hopelessness. I *see* no future. There really is nothing. I've thought of ringing someone. How? What do you say?

The implication is that he was thinking of calling someone for help. But Osborne always refused to see a shrink. D.S.J. Maw, the consultant physician who treated his diabetes in the mid-Eighties, became Osborne's friend and suggested that he consider seeing a psychiatrist during one of the wintry periods of unbearable grief. "He didn't react with any enthusiasm, and he hated the idea of being treated with pills," Maw told me. "He didn't like taking insulin injections for his diabetes, but he knew that he needed them. On the other hand, he knew his depressions were cyclical and that he'd come out of them."

Like many artists, Osborne was superstitious about therapy, fearing that those twin pillars of a well-adjusted life, analysis and drugs, would block creativity and affect his writing.

"John felt that inspiration comes from God and don't bugger about with it," Helen Osborne told me. So he resisted psychiatry, though the long shadow of his father's death threatened to paralyse him. He believed with Martin Luther that words are closest to God – thereby conferring an untouchable power on their sanctity. (*Shrunk* to him meant lessened in substance, diminished, made smaller. Give us the chaos of big, unfathomable things!) I have read earnest articles arguing how the problems of anguished dramatic heroes like Jimmy Porter, Willy Loman and James Tyrone, wrecked by rage and failure and booze, would have been solved by Prozac and a prescription or two of lithium. But who would have been interested in their sedated stories?

We might as well recommend a marriage counsellor for Hedda Gabler, or a therapist for Hamlet and his too well-known Oedipal complex. Osborne came from a generation in England that was embarrassed by therapy and even ashamed of it. Cynical about shrinks and their jargon anyway, he was temperamentally unsuited to confess all to a mute stranger in a neutral room, and confess all that he might yet come painfully to know.

With other writers, despair can generate creative power, and through it, catharsis. Leon Edel pointed out that depression drove T.S. Eliot to write *The Waste Land* when he thought his own life was wasted, and that Virginia Woolf's novels were a last-ditch defence before "relapsing into her manic state when they were done". But Osborne's immobilizing depressions were akin to William Styron's ravages of melancholia that he described movingly in his 1990 memoir, *Darkness Visible*. Osborne read the book, given to him by Helen who hoped it might help him. He recognized the symptoms of his own anguish, though Styron's illness was more traumatically dangerous.

Osborne's depressions came and went and worsened over the years like a poisonously unwelcome house guest at Christmas. Styron was sixty, a heavy drinker who had given up alcohol several months before he awoke to find himself spiralling toward a state of such mental torment, it enveloped him like a shroud and threatened his life. He belatedly found that the early death of his mother was the most crucial factor in his condition – as the early death of Osborne's father appears to be in his.

"The genetic roots of depression seem now to be beyond controversy," Styron wrote. "But I'm persuaded that an even more significant factor was the death of my mother when I was thirteen; this disorder and early sorrow – the death or disappearance of a parent, especially a mother, before or during puberty – appears repeatedly in the literature on depression as a trauma sometimes likely to create nearly irreparable emotional havoc. The danger is especially apparent if the young person is affected by what has been termed 'incomplete mourning' – has, in effect, been unable to achieve catharsis of grief, and so carries within himself through later years an insufferable burden of which rage and guilt, and not only dammed up sorrow, are a part, and become the potential seeds of self-destruction."

Osborne's unresolved childhood agony looks uncannily like an example of this "incomplete mourning" that could drown and suffocate as each New Year approached, even when life itself appeared to be good.

November 1962

I really have been fortunate. People seem to smile on me more than ever. Sick pain so much of the time. It's all I can remember or think of: pain. And ending up alone.

3 December 1973

I don't think I have ever known such despair as this. It is inescapable, yet I am learning the everyday techniques of it. Out of it comes a kind of probing faith in chaos. I have thought of dying. I could drink myself to death – if I'm not doing so already . . . Perhaps this living is the most perfect form of death. Perhaps this *is* holy dying. Death itself is a deluding swindle. Love, marriage, physical longing – intense this week even among the numbness – my childhood, my past, England, the wars, the partings, the farewells, the deaths, the imminent dyings, all seem like a shining despair.

8 December 1989

Write it down – even if you're in the last stages of madness.

4 November 1993

Well, on to December! The death, that time of year . . .

Osborne's father is a figure glimpsed, never quite seen. He appears through a filter like a shadowy silhouette in a recurring dream. The father who died of TB at thirty-nine is never in focus, except for the most important thing about him – his love for the son and the manner of his dying.

Osborne remembered his appearance clearly enough, though he was ten when he died. He tried to remember his voice. When he was in his thirties, he met the father of a friend who spoke with a light Welsh accent. "That was my father's voice," he later remarked, as if still yearning for the essence of him.

Osborne was nine years old when he and Nellie Beatrice were seeing his father off on the Continental Departures platform at Victoria Station on his way to a sanatorium in Menton (paid for by Thomas Godfrey's Benevolent Society) and another "exile of pain".

"Take your mother to the pictures, son, and then go to Lyons Corner House," said his dad, giving his tearful boy a ten shilling note as he leant out of the railway carriage. Forty years later, Osborne remembered his appearance that day:

His hair was almost completely white (at this time he would have been thirty-eight). But it had been that colour since his early twenties. His skin was extremely pale, almost transparent. He had the whitest hands I think I had ever seen; Shalimar hands he called them. ("Pale hands I love beside the Lethe waters of Shalimar." It was one of his favourite Sunday ballads.)

But the impression of this ailing man changes surprisingly. The long, pale fingers of his beautiful hands were badly stained with nicotine. He washed his hands obsessively, "like a pussycat". He manicured them fastidiously, too, with a tiny pair of clippers he kept in his waistcoat pocket. He was meticulous in other ways – about the state of his cuffs and collars and his brightly polished, papery shoes. Yet his shabby, hand-me-down blue striped suit – the only suit he had – was rumpled, his bowler hat and raincoat greasy and "mourning black". To his distress, his wife threw the old bowler away in the dustbin and he bought it back the following week for a couple of bob from the dustman who was wearing it.

"In all, he must have seemed a little like a Welsh-sounding, prurient, reticent investigator of sorts from a small provincial town," Osborne observed on a jarring note.

The sketch created – even one drawn by the son who adored the father – is of a down-at-heel and defeated man. The image in Shalimar purity of his father, tall, stooping and frail, is one of failure.

He was ill for most of his life. Asthma kept him away from school throughout his childhood. In adulthood, in the shadow of unemployment during the Thirties, he became an invalid brought down by tuberculosis.

"He was a man who, most of his life, had very little control over it," Osborne told John Freeman in a 1962 BBC TV interview. "He always seemed to be in the control of other people. It always struck me very strongly." Even so, he described him as "a man of tremendous strength, tremendous integrity . . ."

He romanticized his luckless father as he tried to piece together the fragments of his childhood memories. "He may have conformed consciously to what was then a popular idea of the aristocratic tramp," he recalled later. Osborne identified with him, and his heart went out to him. He said that he was the only adult throughout his childhood who cared about him. "I loved being out with him and holding his hand in the street. Perhaps he liked having me with him. For a time I was a rather dandyish, yes, bohemian-looking child dressed in a black beret and large velvet bow-tie. We must have looked bizarre walking down the street together."

Osborne rejoiced that the one unforgettable feast on his calendar was 8 May. His father, Thomas Godfrey, known as Goff or Geoff, was born on 8 May 1900, and *Look Back in Anger* opened at the Royal Court Theatre on 8 May 1956. The published version of the play is dedicated to his father. Thus the two birthdays were always linked for him – a cause for celebration, or conscience.

Father and Son

8 May 1966

Thought about the old man and him looking at me with his blue eyes. "Look Back" seems further away still. I *must* make it. I must not be cautious. I must invent. I must improvise. I must love.

His father's side of the family, the Welsh Osbornes, were baffled by the cockney Groves. "Their value system was quite different," Osborne wrote in 1957. "What impressed me most when I was a small boy, about my other grandparents, and all my father's relatives, was the calm that surrounded them. Not only were their voices soft, but they actually *listened* to what you were saying . . . Besides, my father and all his family were particularly gentle. There were no fights, few rows, hardly ever any tears. Whenever there was an argument, it was nearly always about *income* and mostly characterised by gravity and long stretches of silence."

His mother's working-class roots contrasted with those of the more genteel Osbornes whose bitterness was caused by their shameful descent from the moneyed middle-class to the impoverished lower class. As Osborne put it, they doted on their own defeat.

In their resentful way, his paternal grandparents were distant cousins to the middle-middle class of the Comstock landless gentry in George Orwell's *Keep the Aspidistra Flying*. They lived a life of unshakeably rigid, ritualized order in which nothing ever happens. Appearances were maintained like exotic fruits in a silver bowl; disappointment was their calling card. "Disappointment was oxygen to them," Osborne concluded lethally about both sides of his family. But the resentment on the Osborne side was born in lost entitlement – the deathly grievance of having been cheated since birth.

It began with terminally lazy Grandpa Jim, who owned a thriving jeweller's shop in Newport, but lost the business entrusted to him by his mother when he preferred to watch cricket all day. Downwardly mobile Grandpa Osborne, like his feckless opposite number Grandpa Grove, had gone and lost it all.

Still, Grandpa Jim's brother was Mayor of Newport and Chairman of the Conservative Association. His brother, Tom, exaggerating his deafness to shield himself from the boastful yammering of his bejewelled wife Lottie, prospered too. Tom and Lottie had retired like characters in Terence Rattigan's *Separate Tables* to the sheltering aspidistras of a nice hotel in Bournemouth. Auntie Lulu lived in leafy grandeur in East Cheam with her self-important husband – a wealthy accountant, whom Osborne remembered "looked obscenely exposed without his bowler hat, like a turtle

47

without its shell". "Wormy little bank teller," Thomas Godfrey called him, contemptuous of his airs and graces.

Unemployed for as long as anyone could remember, Grandpa Jim, the cricket-loving slacker, became more of an unpaid family retainer, a docile odd-job man about the place, cowed as a dignified butler. Even Nellie Beatrice patronized him, giving him a shilling from time to time, like a tip. His grandson was fond of him, though – "poor neutered old dog", said Osborne.

On the other hand, he compared his withering grandmother, Annie, to Mrs Danvers in *Rebecca*. The "gentle" side of the family seems not to have included iron-willed, puritanical Grandma Annie Maud Osborne with her "eyes half-shut like a smug fakir" sucking through her dentures on her home-made treacle toffee with her feet up on the pouf. She was the surrogate parent to Osborne's detested cousin Tony, her favourite grandchild. Her slothful, sacrosanct routine of afternoon naps, according to Osborne, would be followed by the uninspiring rigidity of early nights in Stoneleigh with Warwick Deeping, whose popular novels she enjoyed.

On Sunday mornings, the young Osborne always accompanied his father to see Annie Maud, who lived close by. "This weekly visit to his mother was something he dreaded and it was not difficult to see why," he wrote. "Her dismissive skill was subtle and brutal, sometimes no more than a thin smile, a watery upward look or an amused intake of breath, a scanning cauterising instrument which rendered any endeavour puny or extravagantly indulgent. Her son was her prize victim."

Thomas Godfrey's crime was his illness and his youthful ambition to become an artist. Yet Osborne continued to visit her dutifully until her death. "She hardly ever spoke of him for nearly twenty years," he remembered, "and when she did there was always a bitter dismissive note in her voice, even when she seemed about to soften into nostalgia about the clothes he wore as a child or the things he had painted or written instead of going to school or playing games. Often I wanted to attack her violently for having murdered his spirit and helping to kill him. But I never did, and we left each other alone."

He empathized with his beaten father in this family of hated matriarchs. But one constantly resurrected incident hardened him against his belittling grandmother for ever. When his father was twelve, he won first prize in a drawing competition sponsored by the *Daily Mail* – a round trip by boat to Cape Town. Thomas Godfrey was always frail, a chronic asthmatic, and the journey was felt to be too much for the boy. But eventually, he was reluctantly allowed to board the steamer bound for Cape Town. A few days out in the Bay of Biscay, he suffered a violent attack of asthma and was hospitalized in Lisbon before being shipped home with the bill of several hundred pounds.

"He was never allowed to forget it," Osborne wrote bitterly. "The account of the family borrowings and scrapings inflicted by his unhappy prize was repeated to him until he died and still recalled afterwards. Like a mark of inner folly the prize caught up with him in death, as she knew it would."

She got the money back when her son died almost thirty years later, shabbily suing for what money was left from an old insurance policy – all he had. "I never heard her say a kindly word to him or of him," Osborne concluded. "When both her children died, both in their thirties, she spoke only of the bitter injustice of her daughter's early death."

The daughter, Aunt Nancy, had married a Welshman from Newport named Porter who prospered in West Africa and became a director of Unilever. Their child was Osborne's loathed cousin Tony, who rose to be Assistant Chief Probation Officer for Cheshire. Osborne borrowed his surname for the hero of *Look Back in Anger*.

"Yes, it is a claim to fame, I suppose," Tony Porter, a thoughtful, amiable man, said when we met. I'd gone to see him at his home in Cheshire. In his late sixties he had the look of a burly ex-rugby player – his grandfather on the Porter side had played professional rugby for Oldham – but he offered another explanation. "We run to fat the Porters do," he explained blithely. "An aunt once told me, you've got the Porter failing – a big fat bottom and big fat face." And at that surprising pronouncement, he made us both a big fat pot of tea.

He and his wife of some forty years had attended Osborne's memorial service and thoroughly enjoyed it. Afterwards, they went to see *Blood Brothers* in the West End. The last time Tony met Osborne was at the funeral of Grandma Osborne in 1958 when the family gathered in her flat over Tesco's in Stoneleigh. He wasn't one, he told me, to bask in another's limelight.

Cousin Tony was fifteen months younger than cousin John. They used to play together once a week in Stoneleigh until they were eight or nine years old. He pointed to a small scar just beneath his left eye. "See this scar? John did that when I was six. He threw a stone at me. My father used to say, 'I see you've still got that bloody scar John Osborne gave you.' He was furious about it. I can remember a doctor with a huge ring on his finger stitching me up. We were on a Sunday walk with John's father and my grandfather was with us when John threw the stone at my eye."

He added, unconvincingly, "I don't think he did it on purpose."

I reminded him of a few things his cousin had written about his childhood self and he listened solemnly, taking each insult in stride. "Tony was an ingenious and malevolent schemer, proudly encouraged by his grandmother, to whom he was undoubted heir apparent. No one, child or adult, was allowed to challenge his domain or his tantrums, flagrant lying and dwarfish bullying. I was repeatedly instructed by my mother never to retaliate whenever he surprised me with his armoury of kicks, finger twistings or rabbit punching. Having disabled me with one of these, he would howl off to Grandma, accusing me of his own offence. He was always believed. Later of course I found it to be a common technique among adults, particularly in marriage."

"Pity I grew up," he responded dryly.

Even so, he implied the picture might be close to the mark, pointing out reasonably that he didn't think he need apologize for what he was like when he was six or seven years old. His memory of cousin John was more sympathetic. "He always seemed a sad, quiet boy. I don't think he was terribly happy, that's my recollection. He wasn't strong physically. But I can remember him arguing one day with a group of boys when he was eight or nine. He was useful with words even then. I didn't even know what it was about, but he got very angry with me because he wanted me to take his side. He thought I'd let him down. When I met up with him just after he left school, I was very impressed. He seemed so sophisticated! He was older than his years. He was wearing a bow tie and lent me a copy of *Lady Chatterley's Lover*. He seemed to know a few things. When he was very young, he was a sad child, a loner."

Porter told me that Osborne's view of his sourpuss Grandma Osborne and her sweet, washout of a husband was similar to the impression his own father had of them. But his perspective differed. "They were a miserable lot," he conceded. "But they had something to be miserable about." Money was always an issue. They pawned his mother's engagement ring after she died and never redeemed it. "They were people who felt they'd seen better days and that the world owed them a living," he explained. But they were his surrogate parents, and he loved them. They were all he had, and in a crucial way, he was all they had. He was their meal ticket.

His absent father paid the Osborne grandparents to look after him. Porter was an only child of the 1930s like Osborne, but his childhood of abandonment took a different path. His mother would visit his father at work in West Africa for a year at a time, before her death from peritonitis when Tony was seven. His father came home to visit every two years. So he lived with his grandparents, who raised him, and he saw something of Thomas Godfrey during his weekly visits. In time, he went to a Welsh public school, his absent father paying the fees. During the war, he was evacuated to the Isle of Man for five years to live with an aunt he scarcely knew. He next went to Sandhurst, destined to become a professional soldier, but he too contracted TB and was invalided out. Eventually, he went to Leeds University to study sociology.

He called Thomas Godfrey "Uncle Goff", remembering him as a man who was always ill – a kindly figure from his childhood whom he glimpsed in his sickbed at the grandparents' house. Yet his home was only a short walk away. Why wasn't he there? It was further evidence, if any be needed, that his marriage to Nellie Beatrice was unhappy.

According to Porter, Thomas Godfrey was also a drinker who would disappear for days at a time. When reconciled with Nellie Beatrice, he avoided going home. Osborne explained that his father would sooner spend Friday evenings in the scullery with Grandma Osborne than face the black looks of his wife, or he'd linger over a glass of port at Grandma Grove's house and join the "Press Boys" in the Fleet Street pubs. "He would return home with comics for his son together with a peace-offering half-pound box of Terry's Brazil nut chocolates for the implacable Nellie Beatrice," Osborne wrote. "And after supper and doubtless full of Waterloo buffet whisky, Guinness or Moussec, he would sit at the upright piano and sing." There would be hymns and popular songs like "Red Sails in the Sunset", and a big repertoire of Music Hall favourites.

In the anarchy of Osborne's 1972 play *A Sense of Detachment*, there's an old man known as Father who returns from the dead like a ghost of the Thirties to entertain everyone on the piano. He's the Edwardian spirit of Thomas Godfrey.

Porter continued: "My father liked him. He said he was a nice, cultured man and he felt very sorry for him. He told me that he would have gone on the booze, too, if he'd been as ill as him. John's dad was a talented man who took refuge in drink and perhaps he was frustrated by old Nellie Beatrice. He had some good jobs as a commercial artist, but of course he lost a lot of them through ill health. My grandmother told me he created a very successful advertising campaign for Virol – stuff you push down kids' throats to make them fit. It was popular in the Thirties. John was used as the model for the sickly child who gets better."

Before my meeting with Tony Porter ended, he took out a family photograph – the only one I was to come across with Osborne and his father together. It was taken in the early Thirties, he said, and he believed his own father took the picture. The family are posing stiffly in the back garden of Grandma Osborne's home. It must have been a Sunday, when Thomas Godfrey always visited his mother. The group appears to be dressed in its formal Sunday best.

All faded photographs are melancholic, but this family portrait was a grim *memento mori* with one survivor, cousin Tony. The stiff, formal figures surrounding the frosty Osborne matriarch appear strangely tense. Porter looked at the picture over my shoulder, identifying each one. There he was. The sixteen-month-old miniature version of himself, a chubby little chap with neatly brushed hair and white socks and sandals, is seated in Grandma Osborne's polka-dot lap. She's holding him, sitting upright in a wicker chair at the centre of the picture – a grey and angular figure, stern and Victorian in her black choker.

"There's my grandfather Porter," he said, pointing to the image of the former professional rugby player. He's standing to the left of Grandma Osborne and no one in the group is animated except for this burly, pleasant-looking man in his tweedy three-piece suit. Standing to his right is Porter's attractive mother in her late twenties, who seems to be forcing a thin smile. She looks like a younger version of her mother, Grandma Osborne.

I easily recognized John Osborne, though he's about three years old. He's standing behind a toy terrier dog. "Sweet little boy," said Porter. Yes, but a serious one, too; soft in his pullover with his fair hair combed neatly for the occasion like his cousin's. He looks puzzled by something and even troubled as he peers out. Perhaps it's the camera.

Two more figures remained. "That must be his father, Thomas Godfrey," I said, and pointed to the man kneeling to the right of "the sweet little boy". I assumed the other figure was Grandfather Osborne.

But to my astonishment, it was the other way round. I had mistaken Osborne's ailing father for the grandfather. It still shocks me. Thomas Godfrey, then in his early thirties, looks like a grey old man. Grandpa Osborne looks younger than his own son, with his snappy, stiff white collar and silvery hair.

But there is the tragic reality of Osborne's father, wan in his round spectacles, his hair matted white, his whole demeanour tired, ill and defeated. He has a moustache. We can see the long fingers of a bony Shalimar hand leaning against the wicker chair. His pose is recessive. He's crouched in half-shadow just behind his boy, as if hiding in shadow, gravitating there.

6

The Naked Christ

Those hours after he died, when I was dragged back from the corpse, the hatred between us.

Osborne notebook entry, 1953

Osborne's lifelong lament for his father was for a man he never really knew.

Tuberculosis itself was viewed as a death sentence – in Kafka's chilling description, "the germ of death itself" (Kafka died of TB). In *Nicholas Nickleby*, Dickens described it as the "disease in which death and life are so strangely blended, that death takes the glow and hue of life, and life the grisly form of death . . ." Known as "the white plague", it was widespread in both England and America until a cure was found with streptomycin in 1944 and the introduction of isoniazid in 1952. TB was a contagious bacterial infection of the lungs – Osborne's father was left with one lung – passed on by close contact and tainted by a shameful social stigma. Though the rich died from TB, it was known as the disease of the poor. The causes were thought to be urban overcrowding, dank living conditions, poor food, bad hygiene, foul air. "No Spitting" signs in pubs and streets were a consequence of TB.

A leading American doctor, who caught it from a patient's cough, compared its stigma for me to the fear and superstition caused today by AIDS. You avoided people with TB. Its chronic symptoms were emaciation, fever, and the wracked coughing up of phlegm and blood. Blood on the handkerchief was the fate of Osborne's father. The "cure" was isolation from the community, restful mountain retreats, healthy diet, fresh air. Thomas Godfrey's Benevolent Society paid for his visits to various sanatoriums, and for some of his household bills, too. The word "sanatorium" implies "sanitize" – cleanse. But TB was incurable and survival was down to great luck.

As a child, Osborne knew of his father's agony. He saw him bedridden at home, and understood the pain he was in. He would wave his dad off sadly on his journeys to the sanatoriums and "exile". He was a witness to his convulsive dying. Yet the subject of TB is scarcely mentioned in his memoirs and nowhere at all in the notebooks.

Osborne never acknowledged the shadow that tuberculosis surely cast over his mother, who lost both her husband and daughter to TB and must have feared for the life of her only son. Nor did he confront the nature of the disease itself. He acknowledged only that his mother told him his father had "dry TB" not "wet TB" – "so Dad's germs did not buzz around in the air like filthy moths," he noted frivolously. "They stayed, presumably snugly, inside him in little sachets like dried cigarette tobacco, almost hygienic germs."

There would have been some consolation in his father's "dry TB". It meant that he couldn't infect other people. But how would wary strangers have known? And would they have trusted the diagnosis? Osborne's remark is consciously flippant with its passing reference to his father's "presumably snug" germs, and it was written in the context of Nellie Beatrice's obsession with hygiene – even with "almost hygienic germs".

"Even the doctor's tea cup was sterilised," he wrote. "His patients' germs must have been jumping like fleas from it. The sight of children sharing the same bottle of Tizer or, worse, milk, made her almost delirious. If ever afflicted by raging thirst I was driven to share a bottle, I was to wipe the top of it as vigorously as possible, but only if boiling water were unobtainable."

Nellie Beatrice's germ phobia continued after her husband died. But every schoolchild of the day was warned against sharing milk bottles. Her fear mirrored society's as a whole. Given the family history, her excessive concern grows wholly understandable.

When Thomas Godfrey died, however, she insisted their ten-year-old son go into his bedroom to view him in his coffin.

"The smell in the room was strong and strange," he remembered, "and in his shroud he was unrecognisable. As I looked down at him she said, 'Of course, this room's got to be fumigated, you know that, don't you? Fumigated.'" She pronounced it *frumigated*.

Her panicky insensitivity toward the traumatized boy is one thing. The drastic fumigation was a necessary humiliation – primitive as the aftermath of a TB death had always been. In her admired essay *Illness as Metaphor*, Susan Sontag compared it to cholera – pointing out that the common practice of burning the clothes of someone who died of TB was no different to the aftermath of a cholera death. (Sontag's father died of TB, but curiously she made no mention of it.) She went on to quote the description of the clean-up following the death of the consumptive Keats:

"'Those brutal Italians have nearly finished their monstrous business,' Keats's companion Joseph Severn wrote from Rome on March 6 1821, two weeks after Keats died in the little room on the Piazza di Spagna. 'They have burned all the furniture – and are now scraping the walls – making new windows – new doors – and even a new floor.' But people could believe that TB was inherited (think of the disease's recurrence in the families of Keats, the Brontës, Emerson, Thoreau, Trollope) and also believe that it revealed something singular about the person afflicted."

Osborne's father – the artistic father of a writer, after all – was at least in renowned company. The TB roll-call also includes Chekhov, Shelley, Poe, Simone Weil, Robert Louis Stevenson, Sterne, Beardsley, Eric Blair, Chopin, Thoreau, Watteau, Katharine Mansfield and D.H. Lawrence. Thomas Godfrey's "singularity" was in his stoic suffering.

Illness is what we know most about him; illness makes him "interesting". Osborne romanticized his adored sister who died in childhood, imagining her angelic protection had she lived. He idealized his dying father as his saviour-protector in the battles with his mother. The loving bond between father and son was locked in a time capsule. It was never tested by the passage of time, by rebellious adolescence or everyday contact. His father was the suffering artist manqué who was absent by choice as well as illness. He was the remote, saintly victim of ill-fate and a bad marriage. His son never knew him when he was carefree or fit or hopeful. There were reprieves, that's all.

"Identity: Identity of childhood often seems more defined than recent pleasure or grief," Osborne wrote in the 1980s like a man sifting through sand for a sign, some saving grace that something tangible came before. "A delusion perhaps, but an attempt to salvage some*thing* of the derelict past. So that I can say I *was* there. Instead of where am I now? Among ravages of present turmoil . . ."

He *was* there with his father, who took him for walks in Bishops Park and by the river, using his walking cane stylishly to hand on the funny Countryman Tramp's Walk taught to him by his own father. His dad took him on outings to the Victoria and Albert Museum and Lyons for tea, to the Zoo, St Paul's, Westminster Abbey and Hampton Court. ("I loved being out with him and holding his hand . . .") He made his boy laugh during a visit to the Tower of London, singing a Music Hall song of Stanley Holloway's about Anne Boleyn entitled "With 'er 'Ead Tucked Underneath 'er Arm". He took him to his favourite pubs – the Spotted Horse in Putney High Street, the King's Head in Fulham Palace Road – though it couldn't have been much fun for a boy of seven or eight moping about outside smoky rooms waiting for him to have his fill of Guinness.

And on Saturday nights, father and son would go eagerly together to the Shepherds Bush Empire, working-class mecca of Music Hall. There's a sense of occasion to those Saturday night treats – the absent father picking up his excited boy to take him to the packed theatre, which would lead in time to the invention of the desperate entertainer and symbol of declining England, Archie Rice. "Don't clap too hard," Archie warns us, "it's a very old building."

Osborne remembered his father solemnly teaching him the "Facts of Life". An accomplished draughtsman, he carefully drew male and female figures and began explaining the functions of them both. But to his amusement his squeamish son rushed out of the room to be sick before the lecture was half finished.

"What did you want to start telling him all that for?" Nellie Beatrice moaned. "You know what he's like."

Father, like son, had always wanted to become a writer. When Osborne spent his year in bed with rheumatic fever, he subscribed to a correspondence course conducted by the important-sounding British Institute of Fiction Writing Science. Its secret, apparently, was a belief in scientifically proven methods of fiction writing. He was then twelve years old. Not daring to send in his own efforts, he submitted two short stories by his father, who had died two years before. Was it an attempt to give them legitimacy – to prove that his father had talent? One story was about a small boy's obsession with a Great Western steam engine, and he immediately recognized that the other was about himself. It was entitled "Mouse Pie". "Eating mouse pie" is a folkloric Welsh cure for bed-wetting.

His father nicknamed him "Skipper". Osborne's childhood ambition of becoming a veterinary surgeon had been replaced for a while by the Royal Navy. When Thomas Godfrey was away ill in sanatoriums, he wrote him dozens of postcards with careful, elaborate drawings on one side, fancifully addressed to Captain John Osborne RNVR or Paramount Chief Big Feller Osborne. The cards, written neatly in green ink, were treasured. On one of them, his dad had drawn a skipper in a sou'wester and huge oilskins staring up at a giraffe who's saying: "Come up and see me sometime!"

Others were more like saucy Donald McGill postcards: "Dad's had his bum shot full of gold today so he's never been more valuable. The nurse is German and a proper Hun she is. Must be Mrs Hitler!"

He invented words for fun in a private language between them. He sent his boy a racy card from a sanatorium when Osborne was three years old and Nellie Beatrice must have read it to him: "Got up seven bells. Him feller doctor say the big black Irish bamboo in the next bed is to be shot full of gold! Gold! And they're sending me away! Hooray! See you Waterloo with Mum! Tell her will be wearing bathing costume and bowler hat!"

When Thomas Godfrey was thirty-eight, his advertising agency presented him with an imitation oak clock and twenty pounds, and retired him. He'd been too ill to work for six months. According to Osborne, he felt relieved. "We'll have a week at Margate," he announced, warning his son not to tell Grandma Osborne. "She wouldn't understand."

Reconciled with Nellie Beatrice, his father was game for a last hurrah. "It was the happiest week I can remember with my parents," Osborne wrote. "They were friendly to one another."

They stayed in digs by Margate station. "Morning breakfast was huge and delicious, the landlady as friendly as the best of barmaids, the weather was warm, even the sea. We spent half the day in Dreamland or on the beach, waded under the pier and went to nightclub-like entertainments in the evening, sitting at tables which seemed very grand and grown-up. When I first went to Las Vegas I immediately thought of those evenings in Margate with my parents, of fish and chips and Guinness. And the streams of girls. I had never seen a chorus line before. As they tapped and swung their legs they would sing 'Lullaby of Broadway' and 'Shuffle off to Buffalo', which seemed to be that year's most popular show numbers. I never tired of hearing them."

Strolling along the promenade under the coloured lights, they would look up enviously at the big hotels of Cliftonville and Thomas Godfrey might suggest going in for a drink. But his wife hurried on ahead. "This is where all the posh people stay," she would say. "You can't go in there."

"Rich Jews", Thomas Godfrey added, following on behind.

A few weeks later, they waved him off on his journey to the sanatorium in Menton. He returned home in early 1939 to sit around the house – "fully dressed, but always in his Sherlock Holmes-style dressing gown and large carpet slippers", Osborne remembered, "stroking the cat and reading".

By spring, he was mostly bedridden. By late September, the family was evacuated to Ventnor on the Isle of Wight, away from the London Blitz and where the sea air might help him. There was a sanatorium on the island.

His father was stretchered into a Daimler ambulance drawn up at the backyard. "It was enormous inside with great windows, and looked like a very comfortable hearse," his son wrote. "My mother and I went in afterward and sat down. It was thrilling . . ."

They stayed on the Isle of Wight in a small 1930s-ish house with the name "Mon Abri" (My Refuge). Osborne would later remark that it was a very poor refuge from death.

Its derelict garden faced the English Channel and he described the chill of the bleak, silent island enveloped in a black mist pierced by the whoops of destroyers, the flash of gunfire from the convoy attacks out at sea. "That unyieldingly icy mist must have bitten into my father's remaining lung immediately."

His school was a four-mile hike away in the winter cold. Indulged by his mother and his father's sympathetic doctor, he played truant, as was his custom. He was anxious to be with his father. He was also legitimately unwell for a while, feverish with a bad cough. "He's going to be just like his father," his mother told the school attendance officer.

Nellie Beatrice was unhappy on the island and who could blame her? She would sooner have risked the Blitz and had her own life back at the pub, instead of the bitter loneliness of this freezing "dead-and-alive-hole" and her dying husband.

Her son spent each day with his bedridden father. "We talked and read new books and books we knew already like Dickens, Maugham, Kipling, W.H. Davies, Rider Haggard, Stevenson, Burns, Arnold Bennett, and then he talked about Shaw, but I don't think we ever read any. He admired Lawrence of Arabia and J.B. Priestley, especially 'Angel Pavement', which he read three times . . ." Or the boy played war games alone in his own room with its maps of Europe and the Western Front dotted with swastikas, French flags and Union Jacks.

One day, he met lovely twenty-one-year-old Isabel walking her dog along the empty beach that stretched for miles, and fell in love for the first time since stuck-up twelve-year-old Joan from Stoneleigh. Isabel was engaged to a jolly sort named Raymond and they both took a shine to him. The three of them would set out for regular walks together over the cliffs where the loving couple had a kiss and a cuddle as he watched intently from a polite distance.

"The doctor's nice," he wrote to Mickey Wall. "But he says Dad should go into the sanatorium because it's too much for Mum to cope with. I think Dad wants to go but she says no. Not for Christmas anyway. I was scared stiff when the attendance officer came. He said I'd got to go to school sometime. It's miles to walk, not that I mind that but it's a rotten hole and I don't like to leave Dad on his own with no one to talk to. Even when he can't talk. Anyway, the doctor spoke to him and said my nerves weren't up to it for the moment and the inspector said we'd see what happened in the New Year."

Toward the end of November, an ambulance took his father on a stretcher to the big, shadowy Edwardian sanatorium on the island. Mother and son accompanied him, helping him into his wheelchair when they arrived. They saw grand verandahs facing the ocean where patients coughed in their iron beds overlooking the black mist.

"They wanted him in for Christmas, but I wouldn't have it," said the exhausted Nellie Beatrice after meeting the doctors.

They returned to their rented house where she told her disbelieving son that his father had six weeks left. "Six weeks to *live*, do you understand?"

"Will he be alive at Christmas?" he asked urgently, and fled to his room.

Osborne was determined to give him a nice Christmas present – "something to keep him going, even alive", he promised himself. His father told him there was a new series of books called Penguin and he'd like one.

He dashed out to buy him four from his savings – *Ariel*, the Shelley biography, *Death of a Hero* by Richard Aldington, *A Safety Match* by Ian Hay, and *Gone to Earth* by Mary Webb. He didn't live to read them.

His father's Christmas present to him was a *Boy's Own Annual* for 1940 inscribed: CHRISTMAS 1939. TO SKIPPER. LOVE DAD.

There was also a Hurricane glider and, best of all, a small model yacht. On the mast was a label with the words written on it: DON'T FORGET WHAT I TOLD YOU: THE ROYAL NAVY ALWAYS TRAVELS FIRST CLASS. IT'S THE ONLY WAY. LOVE, DAD.

He managed to come down from his bedroom for Christmas dinner. Osborne remembered the image of him as "thinner and paler than ever, with a heavy growth of beard, almost like a very frail prophet in his dressing gown". The dinner was a bleak affair. He could hardly eat anything at all. "Try and eat it up, Dad," said Nellie Beatrice sympathetically.

They listened to King George VI stammering bravely through his Christmas Day speech on the radio, and toasted him in Moussec – "the champagne of the poor", Thomas Godfrey always said.

"The King!"

"And beating the Germans!"

They toasted him sitting down, his father explaining that it was the traditional custom in the Royal Navy.

"Eating my own dinner eagerly," Osborne remembered, "I was suddenly overcome with a panic sense of loneliness that I felt had descended on me for good. Sitting between my father and mother I burst into tears . . ."

"What's he grizzling about?" his mother asked irritably.

"Leave him alone."

About two weeks after Christmas, his father went blind.

His son was reading in the kitchen when he heard his mother screaming from the bottom of the staircase. "I ran to see what was happening and stared up to the landing where my father was standing. He was completely naked with his silver hair and grey, black and red beard. He looked like a naked Christ."

He fell headlong down the stairs on top of them. And mother and son carried him back to his room.

He died soon afterward on 27 January 1940.

"Those hours after he died, when I was dragged back from the corpse, the hatred between us," Osborne recorded cryptically in his 1953 notebook.

According to Helen, he blamed his mother for not caring enough about him, for wanting it all over and done with. "His death was inevitable for her," she explained, "but not for him."

The hatred of his mother was sealed that day over the corpse. Osborne felt, in so many words, that she had killed his father.

The only letter from Thomas Godfrey that survives was written just five weeks before he died to Grandma Osborne from the Isle of Wight as Christmas approached.

Dec 21st, 1939

My dear old ma,

Very many sincere thanks for your characteristically affectionate and sympathetic letter; it was good to hear from you again old dear, as I have sorely missed the scandalous chats we used to have over a glass or two (or even more!) in the good old days of yore. Everything seems to have got very melancholy and cheerless for us all these last few years, doesn't it?

With all my love, and very best wishes.

Your affectionate son,

Geoff.

He added an afterthought in the spirit of his naughty seaside postcards:

PS. In case of any trouble with police for you over the holiday in the black-out, am sending nice clean pair of knickers as my little gift! Here's lookin'!

So Thomas Godfrey *was* fun – "Here's lookin'!" – or he was trying his best to be, when he wrote irreverently from his deathbed to tease his old battleaxe of a mother. He was sceptical by nature, but he seems a forgiving, kind-hearted man. He was making his peace with her, though she hadn't troubled to visit him during his last days. There's a jaunty Edwardian lilt to the brief farewell, and regret for the cheerless last years.

A note on the back of the letter is dated 1957: "Dolly, this last letter before he died. Bless him." Dolly was the family nickname for Nellie Beatrice; 1957 was the year Thomas Godfrey's mother died. So she had passed the letter on to Nellie Beatrice. The letter itself is quite fragile. It has been opened and folded many times, read and re-read obsessively over the years. It was never left forgotten in a dusty drawer. Perhaps it was Nellie Beatrice or Grandma Osborne who kept re-reading it. But neither of them grieved over Thomas Godfrey. It was his son. He was the one who cherished the letter, reading it again and again, salvaging the connection to his father's distant voice from memory's wreckage.

". . . have you ever watched somebody die?" Jimmy Porter asks Helena without warning in *Look Back in Anger*.

Helena is his wife's best friend and his future lover. He's goading her, sensing blood, putting her superior, refined, *coping* upper-class English manner to the test, as he always does with Alison, his reticent wife. Jimmy Porter goes in for special pleading, but his festering wounds have never healed.

JIMMY: I said: have you ever watched somebody die?

HELENA: No, I haven't.

JIMMY: Anyone who's never watched somebody die is suffering from a pretty bad case of virginity . . . For twelve months, I watched my father dying – when I was ten years old. He'd come back from the war in Spain, you see. And certain God-fearing gentlemen there had made such a mess of him, he didn't have long to live. Everyone knew it – even I knew it. But you see, I was the only one who cared . . . My mother looked after him without complaining, and that was about all. Perhaps she pitied him. I suppose she was capable of that. But *I* was the only one who cared! Every time I sat on the edge of his bed, to listen to him talking or reading to me, I had to fight back my tears. At the end of twelve months, I was a veteran. All that feverish failure of a man had to listen to him was a small, frightened boy. I spent hour upon hour in that tiny bedroom. He would talk to me for hours, pouring out all that was left of his life to one, lonely, bewildered little boy, who could barely understand half of what he said. All he could feel was the despair and bitterness, the sweet, sickly smell of a dying man. You see, I learnt at an early age what it was to be angry – angry and helpless. And I can never forget it. I knew more about love . . . betrayal . . . and death when I was ten years old than you will probably know all your life.

At ten, Osborne already knew the terror of death, and felt for the first time what he later called "the fatality of hatred". Even when life turned golden for him, the unbearable memories of those times long ago would return in the dread of each approaching New Year. Christmases would be plentiful as if by decree, but the feeling of abandonment would always permeate him in the angry injustice of betrayal and tears of bewilderment.

Osborne told his future wife, Helen, about the death of his father in the first months of their relationship, and significantly the date was a New Year, January 1977. They were at his Edenbridge home in Kent. He wanted to confide in her about his father and perhaps to warn her. He was telling her, in effect, "This is who I am."

He was then forty-eight and he cried when he told her. His emotions were always close to the surface, closer than anyone she had ever known. "He wasn't ashamed of emotion," she explained to me quietly. "Nor of his tears. He'd get upset and weep. He cried quite often – but then, there was the opposite of his laughter and pleasure in life. He would talk about how his enthusiasm for writing and reading came from his father, and how he loved him and relied on him. When he talked about his death, he remembered feeling a fantastic loneliness, and a fear of being alone that never left him. He was absolutely vivid about it. He gave me the strong impression of a small, very vulnerable, not very healthy child having to deal with something horrifying. He had no one to turn to. He couldn't understand that his mother wanted it all over. She wouldn't even talk to his father. She just left him there in his sickbed. Her irritation with him dying, the haste to get the coffin off the Isle of Wight. It would have been hard enough for anyone. It was a brutal thing for John."

Helen was left fearful when he first talked to her about his father. The past seemed just as real to him as the present. She found herself walking alone to gather her thoughts, to try to deal with his sadness calmly. She would do anything to help him. But she came to dread the times when he talked of his father's death. It signalled the spiral into despair beyond help.

"But I always knew he would come out of it eventually," she added, describing his return to "the shining world" of answered prayers. "So did John. He would say when he felt good again, 'It's so wonderful! It's *gone!*'"

7

Why Ozzy was Expelled from School

*Even then I had the notion that I could unerringly smoke out the
prigs, hedgers and dissemblers.*

Osborne on his school days

Osborne was sent at fourteen to Belmont College (now closed) in rural
Devon, his father's Benevolent Society paying the fees for a wartime bargain-
basement education in the summer of 1943. It was many rigorous middle-
class steps up from the cheerless local schools he'd known in London and
Stoneleigh. Even so, he described Belmont as suffocating in its "timid trappings of a fake public school for the minimum expense" – a miserable
destination for "a collection of washouts, staff and pupils alike".

Already affecting an actorish style from his early teens, he took an instant
dislike to the headmaster for his exaggerated upper-class accent. "Skol" for
school, "haice" for house "naice" for nice. ("What a naice haice!") He nicknamed Mr Heffer "The Prig Farmer", scoffing at his "braying, pedantic
vowels and dowdy, prissy appearance that sniggered rather than proclaimed
his calling". Yet the adolescent Osborne disguised his own cockney accent
at Belmont – feigning posh to camouflage his lower-class roots just as he
would adopt classless showbiz camp as his accent of choice when he became
an actor. He told everyone at school that his late father had been an "artist"
– a vague badge of honour, a neutralized heritage.

He seems to have been liked by his fellow students. "I remember you as
one of the more pleasant boys at school," Sheelagh Darling (née Glover)
wrote to him fondly forty years on. "There were some wretched little things
then. Your nickname was 'Ozzy' . . ."

"Ozzy" was often in trouble. "I was in his form and remember him well,"
a Sidney Hillman of Yelland, Nr Barnstaple, wrote to the *Sunday People* on
20 October 1957. "When we heard that Osborne had been concerned in
a flying fists incident we were not surprised."

He was caught drunk after reeling tipsily back to school from the town's station bar with a few other boys, singing as they went. He received nine strokes of the cane from Mr Heffer. He also earned the headmaster's displeasure by falling in love with his niece, Jenny, who attended Belmont Day School. A lifetime later, he remembered them both holding hands on chaste walks together along the shore at Instow where crafts were preparing for the Normandy landings. They wrote each other ardent letters, but Jenny's were discovered when he somehow managed to lose them in school. "They're love letters, sir," said the snitch to the reddening Mr Heffer. "From your Jenny." And so poor Jenny was packed off to another school before she could succumb to the disgraced J. Osborne's probing embraces.

The balm of boys seems not to have been widespread at Belmont. But girls were his fancy. "Imprisoned in this dream of girls and married women, of looking up skirts on tennis courts and lying beneath hedges," he recalled happily, "each new term brought its challenge, recharged, more urgent and impatient." He might score a Durex – he named it "the rubber badge of courage" – off a GI striding confidently through town like a friendly alien. He had to content himself with fantasizing about flighty, married Matron – "crisp and crackling in her white overall" – who was lusted after by almost the entire school. "Sex filled our days if not our nights," he wrote. "Even bovine Devon maids who waited on us in the dining room were coveted itchily under the tablecloth as they bent over us, revealing the elastic Plimsoll line of desire."

It wasn't all work, however. He was a soloist in the school choir ("Old Man River", "The Lord High Executioner"), he acted in school entertainments and sketches, he played school cricket quite stylishly, he even boxed for the school, and he won a literature prize.

"English – excellent," went an early report with the headmaster's initially enthusiastic endorsement: "Progressing rapidly. His application is highly commendable."

"English – excellent", his report for 1944 acknowledged again, but the headmaster was beginning to have Room For Improvement doubts. "He must work more steadily," he commented tersely, as headmasters do.

"Literature: promises well," went the last report. "Maths: not his strong subject and is inclined on that account to think it does not matter." But the headmaster's concluding remark was now expressed in the traditional teacher's argot designed to breed resentment for life. "Although he worked well, in all other things he has disappointed."

Osborne would soon be expelled from school for hitting the headmaster. We must first consider, however, how he came to box with surprising effectiveness on the school team, scoring a technical knockout over K. Reynolds. The classic straight left of the English gentleman boxer had been taught to him by Grandpa Osborne, who also gave him lessons in socialism. "A socialist," Grandpa advised gravely, "is a man who never raises his cap to anyone." He took it to heart.

Considering his poor health as a child, however, he was an unlikely boxer. He was squeamish about blood – possessing, he confessed, "a spinsterly sense of survival". But when threatened by school bullies, he instinctively retaliated – pitching in against overwhelming odds. In that pugnacious sense, Osborne never changed. His best form of defence was invariably attack, the pre-emptive strike (or flight).

He applied his quixotic boxing tactic to the theatre, and invited punishment. "If somebody doesn't walk out," he wrote about his plays in an unusual 1975 programme note, "I always think I must be losing my touch." He boasted that he was the only dramatist ever to have been pursued by a mob, or to be booed in Brighton on a Thursday matinée attended by five old ladies and a dog when even the dog howled. In the goading, sometimes pornographic *A Sense of Detachment* he even invented a character to heckle his own play. "Load of rubbish!" yells the heckler from a box. "Get it off!"

The slamming of upturned seats was music to Osborne's ears. Or so he wanted us to believe. His bravado disguised his thin skin: he was ultra-sensitive to criticism. At the same time, he relished a theatre of uproar and audience provocation – anything but the weary weight of the polite response – as a boxer lurching headlong into the action hopes for a sensational knockout.

He didn't floor the headmaster with Grandpa Osborne's gentlemanly straight left, however. The damage was done, according to Osborne, by a reflexive haymaker of a right hook into Mr Heffer's moustache that sent him flying over the cocoa urn in the school canteen.

But a decade later – when Osborne had become a precociously famous dramatist on both sides of the Atlantic – a dispute arose with the school authorities over how, and where, the blow actually happened.

The *Sunday Express* informed the nation on 4 October 1957, the reason why the new headmaster of Belmont College, a Major A.J. (Paddy) Reynolds, was breaking his long silence on the sensitive matter. "It's because of those disgraceful things he's been saying about the Queen," the indignant Major told the *Express* reporter before going on to describe what really took place that fateful day:

"It was in the second year that the trouble started. Osborne got three other boys of his own age under his influence and started a reign of terror

through the school. Mr Heffer found it almost impossible to control him."
The Major then went on to testify how Osborne had blundered into the
headmaster with several bottles of cider in his pockets and refused to hand
them over. He was therefore called up in front of the entire school at
morning assembly the next day. "He came forward and Mr Heffer asked
him a question. He gave a most insolent answer. Mr Heffer slapped him
across the face. Osborne immediately struck him back – to the confusion
of everyone in the place."

Defending his sullied reputation from glittering Broadway, where his wife,
Mary Ure, was starring in *Look Back in Anger*, Osborne stood 150 per cent
behind his story. Interviewed in New York, he insisted that the incident
hadn't taken place during morning assembly at all, but in the canteen when
he was innocently sipping evening cocoa. According to his steadfast version,
a few other boys had gathered round the radio with him and were listening
to Frank Sinatra by the cocoa urn when the headmaster suddenly blundered in furiously. "He strode over to the wireless and turned it off, looking
round, defying a response," Osborne clearly recalled. "Seeing my upturned,
smirking scorn he lunged forward and slapped me very hard across the face."

It was then that he instinctively retaliated with the deadly right hook
to the moustache. "Slowly, dripping blood and cocoa," Osborne went on,
"he rose to his feet, to my infuriated dismay, helped by several boys. He
swayed and quivered. 'Go to the sanatorium . . .'"

And there we have it. But whichever version we accept, one thing is
beyond all conceivable doubt. Osborne decked the headmaster. Thus his
schooldays ended ignominiously soon after VE Day in the summer of 1945.

When he hit poor Mr Heffer the fifteen-year-old Osborne fulfilled the
fantasy of every cowering schoolboy who's ever been humiliated by untouchable authority. But my strongest hunch is that the turning point for him
wasn't being expelled from school. It was being treated with condescending
indifference when he asked Heffer if there might be a chance of his getting
a place at Oxford.

He had even toyed with the idea of becoming a historian. His formal
education, such as it was, had been characterized by absenteeism and illness.
(Even his first term at Belmont was spent alone in the sanatorium with
measles.) But Osborne the schoolboy rebel was secretly a conscientious
student. He had taken six General School Certificates at Belmont and
passed them all. He was bright enough to go on to university, and he was
ambitious. But the headmaster only looked amused at his Oxford hopes,
wincing at his presumption. Osborne noted curtly that Heffer advised him

that, with his enthusiasm for English and his father's background, a career in journalism was more practical.

England's post-war temples of privilege were as closed to him as a fortress nailed with the warning KEEP OUT. Educated at Belmont on charity, he was eligible for third class only, never first. ("First class all the way, Skipper!" his father always advised.) Schooled in the discipline of disappointed expectations, he should have known that his Oxford ambitions were considered laughable – worth a snigger from the shop-soiled elites of the minor public *skol*. It would take *Look Back in Anger* to declare open warfare on the divine rights of the conning chinless wonders of England's self-perpetuating Establishment.

In his major 1964 play, *Inadmissible Evidence*, the anti-hero, Bill Maitland, is a forty-year-old lawyer who's cracking up and put on trial for his life before a judge:

> BILL: No, but I never seriously thought of myself as being brilliant enough to sit in that company, with those men, among any of them with their fresh complexions from their playing fields and all that, with their ringing, effortless voice production and their quiet chambers, and tailors and mess bills and Oxford colleges and going to the opera God knows where and the 400, whatever I used to think that was. I have always been tolerably bright.
>
> JUDGE: Always been?
>
> BILL: Bright. Only tolerably bright, my lord. But to start with, and potentially, and finally, that is to say, irredeemably mediocre. Even at fifteen, when I started out in my profession.

8

The First Father Figure

I have thought of you consistently for over forty years now. You were
the first person who ever offered me friendship or affection.
                    Osborne letter to his former editor, Arnold Running,
                                                    6 February 1992

Osborne became a man in search of fathers, and the loss of his own led
to protective surrogates who understood him and were steadfast in their
affection.

His most important father figure in adulthood was George Devine, artistic
director of the Royal Court, who discovered him and became his mentor.
The puritan, Oxford-educated Devine was patriarchal by nature, a school-
masterly figure who was forty-three when the twenty-six-year-old Osborne
met him, though he looked older. "If I didn't have white hair and smoke
a pipe, nobody would pay any attention to me," he liked to say. On the
other hand, that porcelain beauty Vivien Leigh once chided him: "I was
always very fond of you, George. But I could never stand that fucking awful
pipe. If you'd been married to me, you would have had to smoke it outside
in the garden!"

Devine died of a heart attack at fifty-three. As we've seen, Osborne
sometimes recorded in his journals on the anniversary of his father's death:
"My father died today." The only other comparable entry is, "George died
today."

A father figure he would have liked to have had was Laurence Olivier.
But Osborne was too in awe of him, and Olivier was too emotionally remote.
Olivier had other roles to play. A better candidate was that cuddly English
eccentric John Betjeman, then the Poet Laureate. They became good friends
not least because of Betjeman's romantic love of a vanishing England. They
sang Music Hall favourites round the piano together – as the young Osborne
had done in childhood with his father.

But he would remember his first surrogate father with touching gratitude all his life. Arnold Running was a Canadian journalist living in London who edited a Fleet Street trade journal called *The Miller* when the teenage Osborne became his subversively idle assistant. Running was twenty-nine – too young to be cast in the role of father figure, perhaps, but not to the needy adolescent he took under his wing. "He was extremely handsome, I thought," Osborne wrote about meeting him for the first time. "A little like an American footballer version of my father."

Before Osborne fled reality for a life in the theatre, he became that despised thing, the object of his own derisive furies, a journalist. The fifteen-year-old Osborne left school and became an intrepid reporter for a trade journal named *Gas World*.

It wasn't quite so exciting as it may seem. His father's charitable association – "Dad's Society", he called it – had come to the rescue again and arranged the job at Benn Brothers, which ran several trade journals from the fringes of Fleet Street. Glanville Benn, known benevolently as "Mr Glanville", was the chairman of the Society as well as chairman of Benn Brothers whose drab inferiority, Osborne claimed, set it apart from the big boys on Fleet Street and reminded him uncharitably of cut-rate Belmont College. "Mr Glanville" and his brother Sir John – known as "Mr John" – were the sons of the conservative Sir Ernest Benn whose brother Wedgwood Benn, later Lord Stansgate, was the father of socialist Tony Benn. Osborne the novice reporter began work for the meticulous Mr Silcox, editor-in-chief of *Gas World*, who proudly displayed PRESS on the windscreen of his baby Austin.

Osborne had dutifully learned shorthand and typing at Clark's College in London before joining the firm. Occasionally, over many years, he was still scribbling brief notes to himself in shorthand; his plays were always handwritten in Reporters' notebooks.

Among his duties at *Gas World*, he wrote the copy for a column entitled "Round the Showrooms". His first byline was "Onlooker". In his 1980s draft manuscript for a second autobiographical film that was never made, there's a scene that involves a reproduction of one of his "Round the Showrooms with Onlooker" columns. In the 1940s, they used to display desirable new gas fittings in the plush foyers of Odeon cinemas. The story – in effect, the first professional writing of Osborne's career – reads:

"Choice of the week. Seen here – the foyer of the Odeon Cinema, Loughborough, with manager Mr J.R. Shanks beside the imaginative display of latest gas industry innovations. Why not contact the manager of your local Odeon? ONLOOKER."

Forty years on, he was sending jokey postcards to friends signed, "John Osborne, Deputy Ed. Gas World". He didn't actually reach those heights, but went on to work instead for Arnold Running at *The Miller*, another Benn Brothers publication, which published learned technical and historical articles about the milling process and windmills. He asked to work for him. The Canadian with the long hair was different from the rest. He was the only management figure who ate in the canteen.

Arnold Running was almost eighty when I met him at his home in Brampton just outside Toronto, and still a fine-looking man with his full head of hair and grey beard hinting at the bohemian. He looked alert and welcoming, peering at me with his glasses perched on the end of his nose. His wife, Pamela, formerly one of the leading breeders of wire-haired fox terriers in Canada, came bustling into the sitting room with coffee and cakes. They had been married for fifty-six years and when they told me, they laughed at the wonder of it.

"We can't remember something that happened five minutes ago. But fifty years ago is no problem," Mrs Running announced cheerfully.

They both knew the seventeen-year-old John Osborne. What was he like, I asked eagerly. Mrs Running jumped in. "He was very slim and tall and had spots all over his face. Terrible complexion! Well, he did, Arnold."

"He was an awkward teenager when he came to work for me," Arnold Running explained amiably. "And I liked him from the start. He resented the Benn Brothers connection with his father's charitable association. He proudly didn't want to be beholden to anybody, no doubt about it. He used to carry the *Daily Worker* with him everywhere just to irritate everyone."

In those days, he explained, management went to the office wearing bowler hats. "But John made out he was a socialist! I never saw him even read the *Daily Worker*. I didn't see him *open* it. He also had a very lah-di-dah accent, which I used to tease him about. He'd put on this godawful accent. He wanted to impress people, I suppose. But he was as smart as a whip. He was always scribbling down thoughts and words into little notebooks. We had this giant encyclopaedic dictionary in the office and when John came into work, he would spend an hour copying dozens of words out of it and take them home to learn. He did it every day. I used to say to him, 'I don't even know what they mean.' But he loved the big words, and he learnt how to use them."

The notebooks from Osborne's days at Benn Brothers no longer exist, but the lists keep recurring throughout his life. When he became a mature wordsmith, he exercised his muscle by copying out words from solid dictionaries as a pianist ritualistically practises his scales. In earlier years, he was literally learning the English language. In a small 1952 notebook, for example, he had copied the words that appealed to him from A–Z, sometimes noting their meaning. You can sense him rolling them round his tongue pleasurably, an apprentice connoisseur:

"Acolyte, addled, alchemy, blancmange, bumbling, burgeon, bollocks, clammy, coverture, cluster, conk, confluence, daffy, diddle, dropsical, encyclical, eviscerate, galumanfry, grail, huckster, impeachment, ingle-nook, jerk, knoll, liturgy, libation, neophyte, nibble, nobble, overlords, pasquinade (satirical writing), pimp, poleaxed, quiddify, roystering, ram, sophistry (fallacious reasoning), servitude, squirrel, skulk, tumid, umbilical, vomit, windbag, yaw (deviate)."

He yawed from working on his weekly windmill articles to write short stories at his desk and wrestle his boss's flighty secretary, Josie, to the floor in her short green skirt. Work wasn't demanding at *The Miller*, and Arnold Running indulged his protegé, encouraging him to try his luck at writing a novel – as Running himself was – and lending him his favourite books, almost all of them American (Melville, Hawthorne, Hemingway, Thomas Wolfe, Eugene O'Neill, John Dos Passos). The Runnings made him welcome in their home off the King's Road, Chelsea, and he continued seeing them when he left Benn Brothers after a year to become an impoverished actor.

"Well, he needed the meals," explained Mr Running, showing me a poem the nineteen-year-old Osborne had read to him all those years ago over dinner. Dated spring 1949, the early poem is untitled, but dedicated solemnly, "To my fellow artist."

He laughed to himself. "I was no artist! But he was sentimental, you see. Can you understand it?"

I couldn't. Neither of us could.

> We are plain men, you and I
> except at our fingers' patient
> pacing is our vagitus always

I fell at the first verse over the word "vagitus". And none of my dictionaries even list the word. I took to searching for it in the dictionaries of friends, but without success. Yet I felt certain that this student of words wouldn't have invented "vagitus" or made a mistake. Then I found its meaning at last in Sir William Smith's *A Smaller Latin–English Dictionary* (Third Edition, London: John Murray, 1933): *Vagitus*, us. m (vagio), a *crying, squalling* of children. Also *vagor*, the *cry* or *wail* of an infant; *vagio* of children, to *cry, squall*.

So the poem, dense, romantic, over-written, speaks of men who are "plain" and simple ("you and I") except in their writing ("fingers patient pacing") that cries out like children ("our vagitus always"). It goes on earnestly, "We are the men in possession of the soul's home . . ." The poem is the teenage Osborne's self-conscious acknowledgement of one struggling artist to another.

I learned a number of important things about him from the Runnings. He was starved for affection and encouragement. He was quick to resent even implied criticism, but could be just as angered by flattery. He was invariably generous – buying gifts for all, particularly at Christmas. (Perfume for Pam, whisky for Arnold.) "He'd spend all his birthday money on everyone else," Running said. "And have damn all left." He was possessive. "He looked on Arnold as a father figure and he seemed to resent me being there sometimes," Mrs Running pointed out. "He made me laugh, but I think he could get jealous of me. He was very insecure."

Perhaps none of us ever changes in the essentials, but in these aspects the young Osborne they knew differs little from the adult he became. He was later possessive with George Devine and Olivier; so, too, with the director who became his brother figure, Tony Richardson, when Richardson married Vanessa Redgrave. He was always generous with gifts and hospitality, as well as offers of financial help, even to strangers. He remained thin-skinned and easily wounded, lashing out at criticism. He would say of a wife, and even his daughter, that they were "cold" and the relationship would be over.

I learnt, too, that he always carried with him the postcards his father wrote to him a few months before he died. "After we'd been working together for a while, he'd take out these cards and read them from time to time," Mr Running told me. "He wouldn't let me read them. But he'd say, 'They're from my father.' I knew he was obsessed with him. He carried them with him in the inside pocket of his jacket, and got quite teary-eyed whenever he talked about him. The cards were written to him when his father was in the sanatorium in France. He just worshipped him. He felt that his mother ignored him and wrote him off, and that his dad was painfully lonely. John put on a rough exterior, pretending he had no use for anybody. But he loved people. He loved his father."

He kept the postcards, talismans of his dying father's love, until his early thirties when they became a casualty of the marital wars with Mary Ure, who refused to return them.

The father had a drink problem, Mr Running confirmed. He didn't hear it from Osborne, but from the chairman of the company, Glanville Benn, who knew the family history from the firm's charitable association. The sick, beloved father was a drinker, taking solace in the pub with his Fleet Street cronies, or in lonely obliteration.

And Nellie Beatrice? "He ran his mother down all the time," he said.

"I used to say, 'John, you don't *hate* your mother.' And he'd say, 'I do hate her.' He remembered her black looks and snide remarks more than any encouragement. He told me she poked fun at him in front of friends and strangers. He was convinced she'd treated his father badly. But when I met her, she seemed a nice enough old girl and I liked the woman even if she didn't talk too brightly."

He was the go-between for mother and son when Osborne decided to work in the theatre and enlisted his support. Always in Osborne's corner, Arnold Running was all in favour of his new career. "You're too full of highbrow horse shit for Fleet Street. You better get rid of it someplace else," he told him. But Nellie Beatrice was opposed. ("I never did stand in John's way," she told the press proudly in the 1960s.) "She thought the theatre wasn't a respectable profession and he'd starve to death," he explained. "She was very distressed about John leaving us."

He charmed her by promising that if it didn't pan out for her boy, he could always come back to work at Benn Brothers. According to Osborne, a sly appeal to her vanity won the day. "Well, you see, Mrs Osborne, the little bastard's a kind of genius in my humble opinion."

"Oh," Nellie Beatrice simpered. "Daddy would have liked to have heard you say that, Mr Running."

Why did he need his mother's blessing in the first place? Why didn't he just pack up and leave? However much he loathed his mother, he always needed her approval in the unwinnable lifelong war between them.

We talked about the Osborne they knew for the rest of that pleasant day in Brampton, and they enjoyed remembering him. They had known him from his Benn Bros days until the Royal Court premiere of *Look Back in Anger* in May 1956. Two weeks after the play opened, they returned to live in Canada. The move had been planned for some time. "He couldn't understand how anyone could leave England," Mr Running pointed out.

He remembered sitting behind Osborne during the play. "At the intermission he came rushing out wanting to know what I thought about it! I felt proud to know him."

It wasn't for everyone, though. "I couldn't relate to it," Mrs Running confessed. "It seemed rather sordid to me. When I go to the theatre I like to be uplifted."

74

Arnold disagreed. "It just held me spellbound," he said. "The intensity of the language, for one thing. I don't think too many people can dispute the fact that he was a brilliant bloody writer. I've always thought he was the greatest dramatist of the century. You might say, 'That's a bit strong.' But that's what I think."

The last time they saw Osborne was in New York for the US premiere of *Look Back* in October 1957. He was now a famous man, acclaimed as the dramatist who changed the history of British theatre, and celebrated on both sides of the Atlantic. Mary Ure was starring in the play on Broadway, and she joined them for lunch.

"I don't think she said more than ten words the entire meal," he remembered. "Do you know what John said to me afterwards? 'Never marry an actress!'"

He married three actresses, of course. As the playwright-hero of Tom Stoppard's *The Real Thing* puts it, "To marry one actress is unfortunate, to marry two is simply asking for it." And three? Very, *very* careless.

"She was beautiful, though," Mrs Running added.

"I couldn't see it. She had a moustache."

"She *didn't*, Arnold."

He recalled a walk with Osborne in Central Park. "He talked about writing *The Entertainer* for Laurence Oliver. And he told me how much money he was making. And he couldn't believe it and I couldn't believe it. He was looking after his mother, too. He was paying her a salary! He also wanted to know if I was all right financially. I said, 'I'm doing fine, John.'"

Osborne subsequently sent him the published editions of his plays, and they corresponded for a while:

18 December 1957

My dear Arnold,
So glad to hear you and Pam are still all right in that horrible provincial hole you live in with all those bloody dogs . . .

8 October 1959

My Mum is alright, thank you very much. She is still as dotty as ever, but money in the bank seems to agree with her, and I have bought her a dog which has taken her off my back to an unbelievable extent . . .

We are having a General Election today, and once again I'm going off to vote for Labour. The Tories are almost certain to win. Emigration anyone?

Before long, they lost touch. But towards the end of Osborne's life, the correspondence began again with an exchange of photographs. Osborne sent his books and plays too, with photos of Helen ("The Warrior Wife") and pictures of the Shropshire house, labradors romping in the grounds. "Why don't you come over here and get some CULTURE?" he wrote on a breezy postcard of a 1940s chorus girl signed "Deputy Ed. Gas World".

6 February 1992

Dear Arnold,

. . . I have thought of you consistently for over forty years now. You were the first person who ever offered me friendship or affection. Apart from that you were always a delightful companion. I am hideously in debt to the Internal Revenue, but if I should make any money this year, I shall send you the fare to come over and have a holiday. I'm sure you wouldn't refuse. I owe it to you.

Apart from that, we live in a vast (to me) Regency House (30 odd rooms) in 30 acres right on the Welsh border. It's what I always wanted.

My dear Arnold, I am so gratified, relieved and exhilarated by your letter. Please let me know when you get the book.

As ever,

Your one time teenage friend.

Love, John.

But then his letters took an increasingly disturbing turn:

30 June 1992

Dear Arnold,

. . . I'm afraid this is just a scribble as I'm recovering from a nightmarish few weeks/months/3 years of getting my new play on. [His last play, *Déjàvu*.] I certainly do attract concerted malignity. I thought it might have abated after nearly 40 years, but no . . . Usual feeling of utter degradation and squalor . . . *Why* did I become a writer? It seems to bring little pleasure to others, and to me, mostly hatred and notoriety.

2 June 1993

The last few weeks have been horrendous, possibly the worst – well, almost of my life. I've been too dispirited to write even a postcard to my friends. In the happy phrase here: "I can't write fuck on a shutter." I seem to have a complete failure of nerve. I can't put a decent sentence together, let alone attempt a book or play. At present I'm supposed

to be writing a film for the tercentenary of Henry Purcell, a personal
hero, but I've no idea how to put it together. I need the money
desperately . . . What fugitive reputation I have left is about to go up
in very public smoke.

26 June 1993

Frankly, if it weren't for Helen, I would have long ago taken a weekend
in Brighton, dined off a bottle of Roederer Cristal Brut and a Pichon de
Longueville '76, some malt whisky, and jabbed myself several times with
several hundred units of insulin and walked off the pier into the Sea.

9

The Apprentice Actor in Search of a Home

Own wardrobe and dinner jacket. Start immediately.
No fancy salaries and no queer folk.
1940s advert in *The Stage* offering actors work

The theatre became home and sanctuary to Osborne when he fled his mother. A world of make-believe was his refuge from nagging reality, an actor's life for him the beginning of his own re-invention of himself.

We've seen how he adopted a spindly theatrical air from his early teens, fancying himself as a bohemian outsider in the romanticized, dandyish image of his father. His love of the intoxicating possibilities of theatre was first ignited by those stage warriors in nonconformism, the great Music Hall artists who mesmerized him as a child. He had performed in school entertainments and written short stories from the age of twelve. He was still writing fiction and poetry during his time at Benn Bros, sneaking off to the West End theatre during the day. The image of this apprentice writer hunched over the fat office dictionary suggests that he might have become a novelist. As a teenager, he fantasized mistily about leading the solid literary life of a successful novelist (with devoted family and dogs). Yet the catalyst to his flight into theatre happened in an unlikely way.

When he was eighteen and living with his mother in surly, bookish isolation in Stoneleigh, Nellie Beatrice encouraged him to venture out to Saturday night dances in North Cheam. The word "teenager" didn't yet exist in 1940s England, but we can easily picture him alone and awkward at the dance, hoping to get lucky in his best suit. He was lanky and uncomfortable in his own skin, yet he felt morosely superior to the indifferent local girls across the empty dance floor during the ritual stand-off between opposing armies in the night. Easily discouraged, however, he would slope off after one hasty beer, too timid to approach anyone. He couldn't even dance.

He joined a local dancing school advertised in a shop window framed with lace curtains. Its name was a mouthful: The Gaycroft School of Music, Dancing (Classical, Exhibition and Modern Ballroom), Speech, Elocution and Drama. The first Angry Young Man at the dawn of the age of rock 'n roll was schooled, it turns out, in the sequinned *Come Dancing* arts of the paso doble, the samba and the ever-popular quickstep. After a few lessons, he found that his confidence increased with every slow-slow, quick-quick, slow. There were also fetid foxtrots with his heavy-breathing dance teacher, Betty, the married daughter of the Gaycroft School proprietor, Mrs Elizabeth Garrett, who took as much of a shine to him as her Betty. It was Mrs Garrett who encouraged him to become an actor.

There was also another important turning point when the impulsive Osborne found himself engaged to be married to one of his dance partners. Renee Shippard of the Halifax Building Society was among the few pupils at the school who were his age. He remembered first noticing her smiling at him bashfully as they both awaited the 8:17 train into the City at Stoneleigh Station. They met at the dance class.

"Sex itself was the most unobtainable luxury in the winter of our post-war austerity," he wrote of his exasperatedly chaste youth, describing how he and Renee eagerly settled for "snatched pelvic felicities during the Quickstep" and what he later came to appreciate as "The Dry Fuck On The Floor". Before long, they were seeing each other almost every evening, if only for a kiss goodnight on her doorstep as Mrs Shippard advised them coyly, "Now, now. You don't want to get tired of each other too soon, do you?"

Led by the nose by girlish Mrs Shippard, he bought Renee an engagement ring from Bravington's in the Strand, where he noticed that Jill Bennett, who would be his fourth wife, was then making her theatre debut in a William Douglas-Home drama in the West End. He borrowed the £12 from his mother for the cheap diamond ring, known in the trade as an "illusion setting".

What was he thinking? What was she? He was the marrying kind even then, it seems. Yet the two of them had little or nothing in common save for their frustrated, fumbling desire. Osborne had been excused the compulsory two-year national service in the army – the examining medical officer reeling at his history of poor health. He was free to go his own way, yet here he was, tying himself giddily to marriage and a nine-to-five job in suburban bliss as his future bride went window-shopping with her mother for three-piece suites in the High Street. He had no real prospects. He was earning £4 a week at Benn Bros. He had just turned eighteen.

"I had not dissembled my doggy, lecherous, sentimental feeling for Renee," he offered in lame explanation of the engagement. "But I knew also that it was fired by a wholly selfish desire for flattery and comfort."

It was more than that. Throughout his unruly life, Osborne could seem like an orphan in search of a home in a secret pact with the conventional. The nonconformist was drawn to shelter, constancy – until the wrecker's ball. He needed comforting stability, yet he detonated it. In his life and plays, the roof is always falling in – or worse, it's about to. There's a sense of imminent collapse, as if he courted it.

> GEORGE: Look at that wedding group! Look at it! It's like a million other grisly groups – all tainted in unbelievable pastels: round-shouldered girls with crinkled-up hair, open mouths, and bad teeth. The bride-groom looks as gormless as he's feeling lecherous, and the bride – the bride's looking as though she's just been thrown out of an orgy at a Druids' reunion! Mr and Mrs Elliott at their wedding. It stands there like a comic monument to the macabre farce that has gone on between them in this house ever since that greatest day in a girl's life thirty-five years ago.

> *Epitaph for George Dillon*, 1955

Meanwhile, clamped to thrusting Betty during another sweaty samba lesson at the dance school, his thoughts turned to acting. Encouraged by one of the older dance pupils, he joined an amateur dramatic society in Leatherhead, directed by a merry-sounding lady named Terry Tapper. He even persuaded its obliging members into producing Noel Coward's frothy *Blithe Spirit* instead of the gloomy symbolic drama they were rehearsing at the time, one of J.B. Priestley's metaphysical "time plays" entitled *I Have Been Here Before*. Though the amateur Coward production was abandoned after a few weeks' muddled rehearsal, he claimed that he impressed everyone by giving an astonishing reproduction of Rex Harrison's performance in the film version of *Blithe Spirit*, which he'd seen about half a dozen times.

His Rex Harrison impersonation was admired as "professional". Renee's mother had even gushed that he looked and sounded exactly like him, which he was almost willing to believe. Suave, elegant, sophisticated "Sexy Rexy", last of the gentleman actors, would have been a perfect new persona for the lower middle-class Osborne. Rex Harrison was so effortlessly supe-rior, it was said that whenever he exited the stage he looked as if he were about to leave a tip for the rest of the cast.

Flattery encouraged Osborne into believing he could become an actor. When Mrs Garrett told him that he looked like Leslie Howard and should go into films, he believed her. The young Osborne did bear a resemblance to him. But he would have preferred to be Rex Harrison. So would Leslie Howard. It was enough encouragement, however, for Osborne to have his photograph specially taken by a High Street wedding photographer and sent out to various agents. His photos were even mounted and displayed in the Gaycroft School window behind the limp lace curtains – an advertisement for himself, a suave invitation to the dance.

The breakthrough came soon afterwards when he went for an interview with a campy theatre producer called Mr Michael Hamilton, who was busy moving into a block of Edwardian flats near Harrods.

"Mr Hamilton?" Osborne enquired, shifting uneasily as the removal men bustled in with the antique furniture.

"This is she," he replied.

Michael Hamilton of Barry O'Brien Management was the first man he'd ever met who was openly camp. "Camp was then something ineffably mysterious or misunderstood," Osborne wrote, "a source of incomprehension and derision to most of the British Public who thought it was merely a synonym for homosexual behaviour, effeminacy, decadence or drag." But the impressionable teenager believed it would announce his contempt for dull conformism and might even give him "an aura of poetic authority". He saw in its nonconformist style the transformation of his tepid personality.

Osborne's showbiz camp, like his accent and taste, was carefully acquired. He was self-educated and he was self-invented. He had changed his cockney accent at boarding school in order to belong to the solid middle class. But showbiz camp transcends all the pigeonholing and snobbery of the system. It exists in a class of its own that can't be categorized. Laurence Olivier, the son of a clergyman, was deliberately campy with his effusive "dear hearts" and "darlings" and lordly low humour. He used it as a form of greenroom freemasonry. Robert Stephens, the son of a shipyard labourer (and a friend of Osborne's), was so extravagantly affectionate that he was described as "the original liposuction". He used camp for the fun of it. But where could we place Lord Olivier and Sir Robert Stephens, or a thousand other actors, in the unwritten hierarchies of birth?

At worst, showbiz camp breeds a mincingly exaggerated luvviedom for queenie crimpers, effeminate dressers to the stars and high-camp entertainers. At best, it's a classless neutrality of style. Showbiz camp makes it impossible for others to know exactly who you are. It functions as a covert leg-up the social ladder by suggesting the style of the sophisticated upper class, while glamour and success provide the sheen of a showbiz aristocracy.

Charles Wood, a long-time friend of Osborne's – and the writer of such well-regarded plays as *Veterans* and the Falklands War TV drama, *Tumbledown* – offers a fascinating insight into the invention of the "showbiz class". Wood, who was approaching seventy years old when we met, grew up in the tattier provincial rep theatres in which all his family worked. "My parents were working class," he explained, "and my mother was on the stage as soon as she could walk. She had no education whatsoever. But ask her to speak posh and pretend to be upper class onstage – and by God, she could do it! I'm sure John and all the others got their accent from the upper-class roles they played. It all developed through impersonating toffs onstage."

All kinds of people re-invent themselves – but only the actor re-invents himself nightly. And actors have always migrated socially, like upwardly mobile Shakespeare, travelling from vagabond actor and apprentice playwright to English Gentleman with his own coat of arms and one of the grandest houses in Stratford. Noel Coward's silk dressing-gown image of a born uppercrust dilettante drenched in martinis was a wonderfully *soigné* sham. (He was the son of a Teddington piano salesman.) So Osborne's light showbiz camp and carefully cultivated Savile Row elegance would always camouflage his own lower-class roots.

The outcome of the meeting with his new hero, Mr Hamilton of Barry O'Brien Management, was that he was hired for £7 a week as an assistant stage manager on what was then called a Number Two tour of a post-war potboiler entitled *No Room at the Inn*. It was a popular melodrama about wartime child evacuees farmed out to wicked foster-parents. His duties also included understudying five actors aged twenty-one to seventy, as well as tutoring the child actors in the company each morning, although he had no teaching qualifications. He had no qualifications for anything.

And I would say that for the first time in Osborne's life, he was carefree, and happy. He was on his way to a new life, and he was free of two millstones – his mother and his fiancée. He callously broke off his three-month engagement to Renee by letter while on the road. He seems to have told her in a complex spiritual way that he was undergoing a religious conversion and must go to Spain. A monastic order was involved.

The good news about Number Two tours was that they weren't Number Three. A Number One tour, on the other hand, played all the leading theatres in the major cities. It's good to be Number One.

Osborne, who remained an unknown actor for seven miserable years, never got higher than a Number Two, sinking to a Number Three and worse. Theatre itself had its class structure. The phrase "legitimate" theatre (West End drama; art) implies the "illegitimate" (Music Hall novelty acts; Lancashire comedies). In the now vanished system of the smaller repertory companies of England, the lowest rung on the ladder was known as a Fit-Up. A Fit-Up tour could mean playing in a different small town every other night, which Osborne also experienced, glad of the work.

With its overripe twice-nightly performances, *No Room at the Inn* toured forty-eight cities and towns in a year. Osborne's 1948 pocket diary – inscribed with the name he preferred then – "Osborne J. James" – reads like a crowded railway timetable of Britain: The Empire, Sunderland; the Grand, Leeds; the Opera House, Manchester. The touring venues also included Blackpool, Southport, Norwich, Newcastle, Torquay, Morecambe, Scunthorpe, Glasgow, Grimsby – and on, as Osborne lugged his suitcase up foggy Station Road.

Almost every leading actor in England has experienced the highs and lunatic lows of the English rep system. Reps were nevertheless the backbone of the theatre since their honourable inception at the turn of the previous century with the original Royal Court of Harley Granville-Barker and G.B. Shaw. Birmingham Repertory Theatre alone was the prestigious showcase for the younger Olivier and Ralph Richardson, Derek Jacobi, Michael Gambon, the twenty-three-year-old Paul Scofield, and the unknown Albert Finney (who understudied Olivier). Vanessa Redgrave began her career in rep at Frinton-on-Sea; Rosemary Harris toiled at the Roof Garden Theatre, Bognor Regis; Judi Dench was at Oxford; Dorothy Tutin at Bristol and Fiona Shaw at Bolton. Of all the gin joints in all the world, Butlin's Repertory Company on the Palace Pier in Brighton was the training ground for Eileen Atkins.

"All the plays were cut to an hour. It was the longest anyone could sit it out in the audience," Atkins told Kate Dunn, the author of an affectionately written book on the great days of rep, beguilingly entitled *Exit Through the Fireplace*. "If you hadn't finished when the hour was up, a huge bell rang to tell the audience to go onto the next thing, which was bingo or pony racing. It was marvellous training for not letting the play spread, you had to stick to what you'd rehearsed. When the bell rang people just walked out, whether you'd finished the play or not."

During long winters travelling from rep to rep on the road, the local public libraries were warm havens where Osborne wrote his first plays. In summer, the seaside piers became his open-air office. When he was playing a small role in lowly Morecambe Rep in 1955, he wrote most of the second act of *Look Back in Anger* sitting in a deckchair at the end of the pier.

A different play would be performed in rep each week, or even twice weekly. Impossible though it is to imagine, there were companies that produced three different plays *every* week. Small wonder the sets wobbled and lines of dialogue were stuck to the back of the furniture onstage. There were times when the panicked Osborne wasn't certain which play he was even appearing in, or why.

On 15 March 1952, the *New Statesman* published a heated, somewhat garbled letter from a repertory actor protesting the dire state of England's theatre. The writer is the unknown John Osborne:

> The general policy is reactionary to say the least of it.
>
> Even the plays they present (under admittedly difficult conditions, which, however, they resolutely do nothing to overcome by decent endeavour) have changed little in twenty years. Indeed, so often they are the very same plays, only too familiar to any actor who has had the experience of working in these play factories, which turn out their perennial and vulgar farce-drama-thriller cycle twice nightly to audiences who would be as well served by a nude review.

Every company had its Officer Class (leading actors) and Other Ranks (Osborne). There were early band calls and steam engines. "All trains change at Crewe, change at Crewe for all points North!" There was the dusty cosiness of actors' digs Osborne remembered fondly for their sunny messages scrawled in the Visitor's Book: "Thanks again Rosie for a grand week. Usual lovely grub, lashings of it and plenty of good old giggles. Here's to the next time!" The going rate was £3 a week, breakfast, tea, and supper after the show. Faded photos of the stars were displayed on the piano in the parlour and an actor staying the week might get his leg over the landlady if he wasn't careful. There were hissing gas fires and rules for the bath geyser, bumpy single beds and satin eiderdowns. There were the dragon landladies – "We'll have none of that in *my* house" – and the softer, maternal stagestruck ones who turned a blind eye to "guests" after deferring, for the sake of propriety, to the master of the house who was preoccupied studying the racing results in front of the coal fire. "*I* don't mind but I'll have to ask the old bugger first."

"And the curtain will rise in two minutes," went the breathy, ritual announcement, as it still does. "Ladies and gentleman, please take your seats. The curtain will rise in two minutes. That's two minutes. I *thenk yew*."

The advert "No fancy salaries, no queer folk" was the theatrical equivalent to the warning posted in pubs, "No children, no dogs, no Irish." But in practice, the theatre has always been open to outsiders. Theatres are traditionally tolerant and well-lit inner worlds, which is why Cromwellian despots close them down in a political crisis and the Lord Chamberlain of England used to censor them. But the astonishing post-war injunction that actors must provide their own clothes for the roles they played helps our understanding of the entire era. "Own wardrobe, own dinner jacket. Start work immediately." Nothing tells us more about the state of the post-war theatre that Osborne now entered and would rebel against – or about class-ridden England itself.

The rule of all repertory companies was that the management provided only period costumes. The male actor was contractually required to supply his own wardrobe for contemporary plays – invariably a blazer, sports jacket, grey flannel trousers, a formal suit and a dinner jacket. Actresses had to supply such essentials for themselves as a cocktail dress, riding kit and a tennis outfit.

The generic upper middle-class wardrobe makes it clear that although the plays might be different, they were all the same. Frozen in a bourgeois time capsule, they were given the collective name of "The Loamshire Play". Loamshire could be found in a mythical part of England not too far from Hampshire, Hereford and Hertford where hurricanes hardly happen. Loamshire stood for the safe drawing-room dramas and romantic comedies, the traditional farces and murder mysteries that defined the theatre of England.

Stoppard satirized the dead hand of the genre in *The Real Inspector Hound*. "Hello," says the cheery maid answering the telephone in the opening scene. "The drawing room of Lady Muldoon's country residence one morning early in Spring . . ."

10

What is Truth and What is Fable?

I attract hostility. I seem to be on heat for it.
Epitaph for George Dillon

When Osborne first met George Devine, finding him forbidding with his tang of Beaujolais and priestliness, he listed his experience in bottom-drawer reps like previous convictions: Kidderminster, Ilfracombe, Bridgwater, Sidmouth, Leicester, Dartford.

"Almost a Shakespearean sequence," he noted about them dryly. "Talbot, Gloucester, Hereford, Warwick, Northumberland. 'My Lords, ill news from the north. Kidderminster is dead and Bridgwater fled!'"

How bad an actor was he? Osborne said of himself that he shone like pinchbeck in flashy roles like so many second-rate actors. "I've never taken myself seriously as an actor," he confessed. "And neither has anyone else." But eyewitness reports differ.

He appeared in four Royal Court productions during the first, crucial year of Devine's leadership. It was Devine's way of helping his protégé financially at first, and then of keeping him close to the company. ". . . and who should turn up, wearing false sabre-teeth and a hairless dome, but John Osborne, ruthlessly funny as the Custodian of Ancient Offices!" wrote Tynan, reviewing Nigel Dennis's mad social satire, *Cards of Identity*, in May 1956. "The Royal Court's captive playwright stands out from an excellent cast."

Tynan was still rolling merrily along on the *Look Back in Anger* band-wagon from earlier that month, and *Cards of Identity* itself (with the young Alan Bates and Robert Stephens) was booed off the stage. Still, that's two thumbs up from England's premier critic for Osborne's first appearance on the London stage.

Laurence Olivier, a friend of Devine's, saw *Cards of Identity*, too, but his response was more slyly diplomatic. "You're my kind of actor," he confided flatteringly to Osborne backstage. "You like hiding behind make-up."

Olivier (who frequently hid behind a false nose) added that he was preparing a film of *Macbeth* and suggested Osborne would be perfect as the English doctor. The role of the English doctor isn't easily found, however. He has five lines in Act IV Scene III – even fewer than the Scots doctor in Act V Scene I.

"Oh dear, oh dear," Alan Bennett murmured, blinking at me through his glasses as he remembered an Osborne performance. "He was terrible."

"What is truth and what is fable?" goes the deeply philosophical question in Bennett's *Forty Years On*. "Where is Ruth, and where is Mabel?"

"I was worse," he added candidly about his own appearance with Osborne in the 1964 Royal Court revival of the Ben Travers farce, *Cuckoo in the Nest*. "But John was *terrible*." Osborne was making, in effect, a guest appearance as Claude Hickett MP, the blustery father of the girl who elopes. One of Hickett's memorably indignant lines is, "What the devil do you mean, sir? How can you spend a night in a lady's room '*in a way*'?"

Alan Bennett, who seems to have played more vicars than vicars, played the role of the vicar. "John had this red colonel's face and looked as if he was exploding," he said. "Nicol Williamson had the lead comic role, but he wasn't really a comic actor. It was hopeless. We chilled the audience. The thing is, nobody could remember their lines . . ."

That solid yeoman actor Nigel Davenport, a man who when the whisky flows looks as if he might knock you through the wall for sport, knew Osborne in the early days of the Court. They first met when they shared a dressing room during a television production of a downmarket police thriller in 1955. He played the sergeant and Osborne was the police constable. It was directed by Tony Richardson, the future director of *Look Back in Anger*, who was President of the Oxford University Dramatic Society when Davenport was his Secretary.

"What stuck in my mind was that Osborne was a vegetarian," Davenport told me. "The first words he said in the dressing room were, 'Do you want any of this date bar crap?'" He laughed heartily as he remembered. "He didn't have a pot to piss in then. He was *potless*. I liked him instantly. He didn't have that superior cleverness I met at Oxford. He was completely without any bullshit, intellectually sharp, pleasant, jokey, a bit campy. Well, we all were. 'Hello, *daaahling*.' All that nonsense. He was very funny in over-the-top roles. Probably a good *farceur*. I think it allowed him to hide."

Alan Bennett mentioned Osborne's offstage theatricality. "It was to hide his social background," he said in his uncompromised Yorkshire accent.

"Hello! Hello, there! Hello, me old darling!" Frank Middlemass was saying over the phone when I introduced myself. I'd called this well-liked veteran actor, who acted with Osborne in Bridgwater as far back as 1951, in the hope of meeting him. "Let me consult my diary," he confided gravely.

"What luck!" he announced after a suitable pause. "I'm completely free."

He turned up for a drink, looking sunny in his immaculate summer suit, and I recognized him from a thousand roles. He had twice played Billy Rice, the decent Edwardian father of Archie in *The Entertainer* and the play's symbol of a lost England. In younger days, Middlemass left the army after eight years' service (he was a half-colonel) to become an actor. "If you came from my family background, the idea of going on the stage was the equivalent of going on the streets, whether you were man, woman or dog," he explained. He shared digs with Osborne in Bridgwater. They used to swap their Loamshire outfits, pooling their resources for stage appearances. Osborne borrowed his demob suit.

"None of us had a bean," he remembered happily. "But I thought John had natural style, a sort of languid elegance. He was extremely good-looking, which made me green with envy. He had very nice hair, darkish blond, not curly, but wavy, very good hair, like a cap on his head. The sort of hair one admires."

He beamed and went on: "He used to laugh at all my middle-class Tory pretensions. I'd say *scorn* was the word, really. He was a natural rebel and I'm not. But I adored him. I thought he was marvellous, although I had no idea how brilliant he really was in those days. He persuaded me to become a vegetarian. Well, I thought I'd give it a whirl. But it didn't suit me at all. Every time a door banged, I fell on the floor and burst into tears. I had to pull myself together with sausage and chips! Oh, I loved John to death. He made me laugh all the time. He thought the perfectly sweet, very nice couple who ran the company were awful."

And Osborne, the actor? "I don't think he was terribly *interested* in acting," he responded guardedly. But he quickly added, "He could be very good though. I remember he could be hysterically funny in farce."

Michael Blakemore – the veteran director of Michael Frayn's *Copenhagen*, among many award-winning productions on both sides of the Atlantic – began as an actor and shared a dressing room with Osborne in Derby during the early Fifties when they both played supporting roles in Noel Coward's *Relative Values*. As unknowns together, they talked a lot about the rep system and the depressing state of English theatre. The one thing an actor in England had to be able to do in those days, Blakemore stressed, was act upper-class. Drama schools taught working-class actors to "talk posh". But Osborne couldn't really do it. In a sense, he couldn't bring himself to do it.

"We played upper-class roles week in, week out in the Coward and Rattigan plays, in Somerset Maugham and many others," he explained. "But John played it deliberately camp, and it limited him. He was a character actor and not a bad one. He could perform an audaciously funny parody of an Establishment figure, but his camp wasn't upper-class. It was an exaggerated version of it."

It's as if the contemptuous Osborne was appearing in the wrong plays – as if, in his over-the-top version of the Loamshire classes, he was satirizing the roles he had to play. If so, it's a form of ironic sabotage only the greatest actors can get away with.

But Peter Nichols, the writer of such classic English dramas as *A Day in the Death of Joe Egg* and *Privates on Parade*, was impressed by Osborne's daring when they were actors together. He was struck, firstly, by the unusual "sneering quality" he brought to the role of the butler in William Douglas-Home's *The Reluctant Debutante*. Osborne's surly butler, doubtless despising the tweedy toffs who employed him, made his surprising appearance at Frinton-on-Sea Summer Theatre. Nichols had just joined the company when he learnt the management was about to let Osborne go.

"They said, 'We're getting rid of this bloke, he's no good at all'," he told me. "But I didn't think so. I told them I thought he'd got an extraordinary quality. I don't know whether I had anything to do with it, but he did stay on for a while. We played together in Agatha Christie's *Ten Little Niggers* [since renamed *And Then There Were None*] as well as a 1940s farce called *See How They Run*, and after that I think he left."

He still had the programme from *See How They Run*, "the riotous comedy by Philip King" that played in Frinton from 3–8 August 1953. The action takes place in the vicarage in a Merton-cum-Littlewick. Nichols played a Lance Corporal Clive Winton, and Osborne was cast as a character mysteriously named The Intruder.

"That's exactly what he was," Nichols pointed out, looking pleased. "He came into English society as The Intruder, and he put a bomb under the whole bloody thing!"

Osborne all but gave up stage-acting in the mid-Fifties when he no longer needed to act. His low status throughout the fruitless years in rep never changed. He was a pirate in *Treasure Island*, a kilted Scot in *Castles in the Air*, a GI in *Love in Albania*, a medical student in *The Wind and the Rain*, and a medical student again in *White Cargo*. "It was like being the hind legs of a pantomime horse," he noted, as much about the plays as the parts.

He played the prefect Loder in the first episode of the beloved Billy

Bunter TV series about the greedy guzzler of Grayfriars. He continued playing supporting roles in staple rep fare like *Charley's Aunt, Murder at the Vicarage, Dr Jekyll and Mr Hyde* and we have his Orlac with the murderer's mitts in *Duet for Two Hands* at Ilfracombe Rep. An unknown actor named Anthony Creighton ran the small company there, but it soon folded. Creighton – "with his reveries", Osborne wrote, "of sausage, mash and diamond tie pins" – would write two early plays with him. He was a decorated bomber navigator who attended RADA after the war and toured in an RAF drag show directed by Terence Rattigan, who was Creighton's lover for a while. The RAF show was a precursor to all-male 1940s favourites like *Boys Will Be Girls* and *Soldiers in Skirts*. Rattigan cheerfully performed in one of them wearing a tutu and waving a wand as the band played the Music Hall gem with the rousing lyric, "Nobody loves a fairy when she's forty . . ."

Osborne teamed up with Creighton again in June 1950, to start another shoestring company at Hayling Island, the small resort on the Hampshire coast that was the site of his drunken Hamlet. Another of their disastrous productions was a new Yuletide version of *Aladdin* written by Osborne, who doubled in the roles of Abanaza and the Dame opposite Creighton's tipsy Wishee Washee. It must be the only show in theatre history to have closed during the intermission of its opening night.

The restless audience, which was small enough to begin with, failed to return for the second act, except for one bewildered old-age pensioner who had to be sent home. "Those who have never appeared on the stage," Osborne concluded about the *Aladdin* debacle, "will never know the living presence of silence."

The company notepaper was headed ambitiously in boldface: "The Saga Repertory Group Directors: Anthony Creighton, John J. Osborne." But they soon had to fold that tent, too, with the twenty-one-year-old Osborne ineptly in charge of the books and fleeing the taxman like Archie Rice.

He then branched out on his own – crossing paths with the unknown Harold Pinter, who also started out in theatre as a humble rep actor with the stage name David Baron. England's two foremost dramatists of the post-war era learned their trade from acting. In his *Life and Times of Harold Pinter*, Michael Billington relates amusingly how Pinter's old school chum from the East End, Henry Woolf, wrote to him asking if he should take up the acting lark, too. "What do you want to go into this shit-house for?" Pinter replied from the road.

Osborne, slogging simultaneously round the lowly reps of England, felt the same way. But he maintained that the midnight grind of learning lines in bad plays gave him an intimate lesson in playwriting. In that sense, he resembled Eugène Ionesco who said that he started writing for the theatre because he hated it. Osborne found that Somerset Maugham, for example, was extremely difficult to learn, blaming his language for being "dead, elusively inert, wobbly like some synthetic rubber substance", Bernard Shaw's plays always gave him trouble. "Try *learning* them, Mr Billington," he wrote to the *Guardian*'s distinguished drama critic about Shaw's plays of "posturing wind", challenging his view that Shaw is the greatest British dramatist since Shakespeare.

Told in his youth by his grandfather that he would be the next Shaw, Osborne loudly rejected the imposed role model for the rest his life. His grandfather had even called him "Sonny" – Shaw's childhood nickname. But his longstanding bias was at least based on personal experience. By the time he was twenty-five, he had appeared in eight of Shaw's plays, including *Heartbreak House* (which he brazenly dismissed as "Chekhov-for-philistines"). He acknowledged only one possible exception in the Shaw canon – *Pygmalion*, in which he appeared during a third-rate Arts Council Fit-Up tour through the Welsh valleys in 1954 as Freddy Eynsford Hill. Forever the Freddy, never the Higgins . . . Pleased with his *Pygmalion* performance, however, he generously concluded that it proved you can't make bricks entirely without straw.

He made light of those bitterly unhappy years when he became a successful playwright and romanticized his time as an actor. He had always enjoyed the company of actors and their battle-scarred high spirits. When *Luther*, starring Albert Finney, was staged in Paris before its Royal Court opening in 1961, Osborne went along for the ride with his beautiful mistress, costume designer Jocelyn Rickards. But he couldn't resist drinking till dawn, swapping stories with Finney and the rest, leaving his beloved sleeping alone in their Paris hotel.

"Chilled with poverty, steeped in contempt," Hazlitt wrote of actors, "they sometimes pass into the sunshine of fortune, and are lifted to the very pinnacle of public favour; yet even there cannot calculate on the continuance of success . . ."

But there was no "sunshine of fortune", no rewarding pinnacle of favour or recognition for Osborne. His early struggles were hard and demeaning. He was frequently unemployed, "resting". Never a joiner, he was fired from three companies. His fruitless actor's life was one of anxiety and humiliation, or the dole. Until *Look Back in Anger*, he had delivered the mail from Blythe Road Post Office in London every Christmas for eight years.

His acting was at best a pyrrhic victory of mediocrity over cruel rejection.

He was like the frustrated actor-dramatist fighting for his life in his 1955 play *Epitaph for George Dillon*:

> I attract hostility. I seem to be on heat for it. Whenever I step out on those boards – immediately, from the very first moment I show my face – I know I've got to fight almost every one of those people in the auditorium. Right from the stalls to the gallery, to the Vestal Virgins in the boxes! My God, it's a gladiatorial combat! Me against Them! Me and the mighty Them! Oh, I may win some of them over. Sometimes it's a half maybe, sometimes a third, sometimes it's not even a quarter. But I *do* beat them down. I beat them down!

The theatre, as yet, was far from becoming his longed-for home and refuge. He could write sentimentally in *A Better Class of Person* about the vagabond gypsy camaraderie of his rep days: "Feelings were open, often raw, and most frailty smiled on or laughed away." But his despairing letters to Anthony Creighton are much closer to the hostile truth:

Bridgwater 1951

> Their work is like their approach – hearty, vulgar, depressingly and doggedly efficient . . . I have nothing in common with them.

Derby 1954

> Playing old man of 65 next week. [He was 24.] Furious about this. I've had it shoved on to me because no one else wants to play it. How I hate this fucking hole. I've had a raw deal right from the start. The bastards just don't like me.

11

Aunt Edna's Knitting Needles

> The English Theatre isn't merely dying, it's being buried alive to the sound of Aunt Edna's knitting needles.
>
> Osborne notebook entry, 1953

Osborne's compensation for his failure as an actor was to write great whopping roles and imagine himself performing them brilliantly. It's why the leading parts in his best plays are all male, and why their monologues of blistering contempt and desperation revel in star actors – among them, Laurence Olivier, Albert Finney, Nicol Williamson, Ralph Richardson and Paul Scofield. Jimmy Porter, Osborne's Angry Young Man railing against the unfairness of the world, could easily be an out-of-work rep actor. His job running a sweet stall is the least convincing thing about him. Jimmy Porter is someone who wants to be heard at all cost, and recognized:

> "One day, when I'm no longer spending my days running a sweet-stall, I may write a book about us all. It's all here. (*Slapping his forehead*) Written in flames a mile high. And it won't be recollected in tranquillity either, picking daffodils with Auntie Wordsworth. It'll be recollected in fire, and blood. My blood."

If we now look closer at the England that stifled and enraged people like Osborne, we'll see more clearly what had to change.

The West End theatre that fed the rest of the country with its contented Loamshire diet was ruled absolutely by the Machiavellian Hugh Beaumont, known to all as "Binkie". That cockney free spirit of the theatre, Joan Littlewood, defined his sprawling West End kingdom as "the labyrinth where the minotaur Binkie Beaumont lurked". Beaumont, managing director of HM Tennant, was the most influential and feared producer of the post-war era. On the opening night of *Look Back in Anger*, he would walk out at the interval in disgust.

Sir Tyrone Guthrie called him "the iron fist wrapped in fifteen pastel-shaded gloves". Osborne, as we might expect, went further, describing him as the *éminence lavande* of English theatre whose "Binkiedom" was "the most powerful of the unacceptable faeces of theatrical capitalism".

In fact, he admired his elegant "Fortnum & Mason" productions for their star actors and polish. It was the theatre Osborne was raised on, civilized and above the fray – an antidote to the austerity of post-war England. Beaumont's signature style *avoided* contemporary reality. The star actors appearing in his glamorous, handmade productions included Noel Coward, John Gielgud, Ralph Richardson, Peggy Ashcroft, the two Dames, Edith Evans and Sybil Thorndike, and the theatre royalty of Laurence Olivier and Vivien Leigh. Terence Rattigan, a close friend of Beaumont's, was the house playwright, and Cecil Beaton a favourite set designer. (Beaton was also portrait photographer to the Royal Family.) "And a highly respectable, professionally adept, and very profitable business it was," Osborne conceded.

Nor was devastated post-war England the cultural wasteland it was often claimed to be by the restless new generation of the Fifties and later. It was both escapist and nurtured a seed of renewal among the ruins. Peter Brook's *The Empty Space*, while famously proposing a break with deadly tradition, pointed out even-handedly:

"The theatre of the late 40s had many glories: it was the theatre of Jouvet and Berard, and of Jean Louis Barrault, of Clave at the ballet, *Don Juan*, *Amphitryon*, *La Folle de Chaillot*, *Carmen*, John Gielgud's revival of *The Importance of Being Ernest*, *Peer Gynt* at the Old Vic, Olivier's *Oedipus*, Olivier's *Richard III*, *The Lady's Not For Burning*, *Venus Observed*; of Massine at Covent Garden under the birdcage in *The Three-Cornered Hat* just as he had been fifteen years before – this was a theatre of colour and movement, of fine fabrics, of shadows, of eccentric cascading words – it was a theatre of a battered Europe that seemed to share one aim – a reaching back toward a memory of lost grace."

But who was this cultivated nostalgia for? Not Osborne's class-conscious generation, nor anyone under thirty. The young, as a rule, didn't even go to the theatre.

The two leading reviewers of the day, the leftish atheist, Kenneth Tynan at the *Observer* and the older, conservative Christian Scientist, Harold Hobson at the *Sunday Times*, were frequently locked in critical combat, as prizefighters need worthy opponents to make a fight memorable. But the two rivals with such contrasting taste were in uncharacteristic agreement in their diagnosis of what ailed England's theatre.

"I came back to a country," Hobson wrote after a 1952 theatre trip to Paris, "whose newspapers are mainly filled with tidings of war, insurrection, industrial unrest, political controversy, and parliamentary misbehaviour; and to a theatre from which it seems to me, in the first shock of re-acquaintance, that all echo of these things is shut off like soundproof walls."

"We need plays about cabmen and demi-gods," Tynan wrote two years later, "plays about warriors, politicians and grocers – I care not, so Loamshire be invaded and subdued. I counsel aggression because, as a critic, I had rather be a war correspondent than a necrologist."

There was an extraordinary post-war influx of French drama that neatly avoided having to deal with the reality of England at all. The Francophile mood was personified by the *Sunday Times*'s Hobson, whose swooning infatuation for the French actress Edwige Feullière became better known than Feullière herself. The lecturer and playwright, Dan Reballato, reminds us in his book, *1956 and All That*, that in a single London season in 1954 – just two years before *Look Back* – an astonishing seven Jean Anouilh dramas were playing in translation, while Jean Giraudoux had an estimated eight major productions.

In addition to the dominance of Anouilh and Giraudoux, there were the imported plays of Cocteau, Marivaux, Camus and Sartre – and latterly the revolutionary new work of Genet, Ionesco and Beckett (if we count the Irishman Beckett, who wrote in French), as well as several minor French playwrights.

Where was the new English drama? The surrender to France reveals less a transformation of insular English taste, more an enfeebled national culture unconfident in its own identity. It was as if the country were living in fear of the truth about itself. Francophilia reached such fashionable heights that high-minded literary reviewers routinely wrote in chunks of French. *Mais regardez le following, s'il vous plaît*:

> JIMMY: I've just read three whole columns on the English Novel. Half of it's in French. Do the Sunday papers make *you* feel ignorant?
> CLIFF: Not 'arf.

> *Look Back in Anger*

Osborne opposed the French because they weren't English and he opposed England's leading dramatists because they were *too* English. There were the popular Thirties and Forties plays of J.B. Priestley, the portly, pipe-smoking socialist who would be parodied by Jimmy Porter in *Look Back*: "He's like Daddy – still casting well-fed glances back to the Edwardian twilight from his comfortable, disenchfranchised wilderness . . ." Rattigan and Coward were still the dominant forces until the mid-1950s – though Rattigan's first success, *French Without Tears*, dated back to 1936, and Coward's best work shone from the 1920s to the 40s. The West End verse dramas of T.S. Eliot and Christopher Fry were another staple, while established lightweight figures like Emlyn Williams and William Douglas-Home still flourished.

Emotional understatement was the defining English style, a dry reserve worn lightly. "You mustn't be serious, my dear one, it's just what they want," Elyot advises Amanda in Coward's 1930 masterwork, *Private Lives*. "All the futile moralists who try to make life unbearable. Laugh at them. Be flippant. Laugh at everything, all their sacred shibboleths. Flippancy brings out the acid in their damn sweetness."

Coward's urbane message is a deft defence of living your own life in the teeth of prissy disapproval. One rises above bourgeois convention by appearing not to give a hoot. Coward's mask of inscrutability, which he liked to say gave him the look of a heavily doped Chinese illusionist, could make anything even remotely serious seem dull. What does Elyot Chase in *Private Lives* actually do for a living? Nothing. But he does it terribly well. And Elyot and Amanda? They "do" pleasure, together.

"Let's be superficial and pity the poor philosophers," goes the unapologetic Thirties message of *Private Lives*. "Let's blow trumpets and squeakers and enjoy the party, as much as we can . . ."

In the plays of Coward and Rattigan, love is invariably *thwarted*, sex unmentioned, emotion discreetly repressed. As gay men, they had good reason to be circumspect in an age when homosexuality was still an imprisonable crime. Coded evasion was a tactful, necessary style. But reticence has always been a defining English characteristic, the national temperament innately one of restraint. Subtext is all. We must often deduce what the reserved Englishman really feels by what he leaves unsaid. But Osborne left nothing unsaid. He set out to write plays in which it was impossible to tell a lie.

The day would come when he would shout unembarrassed from the rooftops to a drab and disillusioned post-war England:

"Oh heavens, how I long for a little ordinary human enthusiasm. Just enthusiasm – that's all. I want to hear a warm, thrilling voice cry out Hallelujah! . . . Hallelujah! I'm alive!"

Jimmy Porter, *Look Back in Anger*

In rainy contrast, the peculiar English psyche often seems more at home in damp defeat. The culture of complaint – a satisfying *rant* – is an English speciality. As Stephen Fry put it, "Perhaps we are the only people who take *freude* in our own *schaden*." The pursuit of happiness is a brazenly optimistic American invention whereas stoicism is England's proud bulwark. D.H. Lawrence – an early influence on Osborne – longed to feel the intuitive, celebratory "gladness of life" among the British. Osborne's furious new voice was un-English in its unrestrained feeling and passion. If we're going to moan, he announced, let's make it count. In that thrillingly emotional sense, he became the country's post-war hammer. The brittle, polished surfaces of Coward, like Wilde's elegant flippancy, the fizz of Shavian intellect and the artifice of the pre-*Look Back* era, were still used to deflect openly expressed emotion. "Shaw avoided passion almost as prudently as Coward," Osborne argued. "Frigidity and caution demand an evasive style and they both perfected one." Emotional display, like speaking your mind, like a little ordinary enthusiasm, was considered socially awkward, incorrect, a gaffe.

"Certainly, a recurrent motif in mid-century plays was the avoidance of emotional display," Rebellato, among many commentators, confirms, citing Coward's 1947 *Peace in Our Time* in which a married couple bids a heart-felt farewell to friends –

NORA: Good luck to you both – always.
(*She dabs her eyes*)
FRED: Now then, Nora – none of that.

A stiff upper lip is the trick, if appearances are to be well-maintained. Terence Rattigan was the most commercially successful dramatist of his time and his 1940s dramas are among the most enduring. Most of us know *The Winslow Boy* with its rousing theme of wrongful accusation and the price of justice, or *The Browning Version* with its wronged minor public schoolteacher, Crocker-Harris ("the Himmler of the Lower Fifth"), and its touching portrait of cringing failure. Both grew out of middle-class Edwardian domestic drama (and melodrama). Rattigan's most admired play, *The Deep Blue Sea* of 1952, is a modern tragedy of love, sex and attempted suicide. Yet sex and suicide are never explicitly mentioned, and the heroine's illicit love affair is tastefully described as "something far too big and confusing to be tied up in a little parcel called lust".

Now then – none of *that*.

Rattigan even argued against any alternative to the drawing-room dramas of his time. "I don't think ideas, *per se*, social, political or moral, have a very important place in the theatre," he announced in a 1950 *New Statesman* article that roused the dying Shaw to vigorous opposition. "They definitely take third place to character and narrative, anyway."

There goes Samuel Beckett and all plays of political and social consequence. Rattigan – educated Harrow and Trinity College, Cambridge – was
arguing for the supremacy of the storyteller's traditional craft at which he
was a master, but he couldn't see beyond his own bourgeois audience. Arthur
Miller – born in Flatbush, Brooklyn – described the West End theatre he
saw while visiting London in 1956 as "hermetically sealed off from life"
and named the single exception of *Look Back in Anger*. It was for him the
only modern British play.

"I couldn't connect with the people on the London stage until I saw
Look Back in Anger," he re-affirmed for me. "I felt I know those people. I
felt I understood their anger and fears, and they shed more light on England
than anything I'd seen."

Rattigan went on to uphold the theatre's cocooned state with the notorious creation of his beloved Aunt Edna as the conscience of England.
"A nice respectable, middle-class, middle-aged maiden lady with time on
her hands and the money to help her pass it," he described her famously.
"Let us call her Aunt Edna."

Rattigan introduced her to the world in the introduction to the 1953
second volume of his *Selected Plays*, and he would come to regret her immaculate conception. With her untroubled, unchangeably genteel tastes,
maidenly Aunt Edna became an English joke. Rattigan explained that she
didn't possess "much knowledge or discernment".

"She is, in short, a hopeless lowbrow," he said, adding without irony that
the dramatist who displeases her "is utterly lost".

But it was Rattigan who would soon become lost in changing England
– discarded like an old-fashioned relic along with Noel Coward et al., while
Aunt Edna, personifying everything that was unacceptably, smugly shallow
about England's class-bound theatre, would help usher in the new era.

Osborne and his angry generation were incapable of playing Aunt Edna's
civilized, well-bred game of being acceptably, respectably *nice* in order to
get time off for good behaviour. They didn't have time to be nice.

"The struggle to *please* above all," Osborne wrote in his 1953 notebook,
relishing his theme. "There are so many people twisting themselves into
thrombosis and neurosis in the almighty effort to please. My aim is not to
please, but to stimulate, not to flatter and lick but to needle and insult as
cheerily as I can. Surely, you don't want sugar all the time. A little sour
can settle the stomach . . ."

Coronation Year had just passed, crowning the old hierarchical values
of mythic England and certainty of Empire in a show of national unity.

"The gold filling in the mouthful of decay," Osborne later scorned the Royals – notoriously dismissing them as "the last circus of a civilisation that has lost faith in itself" in an age when royalty still stood above criticism and mockery of the Crown was even considered treasonable.

"They seem to think I'm a sort of juvenile delinquent, the result of an undesirable background," he boiled over in his notebook. "Give him a normal, reliable theatrical home, and you'll find he can behave as decently as anyone else. Above all, they suspect passion. Nothing will surely mark you down as a literary raggamuffin than coming out with an *attitude*. Playwrights, they feel, should be like the Royal Family, above the brawl and conflict of life, of life as we know it, anyway."

He was still a struggling twenty-three-year-old actor three years away from *Look Back in Anger*. But the following seething entries in his 1953 notebook struck me as revelatory. They amount to an uncompromising battle plan from an unknown dramatist in training for the future – a private manifesto in reply to Rattigan's public one:

> English Theatre isn't merely dying, it's being buried alive to the rattle of Aunt Edna's knitting needles. Aunt Edna herself is one of a long line of swindles handed down on tablets of white tiling from the summits of Shaftesbury Avenue and Charing Cross Rd. She is merely the New Testament Version of the old fundamentalist religion of theatrical management with its dread of the original sin of being articulate. Aunt Edna, poor thing, is the latest, self-conscious and uneasy Messiah who brings the glad tidings of What the Public Wants. Public taste is *created* – never forget that.

Yet radical change had been happening in the American theatre since the 1930s – reminding us how cut off the England that raised Osborne really was. There were as yet no snarling anti-heroes with the wrong accents on the London stage. There was no English version of Eugene O'Neill's conman evangelist Hickey and his self-deluding bar-room bums in search of salvation, no mythic working-class salesman Willy Loman – a "low man" – to represent a country onstage. There were no emotional protest plays from a Clifford Odets urging audiences to rise up against an unfair world, or poetic tender mercies of a Tennessee Williams to sing a different song.

The only voices heard onstage were uniformly upper class, the accents plummy Oxford or standard BBC. With its rigid rules of acceptable spoken English, the stuffy BBC was itself an uncritical endorsement of the Establishment and the elitist status quo. The TV stood in its oak cabinet in a corner of middle-class homes like an obelisk, and the news was solemnly read in evening dress. It was even read in black tie on the *radio*. The BBC news was the sacred word of a divine power. The panel members of *What's My Line* – the most popular TV show of the Fifties – also appeared in evening dress, like Edwardian gentry treating the staff below stairs to Christmas charades on Boxing Day. Until the introduction of commercial television for the masses in 1955, the paternal BBC had the cultural force of a monopoly in unruffled smugness leading the nation in "good taste".

The working classes were also excluded from the English stage – unless they were servants and lovable "characters"; or foreigners (American, German); or Irish (cf. foreign or *quaint*). Sean O'Casey's great Dublin trilogy of 1920s working-class dramas remain Irish to the marrow of their bones, whereas the middle-class Irish dramatists – Congreve, Sheridan, Wilde and Shaw – have always been treated as honorary Englishmen by middle-class Englishmen. Crucially, D.H. Lawrence's ground-breaking dramatic poems of working-class life in turn-of-the-century Nottinghamshire remained largely ignored until the Royal Court director, Peter Gill, rediscovered them in the late 1960s. The outcast lower orders were the Eccles cakes of English drama confined to homey supporting roles where they could do no harm, cast as the ever-friendly copper, the unflinching loyal butler, or the adorable cockney maid played by a refined RADA actress in curlers speaking "stage common": "Will that be all for today, Miss, or may I be awf 'ome?"

In a neat form of class revenge, there were the traditionally broad working-class comedies from the north of England that portrayed anyone upper class as either a villain or a fool. Their muscular language used archaic words like "wench", "thine", "thy", "dost" and "ye" ("I'm well rid of ye!"). The gormless end-of-the-pier comedies with risqué titles like *Jack the Lad* and *My Wife's Lodger* were akin to the Chitlin circuit of cheap entertainments that toured America with ghetto stereotypes for the black underclass.

The better northern dramas, going back to Stanley Houghton's *Hindle Wakes* at the turn of the century, were known historically as the "Manchester School" of social realism. I grew up in Manchester, so bear with me. There are those who insist that Harold Brighouse's classic north country comedy of 1915, *Hobson's Choice*, is an underlying analysis of class-ridden England, a proto-feminist tract, and the equivalent to a lost Rembrandt. But this Manchester yarn about the tyrannical – yet lovable – tippler Henry Hobson and Maggie, his plucky daughter in the Salford shoe trade, is little more than an endearing fable about a Big Bad Bear, a Cinderella and a Simpleton. Our 'Enery, or the Big Bad Bear, gets his come-*oopance* when blossoming

Maggie, or Cinders, finally makes a man out of her daft husband Willie, the shoe-making Simpleton of Salford. Hobson is humbled – 'Obson is 'umbled – and everyone lives happily ever after! Why, it's *nobbut* a comforting pudding of a play – a nice "slice" of working-class life for tourists with clogs on.

No, the characteristic dramas that Osborne came to know intimately as he waited impatiently in the wings held up a well-polished mirror to the *haut bourgeoisie* in the audience.

Noel Coward's 1951 *Relative Values* actually parodied social equality. His 1956 *Nude with a Violin* took even shakier aim at the modern art movement in the same year that *Look Back* took lethal aim at England itself. T.S. Eliot – whose verse plays *The Family Reunion* and *The Cocktail Party* were set in grand country homes – urged audiences to listen to poetry "from people dressed like ourselves, living in houses and apartments like ourselves". The theatre even made the bourgeoisie feel literally at home: tea could be served on a tray to your seat in the stalls.

But the real world, the dangerous, dismal world beyond the velvet curtain, proved distressingly different. Change was coming and the Fifties "silent generation" would give it voice. Until then, post-war England was a pinched and deprived place to live, a censored society in mean-spirited ways. It was the only country in the free world to tolerate state censorship of its theatre. Homosexuality was still a crime. Though a Soho demi-monde existed, public figures such as Lord Montagu, John Gielgud and the choreographer John Cranko, were notoriously victimized and arrested. (The Homosexual Reform Act wasn't passed until 1967.) Capital punishment by hanging was still in place. Abortion was mostly illegal. Food, clothes and petrol had been severely rationed. The licensing laws confined the masses to strictly regulated drinking hours in pubs "for their own good". Sundays were always bloody. It's no coincidence that *Look Back* takes place during the torpid coma of another wet Sunday in England with the pubs closed and nothing to do and nowhere to go.

"I believe we started out with hope. And hope deferred makes the heart sick, and many hearts are sick about what they see in England now," Osborne wrote of the joyless Fifties. "There are bad times just around the corner," Noel Coward sang in his jaunty ditty of national despair. "The horizon's as gloomy as can be . . ." What use Aunt Edna's myopic view from her plush seat in the stalls with a box of Quality Street nestling contentedly in her lap? Post-war England was virtually bankrupt and the jubilant, patriotic high of the 1953 Coronation was more like a last-gasp glory of a once invincible Empire. There were dole queues and most of the population wore shabby clothes that were always dark – to hide the dirt caused by the miserable pea-soup fogs that choked and blackened the country, particularly in the demoralized industrial north.

Simply put, a West End theatre still dressed in dinner jackets and cocktail dresses was a theatre utterly out of touch with Osborne's England.

12

The Apprentice Playwright in Search
of an Audience

Am I wasting my own and other people's time?
Osborne submitting an early play, 8 July 1953

Look Back in Anger is often seen as Osborne's first play, for nothing succeeds like overnight success. Yet four full-length plays were completed before the 1956 breakthrough, although only one of them – *Epitaph for George Dillon*, written with Anthony Creighton in 1955 – has become known. It's the story of a failed actor-playwright who sells out for crass success.

Two years before he completed *Look Back*, Osborne was writing to Richard Findlater, the influential drama critic of the left-wing weekly *Tribune*, cravenly hoping to be noticed.

23 April 1953

Dear Mr Findlater,
I feel that I must write and tell you how much I enjoyed your lecture last night . . . I was hoping that I might have the pleasure of a few words with you afterwards, but I was headed off.

He eventually persuaded Findlater to meet him, and submitted an apprentice play:

8 July 1953

Dear Mr Findlater,
Thanks so much for the tea the other afternoon. I am sending the M.S. to you as I threatened. I nearly sent several, but I thought it was hardly fair. This one should at least give an idea. I wrote it six months ago, and it's not the play I should write now. I've gone the wrong way

about it. Anyhow, I'd be so interested to hear what you think . . . I really do wonder. Am I wasting my own and other people's time?

He began writing his first play, *Resting Deep*, in the dressing room of the Empire Theatre in Sunderland when he was eighteen years old. Playing small roles had its advantages. It meant he always had time to write backstage during the performances.

He later described the novice play, whose script hasn't survived, as a crude melodrama about a Welsh loon who's an unrecognized poet. It was rewritten in partnership with Stella Linden, the leading lady of the touring wartime saga *No Room at the Inn*, who became his first lover. Having jilted his fiancée, Renee Shippard of the Halifax Building Society in Stoneleigh, he lost his virginity to Stella, who was twelve years older than him. Osborne was unembarrassed to recall the awkward start to their affair by describing an expensive pair of yellow poplin pyjamas he'd bought from Simpson's of Piccadilly for a special occasion. But when he came to bed proudly wearing them for Stella, he was so overcome with emotion that he burst into tears.

Thirty-year-old Stella Linden took her nervous apprentice under her firm, protective wing. "Even in adolescence, she could never have strived as an eternal slip of a girl," Osborne wrote about her. "Stella was a woman, all right, with a pelvic arch like the skull of an ox, a slippery slope of hips, and the shoulders of a Channel swimmer."

Strapping Stella was married to a homosexual, Patrick Desmond, a sometime producer, actor, agent and play doctor. Osborne later based the character of the seedy theatre producer, Barney Evans, in *George Dillon* on him. Here's Barney advising Dillon, the future playwright:

BARNEY: Dialogue's not bad, but these great long speeches – that's a mistake. People want action, excitement. I know – *you* think you're George Bernard Shaw. But where's he today? Eh?

Stella's husband obligingly paid the rent for his wife and the smirking, adolescent Osborne to live together for a year in Brighton at 7a Arundel Terrace. Raffish, Regency Brighton, smelling of sea, sex and cockles, would be forever his Mecca of the dirty weekend. "To shudder one's last, thrusting, replete gasp between the sheets at 4 and 6 o'clock in Brighton," he wrote, "would be the most perfect last earthly delight."

It was Stella, an evangelistic vegetarian, who converted him to the cause, hoping that nut cutlets would cure his acne. She also gave him dogged playwriting lessons souped up with the Victorian niceties of Sir Arthur

Wing Pinero. With the addition of bad jokes and a fashionable hint of T.S. Eliot theology, the rewritten *Resting Deep* was retitled *The Devil Inside*.

Unemployed for most of his carefree Brighton year, Osborne toiled as a reluctant dishwasher, and the hot affair eventually cooled with their abandoned second play, a formula family saga entitled *Happy Birthday*. She left him for another young actor while on tour.

But there's a semi-happy end to his playwriting with Stella. On Easter Monday 1951, *The Devil Inside* played for one week at the Theatre Royal, Huddersfield. It was produced by Stella's husband, and the twenty-year-old Osborne was seated anxiously in the stalls to see its world premiere as he held hands with his co-author and ex-lover. The mixed review in the *Huddersfield Examiner* complained about "the argy-bargy on religion in the third act, which comes at the wrong time", but the audience reception at the end seemed friendly enough and Osborne remembered that when he returned to live with his mother in Stoneleigh and look for acting work again, he could at least say that he had witnessed his own play – or a ghost of it – performed in a professional theatre. His share of the royalty for the week in Hudderfield was nine pounds.

There's a surprise coda. Twelve years later, *The Devil Inside* was revived in 1962 at the Pembroke Theatre, Croydon, when Osborne was the most successful dramatist in England. But he had his name on the billing changed to "Robert Owen", and the play was re-named once again, becoming *Cry for Love*. The local drama critic, a Donald Madgwick, described the unknown Robert Owen as "a dramatist of great potential of whom we ought to be hearing a great deal more in the future".

His second play, provisionally entitled *The Great Bear* or *Minette*, was written in 1951 when he was once again "resting". The near-unreadable manuscript of *The Great Bear* or *Minette* appears to be a Dante-esque love story with erotic undertones. It's written in blank verse inspired by T.S. Eliot's modern-dress verse plays, which Osborne later lampooned as evenings of faux myth and theology dressed up in tweed skirts. Intriguingly, the novice play contains early intimations of the derided Bears and Squirrels scenes in *Look Back in Anger*. At the top of the script, he's upped the anthropomorphic ante with an introductory note attributed to Baudelaire:

"Minette, minouette, minouille, my pussy, my wolf, my little chimpanzee, you big baboon, you big snake, my gloomy little chimpanzee. Such verbal whimsicalities as those – animal nicknames used too many times – are evidence of a satanic side to love. Are not devils shaped like animals?"

The discovered manuscript shows us how far Osborne still had to go. As the curtain rises, the scene is set with the heroine, Cornelia, described as "thoughtfully pushing a few green vegetables and plants into a large basin. Beside her on a low stool are a large worn teddy bear and a toy squirrel."

"Bear! O Bear! Bear!" she cries, talking to them "to heal the bitings of this little beast".

Enter the hero, a poetic figure named Owen (who became Osborne's mysterious pseudonym "Robert Owen"):

CORNELIA: You lovely bear.
  You look ferocious rouged
  abruptly from your chair. Come here
  and kiss me. My mouth is watering for you.
OWEN: My squeaking, squeakful squirrel.
  (*He comes over and kisses her.*)
CORNELIA: Your tongue was thinking of the men, you beast.
OWEN: And so was yours, my sweet.

Osborne claimed that he wrote two verse plays before *Look Back in Anger*. If so, the manuscript of the second has been lost, fortunately. Though we ought to remind ourselves that he was just twenty-two years old.

His third play, an assault on McCarthyism entitled *Personal Enemy*, was co-written with Anthony Creighton and completed in 1954. The McCarthy trials in the USA were at their height and he spent several weeks in the American Library in Grosvenor Square, poring over manuscripts of the Un-American Activities Committee. The play was based on Creighton's own melodramatic plot, but whatever its merits, it never stood a chance. *Personal Enemy* dealt with a McCarthyite witch-hunt in which two of the characters were smeared as traitorous homosexuals. In 1950s England, even the suggestion of homosexuality was outlawed onstage. The high-ranking member of the royal household quaintly known as the Lord Chamberlain decided what was "acceptable", and the outcome was frequently a farce. As Dominic Shellard points out in *British Theatre Since the War*, the Lord Chamberlain could thus rule that in Tennessee Williams's *Suddenly Last Summer*, cannibalism is more acceptable than the implication that the cannibalized man is gay.

It wasn't until as late as 1968 that theatre censorship was finally abolished in England (just before the opening of the Vietnam-era rock musical *Hair*). Until then, the Lord Chamberlain's absolute power had been entrenched since the Theatres Act of 1737. Why Osborne and Creighton didn't see the obvious risk they were taking with *Personal Enemy* must be put down to naivety, or to too much trust in the only producer who wanted to stage the play, fly-by-night Patrick Desmond of Osborne's Stella days.

Censorship would become one of Osborne's fiercest battlegrounds, as if he were on a personal mission to do away with the Lord Chamberlain. The tragi-farce of the Lord Chamberlain's Gilbert and Sullivan world, created in social privilege, weaned on self-preservation, has much to add to our understanding of Osborne's England. His office represented the Establishment at mandarin work, the alien, inherited enemy within theatre itself ruling without checks and balances from a wisteria-clad tower at St James's Palace. Until 1991, the files of the Lord Chamberlain and his staff were withheld from all public scrutiny. The official censor (and self-censorship) were the insidious stumbling blocks to all change.

The 11th Earl of Scarborough held the office in the early Fifties. Scarborough, educated at Eton and Oxford, was a former Governor of Bombay and the author of a history of the 11th Hussars. His successor was Cameron Fromanteel, 1st Baron Cobbold, educated at Eton and Cambridge, Governor of the Bank of England, High Sherriff of the County of London, permanent Lord in Waiting to the Queen, and husband of a daughter of the 2nd Earl of Lytton. As the high-ranking official in charge of the Royal Household, the Lord Chamberlain's duties included – and still do – the care of several hundred royal swans, supervising entrance to the Queen's Lawn at Ascot, the administration of royal weddings, and the granting of coats of arms to the makers of Royal marmalade.

Every new play had to be submitted to him in order to be granted a licence for performance. No formal rules of censorship ever existed. (Rules can be changed for the better; vagueness is the censor's secret weapon.) How the Lord Chamberlain was considered qualified to assess plays is to miss the point. G.B. Shaw – whose moral debate about the merits of prostitution, *Mrs Warren's Profession*, was banned for thirty-three years – argued, correctly, that the unwritten rules of the censor's office simply codified the prejudices the Lord Chamberlain represented.

No criticism of the Crown or Church was therefore permitted onstage. The Lord Chamberlain represented the Crown and the monarch was the head of the Church. Nor was any criticism permitted of government leaders or pillars of society (dead or alive), unless they were from unfriendly nations (which for a time excluded Hitler, until he became less friendly). All sexual references deemed offensive were censored, including the words "shag", "bum", "balls" and "fairy". Until 1950, the words "abortion" and "syphilis" were unacceptable. Just twenty years before, it was "hips" and "breasts". Two characters in bed together were still taboo, although bed scenes were, of course, as old as *Othello*.

In other puritan words, the Lord Chamberlain represented the entrenched traditional values and hypocrisies of middle-class drawing-room decorum. He protected the "lower orders" from moral corruption and radical ideas. He maintained the politically innocuous, neutered netherland of the unconquerable Loamshire play.

His lordly paternalism was no different to the government prosecutor's renowned instruction to the jury during the 1960 trial of the unexpurgated edition of *Lady Chatterley's Lover*: "Is it a book that you would have lying round your own house? Is it a book you would even wish your wife or your servants to read?"

It was possible to appeal the judgment of the Lord Chamberlain, but the Lord Chamberlain judged the appeal. Every new play was read by a lay Reader, who then made recommendations to one of two senior examiners known as Comptrollers, who were the direct link in the chain to the Lord Chamberlain. The Comptrollers were mostly retired military men, ex-guards officers and showbiz-loving colonels with titles and names like Lieutenant-Colonel Sir St Troubredge of Vincent. A courtly letter written on crown-embossed notepaper would be sent to the dramatist or his producer stating the cuts and changes required: "I am desired by the Lord Chamberlain to write to you about the above play . . ."

The Lord Chamberlain thus maintained public order, morality and good manners – and, by definition, the entrenched status quo. With its homosexual theme, *Personal Enemy* was censored beyond recognition. Making matters worse, Patrick Desmond, its producer, had blundered badly by putting the play into rehearsal before even hearing from the Lord Chamberlain. Four days before it was due to be performed by the White Rose Players of Harrogate, he was summoned to the censor's office, and he took the twenty-four-year-old Osborne along with him.

Their accounts of the meeting differ somewhat. Patrick Desmond's is a model of restraint and resigned acceptance, in spite of the fact that the play had been savaged by the censor. Whereas Osborne tells us that after a liquid lunch in the Salisbury pub on St Martin's Lane, they had a much jollier session with a "guards officer" type at St James's Palace who just ticked them off like naughty schoolboys and made it clear the play was unacceptable. The censored *Personal Enemy* opened at the Opera House, Harrogate, on 1 March 1955, and was never heard of again.

Epitaph for George Dillon, the second play Osborne wrote with Creighton, was completed shortly before *Look Back in Anger*. It was turned down by everyone, including Patrick Desmond.

On the wave of *Look Back*'s success, however, the Royal Court produced it in 1958. The play has dated and is rarely staged, though some reviewers have always regarded it highly. A critically well-received new production opened in London's West End in autumn 2005, starring Joseph Fiennes as Dillon. For our purposes, however, it's more of a portent. *George Dillon* reveals the first signs of Osborne's authentic voice.

The shiftless hero is a struggling actor-dramatist sponging off a lower middle-class family in Osborne's despised, droopy suburbia. Painted china ducks are seen in synchronized flight on the wall of the sitting room where a prized cocktail cabinet is venerated like a private altar. Dillon's spoken thought that brings the first act to its witheringly abrupt end is one of the great curtain lines. "You stupid-looking bastard," he says, looking steadily at the framed photograph of his landlady's beloved son who was killed in World War II.

George Dillon is Osborne's modern anti-hero in the making – the lacerating, bruised outsider whose strawberry mark is self-disgust and doubt. The name "Dillon" evokes an outlaw spirit. Paranoia and painful isolation are part of his condition. His eyes are weary, threatening dead-ness. The appetite is there, but life – the simple, unattainable achievement of feeling gloriously alive – defeats him. Dillon will throw in the towel and sell out; Jimmy Porter will go down swinging in the mud. Both of them are fiery neurotics betrayed by treacherous, loving wives, who fail to live up to the romantic, unbreakable *promise*. Both are tormented by the mortal fear of never making it in this mediocre little world.

Yearning to be a respected playwright, Dillon has all the symptoms of talent, but his crippling doubts reflect Osborne's, then and later.

RUTH: Perhaps you have got talent, George. I don't know. Who can tell? Even the experts can't always recognise it when they see it. You may even be great. But don't make a disease out of it. You're sick with it.
GEORGE: It's a disease some of us long to have.

The initial idea for *Epitaph for George Dillon* came from Creighton. They wrote separately – cobbling the script together in less than three weeks. Creighton concentrated on the expository opening act, while Osborne worked on the character of the shoddy entrepreneur Barney Evans, and the entire George–Ruth duologue of Act Two. After the play was first rejected, its route to the Royal Court, and subsequently to the West End and Broadway, was unusual.

Osborne offered it to George Devine at the Court after he accepted *Look*

Back in Anger. But Devine found it inferior and tactfully turned it down by the prudent device of never mentioning it. Then the Oxford Experimental Theatre – the university group – wrote to the newly famous playwright asking if he had a neglected play in the bottom drawer. They were the first to stage it. "Every newspaper sent one of its predators to see it and the response seemed to suggest that it might be a superior version of *Look Back*," Osborne wrote. "Certainly, it sorted out the Philistines from the Boys, and the Royal Court perversely decided to stage it."

He never made any claims for the play – least of all that it might be preferable to *Look Back in Anger* – and grandly didn't trouble to attend its opening night at the Court. (He was in New York.) But when the favourable reviews came in, he was happy to jump on his own bandwagon.

He remained defensive about Creighton's contribution. *Epitaph for George Dillon* was Creighton's one claim to fame, and, though he wrote another play or two, he was never heard of again. "Critics were to point out that someone called Anthony Creighton had imposed a discipline on me which I had been unable to exercise on myself in the writing of *Look Back in Anger*," Osborne wrote churlishly. "The typing was indisputably all mine . . ."

To his irritation, it was often claimed – and still is – that his co-author must have influenced the sympathetic portrait of Ruth, the play's heroine. She's an untypical Osborne woman in that she is, uniquely, someone who's capable of giving the uppity protagonist a smack in the mouth. She's his equal.

Ruth, the humane, courageous older woman trapped in suburbia, is herself an outsider – an ex-Communist who formerly loved a young writer. She's the born giver, as Tynan said, who slowly recognizes in George a born taker. She's a lost soul like him, and in a different life, she might have been his saviour. Perhaps Creighton had a hand in creating her. But it's unlikely. They wrote their scenes separately. But Osborne also wrote about his source for Ruth, and he never published the full account that I was now able to read.

All the lower middle-class members of the family in the play have their counterparts in Osborne's own family – with the exception of Ruth. She was based on a middle-aged spinster named Helen Henderson who ignited an unusual affection in him that grew from their first encounter.

Creighton had first met her when, unemployed in the theatre, he was working at a debt-collecting agency in Oxford Street where she toiled in a menial job. He introduced her to Osborne, who was then twenty-three or so. Osborne made clear that his attraction wasn't erotic – as the undercurrent between George and Ruth is in the play – although the feelings Helen Henderson aroused in him were emotional and hypnotic.

"She was small, frail with a fine, slightly pinched face with a gentle intensity that often seemed to me hauntingly beautiful," he wrote of her in his middle-age. She had a Scots accent and her low, rhythmic voice had mesmerized him. "It was the sound of a bruised, reflective spirit, easily startled and put in flight. I guessed her to be about fifty but she resembled a young girl more than anyone I had ever met. If this seems like an over-romanticised remembrance of her, it may well be, but she did have the rarest presence, which, to me, she always left behind her like some gentle imprint. Illusory or not, it was always the effect she had on me, one that filled me with a disturbing, irrepressible, thwarted tenderness."

He went on to describe how she lived in a small north London flat with her sister, also a spinster, and a retired civil servant. She was an active, lifelong member of the Communist Party – as Ruth had been in the play – but was losing heart in the cause when they met in 1954. She seemed wounded in an unspoken, inconsolable way that reminded him of his father. He therefore felt protective towards her, indebted in a sense that he could never rationalize. When he became successful, he was able to help her and persuaded her to leave her miserable job at the agency to become his secretary.

By then, he was married to his second wife, Mary Ure, and Helen began work in a small office of their home. Yet he knew from the beginning that she possessed no secretarial skills whatsoever. She couldn't type or take shorthand. She tried her best to learn typing, but he was soon typing the letters himself after she went home. She grappled unsuccessfully with shorthand and he felt relieved when she agreed that it wasn't really necessary for the job. She was too polite to field telephone calls as he mimed frantically in the background that he wasn't home.

She persevered for a year or so. But by then the strain of coping with his increasingly chaotic life became too much. However hard he tried to placate her growing panic, it was obvious the job had degenerated into a charade. There was no choice but to let her go back to the Oxford Street treadmill, which she did for a while, until they sacked her. She then spent the long days with her sister, but ventured out little. He described meeting her occasionally when the remains of her old vitality would smoulder and his hopes would revive. But they faded with each encounter. Before long she died, and, according to her sister, without complaint.

"I knew very little about her," he concluded his memory of her. "And if there was little to know, perhaps it was because she was so little regarded.

She committed the unthinkable error of the age of not demanding attention and got none, except for a factitious life imposed on her anonymity in a second-rate play."

13

First Love, First Marriage

Pamela: the ultimate illusionist.
Osborne notebook entry, 1985

Early in 1951, Osborne was a lowly member of the Roc Players in the back-water town of Bridgwater in Somerset, when he fell in love with Pamela Lane as they acted together onstage. The promising young actress who would become his first wife was almost twenty-one, a local girl who trained at the Royal Academy of Dramatic Art and had now returned home to join the small company as an assistant stage manager. It wouldn't be too long, she hoped, before she would return to London. She was the daughter of a respectable middle-class draper and a mother who came from minor rural gentry, but with her defiantly cropped red hair, she possessed a rebellious streak. She had passed up a place to read English literature at Durham University to become an actress against the wishes of her conventional parents, who rarely went to the theatre. They would have preferred her to settle down and marry the local solicitor or doctor.

Osborne, himself twenty-one and eager for work after the debacle of his Yuletide *Aladdin* at Hayling Island, was playing a small role as a young man in the Roc Players drawing-room comedy entitled *My Wife's Family*. The curtain went up to reveal him with his arms round the housemaid, played by the ingénue, Pamela Lane, locked in a kiss.

"There was no calculation in my instant obsession, no assessment, thought of present, future comfort or discomfort," he wrote extravagantly of his smitten younger self. "I knew that I was in love as if the White Plague [tuberculosis] had claimed me earlier than I had calculated. I waited for the curtain to go up, holding in my arms this powerful, drawn up creature, dressed in a green maid's uniform of all things. Life was unimaginable without her matching green eyes. Pamela's emotional equivocation seemed so unstudied that I interpreted it as ineffable passion. It was as if she had once known a secret divinity that in time would reveal itself and her."

The young, impressionable Osborne, an impulsive romantic, fell for the young actress he would brood about all his life as "the ultimate illusionist", and it happened within the illusion of theatre itself where nothing is ever quite real. Years after the wreckage of his marriage to Pamela, he was still trying to unlock her mysterious source as if he could never grasp who she really was. He was obsessed by the cool, enigmatic beauty of his first wife, but she always eluded him, as Alison's measured middle-class way in *Look Back in Anger* defeats the enraged Jimmy Porter in his battle to possess or destroy her.

> "I want to stand up in your tears, and splash about in them and sing. I want to be there when you grovel. I want to be there, I want to watch it, I want the front seat. I want to see your face rubbed in the mud – that's all I can hope for. There's nothing else I want any longer."

There can be no doubt that Osborne fell in love with Pamela Lane at first sight. From their first meeting, he was bewitched by her wilful independence, her fiery red hair and the sphinx-like allure of her huge green eyes. He fancifully took red hair to be "the mantle of goddesses and priestesses who craved not obedience, like Ayesha, but a siren enjoining flight up into the firmament of life itself". As if that weren't flighty enough, red hair was also "the copper-headed helmet of destiny of those who would hurl their challenge against the very centre of creation and, having struck, plummet and explode upon a disbelieving world. It was lifted by the winds from the north-east, breathing like warspite Hotspur . . ."

Stop! (one surely thinks). He's on a roll, riffing jazzily in his overheated solo before the mythic red-headed goddess of his dreams. "It was the shade of the imagination's crimson twilight, punitive and cleansing, the colour of communing voluptuaries, of pre-Raphaelites, Renaissance princes, of Medicis and Titians, of Venice and Northumbria, of bloodaxe and vengeance, Percy and Borgia, of Beatrice – Dante and Shakespeare's – of hot pretenders and virgin monarchs. A red-haired Doris Day was unthinkable."

The pert blonde is unquestionably preferable for the role of the girl next door. But Osborne never married the girl next door. Which crash-and-burn redheads wildly plummeting and exploding like meteors in the firmament could possibly live up to his romantic illusion of love? (Not Pamela Lane, nor his redheaded third wife, Penelope Gilliatt.) Then there was the imagined fantasy life with his first love in those stricken moments in each other's arms onstage that he remembered as "unimaginable without her green eyes" which mysteriously "mock or plead affection".

Yet the first thing I noticed about Pamela Lane when we met was that her eyes were pale blue. Her red hair had turned grey, but the colour of her wide, engaging blue eyes had never changed, she told me.

For a while their marriage was happy enough, although they were frequently apart when she was acting on the road and he stayed behind looking for work in London. Her career blossomed from the start, and he grew to resent her success as she overshadowed him. When they acted together at Derby Playhouse, to his chagrin he was even known as "Mr Lane".

Alan Bates – whose breakthrough role was to play Cliff in the first production of *Look Back in Anger* – saw Lane act a number of times at Derby when he was a teenager and remembered her as a gifted actress. Osborne's acting made no impression on him. But when he later auditioned for his role in *Look Back*, he recognized its unknown dramatist lurking backstage.

A working actress all her life, Lane was always well regarded but stardom eluded her. She never had the luck. It takes good fortune to make it anywhere, but the theatre makes a fetish out of luck. In those early days, however, she soon became a leading actress in repertory and seemed destined for great things.

"We were so ridiculously over in love," Osborne said of their mutual infatuation, quoting from *Private Lives*.

"I remember thinking when we first met, now here's a surly sod," she told me. "But he had flair and blazing ideals, and we were married in three months. We were just potty about each other."

When I asked her to say more about the "surly sod" she impulsively married at twenty-one, her response took me by surprise. She said that it was like Alison's explanation of why she married Jimmy Porter in *Look Back in Anger*.

HELENA: Why did you –
ALISON: Marry him? There must be about six different explanations . . . I knew I was taking on more than I was ever likely to be capable of bearing, but there never seemed to be any choice. Well, the howl of outrage and astonishment went up from the family, and that did it. Whether or not he was in love with me, that did it. He made up his mind to marry me. They did just about everything they could think of to stop us.

HELENA: Yes, it wasn't a very pleasant business. But you can see their point.

ALISON: Jimmy went into battle with his axe swinging round his head – frail, and so full of fire. I had never seen anything like it. The old story of the knight in shining armour – except that his armour didn't really shine very much.

Look Back in Anger was based on the breakdown of Osborne's marriage to Lane. Its plot was influenced by Tennessee Williams's *A Streetcar Named Desire*.

In both dramas, a refined upper-class woman has married into the lower class. Stanley Kowalski/Jimmy Porter has blowtorched his way into "society". Each wife is brutalized by a furious outsider who wants to bring her down to his animal level. And in each play, Another Woman intrudes in the role of the wife's genteel sister/best friend whose façade of propriety is shattered when she's raped/seduced by the hero.

Look Back is written in the rhetoric of war. (Class war, marital war, sex war – a potent brew.) Women wear their men's colours in the play like loyal foot soldiers. Both Alison and Helena, the mistress who replaces her, wear Jimmy's shirts as if draped in the Porter flag of allegiance. Osborne called Pamela his "unique prize" to be carried off in the bloody war to end all wars against "Mummy". "Mummy" is Lane's disapproving mother, who is demonized in the play as the kind of righteous upper-class hypocrite demanding the battle be fought by Queensberry Rules while kicking you in the groin.

JIMMY: Mummy locked her up in their eight-bedroomed castle, didn't she? There is no limit to what the middle-aged mummy will do in the holy crusade against ruffians like me. Mummy and I took one quick look at each other, and, from then on, the age of chivalry was dead.

Lane's parents were implacably opposed to the marriage. "They'd never met anyone like him before," she told me. "They'd never been *spoken* to like that before." Yet Osborne didn't regard her father bitterly, and the two of them even liked each other grudgingly across the great divide. Mr Lane, himself the son of a West Country master draper, had been a dashing flying officer and hero in the Great War. "Mummy" was the armour-plated war leader marshalling all forces in the bloody cause of stopping the marriage. The twenty-one-year-old Osborne wrote emotionally to Anthony Creighton from the Bridgwater battlefront.

Repertory Theatre,
Bridgwater
May 1951

And now – to tell you of the terrible nightmare of the last few days. I
hardly know where to begin. Horror has heaped upon horror. Rage, tears,
disgust and utter havoc have been mine in a way I have never known
in a short speck of time that I shall remember as long as I live. It has
all been so sordid and horrible. I can only give the merest outline, but
here goes . . .

His "merest outline" ran to eleven pages of escalating hysteria. The first
page sets the scene:

Last Thursday it began. I was summoned down to Pam's house in the
afternoon. I went down determined to be completely ruthless and uncompromising. And I was. The family tried to attack me with everything,
of course, but they had never met anything like me before, and I scattered all before me. They tried abuse, cajolery, remorse, tears, appeals to
my better nature – the lot. I knew just how to deal with it. I stamped
on it. I told them frankly that I knew they hated me and everything I
stood for (they even dared to timidly deny it) and that I hated them. I
said that I loved Pam, admired her and believed in her, and would take
her away from all the things here that threatened all her fineness . . .

He went on to write that "the bastards" who ran the theatre were plotting his downfall by threatening to blacklist him. Then he told of a ghost
from the past, Lynne Reid Banks (who would later write the best-selling
novel *The L-Shaped Room*) blundering into the scene. She was a new recruit
of Pamela's mother in the campaign against him. "In the evening, to my
HORROR, who should arrive at the theatre but LYNNE. We looked at each
other with open loathing."

Reid Banks had been at RADA with Lane and was one of the three
plummy-voiced actresses who were members of the shambling Saga
Repertory Company with Osborne. He disliked her on sight, finding her
snootily prim and disapproving – "a professional virgin" who was later able
to detect "the smell of male squalor in either cock-happy Copt or free-
crapping labrador." "Some men will put it in a brick wall," he said about
her uncharitably.

The letter next related how Osborne gave in his notice at the theatre.
Pamela did the same. But she recanted under pressure. "Oh, I can't begin
to tell you a fraction of the whole terrifying business," he went on, describing

his loved one locked up in purdah with Mummy. (Jimmy Porter's princess "locked up in the eight-bedroom castle".) "I managed somehow to smuggle a letter into Pam's house through the Assistant Stage Manager. I swore to myself that if it was the last thing I did I would get her out at the soonest possible moment away from all this squalor."

The outraged letter concluded with the Lanes accusing him of going after Pamela's money. A small legacy was due to her.

A paltry 2,000 – useful God knows, but I wouldn't suspect my worst enemy of these motives . . . The bloody oafs. Those kind of people are natural born fascists. Surbiton's own supermen – blind, intolerant and stupid. Quite without scruple. God, how I hate them . . .

Then comes the crunch:

We have thought the whole situation out very, very carefully. And we have reached one decision. It sounds quite, quite mad I know. But I know – oh God I do know – that it is RIGHT . . . We are going to get married as soon as we possibly can.

Only days before the marriage, Pamela was still writing to him in secret. Straining to be tactful, she pleaded with him not to antagonize anyone further:

Bridgwater
8 June 1951

Darling, it's not that I don't trust your instinctive knowledge of how to behave in any situation which might arise . . . I'll try to tell you all about it when they let me see you again. Until then, just trust me enough to know that you must follow the small points of advice I'm going to give you. They're the only things that can save us. A repeat of what I said over the phone this morning – please, please don't antagonise anyone in the company. IT WON'T HELP. Don't try to defend me in anything they may say about me. Just know that whatever happens I love you more and more through all this. Pray God gives you courage and strength to deal with whatever comes along. I'm with you and closer to you than ever. My everlasting and enduring love.

But events then spun out of control in a last-ditch attempt by the Lanes to stop the marriage. In another letter to Creighton, Osborne related how Mrs Lane had now accused him of being homosexual.

Repertory Theatre
Bridgwater, 1951

When troubles come they come not in single spies, but in battalions –
the big gun she [Pamela's mother] brings up against me is that I am
QUEER. Yes!! Or as she puts it: a NANCY BOY. She points to my
long hair, the dying Keats face and body, my complete oddity, my affect-
edness, effeminacy – even Vicky!! [His dog, a dachshund.] The rest you
can imagine – that a daughter of hers should be seen with anyone as
low as that. And so on and so on. I'll confess it all made me feel a little
sick and ill. Pam was horrified, virulent and firm . . .

Dying Keatsian appearance or no, we can imagine the immature, long-
haired Osborne mincing merrily down Bridgwater High Street *being* actorish.
Vicky the dachshund wouldn't have helped. Osborne's idea of an actor was
to act one. (But he wasn't a good actor.) He set out to shock and rile the
1950s small-town conservatism of the Lanes, and his provocative notion
of bohemian camp did the job. At the same time, the parental holy war
against him only made him more determined to carry off his Juliet. "Some
people do actually marry for revenge," says Alison in *Look Back*. "People
like Jimmy, anyway . . ."

"It never occurred to me he could be gay," Lane told me. She didn't
seem in the least defensive about it. "At RADA I lived in digs with gay
actors. I was also used to people being camp. I recognized camp in John.
He was actually rather fond of men and he was tactile with everyone. But
he was exclusively heterosexual."

Osborne and Pamela Lane, I assumed, had been infatuated lovers since
they met. "You're wrong to suppose that," she said, and volunteered they
hadn't slept together until they married.

"You know, it's funny," Alison confesses to Helena in *Look Back*, "but
we never slept together before we were married."

"All well on the night, I trust?" I ventured.

"Indeed," Pamela replied.

Osborne cheerfully claimed the reason Lane's parents were convinced of
his homosexuality – and had him trailed by a private detective to prove it
– was that they'd seen an actor in the company fumbling with his knee
under the table in a local tea shop. "You don't know *what* you want, dear,"
the actor cooed hopefully.

The private detective drew a blank. The intervention of Lynne Reid Banks
poured oil on the fire when she turned up in Bridgwater to accuse Osborne

of being gay. In correspondence with me from her home in Dorset in February 2002, she admitted after quite a struggle with her uneasy conscience, however, that her accusation all those years ago was false. She had plotted with the seething Mrs Lane to persuade Pamela to call off the marriage.

Mrs Lane had never met Reid Banks, but she knew of the RADA connection with her daughter and telephoned her urgently in London. "She sounded absolutely frantic," Reid Banks told me. "They begged me to come down secretly and try to persuade Pam that he was a homosexual. They said I had it in my power to save her from a disastrous marriage."

Banks was young and silly, and the cloak-and-dagger aspects of the affair must have appealed to her. There's also a sense of retribution for the way Osborne had taunted her during their days together in the little rep company. "We didn't get on before this. It was a class thing . . ."

She had one speculative theory, however, that Osborne might in fact be gay. Visiting Hayling Island, she was struck by his bizarre appearance in a modern American play by John van Druten (possibly *Voice of the Turtle*). "It called for a clean-cut juvenile lead, and there was John with his bushy hair swept up in a precursor of an Afro and very heavy make-up embellished with green eye-shadow. It was the eye-shadow that startled me."

Never judge a man by his eye-shadow. Osborne, the attention-grabbing novice actor, performed many a contemporary role, it seems, as if appearing flamboyantly in a Restoration Comedy. But, his future wife told me that she contemptuously dismissed the allegation. Reid Banks remembered her saying, "That's just my parents' mad idea. They think all actors are nancy boys."

Osborne was to get even with Lynne Reid Banks in his own way. Attending a house party she gave in London when he had become a famous dramatist and she a well-known writer, he took gleeful schoolboy revenge on her. He offered her a smoked salmon and cream cheese sandwich in which he'd gone to some trouble to carefully insert a used condom. "The unbelieving repulsion on her face, the prig struck by lightning," Osborne remembered with delight, "was fixed forever for me, like Kean's Macbeth."

John James Osborne and Pamela Elizabeth Lane were married at Bridgwater Parish Church in the County of Somerset on 23 June 1951. "Lusting for the slaughter," as Jimmy Porter describes his own church wedding.

The description of the wedding in *Look Back in Anger* mirrors the near-farcical reality down to the triumphant image of vanquished Mummy slumped over her pew – "the noble, female rhino, pole-axed at last!"

Osborne, not even knowing how to get legally married, had to visit the public library to look up the rules of the game in *Whitaker's Almanack*. They planned to wed in secret, but the registrar in Bridgwater was a friend of Mr Lane's and they were nervous he'd spill the beans. So a church wedding it was. They hurriedly bought a special licence, at a cost of four pounds – half a week's salary – enabling them to be married in church within three days. The sympathetic local vicar agreed to marry them on a Saturday morning at 8 a.m.

The ungodly hour wasn't just a matter of secrecy. They had a rehearsal at 10 a.m. According to Osborne, the vicar lost his nerve at the last moment and contacted the Lanes. Pamela's account differs a little. Her father learned of the wedding through a member of the parish council and tried to persuade the harassed vicar not to marry them. The Rev. Hughes-Davies remained steadfast, however, and the Lanes turned up uninvited on the big day determined to do the right thing even though they were all at war.

Jimmy Porter describes his best man as "a chap I'd met in a pub that morning". In real life he was the convivial Frank Middlemass, Osborne's one good friend in the Roc Players company, who was sworn to secrecy and terrified it would all go wrong. "It was not a happy day," he told me glumly. All he could remember about it were the parents seated at the back of the empty church with the mother having hysterics.

The bride was married in the best frock she wore for her RADA audition. The groom was in his usual frayed jacket and cords. She called it his "Dylan Thomas look".

Nellie Beatrice wasn't invited to the wedding. Perhaps Osborne's initial reluctance to tell his mother about the marriage can be explained away by the need for secrecy on the wedding day. He would also have dreaded her belittling mantras: "What do you think a girl like that could see in you?" "Don't get above yourself . . ." In class-bound England, he *was* getting above himself. He was on the make. As long as he remained an anonymous actor and playwright, however, he was still too insecure to risk his mother's disapproval.

Throughout the marriage, he nevertheless continued visiting her for their ritual "Black Monday" outings. He wrote to her while acting on the road, sending a little money each week, flowers on her birthday. (She sent him back food parcels.) Yet his mother didn't even learn of the marriage until five years later. Osborne had no choice but to tell her when his divorce and subsequent marriage to Mary Ure were about to make headline news.

His first wife never met the humiliated Nellie Beatrice, and she didn't think it worth the risk. The thorny subject was taboo at home and could be explosive. "Whenever he spoke of her, it was always of someone who blighted his father's life," Lane explained. "I'm fairly sure that he didn't want her to put a curse on the marriage. He saw her as a sentimental tyrant and felt that I might be infected by her in some way. He had a very super-stitious feeling about his mother's influence on his affairs generally. He thought if anything went wrong with his life, Nellie Beatrice had somehow cast her spell over it. It's an extraordinary delusion for an intelligent person, but he had it."

After the wedding ceremony, the first Mr and Mrs John Osborne went off to their 10 a.m. rehearsal at the theatre, followed by the Saturday matinée and evening performance. The father of the bride, still trying desperately to do the decent thing, insisted on giving a little wedding lunch at the local hostelry usually frequented by the town's Masons and Rotarians. His new son-in-law remembered the four of them having pilchard salad and light ale in almost complete silence "apart from the occasional sob from the mottle-necked Mrs Lane". Even the more forgiving Pamela described the occasion to me as "grisly".

Later that wedding day, the artistic director of the Roc Players, who had always been firmly opposed to the marriage, threatened to shoot Osborne with his army rifle. In return, the giddy groom handed him a week's notice on behalf of "my wife and I".

He had carried off his "unique prize", but in the stagey haze of melo-drama nothing rings true. The marriage certificate in his back pocket was triumphant proof of his victory and the ultimate "up yours" to defeated, pole-axed Mummy. The defiant act of getting married was all that mattered. As if in exhausted reflex, the newly-weds even went their separate ways after the evening performance. Osborne described how, overcome with boozy exhaustion, he saw his bride back to her parents' home on their wedding night, and to his relief, he was not invited in. He returned to his digs where his motherly landlady, who was fond of him, greeted him in tears and told him what a wicked boy he'd been.

The following Sunday, the week's notice played out at the theatre, they left for London where they spent their first night alone in a small, dingy hotel on the Cromwell Road. They had twenty pounds between them. Although the weary Mr Lane dutifully saw them off at Bridgwater station, Pamela would be estranged from both her parents for many years. Before the newly-weds left, Osborne slipped Mr Lane a letter promising he would always love and take care of his daughter.

14

First Divorce

I suppose the fact is, quite simply, that I can't bear the thought of
having to go on living with her at all.

Osborne letter to Anthony Creighton, 1954

When Pamela Lane first saw *Look Back in Anger* shortly after it opened at
the Royal Court Theatre, the marriage had been over for almost two years
and she had the surreal experience of seeing it reinvented onstage. Yet she
found herself admiring the play that gave such passionate voice to the kind
of theatre they had talked about so often during their marriage, and it
disturbed her. The details might differ, but she could not have failed to
recognize the sources immediately.

"Oh, no," she remembered thinking with a sense of dread even as the
curtain rose. "Not the ironing board." The play's symbolic relic of domestic
bondage in the unemancipated 1950s ranks almost as another character
projecting the unspoken role of the heroine's silent attrition. We must
remind ourselves that even the sight of an ironing board onstage was considered remarkable at the time. Alison's opening line as she irons is an absent,
"What's that?" Her second, "I'm sorry. I wasn't listening properly." Isolated,
coiled Jimmy must bully and needle a reaction out of her at all cost. (He
needs an audience as much as love; so did Osborne.) Alison's power and
secret weapon is her self-protective shield of withdrawal.

In an admiring essay on Tennessee Williams, Osborne wrote of his own
belief that theatre is "the art of the more so". Like Williams, he preferred
plays writ emotionally large. *Look Back in Anger* – his most autobiographical play – thus exaggerated and distilled reality, turning marriage into a
blood sport while the two protagonists are based on real people, only more
so.

"To be as vehement as he is is to be almost non-committal," Osborne
wrote of his alter ego, Jimmy Porter. The refined Alison – "tuned to a

different key, a key of well-bred malaise", as he described her – keeps the shaky peace in the ferocious class war and turmoil between them with every stoic swipe of her iron. "Oh, I *loved* ironing," Pamela Lane told me sarcastically. But there was one crucial difference between her and her fictionalized self. She would have thrown the ironing board at Jimmy Porter.

She did, in a sense. When they first met, Osborne described her as a female version of himself. Their temperaments were opposite, but they shared a combative streak, a survivor's instinct. They were both rebels in their own wilful fashion. From the beginning of their illicit infatuation, detached, enigmatic Pamela Lane had shown an articulate obduracy. When they were first married, she read his second play, the bloated verse drama *The Great Bear* or *Minette* and judged it "D and B" – shorthand between them for "Dull and Boring". He agreed with her verdict, although those stinging little words "D and B" would haunt him. Fearing her hanging judgment, he hid the script of the 1954 *Personal Enemy* from her, though by then the marriage was in turmoil.

Pamela was no simpering pushover as *Look Back*'s Alison is often mistaken to be. She was uncowed by John Osborne before he became "John Osborne". After all, she defied everyone by marrying him and she defied him in the end by leaving him.

When the newly-weds fled Bridgwater for London, they couldn't afford their own home and eventually moved into one of Anthony Creighton's two rooms just off Brook Green in Hammersmith, sharing his chintzy sitting room for a weekly rent of two pounds. The *ménage à trois* at 35 Caithness Road is mirrored in *Look Back* where Jimmy and Alison share their flat with his best friend, Cliff, the loyal Welshman. Osborne based him loosely on Creighton, who was nicknamed "Mouse".

"He gets more like a little mouse every day, doesn't he?" Jimmy says teasingly about Cliff, who is the peacekeeper in the play. "He really does look like one. Look at those ears, and that face, and the short little legs."

"That's because he *is* a mouse," replies Alison.

Osborne nurtured hopes of re-forming the disastrous Saga Repertory Company with Creighton as producer, and he had in mind that Pamela Lane would join them from the beginning.

12 June 1951
Bridgwater

As far as Pam is concerned with the future with Saga. I *know* – we know it will be all right. She is so wonderful, old son. Dear, dear Mouse, thank

God for us all, beautiful, talented, intelligent people. I can't wait for you to start producing Pam. Believe me, apart from the fact that I am completely, irrevocably in love with her, she has such promise theatrically and that "star quality" I know you will recognise. Admittedly, she is a bit tall, but so are many others . . .

His love for her was otherwise unqualified. "She has all the world's passion," he wrote again to Creighton. "Pam and I are so terribly, incredibly in love. She is so good and kind, my old friend. I know you will get on well."

They did get along and she became fond of him. They shared the same dreams of making it in theatre, and the three of them could live cheaply together. They were pragmatic vegetarians making do on deprivation, as the British will. There was still food rationing and they could barter their meat coupons for more cheese. Osborne, an obsessive list-maker all his life (words, useful phrases, enemies), fussily kept a laundry list of the precise weekly cost of everything – razor blades, herbs, envelopes, cigarettes, sticks of greasepaint, mother. (He sent his mother ten shillings a week and a pack of cigarettes.) He would hope for work here or there around London while his wife, a leading lady on tour, earned £10 a week and sent him back three or four pounds. She had to pawn a ring; he almost pawned the typewriter.

When she unexpectedly sent him a pound from the road, he telegrammed back as if it were a lifeline: "ECSTATIC THANKS FOR CASH. BLESS YOU. SO BLEAK WITHOUT YOU. LOVE TEDDY." Remember, her nickname for him was "Teddy" or "Bears"; she was "Squirrel" or "Nutty".

Derby,
8 Dec 1953

Darling much-missed one,

I think I'm preggers again. So I've got at least a baby bear to keep me warm. Lovings and blessings, sweetheart –

Nutty

P.S. How's Mouse? Is he feeling better now?

She became accidentally pregnant twice, but no child came from the marriage. "The first time was a miscarriage, and by the second we were riding a very rough road," she said. "I wanted to go on acting."

"If only you would have a child and it would die," Jimmy Porter curses the pregnant Alison during the marital wars in *Look Back*.

Pamela Lane was the breadwinner. She got Osborne work.

4 January 1954
Derby Playhouse

Darling Treasure-bear,
I'm rather taking it for granted that you want to come here. I wish it could be as leading man . . . Wish there was a job for Mouse, too, but, at least if he feels lonely in town, he can come and stay here whenever he likes.

"Trying to get old Bears work in Derby," she wrote optimistically to him again, and the marriage thus far seems loving and inescapably, cosily fey. "Oh darling, I did miss you more than ever over Christmas," she wrote to him some two years after they married. "Such a cold end to the festivities climbing into an empty bearless bed. I've got your *beauooootiful* Christmas Bear card on my mantelpiece. My beautiful furry lover, it *shall* be the last Christmas apart if I can help it. All my love, Nutty."

She was naive about money, and perhaps they both were. When she did inherit the £2,000 legacy that her parents had accused Osborne of marrying her for, he came up with a surprising proposal. Although the money would have kept them both comfortably for a good two years or more, she ended up investing it in a small hotel in Salisbury to be run by Osborne's favourite Uncle Jack. Thrice married, one-armed Uncle Jack – the roguish soldier of fortune who was run over by his own ice cream van in Southend – was on his uppers again.

"Can't we help him in some way?" Osborne asked his wife sweetly. Uncle Jack installed his girlfriend, known as Chips, to run the place as manager and wife. But Chips preferred to spend her time behind the bar, and so did Uncle Jack. The doomed hotel was named Claridge's – "biggest misnomer of all time," Lane told me, laughing.

Why did the marriage fail? One explanation is their lengthy separations. Work frequently took her away and it became a weekend marriage. She told me that he wanted her to give up her career and stay at home.

"He wanted you to be a housewife?"

"He said he did."

It wasn't unusual for actresses to abandon their careers for marriage in the Fifties, however. A domestic role for middle-class ladies was still more the unliberated norm. But she was the one who paid almost all the bills while he was unemployed and struggling with his plays. He couldn't even find an agent willing to represent him. No one, Osborne confessed, could compound his terror of isolation with such finality as Pamela, his "prize possession". He came to see even her presence as a reproach, infesting his

First Divorce

uncertainties and sense of failure. She wouldn't, in any event, abandon the
stage for him. "Pusillanimous", as he mocked her when the marriage turned
sour, wouldn't cave in to his needs.

"Pusillanimous. Adjective. From the Latin pusillus, very little, and
animus, the mind. (*Slamming the dictionary shut.*) That's my wife, that's
her, isn't it? Behold the Lady Pusillanimous. Hi, Pusey! When's your next
picture?"

Look Back in Anger

"My separation from Pamela had no consolation now that I was not
working," he wrote. "There was no thought of prizes, only loss. I was
absorbed in loss, unmistakable loss, inescapable loss, unacceptable to all
but gamblers. It still needed the croupier's nod, the bland confirmation
from Pamela herself."

The croupier's nod, that mortal signal to the crushed loser that the time
has come to slink away from the gaming table, came when his wife eventually confirmed she was having an affair.

She had now got him work at Derby Playhouse and the serious rifts
between them began when they first worked together in Derby. Having
joined her there, he found himself bewildered and sick with disbelief that
she had turned away from him without warning or explanation. He wrote
about it to Creighton, his only friend, two and a half years into the marriage.

Derby
[Early 1954]

You see, ever since I have been up here, she seems to have gone out of
her way to deliberately treat me like a stranger. She has given me *nothing*
– not an ounce of warmth or spontaneous affection. I just don't know
what is in her mind – but it's almost as if she's set out to break me. I
feel so stupid, too, for I'm sure the whole company must have noticed
it. What had I done? Had I never meant anything to her? She has very
little to say, except this: *I had to realize she was very different when she
was working!* That THE THEATRE meant so much to her etc. Yes! That is
the honest truth! I couldn't believe my ears. If she were leading lady at
the Old Vic, it wouldn't excuse her treatment of me. But weekly rep in
Derby! How can anyone expect to be an artist with such meanness of
spirit? Good God, you must have HEART, above all things. That is what
I believe, anyway.

The letter then escalates in bewilderment and loathing:

Watching her fool about at the dress rehearsal today, giggling and laughing helplessly, I can only think she's the biggest PHONEY ever to walk. A PHONEY. She says she wants PEACE. I replied, justly I think, that she's never known anything else. She says I shouldn't have married her if she was cold. How was I to foresee anything like this? It's a nightmare to me. I cannot believe it is happening to me. I feel ill and dazed. She doesn't even have a twinge of regret, not an ounce of remorse, absolutely no inkling of compassion. I am so low, so humiliated, so ashamed. I hate and loathe the very sight of her. My bowels turn over every time I think of her. Everything has simply collapsed round my ears – God knows it was little enough! Everything, everything has turned utterly sour and terrible.

He was suffering from recurring migraines during this time and had broken out in a body rash too. When he found himself overcome by a sickening toothache caused by an abscess, Pamela arranged an urgent visit to the local dentist before the show that night. He didn't yet know that she was having an affair with the dentist. Two back teeth were removed, after a struggle. "You've got teeth like a horse," he remembered his wife's lover saying to him chattily while he leaned on his chest before wrenching them out.

As if that weren't agony enough, the dentist wasn't any old philandering flosser of Derby. He was on the board of the theatre. Osborne had already been made the town cuckold, it seems. But the story gets more farcical. While all this was happening, Osborne was playing the supporting role of the dentist in G. B. Shaw's *You Never Can Tell*. It was another reason for him to hate Shaw.

There's an old theatre expression about infidelity: "It doesn't count if you're on tour." This counted. Osborne had been faithful to his wife and a brief compensatory fling he would have with another actress in the company seems to have been little comfort. For him, disloyalty would always be one of the deadly sins, though he was unfaithful to all his wives and lovers.

ALISON: It's what he would call a question of allegiances, and he expects you to be pretty literal about it. Not only about himself and all the things he believes in, his present and his future, but his past as well. All the people he admires and loves, and has loved. The friends he used to know, people I've never known – and probably wouldn't have liked. His father, who died years ago. Even the other women he's loved. Do you understand?

Look Back in Anger

"I think John was a man you would be bound to let down in some way," a friend of Osborne's told me. "Once you've introduced the necessity of loyalty, somebody's going to be treacherous."

But he had been weaned on loss, as if born with some ill-defined fear that people like him would always end up dispossessed. The painfully isolated heroes of his plays are never able to transcend their anguish, like Archie Rice dreading the hook and oblivion, or the meltdown, middle-aged lawyer Bill Maitland who's put on sweaty nightmare trial for his life, or Jimmy Porter bitterly mourning "the wrong people going hungry, the wrong people being loved, the wrong people dying".

Osborne dreaded loss – a legacy of his father's death – and loss seeps through his plays. Its ugly sister, rejection, would forever be expressed by him in the language of the disenchanted as unforgivable coldness. In his 1953 notebook, we find him already "looking back" darkly: "When I look back on the short years of my life I can see all my personal relationships as an unbroken series of defeats, every one of them bitter and bloody."

At twenty-four, his wife's rejection left him helpless. He was unable to cope with infidelity. (Who can?) But the hypersensitive Osborne would always be an emotionally vulnerable man. When threatened, his animal instinct turned savage, while his wife's betrayal, as he saw it, left him keening in utter confusion and self-pity.

Derby, Sunday
[Early 1954]

I cannot believe that this can have happened to me. It is too cruel, too unbelievable that life could be so wantonly treacherous and destructive. But it *is* true. It is true. Oh, Mouse, I know I must sound incomprehensible. But I am so *hurt*. I am beaten up and mangled. I *am* trying to gather myself together. I am trying to reconstruct a future for myself. I have not given up. Believe me. But try to understand how I am feeling.

The marital rows turned violent. Before and after her affair, according to Lane, he sometimes hit her and she fought back. She suffered from asthma – a condition she kept secret during her acting days – and in his fury, he would pin her to the floor and blow cigarette smoke down her mouth as she struggled to get free.

"He knew what would hurt me the most," she told me. "I literally had to fight back with all my strength. I felt I was going to die, actually. I really did. All of that time at Derby. I felt he was murderous toward me."

His violent emotion and sorry state are clear from a stream of other letters he wrote to Creighton, offering us a running commentary on the marriage as it fell apart:

"I just can't conceal my hatred and disgust any longer." "Every time I look at Pam I could beat her head in." "I cannot bear to touch her." "When I think she might have had my children – it makes me ill." "I simply long to knock her down every time I look at her." "Last Sunday I felt suicidal. Sundays I detest her twice as hard. When I got back to the flat last night I simply couldn't help myself crying." "I want to wipe it all out, but I can't." "All my confidence gone, everything." "She must have been born with disloyalty in her heart." "I just want to see the back of her."

Yet he stayed, and so did she. They both clung to the wreckage, like the mythologized version of themselves – Alison and Jimmy in *Look Back in Anger*. "Hope is too cruel to desert one utterly," he wrote to Creighton as if apologizing for his weakness. He resolved constantly to leave, yet he lingered in Derby for months in the hope and lost cause of saving the marriage even after she fled on holiday with her lover to Switzerland that summer.

> My dear,
> I must get away. I don't suppose you will understand, but please try. I need peace so desperately, and, at the moment, I am willing to sacrifice anything just for that. I don't know what's going to happen to us. I know you will be feeling wretched and bitter, but try to be a little patient with me. I shall always have a deep loving need of you.
>   Alison
>   Letter to Jimmy Porter, *Look Back in Anger*

Those were Pamela's own words, Osborne noted bitterly, as surely expressed as she judged his early writing "dull and boring". "Deep loving need!" Jimmy Porter explodes at Alison's farewell note. "That makes me puke! She couldn't say 'You rotten bastard! I hate your guts, I'm clearing out . . .'"

But his motives for staying were suspect. "At least I can live at her expense up here and save some money and fuck off when it suits me," he confessed to Creighton. "My only thought now is what I can get out of her."

Accused of marrying her for money, he now set about fulfilling the prophecy. Uncle Jack's Salisbury hotel was up for a fire sale. The impoverished Osborne was hanging in for the money.

Now: this is going to change my plans I think. Let me know what you think about it. But my own feelings are this: Pam will have at least £1000 in her pocket in a few months time, and I feel quite unscrupulous about trying to get my hands on at least some of it. I will go through some form of truce for the sake of some recompense. I think she owes me something, and I'm determined to get it somehow. Afterwards, when it suits me, she can go hang. I know how horrid and unpleasant it all sounds, but I am driven to it.

Driven to it? He was aware, at least, how low he'd sunk. "Life is so SHABBY here, Mouse. Spiritually shabby, I mean. Do you understand? I feel very much a tramp."

But he ultimately left the marriage humiliated and penniless, as this letter to his wife shows. It was written three months after they separated:

13 February 1955

Thank you very much for the two pounds. A sudden inexplicable fortune out of the blue – I am very grateful indeed . . .

Make no mistake – for the money I am sincerely grateful. But your setting up as a kind of emotional soup kitchen to your grubby husband is something else. If you had any understanding – and not simulated – feelings at all, you must know what a bitter taste this kind of watery gruel must have. What you may put in a registered envelope and send to me, I accept but spare me the cheesy charity of your feelings. Again, thank you for the money.

His merciless contempt for her was uncontrollable. "That bitch, that pusillanimous, sycophantic, snivelling, phlegmish yokel, that cow . . ." he wrote again to Creighton from Derby. "Fortunately, I've ceased to care what happens to her."

Even her talent was put in jealous contention. "Madam is busy learning her part – The BIG ACTRESS that one, devoted to her A-R-T. She makes me puke." "I still believe I could teach her a thing or two. Of course, I would never dare to *presume* . . ."

He attacked her vindictively into sleepless nights. "We go to and return from the theatre separately, sleep separately. Last night the horror of it all was too much for me and I kept her awake, calling her all the cruel, vicious names that have stimulated my loathing, my humiliation and rage. She could say nothing – only long for me to shut up and let her go back to sleep."

He put her on trial even for the past, fighting old battles long since won. (The Bridgwater wars, Mummy, Lynne Reid Banks.) "Cancel and pass on," goes the motto of the bullying Captain in August Strindberg's grotesque tragi-comedy of a rotten marriage, *Dance of Death*. But Osborne never could "pass on". (Nor could the Captain.)

He scribbled this thumbnail portrait of his paranoid obsessiveness in his notebook – a dry run for a passage in *Look Back*: "I go through all the drawers, the trunks, the cases, in the bookcase. To see if there's anything of me somewhere, a reference to me. I want to know if I'm being betrayed and I don't know it."

And, finding clues, he gloated over the crumbs of victory:

Derby
[Late 1954]

. . . I told her how contemptible and weak she was to go plotting among my old enemies (and enlisting new ones). She tried to bluff her way out, but I had her trapped. I brought out that trump card I've kept all this time: the letter she wrote to Mummy all those months ago. Was she *shaken*! I called her a snivelling bloody Judas and so on. By this time I knew I'd got her up against the ropes, and I was enjoying every moment of it. A few more blows smashed home and it was a knockout. She was sobbing her heart out, and I was obliged to try and comfort her . . . The fact is that it was a very real triumph for me. I was able to break her like a stick in my hands and every moment was joy – an empty joy, no doubt. But there it is.

So the story of Osborne's first marriage, begun in romantic infatuation when they were both twenty-one, ended wretchedly three years later.

It seems impossible to imagine they could be reconciled in any way, yet they would maintain a friendship for many years after the marriage was over. When Pamela Lane's career faltered in the 1960s, she turned to her ex-husband, who helped her financially for the rest of his life.

Osborne lingered in Derby for nine months in all, even returning to the company for another season, until they finally parted.

Eight months later, he recorded in his 1955 Pocket Diary:

4 May: Began writing *Look Back in Anger*.
6 May: *Look Back in Anger*, Act I finished.
17 May: Act II, Scene 1 finished.
3 June: *Look Back in Anger* finished.

15

A Subject of Scandal and Concern

JOHN OSBORNE'S SECRET GAY LOVE – banner headline advertising exclusive interview with Anthony Creighton who declares he was Osborne's longtime lover.

Evening Standard, 24 January 1995

When Osborne and Pamela Lane separated, she moved out of the Hammersmith flat they shared with Anthony Creighton, and soon afterward, Creighton invested a small inheritance in a creaky old Rhine barge on the Thames. It was Osborne's idea. The M/Y *Egret* was moored in the Cubitt Yacht Basin beside Chiswick Bridge, and the two friends moved in just before *Look Back in Anger* was finished.

"My entitlement to forty-two shillings a week dole money had lapsed, but my expenses were minimal," Osborne wrote. "My half contribution to the mooring fee was ten shillings. Calor gas was cheap for the galley, and we used paraffin for the ancient heating-stove."

That inert late summer, waiting anxiously for the telephone to ring with news of his new play, he painted the boat in nursery-like colours and still forlornly hoped for a reconciliation with Pamela. Every major theatrical management and agent would reject the play (including Margery Vosper, the literary agent who eventually represented him). Even Patrick Desmond returned the dog-eared manuscript of *Look Back* with a reproachful call: "I mean, this simply won't do *at all.*"

Seething at the rejections, he kept painting the M/Y *Egret* from stem to stern as Creighton, also an unemployed actor, sunbathed on deck, cooked vegetarian meals and hoped for news of work. They picked plentiful nettles from the river bank and stewed them. "Combined with the occasional Nuttelene health-shop fantasy like 'Risserole'," Osborne remembered with homespun expertise, "or the lusty-sounding 'meatless steaks' and as much New Zealand cheddar as we could afford, we just managed to avoid actual hunger."

His published version of *The Entertainer* is dedicated to Creighton in memory of such hard times:

> To A.C.
> who remembers what it was like, and will not
> forget it; who I hope, will never let me forget it
> – not while there is still a Paradise Street and
> Claypit Lane to go back to

He never made any secret of their friendship. The two of them turned up together at dinner parties from the earliest days of the Royal Court. William Gaskill (who would become Devine's chosen successor) met Osborne for the first time at Tony Richardson's flat before *Look Back in Anger* was produced. Like everyone else at the newly formed Court, he was curious to meet the unknown dramatist. "I suppose I had imagined a shaggy-haired, open-necked intellectual," Gaskill recalled. "John arrived in a blazer and bow tie, very neat, a bit flash and accompanied by his flatmate – or rather his boatmate – Tony Creighton, who was diminutive and prissy and wore a kilt. It emerged that Osborne and Creighton were both vegetarians. Were they also gay (or queer, as we said then)?"

"A lot of people assumed we were lovers," Osborne admitted with typical brazenness, adding that the rumours didn't bother him much. His candour only fuelled the speculation, of course, but he couldn't help himself. By temperament, he was an open book on his own untidy, improvised life – a privately vulnerable man who made himself publicly immune to scandal by seeming to hide nothing. He pre-empted sleuthing biographers and gossip by creating the gossip for us. The single exception was the descent into darkest depression he hid from outsiders when life itself hid from him. Even so, a handful of people knew of his depressive side. The rest of his life seems to contain no skeletons or subterfuge, and his biases are well known. This is a man, after all, who could joyfully declare in all politically incorrect mischief: "Whatever else, I have been blessed with God's two greatest gifts: to be born English and heterosexual."

The American essayist Cynthia Ozick has written engagingly about the thorny question of biographical revelation and sexual secrets, siding with Lyndall Gordon – the biographer of both Henry James and T.S. Eliot – who believes "the deeper the silence, the more intently it speaks". James and Eliot were both massive pillars of their own fiercely guarded privacy, and both, it's assumed, therefore had something to hide. Perhaps. But the deeper the silence, the more intently an honest wish for privacy also speaks. The man who places a high value on discretion needn't be suppressing guilty little secrets. He might simply be exercising his fundamental right to a private life.

The chronically reticent Henry James nevertheless believed that the artist permeates "every page of every book from which he sought to assiduously eliminate himself". The artist is therefore bound to be found in his work. But from where I sit, chained to my desk, if the work tells us all there is to know about the artist, there would be no need for biographies.

An artist like Osborne, however, thrived in a confessional culture of personality where becoming known is the name of the game. After Wilde, Shaw and Coward, few English dramatists in modern times have achieved more public celebrity than him. Walt Whitman, first icon of American individualism, proclaimed "the destiny of me"; Osborne's renegade hero, Colonel Redl, declared himself "a patriot for me". What, then, if the man who set out to write only the truth lived a lie?

The issue of Osborne's homosexuality was raised by his old friend Creighton, who emerged from the shadows to tell all just after Osborne died. "The playwright John Osborne took one secret with him to the grave," the Evening Standard's interview with him in January 1995 announced with a roll of drums. "This inveterate despiser and mocker of homosexuals never said a word about one of his rare love affairs that was happy, enduring and did not finish in a flurry of recriminations: the affair was, it now emerges more than forty years after its inception, with a man . . ."

Give the English a whiff of the illicit and, as a rule of thumb, they find it irresistible. Not since Dr Aziz and the burning question of what really happened with Ms Quested in the caves of Chandrapur had there been such a fuss. It's always possible, of course, that Osborne had a cuddle with Creighton after a meatless steak on a Saturday night. People are only *human*. Angela Fox (indomitable mother of actors James and Edward, and producer Robert) knew and liked Osborne from his earliest days at the Royal Court. "Be sensible, dear," she advised me as I looked into the evidence. "What do you imagine young men living together on boats *do?*"

"You think I am, don't you? Well, I'm not. But *he* is!"

Archie Rice, *The Entertainer*

Osborne encouraged conjecture about his sexuality. He was the one happy to tell the stories – against himself, if you like. "How queer *are* you?" he gleefully reported Noel Coward asking him over "a very, very light omelette" during dinner for two at Coward's Chesham Place flat.

"Oh, about 20 per cent," Osborne replied, quite obligingly.

"Really?" said "The Master". "I'm about 95 per cent."

He must have given the other 5 per cent to his agent. But the more Osborne relished telling the Coward story, the more his own percentages rose (reaching a high of 45 per cent on a good day). "Oh, do stop it, John. You sound *just* like a queer," Mary Ure chastised Osborne whenever he lapsed into showbiz high camp. When she was starring in *Look Back in Anger* on Broadway, she attended a party alone where the director Elia Kazan of *On the Waterfront* made a clumsy pass at her. "I hear your husband's a fag," Kazan said.

"It was quite believable," Osborne blithely explained. "There was a teasing softness of style in the English male that baffled and even outraged these guardians of acceptable mannerism. The ambiguity of English maleness was not merely un-American but downright provocative. Mary had given Kazan a good Yankee smack in his Armenian face, which turned her into an instant heroine, an exemplar of the firepower of the frontierswoman."

When they later attended a party for *The Entertainer* on a private yacht sailing up the Hudson with the host, Laurence Olivier, who was jauntily dressed as a naval commander, one of the guests at the glamorous gathering was Kazan. Osborne, to his wife's dismay, immediately went over to introduce himself while giving an impersonation of a raging queen.

He camped it up most when he first visited America – the better to disturb the puritan natives, we assume. Osborne argued on a favourite, goading topic in a 1992 *Spectator* column that the femininity of leading English actors mystifies the hygienic demands of Americans in the face of human complexity. "They need reassuring safeguards against it, like the cleanliness-guaranteed seal straddling the lavatory seat."

On the opening night of *Epitaph for George Dillon* on Broadway, co-author Creighton appeared in his kilt accompanied by a male lover, while Osborne swept merrily down the aisle arm-in-arm with a gay black tailor who'd introduced him to nightlife in Harlem. His showboating style would have caused a stir even today, for the godfathers of Broadway have always been as straitlaced as a vicar's tea party. Osborne's new friend, the bespoke tailor, was part of his New York entourage that also included a faux bodyguard – the muscular, proudly heterosexual actor Robert Webber, who came out of the closet toward the end of his life.

Why did he play these childish games, provoking scandal and rumour along the way? I'm as sure as I can be that we have the explanation in the inspiring form of the man he worshipped fiercely from childhood, Max ("The Cheeky Chappie") Miller. The king of Osborne's beloved Music Hall, a formative influence, was decidedly camp.

Max was as devoted to his long-time wife as he was to his long-time mistress, but he presented an image onstage of carefree sexual ambiguity. He was rude, he was racy, and he didn't give a damn. His entire risqué act was about sex and girls who will, and girls who won't. James Agate reminds us in an admiring review that a dirty mind is a perpetual feast, and Tynan compared him to a man unzipping his fly in a nunnery. Max would bounce exuberantly onstage to his signature tune, "Mary from the Dairy", and announce to one and all, "I'm ready for bed . . . anybody?"

Yet he appeared like a campy Pierrot in a coat of many colours and enormous plus-fours decorated with a mass of daisies, teasing and goading his adoring audience. "Miller's the name, lady!" he'd say, doffing his snappy white trilby with a knowing beam to the gallery. "There'll never be another, will there? They don't make 'em today, ducks."

Osborne saw him as an antidote to English drabness, and he first mimicked his flashy style as a twelve-year-old, defiantly showing off a prized yellow cardigan he wore in tribute to his hero. He remembered that he was jeered at in the street as a nancy boy as he hurried home blushing along the Fulham Road. Later in life, he could be seen wearing ludicrous plus-fours and buckled shoes during fashion-conscious parades along the King's Road – less early Blimp, as some thought, more post-modern Max. "You could see his wig join from the back of the stalls, and his toupee looked as if his wife had knitted it over a glass of stout before the Second House," he lovingly described Miller. "His make-up was white and feminine, and his skin was soft like a dowager's. This steely suggestion of ambivalence was very powerful and certainly more seductive than the common run of manhood then."

In this game of appearances, it's implied, only a confident man messes knowingly with manhood. "Oh, you wicked lot!" Max always protested to his audience with mock innocence. "You're the kind of people who get me a bad name."

But this is the point, according to his expert biographer John M. East. "Maxie", as Osborne affectionately called him, would often mince his way absurdly toward the backcloth, hang his silk coat on an invisible hook, and protest: "I know what you're thinking, but you're wrong."

At other times, he liked to place his left hand with ridiculous suggestiveness on his hip, staring out defiantly at the audience to enquire: "What if I am?"

And that's it. That was Osborne. His joke on sexuality owed everything to his taunting hero and ambiguous showbiz god, Max Miller – the pointing star, he always maintained, to his own sense of mischief and theatrical daring.

"Hey, lady! What if I am?"

*

But that still leaves us with Creighton's claim of their long-standing affair.

"It was a love affair, a good, happy, mutually supportive and enduring relationship," the seventy-two-year-old Creighton told the *Evening Standard*. He described it as a sexual relationship that began before Osborne's marriage to Pamela Lane, continued into his next marriage to Mary Ure, and finally ended after some fifteen years with his marriage to Penelope Gilliatt in the mid-Sixties. He added that he last saw Osborne only a few months before he died on Christmas Eve in 1994.

If it's a true story, it's surprisingly true. If Osborne were homosexual, or bisexual, the chances are we would have known about it long before Creighton's story. We might also wonder why no other male lover of Osborne's has emerged in over forty years. Creighton stands alone, and the *Evening Standard*'s sensational story is uncorroborated.

There are a number of other troubling aspects that invite scepticism. The story was written by the *Standard*'s drama critic Nicholas de Jongh who, only a month previously, had described Osborne in his obituary of him as a "repulsive", "disgusting", "distinctly minor league" dramatist. De Jongh wrote: "He was famously and consistently homophobic, and according to Freudian theory his anti-homosexual vehemence could be read as an attempt to suppress what was struggling for expression in him."

Having undertaken what he describes as a long search for Creighton (who was presumed dead), he reports Creighton saying, "In his plays and journalism John subjected homosexuals to derision, contempt and malice. And I think people should be able to appreciate that *Patriot for Me*, which stigmatises homosexuality, is a projection of his own self-hatred."

Creighton and de Jongh – keen Freudians, both – coincidentally state the same projection theory against Osborne in startlingly similar terms. But de Jongh adds another reason why Creighton has come forward to tell all: "[He] also understandably wants to expose what he believes to be the playwright's treachery." Leaving Creighton to explain: "I think John was a hypocrite. In his autobiography he 'outs' me with contempt – and without my permission. Yet it was he who had a homosexual affair with me."

It doesn't hold up. Osborne first "outed" Creighton when he wrote about him in his first autobiography in 1981. We are being asked to believe that Creighton waited fourteen years to make his wounded protest.

The *Standard* interview was conveniently published a month after Osborne's death when he could neither reply nor sue. It was known that during this time, Creighton was shopping Osborne's letters around for a potential book sale. Then again, de Jongh tells us that the interview took place when Creighton at last made contact with him "after a search which took months". Yet all the intrepid drama critic needed to do in his quest for Creighton was telephone him at home in north London – as Helen Osborne did. When she read the *Standard* interview, she was still grieving badly over Osborne's death and called Creighton to give him a piece of her mind. They had never met. She got his number from Osborne's literary agent.

De Jongh points out, correctly, that nothing had been heard of Creighton for so many years that theatre people thought he had long since died. Osborne believed so, too. He always maintained that he last saw Creighton on the opening night of *A Patriot for Me* in 1965 and that he might have gone to live in America and subsequently died there. He imagined he must have died because for some thirty years he hadn't picked up his royalties from *Epitaph for George Dillon*. Permission to produce the play had always been left in Osborne's hands. The royalties were modest and kept in separate accounts. But Creighton had never collected his money from the Faber edition of the play, either.

And here's the twist: when *Epitaph for George Dillon* was broadcast on Radio 3 on 22 January 1994, a year before Osborne's death, his literary agent, Gordon Dickerson, received a call from an Anthony Creighton wanting to know how he could collect his royalties.

"Good God! We all assumed for years he was dead," Helen Osborne remembered. "He wanted his *lolly*. John was astonished when he turned up. He was just amazed."

So they knew Creighton was alive a year before de Jongh found him after his "dedicated search". And that was all there was to it, Helen explained, until the day she travelled from Shropshire to London for a meeting at the Garrick Club with Melvyn Bragg and Dominic Lawson, among other friends, to plan her husband's memorial service. "There's something we have to tell you," one of them said to her when she arrived, and she was shown a copy of that day's *Evening Standard*.

When she returned home to Clun, still upset and stewing over Creighton's accusations, she got his telephone number from Dickerson and impulsively called him. She told him in no uncertain terms there wasn't a word of truth to his story – and he knew it. Nor could he have visited Osborne before he died. Because no one visited him. The doctors allowed no one to see him as she stood vigil by his bedside. "How *could* you?" she protested to Creighton through her grief. But there was only silence, until he put down the phone.

*

From the outset, Osborne appears miscast as someone who lived a lie. On the contrary, he was a man incapable of keeping a secret. His transparency was apparent to everyone who knew him.

Jocelyn Rickards was his lover during and after the marriage to Mary Ure – the period Creighton maintained his affair with Osborne was still flourishing. Creighton told de Jongh, "I'm sure it did not occur to Mary, who was a splendid, spirited girl, that John and I sometimes slept together . . ."

"Dolly", as Osborne nicknamed Rickards, remained his friend and confidante for some thirty-five years until he died. "He would have told me about it," she confirmed about any affair between Osborne and Creighton.

How could she be so sure? "Because he couldn't keep his trap shut about *anything*," she explained, and roared with laughter.

I ought to add that at the height of Osborne's three-year romance with Rickards, during which they shared a flat in Lower Belgrave Street while he was still living with Mary Ure in Woodfall Street, Chelsea, he was also having an intense affair with the married Penelope Gilliatt (who would be his next wife), together with various other flings with women, as frequent as hot dinners, according to Rickards, and a loving, long-standing affair with an upmarket Swiss hooker named Francine. "John, my darling," Francine wrote to him one day from her London address. "Why oh why did you leave me, why do I feel so close to you, why do I still believe in miracles, why is my name Francine?"

So he had a lot on his plate.

When Osborne and Creighton lived together on the Thames houseboat, the Runnings had them over to their Chelsea home quite often for supper. They knew Creighton was gay and, though not everyone took to him, they liked him. "But I never thought of them that way for a minute," Mrs Running explained. "We didn't think much about gays in those days, either. We used to call them 'pansy-boys', particularly in the chorus. All my best friends in the dog shows are gay. Very nice people."

Arnold Running was patiently awaiting his turn. "John certainly didn't seem gay to me," he said. "He was always chasing women – my secretary included." She was Josie of Benn Bros, pinned in her short skirt to the office floor by the fumbling sixteen-year-old Osborne. For good measure, Mr Running mentioned various Osborne girlfriends he'd met. There was the daughter of the ballroom-dancing teacher who taught the tentative Osborne his first vigorous paso doble, and the jilted fiancée, Renee Shippard of the Halifax Building Society, abandoned for a life in the theatre. A clergyman's daughter, whose name he couldn't recall, was another fiery wing of desire. Then there was the eighteen-year-old Osborne's first love, strapping

Stella of Brighton. "When John was at Benn Bros, he carried a raincoat down the street with him, even on a sunny day," Running added unexpectedly. "It was because he had an erection! Not for men. For *women!*"

The things we learn. But though the protective, good-natured Runnings remind us of Osborne's blossoming adolescence, Osborne had yet to meet Anthony Creighton, and when he did, he might have hidden any affair with him from his surrogate parents.

Pamela Lane was in a prime position to know what might have gone on. After all, she and Osborne lived with Creighton under the same roof in the small flat in Brook Green. The three of them palled about together. She told me she was amazed and offended – "gobsmacked" – by Creighton's story. She was adamant there was nothing in it.

"But hadn't Osborne everything to hide?" I insisted. They were often separated during the marriage. How could she be certain nothing happened when she wasn't there?

"Because," came her emphatic response, "he would have used it against me."

It rings all too true. We've seen how Osborne threw everything at her when she turned away from him. He spared her nothing in his attempts to destroy her. "He would have used it against me out of spite," she emphasized. "It would have surfaced in the rows between us."

Osborne lived with two other men beside Creighton. The first was gentlemanly Frank Middlemass when they shared actors' digs together in the early days of Bridgwater rep. That was the period when Creighton says his affair with Osborne began.

"Any clues?" I asked Middlemass.

He dismissed the rumours. "I knew that Creighton was absolutely devoted to John, but I would be surprised if they had an affair. John was always very keen on the ladies. I wouldn't have thought he had time for fellas. He was smitten by Pam, although her parents thought he was as camp as a row of tents."

"They thought he was homosexual."

"They were wrong."

The tone of Osborne's letter to Creighton from Bridgwater describing how Pamela's mother had accused him of being homosexual is one of outrage. "The big gun she brings up against me is that I am QUEER. Yes! Or as she puts it a NANCY BOY . . ." If he were having an affair with Creighton at the time, this would have been the letter for him to allude to it. He might have written of the despised Mrs Lane's accusation something truculent like, "If only she knew!" But he doesn't refer to any affair with Creighton here or in any of their correspondence.

He also shared a rented flat in Hertford Street during the early 1960s with Tony Richardson – the wired, gangling director of *Look Back in Anger, The Entertainer* and *Luther* described by Osborne as "just a few pence short of genius". Osborne used the London service apartment, with its fridge filled with Dom Perignon and oranges, for his trysts with Penelope Gilliatt. But when the bisexual Richardson met his future wife, Vanessa Redgrave, their mutual ardour kept wrecking the place – leaving the astonished, fastidious Osborne to pick up the pieces of broken furniture among the empty bottles of champagne and mysteriously torn curtains. When Richardson later married Redgrave, he moved out to lease a charming little house with priceless antiques in Eaton Mews North, inviting the wary Osborne and the delighted Gilliatt to share it with them. They did move in for a while. But the same passionate pillage happened again. This time, Richardson received a solicitor's letter from the owner. "I mean, Johnny," he protested indignantly to Osborne on being sued for the cost of all the damage, "don't you think it's a disgrace?"

He loved Tony Richardson if only for the laughter. Two men of their generation sharing the same roof – or the rent of a leaky boat – wasn't particularly suspect or "strange". Richardson was a born Machiavellian and their lifelong friendship was turbulent – "a scabrous *mariage blanc*", Osborne described it. But he was unembarrassed to write on Richardson's death that the man had pierced his heart inexorably.

Tony Richardson died of AIDS in California in 1991, and his memoirs were published posthumously. About Osborne and Creighton, he wrote:

> They were living on the dole, in near penury. The barge was the cheapest accommodation they could find. It was narrow and smelly (from the stench of cabbages – they were both vegetarians at the time), and its gloom was relieved only by posters of Marlon Brando in *The Wild One* and *Julius Caesar* and other American muscled movie stars. All this made for instant speculation that they were homosexual lovers. This was never true of John – quite the opposite – but he was prepared to accept the care and attention that Anthony lavished on him, clucking and fussing like some mother hen . . . We gradually became friends, but it was a long time before his guard and his mistrusts were overcome.

When I met the director William Gaskill, he remembered the whispered consultations about them in Richardson's kitchen when they asked each other about the odd couple in their midst, "Do you think they're queer?" There they were – the tall, flash Osborne who had just had *Look Back in Anger* accepted, and the small, mousy Creighton, camp in his kilt.

"What did you think?" I asked.

"*Nah,*" this calm, modest gay man said and smiled. Gaskill was sixty-eight when I met him, bearded and handsome with his long hair tied in a ponytail. Nowadays he mostly teaches and paints, secure in his reputation as one of England's finest directors. When he was artistic director of the Royal Court, he produced three of Osborne's later plays. He made his debut in his twenties directing *Epitaph for George Dillon* at the Court and in the West End (where it was a modest success) as well as on Broadway (where it was a *succès d'estime* or prestigious flop). He enjoyed Osborne's company and expressed irritation at Creighton, finding them an odd combination. He was certain they were close, however. "There was quite a lot of emotional dependency between them," he said. "But one has a sense of these things. We all knew Tony was gay. But John? I never got any sort of hint of it from him."

There's no doubt how much Osborne cared for Creighton, as Gaskill sensed. The emotional dependency between them is evident in the cache of letters that has given us a detailed insight into his first marriage. Osborne wrote some 122 letters and cards to Creighton between 1951–1958. Most of them were written from Derby during 1954–5 when the marriage to Pamela was cracking up. He wrote once and even twice a week, often scribbling them in his near-indecipherable scrawl between acts in the dressing room. "Must go now, me old son," one letter ends abruptly. "Wanted on the stage." He corresponded from his digs, describing his loathing for his wife as she learned her lines in the same room. The letters themselves were no secret. "P.S. Pam sends her love . . ."

He signs off, unusually, "Johnny". As far as I know, the only people who called Osborne "Johnny" were Creighton, Tony Richardson, Olivier, Penelope Gilliatt (who, to his irritation, called him "Muddle-headed Johnny") and Gilliatt's sister, Angela. "Must go, Mouse. All love, Johnny," he closes typically. "Bless you for everything. Thinking of you very much. All love . . ."

The letters reveal that his feelings for Creighton were remarkably, affectionately open, his emotional fragility and reliance apparent. "Bless you, Mouse, and thank God I can always turn to you in my every state and condition." There's the commitment of a fraternal blood knot between the two friends, and there are times when Creighton seems to be the despairing

Osborne's only lifeline. "Thank heavens for you, dear Mousie. You are founded on rock really. I trust you."

The star witness in de Jongh's murky exposé – his only witness apart from Creighton himself – is a single letter from Osborne prominently quoted in italics. He seems to have found nothing compromising or worth quoting from the other 121 letters and cards. For his purposes, this one example offers conclusive, damning evidence of the affair. Written en route to Derby in 1954, at first sight it appears to be an intense, tearful love letter:

> My dear Mousie,
> Here we are, and another of those terrible farewells that I can hardly bear – you know what a sickening softie I am. Once again you will have to endure these last minutes of gibbering on the platform, when I shall be stupid, inarticulate and – as always – close to tears. And so, I must simply and quickly tell you how I hate to leave you.

De Jongh has cut the following lines, however:

> Admittedly I am going away to a place that is near-familiar, and to Pam. Whatever distress she may have given me, it has been mainly because I love her very much – but you know that. I know that I go away to something, and to someone. I have that, and I am very lucky.

Osborne was then twenty-three years old and his emotional fragility will always strike us as extraordinary. The reason he's upset, however, becomes clear with the missing paragraph. He's leaving the safe haven of 35 Caithness Road with Creighton for the turmoil of his love for his wife. Whatever the problems with the marriage, he's saying of himself that he isn't alone, he at least has a job, and he feels badly for his luckless friend.

De Jongh then picks up the text of the letter with the next paragraph:

> It is so easy for me to feel that I am leaving you behind – and with nothing, with no one. But let me just say this. It hurts me terribly to have to leave you. But you know that I am not deserting you – in any way. That would be impossible for me. I suppose I don't need to "sell this to you". You have known me long enough, and I don't think I have ever betrayed you. Any future I may have would be unthinkable without you sharing in it.

The principle of loyalty with Osborne was absolute. (Until, from his point of view, it wasn't.) He would never desert or "betray" his closest friend. It was unthinkable even when Osborne became famous. At the same time, he feels responsible for him. In many of the other letters, he's promising never to abandon him. He's constantly reassuring Creighton of his support and love.

The next paragraph is quoted out of context at the top of de Jongh's story. The reason is obvious. The intimate words appear to establish the affair:

> My love for you is deeper than I could bear to tell you to your face. It is so strong and indestructible. Never be in doubt about this or my loyalty.

But de Jongh has cut a key line. The full text reads:

> My love for you is deeper than I could bear to tell you to your face. *I know it is not what you need or really want,* [my italics] but it is so strong and indestructible. Never be in any doubt about this or my loyalty.

The concluding paragraph has also been cut – airbrushing out the innocent reason for Osborne's letter in the first place.

> Going away like this may seem like the crowning failure, the end of our immediate plans. [The plans were to re-start their failed Saga Repertory Company.] But try not to believe it, my son. This is the interval. The curtain will go up later on – just as we planned. My dear friend, you have a great, great heart, and you will not fail it.
>
> Bless you always,
>
> Johnny.

He's saying in the most supportive way, "Don't give up." The friendship cannot give Creighton all he wants, but he can confirm his steadfast support. He encourages him in letter after letter in the same open-hearted way, vowing they'll both make it: "The firm of Creighton and Osborne will be back in business very soon – and twice as good as ever," he reassures him on another occasion. "We *will* get decent jobs, we *will* get our own theatre once again . . ." Creighton was mostly unemployed during this entire period. He rarely seems to have found work as an actor and Osborne sends him what help he can scrape together – ten shillings, a pound, a packet of cigarettes, extra money to pay for an advert in the actors' directory, *Spotlight*. "Try and keep going somehow. You know I'm with you," he writes again. "Don't give up." It's as if he were sending the message to himself. "Don't give up . . ."

Unless we find friendship itself suspect, the letter published in the *Standard*, before de Jongh made his cuts, proves that Osborne loved Creighton as a friend. There's no sexual content in any of the correspondence. When

Creighton writes in crisis, Osborne reassures him of his unrestrained love while again alluding, tactfully, to the absence of any physical relationship between them:

> I will say what I have repeated to you so often: I am always with you at all times and wherever the years and circumstance may take us. I love you – inadequately for your great needs, and almost entirely without physical passion – but with a passion stronger than my body could ever know. *When you read this, know that it is the truth.*

Another letter refers to "this unique relationship of ours" that nothing can knock down. "My dear, dear Mousie, we have created something very fine and splendid. Thank God for us both."

And here he's reassuring Creighton once again after breaking the news of his forthcoming marriage: "*Don't, for God's sake, let this horrify you.* Your place in my heart has never been so real, secure or assured . . . I have been honest with you at all times in the past, it is always like that. It can be no other way."

The Osborne–Creighton correspondence informs us crucially that Osborne saw Anthony Creighton as his only family and the room he rented from him at 35 Caithness Road as his only home. "I've been thinking how damn lucky I am to have a home to come back to. I don't just mean a roof and comfortable surroundings. I mean 35 and all it means, and you. It's my family, if you like – all the family I have in the true sense. How utterly different returning to London would seem without that little indestructible corner."

He was like a homeless orphan who adopts an imagined older brother for shelter. (Creighton was six years older.) He was considerate to Creighton's mother, too – he nicknamed her "Tony's Mum" and she became the replacement for wicked Nellie Beatrice hunched over the *News of the World* with her gin and tonic. He teases Creighton about his various boyfriends: "Keep me up to date on *all* developments." He's fey: "Only three more weeks. Eeek!" He's knowingly campy: "I'd like to get myself a pair of jeans, only I'd like some of those tight fitting ones. (Get me!)" He's protective: "I just don't want you to feel you've sold yourself into slavery," he writes when Creighton has had to take a job at Wall's Ice Cream.

They propped each other up in mutual desperation. He writes about searching for acting work for Creighton while cursing his own "shitty little parts" and "life of fuck-all". Preparing an overambitious audition for the Old Vic he moans, "Why do I bother?" but sends on his chosen text for support. *Henry VIII*, Act III, Scene II, Wolsey's speech: "So farewell to the little good you bear me, farewell, a long farewell to all my greatness."

Creighton sends him the *New Statesman* and *Tribune*, a weekly ritual between left-leaning friends. "Thanks for the *Tribune*, old son," Osborne responds. "Most interesting again. Up the old Red Flag!" "If only Orwell were alive, or Shaw even, or Wells. Priestley is discredited and unpopular, [Bertrand] Russell is an old man and too remote from the brawls of public literary life. What a deep and bitter division there is in this country. There's no one to take the lead, no one to jolt and inspire the angry ones among us . . ."

Four of the letters attack the outcome of the notorious Montagu trial, describing it as a "witch hunt" and "a grisly, tragic farce". Under the laws prohibiting homosexuality, Lord Edward Montagu of Beaulieu and Peter Wildeblood, the diplomatic correspondent of the *Daily Mail*, were tried in 1954 for "acts of gross indecency" involving two RAF servicemen and sentenced to eighteen months in jail. "Martyrs in the cause of tolerance and enlightenment," Osborne, the so-called homophobe, protests. "What a travesty it is."

He writes enthusiastically that he's taken on all the leading Elizabethans and Greeks at the local library. He laps up Orwell's *1984* ("magnificent"), the new work of Genet ("I am intrigued by this man Jean Genet"), Angus Wilson's *Such Darling Dodos* ("It's wonderful. Have you read it?"). Between appearances onstage, he's in the dressing room listening to radio concerts on the venerable Third Programme – Vaughan Williams, Bach, early English keyboard music, Purcell – musical tastes that never changed. He tunes in regularly to that inspired liberator of BBC stuffiness "The Goon Show". He also reports on the actor's universal pastime – movies in the afternoon. "Saw *The Robe* yesterday. *Terrible!* Cinemascope is a dead loss." "Went to see *Genevieve* again – on my own – couldn't resist it." "Just got back from *Calamity Jane* with – yes! Doris Day. She's *adorable*." "Seeing *Heart of the Matter* tomorrow. Am saving it."

Letter after letter piles up on the wreckage of his marriage. "I'm sorry, Mousie, this is all me, me, me." The prurient reader might jump on his warning, "Don't leave this lying around" – until we realize he's hidden a little money from his wife that he's sent to help Creighton out of a mess. "For heaven's sake, don't go without food . . ." Osborne himself is so impoverished that the shoemaker in Derby returns his shoes as beyond repair. He would like to telephone Creighton, but daren't: the phone is about to be cut off. On the one hand, he's riding round town on his bike like a carefree student. On the other, he's gloomily observing himself at home lingering over a pot of sticky tea like a petulant old man. "I steal (yes steal!) pieces of bread, hide them in my trunk and eat them when she's out. At 24, I am an eccentric."

There's his youthful bluster: "Oh, Mouse, if only I could live without *women* – what an echo of the ages!" There's a warning sign of his "disabling inheritance of bloody melancholy": "I am dead, dead, dead. Something please bring me back to life!" "If only I could start afresh. I am a young man still, and I feel I should be living a young man's life." There's the longed-for lurch of hope when an agent takes an interest at last in one of the plays: "This is the moment! I'm so confident . . ." But after weeks of uncertainty, the agent backs out. And always, the encouragement and affection for his friend in the wilderness: "Be confident, dear Mouse . . . Don't give up."

When I telephoned Creighton to arrange to see him, he took me by surprise. "Are you prepared to make an offer?" he enquired.

It was the last thing I had anticipated. I was locked in time past when he was young and life still held out some hope for him. But he had become an old man in the intervening years and he sounded like a toff down on his luck. I must have registered my distaste. "Now you've embarrassed me," he said, adding coyly, "I don't want to appear cheap." But without payment, he insisted, there could be no meeting, and he named the sum of £300.

I was too curious to see him and reluctantly agreed. The sum itself seemed quite low, although it was big enough for me. But my visitor that summer afternoon would shock me in other ways.

He was now seventy-four, tanned from the sun, and dressed informally in a checked shirt, neat corduroys and sturdy walking shoes. The man Osborne nicknamed "Mouse" seemed scarcely taller than five feet or so. He lived alone, he told me, and quite contentedly. He had given up the theatre long ago to become a night-school teacher (though at which school or where, he wouldn't say). He seemed nervous – glancing at notes he had brought along with him. He had prepared what he had come to say.

This wasn't the confident, articulate man presented by the *Evening Standard* three and a half years before. Then and now, there were muddled details, but his memory lapses struck me as serious and there was a troubling blankness behind his eyes. He talked comfortably about certain things, however, relating a good deal about the early days. He told how the eighteen-year-old Osborne first acted in the little company he ran and would write in his notebooks during rehearsals, and how Osborne cursed Nellie Beatrice because he believed she killed his father. And before long, he was describing how he and Osborne shared a flat before the marriage to Pamela.

"As friends or lovers?" I asked.

"No, we were together as friends," he answered, going on to explain that he thought if Osborne wanted to write plays he had better stay in his flat and get his work done. I let it go for the moment as he next described living happily with Osborne and Pamela in Hammersmith. He sometimes heard her crying, he told me.

Then he paused and confessed, "It was a friendship of the spirit with John. That's all it was, nothing more."

He was withdrawing his story.

"Are you saying you were never lovers?" I asked him.

"Yes. I'm saying, no. Never," he replied.

Before our meeting ended, he would confirm several times that the affair never happened. Nor had he seen Osborne before he died, as the *Standard* claimed. He last saw him on the opening night of *A Patriot for Me* some thirty-five years earlier – exactly as Osborne had always said.

Following the success of *Look Back in Anger* and the marriage to Mary Ure, Osborne stood by Creighton. "I'm going to be RICH. I'm going to get such a kick taking you round this city one day," he wrote to him exuberantly from New York. "I miss you as ever. SCREW ENGLAND!"

Osborne helped a number of people financially and his old friend was one of them. He virtually kept Creighton for seven or eight years, paying almost all his living expenses until he became a problem. Creighton wrote to him gratefully, "I shall not forget – ever." But although he enjoyed a fleeting moment in the sun with *Epitaph for George Dillon*, he fell on hard times and the begging letters kept coming. "It makes me cringe to have to do this . . ."

He developed a drink problem – since cured, he told me. But on the opening night of *A Patriot for Me* at the Court, he drank too much and became a nuisance. He didn't offer me any pseudo-Freudian analysis about the play's alleged homophobia. He was drunk! At the curtain call, he loudly criticized the actors to Osborne. "It scars me for life," he murmured, blanching at the memory. There had been other foolish incidents, but this was the last straw. He was thrown out of the theatre and never heard of again.

There were no small betrayals in Osborne's life. When a relationship soured badly, so did he. There were times when he was like the unforgiving Timon betrayed by his friends: "Hate all, curse all, show charity to none." He later dismissed Creighton cruelly in the second part of his autobiography as "a cadging, homosexual drunk" and the damage was done.

Why did Creighton lie about the affair? He made several scrambled explanations, but did not mention money. He had been misled, he had been misquoted, he was confused, pathetically misunderstood, out for revenge. "I obviously got carried away with anger," he rationalized, "and I was determined to get back at him." As our meeting ended, I reminded him of all that he had told the *Evening Standard*, and I read two or three of Osborne's letters to him to ignite better memories, cleaner things:

> You are a fine, good, talented and lovable human being with so much to offer and, though you may disbelieve it, with it so much to have offered you. I believe in you and in your strength.

I was glad to turn to a new chapter of Osborne's life when life for him would be changed forever.

16

The Father Reclaims the Son

My loyalty and support in the future, for what these are worth, are yours irrevocably.

Osborne letter to George Devine, 11 May 1956

How George Devine first came to meet Osborne and, in a sense, save him, is a tale that has entered theatre folklore. For the legend of a white-haired, middle-aged gentleman symbolically travelling by river to meet the future suggests a mythic, Conradian journey into the unknown. It wasn't quite like that.

Some time after Devine set out quixotically by rowing boat from his eighteenth-century house overlooking the Thames to meet his future playwright living a mile downriver, his boat capsized. The sight of the English messing about in boats has a way of making them appear comically miscast in the roles they like to play. But that hot mid-August afternoon, with his open-neck shirt flapping round his baggy corduroys, feet firmly planted in his Jesus sandals, pipe clenched between his teeth, the resolute Devine was determined to reach Osborne against the unpredictable, swelling tide.

The nervous playwright himself, fortified by whisky during the long delay, anxiously awaited his arrival as he peered out from the deck of the rickety old Rhine barge. Osborne, pipe clenched between *his* teeth, was wearing his blue Loamshire blazer, club tie and grey flannels from his days on tour as if dressed for an appearance on the balcony of *Private Lives*.

"There's only one place to buy a pipe, dear boy," Devine would later advise his protégé with knowing middle-class one-upmanship. "And that's Charatan's." Osborne thus abandoned his trusty Dunhill to patronize Charatan's. With his first success, he bought his first car – a cream and crimson Austin 100, which he parked outside the stage door of the Royal Court and showed to Devine. "Why didn't you get an Alfa Giulietta?" he sniffed immediately. "That's a *grocer's* car!"

Devine drove a second-hand Alvis – the thinking man's Rolls – proudly polishing its headlights with the sleeves of his jacket. Osborne would own a few cars in his time, including a Bentley and a Cadillac, but the one he kept the longest was his Alvis.

"The blue blazer, saved for and bought in Bridgwater for all-purpose use in Home Counties comedies, seemed to ring out like a leper's bell, begging radical scorn," he recalled, wincing at the memory of his mad choice of costume to impress the beady-eyed Devine. Too late now, he regretted, to change into a *démodé* Left Bank-ish outfit, stale with pastis and Gauloises. Devine could be glimpsed at last, struggling valiantly along the choppy Thames toward him in a borrowed dinghy.

Devine's version of their bizarre first meeting is found in the fragmentary pages of his autobiography, scarcely begun before he died:

"I first met John Osborne after we had read *Look Back in Anger*. It was just what we were looking for – the bomb that would blow a hole in the old theatre and leave a nice-sized gap, too big to be patched up. John was living on a houseboat in Cubitt's Yacht Basin. Due to an error in navigation, I had to borrow a dinghy, take off my shoes and socks, wade out to it and row myself to my playwright. He heaved me aboard, dressed in a smart blazer with shining buttons and well-polished shoes. I don't know what he thought he was going to meet, but he was taking no chances."

A tantalizing question remains, however – and with it, a mystery. Why did Devine insist on going to meet him? We would expect it to have been the other way round. Why wasn't the unknown playwright summoned to meet Devine?

Osborne was surprised by the impatience in his terse voice when he first heard him over the phone arranging the meeting. He knew Devine only from his performance as an endearing, bookish Tesman opposite Peggy Ashcroft in *Hedda Gabler*. His pocket diary of the time reads: "Friday, May 6th: *Look Back in Anger*, Act 1 finished." "Friday, May 13th: Went to see *Hedda Gabler* . . ."

"That was the last time anyone saw George as a fat man," Peggy Ashcroft told his admirable biographer, Irving Wardle. There were two different Devines: Fat Devine and Thin Devine. By the summer of 1955, the newly dieted version had transformed him into a different man. "It was not simply a question of physique," Wardle shrewdly observes. "Something had changed inside him as well. He was not jolly old George any longer."

In middle age, restless with his "new rasping militancy", Devine had become a man who meant business. It would have been usual, then, for him to have summoned Osborne. He was the boss, after all. He worked at that time from an office in his Thames-side home where Tony Richardson, his young associate director, lived in the top-floor flat. Richardson was to direct *Look Back in Anger*, and Osborne could have met him at the house, too. But that didn't happen until later when the director, whose gangly physique was compared to an animated wading stalk, loped into Devine's study to introduce himself with the words, "I think *Look Back in Anger* is the best play written since the war." Why, then, the delay in meeting Richardson? Had Devine even committed to producing *Look Back* when he went to see Osborne? If so, what was stopping him?

There's enough evidence to enable us to reconstruct the decisive events that led up to the first meeting.

We know that in the summer of 1955 Osborne read an ad in *The Stage* for new plays to be submitted to the newly founded English Stage Company at the Royal Court Theatre. He submitted *Look Back in Anger*, typed on Pamela Lane's permanently borrowed Olivetti, a twenty-first birthday present from her parents. Devine and Richardson, preparing their first season, were looking at the work of every playwright of note. Their real purpose, amounting to an unwritten manifesto, was to break with the commercial status quo and make the future Royal Court a writers' theatre.

The National Theatre didn't exist; nor the Royal Shakespeare Company as we know it. There were a handful of small private theatre clubs, but no fringe movement. There was the commercial theatre and little else. Osborne had already sent *Look Back* to every established theatre management and agent. All of them had rejected it.

A phenomenal 750 new plays were submitted to the English Stage Company after the ad appeared. Dipping morosely at home into one of them, Devine read a few pages as if sniffing it out, and took *Look Back in Anger* upstairs to Richardson's flat. "This might have something," he said. Unusually, Richardson read it through in one sitting. His customary play-reading method was to read the first and last pages of a new play, and one more page at random around the middle. "That's *quite* sufficient," he'd say, believing the test told him whether the play was worth reading at all. *Look Back in Anger* proved different. "By the time I was through the first act," Richardson recalled, "I knew, whatever the battles to come, we'd win the war."

Devine then read it immediately afterwards and responded with the same excitement. He subsequently showed the script to his lover, Jocelyn Herbert, soon to become the Royal Court's scenic designer. Herbert was the wife of a prominent London lawyer and daughter of novelist, playwright and politician, A.P. Herbert. Devine's wife, Sophie, was herself a leading costume designer with the design triumvirate known as Motley, but she was ten years older than her husband and the marriage had turned cold. Devine and Jocelyn Herbert were guilty lovers. Though they subsequently lived together in Chelsea, neither divorced their spouse.

"You don't often have the luck to get a play like this," he said to Herbert, handing over the script. As she read it, she saw that Devine had underlined this passage:

JIMMY: It's no use trying to fool yourself about love. You can't fall into it like a soft job, without dirtying your hands. It takes muscle and guts. And if you can't bear the thought of messing up your nice clean soul, you'd better give up the whole idea of life and become a saint, because you'll never make it as a human being. It's either this world or the next.

Today, George Devine's house at 9 Lower Mall by Hammersmith Bridge, displays an English Heritage Plaque on its façade:

George Devine 1910–1966
Actor Artistic Director of the
Royal Court Theatre 1956–65
Lived Here

In the Fifties, it was a thriving little theatrical community. The Herberts lived further along Lower Mall, the Redgraves were nearby, while Anne Piper's house two doors up at number 7 became home to the weekly meetings of the Court's Writers' Group that included Edward Bond, Arnold Wesker and Ann Jellicoe.

When I visited Devine's house, the mystery of why he insisted on visiting Osborne for their first meeting was unexpectedly solved. The playwright and former literary manager of the Court, Donald Howarth, now part-owned the house and had occupied the ground floor in unholy chaos for many years. His first play was inspired by *Look Back in Anger*. His second was submitted to the Court where Osborne, who became a play-reader for £2 a week before *Look Back* was produced, turned it down. "He told me later he thought it was too Ibsen-esque," Howarth explained with a thin smile. "*Very* impressive word, Ibsen-esque . . ." They became friends just the same.

Peter Gill, the playwright and former Court associate director, rented the cool, white, modernist flat where Richardson had lived on the top floor. He first got to know the house as a young inhibited actor visiting the Devines for Sunday lunch and Sophie's ritual teas. The stylish flat has remained much as it was, Gill told me, minus Richardson's South American parakeets. "There was an aviary of about forty exotic birds," he explained amiably. "A toucan, lots of champagne, good-looking people, Casa Pupo goblets . . ."

The day I went to meet Gill, I passed a door about halfway up the winding staircase that had been left ajar in the warm afternoon. I could glimpse an elderly, bearded man seated staring blankly into space within the elegant drawing room that had once belonged to George Devine, while a young man I took to be a minder read a book on the sofa like a Hockney still life. The ghost of a man, I soon found out, had lived with Tony Richardson on the top floor all those years ago.

George Goetschius has always lived in the house, and now owned it with Howarth. A meeting was quickly arranged, and far from appearing subdued, he turned out to be animated and good-humoured. Goetschius was a Brooklyn-born sociologist who worked for the Ford Foundation and ran hospices in New York when he first met Richardson travelling through America on a post-Oxford jaunt. When he later came to live at the house with him, he became the unofficial adviser to the Court. He was privy to its inner councils, advising both Devine and Richardson. I felt in luck meeting him. Goetschius the sociologist was a wry observer of everything that went on around him.

"That boy was a born manipulator," he told me about Richardson. "He knew how to get to the top. Devine made him *legitimate*." He was amusing about Richardson's peculiar, widely impersonated accent. "He loved Hollywood Westerns!" he announced unexpectedly. "It was all part of his love of America and you could tell it in the way he talked. He overcame a slight speech impediment and lost his Yorkshire accent by putting on a *drawl*."

Richardson, the son of a petit bourgeois Shipley pharmacist and upright Conservative Party parish councillor, had been sent to elocution classes as a child to learn to speak like a proper gent. He loathed the class system so much he would eventually flee England for America.

"Osborne's accent was like the Hungarian's in *My Fair Lady*," Goetschius added to laughter. "He made it up himself! He was a *poseur* who changed according to the social situation. That's why you're going to find different John Osbornes," he cautioned me. "Because he was always changing. And every change brought him closer to what he got – a big house in the English countryside and burial in an Anglican cemetery."

Goetschius met Devine informally each week, and was shown the script of *Look Back in Anger* when Osborne first submitted it. He knew immediately it was the play they were looking for. But he told me of one serious, apparently lunatic, doubt he had about its author.

"I heard the authentic voice of an outsider in the play to such an extent that it *couldn't* be English," he explained. "Osborne was knocking the Church openly, he was furious at the Establishment and dull, hopeless England. He was giving it to everyone from all sides. I told Devine he was being fooled. He said, 'What do you mean?' I said, that boy Osborne is from someplace else. I told him *Look Back in Anger* couldn't have been written by an Englishman."

The play that would become indelibly identified with England and the newly-named English Stage Company at the Court was suddenly thrown into doubt. Goetschius thought the blistering emotional fury of the play was so uncharacteristically English it must have been written by an American. Incredulous though it leaves us today, others were struck the same way. The American art critic Hilton Kramer saw *Look Back* at the Court in 1956 and recalls the impact of the occasion vividly. Knowing nothing about Osborne, and accustomed to the traditional reticence of Rattigan and Coward, he found Osborne's furious take on married life so un-English that he couldn't believe it, either. "What! Emotion? On the English stage!" he said to me. "We couldn't believe our ears."

Goetschius explained it was why Devine went to see Osborne that day. He needed to check out everything about his new dramatist on his own turf before committing to the play. He hadn't offered to produce *Look Back* when he tersely arranged the meeting. In fact, Osborne was left anxiously uncertain about the outcome and whether the play would be produced at all.

"It was clear that he was determined to scrutinize his unknown author in his cage," Osborne wrote, though he never learned the real reason behind the visit. Surprised and even perturbed by the grilling he received, he tried to rationalize Devine's probing curiosity. "George sat down on one of the shaky bunks in the main cabin and looked about him. Quickly, I decided that scrutiny was a natural part of his character, that it was not assumed and apparently not censorious. His censure seemed brutal, harsh and intent . . . He interrogated me closely, not only about my professional record but about my past and present personal life."

That done, he finally offered Osborne £25 for a year's option on *Look Back in Anger*.

They were like strange partners in a card game, Osborne observed, and neither the prickly, guarded young dramatist nor his reticent, vinegary mentor were easy men to know. Devine, whose career thrived at the centre of English theatrical life, came from another world.

He had turned himself into a theatrical figure when he was at Oxford, parading about the place with his silver-topped cane and wide-brimmed hat. Devine became President of the Oxford University Dramatic Society – an influential route into the professional theatre. But he was self-invented, like Osborne. He was the unhappy child of an ineffectual bank clerk and a mentally unstable mother. A kindly, eccentric uncle who was headmaster of Claysmore gave him his respectable private-school education. But it was Oxford that made him. Rattigan was an old friend of Devine's from Oxford days. Gielgud took an interest in his student career and directed *Romeo and Juliet* for him when he was President of OUDS. Peggy Ashcroft played Juliet, Edith Evans was the Nurse (and Devine the portly Mercutio).

He became an Establishment insider who worked in the West End among a golden circle of actors – Olivier, Gielgud, Ashcroft and Redgrave among them. But he was never the insular Englishman. The turning point of his life came when he met his own mentor, Michel Saint-Denis, who in turn had studied at the feet of his visionary uncle, the experimental director, Jacques Copeau of the Théâtre du Vieux Colombier in Paris and Burgundy. ("All that Copeau jumping about," sniffed Tony Richardson, who looked to the modern theatre of New York for inspiration.) Saint-Denis and Devine founded the London Theatre Studio in the Thirties, and the two of them and Glen Byam Shaw opened the Old Vic Theatre Centre in 1947 with its own school, children's theatre and experimental stage. Joan Plowright was among its graduates.

Devine's education in European theatre and theory was anathema to Osborne's stubborn, gut Englishness. He spoke fluent French. Samuel Beckett was a close friend. He was open to the new post-war drama of Brecht at the Berliner Ensemble and the avant-garde theatre of Genet and Ionesco. The original blueprint for the Court was closer to a European theatre of ideas. "George, we're not going to do *another* of these?" Osborne protested during their skirmishes over Ionesco and the French intellectuals. "Yes, dear friend," he would reply, "I'm afraid we *are*."

"He thought they were good. I couldn't abide them," explained Osborne, who tended to dismiss all things French as "Frog wankery". "But he could maintain my reaction patiently, even though he was not a patient man. He could contain and comprehend many different things: that was one of his strengths. It wasn't that he was weak and compromising; he could be brutal and dismissive, and he went for what he wanted. But he had a special kind of tolerance. He suffered talent gladly."

Devine was the patriarch of the Royal Court who broke with his own bourgeois past. When he returned to London after five wasted years in the army, the dominant drawing-room theatre of the West End was of no use to him. "I have it in my bones that we have got to start on the *young* generation right away," Captain Devine wrote to Edith Evans from Burma in 1945. He returned home searching for new voices and meaning in the post-Holocaust age.

But he functioned best as neither director nor actor. At heart, he was a teacher whose Court disciples saw him as the embodiment of Chekhov's Dorn, the sympathetic doctor in *The Seagull*. He played Dorn memorably toward the end of his life in Tony Richardson's 1965 production, with the young Vanessa Redgrave as the ingénue actress, Nina. *The Seagull* itself is about theatre and writers, and Chekhov's Dorn, like Devine, is on the writer's side. In the opening act, Nina performs young Konstantin's ambitious new play for his glamorous, impossible mother, who is a celebrated actress, famously selfish, and her various guests. The rebellious, unknown dramatist Konstantin is in his early twenties and wants to break with the old-fashioned theatre of his mother's era with its "narrow-minded, predictable ragbag of worn-out routines". Up goes the velvet and gold curtain, he groans, and what he sees sends him running. But his own bloated drama proves a disaster to all except Dorn.

"I don't know – perhaps I'm fooling myself, or I've gone off my head," Dorn says afterwards, speaking to no one in particular. "But I liked the play. There's something in it . . ."

"This might have something," Devine said to Richardson that day when he first showed him the script of *Look Back in Anger*.

"One splendid thing about George," Osborne wrote about this rigorous man, "was that he gave you the impression that whatever seemed to go wrong didn't really matter." Devine took on the philistines with a "fixed-bayonet relish". His support of new writers was an article of faith. It was the adventurer Richardson who invented the quixotic, potentially sanctimonious credo, the "right to fail", and Devine who took it up as the Court's proud banner. "We must support the people we believe in," Devine wrote to his astonished chairman. "*Especially* if they don't have critical appeal."

Against the litmus test of conventional success and the stifling commercial grain, a "right to fail" implies that any artist worthy of the name can fail. The only question is how close the true artist can get to the summit of his imagination. Or, as Beckett gently advised an actor struggling with one of his plays during a rehearsal at the Court, "Try to fail better."

"All of old. Nothing else ever. Ever tried. Ever failed," wrote Beckett in *Worstward Ho*. "No matter. Try again. Fail again. Fail better."

The solid, avuncular version of Devine was perfectly cast in the film of *Tom Jones* as Squire Allworthy, the loving guardian to rascally Tom. But in turbulent reality, the all-worthy Devine was saltier than prim virtue. "There you are, dear boy, take a look out there," he exulted to Osborne as he peered through the curtains on the opening night of *The Entertainer*. He was wearing his battered old velvet jacket and floppy black tie, peeping out at all the fashionable first-nighters and critics. "There they are, boysie!" he grinned, hugging Osborne. "All waiting for *you*. All of us, come to that. What do you think, eh? Same old pack of cunts . . ."

Osborne loved George Devine. They trusted one another in spite of their differences, and Devine protected him from the beginning. He kept his penniless dramatist going with the play-reading job for £2 a week and let him stage-manage auditions for another ten shillings a time in the nine months before *Look Back* was staged. He made him feel good about himself. He gave him *work*. "You see that young man," he'd say, pointing out the unknown Osborne to backstage visitors like an indulgent parent. "He's going to be a dramatist worth watching." He also hired him as a Court actor for £12 a week (understudy duties included; play as cast). The understudy for the role of Jimmy Porter was John Osborne.

There's no doubt that he saw Devine as his substitute father. Richardson and Gaskill, both in their twenties when they joined the Court, also looked up to him as a paterfamilias. But Osborne's needs cut much deeper.

Devine was the successful version of Thomas Godfrey, the *artiste manqué*. He believed in him as Osborne's own father had; he offered him a home; he even had a shock of grey hair like the father. And he would die prematurely at the cursed time of the New Year leaving the bereft Osborne orphaned again.

"Where is the Foundling's father hidden?" wrote Herman Melville, who lost his own father when he was twelve years old and yearned for his protective love all his life. "Where is the one who will say to you, 'I endorse thee all over. Go on.'?"

Devine was that man. He was the one who endorsed Osborne, over and over, and encouraged him to go on. Osborne became the favourite son. No one else among the Court's stable of gifted young writers and directors was so favoured. When the exhausted Devine announced his retirement after ten years to a stunned gathering at the Savoy, Osborne was the only writer he singled out. "The jewel in the crown – our line in the history books –

is Mr John Osborne," he said, believing that without him the Court wouldn't have survived.

Jocelyn Herbert – who was still designing stage sets in her eighties – confirmed for me the love the two men had for each other and how Devine patiently handled his temperamental young protégé. But she herself was rarely at ease in Osborne's company. "John," she'd say to him in exasperation, "I can't help being middle class." She designed three of his major plays – *Luther*, *Inadmissible Evidence* and *A Patriot for Me* – as well as the film of *Tom Jones*. "He was the most self-destructive person I've ever known. There was something in him that seemed to be utterly dissatisfied," she explained. "But he believed in the Court and he believed in George, and he gave him his loyalty, which is where his heart was strongest. He always brought his new plays to George first, even when all the West End theatres were after him."

I knew from a handful of surviving notes from Devine to Osborne how affectionately he thought of him. "My dear friend . . . the way our friendship has grown over the years is vastly important to me." "Above all, John, your card meant the most," he wrote from hospital when he was dying. "My dear John." "My dear boy . . ." But I could find no letters from Osborne to him and none had ever been published. I felt sure that one or more must exist, if only Devine had kept them. Herbert offered to search through the archives she kept at her country home in Hampshire and in time she came up with a gem.

This emotional letter she found from Osborne to Devine was written only three days after the opening night of *Look Back in Anger*:

May 11th 1956

Dear George,

I want first to thank you with all my heart for everything you have done for me, not only in the past week, but ever since you first fished that script of mine out of oblivion. If *Look Back in Anger* is a success on any kind of level, it is your success, your belief, your vision, your integrity that is upheld and vindicated. And, of course, I include Tony [Richardson] in all this. It takes my breath away when I think how much people like you and Tony and Sophie have gone out of their way to give me all they could. You have given me a "home", if you understand what I mean by that, and I feel sure you will.

I remember that a short time ago I couldn't get two pennyworth of anything from anyone – not even a nod of encouragement. No one has ever been so generous to me as you all have. I shall never forget it. My loyalty and support in the future, for what these are worth, are yours irrevocably. Not simply because of my gratitude, but out of my real respect and admiration also.

You have been particularly patient and understanding with me in the last few days. You understood instinctively the sort of person I am, and made allowances accordingly. People like myself really make life impossibly difficult for themselves, and I am afraid that even being aware of the pattern, one can still do very little to change it. At least, I don't seem to be able to, which is pretty frightening at times. Suddenly, this week, I felt more insecure than ever before. I allowed it to knock me sideways. But it *has* passed, I do assure you. Oh, I shall always make grand opera out of my artistic as well as my personal life – there's no escaping that. But I'll not go fundamentally soggy, and forget the real, important things there are to be done. I shall go on writing plays, and play my part in all the things that need so desperately to be done. As George [Goetschius] would say, "Our world will come". But it'll have to be fought for, and with everything we've got.

I didn't mean to write so much introspective shit. Forgive me, but I do want you to know how deeply I feel about all the issues that I know you are concerned about, and how committed I am to them. Again, thank you for everything.

17

Proceed to Texas

What do you – I – want from me?
Osborne note prefacing his MS of Look Back in Anger

The original manuscript of Look Back in Anger is to be found in Austin,
Texas, where it's preserved like a sacred relic of British theatre. Toward the
end of his life, sinking into nightmare debt, Osborne sold his manuscripts
and papers to one of the world's primary literary archives, the Harry Ransom
Humanities Research Center at the University of Texas. Keats and James
are at Harvard; Boswell and Ruskin at Yale; most of H.G. Wells is found
at the University of Illinois; V.S. Naipaul is at Tulsa; and the Brownings
at Baylor in Waco. But 32,676 linear feet of Osborne is to be found in
Austin, where they measure their collected papers in feet like scholarly
undertakers.

"I like the sound of Texas. Texas sounds lavish. Texas sounds *prodigal*,"
announces the lip-smacking mother-in-law of the impoverished writer in
Brian Friel's *Give Me Your Answer Do*. In the play, an unnamed university
in Texas has offered to save the day by purchasing the writer's cherished
private papers, and mother-in-law senses a golden opportunity – manna
from archival heaven or the thinking man's lottery win. Friel's hero – broke
but proud – is conscience-stricken about his unexpected saviour, as if being
tempted to sell off his nice, clean soul. But the Texas university in the play
isn't difficult to identify.

The theatre enclave in cosy exile at the Ransom Center includes the
papers of David Hare, Arnold Wesker and Tom Stoppard. (Though not, as
yet, of Brian Friel.) Osborne is one of the superior pampered guests at the
celestial dinner party for the archival spirits of G.B. Shaw, Tennessee
Williams, Samuel Beckett, Evelyn Waugh, Graham Greene, James Joyce,
William Butler Yeats, D.H. Lawrence, T.S. Eliot, and Walt Whitman –
along with other Ransom Center treasures such as a Gutenberg Bible, the

first photograph ever taken, Arthur Conan Doyle's golf clubs, an initialled Charles Dickens dinner plate, the sunglasses Gloria Swanson wore in *Sunset Boulevard*, and John Philip Sousa's US Marine Band baton.

Orson Welles slyly lampooned the rarefied, cloistered world of research libraries in *Citizen Kane* when Charles Foster Kane's biographer, Thompson, gains entry to the sacrosanct Thatcher Memorial Library of Philadelphia. Walter Parks Thatcher, the Grand Old Man of Wall Street, was Kane's ex-guardian and his unpublished memoirs, locked away for posterity in a bank vault, *might* solve the Rosebud mystery. Welles's fictional library is an echoing mausoleum watched over by a forbidding figure like a witch guarding entry into a tomb. Shafts of celestial light streak through its cathedral windows as the intrepid biographer is permitted to study pages 83–142 of the hallowed manuscript . . .

In Texan reality, the Ransom Center is a welcoming, serious, well-lit place, a cool refuge from the blanket heat outside. Once various permissions and securities had been cleared, I entered a modern room on campus echoing to the pitter-patter of laptops. There, earnest, cross-eyed biographers, deciphering priceless documents in monkish obsession, leave their own lives behind in order to re-live someone else's.

The original, handwritten MS of *Look Back* found there tells us at first sight that Osborne considered six other titles for the play, each one worse than the last. He's crossed them out on the title page leaving the last entry as his final choice:

~~FAREWELL TO ANGER~~
~~ANGRY MAN~~
~~MAN IN A RAGE~~
~~BARGAIN FROM STRENGTH~~
~~CLOSE THE CAGE BEHIND YOU~~
~~MY BLOOD IS A MILE HIGH~~
LOOK BACK IN ANGER

My Blood is a Mile High promises pulp fiction or an early spaghetti Western; *Man in a Rage* suggests a Fifties B-movie; *Bargain from Strength* is surely a trade union pamphlet. Osborne was unembarrassed to scan for a result, it seems, like an actor haphazardly trying out different choices in the privacy of a rehearsal room. Tynan, the play's most enthusiastic champion, objected to the title of *Look Back in Anger*, telling Tony Richardson before the opening that it had to be changed. It reminded him of a second-rate musical that was playing in the West End, *Cage Me a Peacock*.

The title *Look Back in Anger* wasn't new. It was used in 1951 for the autobiography of a disillusioned Christian social philosopher, Leslie Paul, who lost faith in Soviet Russia during the 1930s. But the title of the play might also have been inspired by Francis Bacon's revised *Essays* (1625 edition) in which Bacon writes *Of Anger* and how "the Naturall Inclination, and Habit, *To Be Angry*, may be attempred, and calmed":

> There is no other Way, but to Meditate and Ruminate well, vpon the Effects of *Anger*, how it troubles Mans Life. And the best Time, to doe this, is to *looke back vpon Anger* [my italics], when the Fitt is thoroughly ouer.

The *Look Back* phenomenon turned the title into a timeless, all-purpose catchphrase. "Look Back on the Year"; "Look Back on the Decade"; "Look Back on the Century"; "Look Back in Sorrow"; "Look Back on Osborne . . ." Forty years on, an Oasis hit song was entitled "Don't Look Back in Anger".

The cult label "Angry Young Man" or "AYM" entered the English language newly minted. "Rock 'n roll" first entered in 1953; "Teddy Boy" in 1954; "Angry Young Man" or "AYM" in 1956; "miniskirt" in 1965; "yuppie" in 1984 (and "Blairite" in 1997). Osborne attributed the invention of the AYM phrase to the part-time press officer of the English Stage Company, George Fearon, who disliked *Look Back in Anger*. "I suppose you're really an angry young man," he told Osborne disapprovingly. We assume a light bulb (Thomas Edison, 1879) must have gone off inside his head.

The conformist Fifties became known as "The Angry Decade". But anyone who was even irritable seemed to qualify for AYM membership. Nigel Dennis who wrote the social satire *Cards of Identity* – which became an early Court play – was categorized as an Angry Young Man, although this mild-mannered writer and father of two children was over forty. The smart, opportunistic publisher Tom Maschler of Jonathan Cape, while indignantly protesting outrage at low journalistic catchphrases, encouraged the cult with the publication of *Declaration* as an instant AYM book in 1957. Written by so-called Angries like Osborne, Tynan, Colin Wilson (of *The Outsider*), John Wain and Lindsay Anderson, the contributors also included an honorary AYM for the occasion, Doris Lessing.

Kingsley Amis, then in his twenties, refused to be buttonholed in their company, harumphing like a middle-aged geezer: "I hate all this pharasaical twittering about the 'state of our civilization'." The *Declaration* writers themselves ended up attacking each other, appearing to have little in common, including their anger. But the phenomenon flourished and Osborne would describe the AYM label as a millstone round his neck for the rest of his life.

The original MS of *Look Back* contains some thiry pages of scribbled notes prefacing the text of the play itself. Plot lines and haphazard bits of dialogue are mixed in with bitter echoes of Osborne's first marriage as if he's firing himself up for the task ahead. He's numbered thirty-seven brief observations about Jimmy Porter. ("There's old Porter – off to the battle-field, swinging his club.") And another thirty-two about Alison. ("Her life is the *great unsaid*.") He prepared his plays carefully and wrote them swiftly. The preparatory notes for *Look Back* amount to messy streams of conscious-ness like the entries in his private notebooks. The discovery as I read them was that I couldn't tell whether Osborne was talking about himself or Jimmy Porter.

He slips into the first person singular until it's impossible to tell the two of them apart:

We must concern ourselves with him, with his feelings. What about mine? Who considers mine? The importance of grief. What *they* did to me.

They all hate me. And I hate them. Do you think I have always been like this? I have not. She has made me like it.

The dentist . . .

She just devours me whole every time, and lies back like a puffed out python to sleep it off, as if I were some over large rabbit. That's me . . . She'll sleep on, until there's nothing left of me.

Dull and boring she says. Dull and boring! I wanted to be loved. Your touch is like a gelding iron. You make me impotent. I can't work. I can do nothing. Only goad you into working more refinements of torture. I have seen death and sickness. I have watched them day by day. What do you know of these things?

If only I could make her crawl . . .

Oh, don't take his suffering away from him – please. It's all he's got. What do *you* – I – want from me?

The MS of the handwritten script itself held the biggest surprise. There's so little evidence of any serious revisions or creative struggle, it's as if he's written the entire play spontaneously on the wing. The changes made along the way are so insignificant, that the 275-page script of *Look Back* must have poured out of him as he heard it in his head.

He's written it like a jazzy improvisation. Alison points out that Jimmy had a jazz band at college and wishes he still had one. His bluesy trumpet riffs throughout the play are as much a metaphor of alienation and protest as Sam Shepard's cool saxophone became the signature of lost causes in the American wilderness. The music of England's 1950s generation was jazz – traditional New Orleans and blues for Osborne. Two of his contemporaries, Kingsley Amis and Philip Larkin, were sometime jazz critics – *serious* students of a liberating new art form. I'm reminded that the great Artie Shaw, foremost American intellectual of the clarinet, talked about creating jazz this way:

> Here's this clumsy series of keys on a piece of wood, and you're trying to manipulate them with the reed and the throat muscles and what they call an embouchure, and you're trying to make something happen that has never happened before. You're trying to make a sound that no one ever got before, creating an emotion. You're trying to take . . . notes and make them come out in a way that moves you. If it moves you, it's going to move others . . . Very rarely does it happen, and when it does you remember it for the the rest of your life.

Osborne's writing process was spontaneously the same with all his plays except for one, *Déjàvu*, his last. There are only about a dozen changes to his 355-page script of *A Patriot for Me*. The orginal MS of *Inadmissible Evidence* contains one of the longest speeches ever written, but there's little more than a handful of alterations throughout the entire script. "The problem is, John doesn't write a play," Devine once told Peter Hall, "he *shits* it out – and it just lies there in a great steaming heap."

If so, it was a problem he was glad to have. During the first rehearsals of *Look Back*, Devine and Richardson both tried to get their young dramatist to trim the lengthy script and make a few changes. But they couldn't persuade him. Once a play was out of him, he was basically incapable of changing it. From the beginning, he could no more write to order as compromise on a principle.

The producer Donald Albery offered to transfer *Look Back* to the West End in 1956 on condition that Osborne cut the widely criticized "bears and squirrels" sequence that closes the play. Even Tynan and Hobson had found it as winsome as anything out of J.M. Barrie. We might anticipate most first-time playwrights conceding – jumping at the opportunity of a lucrative transfer. Osborne refused, and a West End production of *Look Back* had to wait another nine years.

He was implacable, but was he wrong about the dangerous device of silly love in his play? I've seen productions of *Look Back* when the escapist whimsy of Jimmy and Alison is more like the last gasp of lovers clinging to the wreckage. The warring couple – we know it – will have no future together after the curtain comes down. The now famous "bears and squirrels" scene needn't be at all sentimental – provided we sense the hidden steel traps lying in wait.

Osborne protected his plays tenaciously – yet, once written, it's as if they took on a separate identity for which he wasn't really responsible and could therefore do nothing about. When he became successful, he still continued writing his plays by hand in the notebooks, and his secretary typed them out. But he never troubled to read the clean copies. Sonia McGuinness was his secretary from 1961 to 1971, the decade that coincides with his golden period. Very occasionally, she told me, he might refer to notes and add a few lines of dialogue as she typed out a script – but he dictated the additions to her off the top of his head. Later on in the process, he would check through the galleys of the published version with her – but again, he very rarely made any changes. The play was out of his hands – *done* the moment he wrote it, trying to make something happen that had never happened before.

18

Critics

This first play has passages of good violent writing
but its total gesture is altogether inadequate.
The Times review of *Look Back in Anger*, 9 May 1956

The critics – a strange, parasitical species, Osborne declared, that should
be regularly exposed like faulty sewage systems – were at first out of tune
with *Look Back's* message. Were they as hostile as myth – and Osborne –
would have us believe? It is always the bad reviews theatre people remember
the most.

Of the fourteen daily reviews, twelve were negative and only two positive. Some of the naysayers tossed the newcomer a bone, but the label
"promising" is no consolation to the playwright who believes he's arrived.
The critical "yes, but" amounts to the dismissive "not really", and no artist
can take lasting solace in the cold comfort of a mixed review. Jimmy Porter
waves the flag for himself with his "Either you're for me or against me."
There could be no half-measures for his creator, either. But if we put a
kinder spin on *Look Back's* critical count, we're still left with seven negative, five mixed and only two clearly in favour of the dramatist who enjoyed
– it's also claimed – the most celebrated theatrical debut of the twentieth
century.

"The First Night audience, if they were conscious," Osborne remembered sourly, "seemed transfixed by a tone of voice that was quite alien to
them. They were ill at ease; they had no rules of conduct as to how to
respond. The obvious one was to walk out, which some did, but with only
a vague idea why. Boredom and anger may have contributed, but mostly
they were adrift, like Eskimos watching a Restoration Comedy."

But he wasn't in the best state to judge the Eskimos. As the evening
wore on, he got so drunk with tension that he could recall little more about
it beyond a blur.

We can help him out a bit. According to one of the Court's council members, Oscar Lewenstein, who was sitting in the front row of the dress circle next to the glazed Osborne, the audience response was divided between stony silence and enthusiasm. But it was far from a triumphant opening. The Court was surprisingly less than full. Osborne, sensing doom at the curtain call, left the theatre after the ritual he described as "the playwright's lap of dishonour" when he visited the cast in their dressing rooms. He subsequently ended up at the Jacaranda nightclub, not far from the Royal Court, in the company of a few actors and Peregrine Worsthorne. The columnist and former editor of the *Sunday Telegraph* described how the champagne-filled night was less to celebrate a first-night triumph than to cheer up the author after a less than rapturous reception of his play.

"It was a drunken night and when the massive bill arrived it became clear that neither John nor any of the actors had a bean between them," Worsthorne recalled. "Fortunately, one of our number – Kenneth Bradshaw, now Sir Kenneth, then a junior clerk at the House of Commons – took charge. Looking round at the other two or three non-actors present, all of whom had served during the war, he said authoritatively: 'Fall out the officers!' By which he meant it was our duty, as relatively the more responsible citizens, to pay."

Osborne remembered awakening in the barge on the Thames the following morning – Judgment Day – still dressed and hung-over, with only a hazy recollection of having kissed an affectionate, plump girl goodnight. He crept ashore across to Mortlake, where he bought all the dailies and walked back reading them with a sickening feeling.

"This first play has passages of good violent writing, but its total gesture is altogether inadequate," went the dismissive opening line of *The Times* review. The *Daily Telegraph* facetiously recommended that Jimmy Porter should have gone to a psychiatrist rather than a dramatist – "not at any rate to one writing his first play". The *News Chronicle* offered watery judgment: "This is an interesting but less than successful offering." The *Evening News* took no prisoners and called it "the most putrid bosh". *The Star* looked forward "in high hope" to Osborne's next play, but found Porter "a caricature of the sort of frustrated left-wing intellectual who, I thought, died out in the war". The *Daily Mail* welcomed a new playwright of "outstanding promise", and then dismissed Jimmy Porter as "basically a bore". The *Manchester Guardian* also welcomed "a potential playwright at last", and then dismissed the play with, "Numbness sets in."

"We should be frank about this," wrote the frank critic and theatre historian J.C. Trewin in the *Birmingham Post*. "If more plays like tonight's *Look*

Back in Anger are produced, the 'Writers' Theatre' at the Royal Court must surely sink." The *Daily Worker* offered no comfort: "John Osborne starts rich in promise but lets us down with a sickening thud." And, among the crushing pile, the *Evening Standard* called the play "a failure", "a self-pitying snivel", and concluded in the condescending tone of a schoolma'am giving a naughty boy a slap over his outstretched hand: "When he stops being angry – or when he knows what he's angry about – he may write a very good play."

At least no one said, as George S. Kaufman did of a Broadway opening, "I saw the play at a disadvantage. The curtain was up." But those thumbs-down reviews of *Look Back* with their humiliating buzzwords – "failure", "putrid", "inadequate", "bore", "caricature", "sickening" – were a devastating blow to Osborne's hopes and those of the newly-founded Court.

The two positive reviews that bleak day wouldn't be enough to tip the balance. One was a short, breezily enthusiastic review from a young critic, John Barber, in the *Daily Express*: "It is intense, angry, feverish, undisciplined. It is even crazy. But it is young, young, young." The other positive review was the kind of rave review Osborne must have dreamt about for years. "This arresting, painful and sometimes astonishing first play by Mr John Osborne . . ." went the opening words of Derek Granger's long, admiring review in the *Financial Times*. Granger was the first to recognize *Look Back*'s contemporary significance, burying a few quibbles about its rawness to hail "a play of extraordinary importance. Certainly it seems to have given the English Stage Company its first really excited sense of occasion. And its influence should go far . . ."

But the *Financial Times* didn't possess enough clout with theatre audiences to turn the tide, and Devine knew it. Osborne recalled that when he went forlornly to a meeting at the Court after reading the damning reviews, "George attempted to brace me up but his own disappointment seemed clearer and more stricken than my own." In fact, Devine believed the future of the Court itself was now in serious jeopardy.

"Well, what on earth did you *expect*?" Tony Richardson said to them both, feigning astonishment at their disappointment. "You didn't expect them to *like* it, did you?" It was his scornful, stoic reaction whenever anything went wrong in life in the unwinnable war against the philistines. "What did you expect?"

Osborne remembered desultory talk of being "saved" by the Sundays, but without conviction. He saw the Saturday night performance of *Look Back* believing it would be its last. The following day he walked over to the Mortlake newsagents once more, and read the *Observer* and the *Sunday Times* on a bench:

I doubt if I could love anyone who did not wish to see *Look Back in Anger*. It is the best young play of its decade.

Kenneth Tynan

. . . he is a writer of outstanding promise, and the English Stage Company is to be congratulated on discovering him.

Harold Hobson

Tynan's endorsement with its astonishing protestation of conditional love – "See *Look Back in Anger* or I won't love you!" – was the critical turning point, and the more restrained support of Hobson the icing on the cake. The *Sunday Times* had bestowed its Good Housekeeping Seal of Approval on the Court, and the *Observer* had embraced the play as "all scum and a mile wide". Tynan – the illegitimate son of a laundress and a Birmingham businessman – wrote triumphantly, "The Porters of our time deplore the tyranny of 'good taste' and refuse to accept 'emotional' as a term of abuse. I agree that *Look Back in Anger* is likely to remain a minority taste. What matters, however, is the size of the minority. I estimate it at roughly 6,733,000, which is the number of people in this country between the ages of twenty and thirty."

In her admiring essay on *Look Back*, the American critic and novelist, Mary McCarthy – Osborne's first major transatlantic champion – made a surprising link between Jimmy Porter and another angry young man who couldn't cope, Hamlet. Tynan, among others, made the same connection. But neither of them could have known that Osborne always kept his well-thumbed acting edition of *Hamlet* with him like a talisman – where he had crossed out all the other parts leaving Hamlet to go it alone, in effect, without a play. *Look Back in Anger* was the play he put in its place.

McCarthy's case for *Hamlet* isn't so fanciful. She sees Cliff, the working-class Welshman, as Jimmy Porter's loyal Horatio; Alison is the brutalized Ophelia who's the innocent product of a corrupt Establishment; both Ophelia and Alison are victimized by a paranoid hero pre-empting betrayal; Alison's brother Nigel is her Laertes; and her plotting mum is the pompous ass Polonius lurking behind the scenes for any damning evidence *against*.

"Both Hamlet and Jimmy Porter have declared war upon a rotten society," McCarthy wrote. "Both have been unfitted by a higher education from accepting their normal place in the world. They think too much and criticize freely. Jimmy, like Hamlet, might have become a species of courtier or social sycophant; that is, he might have 'got ahead'. Critics complain that he ought to have found a job, instead of torturing himself and his nice wife by running a sweet stall. Hamlet, too, might have settled down to a soft berth in the Court of Denmark, married Ophelia, and waited for the succession. Hamlet's tirades and asides are plainly calculated to disturb and annoy the Court. He too cannot stop talking and, like Jimmy Porter, who practises vaudeville routines, he turns to the players for relief from the 'real' world of craft, cunning and stupidity. Both heroes are naturally histrionic, and in both cases the estrangement, marked by histrionics, is close to insanity. Both have no fixed purpose beyond that of awakening the people around them from their trance of acceptance to the horror and baseness of the world . . ."

And both – I would add – are haunted by a father whose death must be avenged.

The celebrations that took place that Sunday at Devine's local pub in Lower Mall, when the belated, glowing reviews appeared to save the day, were premature. The newly crowned Osborne was now interviewed and photographed by *Picture Post*. Tynan – who, at twenty-nine, scraped under the wire of his own youth culture – was also a script editor at Ealing Studios and invited him to lunch to discuss writing a film. Hollywood producers were leaving urgent messages from the Dorchester. But despite the last-minute critical acclaim, *Look Back in Anger* continued playing only to disappointing business.

The reason became startlingly clear. The untapped younger generation didn't go to the theatre. It watched television, and it was television – theatre's deadly competitor – that would turn Osborne into an overnight sensation.

Everything changed when Lord Harewood introduced an eighteen-minute excerpt from the play on BBC TV as if the Establishment were now blessing the enemy within. Michael Halifax, the first stage manager of the Court, witnessed the startling transformation. This distinguished, kindly man had long ago searched with the excited Osborne among Shepherd's Bush junk shops for the props and furniture for the original *Look Back* production, lugging a bed and an ironing board back to the Court in an ancient 1930s Beardmore taxi. No one knew whether the play would make it, he confirmed. But after the TV extract, the theatre was immediately filled with young people – all in their late teens and twenties. Now joined by the middle-class intelligentsia, they were the ones who transformed the play and the Court into national symbols of change.

"You knew something important was happening not only in the theatre, to the theatre, but to England itself," said Keith Waterhouse, the dramatist of *Billy Liar*, who was there, aged twenty-six, on *Look Back*'s second night. The number of people who claimed to have attended the opening night, Osborne always had fun pointing out, could have filled the Albert Hall.

19

Context is All

Don't let the bastards grind you down.
Saturday Night and Sunday Morning, 1960

George Devine's drawing room at 9 Lower Mall overlooked the Thames and offered his guests a perfect view of the annual Oxford and Cambridge boat race. Devine liked to hold a little party to watch the big event and, like him, his Royal Court lieutenants – Tony Richardson, William Gaskill, Lindsay Anderson and Anthony Page – were all Oxbridge men.

"Oxford or Cambridge?" Anderson asked Osborne as they waited for the boat crews to turn into view.

"Neither," he replied.

Osborne was self-educated, and Jimmy Porter went to a white-tile, red-brick university. The uncompromisingly working-class playwright Alan Plater, son of a shipyard worker, demurred about an important question of class. "The one lunatic thing pinned on Osborne is that he was a kitchen-sink, working-class writer," he pointed out to me. "It's just a lot of bollocks. None of his plays is working-class. Jimmy Porter isn't a working-class lad, either. He's first-generation, university-educated, emerging *middle-class*. Let's get that straight for a start."

Porter, the graduate drop-out, belongs to the newly educated generation of England who were dismissed notoriously by Somerset Maugham as "scum". The surly reaction of the old guard to the new can be measured by the resentful fogeyism of Maugham and Harold Nicolson, the art critic of *The Times* who prophesied, "The dandies of the new generation will have dirty fingernails." Rubbing salt into the blue blood of Nicolson's wound, Osborne went on to dress like a dandy with clean fingernails, and Tynan, the dazzling peacock of his Oxford generation, would describe Osborne as the dandy with a machine gun.

The early Oxford bias at the Court is deceptive. Among the second wave of associate directors, John Dexter – who would become a key figure in British theatre and director of the Metropolitan Opera in New York – was the working-class son of a coal miner. (Osborne knew him at Derby rep and recommended him to the Court.) The Court's literary manager playwright Donald Howarth, went to night school and fried chips in a Manchester fish-and-chip shop. Howarth, Gaskill and Richardson had all known each other since childhood in Yorkshire. Gaskill, the son of a grammar-school teacher, was born in Richardson's home town of Shipley. (Richardson recommended him to the Court.) The Oxford bias under Devine's leadership wasn't the traditional product of wealth and privilege it seemed. The Court's bright scholarship boys now joined forces with the emerging generation of working-class dramatists and actors to create a new elite.

Look Back in Anger led the way – but a crucial difference had been made by the new 1944 Education Act when it created state-aided scholarships to universities and drama schools. The Act ensured that education no longer remained the fortress of the privileged. It held out the promise of trans-forming the social landscape by creating opportunity for the excluded working class, while giving birth to a new meritocracy of talent and a newly educated audience for the theatre. Osborne's generation was its first outcome.

A dynamic school of working-class actors emerged in the Court's early years. Albert Finney, son of a Salford bookie, became an international name with Osborne's *Luther* and Karel Reisz's 1960 *Saturday Night and Sunday Morning*, produced by Woodfall, the film company founded by Richardson and Osborne. Finney attended the Royal Academy of Dramatic Art with Alan Bates (the first Cliff in *Look Back* and Archie Rice's son in the film of *The Entertainer*), along with Peter O'Toole, whose first sensational stage role was as a squaddie in Willis Hall's *The Long and the Short and the Tall* at the Court. Tom Courteney of the same RADA generation became a star with Tony Richardson's *The Loneliness of the Long Distance Runner*, also produced by Woodfall. There was Kenneth Haigh, the first Jimmy Porter, and Richard Burton, who played Porter in the film of *Look Back*. The Court's first home-grown female star, Joan Plowright, was Archie Rice's daughter in the film of *The Entertainer* and more famously the idealistic working-class Beatie in Arnold Wesker's *Roots*. Rita Tushingham's break-through role came with Woodfall's film of Shelagh Delaney's Salford classic, *A Taste of Honey*. Robert Stephens, son of a docker, became a rising star at the Court with Osborne's *Epitaph for George Dillon*. For good measure, Stephens's understudy as Dillon was the unknown actor named David Baron, aka Harold Pinter, son of a Hackney tailor.

Middle-class actors just out of Oxbridge and RADA even pretended to be working-class to get *into* the Court. The new plays demanded a new kind of actor. What use the bedsit battleground of *Look Back in Anger* to a John Gielgud?

"When I saw *Look Back in Anger*," Gielgud declared, sensing change in the air, "I thought my number was up." The old ruling elite was on the defensive. Noel Coward lost his insouciant touch when, aged fifty-seven, he noted feebly in his diary about *Look Back*, "I wonder how long this trend of dreariness for dreariness sake will last." Olivier, whose regal tendency, Osborne slyly observed, was to regard himself as a bequest to the nation, at first dismissed *Look Back* as "a travesty on England".

The bewildered Terence Rattigan spent more than two hours protesting to Devine, his old Oxford friend, as to why *Look Back* couldn't be a success.

"Well, it is," Devine insisted. "And it's going to make the Royal Court possible."

"Then I know nothing about plays," Rattigan replied.

"You know everything about plays," Devine told him. "But you don't know a fucking thing about *Look Back in Anger*."

In his biography of Devine, Irving Wardle made it clear that Devine understood the cautiousness of the English temperament and its resistance to change. "I knew my country," Devine said, "and I knew that we ourselves had to become part of the establishment against which our hearts were set."

Osborne was eased into the Royal Court's first season as if by stealth. The opening production of *The Mulberry Bush* by novelist Angus Wilson was an unexciting compromise and had previously been produced at the Bristol Old Vic. (It was Wilson's first and last play.) The second production was the solid bet of Arthur Miller's 1953 political parable, *The Crucible*, which also came via Bristol. Then came the big gamble of *Look Back* – but it was followed like decompressed air by a conventional evening of two one-act verse dramas by the Establishment poet, Ronald Duncan, a some-time West End dramatist and leading disciple of T.S. Eliot.

The so-called revolutionary Court was in fact "born in the ashes of the old literary theatre", as Tony Richardson described it. The elitist, High Church Duncan played the leading role at its uncomfortable birth until usurped by Devine, who regarded all verse dramatists as "absolute shit" and nicknamed him the "Black Dwarf" because of his short stature and allegedly poisonous spirit.

We couldn't invent the unlikely cast of characters who founded the theatre where Osborne would thrive. Duncan had previously run a festival

1 Family group around Grandma Osborne (seated), *clockwise from top left*, 'Grandpa' Porter, Nancy Porter (John's aunt), Grandpa Osborne, John, Thomas Godfrey Osborne (John's father), Tony Porter (John's cousin, on Grandma's knee).

2 John's sister Faith (Fay), who died,
like their father of TB.

3 John Osborne as a child,
dressed to kill.

4 John, *left*, with his mother
and cousin, Peter Grove,
at the seaside, *c.* 1946.

5 Osborne hamming it up in repertory at Derby, with his first wife Pamela Lane, *left*.

6 Osborne, as modest young playwright, on the barge on the Thames
that he shared with Anthony Creighton, 1956.

7 The first production of *Look Back in Anger*, with *left to right* Kenneth Haigh as Jimmy Porter, Alan Bates as Cliff Lewis, Mary Ure as Alison Porter, June 1956.

8 The leading actor and the playwright: Kenneth Haigh and John Osborne outside the Royal Court when *Look Back in Anger* opened, 1956.

9 John Osborne
marries his leading
lady, Mary Ure,
11 August 1957.

10 Osborne and
Ure march to
'Ban the Bomb',
September 1959.

11 The golden couple,
John Osborne and Mary Ure.

I'll walk beside you
Francine

12 Osborne's Swiss-French mistress,
Francine Brandt.

13 Max Miller, king of Music Hall and Osborne's hero.

14 Laurence Olivier as Archie Rice in *The Entertainer*, 1957.

15 The young Albert Finney plays Martin Luther, 1961.

16 Playwright as teddy
boy and dandy, c.1965.

17 The successful
playwright in his
Belgravia home, 1965.

in backwater Devon with the rustic name of The Taw and Torridge Arts Festival, launched with the help of Benjamin Britten, J.E. Blacksell (a Barnstaple schoolteacher) and Lord Harewood, the opera devotee and first cousin to the Queen.

At that time, the Royal Court was leased to the property developer, Alfred Esdaile, a retired Music Hall comedian and pioneer of non-stop variety, who sported a monocle and spats. Esdaile was also the inventor of the stage microphone that mysteriously rises and falls through the floor on command. His general manager was a Communist Party idealist named Oscar Lewenstein, a son of Russian emigrés who would become a leading independent producer and eventual artistic director of the Court.

Thus, the ex-Music Hall comedian, the card-carrying Communist, the royal, liberal Lord, the maligned Black Dwarf, and the evangelical Devine were all about to converge with the future Chairman of the English Stage Company – a Manchester businessman with no apparent interest in theatre.

Duncan, ambitious for a resurgence of his verse plays in London, had gone in search of his own theatre base. Devine, in search of a theatre, too, had already met Esdaile and Lewenstein, but the price of leasing the Court was then too high for him. Enter the wealthy, newly retired Neville Blond, Manchester businessman and government adviser on trade who was married to a Marks & Spencer heiress. By all accounts, the future Chairman of the English Stage Company not only had no interest in the theatre, he would fail to acquire one. He coveted a knighthood (which he never got) and he was a rough diamond. "Don't tell anybody," he whispered to Osborne, furtively handing over a bundle of cash to the penniless playwright during the first days of the Court.

Blond had first been recruited by Duncan's men to raise finance for a lease on his London showcase. When they approached the Court, a deal was eventually on, but the influential Lewenstein nominated Devine as artistic director of his newly named English Stage Company. According to Wardle, the determined Devine then gave Duncan the impression that he was in complete sympathy with everything he stood for, and the die was cast for a bloody battle for control of the Court.

It could also seem as if nothing had ever changed. Aunt Edna was still able to get her pot of tea and a nice slice of Dundee cake served to her seat on matinée days. The original programme for *Look Back in Anger* advertised, in its cosily reassuring way, "Afternoon Tea. A Special Service (freshly made for each order) is served at Matinees in all Saloons and in the Auditorium. To facilitate Service, Visitors are kindly requested to order in advance."

As the curtain descended on *Look Back*'s premiere, BBC Television was showing the visit of Queen Elizabeth the Queen Mother to the Royal School of Needlework Loan Exhibition at Marlborough House, followed by the Weather Report and the playing of the national anthem.

Chairman Blond and his first council members attended *Look Back*'s opening night in formal black tie like a night at the opera. The Court's council had its share of aristocrats: Viscount Duncannon, the Earl of Bessborough, Sir Reginald Kennedy-Cox and the Earl of Harewood. As tradition required, the audience at *Look Back* remained standing respectfully at the end of the performance when the national anthem was played on a record. Here was a play declaring, in effect, "The Establishment sucks!" followed by "God Save the Queen". The anthem was still a sacred convention in England's theatres, and even in its strip clubs. Graham Greene, with his gentleman's ginny eye for the seedy, once explained that he had a particular soft spot for the strip clubs of the north of England because whenever the anthem was played, the local businessmen always stood instantly to attention in their raincoats.

The Court sabotaged the tradition until it eventually faded away during the Sixties like a bizarre memory. Sometimes they played the anthem irreverently at the wrong scratchy speed, the wrong time, or over and over again so that no one, theoretically, could ever go home. When I spoke to Lord Harewood about the Court's history, I imagined all this must have left him feeling uncomfortable. "Not really," he replied.

Just as everything within *Look Back in Anger* takes place in uncertain transition – every relationship, the bad marriage, the friendships, even Alison's bewildered father returning home from a lifetime's colonial service in India to a country he no longer recognizes – so England itself was in a state of flux.

The premiere of *Look Back* was only five months away from the crumbling of Empire in ignominious defeat over the Suez crisis in October 1956. The Conservative government's covert, botched invasion of Egypt to regain control of the Suez Canal and the humiliating withdrawal from the battlefield under American pressure was a political debacle that divided the country, and with it, all the old historic certainties were thrown into doubt.

By then, England was recovering economically from the devastation of World War II. "Let's be frank about it," Prime Minister Harold Macmillan declared famously in 1957, "most of our people have never had it so good." Macmillan, the grouse-moor Edwardian who succeeded the broken Anthony

Eden as Prime Minister in the aftermath of Suez, was said to be the smoothest actor since Disraeli. But the people who'd never had it so good didn't include the working class or the Jimmy Porters who felt fobbed off with lies, seething at the eternal privilege of chinless wonders with Old School Ties. The country was still polarized by the class system. Macmillan, the Old Etonian, had succeeded another Old Etonian, Eden (and appointed six more Old Etonians to his Cabinet). For many, nothing had changed.

The two turning points, *Look Back in Anger* and Suez – one cultural, the other political – have become mythically linked in time. "When I was at school in Bolton, we were taught that the year 1956 was the year of *Look Back in Anger* and the year of Suez," Ian McKellen told me. "For my generation, Osborne was a heroic figure." Just as the Suez crisis remains in the collective memory of the British who were there, *Look Back* still holds watershed significance for the generation it first spoke to. There are better plays that came before and after, and Osborne wrote two or three of them, but how we judge *Look Back* today matters less than its first, phenomenal impact.

It's a tantalizing fact that it remains the only play in the history of theatre to have a birthday. Who could name the year when, say, *King Lear* first opened? Or *The Cherry Orchard*, *A Doll's House*, *Long Day's Journey into Night* or *Death of a Salesman*? But within British theatre, 1956 still means *Look Back in Anger*.

The play's flaws are well known. Its sweeping curtain lines and last-minute revelations – a passionate embrace, a convenient pregnancy – can clang like Edwardian gongs reverberating from the standard rep fare Osborne appeared in as an actor. "Never fails," the opportunistic producer Barney Evans advises his novice dramatist George Dillon in *Epitaph*, encouraging him to tart up his earnest script. "Get someone in the family way in the Third Act – you're halfway there."

But if that were all there is to *Look Back*, we wouldn't have heard of it, and if Osborne had been the only Angry Young Man in England in 1956, the chances are we wouldn't have heard of him, either. The play would have died stillborn. If ever a playwright caught the mood of his time, it was Osborne. The play became a national phenomenon because the public was ready to hear what he had to say. It needed to hear it. *Look Back* didn't happen in isolation. It connected to what was already there or boiling beneath the surface.

We see it in the pockets of dissent on several other cultural fronts kicking against the bland propriety of the times – from the irreverent novels of a new generation of writers like Kingsley Amis to socially conscious New

Wave films, the influence of American drama and movies like the 1955 *Rebel Without a Cause*, experimental schools of painting and poetry, the first rock 'n roll invasion and the retro-street fashion of Teddy Boys threatening sombre Fifties greyness like latter-day punks.

In 1945, Evelyn Waugh's *Brideshead Revisited* nostalgically turned the faded myth of England's grand country estates into a national symbol of the old established order. Almost a decade later, the laddish burial of social deference was announced by Kingsley Amis's 1954 *Lucky Jim*. The know-your-place, *civilised* rules of conduct no longer applied to disillusioned drop-outs and university "scum" like Jim Dixon (or Jimmy Porter). The misfits and anti-intellectual meritocrats were the new anti-heroes.

Amis was then a left-wing Oxford graduate with a classless accent. So was his Oxford contemporary, John Wain, whose 1953 *Hurry on Down* had created another graduate anti-hero in revolt against the corrosive system. The novel itself was migrating to the northern and Midlands industrial wastelands led by William Cooper's 1950 *Scenes from Provincial Life*. The best-selling 1957 novel *Room at the Top* by Yorkshire socialist John Braine, celebrated the rise of a ruthless working-class opportunist determined to make it among the north country *nouveau riche*. "You'll not get at my brass via Susan!" fumes the bullying textile magnate during his summit meeting with Joe Lampton at the Conservative Club. But smirking Joe does get at his brass, of course – winning a place at the top table with the glittering prize of the boss's virginal daughter when he puts Susan in the family way.

As the retrograde Loamshire plays once dominated theatre, so the escapist films of the post-war years – *Kind Hearts and Coronets*, *The Dam Busters* – gave way to the British New Wave in cinema.

The founding members of the New Wave were Tony Richardson, Lindsay Anderson and Karel Reisz. The trio of friends, varying in talent, created the Free Cinema movement in 1956 – the year that has come to be seen as a watershed.

We can see how the alliances were made. Anderson and Reisz – the *Kindertransport* child from Czechoslovakia whose parents died in Auschwitz – knew each other at Oxford where they edited *Sequence*, the first ideological film magazine of its kind in England. Like Anderson, Richardson was a documentary film-maker before joining the Court (and was Reisz's co-director of a 1955 documentary on jazz). When Osborne and Richardson couldn't find a producer to finance the film version of *Look Back*, they founded Woodfall Films in 1958 to produce it themselves. Woodfall was the New Wave reflection of the Royal Court and its allies in spirit.

The new socially conscious films elevated working-class life from the sideshow of character parts to the centre of the action – as the post-Osborne plays did. Paul Barker has pointed out that the fierce sexual frustration – the "gin, hot bath and abortion" axis – flourishing within the working-class novels generated the new wave of movies.

Jack Clayton directed the film version of *Room at the Top* in 1958 with silky Laurence Harvey trying to be working class. *Saturday Night and Sunday Morning*, Alan Sillitoe's raw 1958 novel about a renegade factory worker out for a good time – "Don't let the bastards grind you down, that's one thing I've learned" – was filmed by Reisz with Albert Finney in 1960. David Storey's novel about the downfall of a miner who becomes a star rugby player, *This Sporting Life*, was filmed by Lindsay Anderson in 1963 with Richard Harris. (Anderson was also Storey's director at the Court.)

Another Oxford graduate, John Schlesinger, also came to film via documentaries and joined the New Wave. Stan Barstow's 1960 novel, *A Kind of Loving*, the story of a young couple trapped in northern working-class life, was filmed by him in 1962 with Alan Bates. Keith Waterhouse's 1959 novel *Billy Liar* and its Walter Mitty-ish tale of a North Country undertaker's clerk who retreats into a fantasy world called Ambrosia, first starred Finney in the play version before it became another successful Schlesinger film with Tom Courtenay and Julie Christie.

Today, benchmark films of the era like *The Loneliness of the Long Distance Runner* with its elegy of the delinquent Borstal boy who refuses to be bought off by the Establishment, or *Saturday Night and Sunday Morning* and its near romance of working-class life, have inevitably lost their edge. But nowhere could we have a better example of the transformation that took place than these two contrasting films – Noel Coward's classic romance of 1945, *Brief Encounter*, and the 1961 film version of Shelagh Delaney's *A Taste of Honey*. For the Coward is the perfect embodiment of the repressed social climate of its era. It is white, stiff-upper-lip, middle-aged and middle-class. While the Delaney represents the new world of social revolution, race, working-class vitality and youth.

The film of *A Taste of Honey* was directed by Tony Richardson for Woodfall. Osborne, an admirer of the play, bought the film rights for £30,000 of his own money. It tells the story of a Salford teenager, Jo, who finds herself alone when her slag of a mother goes off with her flash boyfriend for a good time. Jo meets a black sailor, they sleep together, and he leaves her. Now pregnant, she moves in with a gay art student who looks after her.

A Taste of Honey is a lament for people who don't stand a chance and a celebration of being different. Delaney wrote it when she was nineteen years old, fed up with never seeing anyone from her own world acknowledged onstage. It was her one successful play. I remember seeing the film version as a schoolboy and how the usually reserved audience cheered when Jo speaks up defiantly for people like her.

"I'm an extraordinary person," she protests to her gay friend in the play's triumphant scene. "There's only one of me like there's only one of you."

"We're unique!" he adds, and the celebration begins.

"Young!" cries Jo.

"Unrivalled!"

"Smashing!"

"We're bloody marvellous!"

As the half-century cracked wide open, the exhilarating spirit of the times was for change and youth. Joan Littlewood, that uncompromising, self-proclaimed "vulgar woman of the people" who first staged A *Taste of Honey* at her own theatre, was a seminal influence in celebrated opposition to the Osborne era at the Court.

Littlewood's story helps us understand the transforming scene. The illegitimate daughter of a cockney maid, she attended the Royal Academy of Dramatic Art but soon quit on the grounds that it was more like a finishing school for debs. She was a romantic idealist whose loyal actors – including the then unknown Barbara Windsor, Harry H. Corbett, Billie Whitelaw and Victor Spinetti (a friend of Osborne's) – were as proudly working class as she was. "I love them," she said about all the actors in her troupe, "the bastards."

Too outspoken for England's theatre Establishment, she was the chain-smoking waif and messenger of rude rebellion who pre-empted the Court's creation with her own Theatre Workshop in 1953. Her "People's Theatre" in London's East End opened for exuberant, risky business at the Theatre Royal, Stratford, a derelict Victorian playhouse reeking of cats. Like Devine, she was unusually influenced by European theatre, including Brecht before Brecht became fashionable. In contrast to her own rackety theatre company, she thought the Royal Court was "very middle-class and proper, like their leader".

There was an edgy competitiveness between the two new companies, with Littlewood the radical, scruffy underdog. But Osborne – for one – gladly remembered "the rollicking Joan Littlewood nights" and her spontaneous, loving commitment. Unlike the Court, however, the Theatre Workshop was never a natural home for writers. Osborne wouldn't have flourished there. Littlewood herself shaped and even re-wrote the scripts and her freewheeling productions improvised off the text. *Oh! What a Lovely War*, her renowned anti-war Pierrot show, ranks among her lasting achievements – along with the early transforming cockney musicals of Lionel Bart and Frank Norman, the discovery of Shelagh Delaney, and the timely new plays of another of her protégés, the unrepentantly drunk Irishman, Brendan Behan.

The Quare Fellow, Behan's tremendous, bawdy drama set in Dublin's Mountjoy prison on the eve of an execution, was premiered just three weeks after *Look Back in Anger* in May 1956 – the defining year that in turn put the Theatre Workshop on the map.

The Quare Fellow made the air less rarefied. The play was a scathing indictment of the death penalty and Behan had artfully modelled its hangman on England's leading executioner, Albert Pierpoint, a meticulous craftsman who enjoyed his job. "The judgment and timing of a first-rate hangman cannot be acquired," Pierpoint, the aristocrat of the noose, once declared.

The free-spirited Behan was an IRA alumnus who had spent several years in Mountjoy prison as a young man. He became a legend in Britain when he appeared drunk during an interview with the stunned Malcolm Muggeridge on BBC TV. Littlewood was gamely by his side propping him up.

Osborne first met him when the Irishman came pounding on the door of his hotel room early one Sunday morning at the Algonquin in New York. "You can always tell the civilization of a country by two things, its whores and its bread. And they're neither of them any good here!" he announced, lurching into the room in search of good company.

They became friends. I don't know whether Osborne ever knew that Behan described *Look Back in Anger* as a play that's "about as angry as *Mrs Dale's Diary*". But he paid homage to his short bohemian life in a wistful 1992 *Sunday Telegraph* review of *The Letters of Brendan Behan*:

"Brendan's life was a balled, a wild outpouring of a pure, forgiving heart, laughing uproariously at the tides of coldness that threatened it from every side. Who is there in Ireland or England to take up his matchless song now when it is most sorely needed to be heard? Perhaps only he could sing it."

Another Irishman, Samuel Beckett, stunned British theatre a year before *Look Back*'s premiere. *Waiting for Godot*, the play that broke all the rules, was first staged in London in the summer of 1955 at the tiny, adventurous Arts Theatre Club on the fringes of the West End. It was directed by Peter Hall, the twenty-four-year-old railwayman's son just down from Cambridge.

The two-act masterpiece – about which it was famously said that nothing happens twice – would have a profound influence on the future of theatre. (Pinter is the British playwright most influenced by Beckett.) *Godot's* two vaudevillian tramps, Didi and Gogo – remnants of the Dublin Music Hall that Beckett loved as much as Osborne loved the British version – pass the time in the wilderness by playing at being alive. "We'll always find something, eh Didi, to give us the impression we exist," is the gently haunting line from the void.

Beckett, the greatest poet of despair who ever half lived, visited Osborne's Belgravia home a number of times during the marriage to Penelope Gilliatt. Osborne not only admired his work, but related to the heroic, dark soul of the man. Beckett, the chronic depressive, possessed the saving grace of black Irish humour. "Nothing is funnier than unhappiness, I grant you that," he says in *Endgame*, the harshest of his plays.

David Hare – who knew Osborne – explained, "It wasn't the plays that appealed to John so much as the man. If I'd said to him, 'Let's go and see this new production of *Godot* tonight,' I probably would have got a dusting." But he vividly recalled him saying, "I wouldn't compare myself to Sam." Osborne saw Beckett as a man apart.

It was *Godot* that reinvented theatrical form whereas Osborne himself flippantly described *Look Back* as "a formal, rather old-fashioned play". Compared to Beckett, he was a traditionalist. *Look Back* has a beginning, middle and end. It also has three acts and two intervals – the structure preferred by the old West End managements of the era. (Two intervals instead of one theoretically doubles the bar revenue.) But it's a formal, old-fashioned play only in the sense that Osborne used the conventional outer form he knew as an actor.

What made *Look Back* thrillingly new among the plays of the twentieth century is that in the blazing heat and vitality of its language, in its unstoppable grievance and need, it spoke directly to England. It was the first British play that openly dramatized bruising emotion, and it was the first to give the alienated lower classes and youth of England a weapon. The immensity of feeling and class hatred that Osborne poured into its traditional outer form was a shock to the entire system and made history.

"What is most disastrous about the British way of life is the British Way of Feeling," Osborne wrote soon after *Look Back's* premiere, "and that is something theatre can attack. We need a new feeling as much as we need a new language. Out of the feeling will come the language."

His urgent message was repeated in the 1957 *Declaration* essay entitled "They Call It Cricket":

I want to make people feel, to give them lessons in feeling. They can think afterward. In other countries this could be a dangerous approach, but there seems little danger of people feeling too much – at least not in England as I am writing.

Those "lessons in feeling" – those extraordinary instructions to a repressed *nation* not to deflect and submerge the quick of its emotion – were addressed to all those who never find the process of living easeful or *certain*, but hard, like the heroes of his plays floundering in discontent and self-doubt find it hard. They were meant for the *un-glib*, for those who yearn in their hearts to connect to some place and meaning in the confusion and hurt of being alive.

If I am biased about *Look Back in Anger*'s place in British theatre history, there's reason to be. All the evidence points to its watershed achievement. On the tenth anniversary of its premiere in 1966, an Osborne Symposium at the Court gathered together a diverse group of leading writers and intellectuals to put the play in perspective. They included the critic George Steiner, playwright John Arden, novelists Alan Sillitoe and Angus Wilson, and director Peter Brook. Wilson believed that "Osborne's passion saved the English theatre from death through gentility." Brook pointed out that with the invention of Jimmy Porter "the world acquired a new reference." And, in a widely quoted remark, Sillitoe concluded that "John Osborne didn't contribute to the British theatre: he set off a landmine called *Look Back in Anger* and blew most of it up. The bits have settled back into place, of course, but it can never be the same again."

The play linked private turmoil to a public view of England – carrying the mantle of "state of the nation" dramas inherited from G.B. Shaw to a new generation of politically engaged playwrights like David Hare, Howard Brenton and Caryl Churchill. Hare – whose plays continue to be a barometer for English life (*Plenty, The Secret Rapture, The Permanent Way*) – is Osborne's most steadfast public champion. For him, *Look Back* "melted the theatre culture" by making change possible.

"To say that *Look Back in Anger* changed the British theatre decisively is not to ignore the good work that went before it," he said, straining at the leash. "Nor to degrade the equally good work that went on around it. But whatever the contortions of historical revisionism, nobody can finally take away from John Osborne the fact that he wrote a play whose social impact was as profound as its artistic effect. He's the gatekeeper. Everyone else came piling through after."

Arnold Wesker, who wrote the classic working-class trilogy *Roots*, described for me how he saw a touring production of *Look Back* when he was a student at film school and sat down to write his first play. Charles Wood read *Look Back* in the wings of his father's rep company while prompting a play, and in his excitement he couldn't put it down. Hare first read Osborne's plays at Lancing College, where he was at school. So did Christopher Hampton – first Resident Dramatist at the Court when he came down from Oxford in the Sixties – who read *Look Back* at Lancing and decided to become a playwright.

Hampton's first play was staged at the Court Upstairs, the theatre's experimental space. "I wrote it when I was eighteen and it was a copy of Osborne, really," he explained. "There was a central character destroying people's lives who never stops talking . . ."

Among many other examples, there's an unexpected admirer of *Look Back* in Sir Kenneth MacMillan, artistic director of the Royal Ballet, who saw the play in 1956 when he was starting out as a choreographer. "Your bombshell made me see that everything in my world was merely window dressing," he wrote to Osborne toward the end of his life.

But if still more evidence of *Look Back*'s place is needed, let's conclude with the consensus of Osborne's favourite target, the critical fraternity, and a sample of the tributes written on his death in 1994:

It was the play that "changed the course of history" according to John Peter of the *Sunday Times*; "a landmark in the history of theatre" for Michael Ratcliffe of the *Observer*. The *Guardian*'s Michael Billington concluded that if Osborne had written only *Look Back* his place in the history books would be secure. "Its premiere at the Royal Court in May 1956 not only put the English Stage Company on the map, but proved to a generation of contemporary writers that it was possible to put contemporary Britain on stage."

Benedict Nightingale of *The Times* was often critical of Osborne, but he had no doubt about his formative influence. He described him as "the father of modern British drama", quoting Stoppard's phrase that *Look Back* made the Court "the place to be".

Finally, Irving Wardle, *The Times* critic for many distinguished years, who came of age during the Devine era, paid his respects in the *Independent*: "Osborne's place, to state the obvious, is Olympian. He, above all other English playwrights of the past half-century, is assured of an historical afterlife." Wardle – who broke with Osborne's later work and was vilified by the wounded playwright in return – concluded magnanimously, "The history of the English stage itself since the 1950s owes more to him than to any other person."

Three Prize Victims

You've been a very silly, silly boy.
Noel Coward admonishing Osborne about his wives

Ever since Osborne's death, however, eager revisionists have been sniping at the significance of *Look Back in Anger* as if there's a guerrilla war going on.

Charles Duff's 1995 *The Lost Summer* is the best-known (and fairest) example of a book that sets out to reverse the popular myth that nothing of much value happened *before* 1956. Among several other books and essays on my shelves, Christopher Innes's *Modern British Drama* revalues *Look Back* as "remarkably derivative" of Shaw, Ibsen and the first act of Rattigan's popular commercial success of the time, *Separate Tables*. *British Theatre Since the War* argues that the real breakthrough wasn't Osborne but Delaney. *1956 and All That* deconstructs the *Look Back* phenomenon along the lines of Michel Foucault. And a scholarly essay in the *Look Back in Anger* "Casebook Series" maintains that Osborne's turning point was really inspired by an obscure 1926 play, *The Best People*, by David Grey and Avery Hopwood, as well as by John Galsworthy's *The Fugitives* (1913).

Duff's *Lost Summer* amounts to a labour of love and part-biography of the forgotten West End producer and director Frith Banbury, a leading light of the pre-1956 era. Various dramatists directed by Banbury are championed – including Rattigan, N.C. Hunter, Wynyard Browne, Rodney Ackland and John Whiting. Whiting, whose 1951 *Saint's Day* anticipated Beckett, is his best example of a neglected playwright of the time. But George Devine admired him. It was Whiting himself who felt out of sympathy with the realistic plays of the Court, and Peter Hall who later produced him at the RSC. Robert Bolt is among the shakiest of the re-discoveries. Bolt, the north country socialist who wrote *A Man for All*

Seasons in 1957, wasn't made redundant by the Court era. He chose to work in the commercial West End and went to Hollywood to write *Lawrence of Arabia* and *Dr Zhivago*.

The lives of successful dramatists of every era are almost always short-lived, however. Changes of fashion in theatre are punishingly swift and unforgiving even as declining playwrights slog on writing past their "sell by" date, even as they're rediscovered and re-cycled in their lifetime to be sent packing to the grave with a knighthood or Presidential Medal of Honour for services rendered.

The disillusioned, middle-aged Osborne who signed his name "Ex-Playwright" knew as intimately as the dramatists he replaced what it felt like to be cruelly discarded. Rejection is democratic; rejection takes everyone down. The sixty-five-year-old Rattigan told *The Times* bitterly that "overnight almost, we were told we were old-fashioned and effete and corrupt and finished . . . There I was in 1956, a reasonably successful playwright with *Separate Tables* just opened, and suddenly the whole Royal Court Theatre thing exploded, and Coward and Priestley and I were all dismissed, sacked by the critics."

Rattigan, living in lonely tax exile in France and Bermuda, wrote six more plays in the next twenty years and licked his wounds in Hollywood. Coward, long since a tax exile in Switzerland, had to survive on the small fortune he made performing cabaret in Las Vegas in the wake of Marlene Dietrich. The plays of J.B. Priestley were in eclipse. "Angry!" he protested to a group of young Royal Court writers in the early Sixties. "I'll give you angry. I was angry before you buggers were born!" T.S. Eliot had already grown disenchanted with theatre. Verse dramatist Christopher Fry wrote a few more plays in despair and also went to Hollywood (where he wrote the screenplay of *Ben-Hur*). When Fry died, practically forgotten, aged ninety-seven in 2005, his plays had been ignored for almost half a century; yet as the "kitchen sink" revolution approached, he had three new plays and his version of Anouilh's *Ring Round the Moon* (directed by Peter Brook) running in London in one year alone.

On 18 November 1999, the weekly Arts and Leisure section of the *New York Times* arrived on my doorstep with its usual thud. But that Sunday morning, I had a particular interest in one of its leading articles. A recent revival of *Look Back in Anger* at the National Theatre had been well received, and a New York production by the prestigious Classic Stage Company was about to open off-Broadway. The *Times* had invited Mark Ravenhill, the British playwright whose own breakthrough play, *Shopping*

and Fucking, was the most talked about of the 1990s, to explain the significance of the Osborne landmark to America.

The title of the article woke me up in a hurry: "Looking Back Warily
at a Heterosexual Classic."

At least the paper was conceding that *Look Back* is a classic. But what's
a heterosexual classic? What is a homosexual classic? *Hedda Gabler* –
straight, gay or indifferent? *Waiting for Godot* – the tragic tale of two men
who couldn't live without each other! And where does this leave *No Sex,
Please – We're British*?

Why, it all makes me nostalgic for the more innocent days when Gore
Vidal was asked if his first sexual experience had been homosexual or heterosexual, and replied that he was too polite to ask. But in his revisionist case
against Osborne, Ravenhill was firstly anxious to dissociate himself from
knee-jerk comparisons that were made with *Look Back* about his own sensational debut at the Royal Court in 1996, and his pique is understandable.
Playwrights before him have long resented Osborne and the golden era that
followed at the Court being thrust on them as the perennial benchmark of
all change. *Shopping and Fucking* has nothing in common with *Look Back*,
except the Royal Court. Its druggy subculture of mostly gay sex and ultra-
violent abuse is a deliberately sordid portrait of the disposable dregs of 1990s
England – an uncompromising metaphor of post-Thatcher youth bought
and sold like rent boys in the kingdom of the lost. *Contra* Osborne, it's
about the death of all feeling.

Ravenhill – who also wrote *Faust is Dead* and *Some Explicit Polaroids* –
wasn't taking *Look Back* as his model. He wasn't even born in the *annus
mirabilis* of 1956. He belongs to the disaffected generation of Irving Welsh's
Trainspotting and the Nineties renaissance in drama embracing the new
school of Irish playwrights and the macabre, comic savagery of Martin
McDonagh's *The Cripple of Inishman*, the cool, urban sexiness of Patrick
Marber's *Closer*, and the agonizing plays and poetry of the late Sarah Kane.
His touchstone is Mamet, Marber's is Pinter, McDonagh's J.M. Synge. In
their contrasting ways, the new Nineties playwrights were in revolt against
the dominance of the politically engaged generation of David Hare and
Caryl Churchill (who, in her youth, had rejected the non-political plays
of Osborne).

Every new generation thus casts off its parents like ungrateful brats.
D.H. Lawrence loudly rejected the heritage of the original Royal Court
elite of Granville-Barker, G.B. Shaw, Galsworthy and all "Irishy people"
(except Synge). "I am sure we are sick of the rather bony, bloodless drama
we get nowadays," he protested.

Ravenhill grudgingly finds *Look Back* "a good, but not extraordinary play" and warns us that "if anyone tries to tell you that the play is the most significant play in modern British theatre, I suggest you pause politely and then continue talking about the weather." (He prefers Rattigan.) He dismisses the iconic status of *Look Back* as the equivalent of a Year Zero and names it "The English Theatre Creation Myth". But who does he claim the '56 revolution was specifically against?

Coward and Rattigan are trotted out again like pet poodles paraded round the show ring at Cruft's – along with Rodney Ackland, the fine, bohemian dramatist who was out of fashion for so many years before 1956, he was never *in*. "Coward, Rattigan and Ackland were homosexuals," Ravenhill informed us with the air of revelation. "Wesker and Arden were hetero-sexuals, and Osborne was – well, very keen to prove that he was heterosexual."

"God help us," Arnold Wesker responded to his new-found role in the '56 revolution. "There's only one category of playwrights who matter – good ones."

But against Osborne's own dissenting grain, he actually admired the best plays of Ravenhill's three prize victims of the '56 revolution. Osborne – the cavalier and roundhead – broke with the elitist status quo that Coward had symbolized since the 1930s, but his theatrical taste was rooted conservatively in the theatre that raised him. He could oppose the superficiality of Coward's silk dressing-gown legacy, yet never waver in his belief that his self-described "talent to amuse" informed and changed the times.

"Mr Coward, like Ms Dietrich, is his own invention and contribution to this century," he wrote in lonely defence of the unfashionable Coward in the mid-Sixties. "Anyone who cannot see that should keep well away from the theatre."

In his 1982 review of *The Noel Coward Diaries* in the *New York Times Book Review*, Osborne indulged Coward's thunderous name-dropping ("The Queen is in Ghana. Princess Margaret is presumably nursing her baby and as happy as a bee") to declare that he wrote "three of the best comedies in the English language" – naming *Private Lives*, *Hay Fever* and *Blithe Spirit*. Far from opposing everything Coward stood for, he also saluted him for penning some of the wittiest lyrics ever written, including "Mad Dogs and Englishmen" and – "cream of them all" – "There are Bad Times Just Around the Corner."

Yet Osborne knew the compliment was never returned. "I detested the play," Coward wrote in his *Diaries* about *The Entertainer* after missing the point of *Look Back*. But Coward was no intellectual of theatre. He also managed to dismiss its three modernist giants, Stanislavsky, Brecht and Beckett. "Mr Beckett has been seeing too many of his own depressing plays," he quipped. "It gets him down, I expect."

Osborne and Coward knew each other. They first met in 1959 when a panicked Tony Richardson rang urgently from Nottingham where he was directing Coward's shaky adaptation of a vintage Feydeau farce, *Occupe-toi d'Amelie* (peculiarly retitled *Look After Lulu*). It was soon to transfer to London as a star vehicle for Vivien Leigh. "I *mean*, you've got to come up," Richardson pleaded. "Noel's determined to be fucking WITTY all the time . . ."

Osborne sniped habitually at Binkie Beaumont's "Lilac Establishment of Shaftesbury Avenue", but no one could have taken him seriously at the time. The minotaur Binkie often had him along to his swanky South Audley Street dinner parties when Coward was present, and Coward invited him to his Chesham Place flat as well as to "Firefly", his home in Jamaica.

"MAY I REITERATE I LOVE YOU" reads a telegram sent by Coward to Osborne on 3 July 1970. But, while expressions of showbiz love often gush, he was more likely responding supportively to one of Osborne's descents into despair. "My dear Noel," he had written to Coward previously. "My melancholia has receded and I've come to London shaking with pious hopes and all kinds of work."

This key Osborne letter, responding to Coward's peevish attacks on the new generation, puts Osborne's opinion of Coward in perspective. He didn't always have "the profoundest respect" for his work, as he writes sentimentally here. (He publicly opposed its emotional frigidity.) But at thirty-six, he's paying tribute to the fading Coward while admonishing him at the same time:

24 May 1966

Dear Noel,

I would like to ask a favour of you. Could you in future stop trashing your fellow writers to newspaper reporters? I have always had the profoundest respect for both what you do and as a unique and moving figure on our landscape. However, I think it is impertinent to pass judgement on other writers in this lordly way. I don't need lessons from you. The skin you inhabit is not mine. In spite of your genius, your opinions on writers are mostly – not always – execrable. You admire middlebrow, cautious hacks because they offer no serious threats. So be it. But please say no more. You may find it hard to believe but there is much good will and kindliness here for you to cherish where you might not expect to find it.

Believe me, with respect and admiration always.

Coward immediately invited Osborne for a peace-making supper at his London flat where he enquired how queer he was and gave him a governessy finger-wagging of his own.

"Never, never trust a woman," he admonished his startled guest, who had just broken up with his third wife, Penelope Gilliatt, and was soon to marry Jill Bennett in a daze.

"But most of your friends have been women," Osborne replied naively.

"Never mind. Don't *trust* 'em, and never, never marry them. Which you appear to do. You've been a very silly, *silly* boy . . ."

The past is as much a key to Osborne as anger.

In 1993 – some forty years after he first saw Rattigan's *Deep Blue Sea* – he wrote to the *Guardian's* theatre critic Michael Billington (nicknamed "Dr Owl" by Osborne) and reminisced about Rattigan's tragedy of romantic love. "George Devine and Tony Richardson and others were very scornful indeed of my respect for the play," he wrote. They saw it as heresy against his credibility at the Court. But Osborne went on to explain how seeing the play had "a very direct bearing" on his first marriage. When he joined his wife as a jobbing actor at Derby Playhouse, she was playing Rattigan's heroine, Hester Collyer, in *The Deep Blue Sea*.

Hester's life is destroyed when her young lover, the RAF pilot Freddie Page, abandons her. "Some of it was quite unbearable for me to watch," Osborne described the shock of seeing his wife in the play. "Most especially because her natural role in life was Freddie Page. I was Hester . . ."

He identified with the betrayed one. He could dismiss Rattigan contemptuously in his 1959 notebook as "The Landseer of British theatre" after Edwin, beloved Edwardian portrait artist of stags and pedigree dogs. Yet he responded favourably to other Rattigan plays, as he tactlessly told the dumbfounded Devine when they first met. "I let slip that I had more or less admired *The Browning Version*," he wrote. "Realizing my error, I hedged that I had no high opinion of *Separate Tables*. Before I had time to compound my blunder on *The Deep Blue Sea*, he cut me short about the patent inadequacies of homosexual plays masquerading as plays about straight men and women."

But the issue was irrelevant to Osborne because the famous play had always spoken to him on its own terms. He could therefore respect the best of Rattigan in spite of the solemn dictates of the Court and his own agenda for change. And, most unexpected of all, it turns out that Rattigan became an enthusiastic admirer of Osborne's plays after the '56 offensive and the shock of *Look Back*.

"Your most persistent fan salutes you once again," he signs off a letter to Osborne in the Sixties. Among other warm letters sent from France and New York to his old adversary, Rattigan advises him never to become a tax exile like himself and diffidently offers to put him up for membership of the Royal Society of Literature. "You can put F.R.L.S. after your name, if you wish." (He didn't wish.) Rattigan also informs him that he's given a twenty-minute interview to the *Guardian* explaining why he believes "you are the best of us," but signs off forlornly, "they didn't use it. Much love, Terry."

He writes this extravagant compliment after seeing *Inadmissible Evidence* in London and then reading the play as if to confirm all he thought:

> 46, Rue des Vignes
> October, 1969
>
> Dear John
> I have to wait until fairly late at night, when enough Calvados and Marc de Boulogne have released this wavering, inhibited pen, to write a fan letter to a fellow dramatist. You don't need encouragement, God knows. But perhaps you don't spurn it. I mean, who does? While the spell is still on me, and unable to sleep at all, I have to tell you that I think it not only your fullest and most moving work, but the best play of the century.
>
> Terry Rattigan

And the third prize victim of the '56 revolution, Rodney Ackland? In fact, Osborne was among the earliest champions of his neglected plays.

It would be more accurate to describe the bohemian Ackland as homosexual except when married. At forty-two, he fell madly in love at first sight with Mab, second daughter of the Edwardian playwright Frederick Lonsdale, and all agree theirs was a blissfully happy marriage for twenty-two chaotic years. After Mab died, he became gay once again.

The author of some thirty plays, Ackland was a victim of prototype political correctness. The biographer and theatre critic Hilary Spurling points out that he came to see himself "with a certain gloomy relish as the theatre's 'Invisible Man' – denounced in an escapist era for insufficient frivolity, persistently convicted in the 1930s and 40s of dealing in offensive truths". In a fairer world, his unsettlingly realistic plays might have found a home at Devine's Royal Court. But the "Invisible Man" was wrongly associated with the *ancien régime*.

The fate of Ackland's notoriously misunderstood *The Pink Room* is a fascinating morality tale of the era and the link to Osborne. The 1952 play takes place in a seedy Soho drinking club based on the real, louche thing – the French Club off Piccadilly – where the drunk habitués and neurotics of the demi-monde become Ackland's stinging metaphor for a hung-over England still clinging to lost illusion. Binkie Beaumont of Tennants rejected the play as distasteful, and Rattigan financed it in the West End with the profits from *The Deep Blue Sea*. Frith Banbury – Charles Duff's hero of *The Lost Summer* – was its director.

The critics savaged the play – none more so than the powerful, right-eous Harold Hobson who wrote with uncharacteristic cruelty that the audience "had the impression of being present, if not at the death of a talent, at least at its very serious illness". The devastated Ackland was scarcely able to write for another decade and would have only one other play produced in the West End.

However, there is a significant and bizarre photograph of Osborne showing him flanked outdoors by a surly quartet, published prominently in the *Sunday Times* magazine of 18 October 1977. The renowned British war photographer Donald McCullin had been amusingly commissioned to take the picture for posterity that celebrated Osborne's declaration of war against drama critics with the official launch of his British Playwrights Mafia.

The bearded, forty-seven-year-old Osborne stares out at us challengingly. He's abandoned his Savile Row chic and seems to be impersonating "Slasher Green", the barrow-boy invention of another favourite Music Hall artist, Sid Field. The butt of a cigarette dangling contemptuously from his lips, he's dressed in a loud striped jacket with a ridiculously floppy pocket hand-kerchief and a kipper tie decorated with sheep. Standing moodily to his left is Christopher Hampton with his hair down to his shoulders like a fallen choirboy, and by his side is the young Welsh director, Peter Gill. Standing to the right of Osborne like a brooding *consigliere* is another young Court director and working-class Celt, Bill Bryden. But the figure next to him is an Odd Man Out, formal and elderly, about seventy years old. He's the penniless Rodney Ackland.

A decade after the picture was taken, Ackland emerged unexpectedly from the shadows again with a new, uncensored version of *The Pink Room* lampooning his critics and free of all sexually coded evasion. Re-titled *Absolute Hell*, it was first staged at the tiny Orange Tree Theatre in Richmond, and produced to acclaim in 1995, four years after his death, with Judi Dench at the National Theatre.

But as we've seen, Osborne was trying to help him from wretched obscurity long before his belated rediscovery in the Nineties. "Once upon a time I wrote a play called *The Pink Room*, but people thought it was a libel on the British," Ackland said in the article written by Osborne to accompany the *Sunday Times* photograph.

In other words, Osborne wasn't opposing him in any way. He was making him a *cause célèbre*.

21

Success

I'd love to have a really enormous Cadillac with built-in dancing girls.

Osborne, *News Chronicle*, 1957

Osborne married Mary Ure at Chelsea Registry Office, a place he would come to know quite well, on 11 August 1957, and all the signs indicate that he didn't know what he was doing.

Their affair had begun soon after the opening of *Look Back* in which she starred as Alison. In effect, he was marrying the actress who played his first wife onstage. "During the civic mateyness of the registry ceremony," he remembered astonishingly, "I couldn't help thinking of Bridgwater and Pamela."

The man who thinks of his first wife while marrying his second gives nostalgia a bad name. It was as if the heady excitement of his runaway church wedding before breakfast held more meaning for him, with the memory of the vicar's bleary-eyed sermon – "He that loveth his wife loveth himself" – and the sight of Mummy slumped over her pew in disgust.

Although the newly famous Osborne, with his beautiful leading lady on his arm, created the picture of a golden couple united in airbrushed celebrity, he was not in love with her. Rather, he conveyed a bewildered lover's foggy despondency at drifting passively into marriage.

"Mary had begun to make arrangements for our wedding with such determination that I wondered whether she might be pregnant and already in dread of brisk finger-counting months north of the border," he later wrote of his Scots wife-to-be. "Like being trapped in an airport queue or in a nightmare at the theatre, one can only pretend that it is all happening to someone else and that a ladder from the skies will descend for the execution of a perfect and daring escape."

At twenty-seven, he was on the road without maps to becoming a serial marrier. Mary was just twenty-four. Although she remained ambitious for her career, her marriage plans reflected the conformist Fifties when extra-marital affairs were still a social stigma.

Osborne's mother was allowed into the wedding this time, and the reception took place at Au Père de Nico, the newly fashionable Chelsea restaurant off the King's Road. Tony Richardson was best man. Devine was there – Nellie Beatrice respectfully called him "Mr Divoon" – as well as Devine's lover, Jocelyn Herbert. So, too, Robert Stephens with his actress-wife Tarn, Anthony Creighton and others. At least half the guests came from north of the border and Osborne remembered Mary's old nanny offering the blushing bride homespun advice after her uncle's jolly toast: "Remember, lassie, if he ever expects, or wants, well, you know what I'm talking about. Don't ever *deny* it to him. That's the secret of marriage!"

It was a bad omen that a little sculpture had been placed on the wedding cake of a bear with a honey jar embracing a squirrel with nuts. Right bear; wrong squirrel. "Honey will flow, the nuts will grow," went the rhyming inscription read by the incredulous Osborne.

Mary Ure had first set out to be a drama teacher in Glasgow after attending the Quaker Mount School in York (Judi Dench's old school) and then the Central School of Speech and Drama in London. Rooted in a large, close-knit Scots family, she was the daughter of a retired engineer who lived modestly in Kilcreggan above the Clyde. One of the dour family sayings – Osborne noted with perverse pleasure – was "Put another woolly on."

As the cynical line in *All About Eve* goes, the wife of a dramatist is the lowest form of celebrity. But she was no simpering starlet. Before *Look Back*, she was already under film contract to Alexander Korda and a favourite of Binkie Beaumont (who discovered her). She had starred in the West End opposite Paul Scofield in Anouilh's 1954 *Time Remembered*, and was a notable Ophelia to Scofield's Hamlet in Peter Brook's 1955 Stratford production. She would soon be nominated for an Academy Award as Best Supporting Actress in Jack Cardiff's 1960 *Sons and Lovers*. She was an exquisite Desdemona to Paul Robeson's Othello at Stratford. Tony Richardson originally cast her as Alison to bring lustre to *Look Back*'s other-wise unknown cast, though Osborne had his doubts. He felt she wouldn't be able to convey Alison's steeliness. "I think you're *quite* wrong," Richardson insisted. "She's a tough little girl from Glasgow."

"He made her sound like a sparky barmaid," Osborne remarked, and the reference to his bartending mother is a jarring comparison. But in offstage reality, he didn't marry "Mary Ure". He married a quite conventional Scots girl with a light Kelvinside accent who was anxious to start her own family.

When they first lived together in her small, chic Chelsea house at 15 Woodfall Street (which gave Woodfall Films its name) he found their new, uneventful life together "oddly settled, almost provincial. We might have been living in Leicester or Harrogate and far from the fiction that was generated about us both."

She was the one who smartened him up, however. He had his teeth capped by her dentist while they were in New York. Cuban cigars and Black Russian Sobranies replaced his stuffy pipe. She took him on his first trip abroad (a week in Spain). His shiny Loamshire blazer gave way to Savile Row.

Charles Wood remembered being bowled over by the first sight of him at an opening night party in the early Sixties. Wood was just beginning to get his plays staged and there was his hero, Osborne, looking absurdly elegant in immaculate evening dress. He'd come on to the party from the opera. "I think I fell in love with him," Wood was unembarrassed to say. "He looked beautiful and it was important that he actually spoke to me. I've remembered that meeting ever since. He told me how much he liked my plays and it meant everything to me. But I also remember the way he took a gold watch on a chain out of his pocket and glanced at it as he entered the room. He looked like everything you'd expect from a leading man entering a Noel Coward play!"

Mary Ure had wanted children from the beginning. "I want to be with you to laugh, to talk and make love to you, and most of all I want your child," she wrote to Osborne soon after they were married. "I want to start it pretty soon in America [during the run of Look Back on Broadway] as I know in my heart this is the right time for us."

She loved him until the marriage foundered on his infidelity after little more than a year. "There are only going to be about three great English writers in this century and you are one of them, my dearest, and all you need is simply inspiration. Baby, I love you so much with all your great virtues and inadequacies. Always longing for you and loving you."

She was described as "Monroesque", though her physical appeal was more refined and delicate. Christopher Isherwood and his young lover, the artist Don Bachardy, knew her in Hollywood. "Don raved about Mary Ure's beauty, finding her much superior to Marilyn Monroe," Isherwood wrote in his 1960 diary. "I agree. You feel she's a really sweet nice girl and not at all dumb, either."

Her closest friend at school and her flatmate in Southwell Gardens during her drama school days, Rachel Powell, found her "lovable and generous-spirited to a fault". Everyone, it seemed, was enchanted by her. She appeared to be carefree and sunny – "as merry as a cockroach in a Kelvinside tea room", Osborne once oddly described her. But, like Monroe, she possessed an emotional fragility that in time grew disturbing.

Paul Scofield sensed it early on. "She was completely charming always," this self-effacing, great actor told me, "and superfically easy to be with – but there was an elusiveness about her, something impossible to contact that I was baffled by, something unrevealed and dormant."

Isherwood noted in his 1960 diary: "I didn't care for Osborne – thought him conceited and grand; now I like him better. Mary's relationship to him is undoubtedly masochistic."

Osborne's fortunes had changed overnight and he liked to maintain that the trappings of faddish fame held no allure for him. In fact, he carefully nurtured a public image of himself from his first success. (He displayed the customized number plates AYM on his first sports car.) His mentor, George Devine, and his first director, Tony Richardson, thought he should be an *homme sérieux* above the fray. But Richardson had been a glittering success since Oxford and the puritan Devine was always a theatre insider. Osborne had spent too many bitterly anonymous years in shadowy failure, and the actor in him now embraced the limelight.

Osborne's anguished soul – the undisguised truth of the man – is found in his plays and private notebooks, whereas the public myth is constantly changing as if he were a Zelig forever morphing into new images and new roles to play. The wiry New Left intellectual with pipe and cravat of the conformist Fifties becomes the faux Coward sophisticate and surly teddy boy with drainpipe trousers of the Sixties, which begets the Beau Brummel with waxed moustache and Chekhovian artist with beard and half-glasses of the Seventies, followed by the late middle-aged dropout of the Eighties and the unruly Falstaff and English country squire of the Nineties.

No journalist ever came away disappointed from an interview with Osborne. He understood how Fleet Street worked from his lowly, improbable days on its periphery as an adolescent reporter for *Gas World*. If he could market a new gas stove, he could market himself – as his baptism into celebrity shows.

3 April 1956: a young reporter, Penelope Gilliatt (later to be his third wife), interviews him for *Vogue*.

22 December 1956, the *Evening Standard* announces its Most Controversial Personalities of the Year are John Osborne, Liberace, Diana Dors and Yul Brynner.

"This way, John. Be a sport, John!" – photographers calling out to him hurrying from court with his lawyer after his divorce from Pamela Lane, 10 April 1957.

The *Daily Express*, 13 May 1957, has an article about Osborne entitled: "What Makes A Woman Attract A Man?" "I like women to be friendly and pretty and gay and chatty. I also like large, silent, peasant types . . ."

On 12 August 1957, headline: ANGRY YOUNG MAN WEDS STAR. In December 1957, *Lilliput* magazine publishes a photograph of Osborne dressed in "a favourite article of clothing". He chooses the traditional emblem of the landed gentry, a Norfolk jacket specially tailored for the occasion.

On 23 March 1958 the *Daily Mail* asks, "Has success spoilt John Osborne?"

"What effect does an English rose have on a stinging nettle?" the *Evening Standard* asks Mary Ure. "I am happier than I have ever been in my life," she replies.

The *Evening Standard* reports on 19 September 1958: "Mr Osborne mellows now he's on £1,000 a week." The article makes an inventory of his success: twelve suits; handmade shoes; a Buick; a Jaguar XK 150; three different companies.

In today's currency, his earnings would have amounted to about £8,000 a week. Not bad for a playwright who didn't even have a bank account until *Look Back in Anger*. But the figure might have been discreetly under-estimated, for a hit play that's a sensation in London and New York then goes on to be staged at big and small theatres all over the world. "Thank God for Germany," Osborne used to say. The royalties from *Look Back* alone came in like an annual stipend for the rest of his life.

By 1958, his first two Royal Court plays were running simultaneously on Broadway – a sign of his phenomenal success. *Look Back*, starring his wife, was at the Lyceum on 45th St, *The Entertainer*, starring Olivier, was at the Royale down the street.

Tynan wrote with wide eyes about Osborne's international acclaim: "In just eighteen months an obscure repertory actor has become one of the most prosperous playwrights of the century, with a weekly income in the neighborhood of £3,500 a week."

Or some £28,000 a week today. Success always exaggerates success – but whichever figure we choose, the newly prosperous Osborne couldn't believe his luck. Even his first modest windfall astonished him – £300 for the German rights to publish *Look Back*. "It was more than my annual earnings for years. Unimaginable," he wrote. "I bought the *Encyclopaedia Britannica* with it."

After carefully checking his box office grosses on Broadway, he corresponded with Creighton like a dazed lottery winner. "The box office is jammed. At this rate, I'll be able to buy cars for everyone soon!"

Later that year, from New York: "Success here is irresistible. When I return I shall be *so* calm and dignified . . . So much I want to do, so much opportunity. I'm going to be RICH. When they don't want me anymore, Osborne is not going to have to worry. He's going to lie on his yacht in the sun with a big cigar and a smile on his face with his chums, and read through the *Encyclopaedia Britannica* from beginning to end."

Generous with money even during the lean years, his pleasure was always to give away *things* – gift-wrapped goodies, surprise treats, cars. He helped a number of his theatre friends by paying their bills and settling their debts. He invariably picked up the tab for everyone in restaurants. He set his mother up. He treated money as if it would never run out. Yet when the film version of *Tom Jones* made him a multimillionaire, he hid a secret money box in his study where he stashed away a roll of banknotes and loose change "just in case".

At twenty-seven, he was such a magnet of interest that he was even impersonated in his own play. Robert Stephens's acclaimed performance as the unscrupulous hero of *George Dillon* was modelled on Osborne's voice and mannerisms. (Nicol Williamson gave another, panicky version of him in the later *Inadmissible Evidence*.) *Hancock's Half Hour*, Galton and Simpson's comic masterpiece of suburban angst, even invented a new character known as "John Eastbourne, the Hungry Young Man".

Mary Ure and the Hungry Young Man were photographed together by Cecil Beaton in his dappled garden (where Beaton described Osborne as an elegant camel). There were soirées at Ken Tynan's fashionable Mount Street flat to meet Cyril Connolly and Peter Hall with *his* film star wife, Leslie Caron. Osborne and Ure were photographed with Arthur Miller and Monroe, and befriended by the Burtons (Richard and Sybil, soon to be followed by Richard and Elizabeth).

But not everyone was impressed by the *arriviste* in their midst. One of Osborne's favourite stories against himself was about a dinner party at Binkie Beaumont's:

"*Now*, Elvira," Binkie said silkily to his old crone of a housekeeper who was grudgingly waiting on Osborne. "Mr Brendan Bracken has just died and his house across the road is up for sale. Don't you think it would be *splendid* if Mr Osborne should buy it?"

She looked down at Osborne disdainfully and replied with an emphatic, "No."

"But why on earth not, Elvira?"

"Because 'e's not *ready* for it yet!"

Osborne sailed to New York on the Île de France for the premiere of *Epitaph for George Dillon*. ("First class all the way, skipper!" his father always told him.) On board, he ended a dreary decade of vegetarianism. But *George Dillon* – his third consecutive Broadway production – opened at the John Golden Theatre in November 1958, and flopped.

He was now baptized into New York's ritual way of handling outcast failure where British compromise (or a mixed review) has no place. New York either celebrates success by popping open the champagne or it kicks you out of town immediately. Sardi's on Broadway was then *the* place to be for opening night parties, and when the negative reviews for *George Dillon* arrived, the place emptied. The cynical waiters of Sardi's – slaves to the judgment of theatre critics as much as anyone connected with a show – didn't even serve food unless the reviews were good. You could get a drink.

Someone shouted at Osborne afterwards, "You've let down England!" But he took the setback surprisingly in his stride. The co-written *George Dillon* had been pulled from his bottom drawer; it belonged to the past. Soon after the unfizzy opening night, he returned to the scene of the crime at Sardi's for a compensatory lunch with Robert Stephens and a few other friends. Marlene Dietrich was at the number-one table, the first banquette on the left. Osborne remembered breathlessly, "As we all tried to direct our attention from one of the century's icons to the menu, a waiter laid down a small salver with a piece of folded paper in front of me."

To his astonishment, there were three words written on it: "Who are you?" Signed Marlene Dietrich.

"Good God!" the others gasped as he passed the note excitedly round the table and Robert Stephens dictated his reply: "My name is John Osborne and may I have the pleasure – no, the honour – of meeting you?"

Back came the waiter with the laconic answer, "Any time." Along with her phone number.

After agonizing about it through lunch, he went over to shyly introduce himself to Dietrich and she even apologized for not recognizing him. But he didn't have the bottle to follow up. He hovered for days over the phone at the Algonquin. "I didn't rise to it," he confessed, "an act of craven timidity I've regretted ever since."

Osborne still kept her note in his wallet many years later. Among the postcards he sent to friends from Shropshire toward the end of his life, one was a photograph of the smokily androgynous Dietrich. "Another lost opportunity," he scribbled by her name.

*

His producer on Broadway was the legendary David Merrick, who was known as "the Abominable Showman". "He liked writers in the way that snakes like live rabbits," Osborne said of him. Yet he produced four of his plays. A modern P.T. Barnum, the scheming Merrick possessed a genius for publicity. As Frank Rich of the *New York Times* related, *Look Back in Anger* was beginning to falter at the box office after only four months, but its fortunes were transformed when a distraught woman in the audience jumped onstage at the Lyceum Theatre and hit Kenneth Haigh's Jimmy Porter on behalf of wronged women everywhere. "The story raged in the newspapers for three weeks before Mr Merrick confessed he had hired the woman for $250," the *Times* reported. "But by then *Look Back* was on its way to running another 15 months on Broadway and the road."

For Osborne and his generation, New York was the tempting New World of ridiculous abundance in the pinched age of British rationing. True, he compared New York's automatic "Have a nice day" to an American version of "Heil Hitler", but that was because he was unused to the kindness of strangers. He lapped up the delights of the city that fêted him as an Horatio Alger success story. It was as if he'd stepped into one of the black-and-white *films noirs* that had transfixed him during childhood. While his wife was onstage at night in *Look Back*, he took in the jazz scene at Eddie Condon's, Toot Shor's, Birdland, the Five Spot and the Apollo in Harlem until dawn. New York was *anything he wanted*. It was a suite at the Algonquin Hotel on 44th St and the miracle of twenty-four-hour room service, a cauterizing Bloody Mary at 11 a.m. and a sauna with Alan Bates at Ziggy's Gym on Broadway and Third to recover from the night before.

New York was where he met hustling Harry Saltzman, who became a founder of Woodfall Films with Osborne and Richardson before going on to make his fortune with the Bond movies. It was during a party in his New York apartment next door to the Waldorf Astoria that Francine Brandt, a dark-haired, stunning high-class hooker, entered the room and stopped all conversation.

George Devine was there, having flown over to New York for a lecture, and he drew Osborne aside. "Now that's the kind of woman you and I could never get near," he told him, sucking lingeringly on his pipe. "Not a chance, dear boy."

Osborne's affair with Brandt began a week later in a pink and green bungalow of the Beverly Hills Hotel, Los Angeles. His wife's 1961 divorce petition named her as one of his adulterous lovers along with a list of their trysts in Montego Bay, Jamaica, during February and March 1958; in the

Hôtel Napoleon, Paris, and in Geneva; and subsequently at the marital home, 15 Woodfall Street.

In his defence, Osborne brazenly quoted St Augustine: "A Stiff Prick hath no conscience." His wife said nothing for the moment, although she knew of his careless infidelity from the beginning. When she returned to London with her suntanned husband after the run of Look Back in New York, they appeared to be the golden couple as before.

In phlegmatic contrast to his life in New York, however, Osborne returned home to that chastising English speciality that cuts all success down to size, the tall poppy syndrome. "The English have a curiously perverted and puritanical attitude to money," he told the Evening Standard, obnoxiously smoking a cigar in his speckled Norfolk jacket. "They think it's somehow sinful to enjoy it."

Outrageous success, the enemy of promise, thus came to Osborne overnight and, with it, all the trappings – an agent, a secretary, various accountants, limited companies, a chauffeur, a tailor, a showbiz lawyer, an upmarket hooker, an ex-directory phone number, a beautiful wife.

His lawyer, the late Oscar Beuselinck, was among the smartest solicitors of his time – a man you would prefer to have on your side – and he was a flamboyant character who was notoriously randy. "Have you ever had it on the kitchen table?" he asked Osborne the first time they met at his offices in Ludgate Hill.

Beuselinck was born in Bloomsbury, the son of a woman known as "Fighting Win" and a father who was a Flemish Catholic chef. "You think I'm Jewish, don't you?" he announced during that first meeting with his clerk, Charlie, in solemn attendance. "Well, I'm not. You should look at my chopper!"

He was a man who liked to lay things out on the table. During the West End premiere of the arty nude revue, Oh Calcutta, he suddenly turned round and shouted to a friend a few rows back. "Well I 'avn't got an 'ard yet, 'ave you?"

You couldn't help liking him, Osborne said, like Max Miller – no inner life to hinder. "If I don't get it three times a day I feel ill. I really do!" All three Mrs Beuselincks were at his bedside when he died. Osborne was best man at his wedding to his twenty-four-year-old secretary and he remained his client for thirty-four years. Beuselinck handled all the divorces. "Got off light there, son!"

Osborne's first chauffeur was in his seventies when I met him – an eccentric, vinegary man named Jimmy Gardner with a bushy white beard and granny glasses. "I was offered a job as a chauffeur to royalty before John

Osborne," he sniffed. "But they pay so little I wasn't even interested."

When he was first approached for the job with Osborne, he was asked to be his chauffeur *and* valet. But he didn't want to be a valet. He subsequently worked all his life as an actor and appeared in supporting roles in Osborne's 1960s double bill, *Under Plain Cover* and *The Blood of the Bambergs*. "I wasn't very good in them," he confided. "But they weren't very good, either."

His father was a jockey. There have been only three triple dead heats in the history of racing, I learned, and his father was in two of them. The gnomish man seated opposite me sipping tea in the living room of his North London home was as small as a jockey, too. And yet, as I pointed out clumsily, he had driven Osborne's gigantic Buick. "I've driven articulated lorries!" he protested.

An American car was an unusual, showy status symbol in 1950s England. It meant you had prospered in The Land of Opportunity – or wanted to. "It was a big, beautiful Buick Sapphire 1957," Jimmy Gardner remembered, "and when John bought it, he wanted to show it off to his mother. But he crashed it on the way. I never saw him drive, though. He liked to be driven, and he liked to sit in the back. Mary always sat in the front."

So the one who needed the prestige sat in the back of the chauffeured car, while the one who was used to it sat up front. When he drove Osborne's mother around on her shopping expeditions, she always sat in the back. "She was quite chatty," he said, "but common."

Otherwise, it was all very democratic. They called each other by their first names and he was asked not to wear a uniform. He joined Osborne and Mary for dinner whenever they travelled long distances together. "If I was just chauffeuring John, he would take me to dinner no matter who was with him. He always had a seat for me at the theatre, too. He never referred to me as his chauffeur. He'd say, 'This is Jimmy.' I loved him. He wasn't vile and brutal and all the terrible things people say about him. He left a profound impression on England, in my view. He understood the English and it frightened them."

In the two years he worked for Osborne, he drove three cars: the black Buick Sapphire, the racing-green Jaguar XK 150, and the custom-built blue Alvis with the Armstrong Siddeley coachwork and gleaming white leather seats. When he announced that he wanted to leave to try his luck as an actor, Osborne took him out to celebrate his new career over dinner at the Ivy. "Mary came along, too, and then we all came back here for the evening. We listened to records until about three in the morning. I've lived here for fifty years."

He showed me a photograph he'd kept of them, autographed affectionately to him by both. And there, in black-and-white close-up, was the fresh, burnished image of their easeful success. The pale and exquisite profile of the blonde Mary Ure, as delicate as a china doll, leans into her wiry young husband, who couldn't look more quietly pleased with himself as he faces the camera with confident intelligence, half smiling.

A private notebook entry from the same period, July 1959, reads:

I am governed by fear every day of my life. Sometimes it is the first sensation I have on waking. Even the thought that I have managed to escape death by waking up. Fear in love. Fear of being deserted, fear of being involved. Fear of getting hurt, of physical pain, of operations and surgeries, of my personal appearance, of spots on my back, over food, of being unable to express myself. Of being afraid at school. The milk bottles. Air raid shelters. The boys in balaclava helmets. I am afraid of the dark. I am afraid of the dark hole and the pain from it which grips me every day: That clenched warning which tightens the dark hole of my inside. It is fear, and I cannot rid myself of it. It numbs me, it sterilizes me, and I am empty, dumb and ignorant and afraid.

22

A Typical Night on Montana Street

> I often confronted problems like an improvising chimpanzee faced with
> the dashboard of a jumbo jet.
>
> Osborne on his chaotic love life

Osborne sniped unflatteringly at his ex-wives in his private notebooks, yet
there's scarcely a mention of Mary Ure. It's as if their marriage didn't count
for anything or failed to leave a mark on him. He treated her cruelly and
she was the only ex-wife he didn't ultimately blame.

"That was squalid," he wrote fleetingly in his 1962 notebook about his
role in the disintegrating marriage. "I was ignoble and my nerve was timorous
and I'd no style, no guts."

He was a man who could be aggressive with women and aggressively
timid. Contrary to his combative Jimmy Porter image, he tried to avoid
personal showdowns (preferring his weapon of choice – the written word,
a blistering letter). He let his aimless marriage to Ure drift indecisively
until she fell in love with Robert Shaw and the break was eventually made.

Their failure to have children was the turning point (". . . most of all I
want your child," she had written to Osborne at the beginning). Ure was
a loving, emotionally vulnerable woman and she was practical and resolved.
Failing to conceive, she took the slavish advice of a New York gynaecologist who recommended an unshakable regime of counting the days,
guidebook sex with contorted illustrations, taking temperatures and even
applying cold compresses.

Osborne subsequently described making love to his beautiful wife as a
"punishing *Kama Sutra* of fertility athletics". Their intimate times together
were planned laboriously in advance.

Ure's closest friend then was the actress Tarn Bassett. She was the first
wife of Robert Stephens and took over the role of Alison in *Look Back* at
the Court. (Ure was godmother to their daughter.) She now lived just

outside Winchester, and when we met, told me how desperate her friend was to have children. "Mary thought the problem was that John was a *vegetarian*," she said and began to laugh gaily. But she also nursed the problem obsessively. "She could be extremely pragmatic. She was always taking his temperature. She used to insist on seeing his poo."

"Why on earth would she do that?"

"She wanted to see if everything was alright. She wouldn't let him flush the toilet until she'd had a look. John thought it was revolting."

He continued to enjoy the uncomplicated sexual freedom of his double life with Francine Brandt. "Probably Mary suspects that I'm having an affair," he wrote to Anthony Creighton soon after the liaison first began in Los Angeles. "For the first time, I'm having a deep sense of guilt. Particularly as this girl – Francine – is becoming a far, far more serious thing than I had ever contemplated. I find – to my horror – that I am constantly wanting her more and more."

He neglected to mention for the moment that she was a call girl. Theirs was an *Irma La Douce*-like story in which the pure-at-heart Parisienne prostitute falls for the unlikely hero. The affair with the French-Swiss Brandt went on for two years. Perhaps she wasn't too brainy, he acknowledged, perhaps she wasn't very sophisticated or even worldly, but he was close to her. "If the whole world hated you I would be glad," Francine wrote to him, "because I would have enough love for you to make up for the world."

She called him "little monkey" and kept his photograph by her mirror. "Presents" – or cheques – were sent to her Geneva address. "Wonderful little monkey – what can I do? Go out of your life? Maybe one day you will know the answer . . . Have a great vacation, rest a lot with me as often as you feel, and let me stay in your heart."

"John darling. Thank you for everything. Thank you for making love to me in this wonderful way, it gave me great happiness. Thank you for your last words and kiss. It gave me back a little confidence in myself (confidence I had completely lost lately). You have made me the happiest woman in the world. If at any moment you feel lonely, please remember me, remember my happiness and my tears. You have made me more romantic than I thought it was possible to be. God bless you, my love. You are the great joy of my life. Francine."

Ure knew of the affair from the start, if only from the New York gossip columns (Walter Winchell's among them). Osborne, a transparent man, was in any case wilfully public about it, as if flaunting the glamorous call girl on his arm before bourgeois respectability. Tarn Bassett held open house with her husband Robert Stephens in their Glebe Place home off the King's Road, but she was upset when Osborne turned up for a party there with Francine. The wayward lives of actors are usually treated with gossipy tolerance among their own, but the compromised hostess was Mary Ure's best friend.

Osborne's high-minded guilty plea describing his behaviour as "squalid" and "ignoble" suggests a puritan conscience. If so, he was a hypocritical English puritan about sexual fidelity. Although he lacked the ocular proof, he was taking peevish, punishing revenge on his wife's suspected infidelities and his goading public parades were meant to wound her. One Christmas, he disappeared to Paris with fun-loving Harry Saltzman rather than join his wife in New York during the run of *Look Back*. "We love Paris, Paris, Paris," they foolishly cabled her like giddy adolescents. "Happy Christmas. See you for the New Year. Love John and Harry."

Yet Ure would not leave him and kept up stoic appearances. There were weeks, however, when Osborne spent more time with his lover than with his wife and it unhinged her core of fragility. There were unpredictable mood swings. She could fly into violent rages and began to drink heavily. When she plunged dazed and naked into the pool at Tony Richardson's Hollywood house, apparently to drown herself, it was because the indifferent Osborne had been staying there with his lover the previous night.

Christopher Isherwood, recording everything in his diary, compared the melodramas at the house on Montana Street in West Los Angeles to a Feydeau farce. Isherwood, who lived in LA, was one of the many guests. Richardson had rented the Hollywood place from Zsa Zsa Gabor who had furnished it entirely in ivory and gold. Included in the rent was an eccentric black maid, Japanese gardeners and a Cadillac. According to Richardson, the black maid hated anyone black and read everyone's letters, selling the information to Hedda Hopper and Louella Parsons. There were parties every weekend – a perfect time for what the notoriously manipulative host called "escapades and adventures and frivolity".

A delighted John Mortimer once told me that the point of Richardson's famously crowded house parties was that sooner or later everyone ended up sleeping with everyone else. But he always pretended never to have invited anyone. "I mean, Johnny," he'd complain in injured faux innocence to Osborne. "*I* didn't invite them, did you? They won't say when they're *going*."

Avoiding writing, Osborne idled away the time during August 1960 at the Richardson house in Los Angeles – or "Sodom in smog" as he called

LA. The West Coast made him feel strangely desolate and tearful, and one day he talked about it with Isherwood who told him he knew the depressive feeling intimately and called it "The Pacific Blues". The only solution, he advised, was to get drunk all day long.

Osborne stayed at the Richardson house with his mistress, Francine Brandt, except when his wife came to stay. Ure was then on tour in Los Angeles with Vivien Leigh in Giraudoux's *Duel of Angels*. When she turned up at the house, Francine had to be hastily bundled out.

Vivien Leigh also came to stay, arriving in her Rolls with her new lover, actor Jack Merivale, while still grieving hysterically over the loss of Olivier to Joan Plowright. En route to Broadway, *A Taste of Honey*, directed by Richardson, was about to open in Los Angeles with Plowright. She was another house guest, but not at the same time as Vivien Leigh. Described by Osborne as an unlikely Wallis Simpson to Laurence Olivier's Duke of Windsor, Plowright was in the midst of her hot affair with Olivier.

George Devine and his mistress, Jocelyn Herbert, also came to stay, along with Zachary Scott, Robert Helpmann, various young studs passing through from Malibu and Muscle Beach, and Simone Signoret, keeping a beady eye on Yves Montand, who was having an affair with Marilyn Monroe while filming *Let's Make Love*.

"Meanwhile, Signoret has been visiting Mary Ure and moaning Yves is having this affair with Monroe," Isherwood scribbled in his diary. "Arthur Miller doesn't care, it seems. Both Simone and Mary shed tears and got drunk. Mary has been rather loving this. She luxuriates in scenes . . ."

Plowright, who disliked Osborne (and vice versa), disapproved of Francine, describing her prissily as a "model" and his "current mistress". But there was a concurrent mistress by then – costume designer, Jocelyn Rickards, with whom Osborne had been having an affair for more than a year.

"I never thought I could miss you so much," he wrote to Rickards from Los Angeles. "I think of you constantly. My love always . . ." "My darling. Do be careful. It means a lot to me that nothing should go wrong. I love you dearly . . ."

Meanwhile, back at the crowded house, Plowright felt uncomfortable colluding in the deception whenever Francine rushed out the back door until the coast was clear. During Osborne's weekends with his wife, there were furious, drunken quarrels between them. Ure was left sobbing hysterically on one occasion as she fled into Westwood Village in the middle of the night. "And how are *you*?" Richardson, lapping it all up, asked Osborne when he returned after searching for her.

That was the August night she later emerged naked from the master bedroom overlooking the pool to drown herself on sleeping pills as her husband and Richardson lolled drinking champagne poolside. "Don't you think we should *do* something?" Richardson eventually asked Osborne, who thought she was just creating a scene. It was the alarmed Richardson who dived in to the rescue.

According to Plowright, however, he wasn't even in the house at the time and it was she who saved Ure by fishing her out of the pool with the help of a friend. She complained that she was dubbed "The Girl Guide" for her trouble.

The basic accounts of both Osborne and Richardson coincide, however, with Richardson's fuller version claiming that Plowright was asleep in bed at that late hour and was awoken by the commotion when he dived nobly in. "A typical night on Montana Street," he said later. But whether he or Plowright rescued Mary Ure, it was as if nothing had happened the following day when Osborne emerged at noon for his first cocktail in the haze of sweltering Los Angeles to find his wife splashing happily in the pool.

Osborne's public parades of infidelity humiliated Ure, but though she retained a certain prideful possessiveness, she otherwise had no complaints about his lovers. She had taken solace in her infatuated love affair with Robert Shaw since they first met in mid-May 1959, and it goes some way to explaining Osborne's cruel treatment of her.

With his black Irish handsomeness, Shaw was then a pushy, promising actor at the Court with ambitions to become a writer. He was competitive with Osborne, and in time he did write a successful play (*The Man in the Glass Booth*, directed by Harold Pinter). He became better known as an international movie star playing menacing, tough-guy roles like the blond Russian assassin in *From Russia with Love*, the gulled gambler in *The Sting*, and the salty dog who's swallowed alive by the terrifying shark in *Jaws*.

Osborne's closest friend, Tony Richardson, played perfidious Cupid between the new lovers. We can piece together the essentials of the night he showed up with Shaw at Woodfall Street for a drink at 2 a.m. and perhaps much later. Both were reeling by then, banging on dustbin lids to awaken the house.

Shaw was a product of the Fifties drinking generation that included Osborne, Richard Burton, Peter O'Toole, Richard Harris, Robert Stephens, Peter Finch and Trevor Howard. Their narcotic was booze rather than drugs. Osborne, steeped in a melancholic's soothing, steady pace from 11 a.m. to bed, wasn't a hellraiser in the macho tradition of his hard-drinking contemporaries, whereas Shaw would virtually drink himself to death. (He died of a heart attack, aged fifty-one, as he stepped from his Rolls in Spain where he lived in tax exile.)

"Where's poor little Mary?" he demanded when Osborne opened the door at Woodfall Street.

She was standing at the top of the staircase in her nightdress – "startled, but not displeased", according to Osborne. Robert Shaw's former agent and biographer, John French, reports that Shaw took one look at her and began to moan with delight rolling on the floor.

"I poured whisky for the three of them," Osborne noted coldly. "They all settled down. Mary happily curled up, knees to her chin, pleased as a welcoming dog. I left them and returned to bed."

Richardson remembered the champagne corks popping within minutes and that Osborne was "furious and truculent, but it was just the kind of escapade that excited Mary". Perhaps. But the decisive moment came when Osborne went back to bed indifferent to the outcome. Shaw boasted to friends he became Mary Ure's lover the following day.

They married and had four children. But her mental problems became more apparent during the marriage. In New York, she was found by Shaw in the middle of the night walking naked in Central Park but could remember nothing about it the next day. She was briefly hospitalized. On another occasion, the police found her on a freezing night naked outside the stage door of the Billy Rose Theatre and escorted her home.

According to Tony Richardson, Mary Ure was a limited actress if judged at the highest levels, but she was the first Ophelia he had seen who conveyed true madness. She was then only twenty-two years old. Peter Brook was her director for *Hamlet* and when I asked him about her acting, he wanted to know what had become of her. I told him how she was unhappily married to Osborne for a while and became infatuated by Shaw who drained her of her vitality. She continued to act occasionally in films and theatre, but grew increasingly disturbed until, at forty-two, she died of an accidental overdose in London.

"And all of that was within her Ophelia," said Brook. "She was beautiful, pure and rudderless. The seeds were already there in her performance."

23

Take My Wife – Puhleeze!

Well, I 'ave a go, don't I? I do. I 'ave a go.
Archie Rice, *The Entertainer*

British theatre – and Osborne in particular – have a lot to thank Arthur Miller for. He paved the unlikely way to Laurence Olivier playing Archie Rice.

In July 1956, Miller accompanied his wife, Marilyn Monroe, to London where she was filming the extremely light period comedy about a breathy innocent abroad, *The Prince and the Showgirl*, directed by her co-star, Olivier. (It was originally a Terence Rattigan vehicle for Olivier and Vivien Leigh in the West End, entitled *The Sleeping Prince*.) Welcoming Miller – nicknamed "Mr Monroe" and "Marilyn's Boy" by Fleet Street – Olivier asked which plays he was interested in seeing.

Miller wasn't yet familiar with the London scene, but he had a link with the Royal Court. *The Crucible* was part of its opening season. He chose to see *Look Back in Anger* because the title intrigued him.

To his surprise, however, Olivier advised him to pick something else – dismissing the play he'd already seen with, "It's just a travesty on England."

Olivier's popular, rousing 1944 film of *Henry V* had personified the romance and glory of being English, and *Look Back* had offended his sense of patriotism *and* theatre – which only made Miller keener to see it. Tickets were quickly arranged for the following night, and Olivier turned up unexpectedly to see the play a second time with him. He was stunned when Miller found *Look Back* a revelation. Anxious to grasp its significance, Olivier asked him twice – during the interval, and again at the end – why he thought it was so wonderful.

Then George Devine took them both backstage to meet his surly protégé. "Do you suppose you could write something for me?" the craven Olivier asked Osborne. Miller said he was laying on the charm so much he could have convinced anyone to buy a car from him with no wheels for $20,000.

The greatest classical actor of the century was about to jump on the Court bandwagon. But Osborne always claimed he didn't write *The Entertainer* with Olivier in mind. The title came from a recording he liked of Bunk Johnson playing Scott Joplin's "The Entertainer". Archie Rice was based on a third-rate comic he'd seen at the old Chelsea Palace dying the death with an impersonation of Charles Laughton playing Quasimodo. There's a kind of heroic, suicidal nobility in a bad comic who goes onstage to face certain derision. The desperate entertainer appearing on the variety bill at the Palace between the trick cyclist and the Irish tenor impressed Osborne with his misplaced, unstoppable valour, a poetic awfulness in defeat.

A great deal hung in the balance with Osborne's next play. Anyone can have overnight success. The hardest thing of all is to sustain it. Devine played a waiting game with his dramatists, never nagging a new play out of them. But early in February 1957, he surprised Osborne by asking how his new play was coming along.

Olivier had been on to him. On the verge of turning fifty, he was a man in search of a new life. His marriage to Vivien Leigh was cracking up, and with it their unbalanced, regal stage partnership. He would fall in love with his young future wife, Joan Plowright, when she took over the role of Archie Rice's daughter, Jean, for the West End run. Olivier in mid-life crisis was also an actor badly in need of fresh challenges. In almost twenty years, he had played only one contemporary role – the debonair Duke in Christopher Fry's 1950 romantic verse comedy *Venus Observed*.

Act Two of *The Entertainer* was almost finished. "I wonder if you've got a part in it for Laurence?" Devine asked Osborne tentatively.

"Laurence who?" he replied in all innocence.

Osborne's generation knew him only as "Larry". Against customary practice, the incomplete play was then sent to Olivier and according to Olivier's own account, "Archie leapt off the page at me and he had to be mine." But that wasn't quite true.

When he read the script, he told Devine he wanted to play Archie's old Edwardian dad, Billy Rice. He'd got it wrong again!

It was an understandable blunder. Billy, the gruff, retired vaudevillian with his hymns and jingoistic songs, is the most sympathetic character in the play. He's the authentic artist who stands for decent old values, Archie is the opportunistic, seedy failure (and worse: Archie knows it). Billy is the showbiz trouper, the good soldier who dies with honour making a futile comeback to save his son from bankruptcy. Archie Rice is given the hook into oblivion while his proud father's coffin is draped in the Union Jack. Olivier instinctively identified with the role that symbolized the lost glory of England.

"When I finished the play, he changed his mind," Osborne commented ruefully. "Just as well – for both of us." It was ultimately brave of Olivier to take on the role of Archie, as Osborne acknowledged. He was the first of the theatrical knights to risk joining the new generation at the Court. In effect, he was theatre royalty embracing the renegade opposition – an Osborne play whose decaying Music Hall setting is a brilliant metaphor for England's post-colonial decline. Archie Rice's number is up, like the once proud Music Halls demolished by the wrecker's ball.

In one of the most troubling scenes in the play, Archie says to his daughter –

"You see this face, you see this face, this face can split open with warmth and humanity. It can sing, and tell the worst, unfunniest stories in the world to a great mob of dead, drab erks and it doesn't matter, it doesn't matter. It doesn't matter because – look at my eyes. I'm dead behind these eyes. I'm dead, just like the whole inert, shoddy lot out there. It doesn't matter because I don't feel a thing, and neither do they. We're just as dead as each other."

When Olivier delivered that ghostly confession, his face took on the hue of a death mask. Archie Rice became one of his legendary roles. (Henry V, Richard III, Hamlet *and* Archie). Osborne marvelled at his uncanny understanding of the character's floundering inadequacy and self-loathing, particularly when Archie appears to be aggressively confident. But years before *The Entertainer*, Olivier had performed a failed comic he named "Larry Oliver" as a party-piece for friends.

"Ladies and germs – a very big hand if you please for the one and only Larry Oliver!" It was as if his very name had been a close call between giving birth to a great actor (Sir Laurence Olivier) or a cut-price vaude-villian (Larry Oliver). England's greatest classical actor saw the smirking, mincing Archie Rice with his dead eyes and deadly, defiant patter as a reflection of his own self-hatred. "It's me, isn't it?" he said within earshot of Osborne and Richardson.

Yet two days after *The Entertainer* opened, the Establishment figure still within Olivier demanded cuts to "all that anti-Queen shit" in the play. "The audience freezes," he told Richardson. "It's disloyal. You and John have had your notices, now we've got to do the fucking thing."

The play implicitly attacked the Tory government and the folly of the Suez invasion. (Archie's soldier-son is killed at Suez.) But an anti-royal line that had slipped by the censor about "the gloved hand waving at you from the golden coach" shocked the royalists the most. Richardson refused to make any cuts (including Olivier's demand to take out a jibe against Eton). But when the play transferred to the West End, Olivier imposed the cuts as part of his new contract. "They didn't make that much difference to the play," Richardson explained sardonically, "but Larry felt he'd bravely defended the Queen."

There was a staggering turn of events before *The Entertainer* was first staged, however. The Court's artistic council vetoed the entire production.

Lord Harewood, a member of the original council, was still incredulous when he told me how the decision to drop the play – and Olivier – came to be made. He voted enthusiastically for the production. But united against him were two purists from the Left and Right: the card-carrying Communist, Oscar Lewenstein and the Christian right verse poet, Ronald Duncan. Lewenstein didn't think much of *The Entertainer* and opposed Olivier turning a Court play into a star vehicle. Duncan disliked Osborne's work and fiercely opposed Devine.

"Well, that makes three in favour and two against," Harewood blithely announced at the meeting, railroading the new production through by including the votes of Devine and Richardson *in absentia*. But, as the opposition pointed out, Devine and Richardson didn't actually have a vote. (Which would soon be changed.)

According to the English Stage Company's constitution, there should have been no appeal. But the next day, Harewood urgently arranged a summit meeting with the dissenters over lunch at the Portman Square flat of the chairman of the Court, Neville Blond.

Chairman Blond would always side with Harewood and argued for the production. "We owe it to the boy," he reasoned (meaning Osborne, we assume). But it was the chairman's common sense wife, Elaine, the Marks & Spencer heiress, who saved the day by joining in the discussion.

"You must be barmy to turn down the play with Olivier wanting to act in it!" she told the dissenters. And so it came to pass that *The Entertainer* went ahead.

It was the first state of England play of its kind, and it led to the preoccupation of British theatre with Music Hall and the metaphor of comedy. Joan Littlewood's 1963 *Oh! What a Lovely War* staged the carnage of World War I in ironic counterpoint to the sentimental songs of the Edwardian halls. Trevor Griffiths used the clueless working-class comics trying to make it in life in his 1970 *Comedians* as a socialist critique of England and a metaphor for change. Peter Barnes's 1978 *Laughter* pushed the metaphor to its outer limits with tap-dancing entertainers in the gas chambers. ("Sing! Everybody sing!") Peter Nichols used Music Hall patter in two of his best plays: the suffering father dispensing comic therapy to his spastic daughter in *A Day in the Death of Joe Egg*, and the enlisted army entertainers on tour in South East Asia in his 1979 *Privates on Parade*.

Thirty years after the premiere of *The Entertainer*, Osborne reminisced about the original production and attacked the critics who claimed that the new "Epic Theatre" of Bertolt Brecht had obviously influenced him. "When the play came out they started on all that rubbish about Brecht," he told Melvyn Bragg. "I've never even *read* one of his plays."

He didn't need to. He acted in one. Six months before *The Entertainer*, in October 1956, he could be seen camping about the stage of the Court playing the role of the stoic Chinese peasant, Lin To, in Devine's wayward production of *The Good Woman of Szechuan*. A very British Peggy Ashcroft played the dual roles of Shen Te and Shui Ta. (Her performance was sho-sho.)

Osborne knew all about Brecht. In August 1956, he'd already seen the first London performance of the Berliner Ensemble with Helene Weigel in *Mother Courage*. The following month, he wrote to the *Sunday Times* comparing Brecht's spare, revolutionary aesthetic admiringly to "the horseless carriage in theatrical technique".

"The Brechtian bulldozer may not be *our* answer," he concluded. "We need to invent a machine of our own. What this may be we shall have to find out. But please don't expect to find it necessarily at work in my new play [*The Entertainer*]. The horse can look an endearing, reliable old thing when you are sweating blood in the workshop."

Osborne remained cautious about Brecht (though *Luther*, his later, episodic history play, was influenced by Brecht's *Galileo*). In December 1955, however – before *Look Back* was staged – Devine had responded to Brecht's suggestion that a British playwright work in collaboration with him in Berlin by recommending Osborne. ("This young chap has the right humour and social feeling and you could mould him as you wish.") Nothing came of it, and it isn't known whether Osborne even knew about it.

But why his stubborn Brecht bluff, feigning ignorance about the man who influenced twentieth-century theatre more than anyone?

Osborne disliked Brechtian intellectualizing. For him, high-flown ideas like "Alienation Theory" or *Verfremdungseffekt* amounted to much the same, less pretentious, thing as the leering Archie Rice announcing directly to the audience that he'd rather have a beer any day. *The Entertainer* didn't *need* Brecht. Osborne had simply used the theatre techniques he'd known since childhood when his father first took him to the music hall.

In Brecht's theatre, the half-curtain within the stage and the placards held up announcing the theme of each scene were said to have accounted for the inner curtain and placards Osborne used in *The Entertainer*. But those same devices had been an English Music Hall convention for more than a century. Archie Rice was a "front cloth" comic – Brecht's inner stage. The number or title of each Music Hall "turn" was displayed on an easel at both sides of the stage so the audience would know where they were in the crowded programme – Brecht's alienation theory.

When Osborne wrote in his preface to the play that "The music hall is dying, and with it, a significant part of England", it was because he mourned that a part of England's heart had gone – "something that belonged to everybody".

For Osborne and others, the golden age of Edwardian Music Hall reflected an entire working-class culture that was on speaking terms with Shakespeare, Kipling, Shaw and the language and beauty of the King James Bible.

He defensively treated sentimentality as a weakness and mocked its gooey centre as deceptively hard, like biting into a sugared almond. But no man can love Music Hall as he did without *being* sentimental. Sentiment was built into the form, his nostalgia for its heavenly sanctuary was the inevitable outcome of its loss.

In a wistful notebook entry, he mentions the loss of England's sense of continuity "when you sang to the only girl in the world to the same tune as your father, his past lighting the torch of your own light."

"If You Were the Only Girl in the World" was one of Osborne's favourite, lilting love songs. His parents sang it. Another was Marie Lloyd's "The Boy I Love (is up in the Gallery)" which Phoebe Rice, unhappy wife to Archie, sings with such sweet sentiment in the play.

The music halls were the last time an audience amounted to an authentic theatre community, for everyone knew the songs and the hallowed routines. The greatest performers became beloved English folk heroes. When Osborne wrote *The Entertainer*, there were only a handful of the old halls left in London. He took Olivier to research Archie at Collins Music Hall in Islington. (It's the site of a Waterstone's today.) Yet there used to be sixty of them between the wars.

The Victorian model was a thriving popular art form with its own rules and imperial pride, its rhyming Kiplingesque monologues and dramatic sketches that became, in effect, little one-act plays (up to thirty minutes in length; J.M. Barrie wrote one). "It is sometimes overlooked that the halls relied so much on undiluted drama," Osborne wrote significantly, "where laughter was interrupted perhaps for twenty minutes at a time by very simple appeals to emotions like jealousy, crude patriotism, lost love, poverty, death."

Music Hall's roots are found in the sing-songs of early nineteenth-century supper rooms that migrated into taverns and then into separate halls with their own stages (just as American vaudeville evolved from beer halls). Osborne's grandparents and parents passed on the routines and songs of the Edwardian halls while Osborne himself caught the tail-end of the great tradition when it became Variety – before wheezing ultimately to its tatty finale with a parade of yodelling accordionists, adagio dancers, underwater escapologists, farmyard impersonators, nude shows and Archie Rice.

"Why did music hall die out?" Alexei Sayle once asked bluntly. "Because it was crap!"

But its authentic Edwardian spirit was arguably more fun – and more *alive* – than anything theatre has known since. Osborne sometimes referred to the cruelty within English nature. Animated Music Hall audiences relished giving a performer the bird. "It was a hard, unyielding world," Osborne wrote about it, and it helped make him – informing his plays and shaping his taste from childhood.

On his first, nervy day at public school, for example, he made a blush-making clanger of style when he failed to arrive in the school uniform like everyone else, but naively chose a loud, checked suit in mad tribute to Max Miller. It got even worse when he decided to play his ukelele for his appalled classmates. The uke – or declassé lute – gets no respect, though it was popularized for a while by the King of Variety, George ("Turned out nice again!") Formby, the sunny plucker of such uke classics as "I'm Leaning on a Lamppost", "When I'm Cleaning Windows" and the ever-popular "Nagasaki" ("Back in Nagasaki where the men all chew tobacky and the women wicky-wacky-woo").

Osborne romanticized the halls as a last refuge of all individualists and renegades of near lunatic virtuosity. After all, who can equal the comedian Douglas Byng who descended onto the stage via a trapeze while singing, "I'm Doris, the Goddess of Wind"?

The titles of the popular songs that Osborne knew tell us a lot about the kind of English humour and sentiment that appealed to him: "Millie the Messy Old Mermaid", "Never Have a Bath with Your Wristwatch On", "Olga Pullofski the Beautiful Spy", "Nobody Loves a Fairy When She's Forty", "Two Lovely Black Eyes", "Britain's Sons Shall Rule the World",

"A Lassie Needs a Pairtner When the Nichts Grow Cauld."

It was the idol of the Victorian halls, Dan Leno, who took the halls to Shakespearean heights, however, with his Hamlet-like soliloquy, "What is Man?" "Ah, what is Man?" Leno asked his adoring audience. "Wherefore does he why? Whence did he whence? Whither is he whithering?"

Osborne compared the curtain up to an "overture to danger" and it defined the pull and intoxication of theatre for him down to the tacky valour of Archie Rice. Nothing was sacred under its roof. The halls radiated freedom for him.

According to dramatist Keith Waterhouse – who shared a common bond of affection for the Music Hall and Variety era – Osborne possessed an encyclopaedic knowledge of scores of their songs and routines. In later years, he used to impersonate the great – and not so great – during their occasional lunches together at L'Étoile in Soho. "He once had a waiter in such stitches he couldn't serve the soup," Waterhouse remembered.

He revelled in the carefree nonconformism of the halls that took aim – as he would – at all groups and types: do-gooders, meddling social workers, all foreigners, the law, politicians, pretentious toffs, the Irish, cross-dressing fruitcakes, dominating wives. The Music Hall comedian – compared by T.S. Eliot, no less, to an enviably popular poet – was traditionally cynical about marriage (a life sentence), meakly perplexed ("The day war broke out, my missus looked at me and said, What *good* are you?"), sexually suggestive ("It's the way I tell 'em, lady!"), gloriously lewd ("I'll tell you one thing," the weak-willed Mrs Shufflewick always announced. "If I'm not in bed by half past eleven, I shall be going home").

Philip Larkin once emphasized how he chose his *Collected Poems* with great care: "I treat them like a music hall bill: you know, contrast, difference in length, the comic, the Irish tenor, the dancing girls." Larkin, the misanthropic poet, was half joking, whereas Osborne, the nostalgic playwright, took the contrasting richness of Music Hall seriously. He could say without irony about Hylda Baker (the north country comedienne who invented a national catchphrase, "She knows you know!"): "I saw her do a straight dramatic sketch between a tenor and a dog act and it was very good. It always obsessed me – how you could draw on that variety of response."

The obsession led specifically to *The Entertainer* and the later anarchic "entertainments" – the whirlwind 1972 *A Sense of Detachment* or the rude 1975 *The End of Me Old Cigar* (the title was taken from a suggestive Music Hall favourite of Harry Champion's). The diminutive Hylda Baker, incidentally, was the living embodiment of Mrs Malaprop. "Ooh," she'd say, folding her arms in typically know-all fashion, "you don't know what I'm talking about, do you? You have no contraception!"

The vivaciousness of language – the *English* language – was a source of pride in the halls. "During the course of my performance tonight," Osborne happily remembered Sid Field telling the audience in his tailcoat and bicycle clips, "I may inadvertently –" Field would then freeze momentarily with the ecstacy of someone who had just tasted forbidden fruit. "I say, do you mind if I say that again? *Inadvertently* . . ."

"He would inhale the sound once more like a fragrant, linguistic ectoplasm," Osborne somewhat over-ripely described Sid Field's eureka! moment. Then he nailed the moment exactly: "He had found himself within a *word*, one of ineffable implication."

Another Osborne hero, the wrecked comic genius, Max Wall, borrowed the worst line in comedy – "Take my wife – *puhleeze!*" – for *The Entertainer*, when Osborne directed him as Archie at Greenwich Theatre in the Seventies. "The Great Wall of China", as Max referred to himself, was a relic of the halls and he relished words like a fetishist holding them up to the light. "The voice is wanly resonant (he uses no mike)," Tynan wrote about him, "speaking volumes of disenchantment except when lighting on an exotic word, italicising it, isolating it for spellbound perfection: 'We can't leave that in abeyance.' (Pause) '*Abeyance.*' (Pause) 'I don't even know what *country* it's in.'"

Pleasure in the silly is the safety valve of the buttoned-up British, and sheer silliness is another Music Hall trademark that appealed to Osborne. It encouraged his appetite for schoolboy jokes, naughty limericks and saucy seaside postcards with fat ladies bent over a bucket and spade showing their knickers.

"*Wait for it!*" the knowing Music Hall comic warned us with the authority of an Osborne monologuist demanding to be heard. "Listen! No, *listen.*" "You'll like this." "Stay with me!" "Here's a good one." "Desist!" "You'll make me a laughing stock!" "Think about it . . ."

Osborne and his godson, Ben Walden, who became a fine actor, talked a lot about theatre together during Walden's regular visits to The Hurst, Osborne's last home. "Everything you need to know about *performance* is in this film," Osborne advised him one day. Thinking it might be, say, Olivier in *Hamlet*, young Walden was surprised as they settled down to watch the vintage 1942 backstage story, *Yankee Doodle Dandy*, starring James Cagney.

Give my regards to Broadway
Remember me to Herald Square
Tell all the gang at 42nd Street
That I'll soon be there . . .

When Osborne first saw the film as a schoolboy, its showbiz sentiment made him burst into tears. Cagney's George M. Cohan speaks for boundless American optimism and possibility, his electric performance springs from the irresistible strut, the verve and swagger, of the true vaudevillian. Cagney, the mythical movie gangster, began his career as a song-and-dance man when he joined a vaudeville act in the 1920s named Parker, Rand and Leach (which became Parker, Rand and Cagney). Leach was a working-class Bristol boy, Archie Leach, who in magical transformation became Cary Grant.

Sooner or later all roads lead back to Music Hall, particularly with Osborne. It goes to the heart of the matter. One of his last visits to the theatre was a pilgrimage he took in 1992 to see a favourite comic, the Liverpudlian Ken Dodd – his sublime "Doddy", last link to the halls, bizarre court jester with a tickling stick – "The size of it!" – inventor of mad mellifluous words ("plumdumptious", "tattifilarious"), prince of corn ("He kissed her neck, a lump came in his throat – it was her earring"), manic Pied Piper ("Come on, missus – let's take all our clothes off and parade past the Town Hall. We'll show 'em!"), high-speed apologist ("If my mother knew I was doing this, she'd be ashamed. She thinks I'm in prison"), and dizzying surrealist ("What a beautiful day for wearing a kilt and standing upside down in the middle of the road saying, How's that for a lampshade?").

A serious student of theatre, Ken Dodd aptly defined Malvolio as the kind of man who stands up in a strip club to ask what time the juggler comes on. He understood the nature of the comedian's war with the audience where no theories can help him survive. "The trouble with Freud is that he didn't play the Glasgow Empire second house, Saturday night," he told me when I interviewed him for an *Observer* profile during the 1960s. He was appearing at the London Palladium then, and by chance, his first words when we met in his dressing room were, "Oh, yes, we've had all the intellectuals in. We've had me dad, we've had the Prime Minister [Harold Wilson], we've had you, we've had me dog, we've had John Osborne . . ."

Osborne saw Ken Dodd's Palladium show three times. One occasion was a Royal Court outing he arranged – a busman's holiday that was his treat (and covert lesson to the Court actors in the group on the secret art of performance). He wasn't disappointed when he crossed the border from

Shropshire to Llandudno all those years later to see the great comic again.
In correspondence with former *Telegraph* drama critic, Eric Shorter, in July
1993, he described how his act "casts this amazing spell" that had him
laughing so much it left him gasping with that same awe he had felt as a
child when he first went to the theatre with his father. What impressed
him most was that it went on for four unstoppable hours.

Doddy took no prisoners that night (or any night). "It did indeed go on
for FOUR HOURS," Osborne emphasized, scarcely able to believe it
himself. "After three, they were carrying the old folks back to their homes.
It was an extraordinary experience. He was actually saying, 'D'YOU GIVE
IN?' And went on . . ."

The difference between Osborne's Music Hall heroes and Archie Rice is
that sweaty, squirm-inducing Archie just isn't funny. He hasn't the talent.
He craves laughter and dies every night in fear of the hook.

"Ever seen an Osborne hero with a dry brow?" David Hare asked,
describing Osborne as "our poet laureate of flopsweat, of lost opportunity,
of missed connections and of hidden dread, of what he himself calls 'the
comfortless tragedy of isolated hearts'."

Hare believes the plays are "what you feel when you wake prickling in
the dark: half-truth experienced as whole truth, intuition experienced as
fact. His characters, quivering, vibrating with life, have no clue how to put
the nightmare away, how to chuck it, forget it, put a sock in it, repress it
or even, for God's sake, how to talk the bloody thing to death. These are
people to whom the fear always returns."

"I am governed by fear every day of my life . . ." Osborne had confessed
in his notebook.

If we had a photograph of the Rice family, it would be of the lower
middle-class Groves – the rowdy, bickering side to Osborne's own family
with their white noise and nagging legacy of eternal disappointment. They
were people who always talked, but never listened. Intimations of Osborne's
warring parents are in *The Entertainer*, too – abused, gin-soaked Phoebe and
her estranged, unfaithful Archie, the artistic failure with his loud dalliances
in pubs. "You wouldn't think I was sexy to look at me, would you?" goes
Archie's non-stop patter. "No, honestly, you wouldn't think I was sexy to
look at me, would you?"

"You're so rich!" Phoebe belittles him. "You're such a big success."

Archie humiliates Phoebe without mercy (as Osborne punished his
mother): "Look at her. What has she got to do with people like you? People
of intellect and sophistication. She's very drunk, and just now her muzzy,

under-developed, untrained mind is racing because her bloodstream is full of alcohol I can't afford to give her, and she's going to force us to listen to all sorts of dreary embarrassing things we've all heard a hundred times before. She's getting old . . ."

Booze plays a strong supporting role in several Osborne dramas – loosening tongues. *The Entertainer* is soaked in gin and draught Bass. (Archie refuses to emigrate to Canada – last chance of salvation in the New World – because the Bass is no good there, because it isn't England.) The more this family of misfits and failures talk and goad and squabble and drink, the more it runs from the truth about itself. "Hold your noise!" Billy Rice shouts.

Clichés are their common currency and camouflage. "You *like* a nice play," Phoebe natters on about her occasional visits to the theatre. "But I can't sit for long" – "clichés dropping like bats off the ceiling", is how Archie describes them. Home and stage are interchangeable for him. They're both horror shows. Osborne explained in the script that whatever Archie says to anyone is almost always carefully "thrown away". It's a comedian's defensive technique that "absolves him seeming committed to anyone or anything." "Still, he could always talk, your Dad," Billy tells Jean grudgingly. "And that's about all."

Archie never stops working the room. He's the grinning life and soul of an exhausted party, the man in the flash suit who can't stop winking at you. But the moment he stumbles onstage – *loses* them – he's finished. Silence from the void beyond the spotlight sentences people like him to death without appeal. Audiences are to be "slayed" as if in mortal combat. ("D'YOU GIVE IN?")

And so he talks, and he can't stop talking, as the hook and the income tax man hover in the shadows. "Did I ever tell you the greatest compliment I had paid to me – the greatest compliment I always treasure?" he asks his daughter one night. It's late and he's half-slewed. He's learned that Mick, his soldier-son, has been taken prisoner at Suez. He's keeping up the act.

"I was walking along the front somewhere – I think it was here actually – one day, oh, it must be twenty-five years ago, I was quite a young man. Well, there I was walking along the front, to meet what I think we used to call a piece of crackling. Or perhaps it was a bit of fluff. No that was earlier. Anyway, I know I enjoyed it afterwards. But the point is I was walking along the front, all on my own, minding my own business . . . and two nuns came towards me . . . two nuns –"

He suddenly falters in mid-sentence. In a devastating moment, Archie trails off. Osborne's stage direction describes him "looking very tired and old" as he looks across at Jean and pushes the bottle at her.

"Talk to me," he says.

Words were Osborne's lifeline as much as the feverish thoughts he scribbled in his notebooks on sleepless nights were evidence to himself that he was still alive. The conviviality of talk and booze was second nature to him. Peter Bowles – who played Archie in the West End in 1986 – described how he committed a serious faux pas when he and his wife were Osborne's weekend guests at The Hurst. When they went off to bed after a late dinner on the first evening, Bowles learned it was a breach of etiquette. They were expected to stay up half the night talking about life.

Osborne was twenty-seven when he wrote *The Entertainer*, and as a writer he was never "quiet". He didn't write neat, understated plays polished to a shine. The messy lives of his chatty, disenchanted heroes are inherently unshapely like the relentless dramas of O'Neill. Plot was never his strong suit. The narrative of *The Entertainer* is overcrowded, important events take place offstage. For the playwright who taught himself the English language by studying fat dictionaries, the sinew and vitality of words, unadorned, uncompromised and direct, are paramount.

"No English-born playwright had put language on the line like this – not decoratively, but to reveal the beat of the human heart – since Lawrence," the playwright and former Royal Court director, Nicholas Wright argues. Though he's discussing Bill Maitland's injured cry for connection and meaning in *Inadmissible Evidence*, he could be referring to any major Osborne play. "It was a revolutionary step, very easily taken for granted now, to assume that language – if only it was sufficiently alive and complex – could *in itself* embody theme. That the story, in synopsis, could be as thin as you like: spoken, it would become profound."

In a surprising scene, Archie Rice describes the power even beyond words – beyond everything, it seems – that only certain music can express. It was the pure, utterly natural sound of a blues singer he heard in some bar once on his travels and he never forgot her singing her heart out to the whole world. Archie, the second-rate English comic, identifies with the holler and pain of the black blues singer. "There's nobody who can feel like that," he says enviously. ("I want to hear a warm, thrilling voice cry, 'Hallelujah, I'm alive!'" said Jimmy Porter.) It was the unforgettable sound of someone like Bessie Smith that Archie heard, and it awoke in him the possibility of strength and solace in an unyielding world.

"I wish to God I were that old bag," he confesses. "I'd stand up and shake my great bosom up and down, and lift my head and make the most beautiful fuss in the world. Dear God, I would. But I'll never do it. I don't give a damn about anything, not even women or draught Bass."

But Archie does give a damn. Al Alvarez wrote of Beckett that in *Godot* and *Endgame* his naked, unaccommodated Man was reduced to the role of an impotent comic "who talks and talks and talks in order to postpone for a while the silence of his own desolation". So Archie blunts his real feelings and apparent indifference is his self-protection. His tinny signature tune, "Why Should I Care?", is an obvious showbiz irony. ("If they see that you're blue/ They'll look down on you/ So why oh why should I care?") The problem with Archie Rice isn't that he cares too little, but too much. When he learns that his son has been killed at Suez, words can't help him, words are no use. He crumples, howling from the depths of his soul and sings the blues.

Archie's last stage appearance and farewell – "Before I do go, ladies and gentlemen, I should just like to tell you a little story, a little story" – is a riddle about a *word*.

The story is about "just a little, ordinary man, like you and me" who awakens one day in paradise. A saint on the welcoming committee tells him that he's now found eternal happiness and asks him what he thinks. "Well," the man says, "I've often wondered what I'd say if this ever happened to me. I couldn't think somehow." And the saint smiles at him benevolently and says, "And what *do* you say, my son?"

"Only one thing I can say," says the little man. And he said it! The astonished saint couldn't speak for a while and everyone in Paradise was stunned. And then the saint threw his arms joyfully round the little man and kissed him, and all the Hosts rejoiced. "I love you, my son," says the saint. "With all my soul, I shall love you always. I've been waiting to hear that word ever since I came here."

Archie's story ends there and he takes his final farewell with a Music Hall joke. ("Let me know where you're working tomorrow night – and I'll come and see YOU.") But what's *the word*? What's the one word that stuns the Hosts in paradise and then has them rejoicing as if someone has told them the truth at last?

Only one commentator has got it right, so far as I know. "The answer is very simple," concluded Mary McCarthy, Osborne's first American champion. "The word is hell."

The demi-paradise of England is really hell and even the Hosts know it. For Osborne's disenchanted post-war generation, the promised Eden never came.

24

Good, Brave Causes

THIS BUS DOES NOT SING
Banner on Royal Court bus travelling with Osborne, Moscow, 1957

The promised, lost Eden was the dismal failure of the Labour Party's post-war government to transform England – Orwell's "deep, deep, deep sleep of England" – and lead the country into a social and cultural renaissance. The "hosts" were the socialist leaders who betrayed the promise with a pat on the broken backs of the little man and an offer of free false teeth on the National Health.

"This is a welfare state, my darling heart," Archie Rice declares bitterly. "Nobody wants, and nobody goes without, all are provided for . . ."

Few modern playwrights – if any – have pulled off the feat of offending both Left and Right simultaneously as Osborne did. It's widely believed that with his overnight success Osborne betrayed the Left, quickly turning to the Right like his contemporary, Kingsley Amis. But is it that simple?

In his youth, Osborne was raised on a weekly fix of the left-wing *Tribune* and *New Statesman*, and contempt for the Conservative Party was in his blood. From 1951 to 1964, there were three consecutive Conservative governments and Osborne could write at the close of the decade that the false dawn of the Left, like hope deferred, made hearts sick.

By then, he was disenchanted with party politics, yet he was still voting Labour in 1974 when he was forty-five (though "with an even emptier heart than usual"). It comes as a jolt to the Osborne myth of Angry Young Man turned brawling Tory blimp that he identified with the Left into middle age. Which party he voted for subsequently – assuming he did – isn't known. (It was about the only thing he kept private from his wife, Helen.) He was said to have turned Thatcherite. But political labels look uncomfortable on a noncomformist.

Osborne, the "little Englander" of later years, apparently became anti-

European like Mrs Thatcher. But he was always a "little Englander". (So was Jimmy Porter.) He was already opposed to Britain joining the Common Market as early as 1967 when the Labour government of Harold Wilson tried to join the European Economic Community. "We cannot pool our sovereignty any more than we can pool our individuality," he protested. "A political idea must grow out of man's need, and that need is not simply economic . . . A nation has to do more than keep counting its change. It has to count the cost of living without meaning."

Mrs Thatcher also loathed the subsidized National Theatre and its artistic director, Peter Hall, while Osborne lampooned the grey monolith as "Colditz on Thames" and nicknamed Hall "Fu Manchu". But he opposed Hall over a play (the foreshortened run of his *Watch It Come Down* at the National with Jill Bennett) whereas the Prime Minister opposed him over a political principle (subsidy of the arts; anti-Thatcher speeches).

Then again, the older Osborne was said to have become a clubland reactionary when he visited town from his Shropshire "estate" like any Edwardian gentleman for his monthly lunch at the Garrick Club (motto: "All the world's a stage"). If so, we must keep in mind that one of the first moves he made with all the success and notoriety of *Look Back* was to join the Savile Club (nineteeth-century haven of Rudyard Kipling, A.A. Milne, Henry James and early TV personality, Gilbert Harding). In younger, AYM days, Osborne was someone who wanted to belong to any club that didn't want him as a member.

By temperament, he wasn't a political animal. His own definition of socialism was idealistic and woolly. "Socialism is the only political system that believes in human beings," he wrote in the late Fifties. "I am not going to define my own socialism. Socialism is an experimental idea, not a dogma; an attitude to truth and liberty, the way people should live and treat each other . . ."

Raised in childhood poverty, he breezily admitted that he got the hell out of "the misery, loneliness and squalor of his life among the working class", as his friend, the satirist John Wells, described it, "straight into the misery, loneliness and squalor of the showbiz aristocracy".

It was really the cultural values of the fawning lower middle class of his mother's family he fled. The social milieu of his plays changed as he changed, but their alienated message remains constant – from Jimmy Porter's dispossessed fury and the fate of Archie Rice, to Luther's tormented defiance of a corrupt Pope and Bill Maitland's open, festering wound, to the tragedy of an ultimate outsider, Alfred Redl, the blackmailed homosexual spy and patriot for himself in the decadent pageant of the Hapsburg Empire.

Early socialist or no, Osborne never identified with the working class except in general terms of the class wars. He could reveal an elitist's contempt for the philistine masses. During the 1970s – when he was still voting Labour – he peered out of his chauffeur-driven Bentley at the crowds along the King's Road and announced to his stunned passenger, "Look at that human garbage!"

Instinct was his wonky compass, particularly in his wayward love life. He reacted to his political times emotionally. His model of social criticism wasn't a statesman or thinker, but Swift's satirical proposal of 1729 to cure the burden of impoverished children by eating them.

"I have been assured by a very knowing American of my acquaintance," Swift wrote in A Modest Proposal, "that a young healthy child well nursed is, at a year old, a most delicious, nourishing and wholesome food, whether stewed, roasted, baked, or boiled, and I make no doubt that it will equally serve in a fricasie, or a ragoust."

In addition to which, children are plentiful throughout the year, particularly in March, and eating them would boost the economy. "It could be the modest opening of some Party manifesto or the dull terms of reference set down in a Government White Paper," Osborne commented on Swift's hairspring daring and genius. "The cant of politics has never been given a more deadly or enduring blow between its beady eyes."

Osborne himself would have made a polemical journalist (and sometimes functioned as one). He felt far more seriously about the fate of English *culture* than has been acknowledged. But his plays aren't overtly political. They offer no "answers". The plays are written from the soul, not from any political point of view. They point to the wound, not the cure.

Only a few months after the premiere of Look Back, Osborne paid tribute in the Observer to the humanity of Tennessee Williams's plays. "Every serious British dramatist is indebted to them," he wrote, identifying with Williams – a depressive, like him, who was haunted by his own "blue devils". In a ringing declaration of faith in the poetic power of drama, Osborne declared that his enduring plays of private fires and public tragedy are "worth a thousand statements of a thousand politicians".

Besides, he would always empathize with the Southern dramatist of lost souls who, when asked to give his definition of happiness, rolled his eyes and replied, "Insensitivity, I guess."

My view is that Osborne was never committed to any political agenda in the first place – Left or Right. With Look Back in Anger, he was labelled a radical socialist and taken up by the Left. But from the outset, he denied any political purpose – rejecting the role thrust on him. "I am not a politician," he announced as early as 1957. "I must make myself clear about this question of identity. I am a playwright, and the only valid statement I can ever make is in the theatre."

He confirmed his stance in the "Declaration" essay: "A writer can express feeling. It takes an extraordinary human being to demonstrate action as well. Most weeks, my own courage allowance doesn't last beyond Monday lunchtime . . ."

When I pointed this out to Michael Foot, former leader of the Labour Party, it made no difference. Foot (who knew Osborne a little and admired the plays) said that he had been galvanized along with the Bevanites on the left of the party by *Look Back*'s message whether Osborne thought in political terms or not. "He came along and expressed all we thought more eloquently than we were doing," he told me.

Poet and critic Al Alvarez – a contemporary of Osborne's – enthusiastically recalled *Look Back*'s first impact for me: "Everyone knows about the young who came of age in the Sixties. But Osborne gave The Silent Generation who came of age in the 1950s its voice – and it was truly liberating. Just terrific! You felt with *Look Back in Anger* that here is someone who knows how the rest of us think and talk."

But the play's critique of England made Osborne a political spokesman for his generation by accident. Harold Hobson of the *Sunday Times* was the first to point it out but, overshadowed by the radical chic of Tynan, no one heard him. Hobson's point was that the Left's identification with the play led to a misunderstanding of Osborne that took his future work hostage. He always maintained there were two different plays within *Look Back*: the play about social anger and protest that Tynan acclaimed, and another, more eternal play about grief and love.

Half a century later, when the class wars are no longer as bloody, *Look Back* thrives more as a drama about the marital wars and the ferment of love. In that sense, Hobson, the tortoise, won the race in the end against Tynan, the hare.

"Yet Osborne's advocates did not see the play so," Hobson wrote in 1984 about the initial response. "They took it to be merely a belligerent document of discontent. They thought so then, and they went on thinking so, and when they later found in Osborne's subsequent plays love and regret and admiration instead of only hatred they thought that he had turned reactionary. They led a protest movement, and they have gone on protesting."

*

JOHN OSBORNE

Nothing tells us more about Osborne's early socialism than his visit to Moscow in 1957. Anyone who can compare Tolstoy's mythic "mother Moscow" to the glum sight of Streatham High Road must be missing something. Osborne in Moscow was missing his English grub for one thing. Complaining like a petulant petit bourgeois about the bad food in the massive barracks of the Soviet hotel named the Stalinskaya, the muddled room service, the endless delays, no running hot water, the washbasins without *plugs*, he couldn't wait to get home.

He was visiting Moscow as part of the British delegation to the Sixth World Festival of Youth during which a production of Look Back was to be staged at the Moscow Art Theatre. The Court contingent included Tony Richardson, Lindsay Anderson (who hoped to film the trip), designer "Percy" Harris of Motley, playwright and producer Wolf Mankowitz and the new ex-Communist, Oscar Lewenstein. Many others had found 1950s Moscow grim beside Osborne, and taken consolation in Leningrad. But he dismissed the imperial city as "a provincial nightmare" and returned home early after only a few days, even skipping the Moscow production of Look Back in the fabled theatre of Chekhov.

He put the blame for his sullen response to everything on his "decadent, Western, superficial perversity". He didn't trouble to contact any underground dissidents or fellow writers during the trip. The sight of the other festival delegates only depressed him as they arrived en masse "overloaded with flowers and fatigue". He recoiled from fellow Brits calling out from their tour buses to the proletariat, "Peace! Friendship!" He seems to have enjoyed Gorky Park and swimming across the River Moskva. But what fascinated him the most was a performance of The Sleeping Beauty at the Bolshoi on his last night.

The ballet itself was of no particular interest. He was riveted by two female claquers on either side of the auditorium who kept milking ovations from the audience. As soon as the applause had almost died during the three intermissions and again at the end, the claquing apparatchiks applauded furiously like clap-happy nannies and got it all going again.

Although he wasn't part of the Court delegation, Keith Waterhouse was in Moscow during the festival and recalled the daily scene for me: "Flag-draped coaches were going to and fro bearing youthful, flaxen-haired delegates singing folk songs lustily. The Royal Court coach came into view. It was draped with a long banner, THIS BUS DOES NOT SING. It made one proud to be British."

Waterhouse went on, "It's my belief that THIS BUS DOES NOT SING sums up John Osborne's political philosophy. Apart from the youthful

232

socialist spasm we all go through, he seemed to be neither Left nor Right, but 'anti'. He only concerned himself with mainstream politics when the issue was intensely dramatic, like Suez. If in later life he gave the impression of being 'blimpish', certainly he worked on this, but to my mind he only began to seem right-wing when the Establishment moved to the Left with all its political correctness, feminism, anti-smoking, and on."

The onus on Osborne to *be* a political playwright is surprising, despite the legacy of *Look Back in Anger*. Most plays aren't political. Which party does *Waiting for Godot* vote for? The committed socialism of Pinter is well known, but it doesn't make *The Homecoming* a political play. The activist socialist Tony Kushner pleads for social revolution in *Angels in America*, but his epic masterpiece of the Reagan era ends by the fountain of the healing angel Bethesda in Central Park with a transcendent prayer for miracles and love. The Rightish Stoppard makes no claims to being a political playwright (though he writes plays about politics). Arthur Miller's *Death of a Salesman* amounts to an indictment of capitalism and the American Dream, but it offers no political solution. Where's the political message in, say, Patrick Marber's *Closer* or Albee's *Who's Afraid of Virginia Woolf?*

Propaganda plays date quickly unless the play transcends the propaganda. Shaw's *Man and Superman* gives the Devil his due as much as Don Juan – making the great play, as Eric Bentley said, "not propaganda, but drama". Brecht's preachy polemics are out of fashion, but the secular, universal message of his finest dramas like *Mother Courage* remains. We could make a case for Chekhov the romantic idealist *and* clear-eyed capitalist. His enduring plays of human frailty and yearning are characterized by their impartiality. Michael Frayn, taking Chekhov as his model, quotes with approval the German playwright Friedrich Hebbel's saying that in a good play everyone is right. Everyone, in other fair-minded words, has a part to play that's worth a hearing. For Frayn, it's a dramatic ideal in search of restrained objectivity. For myself, it's an abdication of the playwright's voice and heart. The personal fires of dramatists like Osborne would be neutered by Frayn's dry social tact.

Osborne's early work challenged the status quo and can therefore be seen as "political". But he wasn't in the conversion game. He was for the unyielding cause of the individual besieged by a conformist world. The politically engaged generation that followed him – Hare, Brenton, Caryl Churchill, David Edgar, Trevor Griffiths – were for the cause of the collective and saw theatre as a catalyst for social justice. But were they politically effective? Their fine conscience plays coincided with the triumph of Thatcherite capitalism.

No *Lysistrata* or *Guernica* ever stopped a war. No play has changed the world. But a play can change the way we *perceive* the world. The question is, how?

One of Osborne's most perceptive commentators, drama critic John Peter, believes that he revealed himself to be "a difficult, attractive, entertaining, observant and cantankerous man; a man who belittled his successes and nursed his grievances; a lover and a tyrant; a sentimental warrior; and one who knew that time lost was to remain time lost, never to be found again". But his political commitment was beside the point.

"Osborne has always been that deeply English thing, the unregimented moral malcontent. People like that are beyond politics. Osborne is not, and never has been, in the business of social amelioration. He carries no embarrassing moral luggage such as public commitments. He has always been essentially a dramatist of private wars, or what Arthur Miller calls the politics of the soul. The outside world of allegiances matters in his plays only in so far as it cripples or corrupts the sense of private justice."

Osborne's questionable nostalgia for the comforting Edwardian twilight of Empire has been taken too literally. He knew it was fake. "Always the same picture," says Jimmy Porter, "high summer, the long days in the sun, slim volumes of verse, crisp linen, the smell of starch. What a romantic picture. Phoney, too, of course. It must have rained sometimes. Still, even I regret it somehow, phoney or not."

The sentimental Edwardian allure is a link to the imagined era of Osborne's father, born at the close of the century. The nostalgia isn't really about the style of the colonial past, but the saving grace of something within the washed-up past that's still of value.

Alison's perplexed, kindly father, Colonel Redfern – "the old plant left over from the Edwardian Wilderness" – is a symbol of decency stranded by history, returning to an unrecognizable England. Billy Rice looks back to a time when the rules were at least known and England's place in the world appeared certain. In *Time Present* (written for Jill Bennett in 1968), the adored offstage father, Gideon Orme, is a dying classical actor of the old school, the only "real thing" in a Disneyfied, showbiz world. In the 1971 *West of Suez*, set on an imaginary subtropical island and former colony, a well-known, elderly writer, Wyatt Gillman (originally played by Ralph Richardson), is a burnt-out Evelyn Waugh floundering in the mediocrity of a violent, contemporary junk culture. In the 1975 *Watch It Come Down*, the dignified, dying biographer representing the older generation is based on Lytton Strachey.

There's a line Osborne throws nonchalently away in *West of Suez*: ". . . as someone said, if you've no world of your own, it's rather pleasant to regret the passing of someone else's."

It's an example of art imitating art. The someone who said it first was Jimmy Porter.

"Still, even I regret it somehow, phoney or not," Jimmy says in *Look Back in Anger* during his unexpected diversion about the old Edwardian brigade and their "tempting, brief little world". "If you've no world of your own, it's rather pleasant to regret the passing of someone else's. I must be getting sentimental . . ."

He sounds defensive. In *Look Back*, and again in *West of Suez* fifteen years later, Osborne is telling us with conscious flippancy that he can't connect to the world. In the kingdom of the lost, a remote fantasy land holds out a promise of salvation, and the demi-paradise of the English imagination is where the lost Eden is found. Osborne's Edwardian idyll is a fantasy.

Richard Eyre, successor to Peter Hall as artistic director of the National Theatre, is among the Osborne critics who look for political commitment in his plays and, failing to find any, dismiss them. (During his reign at the National, he nevertheless produced a revival of *Inadmissible Evidence* as well as Osborne's adaptation of Strindberg's *The Father*.) Eyre mocked early Osborne as superficially Cowardesque in his memoir *Utopia & Other Places*, and bristled at *Look Back*'s notorious statement from Jimmy Porter: "I suppose people of our generation aren't able to die for good causes any longer. We had that all done for us, in the thirties and the forties, when we were still kids. There aren't any good, brave causes left."

"Is there a more solipsistic cry from the post-war years," Eyre protested indignantly, "when the world has become better informed than ever about mass starvation, tyranny, injustice, plague and poverty, than that of Jimmy Porter: 'There aren't any good, brave causes left'?"

He's reflecting a commonly held belief about Osborne's apparent, laconic indifference to the state of the world. As early as 1957, Osborne was defending himself against the charge:

> A great deal of gibberish has been promoted by the words I put into the mouth of Jimmy Porter. These were: "There aren't any good, brave causes left". Immediately they heard this, all the shallow heads with their savage

thirst for trimmed-off explanations got to work on it. They believed him, just as some believed Archie Rice when he said "I don't feel a thing" or "I may be an old pouf, but I'm not right-wing." They were incapable of recognising the texture of ordinary despair.

Osborne knew all about causes. (He campaigned publicly for them, in his own shambling fashion.) But to demand that his alter ego Jimmy Porter swap his despair for a handy checklist of what's wrong with the world is like thinking you can solve the inability of Chekhov's three sisters to get to Moscow by buying them a railway ticket. Ordinary despair, like soul sickness, is born in the disenchantment of unrealized dreams.

Jimmy's malaise was, in fact, exactly in tune with the disillusioned 1950s movement that represented a mass defection from party politics. Known as the New Left, it was a formative influence on Osborne. If we put Jimmy Porter in context, he's a drop-out New Leftist whose father's generation fought against Fascism in Spain and joined the Thirties Hunger Marches. Jimmy's enemy – like Osborne's – wasn't just the Establishment and the Conservative Party, but the ineffectual Labour Party itself.

Several turning points explain the rise of the New Left – the Soviet Union's invasion of Hungary in October 1956 led to the defection of many British Communists from the Party – including the historian E.P. Thompson who began, with others, the extra-party opposition of New Left ideas. The decline of Communism in Britain – "the god that failed" – coincided with the failure of the Labour Party at the polls and the bankruptcy of Old Left orthodoxies. The birth of the expedient modern politician, Left or Right, now blurred the centrist parties into one. The growing cynicism about practical politics, particularly among the young, was symbolized by contempt for quiescent socialist leaders like Clement Attlee – "You Can Trust Mr Attlee" – when he accepted an earldom, or the younger, Oxford-educated Hugh Gaitskell, the prototype Tony Blair in pinstripe trousers struggling to hold the mealy middleground.

The New Left, vague in its humane version of socialism as the younger Osborne was in his, coincided with the New Wave in theatre and thrived primarily as a cultural movement. The two most influential books of the period were cultural landmarks written by New Left literary critics Richard Hoggart (*The Uses of Literacy*, 1957) and Raymond Williams (*Culture and Society*, 1958). Both books were "anti-politics" and both were influenced by Orwell (who, in turn, had influenced Osborne since school). Jimmy Porter's tirades at the stagnation of England's mass culture and the expanding dominance of junk American taste – "It's pretty dreary living in the

American Age, unless you're American of course. Perhaps all our children will be Americans. That's a thought, isn't it?" – owe a debt to Orwell's *Inside the Whale* and *England Your England*.

The Court and the New Left were aligned. *1956 and All That* establishes that Lindsay Anderson, William Gaskill and Wesker spoke at public meetings alongside Hoggart, Williams and Stuart Hall (the editor of the *New Left Review*). Williams and Hoggart – particularly Hoggart – were also influenced by the persuasive cultural ideas of F.R. Leavis, the elitist ogre of Downing College, Cambridge, who vigorously opposed American values and European union. (So did Osborne.) Leavis's Utopian romance of the English country idyll and his open admiration of Lawrence's intuitive "gladness of life" were also shared by Osborne, as well as his sentimental nostalgia for a lost time, a preferred illusion of England's mythic past. By coincidence, one of Osborne's friends in the early Court days, playwright Wolf Mankowitz, was taught by Leavis at Downing.

"Both your houses are infested with expediency, which is why a plague on them," Osborne declared in the *Daily Herald* in 1962, explaining as the election approached why he couldn't bring himself to vote Labour with its numbing "puny bribes and come-ons", or Conservative with its "razor-sharp practice and thug success". (The Liberal Party didn't merit a mention.)

"Friends who were never friends call me blimp," Osborne complained in a 1967 *Encounter* essay (when he was thirty-seven). "To hell with them. It is harder than they will ever know."

He meant life, getting through life was harder than they'll know; labels like "blimp" come easy. That said, there were undeniable times when the middle-aged Osborne's muscle slackened and principle turned into blowhard bias. He admitted he played the fool too often, seeming like "Disgusted, Tunbridge Wells", the mythical colonel who wrote outraged letters to the *DailyTelegraph* from genteel Kent. (To make it worse, Osborne lived in genteel Kent for some time.) But as the *Telegraph*'s conservative columnist Peregrine Worsthorne pointed out: "There were always signs that John Osborne was more a member of the non-party awkward squad than any party whose line had to be followed."

In 1964, for example, Osborne wrote Bill Maitland's opening speech in *Inadmissible Evidence* as an absurdist parody of the Prime Minister's address to the Labour Party Conference. It wasn't widely noticed at the time that Osborne had reproduced many of Harold Wilson's phrases verbatim.

Here's *Inadmissible*'s Maitland, his mind racing, cracking up in middle-age crisis before a High Court judge:

I swear and affirm . . . I hereby swear and affirm. Affirm. On my . . .
Honour? By my belief. My belief in . . . in . . . the technological revolution, the pressing, growing, pressing, urgent need for more and more
scientists, and more scientists, for more and more schools and universities and universities and schools, the theme of change, realistic decisions
based on a highly developed and professional study of society by people
who really know their subject . . . the theme and challenge of such rapid
change . . . in the inevitability of automation and the ever increasing
need, need, oh need for the stable ties of family life . . .

But the Wilson lampoon doesn't mean that Osborne had turned Right.
He was provoked by the Orwellian abuse of language – the Bushite babble,
what he called "the empty fatuity of *peoplespeak*". Scattered through the
notebooks are lists he kept of clichés and platitudes in the lustreless language
of posturing politicians: "Wage restraint"; "quality of life"; "target audience"; "user friendly"; "quantum leap"; "it has generally been recognised";
"bottom line priorities"; "Boom Britain"; "Eurowise"; "We must try to live
together . . ."

In 1964 – the same year as *Inadmissible Evidence* – he was also attacking
the consequences of Tory greed. Had he now lurched back to the Left? In
fact, he was campaigning against the Conservative government and London
property developers for destroying Georgian Mayfair. Osborne the traditionalist in revolt was both rebel and ardent conservationist (of the English
culture, of its language and architecture). But in such ways, he was taken
for a reactionary or tagged a radical when his true place was on the bus
that doesn't sing.

25

Damn You, England

I think John Osborne has gone mad.
      Norman Bell of Thirnscal, letters page of *Tribune*

Osborne's infamous "Damn you, England" letter was published in *Tribune* on 18 August 1961. Provoked by the threat of nuclear war as the Cold War escalated with the Berlin crisis, the ranting letter was written with the rhetorical venom of a goaded pamphleteer. It was written in an age when benign bishops blessed H-Bombs. "The very worst it could do," Archbishop of Canterbury, Geoffrey Fisher, reassured the nation about a nuclear holocaust, "would be to sweep a vast number of people at one moment from this world into the other and more vital world, into which anyhow they must pass at one time . . ."

"Damn you, England" was intended to cause uproar (and did). More than any playwright since Shaw or Wilde, Osborne continued to make news in the public arena. The letter was sent to *Tribune* with its small left-wing circulation – as opposed to *The Times*, say, or the Daily *Telegraph* – because he believed it was the only journal that would even consider publishing such a seditious piece. Its polemics are as raw as its murderous sense of outrage. But of all the indignant speeches that were made against the bomb and all the temperate Letters to the Editor published, Osborne's near-hysterical protest is the one that still burns fiercely.

A LETTER TO MY FELLOW COUNTRYMEN

This is a letter of hate. It is for you, my countrymen. I mean those men of my country who have defiled it. The men with manic fingers leading the sightless, feeble, betrayed body of my country to its death. You are its murderers. And there's little left in my own brain but the thoughts of murder for you.

I cannot even address you as I began as "Dear", for that alone would sin against my hatred. And this, my hatred for you, and those who tolerate you, is about all I have left . . .

I fear death. I dread it daily. I cling wretchedly to life, as I have always done. I fear death but I cannot hate it as I hate you. It is only you I hate, and those who let you live, function and prosper.

My hatred for you is almost the only constant satisfaction you have left me. My favourite fantasy is four minutes or so of non-commercial viewing as you fry in your democratically elected hot seats in Westminster, preferably with your condoning democratic constituents.

There is murder in my brain, and I carry a knife in my heart for every one of you. Macmillan, and you, Gaitskell, you particularly. I would willingly watch you all die for the West, if only I could keep my own minuscule portion of it.

You have instructed me in my hatred for 30 years. You have perfected it and made it the blunt instrument it is now. I only hope it will keep me going. I think it will. I think it may sustain me in the last few months.

Till then, damn you, England. You're rotting now, and quite soon you'll disappear. My hate will outrun you yet, if only for a few seconds. I wish it could be eternal.

I write this from another country with murder in my brain. I am not alone. If WE had just the ultimate decency and courage, we would strike at you – now, before you blaspheme against the world in our name.

But all I can offer you is my hatred. You will be untouched by that, for you are untouchable. If you were offered the heart of Jesus Christ, your Lord and your Saviour – though not mine, alas – you'd sniff it like sour offal. For that is the Kind of Men you are . . .

"I think John Osborne has gone mad," Norman Bell of Thurnscal responded in the letters pages of *Tribune* the following week. On the other hand: "Thank God for John Osborne!" – J.F. Heap of Thetford. "Every true Socialist should roar with applause" – trade union leader Jack Jones. "I never read things written in that kind of language" – historian Hugh Trevor-Roper in the *Sunday Times*. "I agree with every word Osborne writes" – novelist John Braine. "I haven't read the whole thing, but is it that important? – J.B. Priestley.

Osborne's missile – also known as the "Letter of Hate" – was debated for weeks in the national press and editorials were written about it for and against. "The truly significant conflict today is not between rich and poor but between those over thirty-five and under . . . Here is the driving force of deep social bitterness – a basic conviction in the young that the established order neither reflects their faith nor protects their lives" – *Sunday Telegraph*.

The letter wasn't intended as an attack on England, as its critics maintained. It was for the warmongers who are in control of our lives, the ones "with manic fingers" on the switch. "It is for you, my countrymen. I mean those men of my country who have defiled it." Who else – politician or poet – even thought this way? Near incoherent in its blind fury, "Damn you England" was a passionate defence of English soil and its voice belonged to a disillusioned patriot.

"I suppose someone like me isn't supposed to be very patriotic," says Jimmy Porter in a surprising aside.

It was doubly unfortunate, then, that the letter was sent from Valbonne in the South of France, where Osborne wrote it among the olive groves in sybaritic retreat from his countrymen while accompanied by his mistress, Jocelyn Rickards, as his pregnant wife, Mary Ure, gave birth in Welbeck Street Nursing Home. His chaotic love life is one thing. He later admitted only to the laughable postal blunder. The letter of hate had been published in *Tribune* with his address at the bottom and signed thus:

> Your fellow countryman,
> John Osborne
> Valbonne, France

Technically, the letter had been sent from London. Osborne had dictated his scrawled, handwritten version over the phone to his secretary in London and she sent the typed letter to *Tribune*. "Well, this is a rum do," the dismayed Sonia McGuinness thought to herself as she typed it out. Osborne later moaned to her that she wasn't meant to include the South of France address. But she had carefully read the full typed version along with the address back to him before mailing it. There's also the line, "I write this from another country . . ."

"There would be no doubt that I had undergone some kind of brainstorm, to the delight of many and the dismay of my friends," Osborne conceded subsequently. He also critiqued his own rant as politically naive – a "slovenly, melodramatic misuse of my so-called gift for 'rhetoric'". "Maybe so, maybe so," Michael Foot said when I visited him at the offices of *Tribune* (which he once edited). The stooped, eighty-five-year-old icon with his mane of white hair down to his shoulders looked like a Merlin of the Left as we read the library cutting of Osborne's infamous letter together.

"My favourite fantasy is four minutes or so of non-commercial viewing as you fry in your democratically elected hot seats in Westminster . . ."

Foot's eyes lit up at the line as he read on eagerly, warming to the scent of old battles, good, brave causes. And when I remarked at the finish that I had seen the original handwritten letter and it was a complete mess of crossings-out splashed with Ricard in the noonday sun, he was having none of it.

"Well, I don't begrudge him any bloody glass of wine he ever drank!" he exclaimed. "Or any other pleasure he had. He certainly gave pleasure to a lot of us. If we're going to censor writers who criticize their country from abroad, it would be quite a list! John was an honest man. He wrote passionately about what many of us were feeling. It's an honest letter he wrote. Here's to him!" And he raised an imaginary glass to toast his memory.

Osborne also demonstrated publicly against the Bomb, but the role didn't suit him. Whenever he caught sight of the penitential image of himself marching for peace he felt foolish.

His wife, Mary Ure, had a liberal conscience and picketed Downing Street during Nuclear Disarmament Week. Osborne, wary of the perception of "a politicised act of adultery", was faithful to her cause. He dutifully joined her on the picket, tramping reluctantly up and down Whitehall and past the Cenotaph feeling ridiculous strapped to a Ban-the-Bomb sandwich board. It reminded him of the time when he applied unsuccessfully for a job as a sandwich board man for London Transport's Lost Property Office.

"I wished I was touting cheap umbrellas and briefcases rather than self-consciously hawking for peace," he wrote about the experience.

His wife also supported the anti-apartheid movement. "Are these oranges from South Africa?" she would ask the salesman in Harrods Food Hall firmly. If they were, she refused to buy them. Osborne banned all productions of his plays in South Africa, describing the country as a "hideous regime".

But taking part in public demos embarrassed him, as if he'd been cast in the wrong role in the wrong spectacle. He wasn't the sort to hold hands with his fellow countrymen for a rousing chorus of "Where Have All the Flowers Gone?". He wasn't a "We Shall Overcome" type of guy. He saw the *idea* of demonstrations as a worthy act of defiance against politics as usual. (Gaitskell, leader of the Labour Party, opposed the Campaign for Nuclear Disarmament; so did the Conservative Party.) Osborne wrote in his 1962 notebook, "The healthy value of CND and the Committee of 100 [its militant offshoot] was that, allowing for its crowers and lunatics, it did represent some form of saying *no*. It was an incitement to rights of identity."

The Campaign for Nuclear Disarmament started in 1958 and thrived for three idealistic years before its numbers eventually dwindled. (One hundred thousand attended the Trafalgar Square rally in 1960). It was essentially a good-natured, non-party movement – an Easter ritual and chattering classes crusade of Hampstead housewives pushing prams alongside peacenik playwrights, folk-singing clerics, concerned scientists, new sociologists and entertainers. Osborne carried the Court's CND banner, sharing the duties with George Devine, Arnold Wesker, Lindsay Anderson and poet Christopher Logue.

The annual march, said the Court's William Gaskill, was "The Thing To Do". It attracted the liberal Left, but all were welcome in the manner of an English village fête. A banner held aloft directly behind Osborne and the Court contingent read proudly: "The North Hampstead Small Investment Circle".

Other CND notables included: the elderly Bertrand Russell and pacifist Canon Collins of St Paul's – both founders of the movement – J.B. Priestley and Jacquetta Hawkes, A.J.P. Taylor, Rose Macaulay, Michael Foot, John Berger, Vanessa Redgrave, Kingsley Martin and campaigning journalist James Cameron. Harold Pinter watched the march pass by the window of his flat in Chiswick High Road (but didn't join in).

"William Shakespeare, William Blake, we are marching for your sake!" went the chant from the literary set.

Tynan snuck into the head of the march, arriving via cab. Wesker was introduced to his future director, John Dexter, during the march. Jazz bands played; romances blossomed; the future Poet Laureate Cecil Day Lewis wrote "Requiem for the Loving" for CND (with music by Donald Swann).

Osborne was also a member of the radical splinter group, the Committee of 100, led by the now deluded pacifist Lord Russell who had come under the control of an unscrupulous Svengali, the American Leninist, Ralph Schoenman. The notion of direct action made neophytes like Osborne queasy. At Russell's invitation, he attended a meeting when secret plans were discussed to sabotage nuclear stations and official functions like the Opening of Parliament and Trooping the Colour.

"I'd no intention of associating with lunatics intent on disrupting theatricals like the Trooping of the Colour," he objected. "Still less of throwing myself beneath the well-trained boots of British squaddies."

Yet on Sunday 17 September 1961, he was among the Committee of 100's mass sit-down in Trafalgar Square, risking – he timorously believed – six months or more in jail. Describing himself as a reluctant bit player, he had no choice but to attend. He was too big a public opponent of the Bomb to chicken out. But were his panicky fears justified?

In the key letter we have from Osborne to George Devine, he described himself as a drama queen. ("Oh, I shall always make grand opera out of my artistic as well as my personal life – there's no escaping that.") But summonses had already been served on several prominent Committee members, including the frail, eighty-nine-year-old Russell and playwrights Robert Bolt and Arnold Wesker. Summoned to appear at Bow Street Court, they refused to keep the peace on the big day and were sentenced to a month in Brixton jail.

What price the head of the man who had just returned to the country after writing "Damn you, England"?

The Trafalgar Square protest had been banned by the over-defensive Macmillan government on an archaic legal technicality – thereby provoking an inevitable showdown with the police. Came the big day, Osborne, wishing he was back in the South in France, set off in the drizzle via Belgravia for what he called the pantomime. He felt ill, though he looked tanned, carrying supplies of codeine for a thudding headache and a half-bottle of whisky in his raincoat pocket to smuggle into Wormwood Scrubs.

He made his way to rendezvous with fellow protesters in the cafeteria of the National Gallery overlooking the Square. He reported disdainfully, however, that the café was full of well-known people pretending not to recognize each other like figures in an old spy thriller. There was stern Lindsay Anderson among the first-time conscientious objectors of the Royal Court set (minus Devine who had diplomatically excused himself), and there was Vanessa Redgrave in Joan of Arc mood, a nervous Shelagh Delaney, John Arden, Alan Sillitoe, John Neville, George Melly, John Calder (the British publisher of Beckett), and on.

At 3 p.m. Osborne gingerly descended the steps into the Square, joining arms with Doris Lessing. He had spotted her in the National Gallery absorbed by an Impressionist painting. They sat down among the throng on the damp patches below Landseer's lions. The Square was otherwise sealed off with the police massed threateningly around the perimeters. Tynan was filming the event out of harm's way. Osborne's lawyer, Oscar Beuselinck, was close by, though as an "official observer" – a legal minder watching out for his boy and his other famous clients. "Just plead guilty, son," he advised the hung-over Osborne next morning at Bow Street.

A dramatic cry soon went up: "They've got Vanessa!"

Vanessa Redgrave was being carried off by the police to a waiting van. "May God gag all actresses forever," Osborne wrote later.

After three hours had elapsed, he was feeling disappointed that he had yet to be arrested. He was getting cramp in his legs. It must have been from the Lotus position. He whiled away the time slugging his whisky and surveying the scene around him. Trafalgar Square – Osborne's "Theme Park of the Left" – was a stew of Trotskyite anarchists, militant pros, New Leftists, passive resisters, ravers, ingénues and sitting targets. He could see Sir Herbert Read nearby, ailing in his seventies, with a concerned Lady Read by his side. Veteran hardliners were taunting the police as usual, to be roughly handled as usual. "Fascist pigs!" "Bastards!" A mob was trying to surge its way out of the Square toward Downing Street. Many protesters were being dragged off screaming into waiting vans. But there he sat, damp and despondent, and ignored.

By 6.30, it had grown comparatively quiet around the lions. "Rather to my relief, most of my disconsolate companions had dispersed, including Doris," he remembered. "I sat it out, as instructed, and no one took the slightest notice, neither patrolling policeman nor preening pigeon."

At long last, he was arrested. "Mr Osborne?" enquired a dapper police superintendent. Not any old copper on the beat, the superintendent was sporting snappy white gloves and a silver-headed cane. "Mr Osborne?"

He found himself politely lifted up by several policemen to be carried gently to a waiting van. "They've got John!" novelist Alan Sillitoe cried out among the remnants left in the Square. Others took up the shout: "They've got John! Good luck, John! Good old John!"

He had found his role at last. Borne aloft by silent constables, he was Hamlet on his final exit. "I was lowered to the ground as carefully as I was lifted," he recorded the moment pleasantly. Then he walked into an empty police van like an honoured guest, where he remained alone for twenty minutes with the doors of the van left invitingly wide open.

The implication is clear: he was meant to call it a day and nip off home. But for the sake of appearances, he remained in the van in reluctant solidarity to the cause until other protesters were thrown in with him kicking and cursing. They were then all dropped off at various police stations around London with Osborne spending the night in the cell of the Chelsea station at the back of Peter Jones.

The cold, windowless cell didn't bother him. He was content to be alone there, as he had been when he spent hours sitting by himself in the damp Anderson air-raid shelter of his childhood. Presently, a few cursing peace protesters were thrown in with him. "They looked like a group of Millwall supporters tired out from a happy afternoon smashing up the away team," he wrote.

The Trafalgar Square protest provoked one of the biggest mass arrests in British history and he was impressed to discover that he got top billing in the *Daily Express* the following morning: "1,140 ARRESTED INCLUDING JOHN OSBORNE".

"This is a court of law, not a court of politics," the Bow Street magistrate announced gravely to the prisoners in the dock. Mr Bertram Reece, Osborne remembered, smiled at him amiably over his half-lenses like any competent character actor. "Fined. Twenty shillings."

The show was over.

Doris Lessing remembered the Battle of Trafalgar Square and indulged me with amused scrutiny as I read aloud Osborne's account of their meeting that day:

"Then I spotted Doris Lessing poring over an Impressionist painting. I knew her a little and was extremely fond of her. She possessed an extraordinary delicacy and eroticism which touchingly discounted all her White Rhodesian liberal tedium. [Lessing was raised in southern Africa, the daughter of British settlers.] I knew she wouldn't disown me with a vague smile but that she would embrace me, which she did. As we joined arms and descended the steps into the Square, I felt as if I had selected a bride. I cannot think of a public entrance more cheekily stage-managed or carried off with such enjoyment. Doris looked so innocent and sweet underneath that charmless sky that I would happily have married her there on the spot –"

"When can I plunge into this fairly shallow scene?" the deeply unimpressed Lessing intervened.

At eighty, this extraordinary woman whose life has been filled with achievement, had not mellowed. To the contrary, she appeared ageless when we met over coffee and digestive biscuits at her London home overflowing with books and untidy beyond cure. She remembered the meeting with Osborne differently in two or three essentials.

"When he arrived at the National Gallery, everyone was delighted he was there. He imagined slights." (No one "disowned him with a vague smile".) She went on candidly, "We flirted with each other the way we always did. People forget how good-looking John was. He was handsome and sexy and very good company. I descended the steps with him into Trafalgar Square, but I was actually supporting him on my arm. The truth is the man was ill. I can't think of a situation more calculated to turn him into jelly. He loathed it. He hated every second. He sat among a group of people who were protecting him! His lawyer, Oscar Beuselinck, said to me how amazing it was that everybody thought they were going to get beaten up by the police, but John was the only one they felt they should protect."

She rationalized that some people get treated the way they need, or demand. "He suffered a great deal, and his suffering was genuine," she added. "But it's astonishing how he got away with it. After all, everyone has a ghastly time a lot of the time, and yet everyone made allowances for John. We all did. I don't think he could really cope with life. He just wasn't very competent at life."

He knew nothing about politics, she confirmed. "He didn't understand politics at all. There were a lot of people around at that time who were like him. They made lots of political remarks, but that didn't make them left-wing. He wasn't left-wing, he wasn't right-wing. He was just a natural rebel."

Lessing wrote affectionately about Osborne in her autobiography *Walking in the Shade*, without mentioning her brief fling with him, and if I weren't so low I wouldn't be mentioning it now. Though she has remained a leading novelist for half a century, she's a playwright *manquée* who was part of the early, golden Royal Court scene. She wrote two promising plays and was close to Osborne after *Look Back* – which she saw in its first days and dismissed with her diamond intelligence as "a self-pitying whine". She was ten years older than him, a socialist outsider and bluestocking beauty. "Here was a woman who, for all her distrust of the English," Frank Kermode wrote admiringly, "lived in London as Yeats said Verlaine lived in Paris, like a fly in a honeypot."

Lessing was protective of Osborne. She has admitted that she herself was born with skins too few, but Osborne seemed to have no defences at all. She was very fond of him, but he needed too many allowances made, too much attention paid.

"I've never known anybody in my life who was so easily wounded," she told me. "Someone might say something frivolously to him as a joke, and you could see him shrinking from it because it was too strong, too painful for him. He brought out the maternal in women, there's no doubt about it. I wasn't in love with him, and he certainly wasn't in love with me. After all, he was engaged in these calamitous, serious relationships. We had a rapport. It wasn't love, but it was more than a friendship. I had an affinity with John. I don't think he was a misogynist. He was unable to deal with women, which is quite different."

She had always believed that any woman allowing herself to be in love with Osborne must be crazy. Married twice herself, she explained in her autobiography that her views about him were those of a non-combatant. They never fought. "With me he was never anything but courteous and kind. Affable, that is the word. Magnanimous in his judgements. Gentleman

John, that was his real nature – and then something deep and spiteful forced him into venom."

Lessing knew three of his wives and said they were all remarkable women. She thought he found Mary Ure boring. ("She was a good girl which wasn't what he liked.") She described a restaurant dinner when Osborne sniped vindictively at Ure the entire evening until she sat there in tears. "I was there with someone else and we tried to deflect it, but he never let up for a second. He flayed her, just like Jimmy Porter."

She described a hypnotized Osborne later led by the nose to the altar by Penelope Gilliatt. "John was in love with her the way some men are in love, as if they are preparing for a session at the dentist."

The seductive, dangerous Jill Bennett starred in Lessing's adaptation of Ostrovsky's *The Storm* at the National Theatre. Osborne was then on the brink of leaving Gilliatt for Bennett. "She was madly in love with him. But as far as I can make out, he objected to the fact that she was an actress and behaved like one. Lying in bed until lunch time, drinking too much. This is what actresses *do*."

Doris Lessing and Osborne drifted in and out each other's lives over the years, and she thought it strange, as if for an intense period they had become members of an extended family. When they eventually lost touch, she found that she often dreamt about him and was unabashed. She caught the atmosphere of the dreams in her autobiography:

"Now, those were interesting dreams. Straightforward sexual dreams are not interesting: you wake and think, oh, one of those. But there is a kind of dream about a man that is affectionate, friendly, and with a flicker of amorousness, like old lovers meeting, and there is regret and humour and charm. Charm – the main thing; landscapes that seem to smile; nothing to do with ordinary life."

26

The Biggest Floperoo Ever

In Thy great mercy defend us from all the perils and dangers of this night.

Book of Common Prayer

Osborne predicted that the words "ill-fated" would be forever prefixed to his first and last musical, *The World of Paul Slickey*, and he was right. His ill-fated musical opened in the West End at the Palace Theatre on 5 May 1959, to became one of the most spectacular disasters in English theatre.

We needn't dwell too long on what he described as his "tumbrel ride to the scaffold". *Slickey* was intended as an entertaining social satire on venal gossip columnists and the ruling class. Gossip columns then were still dominated by respectful reports about "society" – the social calendar of the Queen, the Princess Margaret Chelsea set, duchesses and debs, hunt balls and the Henley Regatta, Lord Boothby and the Churchill's Club demi-monde. By the onset of the Sixties, however, the old world had been invaded by the roots of today's tabloid culture: former showgirl Lady Docker beaming at a dazzled populace from her gold-plated Daimler; newly rich Labour industrialists like Charles Clore and touchy new celebs like Osborne complaining about all the attention; the arrival of the first English Elvis on the staid English scene, Tommy Steele (aka former merchant seaman Tommy Hicks); Lady Pamela Mountbatten's marriage to a commoner (interior designer David Hicks, no relation to Tommy), followed by the marriage of the Queen's sister to an upper-class photographer (Antony Armstrong-Jones, future Lord Snowdon).

"I shall be interested to see how the show fares," William Hickey commented amusingly in his *Express* column on the eve of *Slickey*'s premiere. "I opened 26 years ago and I'm still running . . ."

If Osborne were due a fall, he couldn't have set himself up for one better. His lead character, Slickey, was obviously based on the *Express*'s Hickey.

(Slickey's first name, Paul, was a nod to Paul Tanfield, gossip columnist of the *Mail*.) His dedication in the script – published to coincide with the premiere – attacked the critics biliously in advance. True, Sheridan's preface to *The Rivals* had belittled the "little puny critics" with their "petulance and illiberality", but at least Sheridan left us *The Rivals*.

Even Osborne's customary blast at the critics was sourly off form. It begins quite promisingly: "No one has ever dedicated a string quartet to a donkey although books have been dedicated to critics." But his sanctimonious conclusion wouldn't raise a hee-haw. "A donkey with ears that could listen would no longer be a donkey; but the day may come when he is left behind because the other animals have learnt to hear."

Yet *Slickey* was admirably bold in its way. Nothing about it works, but in the post-war age of Sandy Wilson's charming spoof of the Roaring Twenties, *The Boy Friend*, it dared to take the British musical further than it had ever been. *Slickey*'s scattershot targets also included corrupt clergymen, dirty debs, death by hanging, Tory dowagers, the tax-dodging stately homes of England, bad West End theatre, stiff-upper-lip British war movies, "sincere" rock stars, moronic public taste and conventional sex. His novel idea that a bad marriage could be miraculously saved by instant sex changes for both men and women is of passing interest. But, as the tactful Hobson commented in the *Sunday Times*, "For the moment, his ambition exceeds his grasp."

Social satire was never Osborne's forte. (Fifteen years later, his lampooning, sub-Restoration frolic about the modern sex wars, *The End of Me Old Cigar*, fell apart.) My hunch is that he meant *Slickey* to be an updated *Vile Bodies*. Evelyn Waugh's perfect 1930 satire of the fashionable bright young things and his Lord Beaverbrook stand-in, Lord Monomark of the *Daily Excess*, is echoed by Osborne's dim, fun-loving aristocrats and his Lord Mortlake of the *Daily Racket*. Waugh has his Miles Malpractice and Osborne his Father Evilgreene. But a glance at Osborne's own lyrics for *Slickey* reveals how wincingly off the mark he was:

"This isn't any madam/I've known lots of girls before/ And, frankly, I've had 'em."
"If I could be a magistrate/you'd have to be importunate."
"She can be as wet as watercress and still be a success."
"The we of me/Is the longing to be free."
And – "This island of phlegm/ It's our staple apology/ Our apophthegm."
Our *thwhat*? "Apophthegm"? It's hard enough to *say*.

I'm just a guy called Paul Slickey
And the job that I do's pretty tricky,
I'm twenty-eight years old
And practically everybody, anybody, anything
You can think of leaves me
Quite, completely
Newspaper neatly
Quite, quite cold.

His initial blunder was to have gone back in time to base the show on an early play – an amateurish comedy of manners he completed in 1955 while waiting anxiously for *Look Back* to be staged. Provisionally entitled *An Artificial Comedy* or *Love in a Myth*, it was turned down by both Devine and Richardson – as tactfully as it's possible to turn anything down – for production at the Court. In truth, they couldn't believe that it had come from his pen. A split with their temperamental protégé was avoided when Court guru, George Goetschius, helped to smooth things over. Devine had even passed on the script to his young associate, William Gaskill, in the hope that he might see its value and agree to direct it, but Gaskill begged to be let off the hook.

The stubborn Osborne then turned the rejected play into his "play with music", *Slickey*, and kept the same cartoon characters (Mrs Giltedge-Whyte, Father Evilgreene, Terry Maroon, and so on). Hysterical blindness often overcomes even the best of people who create musicals. *Slickey* was produced for the West End by the distinguished Donald Albery with the help of an American associate of David Merrick's and three principal investors – a furniture manufacturer with no showbiz connections at all, a stage-struck Russian entrepreneur, and an elderly New York lady with a fat cheque-book. Perhaps in lieu of anyone else with a reputation who was willing to take it on, Osborne appointed himself as director (marking his directorial debut outside of rep). On the advice of his agent, he appointed the composer Christopher Whelan. But no one else seemed to have heard of him, including Osborne, who was also making his debut as the show's lyricist.

He first met his future lover, *Slickey*'s costume designer Jocelyn Rickards, when she had assisted on the film version of *Look Back*. The well-connected Rickards advised him to hire her friend Hugh Casson as set designer and the young Kenneth MacMillan as choreographer for *Slickey*. But Osborne blundered again when he cast the unexciting, though charming, band singer Dennis Lotis to play the magnetic gossip columnist instead of a little-known actor who auditioned for the role, Sean Connery.

JOHN OSBORNE

Among the stunned opening-night audience who were left "quite completely, newspaper neatly, quite, quite cold" at *Slickey's* premiere were the Duke and Duchess of Bedford, Lord Montague, "Bubbles" Harmsworth – socialite wife of newspaper proprietor, Lord Harmsworth – the Profumos, the Marquis of Milford Haven, Cecil Beaton, John Gielgud and Noel Coward.

Booing broke out in the gallery halfway through the show. According to Osborne, his line "God in heaven, it's like a pantomime" was greeted with roars of "Hear-hear!" Another accidental clanger – "What we want is a return to common sense" – received wild applause. At the curtain call, the boos cascaded toward the stage while the most spirited member of the cast, Adrienne Corri, gave the mob a "V" sign and mouthed the words, "Go fuck yourselves." In a gloating last hurrah from the old guard, Coward – and, more surprisingly, Gielgud – were on their feet booing with the rest. "Never in all my theatrical experience have I seen anything so appalling, appalling from every point of view," Coward seethed in his diaries.

Yet Coward had been booed off the stage, too. When he emerged from the opening-night uproar of his own early disaster, *Sirocco*, he was spat at. "Very strong personality," he explained, "irritating success." Osborne's come-uppance was a similar tale of hubris. Emerging tentatively from the theatre, he was booed and heckled – "Bloody rubbish!" – to become the first drama-tist in history chased by furious theatregoers up the Charing Cross Road.

He made light of the reception, of course (though Adrienne Corri remem-bered him in tears at the curtain call). "It's an honour to be booed by certain people," he announced. Two days after the opening, he was denouncing the reviewers to the *New York Times*: "There is not one daily critic in London intellectually equipped to review a play properly." Twenty-five years later, he contributed to Ronald Harwood's enjoyable book collection of triumphs and disasters at the theatre by quoting all the terrible *Slickey* reviews. "This is a sad day for Osborne"; "an insult"; "manifest failure"; "fiasco"; "an evening of general embarrassment"; "unspeakable"; "three boring hours"; "not entirely worthless"; "schoolboyish"; "the biggest floperoo ever . . ."

There's a simple test to measure the scale of *Slickey's* debacle. Had it really hit its targets, the Lord Chamberlain would have banned it from the stage. On paper, *Slickey* was blasphemous and sexually deviant. It should have been red meat to that still powerful, priggish protector of England's virtue, the official theatre censor.

Six years later, in 1965, *A Patriot for Me* was refused a theatre licence

252

and banned for its sympathetic portrayal of homosexuality. *Luther* got bogged down in an absurdist battle over the hero's constipated bowel movements and the Lord Chamberlain's intention to substitute the word "testicles" in place of the heraldic bronze balls of the Medici. "'Testicles of the Medici' would be acceptable," Lt. Col. Penn, one of the Lord Chamberlain's vigilant army men, decreed. The needling skirmishes over *Inadmissible Evidence* were more mundane: the expression "You could stick a bus ticket in there" was censored. Osborne's personal request to keep the word "catchfart" as a vigorous use of the English language found in Chaucer was declined. *The Entertainer* boiled down to a farcical dispute over the naked Britannia in Archie Rice's pier show. Brigadier Sir Norman Gwatkin decided with unintentional humour: "Nudes are allowed by the Lord Chamberlain provided they are motionless and expressionless in the face of the audience . . ."

But *Slickey* openly satirized at least two sacred taboos: the Church and the sanctity of marriage. It wasn't until 1960 that satire came to England with *Beyond the Fringe*, and sex, it's rumoured, arrived with the Beatles in 1963. Yet the Lord Chamberlain, a law unto himself, licensed *Slickey* without much trouble. "This yawning rubbish is recommended for licence," went the sneering internal memo.

Behind the scenes, the honeyed public decorum of the office gave way to know-all amateur theatre critics and mockery on scribbled memos. But while *Slickey* easily passed the censor, there was an extraordinary development that amounted to a Machiavellian plot against Osborne.

One week before the West End opening at the Palace Theatre – as the show tried out in Leeds – the Lord Chamberlain's office received a surprise visit from the owner of the Palace Theatre, Emile Littler, and his partner. They wanted *Slickey* banned.

It was an unprecedented move. The show had received its licence from the Lord Chamberlain. The influential Littler was asking him to revoke it, and Brigadier Sir Norman Gwatkin smelt a rat.

Littler complained personally to Gwatkin that he'd never seen anything so suggestive on the stage before. Moreover, *Slickey* was a "bad play badly produced". Disgusted members of the audience were walking out in noisy protest. Littler feared that when the show came to London the following week, it might cause a riot.

"I may be wrong," Gwatkin reported to the Lord Chamberlain, the Earl of Scarborough, "but I think he's backing a loser and would like the Lord Chamberlain to step in and relieve him of the trouble."

Osborne's shrewd lawyer, Oscar Beuselinck, was already on the case. Gwatkin noted in red ink on an internal memo that same week, "He's got a shyster jew [sic] lawyer knocking around, so don't let's go beyond what we can."

On 5 May – the eve of the West End opening – Osborne sent an impassioned two-page appeal to Gwatkin demanding fair treatment. "Your office seems intent on treating me as if I were the producer of a third-rate nude revue," he protested. ("Which he is," Gwatkin has scribbled in the margin.) "In paying attention to what is without question an infinitesimal and lunatic minority, you are doing a grave injustice, not only to myself, but to the general public and your own office."

"You silly little man," Gwatkin thought to himself, wishing he could respond to Osborne in kind. "But I suppose the best reply is a short acknowledgement," he advised the Lord Chamberlain.

But the Lord Chamberlain couldn't have revoked his licence for *Slickey* even if he'd fallen for Littler's backstage plot. According to the archaic Theatres Act, a licence could be open to question if a show caused a breach of the peace that provoked a police enquiry. All Osborne got was boos and a crushing blow to his reputation.

27

Runaway Lovers

I want to hear about beautiful things
Beautiful things like love
Refrain from *The World of Paul Slickey*

Osborne's affair with Jocelyn Rickards began during rehearsals for *Slickey* and soon after the disastrous opening night he fled England with her, fleeing failure and his bad marriage, fleeing everything in pursuit of enviable, carefree liberty. The fugitive lovers, pursued by the paparazzi, made their escape in his open-top racing green Jaguar, heading for Italy and eventually Naples via the leisurely back roads of France where the reality of his life receded into the distance and he could write that they "fell sated and inflated with food, wine, folly and fresh air into a goose-feathered well of forgetfulness".

Mary Ure, who was in Stratford playing Titania in Peter Hall's production of *A Midsummer Night's Dream*, had long known of the affair. "Jocelyn is my oldest, dearest friend," she told the *Daily Express*. "She and John and I have known each other for years. She was going to Paris – so John said he could give her a lift."

The runaway lovers crossed from Naples to Capri and stayed for three weeks in the sun behind the protective white walls of Graham Greene's house, the Villa Rosario, high up in Anacapri overlooking the Bay of Naples. Greene, an ex-lover of Rickards, once wrote of her that she possessed "an outstanding capacity for friendship – rare in the jealous world of art and letters to which she belongs". Loyalty – the prize that Osborne valued most – was her innate talent.

The daughter of a handsome, wealthy businessman named Bertie, who became penniless, Rickards was an Australian expatriate who arrived in London when she was twenty-four to become a well-regarded painter and costume designer. (She designed, among a number of films, the costumes for *The Entertainer* and Antonioni's *Blow-Up*.) She was known as the lover of famous figures – Greene, A.J. Ayer and Osborne – as her friend Barbara Skelton was known as the lover of famous fatties – Cyril Connolly, George Weidenfeld and King Farouk. Imagining a glamorous café society life of exclusive literary salons and dancing the night away at the Blue Angel and El Cubano, I once asked the gregarious Freddie Ayer – who was described derisively by an unusually jealous Osborne as "the dirty don" and "this pear-shaped Don Giovanni" – what life was like for him when he was with Rickards. "We never seemed to go anywhere," he answered, looking crest-fallen. "We never went *out*."

Until the antisocial Osborne arrived on the scene, Rickards led quite an active social life, numbering among her circle the Connollys, Philip Toynbee, Lucian Freud, Richard Wollheim, Sonia Orwell, Ben Nicholson and the Spenders. But she was always a homebody. A good cook, she preferred to stay at home, and, judging by the photographs of Osborne at the time, she fattened him up. "Jocelyn cooked huge, elaborate lunches, which were followed by long lazy afternoons," he remembered. "Occasionally we went to the theatre, the cinema or a restaurant, but we ventured out rarely and there were few visitors. Most evenings, Jocelyn would curl up with Henry James while I worked or turned on the tele-vision, which she resolutely refused to watch."

His nickname for her was "Dolly" – a peculiar choice. His mother was known as "Dolly". When they set up house together, it also became home to two dogs and two cats, and he feyly gave them the collective name of "The Dollies".

"TOO GLUM RING TONIGHT MISSING ALL DOLLIES OVERWHELMINGLY ALL LOVE JOHN" reads a telegram he sent from San Francisco.

There are too many Dollies in the mixture.

But Rickards offered a secure, cosy domesticity he had never experienced before. She was thirty-three when they first met – six years older than him. The idealized picture of maternal domestic bliss with his older mistress replacing his mother's inadequate love is a tempting Freudian simplifica-tion, particularly as Rickards loved him unconditionally. The comfort of a woman's protective embrace was Osborne's leaky bulwark against aloneness and the tug of defenceless depression. He wrote touchingly about his refuge with Rickards, "It was the first time that I had shared this domestic comfort with anyone."

Some, like Tony Richardson, found her presumptuous or loftily insensi-tive in the name of daring outspokenness, and Osborne privately criticized her later in life for her spoilt, pampered airs. But if she was spoilt, he was the one who pampered her. Comparing her favourably to his first and second wives as "neither sphinx nor tantrum child", he described her as passionately intelligent, emotionally candid, small and dark with wide appraising eyes and an almost comic air of uncombative lethargy that he found immediately attractive.

"Open, ill-natured gossip was one of our devout bounds," he was unembarrassed to admit. "Well, Dolly," his letters to her frequently begin, as if continuing a gossip with her in person. When their affair ended after two and a half years, she became his friend and confidante. He was still writing to her until he died.

They first met when she was living in an Eaton Square flat with her ex-lover, a stylish fellow Austrialian expat, the fashion photographer Alec Murray. Osborne bought a seventeen-year lease on the top three floors of a house at 29 Lower Belgrave Street and Rickards moved in. He found sanctuary there with her while he still lived with his wife in Woodfall St. He kept an office at the second home and would come and go as he pleased.

"Don't be anxious about me," Rickards wrote to him in the early, hazy days of their affair. "Although I shan't cease to be aware that you are not here for even one hour of the time that you are away, I am equally aware of never having felt so utterly and securely loved. Sleep well."

"Oh poor, poor you," Rickards said to me laconically when we met, "having to wake up to John Osborne every day and his five wives too." She was fun and she was sly, and she still spoke at the languid pace that Osborne's mother had described admiringly as "her beautiful speaking voice". In her seventies, she lived in an airy flat overlooking the Thames with the film director Clive Donner, her husband of some thirty years. And there, too, was an attractive woman, their assistant, Sonia McGuinness, who had been Osborne's secretary all those years ago.

In 1961, when she was twenty-six, McGuinness answered an ad in *The Times* and was first interviewed for the job by Rickards who then introduced her to Osborne. "My knees were knocking," she told me. "Because of his name."

Aware of Osborne's thin skin, Rickards never risked telling him that she had walked out of *Look Back in Anger* when it opened at the Court. ("It was all those fucking bears and squirrels," she explained.) In spite of her more usual candour, she remained guarded with him. But it soon became clear during our meetings that she wasn't the type to spare anyone's blushes. "John could be such enormous fun," she said. "When we were in bed together he used to hold his dick like a ukulele and sing George Formby songs."

"Anything we might know?" I enquired.

"Yes," she replied. "'Leaning on a Lamppost'."

Good to learn, at least, that his childhood ukulele lessons hadn't gone to waste. She laughed happily at the memory, and went on, "He was the most complex man I've ever known. He was emotionally immature and fragile, he was tender and scornful. He needed affection and encouragement. He was full of gaiety, but he could reveal little talent for enjoying life. He had a talent for fucking up other people's lives, and his own."

Yet she was devoted to him. He wanted a child with her, but she miscarried at three months. "I wanted a child more for John's sake than my own," she explained. "But he was passionate about it."

Osborne, the father and family man, isn't a picture associated with him. Yet he wanted children with all his wives (though with Mary Ure it was for her sake) and his third wife, Penelope Gilliatt, would give birth to his daughter. But he romanticized family life. It was never real to him, and many years would pass before any of his relationships were even stable. Until then he remained a conflicted, rootless man drawn to the safety of shelter, whose secret pact with the conventional could never be permanent. He needed the domestic ease and security that Rickards, for one, offered. But sooner or later, he became restless or tempted and the roof fell in.

She knew that he was unfaithful to her with a number of women, although it didn't trouble her. "He had more casual sex than hot dinners," she said, "but it did neither of us any harm." Rickards was easygoing and bohemian in style, smoking cheroots with a glass of wine in hand, and she was complaisant. Only when Penelope Gilliatt enters the story was her relationship with Osborne seriously threatened.

Ure was no threat to her. She was indifferent. "I never knew what was going through Mary's head – if anything," Rickards remarked. For two years of their affair, Osborne still lived partly with his wife as the marriage drifted on in mutual apathy. But on New Year's Eve 1960, when he was staying at Woodfall Street, a tipsy Ure casually told him that she was pregnant and went back to sleep. In the early hours of the following morning, as if fated, an electrical fault caused a serious fire and their home was wrecked.

It was the end of the charade of their marriage. He now moved all his belongings into the Lower Belgrave Street house with Rickards, while his wife soon moved into her own house in Cliveden Place, Chelsea. The unresolved question was who had fathered her child.

Osborne was convinced it was Robert Shaw. But his circumspect wife would neither confirm nor deny. "I made a dazed consultation with my diary," he remembered, "laboriously comparing dates of the previous months with my absences in New York, and the likelihood of my having fathered her child seemed far-fetched if not impossible. I needed a woman's expertise in these matters and could only conjecture uncertainty until I consulted Jocelyn."

"I did some swift arithmetic," Rickards told me. "I didn't see how he could possibly be the father. But you never knew with John. He might have had a quickie, of course."

Ure's affair with Shaw was by then an open secret. Osborne's chauffeur, Jimmy Gardner, used to drive her to liaisons with him at a flat he kept behind Sloane Square. (He lived in a family home in St John's Wood with his wife and children.) Their first dinner together was at Au Père de Nico in Chelsea (where the Osborne–Ure wedding reception had been held). Zoe Caldwell, who was acting at the Court then, told me everyone in the company knew about the affair. "You could hardly miss it."

When Shaw appeared onstage with Ure at the Court in Middleton's seventeenth-century revenge drama, *The Changeling*, the audience sensed the electricity between them. Richardson was the director and he cast knowingly to type. Shaw played the working-class servant, De Flores, lusting after Ure's compromised Beatrice-Joanna. Doris Lessing remembered that he delivered the line "I love that woman!" with such passion that "life itself overthrew the play, and everyone applauded."

During the run there were announcements in the press about Ure expecting a baby in the summer, accompanied by smiling pictures of her. But she was still refusing to discuss the paternity of the child, and Osborne visited her that spring at her new home in Cliveden Place to clear the air.

According to his own amazed account, she gossiped contentedly with him about Robert Shaw – about his novel *The Sun God*, how he had introduced her to *Middlemarch* and, finally, his considerable prowess as a lover. ("Not as good as *you*, dear.") Then he followed her obediently to bed.

"I had never made love to a pregnant woman before and she seemed impatient with me in an amused way," Osborne wrote. When she briefly left the room, he noticed a letter, several pages long, left open on her bedside table. He confessed guiltily that he read it, although it seems likely he was meant to. "A quick glance revealed it to be a very explicit and erotic love letter from Shaw, full of excitement about the baby and the mechanics of quickly following it up with another one."

When she returned to the bedroom, he slipped the letter into his trouser pocket while he dressed. He kissed her goodbye and she waved as she settled down to read a magazine. He never saw or heard from her again, except through her solicitors.

*

Perhaps it was inevitable that Osborne would find himself attracted to Penelope Gilliatt. "Penelope had the whitest skin and the reddest of real red hair," Vanessa Redgrave said admiringly. "The Elizabethan poets would have written another five hundred sonnets about her." But for Osborne, fiery red hair provoked the purple prose of fatal attraction. It was "the copper-headed helmet of destiny", "the mantle of goddesses", that had also possessed him fancifully with Pamela, his first wife with red hair.

The new affair began soon after Osborne and Rickards had struck up a friendship with both Roger and Penelope Gilliatt when they attended a few of their fashionable gatherings at their nearby Lowndes Square flat. Since her apprenticeship as a bright features writer at *Vogue* and, later, *Queen*, Gilliatt had become one of the brilliant critics of her generation. Her weekly film reviews appeared on the *Observer*'s arts pages alongside Tynan's theatre column like a star double act.

Gilliatt's husband, a distinguished neurologist, had gained a brief glow of national celebrity for himself and his wife when it was belatedly rumoured that Jeremy Fry, the choice of best man at Tony Armstrong-Jones's wedding to Princess Margaret, had been involved in a gay fling during his youth. The subsequent uproar called for an impeccably straight understudy and Dr Roger Gilliatt stepped into the breach.

As Rickards tells the story, his wife pursued Osborne under her own nose. "Penelope used to come round and it was like having a firework display in the living room," she remembered with undisguised hostility. "She *sparkled* all over." It was as if all these years later Rickards was still staggered by the obvious play that Gilliatt – "glowing in her unpressed azalea-coloured chiffon dresses" – made for her lover. "Whenever she saw him, she lit up like a one-arm bandit when someone hits the jackpot. All I could do was watch it happen."

Though he was a smitten, willing accomplice, Osborne confirmed that Gilliatt's intent was plain: "Even Roger, creased with fatigue from a galley-slaving day at the Middlesex Hospital, must have noticed it, as inexorable as one of his EEG readings."

Then one bright morning, when the page proofs of his new play, *Luther*, had arrived like evidence of work actually done in the midst of his lurching, unfocused life, Osborne invited himself over to Lowndes Square for a celebratory drink with Gilliatt. Shamelessly using that preening ploy of all writers on the make with a future lover, he read aloud passages from his latest work as she listened intently curled up on the floor. Their affair began that afternoon.

He conceded in vague hindsight that his treatment of the tearfully acqui-escent Rickards during the weeks that followed was "probably grotesquely indefensible". But she had no pride in her love for him, she admitted, and would not be pushed into leaving. "For once in his life," Rickards told me, sounding steely, "he had to make a decision."

It was the one thing he could not do without emotional trauma and even collapse. Osborne could be reduced to a ditheringly indecisive state of agony and guilt whenever it came to ending relationships. With both his first and second wives, the decision had been made for him: Lane left him, and Ure went off with Shaw.

When he returned sheepishly to London after a truant weekend with Gilliatt at the "Folkestone Film Festival" – a festival they invented for the occasion – her distraught husband had already been on the phone to Rickards in search of his missing wife. Osborne returned to Lower Belgrave Street to "appraise the state of play", as he put it, while his new runaway lover waited outside. "I think you'd better ask her in," Rickards told him, prepared for the showdown. "She's going to need a drink."

But as Osborne meekly watched the scene unfold like a dazed spectator at the battle, the resolved Gilliatt confronted the pale and obdurate Rickards. "You've got to realize that John and I are in love," she announced, authoritatively propped up against the mantelpiece.

The monkey was back in the machine. The man who compared the way he confronted problems in his love life to an improvising chimpanzee faced with the dashboard of a jumbo jet, didn't seem to know what he was doing again. If he was in love with Gilliatt, he still remained living in the muted domestic bliss of Lower Belgrave Street.

28

Another Perfect House Party

I search out scraps of you, seek out shreds of you. I sit and walk and
lie and I burn for you.
                    Osborne letter to Penelope Gilliatt, 12 August, Valbonne

The tall stone farmhouse in the South of France stood in a remote hollow
among olive groves and sweet-smelling lavender, and they could see the
ocean from the swimming pool tucked into the parched landscape. Osborne
had long planned a summer holiday there with Rickards, sharing the luxurious retreat in the hills of Valbonne with Tony Richardson. It would be
another perfect house party.

La Beaumette, as the house was called, belonged to Lord Glenconner,
one of the Tennant family, and had its own staff. Osborne and Richardson
had rented it for most of August and early September. But Rickards was
now reluctant to go and Osborne had to persuade her out of her sullen
mood of mute attrition. He reasoned with her apologetically that she
deserved a holiday after all the upset, and a break in the sun would do
them both good. He would even arrange for a friend of hers, Jane Sprague,
a fashion model, to join them.

Thus persuaded, Rickards set off with him for the Côte d'Azur in his
convertible blue Alvis, fortified like a chic tank by fifteen hundredweight
of custom-built coachwork. But this time there was no lingering on the
escapist back roads of France as there had been when they first fell in love
and fled London for the sanctuary of Graham Greene's villa in Anacapri.
Many others were also descending on the secluded farmhouse in the hills
where the hyperactive Richardson had already arrived, impatient for drama
and diversion.

Jocelyn Herbert, with two of her children from her marriage to the solicitor Anthony Lousada, was meanwhile driving Richardson's red
Thunderbird from London to the house where her lover, George Devine,

would join them later. There was always an undercurrent of class warfare between the upper middle-class Herbert and Osborne, who mocked her resemblance to Virginia Woolf as a mask of permanently weary saintliness. The Royal Court's distinguished set designer in turn patronized Rickards as "an intellectual's moll", and Rickards herself was never at ease in the controlling company of the feline Richardson.

Oscar Beuselinck was also heading eagerly into the maelstrom, bringing with him his teenage son. "Well, what are we all going to do today?" Beuselinck would ask, patrolling the pool impatiently in his baggy bathing trunks. John Addison, who composed the music for *The Entertainer* and would win an Academy Award for his score of *Tom Jones*, was also en route with his wife and children. Rickards's friend, Jane Sprague, was flying in from her home in Los Angeles. Christopher Isherwood and his lover Don Bachardy were expected before travelling on to Somerset Maugham's palatial Villa Mauresque at Juan Les Pins.

"Well, *I* didn't invite them all, did you, Johnny?" Richardson complained to Osborne when he arrived in the Alvis churning up the gravel. "I mean, what are we going to *do* with them all?"

The top floor of the house was already occupied by the mostly drunk caretaker with his daughter and her teenage sons. Monsieur Voisin looked after the property, and his daughter, Mademoiselle Voisin, was the cook. Rickards described how each morning they would "do" the menus together for the day as though in an Edwardian household. At least, she consoled herself, Penelope Gilliatt had been left behind in London.

But Gilliatt was with them in spirit. A registered express letter from her arrived for Osborne each day from London and subsequently from the Venice Film Festival. There could be two and even three ardent love letters a day. Osborne compared them to food parcels sent to a prisoner of war camp.

"Existing without you is suddenly a half-life," Gilliatt wrote from London. "I find myself absurdly making detours in the car so as to go past the Court and look at the posters and your name there. Oh my love, my love." "The hell with Roger [her husband] in a way, for there's nothing more I can do . . . I long so much to come to you and hold you. Remember how much I adore you, all the time. Nothing deflects it. Nights become restless and brief and days seem interminable. Jesus I long for you." "Hurrah, oops, yelps, two marvellous letters of a heavenly drunk uninhibited doodle have just flopped through my letter box and I hasten (good *Observer* word) to say that I'm absolutely dotty about you . . ."

The unhappy Rickards who, in effect, was running the crowded house, usually signed for the letters from Gilliatt, tipped the *facteur*, and mockingly delivered them to Osborne.

> Biasutti Hotel
> Lido di Venezia
> [August 1961]

My darling one,
I've nothing to tell you except over & over again that I love you & need you desperately. I'm trying hard not to be dragged under again like I was the first week. I love you deeply & furiously & with total attention, & I realize more & more that it has been going on for a *long* time. I'm hanging on by my back molars. My hair would have gone white if the sun weren't turning it a rather crude Lady Macbeth wig colour. I found a note in my box at the Festival today to say that a special *critic's doctor* would attend from 12–1 every day near the Sala Grande & would be sitting in the aisle seat, row H, if one needed him during a screening. I well might. But what shot would inure me from you? I'm saturated with you & anyone who tried to pacify me would meet pretty stiff redheaded resistance.

Osborne left the letters open around the bedroom he shared with Rickards – a copycat case of doing to others as you wouldn't have done to yourself. She responded by telling him firmly that she had no intention of reading them. From then on, he carried the letters everywhere with him in a black briefcase like state secrets. When Richardson asked Rickards what was so precious that it never left Osborne's side, she replied, to his astonishment, "The Collected Letters of Penelope Gilliatt." Richardson, it turns out, had once asked Gilliatt to marry him.

Osborne's love letters to Gilliatt were written in secret:

> Valbonne
> 9 August 1961
> 5:30 am

My darling, darling, it's a whole week, seven outstretched days since I left you. A week and I can't remember a longer one. But you *must* know I feel you as though you are in my flesh. Life without you has become unimaginable, unthinkable. It's early morning, a time that seems specially yours. I can remember the smell of you, the outline of you, the touch of you. The only real news is the news that comforts me all day. I long for you and want you.
Always
J

Valbonne
12 August

These twelve days without you have been extraordinary. For one thing, there have been periods, sometimes for hours on end, when my complete consciousness seems to be paralyzed in my physical hunger for you. I go to bed afire for you, and when I sleep I'm constantly wrenched out of it by you. I search for scraps of you, seek out shreds of you. I sit and walk and I burn for you.

Oh, Penny, my darling, it's so hard to believe, but there's no escaping it. I love you more than I can comprehend, and I want you more and more and urgently than anyone I have ever known.

Unknown to Jocelyn Rickards, he also proposed marriage to Gilliatt from Valbonne.

20 August

My darling love –
I have about five minutes to write this. I've been ill in bed all day. I'm giving this to Oscar [Beuselinck] in the hope he can give it to you before you go to Venice. As you can imagine it's been a hideous nightmare here . . . No time for more. Will write to Venice tomorrow. Don't be depressed by the letter you get on arrival. I've never longed for you more.

    All my love,

    Always,

    J

P.S. Will you marry me? It's risky, but you'd get fucked regularly. Also loved. I *adore* you.

But Gilliatt had left for Venice before the letter could be delivered, and Osborne was therefore compelled to propose again. "When you – we – can, would you please MARRY ME?" (24 August, Valbonne).

ITALY
27 August

Yes yes yes. This must be the first time that anyone has accepted a proposal on a telegram form standing in a Post Office. An Italian widow is leaning over me and asking the date which I shan't ever forget. I'm so ecstatically happy. I can hardly stop myself from hugging her. All my love for always and always. Ask me again and again for the joy of it.

Meanwhile, Devine had arrived in the South of France unable to stop weeping. He was having a nervous breakdown. The strain of running the Royal Court with its needy "tit-swingers" (as Devine called his reliant young acolytes) would soon wear him out completely. But recent wounding events had humiliated him. He was troubled most by the rejection of a friend, a writer he admired greatly, Nigel Dennis. His own production of Dennis's comedy, *August for the People*, had received disastrous reviews at the Edinburgh Festival where Tynan pronounced it a "dead duck". Worse, its restless star, Rex Harrison, had announced his intention of abandoning the production in midstream to play Caesar in the Burton–Taylor *Cleopatra*.

Harrison's contract with the Court wasn't enforceable. There was no choice but to accept the buyout from Twentieth Century Fox's legal battalions and cancel the run. What finally crushed the exhausted Devine, however, was the betrayal felt by his abandoned playwright. "It was hideous to witness his agony at being accused of treachery by one of his most loved writers," Osborne wrote. "The rancour between them would last forever."

Devine was ordered to bed at La Beaumette by the local doctor and put under heavy sedation for ten days. Richardson took characteristic divide-and-rule control by barring Osborne from visiting him. ("You've got to be reasonable, Johnny. You only *upset* him.")

The situation with Rickards – Osborne wrote to Gilliatt – was full of pain and anguish, mocked by its predictability. He admitted he wasn't handling it well. ("But that *will* change.") Rickards' friend, Jane Sprague, was sulkily unsettled by all the incestuous in-fighting at the house and returned home early. Inert with strange forebodings in the soporific heat, Osborne usually dozed by the pool after his first morning cocktail and secretly scribbled his letters to Gilliatt – "It's tough writing to a critic, but then I've never been in love with one before" – or he read drowsily in the shade of the terrace as Rickards napped nearby in a bowered hammock with Henry James by her side.

The bisexual Richardson, who had recently fallen in love with his future wife, Vanessa Redgrave, after seeing her definitive Rosalind in *As You Like It*, was zooming off in his red Thunderbird for mysterious assignations on the beach at Cannes or at parties in Terence Rattigan's suite in the shimmering pink Hôtel Negresco overlooking the Bay of Angels.

After almost two weeks Osborne was suddenly shaken from his poolside torpor while reading the English newspapers Richardson brought back with him from Cannes. Fired up by reports about the frail Bertrand Russell pleading for support for the Campaign for Nuclear Disarmament, he sat down at the stone table on the terrace by the mulberry tree and wrote his infamous, "Damn you, England" letter to *Tribune*.

From then on, the South of France retreat was under siege. Reporters descended on the house. The phone rang off the hook demanding interviews. A Major Colin de Vere Gordon-Maclean, late of the Royal Artillery and veteran of the Malayan jungle, interrupted his holiday in Antibes to protest personally to Osborne. The Major managed to get into La Beaumette with a rifle under his arm, accompanied by his golden labrador, Simla. He found Rickards napping in the hammock and she pottered off to find Osborne dozing by the pool. "He's got a gun and a sweet labrador," she told him, "and he wants you to apologise to England."

"Tell him to fuck off," he replied, and to his surprise, the Major eventually did.

On 31 August, Mary Ure gave birth to a son, Colin, named after her father. Once again, La Beaumette became the target of a media frenzy. Everyone in Fleet Street knew where Osborne was. He wasn't by his wife's bedside in the Welbeck Street clinic.

"JOHN OSBORNE A SHY DAD", "OSBORNE BABY SETS A PUZZLE", went the headlines. "THE STRANGE WORLD OF JOHN OSBORNE – He stays on holiday in France as his son is born in London."

Let's see: Osborne is on a besieged holiday with his aggrieved mistress while having a passionate affair with his future third wife as the founding artistic director of the Royal Court has a nervous breakdown and his current wife gives birth to a son that isn't his. And by now, if not long ago, you will have come to the conclusion that theatre folk are very different from you and me. There's another school of thought that finds them similar, only hysterically more so. Osborne himself subscribed to the Chaos Theory of Love. That is, everything begins and ends in total chaos. It was unfortunate when his new secretary in London naively telephoned Rickards at La Beaumette to tell her the money he needed for his trip to Venice had been arranged. She guessed immediately that he was planning to join Gilliatt at the Venice Film Festival.

He left for Venice leaving her sobbing in the emptying house. "You've simply got to understand, Jocelyn, that your time is almost up," Richardson, ever the realist, told her.

"A nice little holiday?" Rickards asked me rhetorically. "It was the worst time of my life."

Why on earth did she put up with it all? "Well, I was in love," she explained. "Sap that I was."

The elderly Rickards looked suddenly vulnerable, as if even now those foolish, loving days had never been properly resolved. In an early warning sign of what would take its toll on Osborne's marriage to Gilliatt, however, his defection to Venice didn't turn out as happily as promised. What he called his "giddy, romantic lustings" for her at the Europa Hotel on the Grand Canal paled in comparison to her inflexible enthusiasm for all-day screenings.

He ended up moping about the hotel for much of the time, asleep in their bedroom or drinking alone on the terrace. "After the grapplings of a long night," he remembered sardonically, "I did not want to set out before breakfast to watch ideological dramas about peasant passions among Romanian villagers at the turn of the century or Kurosawa's latest."

When he returned to the South of France, Rickards was there to dutifully meet him at Nice airport. He told her what a wonderful time he'd had.

Christopher Isherwood and Don Bachardy had now arrived at the house, trim and tanned from their laid-back, macrobiotic life in California. But the days at Valbonne were coming to an end. "The damp, evening chill had begun to set in, driving us inside as well as within ourselves," Osborne recorded bleakly. "It was as if each one of us wished to escape the others."

He still couldn't bring himself to confront Rickards, making himself ill with nervous apprehension. As the return to London approached, he was often curled up immobilized in their bedroom unable to face anything except the wall. "He is just a great big huge girl," Isherwood concluded in his diary. Bachardy recalled for me the lingering soap opera. "They understood each other perfectly," he said of the Osborne–Rickards affair. "He knew that she was stoically prepared to endure any humiliation as long as she didn't lose him, and she knew that her wet tears would weigh heavily on his guilty conscience."

Some work had been done during the long, clamorous holiday. It was at La Beaumette that Osborne and Richardson hatched the film version of Tom Jones in huddled conference with the recovering Devine (who would play Squire Allworthy, kindly protector to Tom), as well as with Jocelyn Herbert (who took her first film job as costume designer and colour consultant). Richardson offered Herbert a fee for Tom Jones that was the exact price of a Hampshire farmhouse she and Devine wanted to buy.

And it was at La Beaumette that the seeds of A Patriot for Me were sown when Osborne mentioned his sketchy idea for its now notorious Drag Ball scene. Isherwood described the grand drag balls he attended in Thirties

London, and Devine – who would appear in *Patriot* as the bejewelled Queen Alexandra – was no stranger to drag balls since Oxford.

On 13 September, Osborne returned to London by plane with Rickards, abandoning the Alvis like Chitty Chitty Bang Bang in a barn until someone could be found to drive it home. As they made their farewells at La Beaumette, Rickards embraced the entire Voisin family and wept, while Osborne belatedly appeared carrying a Bible.

Isherwood wrote amusingly in his diary about the biblical touch: "Under the circumstances, the effect was that of the execution of a sixteenth century martyr who goes to his death with a proud smile certain of glory."

Later that day, Osborne and Rickards were travelling by taxi from Heathrow when, approaching Lower Belgrave Street, they stopped at the lights by Chesham Place. It was an instinctive decision made before the lights changed, a mad throw of the dice. "I'm sorry, my darling. I'm going to behave rather badly again," Osborne announced shamelessly as he got out of the taxi and disappeared into Chesham Place where Gilliatt now lived.

It was the end of the affair. He moved in with Gilliatt and gave Rickards the house on Lower Belgrave Street. And that Sunday, the man who had recently damned England from his quiet retreat in the South of France made his reluctant way in the drizzle to do his bit for nuclear disarmament at the Battle of Trafalgar Square.

29

The Case of Osborne's Son

Re: Your Domestic Affairs . . . in all the circumstances of this matter,
Colin will never be told that you are his Father.

Letter from Oscar Beuselinck to Osborne, 2 August 1963

We must solve an unexpected mystery: Who is the father of Colin Osborne?
As we've seen, Osborne was convinced it was Robert Shaw.

Ure, in her turn, acted as if the child were Osborne's. Signing her High
Court affadavit for divorce as "Mary Osborne", her sworn testimony of 28
November 1961 declared that "there is one child of the family namely
Colin Murray Osborne", who was "born on the 30th day of August 1961".
In the affadavit, she sued Osborne for child support and custody.

It's possible, even so, that both sides were colluding with each other to
make the divorce easier. Forty-five years ago, divorce was far more complex
than today. An amicable agreement to separate, for example, wasn't sufficient grounds to end a marriage. There had to be a guilty party.

But their divorce wasn't amicable. The proceedings were bitterly hostile,
with each side digging up dirt on the other. Ure had hired private detec-
tives to snoop on Osborne. In a letter to Harry Saltzman, he described the
divorce as "a very squalid brawl" with his now vengeful wife "bent on getting
all she can". There was a reason, then, for him not to cooperate. She's
hinted that Shaw is the real father (the letter left open on the bedside
table), and now she's suing him for years of child support.

Yet throughout the divorce, Osborne never disputed the claim that he
was the father of the child. Playing an uncharacteristic role, he's the dog
that doesn't bark.

After the divorce, Ure quickly married Shaw. They then legally adopted
Colin. In the solicitors' correspondence, however, Osborne treated the child
as his own son. During the adoption process, he even insisted on provi-
sions for Colin's future education and upbringing. "I do not intend to be

270

fobbed off with intransigence," Osborne complained to his lawyer, "and if I get no satisfactory response to this vital question of the child's future, I shall not sign any documents."

A slightly sarcastic Oscar Beuselinck then wrote to Ure's solicitor, "What is proposed as to the child's schooling and education, if any?"

Laszlo Gombos, the Hungarian-born senior partner of the firm of Theodore Goddard & Co. of Lincoln's Inn, replied, "As a matter of courtesy, we can tell you that it is not intended that the child should be brought up according to any particular religion but in view of the fact that he will be sent to Eton or some other leading English public school, he is almost certain to get a good grounding in religious knowledge . . ."

Beuselinck later informed Osborne: "I have today received a telephone confirmation from Mr Gombos of Messrs Theodore Goddard & Co. that in all the circumstances of this matter Colin will never be told that you are his Father."

The smoking gun appears to be in that letter alone. The case is worth re-opening, but let me add that, whatever the letters and documents might say, I think Shaw was the father. Proving it is the story that follows.

We've seen how Ure was eager to have children, carefully planning in advance the best times to conceive from the start of her marriage to Osborne. But they repeatedly failed to conceive and the marriage fell apart.

Shaw's biographer and former agent, John French, defined Shaw as "philoprogenitive" (a word he borrowed from Penelope Mortimer's novel, *The Pumpkin Eater*). It means obsessional about having babies.

When Shaw's affair with Ure began, he was already the father of three children by his first wife, actress Jennifer Shaw. He would have ten children in all, four by his wife, four more by Ure (if we include Colin), one more by Ure's nanny, and a tenth who was adopted. "Shaw didn't have a manhood unless he had children," his agent told me. "It's as simple as that."

Two weeks after he married Ure on 13 April 1963, she gave birth to her second child.

Why, then, did Osborne go along with being named the father of Colin? My hunch is that whatever the ill feeling during the divorce, he took the most expedient route in order re-marry. The principle involved here isn't the paternity of the child, but the practicalities of the divorce. He knew he wasn't the father. He didn't care about the financial cost. His motive was to get the divorce and marry Gilliatt.

They were married on 25 May 1963 (six weeks after Ure married Shaw). There's no evidence that Osborne took a blood test. A DNA test didn't exist in the early 1960s. Blood tests were quite common and inconclusive. They could prove a negative – who wasn't the father (as opposed to who was). But Osborne believed all along that it was Shaw. Nowhere in the correspondence does he refer to Colin as "my child" or "our child". The divorce proceedings were already bitterly contested. Questioning the child's paternity – and his wife's sworn testimony – would have added more fuel to the fire and seriously jeopardize the passage of the divorce.

Also remember that Osborne's lawyer, Beuselinck, was known for his backstage wheeling and dealing. "Leave it to me, son," I hear him saying.

Ure's motive for insisting Osborne was Colin's father is more transparent. It was still a severe social stigma for a child to be born out of wedlock. We're on the cusp of the Swinging Sixties. But the Sixties didn't really happen until the Seventies. A "love child" between showbiz figures wasn't yet the acceptable free-loving fashion.

It was a curiosity of verbal abuse of the era that an army officer could call a recruit any foul and obscene name – except a bastard. (Since more than a few recruits *were* bastards, the abuse was considered too close to the bone.) "This is what it was like then," explained a friend of Ure's, the playwright and former literary manager of the Court, Donald Howarth. "'Decent' people didn't have illegitimate children. They didn't have bastards."

In a stunning twist, Howarth tried to save the reputation of the pregnant Ure when he blundered quixotically into the drama to propose marriage to her. He was the last to know about Shaw, apparently. It was also no secret that Howarth was gay. "Ludicrous, isn't it?" this eccentric, good-natured man said to me, and began to laugh. But the knight in shining armour was in earnest. "I wasn't pretending we were going to have a perfect marriage. It was to save her from becoming a single parent with an illegitimate child. All I knew was that she was getting a divorce and she was distraught. God knows what she really thought when I proposed to her."

What did she say to him? I asked. "She said, 'It wouldn't work, Don.'"

But legally, the child known as "Colin Osborne" *was* legitimate. Ure was ensuring the rights of the child by insisting that Osborne was the father. (And a guilt-ridden Osborne could have been doing the decent thing by going along with it.) According to the 1959 Legitimacy Act, a child born out of wedlock had no legal rights and, crucially, no rights of inheritance. A child could be legitimized, however, if the mother subsequently married the biological father – in this case, Shaw. But how certain was Ure that he would marry her? She therefore hedged her bets, pretended Osborne was the father and ensured the rights of the child.

Ure was playing a manipulative, precarious game. Shaw's truculence aside, there's every reason why she couldn't be certain what he would do. His wife, Jennifer Shaw, was also pregnant. The philoprogenetive Shaw had excelled himself. Both his wife and Ure were pregnant simultaneously.

Meanwhile, Shaw was boasting around town that he was the father of Mary's unborn child. Well, he would. According to his agent, when asked what he intended to do, he replied, "I'll go to the one who gives me the boy!"

Shaw's three children by his wife had all been girls.

Ure's closest friend, the actress Tarn Bassett, told me that Ure confided to her that Shaw was the father and she confirmed that Ure's future with him revolved loopily around gender. "He was absolutely potty about having a boy," she explained. It's why Ure was so distraught during her pregnancy. If she gave birth to a girl, the game was over.

Just over a month after Colin was born, Mrs Shaw gave birth at Charing Cross Hospital on 4 October 1961. Ure was with Tarn Bassett at her Glebe Place home that day. "The telephone rang with the news that Jennifer had given birth to a baby girl," Bassett, who took the call, remembered. "Mary was coming down the staircase and as I began to tell her she said, 'What was it?' A girl. I told her it was a girl, and she fainted. She just crumpled."

It was still uncertain, however, whether Shaw would leave his wife. Bassett knew from Mary Ure that she was "battling like hell to keep him". From everything we've learned, Shaw would have been pleased to have both his wife and lover clinging to his shirt tails. The narcissist in him encouraged melodrama.

Ten days after Jennifer gave birth – 14 October 1961 – Ure flew to Philadelphia with her baby boy, accompanied by a nanny from Orkney. Travelling under an assumed name, "Mrs Fisher", she was nevertheless besieged by reporters at the airport. Asked why she was visiting America, she replied "For a rest." Shaw had just opened in Harold Pinter's *The Homecoming* on Broadway.

The press could only hint at what was going on. ("OSBORNE BABY SETS PUZZLE", "JOHN OSBORNE THE SHY DAD".) If any newspaper had risked naming Shaw as the father of Colin and been proved wrong, the damages from the subsequent lawsuit would have been colossal.

Refusing to say whether she would be meeting Shaw, Ure checked into a Philadelphia hotel. Two hours later, she left in a chauffeur-driven limo for New York. The nanny followed later with the baby.

According to Noel Davis – a close friend of both Shaw and Ure – "Robert

Shaw liked to play practical jokes on the press." Davis, a sometime actor who became a well-known casting director, took on the role of a lifetime in New York. He pretended to be Colin's father.

While Ure was sequestered in Shaw's apartment on Central Park West, he played an American dad proudly taking his baby for a stroll in its pram through the park. "I was a dresser on *My Fair Lady* at the time," said Davis, an amusing man who was born in Liverpool. "I'd take Colin for walkies and change his nappies and each day I wasn't detected was a little triumph."

11 November 1961: Dr Roger Gilliatt files petition for divorce citing John Osborne.

18 November: Osborne best man at Oscar Beuselinck's third wedding.

28 November: Ure responds to Osborne's divorce petition citing Shaw, and cross-petitions citing Osborne as an adulterer with three women (Brandt, Rickards and Gilliatt).

15 March 1963, Osborne and Ure divorced.

"Re: Your Matrimonial Affairs," Beuselinck wrote to his client when the divorce came through. "You are now a free man." He was "at liberty" to marry Penelope Gilliatt, he added, if he could afford it.

In fact, Beuselinck had negotiated a shrewd financial settlement with Ure's solicitor. Her petition for child support was withdrawn – leaving Osborne responsible only for her legal costs. The costs were high, but Beuselinck strongly advised against disputing them. Get the divorce *done*. There had been a change of heart. Ure no longer needed a financial safety net. Shaw was going to marry her.

Three months after the marriage, Shaw quietly adopted the two-year-old Colin Osborne at Amersham County Court in July 1963. In effect, he adopted his own son.

Why did Osborne behave as if he were the father during the adoption process by insisting on guarantees about the boy's upbringing and education? ("I will not be fobbed off by instransigence . . .") Tired of his tactical role, bored with not barking, he was needling the obnoxious Shaw. He was having a last laugh by taunting the newlyweds as the legal charade drew to a close.

Why, then, did Beuselinck tell Osborne "that in all the circumstances of this matter Colin will never be told that you are his Father"? It couldn't be clearer now. He was referring to Osborne as the *legal* father. In the convoluted courtesies of lawyerspeak, Beuselinck was cautiously setting down for the record what he knew about "the tender circumstances" of the case. "Colin will therefore feel, perhaps not without some justification, that Robert Shaw is and always has been his Father."

*

There's a coda.

When, at fifty-one, Shaw died suddenly of a heart attack, Osborne was living in Kent with his fifth wife, Helen. She knew something of the history of the adoption and she was curious. Colin Shaw was then seventeen. Might this be the time to meet him? she asked her husband. But he dismissed the idea.

Her unspoken question was answered for us by Shaw's agent, John French, who last saw Colin when he was in his twenties. "He's the spitting image of Robert Shaw," he explained. "They all look like Shaw, all his boys — exactly the same."

"It's an unmistakable resemblance," Noel Davis confirmed. He watched Colin grow up. "Sweet boy," he said.

30

Spiritual Longing

Crush out the worminess in me, stamp on me.

Martin Luther, *Luther*

Osborne's remarkable choice of Martin Luther for his next play proves at least that an artist's imagination has little or nothing to do with the life he's living. Here was the monkey back in the Osborne machine, his love life in chaos, his future shakily uncertain, and what he's actually brooding about is the ecstatic founder of Protestantism who defied Rome by institutionalizing doubt.

ACT ONE
Scene One

The cloister Chapel of the Eremites of St Augustine, Erfurt, Thuringia, 1506.
MARTIN *is being received into the Order. He is kneeling in front of the*
PRIOR *in the presence of the assembled convent.*

PRIOR: Now you must choose one of two ways: either leave us now, or give up this world, and consecrate and devote yourself entirely to God . . .

When George Devine read that opening page in his backstage warren at the top of the stairs of the Royal Court, his heart must have jumped. Three pages later, there are monks at prayer and then, as they eat in silence at a refectory table, one of the Brothers reads from a lectern about spiritual hunger and penitence.

> "What are the tools of Good Works?
> First, to love Lord God with all one's heart,
> All one's soul, and all one's strength . . .
> Not to yield to anger

Not to nurse a grudge
Not to make a feigned peace
To fear the Day of Judgement
To dread Hell
    To desire eternal life with all your spiritual longing . . ."

Osborne had made the imaginative leap that George Steiner admired him for. He had gone from the parochial domestic world of claustrophobic bedsits and seedy music halls to the public arena of cathedral splendour and world history. After the miserable debacle of *Slickey*, Devine's relief over *Luther* was palpable. When he finished reading the script, he hurried to meet Osborne, greeting him in the street with his arms held triumphantly aloft. "By God, boysie," he cried. "You've done it! You've done it again!"

"I never saw him so thoroughly justified and joyful," Osborne wrote, "like a man acquitted by a torn jury."

Devine excitedly believed the play might save the Court from its usual hovering bankruptcy, and he had a young magnetic actor to shine in the lead – Albert Finney, who even resembled Cranach's bullish, earthy etchings of Luther. His secular prayers would be answered: *Luther*, directed by Tony Richardson, transferred to the Phoenix Theatre in the West End on 5 September 1961, and subsequently to the St James on Broadway.

Osborne's battered reputation was redeemed by a history play forged from Luther's burning pulpit oratory. (Luther's *Works* were in his library at The Hurst.) There's the still shocking swipe at Pope Leo X as "an over-indulged jakes' attendant to Satan himself, a glittering worm in excrement", the "latrine called Rome", the scorching visions of the guilt-ridden, swooning Luther "gorged by God" to the marrow of his bones. "I am a worm and no man, a byword and a laughing stock. Crush out the worminess in me, stamp on me," the self-lacerating monk confesses prostrate before the Cross. "I am alone. I am alone, and against myself."

We are unprepared for Osborne's astonishing turn to Luther, let alone to God. There's almost no evidence of religious faith in his background. Grandma Osborne with her austere, watery smile was a Welsh Anglican, but she was a non-churchgoer. His genteel Grandma Grove was darkly rumoured to be the daughter of a Wesleyan minister, but she never attended church either. His long-suffering, pampered Aunt Queenie was pious High Church and a cream-coloured crucifix hung over her bed, but the suspicion was that it was for show. His mother never went to church at all and his revered father wouldn't let a clergyman near him when he lay dying in agony.

Osborne's only contact with the Church took place opportunistically during childhood when he lived with his mother in Ewell Village and joined the parish choir because it paid one and sixpence a week (plus funeral and wedding fees). He refused confirmation at boarding school and loathed the hectoring school chaplain. As a teenager, he pronounced himself a fierce atheist who read the *Freethinker*.

He thought like a sinner, yet he could write like a believer. Osborne's notebooks from his early twenties to the end of his life reveal a man tormented by suffocating guilt and fear. There had always been flashes of lightning that signalled a Christian conscience.

He was a Lutheran hammer of Church cant in his first, zealous public statements. "There has never been one outstanding moral issue on which the Church has taken a firm, unequivocal stand for simple social decency, let alone for the Gospel," he wrote in the 1957 "Declaration". He compared the C of E to sleazy hucksters and door-to-door salesmen. "The Church hawks around its Jesus Figure like a vacuum cleaner" while God was sold out to the "national swill" of worshipping Royalty.

In his "Letter to My Fellow Countrymen", his parting words of damnation to the indicted politicians who risk blowing up the world were: "If you were offered the heart of Jesus Christ, your Lord and your Saviour – though not mine, alas – you'd sniff at it like sour offal."

His early play, *Epitaph for George Dillon*, took aim at righteous godliness, *Look Back* sniped at a hypocritical clergy, *Slickey* lampooned a corrupt clergy. In the closing scene of *The Entertainer*, Archie Rice's daughter with a social conscience, Jean, asks her uncaring, smugly middle-class fiancé whether he'd ever got out of a train at some godforsaken northern industrial town, gone down a street, and looked around him at the chemical works on one side and the railway goods yard on the other.

"Some kids are playing in the street," Jean goes on, "and you walk up to some woman standing on her doorstep. It isn't a doorstep really because you can walk straight from the street into her front room. What can you say to her? What real piece of information, what message can you give to her? Do you say: 'Madam, d'you know that Jesus died on the Cross for you?'"

When *Luther* first opened, the admiring Tynan wrote that it was asked on all sides why Osborne should want to write about the founder of Protestantism. A play about the tormented Luther was the last thing anyone expected from him. But to greater and lesser degrees, the inner life of every dramatist is revealed in his work and Osborne's best plays poured out of his gut as the notoriously constipated Luther crapped out revelation from his bowels.

Alan Bates – the original Cliff in *Look Back* and a superb Redl in the 1983 revival of *A Patriot for Me* – met Osborne occasionally over many years, and long before his untimely death in December 2003, told me how he once said to him, "I love you, John, but I don't really know you." At which Osborne looked crestfallen. "But you do know me," he insisted. "You know my plays."

Unusually, Osborne prepared himself to write *Luther* as if in training. He had met the future bishop Trevor Huddleston with Devine, and the gaunt, saintly looks of the turbulent priest reminded him of Samuel Beckett. Huddleston was a former Novice Master at Mirfield, the Anglican monastic community in West Yorkshire, and he suggested Osborne might care to stay there. "Take ye heed, watch ye all and pray, for ye know not when the time is . . ."

Osborne, the volunteer penitent, typically described other Mirfield pilgrims during his stay there as kitschy incense-queens and Mary-fetishists laden with liturgical campery who were affectionately known as Walsingham Matildas. His own pleasant week in retreat was spent mostly in alien silence – a silence, he observed, "broken by the sounds of sandalled feet on stone, utensils on wood, and the single bell ringing the offices of prime, terce, sext, none and compline. It was as bracing as the view from my small window."

He also wrote his first television play, whose subject was religious heresy – a dress rehearsal for *Luther*. Broadcast by the BBC and starring Richard Burton, *A Subject of Scandal and Concern* was based on the true story of George Holyoake, a stammering noncomformist and young teacher who, in 1842, was the last man jailed for blasphemy in Britain. Osborne looked down on TV playwrights as "the pavement artists of drama", and this rough sketch for *Luther* has a number of obvious flaws. But the dissenting atheist Holyoake has this in common with the racked believer Luther: both men stand alone and out-of-step with society, and each is utterly incapable of compromise.

Tynan, among many others, claimed that Osborne chose the epic subject of the life and suffering of Luther because he identified with the stubborn working-class rebel and uncompromising advocate for individual conscience. But the popular image of Luther as Christianity's raging AYM – the monkish "malcontent" who defied the Establishment – fits too neatly. (Though Luther, like Osborne, was wrongly hailed as an apostle of social revolution.) Osborne's first impulse to write the play was ignited by something unknown to all but himself. He connected to Luther's anguished soul – to his chronic guilt, physical ruin and self-abasement, to his crucifying doubt and yearning for release.

It counts for little that he now possessed the outer trappings of easeful success or that he had grown handsome. Osborne suffered continually from body rashes, thudding headaches and insomnia. His life would always be governed by wormy self-disgust and unconquerable, clenched fear. "It numbs me, it sterilizes me," he confided to his notebook, "and I am empty, dumb and ignorant and afraid."

The mortal hurt Osborne was born into, the unhealed, unlocked, mysterious *wound* that remained buried in him, would never be made good. The notebooks reveal the tormented playwright in his depression without purpose or identity, empty and cursed. ("The mark is on me!") His despair was like a perverse badge of honour, the price to be paid for the hurt and confusion of being alive. His antagonists were the confident, stylish *copers*, the undamaged, the ones with the answers, the *certain*.

We forget, perhaps, the curse of Job on his miserable, spindly childhood – a childhood lost, never innocent – and the scars left by the hovering death sentence of tuberculosis, the curse of unsightly boils and blisters, terror of crowds, bed-wetting and fainting fits, or the lonely bedridden year with rheumatic fever relieved only by outings in a battered old wheelchair when his mother left him in the street like discarded litter.

"I lost the body of a child, a child's body, the eyes of a child; and at the first sound of my own childish voice," a haggard Luther confesses in the play. "I lost the body of a child; and I was afraid, and I went back to find it. But I am still afraid! I'm afraid . . ."

Osborne resisted psychiatry, believing the quick of him would be traduced and tamed by analysis. Yet *Luther* was influenced by Dr Eric H. Erikson's 1958 psychoanalytic study, *Young Man Luther* (George Goetschius introduced the book to Osborne). Erikson argues that the chronic state of Luther's bowels – "blocked up like an old crypt", as Osborne vividly describes them – explains all sorts of things about his obsessive inhibitions. Osborne portrays Luther memorably in the sinewy language of blood and bone and crap as if doubt itself had to be flushed out of his tormented body, as if the body disgusted itself aching to burn and disintegrate and be cleansed. But this isn't a psychological drama. It's a history play about feverish doubt, faith and religious experience.

Tynan, the Holyoake atheist, insisted *Luther* was influenced by Brecht's *Galileo*, but it was Hobson, the Christian believer, who realized that the last redemptive words left in the audience's mind by the play belong to

Christ. "A little while and ye shall see not me, and again a little while and ye shall see me." If *Luther* is a Brechtian play, it's a poor play. There's no Marxist political content (only a belated, splodgy summary of the Peasants' Revolt offered by an all-purpose Knight). Its episodic tableaux are obviously influenced by Brecht, but the play itself is closer to those popular plays about martyred rebels – Jean Anouilh's 1959 *Becket* or Robert Bolt's 1960 *A Man for All Seasons*. What sets it dramatically apart from them is its extraordinary scalding fervour, its torment and radical despair.

Luther is a drama about the struggle to believe before the blood of the Cross, and it prescribes Osborne's first, tentative steps toward faith and a way out of the chaos. "Oh, Lord, help thou my unbelief!" In the severe words of the play's powerful theologian, Cardinal Cajetan, the terrified Luther is like "an animal trapped to the bone with doubt". Cajetan is a departure for Osborne – a strong advocate for another point of view, a Shavian argument for papal supremacy. "You're not a good old revolutionary, my son," the wise Cardinal tells Luther. "You're just a common rebel, a very different animal. You don't fight the Pope because he's too big, but because for your needs he isn't big enough."

The play's corrupt Dominican friar and preacher, Johann Tetzel, is its ecclesiastical Archie Rice, a shameless Church huckster selling indulgences like bad jokes to gullible fools – "shells for shells, empty things for empty men." A Doomsday scenario permeates the play that was written in the nuclear age. "The Last Judgement isn't to come," Luther warns, but the voice is Osborne's. "It's here and now."

It was no coincidence that in the orginal Royal Court production, George Devine played the role of Staupitz, the kindly, astringent father figure to Luther. Osborne wrote touchingly that he and Devine often walked together in Sloane Square as the Vicar-General of the Augustan Order and Luther stroll in the play arm-in-arm around the garden of the Eremite Cloister in Wittenberg. The exasperated Staupitz knew his man! "I've never had any patience with all your mortifications," he tells his young protégé. "All these trials and tribulations you go through, they're meat and drink to you."

And other echoes of Osborne's life resonate throughout the play. "It was always *you* I wanted," Luther confides to his own father, an unreachable man. "I wanted your love more than anyone's, and if anyone was to hold me, I wanted it to be you."

History tells us that the Cistercian nun, Katharina von Bora, was converted to Luther's doctrines and left her convent to marry him in 1525. And so the play's last scene reveals Luther, the former celibate monk and common rebel, now settled into contented family life and tired middle-age, a father himself.

"Well, *you've* never been so well looked after," his loved, elderly visitor, Staupitz, says to him fondly.

"It's a shame everyone can't marry a nun," Luther replies. "They're fine cooks, thrifty housekeepers, and splendid mothers. Seems to me there are three ways out of despair. One is faith in Christ, the second is to become enraged by the world and make its nose bleed. And the third is the love of a good woman."

31

Third Marriage

Johnny will be forever.
Penelope Gilliatt, c.1964

With Osborne's marriage to Penelope Gilliatt he would enter the most creative period of his life in what appeared to be the perfect harmony of love in a golden bowl. His itinerant, lurching life adapted well to the securely domestic and the birth of a daughter would confirm his happiness. His successful, stylish wife remained besotted with him, he was recognized as England's leading playwright, and great wealth would come his way as if both their lives were blessed. And yet within three years, everything shattered.

Flawed relationships contain laws unto themselves, but not even a perfectionist like Gilliatt could detect the cracks beneath the surface of her own marriage. Osborne was an impulsive lover and any doubts he had were always submerged by his infatuation. But Gilliatt lived for perfection in everything she did and, for her, no marriage could have been more complete than this.

Christmas 1964
For my beloved husband whom I love with all my heart. Thank you for what I know even at the time has been the best, happiest, most exciting year I've ever had. More soon my darling, it will never end. The sight of you touches me always.

She was one of the few people to call him "Johnny". He called her Pen, Nell, or Lady P, sometimes addressing letters to her jokily as "Lady Penelope" with a sketched crown attached. They nicknamed each other "Banks" (though why "Banks" remains a mystery). His loving notes at Christmas and birthdays were usually attached to a gift from Cartier.

December 13 '63

Thank you Banks for my wonderful birthday. I love you so very dearly. You will never know.

John (34 years, one day, six and a half hours approx British G.M.T.)

New Year '63

Darling Banks,

With all my love for the *most* super, clever, funny girl, for 1963, for a super 1964.

Always, J.

Penelope Ann Douglass Conner was the upper middle-class daughter of a Court Sessions judge who took a first at Oxford and a socialist mother who came from a wealthy shipping family. She had always been dauntingly bright. Even as a child she possessed a prodigious memory and could spout Latin and Greek. Her fascination with the rigours of language and arcane meanings eventually irritated Osborne as a form of manic pedantry, though her passion for words was leavened by English whimsy and an astringent wit. It was Gilliatt who wrote famously, "One of the characteristic sounds of the English Sunday is Harold Hobson barking up the wrong tree."

Her parents divorced and she was partly educated in America where her stepfather became spokesman for the Secretary General of the United Nations. She attended exclusive Bennington College in Vermont and studied music at Juilliard in New York, and she might have become a concert pianist. (One of Osborne's gifts to her was a harpsichord.) Her younger sister, the well-known sculptor, Angela Conner, looked so much like her they were often taken as red-headed twins. They were close and Angela looked up to her. When she opened a battered old suitcase to show me the letters her sister had long ago kept from Osborne, she burst into inconsolable tears. "I still love her, you see," she said helplessly.

Conner enjoyed Osborne's company and didn't pretend to understand the few times she witnessed his gratuitous cruelty. She was to give me a number of important insights into her sister. She believed that she never recovered from the break-up of the marriage and loved Osborne until she died. Although Penelope appeared to be a confident, glamorous woman, she was anorexic and had been so since Bennington. A bright, restless student, she never took a degree. She was someone who strived for excellence, but feared never attaining it. "It could be self-destructive," her sister pointed out regretfully. "She always wanted the impossible."

The shrewd American magazine editor Ben Sonnenberg wrote of her, "The great thing about her work, all of it, and about her life, too, is the moving gravity of her feeling for levity." *Festivity*, he noted, was among her favourite words. Lord Snowdon, who knew her well (and worked with her a lot in her early days at *Vogue*), described her as a delightful "mixture of heavy intellectual and juvenile punning, of serious and silly". Some saw her as melodramatic and gushing – an impression bolstered by her vivid enthusiasm and concern. It was unkindly said of her that "Penelope always greets you as if you had suffered a grievous loss." Her friend Kathleen Tynan referred to her "importunate heart". David Astor, the legendary editor of the *Observer*, remembered her as one of his star writers "who was ambitious and emotionally fragile – a butterfly".

She was a workaholic who celebrated the celebrated. Her generous dining-room table was handed on to her sister and round its edges is this brass inscription: "Here once sat together writers Sam Beckett, Harold Pinter, John Osborne and Penelope Gilliatt to whom the table belonged, and Angela Conner Bulmer, Sculptor."

She became film reviewer for the *Observer* and subsequently for *The New Yorker* (alternating with Pauline Kael), yet her sister told me she had passionately wanted to be a drama critic since about the age of ten. Gilliatt reviewed *Luther* for Jocelyn Stephen's *Queen* magazine. ("Written in a language swung like a crowbar, this is the most eloquent and rigorous play that John Osborne has written.") When she later eloped with Osborne, the media frenzy provoked her best article – an onslaught for *Queen* entitled "The Friendless Ones" on the morals of the gossip columnists of the day. It proved more effective than *The World of Paul Slickey*. She was hired by the *Observer* on the strength of it.

The offices of the *Observer* near Fleet Street were then home to a number of gifted individualists and eccentrics lurching about the place after long lunches when Gilliatt swept in one day with news of her forthcoming marriage. Her fiery red hair and flowing dresses tended to announce her. "Guess who I'm going to marry," she said happily to her friend, Terence Kilmartin, the literary editor. Aware of her recent fling with the unreliable Tynan, he was just about to say, "Don't!" when she told him, "It's John Osborne!"

At work in the office next door was the young arts editor of the *Observer*, Helen Dawson, who would become Osborne's fifth wife. She knew Gilliatt mostly through her copy. "Proofs came first," she explained about Gilliatt's obsessive way with work in those pre-computer days. "Penelope agonized over all her reviews. I remember her ringing up with re-writes on the Saturday morning of her *wedding*. Now there's dedication for you."

She also visited Astor that day to tell him the good news. A powerful figure who possessed the unique gift of seeming to be both diffident and stubborn simultaneously, he was fond of her. "I'm going to marry a wonderful man," Gilliatt announced excitedly. "It's John!"

The embarrassed Astor politely enquired, "John who?"

"John Osborne!"

"Don't," he thought to himself as he offered hearty congratulations.

They were married on 25 May 1963, at Hailsham Registry Office, Sussex. She was thirty-one, and he was thirty-three. Tony Richardson was best man (again), Angela Conner was a witness. The reception was held in the garden of Osborne's first country house, The Old Water Mill, in Hellingly, near Hailsham, about sixty miles from London. The low beamed main house was set in several acres enclosed by two tributaries of the River Cuckmere. The idyllic picture on a summer day was like stepping into a Monet painting. A cluster of outbuildings included a cottage, a mill recorded in the Domesday Book and a big, unused granary. Gilliatt worked in the granary, and Osborne in the mill.

When he bought the property, it was an abandoned local tea garden that his ex-lover, Jocelyn Rickards, had found to convert and live in with him. (She never did.) But when Osborne had first stayed there with Gilliatt, there was uproar. The early Sixties remained socially conservative: they were both still married. The upright local citizens of Hailsham demonstrated against the lovers from the front gate of The Old Water Mill.

"DAMN YOU OSBORNE", their placards read. "WE WANT MARY URE." "HELLINGLY ANGRY OLD MEN OBJECT." "It's this damn you, England thing which has got to all our gullets," snuff-taking Mr Fred Livingstone was reported complaining with his indignant wife, Florence, by his side. But some weren't so concerned about the goings-on at the mill. Mr C.T. Freeman explained that he preferred to have John Osborne as a neighbour than a tea garden, and the Vicar of Hellingly said, "I don't single him out as a VIP. I don't know anything about the gent."

In a private letter of 26 September 1961, to William Hardcastle, editor of the *Daily Mail*, J.B. Priestley protested "as one of your regular readers" about the new cult of celebrity and the *Mail*'s pictures of Osborne with Mrs Gilliatt.

If they are merely friends, then I do not know why we are supposed to be interested. If they are more than friends, then why cannot they be left alone? After all, we do not have the private lives of politicians and tycoons served up in this fashion . . .

*

Happy is the serious playwright who sits down to write unserious plays. In July 1962, Osborne's double bill, the satirical *Blood of the Bambergs* and the sexual *Under Plain Cover*, opened at the Court. They were both light comedies about English hypocrisy, and Gilliatt, for one, thought he should have written something weightier. ("You've got it *in* you, darling.")

The first of the two, a blatant send-up of mass hysteria surrounding royal weddings, was prompted by the marriage of Princess Margaret to Antony Armstrong-Jones (and spiced with Gilliatt's backstage gossip). Directed by John Dexter, with Alan Bennett as the Archbishop of Canterbury, it was written at a time when royalty was still treated with hushed, fawning reverence and the only interest in the play today is how Osborne got away with it. Satire of the monarchy was still banned from the English stage lest it incite revolution. But for once, Osborne outfoxed the Lord Chamberlain.

Blood of the Bambergs was a modern version of the Anthony Hope classic, *The Prisoner of Zenda*. One of the Lord Chamberlain's vigilant colonels, St Vincent Troubridge, recognized "the devilish cleverness of this horrid play." "If a licence is refused," he had to concede, "this can at once be presented as a ridiculous banning of the old *Prisoner of Zenda* story sixty years later."

The second half of the bill, *Under Plain Cover*, is much more interesting. It marked the directorial debut of Jonathan Miller and the hour-long play represented a first in post-war British theatre by championing incest and sadomasochism.

Though bondage in book-lined dungeons is nothing new to the British, Osborne took the sexual taboos further. It's a miracle the play passed the censor. "I am sure that a lot of people will swoon with delight at this latest Osborne effluent," pronounced the Lord Chamberlain's comptroller, Sir Norman Gwatkin. "I should think the morals of anyone who pretends to understand what the play is all about will already be beyond contamination; and the remainder will ride the storm unsullied."

Under Plain Cover is about Tim and Jenny, a happily married, ordinary, suburban couple with two little babies, who enjoy fetishistic games of dressing up. Their days are filled contentedly with playing doctor and nurse, mail-order bride and groom, dominating employer and flighty housemaid. ("Any more talk like that and you could find yourself in serious trouble. And you don't want that, do you?" "Oh, no, sir . . .") Only later do we learn that the role-swapping husband and wife are brother and sister.

Until the play drifts uneasily into Osborne's ritual slam at an intrusive, venal press, it raises questions about public morality and privacy – or the right to happiness behind closed doors. But at centre, it's a harmless entertainment that was taken far too seriously by that devotee of spanking,

JOHN OSBORNE

Kenneth Tynan, and if it brought Genet into England, as Harold Hobson claimed, Osborne was more of a wholesome, English public school version lingering over the allure of lingerie.

He'd always been drawn to what he called "the silky, defiant recesses" of desire since his parched schooldays. *Under Plain Cover* cannot be serious. It's basically a prolongued panegyric to women's underwear. There are some forty-five references to the elaborate merits of knicker, panty, bloomer, brief, Directoire, gusset and thread, quality interlock, elastic or open top, school-girl blue, camiknicker and *cornet du bal*. There's the Blakean "The Vision of Knickers that thou dost see, is my Vision's Greatest Enemy." Or as Tim recites lustily to Jenny in the play:

> Knickers, knickers, these are the things to 'ave,
> You puts them on in the bedroom,
> You takes them off in the lav.

Genet was never like this. But then, Genet wasn't raised on English schoolboy humour. Studious scholars of the Osborne oeuvre will note, however, the symbolic significance of women's underwear in his contin-uing nostalgia for a bygone era with its "heavy whisper of descending pink silk", versus his regret at the uncompromising new age of pragmatic moder-nity with its "hard-faced, unembarrassed, unwelcoming nylon".

There's a whispery link between the play and Osborne's private life. During weekend house parties at Hellingly, everyone dressed up in various outfits after lunch. Osborne sometimes appeared sheepishly as a Grenadier Guard and Gilliatt as a bride in white or a nurse. There were lots of outfits to choose from – doctors and bishops, schoolgirls and maids, Queen Victoria and Prince Albert. Renowned directors took turns dressing up as Mary McCarthy. Angela Conner played a Pierrot. But this legacy from the charades of grand country estates was no fetishistic *Under Plain Cover*. Gilliatt's mother was an occasional weekend guest at Hellingly. "She couldn't have been more *proper*," said Angela Conner. "The dressing up was just enormous fun." Others confirmed its innocence, I'm afraid.

The fraternal partnership of Osborne and Richardson had the Midas touch. In the summer of 1963, Woodfall's film of *Tom Jones* was released and it made them both overnight millionaires. Osborne's financial rewards as a playwright paled in comparison. His real money came from the phenom-enal success of the film – a virtual Royal Court production on location.

Directed by Richardson (who had read the Fielding novel at Oxford), Osborne's rollicking screenplay about the bawdy adventures of foundling

Tom endures if only for what Pauline Kael described as its "great lewd eating scene". *Tom Jones* still remains one of the most successful British films ever made. Its rough, unbridled delight in its own Englishness captured the public imagination, making it *Chariots of Fire* or *Four Weddings and a Funeral* of its day.

To discover the profits of a successful movie is to be led by paranoid movie executives on a paper trail into a maze, but this much I've learned: Woodfall produced *Tom Jones* in equal partnership with its distributors, United Artists, for a modest budget of £500,000. According to Oscar Beuselinck who made the deal, when UA's representatives first saw the film, "they hated it and thought they'd lost every penny." But when it opened in London and New York, it broke box office records. The total gross profit in America alone amounts to $37.6 million.

But that figure is deceptively low by contemporary standards. If we take into account ticket-price inflation, *Tom Jones* made the equivalent of $247.7 million today (making it one of the most successful pictures of all time). Half the profits – and more from global distribution – went to Woodfall Films Ltd, jointly owned by Osborne and Richardson.

Neither man was ever "responsible" about money. They were known to be generous spendthrifts. Their deal with Albert Finney, the star of *Tom Jones*, gave him shares in the film's profits – enough to make him an overnight millionaire, too. Oscar Lewenstein, a director of Woodfall, functioned as its associate producer, and according to the miffed Beuselinck, contributed next to nothing but "received riches beyond belief". Osborne also gave George Devine a valuable share in the film. (Devine never earned more than £1,500 a year at the Court.) "It would make nothing but sense," Osborne wrote to him, persuading him to accept, "and no one need know except us."

Tom Jones was nominated for ten Academy Awards, winning for Best Picture (*Lawrence of Arabia* won the previous year), as well as for Best Director, Screenplay and Original Score. Neither Osborne nor Richardson troubled to attend the awards ceremony in Hollywood. They were *above it*. "I've had quite enough of prize-giving at *school*," said Richardson derisively. Osborne disappeared in India with Gilliatt on a tour of Rajasthan. Dame Edith Evans, who played Miss Western, the Lady Bracknell of *Tom Jones*, accepted the Oscar on his behalf.

Though Osborne preferred living at Hellingly, his wife's work took her to London and he purchased a forty-five-year lease on a four-storey town house in exclusive Belgravia at 31 Chester Square. Gilliatt's taste prevailed:

minimalist early Conran, leather and steel furniture, white upon white. Sixteen-foot high copper doors divided the living and dining rooms. They became known as "Penelope's Duomo Doors", after the Ghiberti bronzes in Florence.

John Betjeman and his lover Elizabeth Cavendish were frequent dinner guests at the house, and, like many others, she was struck by the immaculate grandeur of the place. "John lived more grandly than anyone I know," Lady Elizabeth told me at her modest Chelsea semi. (She was discounting Chatsworth, her family seat with 175 rooms. But, still.) Working-class success stories of the Sixties infiltrated the style of the ruling elites, like the young John Lennon living on an estate in Ascot, and Osborne was no different with his two luxurious homes in Belgravia and Sussex, his permanent staff, his chauffeur and live-in couple, secretary and nanny to come.

He bought a Bentley S3. Bentleys and Rolls Royces were the Volkswagens of the new celebrity class. "If you're going to behave like this," I heard Michael Caine warning a restless child in Langan's restaurant one time, "you'll just have to wait outside in the Rolls wiv the chauffeur." Some thought Gilliatt was the one who coveted the Bentley, but she drove a red MG that Osborne gave her wrapped in a ribbon as a surprise Christmas present. The flamboyant Bentley was his. "I used to know him when he had holes in his socks," sniffed the stage doorman at the Court when he saw it.

His bills and receipts from the period reveal other changes in his life – art gallery purchases, gunsmiths, riding gear (he kept horses stabled near Hellingly and rode on the Sussex Downs). There were bills from decorators, tailors and Ladbrokes. His tailor was Doug Hayward of Savile Row. "All the people the working-class boys objected to, they wanted to become," explained Hayward, a common sense man. "They started behaving like them as soon as possible."

Hayward rose to fame in the early Sixties as bespoke tailor to the newly fashionable movie stars and photographers like David Bailey, Terence Stamp, Terry Donovan and Michael Caine. His father washed buses at night for a living. "I've had to polish up my accent a bit," he told me. "Not a lot."

He first met Osborne in 1963 when he went to Hellingly to measure him for several suits. "He was too busy writing to come to London, but I was very impressed by him and I wanted to make his suits. So I said, I'll do one to start with to make sure we're happy. We chatted over lunch and champagne and I liked him a lot. John was very easy to talk to, but she was a strange person, the woman he was married to. They seemed to get on very well, though."

What was strange about her? "She had all the fears and worries of the middle class. You can't change their minds about anything."

As we talked in his Mount Street shop, he went into the back room and found a manilla envelope still on file that was filled with Osborne's measurements and the paper cut-outs of his suit patterns. The cut-outs spilled onto the table like tailor's relics – the remains of Osborne. "He liked to be noticed," Hayward went on. "And he liked unusual stuff. That's the way he wanted to see himself – not totally over the top, but near the edge. I think John would have really loved to have been a very famous star actor."

Then he told me the story of the velvet jacket. Osborne had begun to accompany his wife to the opera at Covent Garden and he noticed that several people in the audience wore velvet jackets. So he asked Hayward to make him one. But he didn't want it to look new. "I want it to look like my father gave it to me," Osborne told him.

In the refinements of class, new is parvenu. But in theatre, designers "break down" newly made costumes to make them look authentically old. So when the velvet jacket was made and the final fitting done, Doug Hayward took it home with him. "I wore it round the house and spilt spaghetti and wine and things down the lapels, and I crushed the elbows and eventually I sent the jacket over to John. He was as pleased as punch."

Osborne liked to say that he changed roles every few years, usually with each marriage. If so, what role was the chameleon playing now? Wolf in Savile Row clothes? Former Angry Young Man morphed into opera-loving Gentleman of Letters? His new life with Gilliatt at Chester Square ushered in a new "A" list cast – architect Sir Hugh Casson, Snowdon, the Oliviers, the Tynans, Leonard Bernstein, Spike Milligan, Peter Sellers and the *Observer* set. But Osborne's old friends were still part of the scene – Devine and Jocelyn Herbert, Richardson with Vanessa Redgrave, Robert Stephens and Maggie Smith, Betjeman and Cavendish, the Addisons and John Copley. Copley became Principal Resident Director of Covent Garden Opera, but Osborne had known him since he was the stage manager of *Paul Slickey*. Ex-mistress Rickards was now married to the painter Leonard Rosoman, and they were dinner guests, too.

Though there was a cook, Gilliatt sometimes liked to do the cooking herself and the results were variable. Prayers were sometimes said after meals. Rosoman remembered seeing Osborne at a Chester Square dinner smothering tomato ketchup all over his fish and when he caught his eye, Osborne blushed.

"It was a glamorous life, certainly," Cavendish remembered. "The food wasn't awfully good. But Penelope was a warm and loyal friend. She wasn't a housewife. She was a terribly insecure person. John's appeal to her was that she liked the idea of him being John Osborne. He didn't like her possessiveness, yet he seemed to need it. Chester Square was *very* unreal. It was like a stage set."

We shouldn't think of Osborne's new life as a constant social whirl, however. While his wife was preoccupied with screenings in London, his days were spent mostly in solitude at Hellingly where he could work in peace with his Great Dane, Western, curled up under his desk. "My dear George," he wrote to Devine. "Honestly, I don't want to see *anyone* at the moment except one or two people like yourself. Certainly the idea of lunch with Arnold [Wesker] makes me want to vomit. Sorry, can you say I'm dying?"

In spite of all the changes and new found wealth in his life, he had already begun writing two major plays simultaneously in an extraordinary creative burst.

6 December 1963

My dear John,
Just a note to ask if you if have any idea at all when you will have "something", as they say . . .
Best love,
G [Devine]

9 December 1963

My Dear George,
In theory, at any rate, you can have *two* for September. I was hoping you would ask.
Lots of love,
J

"Life at Hellingly took on a pattern which I had not expected," Osborne declared, complaining that he was too frequently apart from his wife. But for the moment, the way seemed smooth and gilded. She had become pregnant. He was writing well. The gods were shining on him. When he wasn't wrenching the lawyer in midlife crisis, Bill Maitland, out of *Inadmissible Evidence*, he turned to the sweep of history and the fate of the Austrian spy Alfred Redl in *A Patriot for Me*.

His wife joined him at Hellingly after screening days in London and wrote her film reviews there. His mother visited and Gilliatt made her welcome and called her "Mum". But there would always be tension between mother and son. The more Nellie Beatrice was anxious to avoid a gaffe, the more certain it was to happen. Making conversation one night over supper, she suddenly announced how difficult it was to live with theatre people.

"You have to be careful when you marry someone who works in the theatre," she warned her third daughter-in-law. "You know what they're like."

"But Johnny will be forever," Gilliatt replied, wrapping her arms around her husband. "We'll never, ever part. Will we, Johnny?"

Inadmissible Evidence

> With the first, with friendship, I hardly succeeeded at all . . . With the
> second, with love, I succeeded. I succeeded in inflicting, quite certainly
> inflicting, more pain than pleasure. I am not equal to any of it.
>
> Bill Maitland, *Inadmissible Evidence*, 1964

At over three hours in length, messy and formless and unforgiving, *Inadmissible Evidence* could have been spewed from Osborne's confessional private notebooks where the inadmissible is laid bare. No play of his is more intensely personal. Bill Maitland is Osborne's existential Everyman unravelling in the age of technological revolution and confident new possibility. He's Saul Bellow's Herzog trying to figure out his place and purpose and what it means "to be a man. In a city. In a century. In transition. In a mass. Transformed by science. Under organized power. Subject to tremendous controls. In a condition caused by mechanization. After the late failure of radical hopes."

Inadmissible is Osborne's finest and most disturbing play, and it brings to its peak the art of solitude made public onstage. "He is strongest who is most alone," is Ibsen's renowned line in *Enemy of the People*. But for Osborne, aloneness is a curse, and Maitland is another of his isolated heroes who can find no place in the system – like Luther, Archie, Redl, Dillon and Jimmy Porter, like all his embattled heroes.

This tortured play from the former apostle of disaffected youth is about a seedy lawyer in middle-aged meltdown. It is Osborne's dreamplay of grubby futility and self-loathing in the losing battle against irredeemable mediocrity. It stuns, exhausts and disgusts, forcing us to be witnesses to a man tearing up his life in a long day's journey into night. With his thudding, neurotic headaches and the pills he can never find, Maitland is sunk by the paranoid's squalid, reflexive terror of being judged and found wanting. "His own accuser, his own jailor, his own judge," as Walter Kerr said, he will be found guilty on all counts as his mind races in grasping confusion for mercy.

"I am almost forty years old, and I know I have never made a decision which I didn't either regret, or suspect was just plain commonplace or shifty or scamped and indulgent or mildly stupid and undistinguished . . . I have never been able to tell the difference between a friend or an enemy, and I have always made what seemed to me to be the most exhaustive efforts to find out. The difference. But it has never been clear to me, and there it is, the distinction, and as I have got older, and as I have worked my way up – up – to my present position. I find it even more, quite impossible and out of the question. And then, then I have always been afraid of being found out."

"I never hoped or wished to have anything more than to have the good fortune of friendship and the excitement and comfort of love and the love of women in particular. I made a set at both of them in my own way. With the first, with friendship, I hardly succeeded at all. Not really. No . . . Not at all. With the second, with love, I succeeded. I succeeded in inflicting, quite certainly inflicting, more pain than pleasure. I am not equal to any of it. But I can't escape it, I can't forget it. And I can't begin again. You see?"

It is often claimed that Osborne modelled Maitland on his own solicitor. But Oscar Beuselinck wasn't a complicated, self-hating man. Only Maitland's nudge-nudge flightiness with nubile secretaries rings a bell. "She looks as if she could do with a bit." "You could stick a bus ticket in there. What do you think, Wally?"

In fact, Maitland was suggested by an unlikely source. Osborne had read a letter to a newspaper's Agony Aunt from a distraught woman who said that her husband, a man she loved and admired, was being slowly isolated by the suspicion and dislike he aroused in other people. They seemed to recoil from his presence, and now it was happening to his children and even to his wife until everyone seemed to be turning away from him. "Bill Maitland was born," said Osborne. "It was an overpowering image of desolation."

Osborne connected to the desolation. He identified with the random hostility toward the man because he felt it. The playwright who once said mockingly of his own paranoia that he saw treachery everywhere, was on intimate terms with Bill Maitland.

"I myself am more packed with spite and twitching with revenge than anyone I know of. I actually, often, frequently, daily want to see people die for their errors. I wish to kill them myself, to throw the switch with my own fist. Fortunately, I've had no more opportunity than most men . . ."

Maitland – it's clear – isn't a *nice* man. He's ignominious and he's desperate. In his surly defiance, he excoriates the purblind masses – "the ones who go out on Bank Holidays in the car with mascots in the rear window". He loathes the demeaning mediocrity of life as much as he disgusts himself. Perhaps he sees too much – more than most of us living contentedly in denial, anyway. He wants *more*. But nothing works for him. Taxi drivers with For Hire signs laughably ignore him. He has become invisible. A non-person. Deserted by everyone – the secretaries he screws, his weaselly clerk, his loyal mistress, disinterested teenage daughter, forbearing wife, even his pathetic, frightened clients who come to him for help but in whom Maitland sees only his own pathetic reflection and dread.

Life is too much for this man who longs for some respite and saving grace in the chaos, but who "never said, he hardly ever said, he stopped saying" –

"I love you. It has to be heaved and dropped into the pool after you, a great rock of I-love-you, and then you have to duck down below the surface and bring it up, like some grasping, grateful, stupid dog."

There will always be those who don't "get" Osborne. They turn away from the smell of blood on the page. Critics such as the distinguished American, Robert Brustein, for example, treat *Inadmissible* as another Osborne monodrama lacking "discernible structure" and "coherent progression". (Rhetoric, good; plot, see teacher.) But anguished men like Maitland are not "coherent", nor howls of pain and bewilderment "structured". The dramatist who rejects the sweet geometry of the "well-made play" is not bound by rules if he believes with Yeats that all art begins "in the foul rag and bone shop of the heart".

Inadmissible is a play written from the unruly heart demanding unruly response. For Anthony Page, its original director, Osborne crossed England's boundaries with the play and joined writers like Kafka and O'Neill who found something universal out of exploring themselves unsparingly. "The play creates its own rules," he told me. "It's a dramatic poem about a man's measure – the 'quintessence of dust', the heroic aspiration, passion and fierce irony, and the guilt, weakness and shabby reality."

Written when Osborne was thirty-four, *Inadmissible* opened at the Royal

Court on 9 September 1964, to enthusiastic reviews and accolades for Nicol Williamson's magnificent, defining performance. Tony Richardson was preparing a film of Evelyn Waugh's *The Loved One* in Hollywood (where he eventually settled). Page, still in his twenties when he directed *Inadmissible*, would stage five more of Osborne's plays.

They were unable to cast Maitland until Page asked the little-known Williamson to read for it. Peter Finch, among others, turned the daunting role down. But Page had worked closely with Williamson at Dundee Rep and admired the volatile, hard-drinking Scot. The moment Williamson began his audition at the Court, they knew he was Maitland. Page remembered Osborne walking from the back of the stalls to the apron of the stage as if he were hypnotized. Terror was Williamson's keynote, yet he could mine even the humour of the man within his suffocating panic. At twenty-eight, he was much too young for the role, but it made no difference. "He is old within," said Osborne, who recognized his genius.

Williamson told this extraordinary story about a singular performance of *Inadmissible*:

At the curtain call, he went out to take his bow with the rest of the cast, but they were greeted in terrible silence. He could hear his own clomping footsteps as he walked out to the footlights, bowed awkwardly to the ghostly void and went back into the wings. Then in stunned, delayed reaction, the applause began. The stage manager motioned quickly to Williamson to go back onstage. But he refused. No one knew what had happened. But *he* knew. A little bit of theatre history had been made that night. The fall of Bill Maitland had left an audience in silent awe.

The play turned into an extraordinary prophecy for Osborne. Two years after its premiere, he cracked up like Maitland, ended his marriage to Gilliatt and was hospitalized with a nervous breakdown. His own future had been written into the fictional alchemy of *Inadmissible Evidence*.

When his wife read the script, she wrote an admiring note to him. "The play is extraordinary – very harsh, frightening, desperate. The real authentic stink of an unbearable life in your nostrils. No wonder one rears up like a horse smelling fire. In case I didn't tell you – Nell." She smelt fire and danger, but if she could have known what it portended or told her about his anguished soul she would have been very afraid.

From Gilliatt's point of view, however, the marriage was happy. She wasn't aware that in the days when she was first married to Osborne he slept with his ex-lover Rickards, but that was more of a belated farewell, a ritual full stop. Two years into the marriage, he was sleeping occasionally with his first wife, Pamela Lane. "Once again, easy slide between the sheets," he noted smugly on 3 February 1965. His feelings for Lane would never be resolved. She was his unconquerable first love and in his nostalgia for an innocent past, he was still trying to unlock her secret. It was symbolic of Lane's luck as an actress, however, that when Look Back in Anger was revived at Bromley Rep she was asked to play the part of Helena, the mistress. The director didn't think she was quite right for Jimmy Porter's wife. But Osborne could at least help Pamela Lane financially now, and he gave her a share in the profits of Inadmissible for the rest of her life.

While he complained after he married Gilliatt that he hadn't appreciated her consuming obsession with her work, there had been more than one portent even in the excitement of their first romantic days together. During their clandestine flight to Gilliatt's invented "Folkestone Film Festival", they stayed at a small, nondescript hotel in Sandgate. "Encouraged by its overbearing anonymity, we went straight up to the cold bedroom," Osborne wrote. "There was an air of practical discomfort that could only promote instant sexual revival between the sheets. The bed was our single necessity and, united in intent, we swooped into it . . ."

But they were interrupted within minutes by an asthmatic porter banging urgently on the door. There was a call from the Observer asking for Mrs Gilliatt. Osborne was surprised she had given the number of their secret hideaway to the paper, but last-minute corrections to her copy had to be made and she scrambled downstairs in bare feet and kimono to the only telephone in the place. After a while, she returned to their ardent lovemaking. But twice more the wheezing porter banged insistently on the door like the old porter in Macbeth, and the exasperated Osborne complained she sprang out of bed each time to dispute minute points of syntax and punctuation "just as our own presses had started to roll". No doubt he was exaggerating. But it was the first time Osborne had experienced coitus interruptus over a dangling participle.

Sonia McGuinness, his secretary, saw more of him on average than his wife did. McGuinness, who worked at Hellingly and then Chester Square each day, confirmed about Gilliatt that "absolutely everything revolved compulsively round her work. I think it made him feel secondary. She could never relax. She was married to the Observer."

McGuinness was the first person to read Osborne's plays as she typed them out on her old Adler. "I used to love seeing that notebook on my desk," she said, reminding me that he wrote his plays by hand. "I'd sometimes type all through the night. To see what happened."

She enjoyed the plays? "Yes, but not always. I never told him. I always said they were marvellous."

She loved working for Osborne. He was good to her, informal and unde-manding. Her husband, Mac, was a schoolteacher who worked as a script reader for Woodfall and the McGuinnesses were invited to the house parties – part of the family. Sonia was a docker's daughter and Osborne was pleased to see her dancing at one of the Chester Square parties with the Duke of Devonshire. "Docker's daughter dances with Duke," he whispered to her as they waltzed merrily by.

"Sonia darling – just to thank you for all your care and attention. Bless you. Hold the fort till I get back! Lots of love," goes one of his affectionate notes to her. "To Sonia, for knees-up in swinging Putney. With love."

He kept his writing life separate from his domestic life. McGuinness even signed all his cheques. "He was usually in bed when I arrived at 10 a.m.," she said, describing a typical day. "Then he'd emerge and have his first glass of champagne as if it were morning orange juice. Mornings were his best time. He wasn't drinking excessively then. If he were really engrossed in work, he wouldn't go out at night at all. We'd have an informal lunch together at Hellingly cooked by the housekeeper, a nice old stick named Mrs Lambert. He might have wine or beer. He liked brandy. If Penelope was there, we'd all lunch together. But she was often busy or working through lunch. John would drive me to Eastbourne and we'd have lunch there before he went back to write. He wasn't a snob. He enjoyed company and jokes and gossip and fish and chips."

His wife's tastes were more refined. She would send the staff in search of out-of-season quail. But according to McGuinness (who knew Osborne for a decade), all he really wanted was steak and kidney pud. His taste for plain food never changed. Toward the end of his life, he made a list of the comforting English grub he liked best in his notebook:

"Eels – cooked or jellied, really cold mussels, bacon sandwich, huge mush-rooms, kippers, lamb stew and bacon and beans, asparagus – tinned or fresh, bread and cheese, gherkins, cold meats, bread and butter pudding." He also listed German sausages, but only because he believed they were English at heart, like Handel.

Osborne and Gilliatt were opposites. His secretary found him easy to work for, but she sometimes found his wife's high-handedness and pride impossibly difficult to deal with. Typing out a film review for her one day, McGuinness corrected an uncharacteristic misspelling. But when Gilliatt read through her copy again, she made a scene and insisted the original spelling was correct. McGuinness, a mild and pleasant woman, mentioned that she'd checked the spelling in the dictionary before making the change. "Well, I'm sorry," Gilliatt responded, "the dictionary's *wrong*."

Writing was meticulous agony for this gifted woman, but not for Osborne. He almost never rewrote anything in his plays, while she never stopped rewriting her reviews. To fuss endlessly over a *mere* film review seemed a waste of time to him. She was a serious careerist, whereas to Osborne she was the embodiment of that fretful condition of schoolgirl ambition, a swot. But he felt threatened by her cleverness and rigour, mocking her relish for London's intellectual life as pretentious. His old rival, Professor A.J. Ayer, the pear-shaped Don Giovanni, was a former lover of Gilliatt's. But then, Ayer seems to have been a former lover of half of England.

"Ah well," Osborne wrote with a resigned sigh, looking back on his marriage to Gilliatt in his 1993 notebook (two years before his death). "The greatest shame my poor ex-wife P.G. ever sustained was when she discovered I was not an intellectual. Anyone could have told her. Like so many self-educated, clever people she was hypnotised by academic glamour. A double first was God's own Oscar."

Even her musical soirées were too precious for him. He had an abiding love for fine music. ("Something strong," goes Jimmy's line in *Look Back*, "something simple, something English" – like Vaughan Williams.) But the man who also appreciated the pubby pleasures of singing Gracie Fields songs round the piano with his friends might not be overjoyed at the prospect of another evening with his wife playing Bach fugues on the clavichord. He found her joshing style wounding. She called him "muddle-headed Johnny" (and the thin-skinned Osborne never forgot it). Seeing him engrossed in *The Prisoner of Zenda* with his feet up nonchalantly on the Aga, she didn't realize he was basing a play on it. "Haven't you read *that* yet?" she chided him. "We all read it when we were ten years old."

Such were the everyday niggles of wedded bliss. He thought she belittled him, whereas the much bigger truth is that she loved him and looked up to him. There were differences, but her adoration and her importunate love were transparent. She became pregnant to please him.

"He was absolutely thrilled she was pregnant," McGuinness remembered, although Gilliatt told her and others that she never wanted a child. The pregnancy itself terrified her, repulsing her physically to the neurotic extent that she complained it was like having a rat gnawing inside her body. She ate alarmingly little and was so thin that no one realized she was even pregnant. It was as if her body was in denial. The capable young woman who became the Osborne nanny, Christine Stotesbury – solid and reliable, as nannies are meant to be – told me that she didn't believe Gilliatt was the mother when they first met. She was five months pregnant then. But when they met again three months later, she was astonished to see no difference in her size.

Gilliatt gave Caesarian birth to Nolan Kate Conner Osborne at Welbeck Street Nursing Home on 24 February 1965. According to Osborne, who was there for the birth, his daughter was "rather eccentrically christened Nolan after the wild captain who delivered the fatal order to Lords Lucan and Cardigan at the head of the Light Brigade". He was writing a script for Richardson's 1968 film, *Charge of the Light Brigade*, at the time.

But he was incredulous to learn that when Nolan was older, her mother had told her she was named after a character in an essay by James Joyce. "What an extraordinary, precious, mandarin lie," he fumed in his 1972 notebook. But compare "The Day of Rabblement", an early 1901 Joyce essay critiquing Irish literary theatre. "No man, said the Nolan, can be a lover of the true or the good unless he abhors the multitude" – sentiments with which Osborne would have agreed.

The nanny hadn't heard of either Osborne or his wife when she answered the advert in *The Lady*. ("Own flat. London townhouse".) Christine Stotesbury was a sheltered twenty-four-year-old, a professionally trained nanny who subsequently learned that a surprising number of unemployed actresses had also applied for the job. When I met her, she was fifty-seven, and she still kept in touch with Nolan who was happily married and living in Kent. She found Gilliatt charming when she was interviewed by her. "She asked about my family and what hobbies I had. I told her I'd done amateur dramatics at the local church. I was very naive."

She went to live in the flat adjoining Nolan's nursery and playroom on the top floor of the Chester Square house. (The Osbornes' bedroom was three floors below.) At Hellingly, she stayed with the baby in a cottage near to the main house in the grounds. The formal remoteness is surprising, but Stotesbury pointed out that after the problems of the pregnancy, Gilliatt loved her newborn child.

"They both loved her," she told me, "but I would say that John adored her. I don't want to be unfair, but Penelope always seemed too preoccupied. She liked to keep the baby in her cot with her in her study. But she wasn't maternal. I felt she treated her like a possession. I've photos of Nolan in her arms, but it's not what you felt was natural to her. John held her all the time. He would come upstairs to the nursery every morning while I gave her breakfast. He would often give her a bottle. He was just terribly shy and sweet and excited, and he adored her."

In the months that followed Nolan's birth and the premiere in June of
A Patriot for Me with Jill Bennett, no one had a clue that anything could
be seriously wrong with the marriage – not Gilliatt nor her sister or any of
their closest friends – and Osborne's first child only seemed to confirm his
happiness.

Xmas 1965

Dearest Nell. I love you.
Ever. EVER
John

33

A Patriot For Me

We are none of us safe. This is the celebration of the individual against
the rest, the us's and the them's, the free and the constricted, the gay
and the dreary, the lonely and the mob . . .

Baron von Epp, *A Patriot for Me*

A Patriot for Me is the only play Osborne wrote that began as a theatrical
image. Its notorious drag ball scene was imagined by him years before he
wrote his play about the homosexual officer Alfred Redl who was blackmailed into becoming a Russian spy. A brilliant young Galician and
working-class soldier who rises like a modern meritocrat into the elitist
ranks of the Imperial army, Colonel Redl is a man who "belongs" by
denying his own sexuality and Jewishness. Spies, like actors, live dual
identities. So, too, outlawed Jews and homosexuals. But in drag, all men
are equal.

Based on a true story, *Patriot* takes place in the Habsburg Empire between
1890 and the eve of World War I in twenty-three scenes with thirty-seven
actors. Osborne had read Robert Aspey's melodramatic 1959 biography of
Redl, *The Panther's Feast*. I came across some thirty pages of random notes
in his archives, dated 1.5.61, under the title "A New Play. The Themes of
Homosexuality":

Blackmail
Homophile
Homosexual society is relatively a classless society
I must recreate the experience, and, in doing so, attenuate the pain
The brutality of the thief
The excitement of fucks in Public Places
The Married Queens
Creating a masquerade

Gross Indecency
The Christian View
Deut XV iii 22
Am I a disease?
How about those who are but don't know it
The fear that we may be charged
Oscar
It's so exhausting having to keep up appearances
The scapegoat
Thank God it's out
Wanting to be one's natural self
The emergent queer nation
What is manly?

A *Patriot for Me* opened at the Royal Court on 30 June 1965 – four
months after Nolan's birth and four years after those "Notes for a New
Play" were written – and no scene created more uproar or delight than the
baroque drag ball and what became known as its high Habsburg queerdom.
The script gives a densely detailed, three-and-a-half page description of it
– from the elite officer in wimpled medieval dress, to the Lady Godiva in
gold lamé jockstrap, and the ball's imposing, campy host, Baron von Epp,
costumed as Queen Alexandra and "astonishingly striking with upswept
hair, ospreys in pompadour feathers, a pearl and diamond dog collar at his
neck, and a beautiful fan". For good measure, Osborne also added notes on
six categories of drag, including the particularly feminine costumes of rent
boys, the perfect taste of discreet drag queens like the Baron, and the dykey
theatricality of the more self-conscious rich queens and grotesques.

"You wonder just a little," wrote James Fenton about Osborne's meticulous display of drag artistry, "where he acquired all this information, and
the answer cannot be from reading books about the Hapsburg Empire."

Wondering just a little about Mr Fenton's innuendo, we know exactly
where Osborne got his information. He got it from Isherwood and Devine
on holiday in the South of France in 1961, from the demi-monde of homosexual friends like Anthony Creighton (who performed in early drag revues),
and from ex-lover Jocelyn Rickards, the costume designer, who gave him
all the details of the different categories based on her experience of drag
at the annual Chelsea Balls.

But *Patriot* has always touched a raw nerve in its detractors. Its director
was Anthony Page, but Osborne first asked his old friend Tony Richardson
to direct it and flew out to Los Angeles to discuss the script with him.

"Frankly, Johnny, I'm a bit mystified," Richardson said when they met. "I mean, you'll have to *explain* it to me. What's it all *about?*"

"I had never thought he would put such a question to me," said Osborne, who felt humiliated. A play about a homosexual officer who comes agonizingly out of the closet had been spurned by the bisexual director who never publicly admitted his homosexuality.

Nothing like *Patriot* had been seen on the British stage before. Redl's unfulfilling affair with his Russian mistress, Countess Sophia Delyanoff, is followed by his affair with a young lieutenant, Stephan Kovaks. When the Countess later announces that she's about to marry the Lieutenant, Osborne gives Redl an erotically charged speech that was staggering in its time:

"I tell you this: you'll never know that body like I know it. The lines beneath his eyes. Do you know how many there are, do you know one has less than the other? And the scar behind his ear, and the hairs in his nostrils, which has the most, what colour they are in what light? The mole on where? Where, Sophia? I know the place here, between the eyes, the dark patches like slate – like blue when he's tired, really tired, the place for a blow or a kiss or a bullet. You'll never know like I know, you can't. The backs of his knees, the patterns on the soles of his feet. Which trouble him, and so I used to wash them and bathe them for hours. His thick waist, and how long are his thighs, compared to his calves, you've not looked at him, you never will."

"Why did Osborne write this? What does he mean to say?" Mary McCarthy protested irritably in the *Observer*. The play had touched a Puritan nerve in the liberal American bluestocking. It had *offended* her. "Is it a free translation – or travesty – of the Profumo story?" she asked ludicrously. "Or can it be an anti-militarist tract which boldly declares that if universal disarmament had been established in 1890 none of these Jews and homosexuals would have had to lead a life of glittering pretence?"

Osborne's first American champion appears to have been left unhinged. In any event, McCarthy's concluding remarks about *Patriot* ruined whatever case she might have had: "The chief merit of the enterprise was to give work to a large number of homosexual actors or perhaps to normal actors who could 'pass' for homosexuals."

Among McCarthy's quite normal readers was the astonished Ken Tynan, now Literary Manager of Olivier's National Theatre. He sprang to Osborne's defence – an unexpected turn of events. He hadn't been on the best terms with Osborne since he invited him to write a new play for the National and was surprisingly rebuffed. ("Come and help us make history," Tynan had said to him when they met at a party. "I've already made history," Osborne replied and turned on his heel.) Perhaps, like all playwrights who owe a great deal to a critic, he felt the resentment of a man who borrows money from a friend. Perhaps he just couldn't resist a good line. But the damage was done. Hell hath no fury like a critic scorned. Yet Tynan returned to his old paper, the *Observer*, to defend *Patriot* generously.

"Why did Osborne write this? What does he mean to say?" McCarthy had demanded to know. "Osborne's intention was to show the pressures exerted on sexual deviants by social prejudice; that he was not blaming the queer but the society that outlaws queerness," Tynan replied. "For the first time in Western drama, we are asked to identify with a queer not because he is charming or tragic or a genius but simply because he is queer. And the gaudy, notorious set-piece of the Viennese drag ball is there to make things harder for us – to challenge our liberalism by confronting it with queerdom unabashed and independent, to remind us that the camp world at which we tolerantly laugh is also the world that our penal code imprisons."

It has often been overlooked that there are two ball scenes in the play. The operatic scale of the drag ball that opens Act II overshadows the conventionally straight ball in Act I. The Emperor's court ball at his residence in Hofburg, Vienna, is attended by Redl along with the aristocracy, diplomatic corps, and fellow officers of the Royal and Imperial army. Some of the leading court figures will appear later in decadent drag. But Osborne's point is that Redl belongs in neither world. The same hypocritical, self-perpetuating elites rule them both.

At the Hofball, bantering anti-Semitic remarks drop like light rain in the rarefied air of "perspiring gaiety and pointlessness". At the illicit drag ball, however, Redl doesn't appear in drag but in his formal Colonel's uniform and decorations – the odd man out. "I'm surprised they let you in," says the Baron costumed as Queen Alexandra.

James Fenton's negative *Sunday Times* review of the 1983 revival of *Patriot* with Alan Bates at staid Chichester – "a nasty piece of work about nasty pieces of work" – was right, however, to emphasize that the play's upper-class milieu isn't the kind to call for social justice for homosexuals. "Nor is this play, in any sense, a plea for social justice," Fenton wrote. "One would be surprised to find it on the reading list of any gay studies seminar. This world is distinctly pre-Gay. It is queer."

It's why the high queerdom and camp of the drag ball scene works on its own dazzlingly theatrical level. It remains true to its unpoliticized self: everyone there is a patriot for himself in the unsafe cause of the noncomformist. The title of the play comes from Emperor Francis II's response about one of his junior officers who was described as a patriot: "Ah, but is he a patriot for me?" Gay studies were the last thing ever on Osborne's mind. It's arguable that *Patriot* isn't even about homosexuality as such. It's about sexual ambiguity and outer appearances, public morality and private lives. It's a celebration of the outlawed individual and it's an elegy for the persecuted.

Critics of the play still insist it demeans homosexuals because nothing positive reinforces Redl's tormented life. But where is the "positive reinforcement" in the crumbling, burnt-out life of Bill Maitland? Where is it in the self-lacerating Luther dying daily like St Paul? Such people have no place to go. *Patriot* was written for an England that denied the right of homosexuals even to exist. Redl's ramrod reserve makes him an untypical Osborne hero who in his fearful isolation and pain remains a typical Osborne outsider.

The Lord Chamberlain considered the drag ball scene so shocking that he banned it in its entirety. He wanted to cut the heart out of the play along with its validation and symbol of defiance. "Omit the whole of this scene," went the lofty uncompromising order from the censor. The same applied to the scenes with Redl in bed with another man (or even a woman). "Omit the whole of this scene . . ."

In the era of the defecting spies Burgess and Maclean, the English Establishment personified by that outdated embodiment of privileged paternalism, the Lord Chamberlain, was as hypocritical as the upper echelons of the Habsburg Empire. *Patriot* is an implied metaphor of exclusionary class-ridden England and the Lord Chamberlain's sneering references to "pansies" and "homo-sexuals" (*sic*) sustained a near-farcical atmosphere of legalized intolerance.

His Official Reader for a quarter of a century, Charles Heriot, judged that the play and especially the drag ball scene "would certainly attract all the perverts in London and might even persuade the young and ignorant that such a life might not be so bad, after all".

Assistant Secretary to the Lord Chamberlain, R.J. Hill, advised ". . . presenting homo-sexuals in their most attractive guise dressed as pretty women will to some degree cause the congregation of homosexuals and provide the means whereby the vice may be acquired."

Colonel J.F.D. Johnson, the Lord Chamberlain's assistant comptroller to Colonel Penn, wrote privately: "I have read 'A Patriot For Me' and to give the devil his due the dialogue reads quite well." But the Colonel concluded: "This play looks to me like the Pansies' Charter of Freedom and is bound to be a Cause Célèbre."

Devine even invited Colonel Johnson to visit the Court and see the play for himself. "It is kind of you to invite us to see 'A Patriot for Me', but I am afraid I am rather tied up for the next few weeks . . ." he responded with unintended humour.

Patriot became a *cause célèbre* because Lord Cobbold, the Lord Chamberlain (sometimes known as His Ladyship), refused to back down and Osborne refused to censor his own play. Personal appeals to Cobbold were subsequently made by Laurence Olivier, who wanted to stage the play at the National, as well as by the Queen's cousin, Lord Harewood, and even the Chairman of the Arts Council, Lord Goodman (also the Prime Minister's lawyer). But they and other grandees were turned away. Drama critics joined in the fight. Harold Hobson pleaded the case for not censoring the play on the grounds that he believed it "denounced" homosexuality while demonstrating "homosexual passion with a freedom previously unknown to the English stage".

Osborne had thus provoked the mother of all showdowns with theatre's oldest enemy. The Lord Chamberlain's absolute power, however, was beginning to decline by the liberated Sixties. The Prime Minister, Harold Wilson, and his Lord Chancellor, Lord Gardiner, were both opposed to theatre censorship. The beleaguered Lord Chamberlain's policy on homosexuality had even softened somewhat by the late Fifties with a dual standard: plays could be passed "which dealt seriously with the subject", but they could not show "practical demonstrations of love".

The outcome was that unserious homosexual plays were allowed – like Frank Marcus's 1965 lesbian black comedy, *The Killing of Sister George*, or Joe Orton's sublimely subversive 1964 social comedy, *Entertaining Mr Sloane*. J.R. Ackerley's 1925 *Prisoners of War* is a curious anomaly. Its undercurrent of homosexual passion between two young soldiers couldn't be more apparent – though not to all, including the Lord Chamberlain, who licensed it for production in the West End. Plays with homosexual heroes that passed the censor were otherwise oblique or coded, like Rattigan's derided 1958 *Variations on a Theme*. Coward's *Song at Twilight* – written as late as 1966 – has a blackmailed protagonist, Sir Hugo Latymer, who is obviously based on Somerset Maugham, but the dread word "homosexual" is never mentioned. Rodney Ackland's more blatant homosexual demi-monde was censored. But Shelagh Delaney's ground-breaking 1958 *A Taste of Honey*, with its openly gay and effeminate art student, somehow slipped by the befuddled censor.

A perfect example of a successfully coded British musical is Julian Slade's evergreen 1954 *Salad Days*, whose symbolic magic piano gives lots of people pleasure in parks. The longest-running play in British history, Agatha Christie's 1954 *The Mousetrap*, is clearly a covert homosexual thriller. Christie's baronial Monkswell Manor, where strange, murderous events take place, is a gay coven run by a straight couple. (The married straights, Giles and Mollie Ralston, are the only ones above suspicion of murder.) Christopher Wren, the excitable young guest with long, unruly hair and a peculiar taste in nursery rhymes, great clothes and interior design, is the resident queen. The young woman in sensible shoes who's straddling the fireplace, Miss Casswell, is the dyke with a dubious past described by the playwright as "a manly type". The middle-aged major looks seedily suspicious, rather like the groping major of Rattigan's *Separate Tables*, but he's not nearly as questionable as the flamboyant *foreigner* at the Manor – elderly Mr Paravigini who wears make-up (rouge and powder) and "skips about".

In America, Mae West's 1927 *The Drag* – which she wrote and directed – ended with a drag ball scene in which the hero is openly homosexual. (But the play was closed by the police in its pre-Broadway try-out in Bayonne, New Jersey.) The pioneer in Germany was Frank Wedekind's bisexual *Lulu* in 1894, as well as the hints of gay teenage sex in his *Spring Awakening*. From France, Edouard Bourdet's *The Captive* had a lesbian heroine (the villainness, granted) and ran successfully on Broadway in 1927 with its crowded premiere attended by the Mayor of New York.

America – which had no theatre censor – could be more open-minded than England and was certainly more fun off-Broadway. In the New York of the 1900s, drag balls had even operated at Madison Square Garden and were attended by high society, including the Astors and Vanderbilts. The early 1960s gave birth to Café Cino in Greenwich Village and the unapologetically gay plays of future major playwrights like Lanford Wilson, Robert Patrick Stanley, Tom Eyen and Jean-Claude van Italie.

England fared better on film. The first British film with a homosexual hero was Basil Dearden's well-regarded 1961 *Victim* with Dirk Bogarde as the blackmailed barrister. The first mainstream movie to show two men kissing onscreen was John Schlesinger's 1971 *Sunday, Bloody Sunday* with Peter Finch as the bisexual doctor (and an Academy Award-nominated script by Penelope Gilliatt).

One legal loophole, however, permitted censored plays to be performed in England. Legitimate theatre clubs like London's Arts Theatre and the New Watergate staged plays for members only. The absurdist implication was that a limited audience in a club wouldn't be corrupted by a controversial play, as opposed to the gullible masses in a public theatre. Club performances of censored plays were denied a West End run (unless the Lord Chamberlain relented), but it was the only way England first saw the plays of Jean Genet, Lillian Hellman, Tennessee Williams and Arthur Miller. Miller's A View from the Bridge, for example, was censored because its tough longshoreman, Eddie Carbone, insults fey Rodolpho with a smackaroo on his lips – something, Pauline Kael wrote of the film version, that pleased neither man.

Devine therefore defied the Lord Chamberlain by turning the Court into a temporary club for A Patriot for Me and charged a token sum to join. With its huge cast, it could never recoup its production costs or transfer to the West End. (Osborne paid half the costs himself.) But it could at least open to the public – albeit with a hovering threat of police action. The undermined Lord Chamberlain wasn't yet done. Cobbold, perceiving a threat to the very existence of his office, saw the Court's club performance as an obvious ploy to subvert the law. He now turned to the government's Director of Public Prosecutions, Sir Norman Skelhorn, to uphold the law. The Queen and the Home Secretary were even informed. "If I did not know it to be untrue I should think that the Lord Chamberlain is mad," wrote Hobson in his favourable review of Patriot in the Sunday Times.

The Director of Public Prosecutions stood firm and refused to prosecute. The Lord Chamberlain's folly succeeded only in publicizing the play and sounding his own death knell. Patriot had breached the dam of theatre censorship, "And art made tongue-tied by authority" was freed. The Lord Chamberlain's office would be abolished within three years.

The unforeseeeen problem was how difficult it proved to cast the play. The straight actors turned down A Patriot for Me because they didn't want to be perceived as homosexual, and the homosexual actors turned it down for the same reason. "People were very frightened of appearing in it," its director, Anthony Page, told me. Practically no major actor wanted to be identified with a homosexual role. Christopher Plummer was among several stars asked to play Redl. "He said he would play it if it were rewritten so that Redl was straight," Page explained, still looking incredulous. Apparently, Plummer's wife wanted the hero to be shown as a great lover of women whom the wicked Countess drove into the arms of men.

O'Toole and Burton were among other star actors who turned down the lead. Paul Scofield was tempted, but committed to the Royal Shakespeare Company. Paul Newman sent his regrets for the Broadway transfer (along with his admiration for the play). Page even tried to persuade Marlon Brando to take it on. He had met Brando at a party at Leslie Caron's

London house in Montpelier Square and his magnetic sexual ambiguity would have been perfect for Redl. "I told him he was a beacon for our generation," Page told me with a smile. But it made no difference. Brando was by then lost to movies, anyway.

Devine's biographer, Irving Wardle, makes clear that the production had to be postponed for two months "while the part of Redl rebounded from a succession of nervous British actors" before it was finally accepted by Maximilian Schell. According to Page, however, the handsome, Viennese-born Schell had a pet theory that Redl was really straight *underneath*. The Academy Award-winning actor of *Judgement at Nuremberg* also insisted on playing the sex scenes with his longjohns on. "We tried to get them off him," Page explained. "But he adamantly refused. The audience loved it, though."

An actor who subsequently coveted playing Redl was Robert Stephens – Osborne's original, snarling George Dillon – but the opportunity slipped away. Stephens went to see *Patriot* with Olivier who told him there were only two actors who could possibly play the lead: "You or me."

"Casting bum-boys for the drag ball scene was almost as hard as casting the leads," Wardle concluded. Some thirty actors – including Gielgud, Coward and MacLiammóir – turned down the pivotal role of the Baron. Osborne had originally written it for Devine, who at first was too belea-guered running the Court to accept. "The moment he said he would do it," Jocelyn Herbert told me, "they were able to cast all the others." Herbert was *Patriot*'s set and costume designer. "It was such fun during the fittings for the drag ball scene. All the gays were terribly embarrassed and all the heterosexuals were having a great time."

But Peter Gill, then an assistant director at the Court, demurred. He remembered how all the straights were very busy asking each other about their wives and children. "And how *is* the wife? Keeping well, I trust?" Edward Fox was dressed as a beguiling geisha girl during the drag ball scene. "Loved every minute of it, dear boy," he told me, beaming. Devine's newly acquired hour-glass figure came from a tight lace corset worn under his crinoline. He relished the role of the cross-dressing Baron so much that whenever he was in costume he used the ladies room.

Patriot was to be Devine's farewell to the Court. The previous autumn, he had suffered a minor heart attack – a warning. He took three months' rest and planned to retire on his tenth anniversary as artistic director. He was deeply tired. "The weight of this edifice has driven me into the ground up to my neck, like poor Winnie in Beckett's *Happy Days*," he informed the Court's board. "I am getting out just in time."

For Osborne, Devine's planned retirement was an irreplaceable personal loss, the end of an era for them both. He wrote to Devine during the run of *Patriot*:

30.6.65
A Patriot for Me

My dear friend,
It is very moving for me to watch you in the play. So appropriate, courageous and done with all your usual wit and sheer lucid vitality. You are a very remarkable man indeed. I wish I could express my admiration in a way you would find eloquent and comfortable. Thank you, George, for this, and the last ten years. You have sustained and enriched my life. I feel this will be my last play at the Court. Perhaps we could *both* move on elsewhere later. Please let's discuss it some time.
    As ever, your friend and admirer,
    John

Both Liv Ullmann (one of Ingmar Bergman's leading actresses) and the French actress, Delphine Seyrig, were discussed for the role of the Countess, but it went to Jill Bennett.

"Not keen," Osborne noted about the fateful choice he said had been made by his director. "I saw her being very patronising to her husband, Willis Hall, one night in Beoty's. We'll see."

Bennett's short marriage to playwright Hall had ended bitterly. But that was one of the few times Osborne ever dissembled. His stature as a playwright was so secure that he had casting approval of all his plays. If he wasn't keen on Bennett, she wouldn't have been cast.

His wife was more enthusiastic, judging by her opening-night telegram to Bennett: "I CAN'T THINK OF ANYONE WHO COULD DO IT WITH THIS RECTITUDE DEPTH AND HIDDEN DESPAIR STOP ALL LOVE DARLING — PENELOPE."

"John had never really met Jill before she came to Chester Square to discuss the role," *Patriot's* director, Page, remembered clearly. "But he wanted to see her and was very keen on her being cast. I'm sure he would never have cast someone for sexual reasons. She was right for the Countess. But he was obviously very struck by her."

"So wonderfully common, like Amanda *in Private Lives*," artist Patrick Procktor, a close friend of Bennett's for many years, told me about her. "Watch out!" said Rickards, who saw her as very good company, but a dangerous woman. Bennett was known to be wilful and manipulative. She created public scenes and didn't give a damn. Quick to wound, quick to apologize, she cheerfully put her mood swings down to "Celtic gloom". (Her father was Scots.) When, in time, Osborne announced that he was going to marry her, both Rickards and his first wife, Pamela Lane, cautioned him strongly against. He didn't speak to either of them again until the marriage to Bennett was over eight years later.

Jill Bennett had first wanted to be a ballet dancer. She was petite and striking with a strong mouth and retroussé nose, though she saw herself as plain. She enjoyed telling the story of a recurring dream in which she was asked to appear in Ibsen's *The Wild Duck*. In the dream, she's discussing which role to play when the director says to her, "I thought you'd be absolutely perfect as one of the ducks. You could sit in the wings and go, 'Quack, quack, quack!'"

In truth, Bennett was a glamorous woman with a suggestion of urchin androgyny, ironic grandeur and camp. She was an actress to the marrow of her narcissistic bones. Intuitively smart and amusing, her birthday was on 24 December. "It's quite an honour, I suppose, being born the day before Jesus," she said. She was poles apart from Gilliatt, the reserved intellectual. She compared herself to a highly-strung thoroughbred and in many ways she was. She possessed a dangerously brittle unpredictability, champagne style and a coarse green room wit. Even her severest critics described her as fun, and so she seemed to the impressionable Osborne who had recently settled into the bourgeois conformity of marriage and fatherhood when he first met her.

Who was Osborne a patriot for? He was an embattled patriot for threatened English values – for the English language, for its culture, music, architecture, customs and even its prayers. He was an instinctive patriot for himself – for his own defence against the realm, for outlawed freedom of expression, for unpredictability, individualism and conflicted, private fires. If Alfred Redl could betray his country and remain true to his sexuality – what price a man who betrays his wife? But Osborne's secret fling with Jill Bennett had yet to prove a threat, though he was never very good at "legerdemain affairs".

You live with someone for five, six years. And you begin to feel you don't know them. Perhaps you didn't make the right kind of effort. You have to make choices, adjustments, you have requirements to answer. Then you see someone you love through other eyes. First, one pair of eyes. Then another and more. I was afraid to marry but afraid not to. You see, I'm not really promiscuous. I'm a moulting old bourgeois. I'm not very good at legerdemain affairs . . .

The Hotel in Amsterdam

Yet that ominous reference to "five, six years" of marital forbearance appeared to be holding up with Gilliatt. Eight months after Osborne began his affair with Bennett, he wrote this note to his unsuspecting wife celebrating the anniversary of the first year they met –

25.3.66

Dearest Nell –
Fifth birthday with Banks. You get more exciting and exhilarating and smashing than ever. I know it will be a good year for you. I love you so much.

The one person who knew about the affair from the beginning was Osborne's secretary, Sonia McGuinness. All loyal secretaries know where the bodies are buried. But she couldn't have failed to know about Bennett. Osborne was sending flowers every day to her home at 33 Prince's Gate Mews, Kensington. He asked McGuinness to send them for him! Only later did he naively tell her what was going on. She replied patiently, "I *know*, John." He then confided that he was sexually obsessed with Bennett, but didn't know what would happen.

The new guests at Hellingly and Chester Square now included Maximilian Schell, Nicol Williamson and Anthony Page, but the most frequent visitor was Jill Bennett. She had befriended Gilliatt, and the two of them became so close that Bennett nicknamed her "sister". She was a guest at Hellingly for Sunday lunch and the dressing-up charades. Bennett dressed as a schoolgirl carrying Gilliatt's wedding train.

"She knew what Johnny liked," Gilliatt's real sister, Angela Conner, said. But to her dismay, she suspected nothing. "Jill was delightfully open about *saying* she was a monster. Yet she deceived us all," Conner explained, and her smarting sense of being gulled was still palpable. Yet she didn't blame Osborne for what happened.

"Jill insinuated herself into the fold," she added. "She called Penelope her sister. She was a blatant flirt, but I was very naive in those days. On the other hand, I spent endless weekends at Hellingly and never once witnessed anything wrong in the marriage. There was no slamming of doors, no rows, no tension. I know Penelope was driven by work, but Hellingly seemed like a cocoon of happiness. On the face of it, Jill was a close and loyal friend. Everyone found her great fun. She showered us all with gifts . . . Bastard," she muttered under her breath.

The closest friend to both Gilliatt and Bennett during this period was John Copley, the opera director who had known Osborne since stage managing *Paul Slickey*. Osborne wrote a role for him in *Patriot*: the male counter-tenor dressed as Susanna who sings the Mozart aria at the opening of the drag ball.

I met this frank and amusing man at his elegant London home with his partner of forty years, another John, who was technical director of ballet and opera at Covent Garden. He served us a perfect summer lunch like a grave, silent butler. "So," I found myself saying to them both as the chilled Chablis flowed. "Am I right in thinking you're what your friend John Osborne called a couple of old poofs?"

"Yes! We are!" Copley exclaimed good-naturedly as they both burst out laughing. "We're chaps! John called us two old poofs all the time. But always with affection. We didn't mind. We're chaps!"

Besides, he was glad to tell me how much Osborne had helped him. "He was the most wonderfully generous friend to me. I was seriously injured in a car accident during *Slickey*, but I didn't learn until years later that he was the one who paid all my medical bills. I'll never forget what he did for me."

But their friendship ended abruptly when Osborne left Gilliatt for Bennett. "I know how he felt. It bothers me still. He'd done so much for me. But Penelope was broken when he left her and I felt I should try to look after her and help her through. It was like a death. The life went out of her."

Wasn't he Jill Bennett's closest friend? "Yes, we became great mates during *Patriot*. She took a fancy to me. Fag's moll, wasn't she? She did like gay people. We were at Hellingly a lot together. I think she was an actress about twenty-eight hours a day. She acted in her sleep. She was so convincing that none of us had a fucking clue what was really happening. If only she'd been up front about it. But she used me, she used everyone. John just fell for her, but there was a terrible wickedness about Jill. I never spoke to her again."

Before Osborne left his wife for Bennett, however, his life spiralled out of control like the uncanny self-prophecy of the breakdown in *Inadmissible Evidence*.

34

The Death of George Devine

Hundreds of writers and actors owe their present fortunes and favour
to him. I am in the greatest debt of all.
                        Osborne tribute to Devine, *Observer*, 23 January 1966

A week before the final performance of *A Patriot for Me*, George Devine
suffered a massive heart attack. Feeling tired in the sweltering heat of an
unusually stifling summer, he went onstage that Saturday night to play the
Baron. After his performance, as he wearily climbed the five flights of stairs
back to his office on the top floor, he collapsed and was rushed into St
George's Hospital.

The cast of *Patriot* was so big there were makeshift dressing rooms under
the stage. Jocelyn Herbert had begged Devine to use one of them to change
out of the Baron's tightly laced corset, but he insisted on using his office.
In the black farce of the emergency that followed, the casualty ward of St
George's had an unexpected patient in the bejewelled shape and form of a
drag artist dressed as Queen Alexandra.

In the first few days, however, Devine appeared to be responding to treatment. He was even sitting up in bed writing letters, though with difficulty.

St George's Hospital SW1 [undated]

My dear John,
What a shock, without any warning at all. I really thought I'd had my
chips that night, but about fifty miles behind my head I was obstinately
hanging on, answering their questions with an angry resentful snarl. I
was in an oxgyen mask and my speech was distorted so when I heard
one cry, "How old is he?" "Oh, about 57 or 58." I lashed out 55 with
great venom . . .

But above all, John, your card meant the most. I can't help thinking
I made a balls of it by collapsing. I suppose I should not have gone on

on Saturday night, but the thought of all the flap and Anthony Royle in *my* costume and that packed house and one's innate vanity . . .

Let's talk about a trip somewhere later. Would love that.

From the Baron who went too far.

The prospect of losing Devine had sent Osborne into such shock he could scarcely function. "There is no healing," he wrote to Herbert, abjectly apologizing for one of the stifling moods of depression that had overcome him when they last met. "As you say, when these things come – and they've been regular as long as I can remember – there's no escape . . . Life would not have been the same for me in lots of ways without George. I can only say this to you. Better not go on – there'll be no end to it. I love you both dearly."

He watched the last performance of *Patriot* on 14 August with tears streaming down his face. "Scene after scene, his memory seems to pierce everything, the costumes, the words and, of course, the Drag Ball . . . a silk shirt, an ancient Greek ring, George, our play, our world. Coming to an end. I could scarcely bear to watch it."

At the curtain, he addressed the audience emotionally from the stage and talked about Devine's work at the Royal Court, his hospitalization and recovery, and above all, the unique contribution he had made to English theatre and to English life.

"He made the name of the Royal Court Theatre famous throughout the world; he set standards for us by force of his own rigour and imagination. He had to struggle incessantly against powerful and puny men. All without ambition for himself, only for the art he worked for and the world he lived in. The entire English theatre owes him a special and particular – and I think largely unacknowledged – debt."

In mid-October, Devine was released from hospital and went home, but he knew he was done for. On 17 January, he received the published version of *A Patriot for Me* from Osborne.

Rossetti Studios, London sw3
17 January 1966

My dear boy,

I was so delighted to receive a copy of "Patriot". I can't think of any better person to approach the grave with than Baron von Epp.

He died three days later, on 20 January 1966, aged fifty-five.

*

That day, Osborne was in Newcastle on an escapist jaunt, performing the role of the Narrator in a provincial tour of Stravinsky's *The Soldier's Tale*. His old friend Robert Stephens had flattered him into it and he was glad to get away for a few days. Stephens played the Devil, Derek Jacobi was the Soldier and Sally Gilpin, wife of dancer John, was the Girl. "Mr Osborne," groaned the conductor, "don't you recognise a *downbeat* when you see it?" Not really, he thought. But for the first time in a very long while, he was having fun in his own theatrical milieu.

Exhilarated by the charity performance that afternoon, he returned to his hotel where a message had been left to ring his wife urgently. When she broke the news to him, he scarcely heard another word she said.

Gilliatt was trying to tell him that the *Observer*'s new arts editor, Richard Findlater, wanted him to write Devine's obituary for the paper that Sunday. Coincidentally, Findlater was the former drama critic of *Tribune* who long ago was sent a novice play by the unknown Osborne asking, "Am I wasting my own and other people's time?" The deadline was imminent. Could he manage it? Did it *matter*? he thought to himself bitterly. "I mean, if you can't do it, everyone will understand. I'm sure Richard will." Fuck Richard. "But I do think it should be someone *close*," his concerned wife persisted, "and not just an outsider. Poor Georgie." Fuck the *Observer*. "The thing is, darling, would you like me to do it *for* you?"

He would have it ready by the following morning. "Oh, darling. Poor, darling Georgie . . . Are you all right?" "Yes."

He ordered a bottle of whisky and walked out into the freezing night in a daze. Though he wore his thick overcoat and woolly scarf, he had never felt so cold. "Men were already reeling out of pubs," he recalled, "and, caught in the light of street corners, streams of ale spewed on to the pavement. I had no idea where I was going or what I should do next."

He came across a cinema showing *The Sound of Music*. As a child, Osborne went to see films at his local Rembrandt cinema in Ewell to keep warm and escape reality. The box office had just closed, but they let him in.

"The hills are alive with the sound of music/ With songs they have sung for a thousand years . . ." He numbly watched the entire film. "How do you solve a problem like Maria?/ How do you catch a cloud and pin it down?" He hoped that his muffled shuddering wasn't disturbing the couple next to him.

He blundered out of the cinema and headed for Newcastle station and the night train home. He hadn't eaten since breakfast and the whisky bit into him as he wept and scribbled his eulogy to Devine.

"He was incapable of sentimentality, and I think it is important to stress that this was especially true of his dealings with younger people," Osborne wrote in his obituary for the *Observer* of 23 January 1966. "What was so formidable was his nose for sham in art and people." In the end, he said, Devine was worn down by the "grudging, removed attitude to decent and sustained effort that is such a recurrent and depressive aspect of English life. No one can surpass the Englishman's skill at maiming with indifference." But he went on to add:

> If I give an impression of George Devine as someone disappointed or embittered, I would be quite wrong. His disappointment was minimal, in fact, because his expectation was relentlessly pruned. This, combined with his prodigious, hopeful effort, seemed to make his stoicism heroic and generous, rather than a pinched, carping austerity. These were exactly the qualities he admired and saw in the work of personalities as different as Beckett and Brecht. Perhaps it was a kind of reticence. Strength, gaunt lines and simplicity always excited him . . .
>
> The two big subsidised companies – the National and the Royal Shakespeare – owe a debt to him that is incalculable. Their existence is directly due to him. Hundreds of writers and actors owe their present fortunes and favour to him. I am in the greatest debt of all.

The loss of Devine was the turning point of Osborne's adult life. He was the substitute father who first took him in and supported his plays. He was the one who endorsed him over and over again in a predatory world. Without Devine's protection, he was unmoored and the sun would never shine as brightly again.

"In my own life, January seems to have a gratuitous trick of springing cruelty," Osborne began the *Observer* tribute surprisingly. "Perhaps it is a personal illusion that life at the beginning of the year, like life at the beginning of the day, is harder to bear or contemplate." But that wasn't quite it. He was a man who had always been traumatized by loss and the shadowy beckoning of each cursed New Year signalled the onset of unfathomable depression. His own father had died on 27 January. Devine died on 20 January. The loss of George Devine was bound to Thomas Godfrey, the artist manqué he romanticized and adored all his life.

Osborne was now thirty-seven and the Court was more than his base. It was the only theatre he had known and it amounted to a kind of faith. "You should choose your theatre like you choose a religion," Devine said. The Court had its snobberies (though it was self-consciously the only theatre to give its cleaners billing in the programme). It was clannish in its taste

and violently partisan. Under Devine it was a humanist theatre, not political. But its commitment to its writers was total and its influence seminal.
Compared to the big culture palaces like the National and the RSC, it was
a small club. Two of Osborne's future plays would be staged at the National,
but he never felt he belonged there. He couldn't relate to the corporate
vastness of the concrete monolith he nicknamed "Alcatraz on Thames" or
"The Imperial Theatre Museum".

It's easy to forget how small the Court is. It seats only 400 or so. Marie
Shine was the box office lady for fourteen years, through the Devine period
and beyond. She had two phones in her cramped box office – one for the
theatre agents and only one for the public. "But I was quick!" she told me.
On opening nights, she wore long beaded evening dresses specially made
for the occasion. If the house wasn't full, she put the House Full notice out
just the same. "Well, it looks better!" She watched more or less every
rehearsal of every new play. She dragged actors like Nicol Williamson out
of the pub next door ten minutes before the curtain went up. She knew
them all and she was fond of them all, except Joan Plowright.

"She came up to me in the box office one night and said, 'Two tickets
for Lady Olivier please.' Lady Olivier, indeed! I said, 'Oh, hello Joan. How've
you been keeping?'"

Mrs Shine went on, "I had a big crush on Albert Finney. Very nice man.
John Osborne I loved. The kisses he gave me! I cried my eyes out when
he died. I couldn't believe it. George Devine was a lovely person. Wonderful,
clever man."

"Why clever?" I asked.

"Well, look at the plays he put on!"

Devine's funeral took place at Golders Green Crematorium and nobody
knew what to do or how to behave. Olivier, dressed meticulously like an
undertaker, had assigned himself the role of designated mourner and
solemnly greeted everyone, guiding them to their seats. Beckett got lost en
route. There was some tension in the chapel between those who felt loyalty
to the presence of Devine's wife, Sophie, or to his mistress, Jocelyn. Britten's
War Requiem – specially chosen by Gilliatt – was played inappropriately.

Three weeks later, Sophie Devine, designing a film for Roman Polanski,
died of cancer.

"Something most certainly was over and irrecoverable, although even I
was not yet aware of the bleak landscape that beckoned," Osborne wrote,
"or that loveless times would manifest themselves so swiftly and in such
succession, and continue and consolidate for the best part of the next ten
years. But I already knew that there would never be a place for me to start

again. My Court days were over. It was clear enough as I walked away from the concrete and red roses of the crematorium. Yet I hung around Sloane Square, bereft of intent, for another decade or so before they chucked me out."

35

Breakdown

The psychiatrist: I like him better than I did.
Osborne, Regent's Park Nursing Home,
21 September 1966

Osborne could remember little of the summer of 1966 as he fell apart in a drunken haze of grief over the loss of Devine. Among the more sensational scraps of memory he could recall, he listed these:

"Firstly: a physical, nursery brawl in Chester Square, while Penelope tried to prevent me dragging a suitcase down the staircase."

"Escaping to the Park where I found a shady tree near the Albert Memorial and fell asleep with the suitcase as my pillow."

"Then: rising in the early mornings, sitting alone downstairs in JB's [Jill Bennett's] mews flat, drinking brandy from the bottle."

His fractured memory is shaky. In fact, he hadn't yet left his wife to live with Bennett. His homeless night in Kensington Gardens is closer to the truth about his state of mind. During the lost summer that led to his hospitalization with a nervous breakdown, he saw both his wife and Bennett but he lived with neither of them.

In effect, he went into hiding – unable to deal with anybody. His thudding headaches had returned along with depression and tearful, sleepless nights. Artist Leonard Rosoman remembered a dinner with him when he couldn't stop weeping. There were other occasions, Rosomon added, when he said nothing the entire night.

He fled Gilliatt and Chester Square to live in a house he rented in Egerton Crescent. But he didn't always stay there. He secretly spent days on his own at Hellingly as if hiding out. He sometimes saw his first wife, Pamela Lane, at her Kilburn flat. There were times when he checked into a hotel. He even slept on the sofa in the office of the woman he described as the best agent he never had, Peggy Ramsay. She used to point to it and say to her young playwrights enigmatically: "John Osborne slept here."

He also stayed with Jill Bennett at her Kensington mews home. But his secretary told me there were many times when nobody – including herself – knew where he was. Bennett would telephone her demanding to know.

"I liked her, actually," McGuinness told me. "I found her very attractive and different. I could absolutely understand why people fell for her. But I learned to be wary. One day, early on, she asked me to her house wanting to know where John was. She gave me a glass of champagne and was utterly charming, funny and sweet, saying, 'Come on – tell me.' I said, 'Jill, I honestly don't know,' lying through my teeth. John had asked me not to tell her. 'Of course you know!' she said furiously and then called me a fucking bitch. She was so angry she hurled a glass ashtray across the room and it dented the wrought iron balustrade behind me. It frightened the life out of me, I can tell you. I thought, 'So this is what we're taking on, are we?' She was immediately full of apologies. Jill could change like that in a second. 'I'm sorry, darling,' she said. 'I'm so worried about John. That's why I want to know where he is.' I still said I didn't know. And she said, 'You won't tell anyone about this, will you?'"

It was on 12 June that Osborne moved out of Chester Square, dragging his suitcase with him and leaving Gilliatt desolate.

That Friday, she was correcting the proofs of her *Observer* review by phone when she suddenly broke down sobbing uncontrollably. "Whatever's the matter?" asked her editor, Helen Dawson.

Gilliatt wrote this devastated note informing her mother about the separation –

> 31 Chester Square
> London SW1
> [undated]

John has suddenly fallen in love with someone else, and left three weeks ago. I understand nothing – we were flawlessly happy. He has often been lost to chaos and I've been able to rescue him, but not from this. I can't write anymore. But you should know. Angie [Gilliatt's sister] has kept me alive.

> With love,
> Pen

Her emotional description of the marriage as "flawlessly happy" confirms at least that she suspected nothing was wrong. Only McGuinness and the nanny witnessed Osborne's everyday loneliness. In April–May, Gilliatt went to Positano overlooking the Bay of Naples to work on a novel. Osborne visited her and there's a strong suggestion of a turning point. "Penelope spent all day and much of the evenings tapping at her typewriter . . ."

His affair with Bennett escalated during the weeks Gilliatt was in Positano. He claimed he was having a "sporadic dalliance with J.B.". The truth is he was virtually living with her for most of the time his wife was away. The nanny, Christine Stotesbury, took Nolan to see him at Bennett's house until, feeling guilty and complicit, she refused.

Yet his typically chatty letters to his wife in Italy are warm and loving: "I can't get over all you've done for me and my life. Your presence is all over the place here. Everyone feels it. I love you with all my heart. Be strong and fear not. Banks always prevail!" "*Dying to hear from you.*" "Went mad and bought 9 shirts, a tie and jacket. Flushed with that, went to Sloane Square and bought 5 pairs of shoes. I was like some daft, rich woman cheering herself up. It worked." "This morning *Times* says Naples 61 th [thunderstorms]. Boo! Poor Banks . . . Went with Anthony and Jill to see *Juno* last night. Curious evening. Very much Larry's production – all externals. A [Anthony Page] and J [Bennett] in smashing form and sweet and sort of protective . . ."

He sends her news of Nolan, nicknamed Dokie: "She DANCES beautifully. LEADS, of course." "Nolan looked super."

Shortly before Gilliatt returned to London, he wrote: "Five years. [Since they first met.] It really *is* hard to believe. What a *lot* we've done, Banks." And then: "the next day is our wedding day. Only three years that. What a good day it was. I shall think of you . . . God, I miss Georgie. I love you, Banks."

On his wife's return to London, either Osborne came clean about the affair or she had found out. After the nursery brawl at Chester Square, the distraught Gilliatt tried many times for a reconciliation. This painful, undated letter to Osborne at his "hideaway" in Egerton Crescent was written early that summer.

31 Chester Square
London SW1

My darling – Can I come back to you tonight? Shall I come at 11? I'll be there unless you contact me. I pine for you. I know all this is a *good* idea . . . Our future could be reconstructed. Thrillingly. I know it . . . I yearn for you to be well and yourself again, but ill and divided you are still the same, irreplaceable. Prevent Jill staying the night if you can. She will try. We belong. I want to come to you with all my heart. The things you said were marvellous – no one can ever move me so much. Let us hang on to what we have won in the last three days. It is – well, everything to me, and to you I think.

I have such a terror that I shall never see you again. I can't imagine life or living without you. I've no way of finding you now that Jill has been been told where you are. I am in a state of such longing for you. RING IF YOU CAN. I'm frightened of causing trouble for you.

Your Nell.

On 6 June 1966, Osborne's latest play premiered at the National Theatre and it was a spectacular flop. His adaptation of Lope de Vega's virtually unknown, early seventeenth-century *A Bond Honoured* was an ambitious departure, but he was in no condition to write it.

He worked on the script through Devine's illness and during the aftermath of his death. But his surprising, surly preface to the published script alone reveals no rapport with Lope de Vega's play. He wrote that it had "an absurd plot, some ridiculous characters and some very heavy humour". Worse, he announced that he had no feel for Spanish drama or any particular knowledge of it. "That is why we have the greatest body of dramatic literature in the world," he declares staggeringly on the first page.

Rarely has a playwright so condemned his own work in advance. *A Bond Honoured* – or *La Fianza satisfecha* – was commisioned by the National's Literary Manager, Kenneth Tynan, who almost certainly came across an English version by the American poet, Willis Barnstone, published as part of Eric Bentley's new translations in the *Tulane Drama Review*. Tynan, over-impressed with the soft porn of Osborne's harmless knicker play, *Under Plain Cover*, saw him as the perfect match for Lope de Vega's dark, monstrous study in sadomasochism and sexual perversion.

But the 350-year-old play is essentially a religious work about a sadist's miraculous redemption, and its appeal to Osborne was in its Christian framework. Its existential hero, the immoralist Leonido, opposes all accepted social norms until he's saved by a vision of Christ. "He seeks an absolute freedom," Barnstone wrote, "a nudity, indeed, a form of anarchy comparable to André Breton's free man who would walk into the street firing at random at passers by."

The production, with Robert Stephens and Maggie Smith seated among a circle shrouded in black, was directed by John Dexter. "I played Leonido, a poor benighted creature," Stephens remembered, "who has raped his mother, blinded his father, seduced his sister, assaulted a priest and renounced Christianity. There were not a lot of laughs."

A few critics inevitably saw in its rebellious protagonist a perfect Osborne hero. But Osborne's heroes are wounded souls and their core isn't anarchy, but terror and self-loathing. The script never comes close to Lope de Vega's concept of sin and saintly revelation. All it reflects is Osborne's own turmoil. He hacked three acts down to one, but there's no Christian dialectic – the very reason he took the play on – nor even any evidence of the hero's struggle with evil and redemption. It's an uncharacteristically sketchy effort – not, as Martin Esslin judged in *Plays and Players*, "an abortion", but a mess.

Badly stung by the negative reviews and what he called "the alligator smiles of the fourth estate", Osborne pointed out resentfully that he was paid £250 from the National Theatre for a year's work on *A Bond Honoured* ("less than my wife and I were awarded by the National Assistance Board 13 years ago"). Drama critics, he maintained, deprive playwrights of scarcely making a living.

On 9 June, he fired off this mad telegram to *The Times* critic, Irving Wardle, along with copies to the critics of seven other papers:

> The gentleman's agreement to ignore puny theatre critics as bourgeois conventions that keep you pinned in your soft seats is a thing that I fall in with no longer. After ten years it is now war. Not a campaign of considerate complaints in private letters but open and frontal war that will be as public as I and other men of earned reputation have considerable power to make it.

The only mildly amusing note Osborne struck was his telegram to Herbert Kretzmer of the *Daily Express* explaining the meaning of the word *puny*. Barry Norman of the *Daily Telegraph* cabled Osborne back: "GO ON THEN FIRE THE FIRST SHOT." Wardle at *The Times* responded that he hadn't received any complaints from Osborne when he *liked* his plays. "I don't know what you mean by open war," he added, "but I'm told you used to be a boxer, and if you fancy a gentlemanly British punch-up I'm more than happy to oblige."

Osborne cabled back lamely, "I'M BIGGER THAN YOU BUT I'M SURE YOU'RE STRONGER SO LET'S FORGET IT."

But he never did forget it. When Wardle came to write his admired biography of Devine, Osborne churlishly refused to cooperate. "It's people like you who killed George Devine," was his response.

The breakdown of his marriage now began to escalate out of control.

On 13 June, one week after the debacle of *A Bond Honoured*, a gala night took place at the Old Vic to raise money for the George Devine

Award for new playwrights. Osborne was on the bill with Jill Bennett performing Redl's farewell scene to the Countess in *A Patriot for Me*.

Before leaving for the performance, Gilliatt sent a disturbed good luck note to him:

> George's Award,
> June 13 1966
>
> I think of you constantly and would like to be able to bless you. The people permitted to give blessings are not very substantial people. Anyway, my hand is moving over your head with a love that still stirs the roots of my soul.
>
> Your grieving, fiercely proud
> Nell

The actors taking part in the gala were a Who's Who of British Theatre, and the extracts from past Court productions at the Old Vic brought back their extraordinary original casts. Osborne's place in Devine's legacy was secure. There was Olivier returning as Archie Rice, Finney as Luther, Williamson as Bill Maitland, Kenneth Haigh as Jimmy Porter and Robert Stephens as George Dillon. Alec Guinness played Ionesco's dying king, Jack MacGowran was again Beckett's Clov, and the finale from Arnold Wesker's *The Kitchen*, with Noel Coward as the restaurant manager, included such kitchen staff as Dame Sybil Thorndike, Laurence Olivier, Maggie Smith, Vanessa Redgrave, Geraldine McEwan and Peggy Ashcroft.

But, according to Robert Stephens, the backstage drama between Osborne and his wife overshadowed everything else. He described how Osborne cruelly announced he was leaving Gilliatt for good. "He was talking with Jill Bennett in her dressing room when Penelope, who was sloping around backstage as she was wont to do, knocked on the door. He opened it and said, 'I've left you. I'm going away with Jill.'"

Jocelyn Herbert was seated next to Gilliatt during the performance. "It was macabre," she told me. "She was holding my hand and weeping as she watched John and Jill play their scene. She insisted on watching something that must have been so painful to her. She was even taking photographs of them."

The drama played out onstage had its built-in irony:

COUNTESS: If you leave me, you'll be alone.
REDL: That's what I want, to be left alone.
COUNTESS: You'll always be alone.
REDL: Good, splendid.

COUNTESS: No it isn't. You know it isn't. That's why you're so frightened. You'll fall alone.

REDL: So does everyone. Even if they don't know it.

COUNTESS: You can't be *saved* alone.

REDL: I don't expect to be saved, as you put it. Not by you.

COUNTESS: Or any other woman?

REDL: Or anyone at all.

On 8 July, William Hickey formally announced in the *Express*, "After three years of marriage John Osborne and his wife, Penelope Gilliatt, the film and theatre critic, have separated."

Osborne's own mental state had become alarming. "I'm taking Valium which seems to do fuck all," he wrote to Gilliatt after their separation. "I take sleeping pills and still wake at the same time. I have the same old premonitions of heart attacks and melodramatic god knows what. I've been sick in Eaton Square and fallen dead asleep by the Serpentine for three hours like a part-time washer upper – which I once was. God knows what *you've* done. Anyway: I will be round on Monday. But I need sleep and no telephone and *nothing* for the weekend. Please look after yourself. I don't ask for forgiveness. There is a flaw and the flaw is me."

In early August, the nanny telephoned McGuinness at her home to come to Chester Square immediately. She couldn't get any response from Gilliatt in the bedroom and the adjoining bathroom door was locked. But she could see into the bathroom window from the terrace of Osborne's study opposite. Gilliatt was lying on the floor apparently unconscious.

"To get into the bathroom I had to squeeze through the slats of the terrace of John's study and step across a gap onto the window sill," McGuinness explained matter-of-factly. "It wasn't a problem, except we were three floors up. I was skinny and I could squeeze through and balance on the sill. The bathroom window was open and Penelope was in a semiconscious state with pills scattered on the floor. We called the ambulance. She had her stomach pumped at the hospital, recovered, and that was that."

"I can't imagine life or living without you," Gilliatt had written to her husband. But perhaps it's significant that her semi-comatose body could be seen through the bathroom window. "We never knew whether she was in serious danger or whether it was a desperate cry for help," McGuinness said. "She never talked about it afterward."

*

"This divorce. I'm afraid I cringe from it," Gilliatt subsequently wrote to Osborne. "I will do it, of course, if it's dead in line with what you want. It would be hell, but I will do it if *you* want it. I'd never try to block it. You know that. But of the two of us only you could want it. Not me in 100 years."

Osborne's response is a prelude to his breakdown and hospitalization:

My darling,
Your letter rends my heart. All decisions and I flail in front of them all. I fail you despicably. I fail Jill. I cannot succeed with myself. I see no way out. As you say, all I have to say is "I want it". And no more. I can't bear to think of what life is like for you. Jill is in a panic much of the time. Much of the time it is very good indeed. But I can't keep writing my life off and I don't know how to cope. I can't work – *not* that that matters over much.

I am just desperate with what I fail to do and cannot *do* for anyone. I *was* happy with you, and yet I have gone through this hideous thing. And this hideous thing has been full of comfort and excitement too. Oh, Banks . . . I don't feel equipped. I *am* neglible. I am being so cruel to you both. But sometimes, all the possibilities disappear, and it just becomes a detached nightmare. I owe so much to you. And yet I dread to see you. I must say, at the moment "I want it", and yet it is a partial truth. Can we think of our lives as long and forbearing? Can *you* be?

The other day I nearly upped and went to HOUSTON, TEXAS! I was going to the bank to take out all I could and DISAPPEAR. I just hoped Sonia would pay all the bills for you all and keep her silence. Houston seemed the most horrible choice to make. And a good one. I thought of seeing you today but I couldn't. There *is* a flow: I am going to bed with several Valium and a bottle of whisky. J is doing her best and Sonia is super to me. I don't know how I would have done without her. Hang on to Nolan. Above all, hang on to yourself. You are an extraordinary girl. In the meantime I would set the divorce in train . . .

During the first days of September, Osborne blurrily telephoned his ex-lover, Jocelyn Rickards, who became alarmed. He was at Hellingly alone. It was about 10.30 in the morning.

"It was early in the day and he was already half under," Rickards remembered. "He'd also taken some sleeping pills. He told me he needed to sleep. But I felt frightened. I never thought John seriously considered suicide, although he mentioned it once or twice when he was depressed. I was concerned what the bottle of whisky and the pills might do."

After the call from Osborne, she telephoned McGuinness whose husband, Mac, drove them urgently to Hellingly. When they arrived, the house was locked up. No one was answering. The housekeeper wasn't there. Mac broke in, and the woozy Osborne was eventually roused. Rickards let him talk to her for hours that night and McGuinness alerted Osborne's doctor, Patrick Woodcock, for an appointment the next morning in London.

Dr Woodcock was almost eighty when we met again. I ought to declare here that he was coincidentally my GP during this period, for later events concerning Bennett will bring me briefly into the story. He now lived in France for most of the year, but he still came home to stay in Tachbrook Street where he once kept his surgery. "When I saw John I decided to put him under the care of a psychiatrist in a nursing home for a month," he explained. But he, too, didn't think Osborne was suicidal. He was a willing patient.

"I had the impression he wanted to close the doors on everybody and escape," he continued. "I was dealing with a man in a lot of emotional pain. Creative people with tangled lives go through these phases. I'd say he was cracking up with acute depression."

He managed to get a room for him two days later at Regent's Park Nursing Home. Osborne was still avoiding all contact with Bennett and Gilliatt. The first night, he slept on Rickards's couch at Pembroke Studios in Kensington where she lived with her vigilant husband, Leonard Rosoman. Over dinner, Osborne was quite sober and calm (and hungry). The second night before entering the clinic, he was to stay at the Hyde Park Hotel. But when McGuinness arrived at Pembroke Gardens to take him there, he was legless.

"He didn't know where he was," she said. "My husband piled him into our very small car and we had to be careful about taking him into the hotel pissed out of his mind. But somehow we managed. The porter helped us. Mac tipped the commissionaire on the door and it never leaked out, as far as I know."

His secretary had booked the room under her own name, and she and her husband put Osborne to bed. As they were leaving the hotel, Penelope Gilliatt, alerted by Dr Woodcock, was crossing the foyer. She stayed the night with Osborne and accompanied him to the nursing home the following morning.

Regent's Park Nursing Home – or "Dolly Drops Hotel", as Jill Bennett named it – has long since closed down and there are no medical records to rely on. But Osborne kept notes when he was able, and the accounts of several people I spoke to who visited him coincide.

He was a wreck sedated with Pentothal, Largactil and what he called "other little sweeties". He wept in front of his visitors. A neurological disorder had also left him unable to feel the tips of his fingers. Given coins to identify by touch, he was unable to feel them.

"I've got a cramp round my heart. Usual hypochondria," he scribbled in his notebook when he could hold a pen. "But then it's a bit like the tips of my fingers. And that *had* gone wrong."

"Pills and jabs mostly," he wrote to Rickards as he began to recover. "Bit like bad digs with injections."

"Send sticky buns to the poor demented," he wrote to the nanny.

In his notebook he called the psychiatrist "SYK". (They were the sick ones: "syck-iatrist".)

I told SYK that Jill said all psychiatrists are mad. I wasn't sure whether he was aggrieved or not. He just said, "She may be right". At least he's being a bit more direct. I fancy he has a pretty poor estimation of me. Perhaps I should send him *Bond Honoured* and good old prefiguring *Inadmissible Evidence*.

Jill and I had a very cold discussion last night about whether she was right for me. Usual trite gossip of attraction. It makes her withdraw to a false position and me very, very cautious. I suppose I do ask for a lot. But I grew up craven and timid. All this queen's talk of mother figures gets up my nose.

"My darling," Jill Bennett wrote to him in the clinic. "Thank you for your note . . . Perhaps I should dress up as a nurse and get into the Dolly Drop Hotel and you could lift up my skirt . . . I hope the lowness has passed . . . I'm sure it will be OK . . . My acting is rotten at the minute . . ."

"My darling – Seeing you at the window of the Dolly Drop Hotel – I felt so mean leaving you – you are so brave and I love you and like you and admire you and *everything*. I'm so glad you are better. Chatting in the nursing home is forced on one and I get the feeling one could step out of line very early. I have to see you somewhere else. See you tomorrow. All my love . . ."

Gilliatt, acknowledging at last that the marriage was beyond repair, wrote a virtual farewell note to Osborne:

Banks,

And I shall never meet anyone ever at all like *you*. Gain peace and air around yourself. Take a year. AHEAD – WRITE YOUR PLAYS. It *will* be easy. Part of your pain is that they are waiting to surface. I know it.

She discusses a potential psychiatrist for him when he gets out, one of those recommended by Penelope Mortimer:

He sounds a bit grand and excessively thick, but he picks up what I can tell him of my dear J's temperament and afflictions . . . *Take your time* to make yourself whole. You are J.O. You are yourself. It *will* come back . . . There is support, love, gratefulness for you everywhere. It is the truth . . . Brigid can get hold of me in 20 minutes any time if you are in a panic. Isolation probably best? See Jill without fear of hurting me if you want. I'm far beyond it and the point is to get you well.

Though Gilliatt grieved over her marriage to Osborne for years, she had recovered her shattered self-confidence and poise. "Very strong temperament," she would say in America about Osborne, "very weak character." By mid-September, her friendship with Mike Nichols (then at work on *The Graduate*) had blossomed and she made preparations to build a new life with him and the fifteen-month-old Nolan in New York.

"The psychiatrist," Osborne continued scribbling in his notebook. "I like him better than I did. Although I still think he is vain, prurient, complacent and enclosed. Very interested in himself . . . 'Things fall apart, the centre cannot hold.' Is that right? It feels just right at this moment in time. I feel like a figment. A pretty awful fiction. I take back what I have said about the Irish."

Jocelyn Herbert wrote to him consolingly:

Dear John,
I cannot replace Georgie for you, but you must believe that I will always be around as he would have been – if you ever want or need to see me.
    Very much love dearest John –
    Jocelyn

But he was in his own distracted world:

I said this to the SYK. I don't think the spectrum of invention and possibility is what they want to know about.
"As if a man were author of himself
And knew no other kin" –
Don't know if that's right, either. No Shakespeare. Nor Dictionary. Can't remember what MINATORY means.
What to do? I feel isolated and don't really know whether to go on. I feel an alien in my time and in my country. I *can't* live abroad. Usual

old stuff. I've been lucky. I have been loved. And I have not only been on the receiving end.

FLIGHT

I'm glad Pamela [Lane] wrote to me. Only Mary [Ure] is acrimonious and unloving. But she is an unforgiving girl. Bantam spirit. At least she's happy.

I don't think the SYK recognised it when I said "The time is out of joint".

Everything gone but DREAD.

The false self which everyone accepts, likes, indulges.

I don't know what is real to her and what isn't. Or her to me. Am I a commodity?

A trophy. God, I hope not.

And Nolan?

After five years. Where am I now?

All this clamour.

Not coldness and darkness. But fire. Fire.

RECTIFY, RECTIFY, REMOULD!

36

The Real Thing

You are very sweet about being married so much. I love you for it . . .
Yes, please. I formally say YES. I would like to marry you.

Jill Bennett letter to Osborne, May 1967

Osborne and Bennett were married at Chelsea Register Office on 23 May
1968. That night, his new play, *Time Present*, opened at the Royal Court
with her in the starring role.

He modelled its champagne-drinking protagonist, Pamela, on his new
wife. Bennett played an actress – a stylishly superficial, witty and vitriolic
woman who's a sentimental Tory. For good measure, Osborne also modelled
Pamela's friend and unlikely flatmate, the Labour MP Constance, on
Penelope Gilliatt. Constance is an intellectual socialist with a bulging briefcase, earnest and exceptionally bright, emotionally fretful – a formidable
success. "Constance is very accomplished," Pamela says about her, typically.
"She can cook every sort of cooking, write books, give you an opinion on
anything from Marxist criticism of the novel to Godard, she's even managed
to get herself a child, an ex-husband, and now a well-thought-of lover."

Osborne was fond of saying that his failed marriages followed him everywhere like previous convictions, yet he jumped recklessly into each one as
if he could wipe the slate clean like writing a new play. His wives were too
intelligent to settle for a mere misogynist. They were liberated and self-
made women. But he never spent any time alone. He was always married.
Until he met Helen Dawson, women defeated him. Women drove him
mad. Failure left him raging in marital martyrdom against the species like
that cut-rate Othello, Posthumus, in *Cymbeline*: "I'll write against them,
detest them, curse them . . ." Women failed him – never the other way.
They were Jimmy Porter's devourers. They were Freud's eternally agonized,
"What do women *want*?" They were the marauding women of Saul Bellow's
Herzog who eat green salad and drink human blood.

He seemed happy and relaxed posing for press pictures with his arm around his new bride after the Chelsea wedding. He had grown a handlebar moustache that looked so odd it might have been stuck on. An informed *Observer* reporter first spotted it the year before. "John Osborne has grown a moustache (writes Our Moustache Correspondent). An eyewitness says the moustache converts Mr Osborne from an angry young man into a comfortable-looking, slightly Edwardian major."

In a late Sixties London more accustomed to the trendy Zapata or Chinese Mandarin-style moustache, Osborne's choice amounted to an anti-fashion statement. He was now thirty-nine and she admitted to thirty-seven. Bennett was always vague about these things, although she was officially born in Penang, British Malaya, in 1931, the daughter of a rubber planta-tion owner. Looking at the stylishly dressed couple in their wedding photo, it's impossible to imagine them in jeans, smoking pot or marching in a purple haze against the war in Vietnam. "Don't trust anyone over thirty," went the slogan of the Woodstock generation. But then, *Time Present* scorned the pot-smoking, radical youth culture of 1960s England as if its author had become an overnight, middle-aged sourpuss.

"Thus do the angry young men of 1956 turn into the Edwardian High Tories of 1968, the iconoclasts of yesteryear into the satisfied upholders of established values of today," thundered Martin Esslin (of the defining book, *The Theatre of the Absurd*). For Esslin, history had eerily closed the circle. "Twelve years to the month after Osborne's *Look Back in Anger* opened the new era of British drama, the curtain rises at the self-same spot to reveal his latest play *Time Present*; and what does the curtain reveal? The exact replica of that elegant drawing room set, those elegant uppercrust characters, that creaking exposition, that corny, melodramatic plot that were the birthright and the bane of the kind of dreary play which *Look Back in Anger* was supposed to have finished off once and for all time. And what is more . . ."

As Osborne used to say, "It's *only* a play" (though the play was every-thing to him). *Time Present* reflected his return to living in a showbiz milieu with its upper-class actress-heroine, Pamela, and its great actor of the old school – *the real thing* – dying offstage. But it set out to be more than a superficial throwback to the Coward era. It saw showbusiness as a metaphor for contemporary pseudo-life, like reality TV today, or Andy Warhol's fifteen minutes of fame for all.

"You're all of you in showbusiness now. Everybody," Pamela says triumphantly to Constance. "Books, politics, journalism, you're all banging the drum, all performers now."

Osborne and Bennett were themselves like showbiz aristocrats performing in their own show. They were the fantasy "John and Jill", *folie à deux* stand-ins for "Larry and Viv". They went to the trendy new restaurants in the King's Road, but they were comfortable in traditional showbiz haunts like the Savoy Grill and the Ritz (or the Caprice before it became the unplush place to be). He was known as "Champagne Johnny", and she was known for her extravagance and style, and both of them were in headlong pursuit of happiness. They were seen around town in a chauffeured Bentley and a dashing white Mercedes coupé, and everything they did and said was reported in the press until in the end it was natural for even their murderous rows to be performed in public.

"I think John loves me because he thinks I'm awfully glamorous in the right way," Bennett told the *Daily Mail*'s Lynda Lee-Potter in an interview entitled "I've Met My Match At Last". "And he thinks I'm talented and funny. I'm very bad-tempered. I'm an awful bitch, really, but I'm happy . . . I change with every man I'm with. I was a manic-depressive when I was married to Willis Hall. I failed him dreadfully. He's North Country and he brought out all the melancholy in me. John is so different . . . I've done a lot of immoral things. I thought I was permanently fickle. But with John it all just gets better and better. I think I've met my match at last."

In a *Sunday Express* feature entitled "Why Jill Bennett Has A Fridge In Her Bedroom", she explained, "We practically live in the bedroom," because the fridge was handy for champagne and caviar in the middle of the night. "I'm always waking up John for a light snack and a jolly chat."

And in an *Observer Magazine* interview, "Jill Bennett On Being An Actress. Talking to John Heilpern", she said, "Acting is such a flotsam profession. I'd sooner have been a vet. I'm very fond of animals . . ."

Osborne had two dogs: an English sheepdog and a Great Dane. Bennett had three: a Pekinese and two high-born shih tzus from Harrods. "She arrived at the theatre in the chauffeur-driven Bentley with those fucking little dogs on her arm," said John Standing, who played opposite Bennett in a West End production of *Private Lives*. "She performed at *being* a star."

Tarn Bassett – Robert Stephens's ex-wife – remembered her arriving in a Lagonda at their village home near Winchester when Bennett was still married to Willis Hall. "She used to roar past the little church in the Lagonda and all the cows would stampede. You couldn't get any milk out of them the next day! She wore a black leather helmet with a strap under her chin like Amy Johnson, with a white scarf, black leather trousers and boots. She was just playing another role. She used to squeak into the house in all the leather. She'd come into the drawing room going squeak, squeak,

18 Osborne with Joan Plowright and George Devine, director of the Royal Court and Osborne's father figure, in Rome with Giulietta Masina for 'An Evening with the English Stage Company', 1959.

19 With Vanessa Redgrave, Shelagh Delaney and, on Osborne's left, Doris Lessing, at a nuclear disarmament rally, 1961.

20 & 21 Nicol Williamson, the ultimate Bill Maitland in *Inadmissible Evidence* – the first production, 1964, and the revival, 1978.

22 The drag ball scene from *A Patriot for Me*, with George Devine as the Baron in a ball gown, defying the Lord Chamberlain at the Royal Court, June 1965.

23 Richard Burton and Claire Bloom, stars of the film version of *Look Back in Anger*, take a break from filming, 1958.

24 Tony Richardson, director, and Albert Finney on the set of *Tom Jones*, for which Osborne's screenplay won him an Academy Award.

25 Jocelyn Rickards, costume designer and Osborne's lover and friend.

26 Penelope Gilliatt, screenwriter, film critic and Osborne's third wife.

27 Osborne with baby Nolan, his daughter with Penelope Gilliatt.

28 1968, Osborne
marries another of
his leading ladies,
Jill Bennett,
who starred in
A Patriot for Me.

29 Osborne and
Bennett barely a
year later, when
things looked
less rosy.

30 With his last wife, Helen Dawson, 1981, to whom Osborne was married for over 16 years.

31 Father and daughter, Nolan, aged 13, briefly happy together at Edenbridge.

32 Osborne with Gladstone, in the garden at The Hurst.

33 With Helen, Summer Garden Party at their home in Edenbridge, Kent, early 1980s.

34 Detail from a portrait of the playwright by Anthea Hadley, 1991.

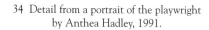

35 & 36 Revivals of *The Hotel in Amsterdam* (*above*) at the Donmar Warehouse, 2004, with Olivia Williams (as Annie) and Tom Hollander (as Laurie); and *Epitaph for George Dillon*, 2005, at the Comedy Theatre, with Joseph Fiennes and Francesca Annis.

squeak. I'd say to her, 'Jill, if you squeak much more I'm putting down mousetraps.' My old dad was potty about her. 'There's my darling!' he'd say whenever he saw her. 'Come and give me a kiss.' And they'd flirt the day away together."

Did she enjoy her company, too? "I did, very much. Jill was the most enormous fun," added Bassett, who was fun herself. "She swished. She would swish in and swish out. I know she could be devious. She was cruel to Willis Hall. She told such outrageous lies that she'd have Robert [Stephens] choking on his food he was laughing so much. She lied about her age, of course, which I always found terribly funny. She could take a decade off and get away with it. Because she *believed* it. She once said to me about her mother, 'Poor Mummy. You see, I was a menopause baby.' A menopause baby!"

In June 1968, Christopher Hampton was sitting on the steps outside the Royal Court in Sloane Square with its new artistic director, Bill Gaskill, when he saw a white Mercedes approaching. His early play *When Did You Last See My Mother?* had been inspired by Osborne, and it was then playing at the Court on Sunday nights. Hampton was still an undergraduate at Oxford. "My God, it's John Osborne!" he thought as he saw him stepping out of the open-topped Mercedes without troubling to open the door. Osborne said hello to Gaskill, who introduced him to Hampton. "He'd seen my play and he was very gracious and said lots of nice things," he remembered. At which point, Gaskill said to Osborne, "Well, John. Do you have any advice for our young playwright here?"

Osborne considered for a moment. "Never marry an actress!" he replied and swanned into the theatre.

In the divorce settlement with Gilliatt, Chester Square went to her in trust for their daughter Nolan, and Osborne bought a fifty-one-year lease on a smaller house at 30 Chelsea Square, off the King's Road. In one of life's delicious ironies, its previous owner was Sir Eric Penn, the lieutenant-colonel who had censored Osborne's plays as comptroller of the Lord Chamberlain's office.

The house had six bedrooms and a separate wing for staff. Osborne added a Nordic solarium and sauna inside – "We understand the floor is suitable as such for erecting a sauna upon it," the Harrods salesman advised him solemnly by letter – and Bennett made the place ultra-modern with wood-panelled floors and ceilings, Eames leather chairs, chrome lights, and impractical white fur rugs dotted with huge pink shells that were used as ashtrays. At one point, there were three paintings of Bennett in the living room – a Patrick Procktor watercolour for the *Time Present* poster, a Leonard Rosoman painting of her in the role of Countess Delyanoff in *Patriot*, and a big Procktor oil painting, commissioned by Osborne, of her lying on a sofa.

It was rumoured that when the marriage turned sour he took a flying leap at the big portrait and put his foot through it. But that isn't quite true. He threatened to. He turned its face to the wall instead.

"Marvellous, unusual looks. Like ski slopes," Procktor said about Bennett, a long-time friend. He lived opposite Lotte Berk's renowned exercise studio where Bennett made a show of working out quite regularly. Procktor described how she kept the Bentley waiting outside Lotte's until she emerged from her exercise session utterly exhausted. She would then be chauffeured across the road to visit him for a compensatory glass of champagne. "I had to practically carry her up the stairs," he said.

Champagne was drunk so frequently at the Osborne home in Chelsea Square that it was referred to as "some". "Care for some?" Osborne asked his guests. Or, "I think we'll have some." The staff included the chauffeur, a housekeeper, maid, gardener, Sonia McGuinness, and Sonny, who was like the camp manservant in *La Cage aux Folles*. He was a transvestite mulatto in a lopsided wig who had a thing about Shirley Bassey. The Osbornes referred to him as their houseboy or butler. One night, they returned home from the theatre to be greeted by Sonny wearing one of Bennett's expensive Jean Muir dresses. But not a word was said, except "I think we'll have some."

Hellingly was sold to Nicol Williamson, and Osborne then purchased a 1907 country house with about fifteen rooms in Edenbridge, Kent. Bordering Chartwell, the house was set in twenty-two acres with an untamed Chekhovian forest of cherry trees, oak, willow and silver birch, and a four-acre lake with its own boathouse where Osborne fished for carp, perch and bream mostly. He let the lake to six rods of the Edenbridge Angling Society. He later had a glassed-in swimming pool and solarium/sauna built onto the house. He sometimes worked in a summer cabin in the gardens and named it Porter's Lodge. The current owners of the property have kept the lodge as Osborne left it – empty, except for a poster of a dog sitting in a chair with the words, "If only I could get the feeling of accomplishment without having to accomplish anything."

When Osborne bought the house, it was already called Christmas Place – an omen. Christmas was the fateful time of each approaching New Year when mortal things happened in his life. Yet he was always happiest there and saw the escape to Edenbridge as his own refuge. When the marriage to Bennett was over and the division of the spoils took place, he kept the house in Kent and never lived in London again.

In spite of his urban polish and flashy public image, he remained a countryman at heart. He had preferred living in quiet isolation in Sussex to London. Toward the end of his life, he went to live in a remote part of Shropshire bordering the land of his father. In the early Seventies, Kent wasn't the commuter belt it's since become. It was still "England's back garden". Osborne kept an article about it written in 1970 by one of the *Observer*'s great journalists, John Gale: "Not 30 miles from London, mainly in Surrey, but touching Kent and Sussex, is a rectangle of flat land between Lingfield and Edenbridge. It reeks of cows and mangel-wurzels and echoes to the sad cry of peewits. Poplars line the ponds and the small brown River Eden which smells of mud and fish. Rooks and gulls wheel above the bare elms and the plough."

The article ends, "Return to London through Edenbridge and Crockham Hill. At Crockham look back: if the weather is clear you get a magnificent view of the county you have just left. Take the B269 to Limpsfield and then Titsey Hill. Before Warlingham turn off north-north-east on the minor road that eventually brings you into London by West Wickham. It is an excellent route through real countryside of meadows and Friesian cows right up to the concrete and double-deckers."

On 6 October 1990, many years after her marriage to Osborne had ended, Bennett committed suicide. The year before she died, she asked her secretary, Linda Drew, to destroy all Osborne's letters. "I did my duty," Drew explained. But there remains a love letter from him to Bennett in a play. In *The Hotel in Amsterdam* – written in tandem with *Time Present* – there's a declaration of love that at least suggests the finer, real thing about Osborne's feelings for her.

The play's disillusioned writer-hero, Laurie – Osborne's alter ego – suddenly confesses to his best friend's wife, Annie, that he's fallen in love with her. The role of Annie was written for Bennett and the scene is the most memorable in the play. Its unexpectedly tentative heart amounts essentially to ten melting words that were spoken by Paul Scofield's Laurie in a way that conjured a miracle of stage poetry out of the banalities of romantic love.

Because . . . to me . . . you have always been the most dashing . . . romantic . . . friendly . . . playful . . . loving . . . impetuous . . . larky . . . fearful . . . detached . . . constant . . . woman I have ever met . . . and I love you . . . I don't know how else one says it . . . one shouldn't . . . and I've always thought you felt . . . perhaps . . . the same about me.

"Such sad words," Scofield said surprisingly as he recalled the extraordinary scene for me. "Dashing, friendly, impetuous, larky . . . It's as if these qualities were the ones he had always been deprived of."

So we have a taste of Osborne's romance with Jill Bennett and how he first felt about her before the illusion of love was broken. But in *Time Present* he parodied the tricky epistolary form in a speech delivered by the cynical heroine.

I tried writing love letters to someone. For quite a long time . . . I don't know what I can go on saying. I love you. I need you. I want you. I ache for you. I need you beside me and in my bed. Don't let's part like this again. It's more difficult than I can bear. It's never been like this in my life before. I never thought it could be . . .

"I told you not to expect super love letters," Osborne wrote apologetically to Penelope Gilliatt in Venice during the first infatuated days of their affair.

"I know what you mean about clichés etc regarding being in love," Bennett wrote to Osborne from film location in Turkey, "but it's impossible not to use them. I use them all the time and I don't care. I'm wildly, hopelessly in love with you & I'm out of my mind with delight and gratitude to you and God . . ."

During June–July 1967, she was in Istanbul and Ankara playing a small role in Tony Richardson's *The Charge of the Light Brigade*. Osborne, who wrote the original script, had argued so bitterly with Richardson over the film that they did not speak to each other for years. Bennett was in Turkey to play Mrs Fanny Duberly who bravely follows her husband through the military campaign.

She wrote to Osborne every day.

Turkey,
May–June, 1967

John, we are lucky, aren't we? And we do *deserve* it – I honestly don't think people feel like we do . . . Thank you my darling for taking your clothes off. The best thing you ever did . . . and we *are* good friends as well as super lovers . . .

My body aches for you . . . I wish I was pregnant. There I've written it down.

Actually, Daisy is a super name for a girl. Daisy Osborne – divine.

My dearest darling love, I never thought in my imaginings that anything like this could happen to me. When Willis [ex-husband Willis Hall] and I split, I thought that was it. I would never really have a chance to love properly or be loved, and I never dreamt I would be loved by someone so unique and special. I do thank God and you and fate. We have proved we can do anything and we shall. We awake so much interest from people and care and affection and also envy and jealousy. I notice it daily. Your pottily in love Gypsy.

Remember the rules, please. I do.

You made Hellingly work for me. It could have been impossible, especially me being such a friend of Penelope's . . .

Darling, won't it be SUPER when I get home and we are together again. Yes, we are very well known lovers. John G [John Gielgud who played Lord Raglan] is *mad* for us . . .

When Doris Lessing knew Osborne and Bennett at the beginning of their affair, she noticed even then "rumblings of thunder in the wings". It becomes apparent in Bennett's love letters to him from Turkey.

My love. How are you? Are you OK? Are you working? Fucking awful, boring day. No letter, so was sad.

How I feel. LOC. Lack of Confidence. SOD. Slough of Despond . . .

Golly. Let's have a super glamorous life – we are geared for it – help me – I need you . . . you are so loved by so many and so admired. All will be *well*. Your Baby.

TR [Tony Richardson] says how tough I am – if only he knew!! I feel like jelly – High Tension – lack of confidence is what I am suffering from – I feel as if I haven't acted in years – I never do a play . . . I would love to do something decent again. It's been too long – this film is rather draggy – small parts are HELL. Oh my darling . . .

The rules are very good & we are very good friends as well as super lovers. Remember that well.

Dearest loving John, I want things to work too. I believe they can and will. I know how you feel about the dangers especially with the pasts we have had – but let's look forward not back . . . I know when you revile and abuse me that it hurts as much to do it as to receive, and I do it to you. But things will get better. I promise. We get closer every day . . .

First, John, do not ever apologise for writing to tell me how you feel however vile and shabby it is . . . I feel desperately unhappy that I am so far away and can't comfort you, and most of all that you should feel so bleak. There is nothing shabby about you, nothing you have done is shit, the past 10 years have not been a waste. Your life has been marvellous and is going to be more so. Of course you get withdrawal symptoms sometimes and feel lacking in courage. Anyone who is imaginative and creative does. I know I do . . . Of course you're a manic depressive. So am I. We can't help it. But my darling it does pass, doesn't it?

Osborne proposed marriage by letter to her in Turkey – as he had by letter to Gilliatt in Venice – too bashful, perhaps, to propose in person. Bennett responded:

Dearest playwright,
. . . You are very sweet about being married so much. I love you for it, and for being slightly inhibited about it. *Don't be any more*. It's passed . . . Yes, please. I formally say YES. I would like to marry you.
Now I must ask you. I have wondered about it often. In the beginning when you talked of it and it seemed a wild dream I was scared as you know, and since then many conflicting thoughts although I've *felt* married this past year. But all that (I mean the conflicting ideas & the fear) is past. Will you marry me?
I am depressive, imaginative, over emotional, slightly comic, tip tilted nose (fuck them!), brave, fearful, over romantic, soppy, sexy, passionate, wilful, patient when required, athletic, industrious. I love to work and to act, potty about the theatre, bitchy, abrasive, loyal, constant, puritanical, I have a Jewish house, a super Ma and Pa, a second hand car & a mad gynaecologist, a very brainy dog, am in love with my horse, I drive, I can't sing, my cooking is a disgrace except for tomatoes & mushrooms on toast, but am willing to learn anything from you – oh and I'm mad about clothes yours and mine, I dress quite well, am really gregarious, a chatterer and a champion cuddler, FRIENDLY & LOVING. Will you have me? I'm rather resented sometimes and it can be misjudged. ANSWER PLEASE. And I have a temper, as you know. I've never proposed before. It's lovely.
Your Jill.

Bennett's performance as Pamela in *Time Present* won her the award for Best Actress of the Year, and the now forgotten play transferred successfully to the West End. But if we assess great actresses by the defining, benchmark roles we remember them by, Bennett wasn't an actress in the same league as her contemporaries, Judi Dench, Maggie Smith or Vanessa

Redgrave. (In *Time Present*, Redgrave is blatantly satirized by the envious Pamela as the loopy star actress Abigail, a myopic Tinkerbell who's in love with Castro.) Bennett was a driven actress whose appeal was dependent on her personality. Michael Blakemore, who directed her, maintained that she succeeded by dint of her personality alone. She belonged to a West End tradition – as opposed to the Court's – where she was admired for her elegant high comedy and fragile glamour. She lived for acting, yet she suffered from bad stage fright. She shook with fear waiting in the wings to go on. Yet once onstage, she appeared nerveless.

"She wasn't a great actress, but she could be an excellent one," said Anthony Page, who directed her in several Osborne plays, and his adaptation of Ibsen's *Hedda Gabler*. Bennett's desperate Hedda, trapped restlessly in a pointless life, was her best performance. She understood her: caustic, restless Hedda, the free spirit manqué longing to defy bourgeois convention, and the first tragic heroine in dramatic history whose calling card is boredom.

Time Present was Osborne's present to Bennett. When he read it to her, she fell fast asleep two-thirds of the way through Act One. (He gamely put it down to his acting.) Criticized for writing leading roles only for men, he set out to write a leading role for a woman in *Time Present*. He confided to a friend, "It may not be Cleopatra, but it's a start."

The outcome was that he ended up creating a female version of himself. Worse, the fury of the authentic Osborne hero was now replaced by actressy, middle-class complaint – about high taxation, avant-garde happenings, stoned hippies, modern art movements, boring politicians. There's a newly precious preoccupation with "style" and good taste, and what's "proper", "common" and "vulgar". ("I think excessive effort is vulgar," Pamela announces in flippant, Cowardesque mood.) Nostalgia itself has become a style – though in some ways it's the fascination of the play.

The one real way of life and real way of acting in the heroine's rudderless, sham life is represented by Gideon Orme, the great classical actor from another era who's dying offstage. Toward the end of the play, Pamela lingers over Orme's mementoes – faded theatre posters and photos, old programmes and scripts – things only a sentimental theatre lover would appreciate. "He was big in all of them. Even when he was bad," Pamela says fondly of the various productions he starred in. "Here we are," she adds, naming another, "'The Real Thing'."

The title of what sounds like an Edwardian potboiler pre-empted the title of one of Tom Stoppard's best plays, his 1982 *The Real Thing*, whose subject is love, illusion and make-believe in the theatre world.

Pamela reads aloud from Orme's tattered old script. "'I *want* your life. Ella, oh Ella, you are a magnificent woman. A gem.' 'And so are you, David. All that a woman could ever want. A real gem. Not paste. But the real thing, David. The real thing.'"

"Perhaps it should have been called 'A Real Gem'," suggests the literal-minded Constance.

"No. 'The Real Thing' was better," Pamela insists. "Oh, here's one of his great flops. His own adaptations of the 'The Brothers Karamazov'. Lost all his savings in that . . ."

In the fiction within *Time Present*, Gideon Orme is Pamela's worshipped father. In life – real life – he was Osborne's tribute to Jill Bennett's first love, a famous actor of the old school, Sir Godfrey Tearle. He was some forty years older than her when they became lovers. She was just out of RADA playing walk-ons in the Shakespeare Memorial Theatre company's 1949 season at Stratford. Tearle, the son of a nineteenth-century actor-manager, was a star actor blessed with what used to be called matinée idol looks. After a performance, adoring women in the audience pelted him with flowers.

In 1983, the marriage to Osborne over, Bennett published a memoir of her love for Tearle, *Godfrey: A Special Time Remembered*. It was ghosted by the prize-winning novelist, Suzanne Goodwin, who had first met her during that 1949 Stratford season. John Goodwin, her husband, was then the theatre's press representative, and he told me, "I adored Jill ever since I saw her backstage at Stratford walking down a corridor wearing nothing but a straw sun hat and high heels. Stark naked, my dear. And lovely! She was a little bit of a show-off."

His wife laughed lightly, seeming unsurprised. She remembered Bennett affectionately, too. When they worked on the Tearle book together, the champagne flowed so freely that she had to pour hers into a teapot or a potted plant whenever Bennett wasn't looking. Her husband reminded her that when she was in hospital, Bennett sent her a case of champagne. "To the amazement of the nurses," his wife added. "But she was always ridiculously, flamboyantly generous."

"You are supposed eventually to get over love," the memoir of Tearle begins. "Nobody can pine forever. It becomes a self-indulgent invention, like Queen Victoria keeping rooms full of Albert's clothes, or Miss Havisham in *Great Expectations* stopping the clocks and letting mice eat the wedding cake. So what I am writing will look far-fetched and even impossible. Yet it is the plain truth. I never have got over the man I loved when I was very young."

The Real Thing

Written eight years after her marriage to Osborne ended in turmoil, the book is dedicated:

For Orme
The real thing

The dedication perplexed those who didn't know the play. Who was Orme? In *Time Present*'s invention of love, the fictional Gideon Orme is Godfrey Tearle. Osborne's shadow still hovered over Bennett's life. The message was meant for him. He was never the real thing.

37

My Dear Tony

So, don't speak to me about "loyalty based on truth and knowing each other." You have blasphemed against this principle every day of your life.

Osborne letter to Tony Richardson, 10 May 1967

The Charge of the Light Brigade created a fraternal blood feud between Osborne and Richardson that ended their friendship for many years. The outcome of the breach was that they never collaborated with each other again, their partnership in all the Woodfall companies was dissolved, and Richardson contemplated suing Osborne for libel.

Osborne's cluster bombs of invective when crossed were well known, as was his view of Richardson as a Machiavellian schemer. Whatever their mutual differences and flaws, the two men had been like brothers in each other's confident, sparring company, fizzing with the swagger of talent and success. Osborne even begged his friend not to leave England on the Isherwood–Hockney road to "blue skies and buggery in California". But the trouble between them was caused by *The Charge of the Light Brigade* when they quarrelled almost continuously for two years over the script.

"TR is hell-bent on making an anti-war film," Osborne wrote. "Oscar Lewenstein [a director of Woodfall Films] looks as glum as he did in the Acapulco brothel. I am losing heart . . ."

"You must tell me what you want," he announced sourly to Richardson during the umpteenth script conference on a yacht in the Greek islands. "I am here at your bidding like a tailor and cutter." Though they had worked well together on *Tom Jones*, the director's medium of making movies was basically alien to Osborne. During his divorce settlement with Gilliatt, he asked his lawyer to make certain all his finances were in order so he wouldn't have to take on another film. Hollywood money was only welcome when badly needed. But the dramatist who never rewrote anything in his plays had no appetite for collaborative *drafts*.

Charles Wood, the playwright and friend of Osborne who eventually took over the screenplay of *The Charge of the Light Brigade* at Osborne's suggestion, has written several successful films – the Beatles' *Help*, among them – and he's also written many that never got made. "It's better *not* to get them made," he explained dryly. "They have to keep paying you for the drafts."

Richardson nevertheless said that Osborne was as passionate about *The Charge* as he was. The serious problems began with a lawsuit accusing Osborne of plagiarizing Cecil Woodham-Smith's masterly popular history, *The Reason Why*. The rights to the book were owned by the movie star, Laurence Harvey, who claimed he intended to produce and star in his own version of the book. Harvey was represented by Lord Goodman, considered the most powerful lawyer in the land.

Richardson and Woodfall – backed by United Artists – quixotically decided to defend the suit. But a preliminary judicial hearing in February 1967 went disastrously wrong. The case hinged on the distinction between a writer's use of historical events versus details taken from another author's work. Though there was evidence to bolster both sides, the hearing went against Osborne. According to Richardson, "he had helped himself liberally to stylistic phrases and descriptions in *The Reason Why*."

"I've plagiarised no one, only myself," Osborne argued back. But Richardson pointed out that when he was confronted with the evidence he grandly murmured something about Brecht helping himself to Shakespeare. (Brecht adapted *Coriolanus*. So would Osborne.) In May, the filming of *The Charge of the Light Brigade* was about to begin in Turkey in a valley twenty miles from Ankara. Unless they abandoned the film, there was no alternative but to settle the lawsuit.

Laurence Harvey – who now had Woodfall over a barrel – agreed to a small role in the film for a fee of £60,000 plus a percentage of the profits. (In the end the film flopped and there weren't any profits.)

"I think I have had a really raw deal over 'The Charge'," Osborne wrote to Oscar Beuselinck on 20 April 1967. "I've come in for all the calumny, done the basic work, won't be paid for it and won't even get credit for what I've done. Will you please ask Tony what, in these special circumstances, precisely – repeat precisely – my credit is to be. I would like an early reply to this question as my decision to play in the film may hinge upon it . . ."

He had returned to acting from time to time, and was to have played a cameo role as the peacock Prince Radziwill who dashingly escapes a group of wild Cossacks. But Richardson had given Osborne's role to Laurence Harvey. The offer of an alternative role was refused. It mattered little to Osborne – assuming he ever knew – that Richardson shot Harvey's scene with no film in the camera.

On 6 May, Osborne asked for his name to be removed from the film. Richardson replied immediately –

Ankara, Turkey [May]

My dear John,

I am sorry you feel so bitter. I feel bitter in some ways too but they're not the most important ones. The trouble is that you have a one-way morality as far as films are concerned. You don't really like writing them, you don't give of your whole heart but you expect other people to treat what you do as if it was one of your own plays. You don't really value the writing in the same way but you can't bear others not to.

I'm sure this probably won't help our relationship only exacerbate it because I feel increasingly that what you want from a friendship is not real loyalty, which is based on truth & on knowing each other but sycophancy and adulation which I can't give and despise anyway.

I was going to write that my basic regret is that I asked you to do the script in the first place – but it isn't finally true because what you really created I am going to make – the characters of Nolan and Mrs Duberly [Jill Bennett's role] – the relationship of Clarissa and Norris – the shape of the battle & above all the feeling you conveyed about the subject and the history. This may not be on paper at the moment but it is with me – & what I hope will finally be on the screen.

I am just going off to shoot for the first time – amongst much chaos & some bad shocks. I hope your present feelings will change soon. Whether they do or not won't change mine. I love you. Please come out if you can.

Tony

Osborne's typed, four-page response takes the breath away. Richardson ignited a tinder box not because he questioned Osborne's commitment to screenwriting, but because he had questioned his loyalty. Richardson's subsequent peace offering and expression of love counted for nothing. Loyalty was Osborne's byword. His unstoppable, merciless response is published here almost in full. As character assassinations go, it's a model.

10 May 1967

My dear Tony

Yes, I am bitter. But not in any surprised or consuming way. Why you would have similar feelings eludes me altogether. I am principally bitter with myself for allowing myself to get caught up in an enterprise which is entirely burnt out for me and without any profit or pleasure whatsoever. After all, I have known your character long enough to be unsurprised by the over familiar process of your deft exploitation of those unfortunates who regard themselves as your friends. It is the most commonplace joke about you and has been for years past. As one would expect, your letter is very adroit. Predictably, you manage to sound innocent, rational and ill-used. In some ways you are indeed an innocent. Consequently, you have long since arrived at a condition where your elaborate politickings contain instant automatic rationalisations . . .

What I object to is *your* approach to film making. I abhor the way you scavenge and use and misuse the talents of others – not merely writers – with mocking vampire contempt. I have never expected my work to be regarded as holy writ. (Indeed I was surprised to find how literary your final script has become.) But I was dismayed, disheartened and a little humiliated when I read this new version. It could hardly have been a clearer repudiation of what I had already done. But this response from me I knew to be at the heart of your intention from the outset . . .

I am grateful to my own instinct for not having squandered more time on a script when the outcome could only have logically been the same. I have been used, and used calculatedly. Doubtless in ways that I shall never even know about.

The incidentals are endless. You can scarcely imagine I was unaware of the small pleasure it must have given you to toss the poor crumb of Radziwill to a drab blackmailing little whore like Laurence Harvey? And for dessert to offer me a part in a script which you knew full well would only be at the least depressing and disappointing to contemplate. The triviality of these manouevres is the very sweetness of the contempt and power you feel and express . . .

Your glib reference to friendship is mildly staggering but not in the light of your character. I have never demanded "sycophancy or adulation" from anyone. Admittedly, I now have less friends than a handful. But it is a bizarre accusation from you, hedged in as always by conmen, camp followers, eunuchs, pimps, procurers of all things procurable,

349

and archetypal mercenaries and globe trotting bum boys.

As for what you say about my loyalty, this is another smooth incantation. Like so many other things, you flail away mimicking the tricks of it because you are sick with the knowledge that you have none to call upon. It is a dead nerve and none of your powers of intellect and resolution can ever give proper life to it . . .

But you shouldn't evoke friendship. Don't, above all, pretend to an ethic of truth between yourself and anyone. One of the main and recurring reasons why it has been almost impossible to establish any honesty of contact with you lies in a simple fact: that a large number of your devoted friends have been burdened with the necessity of an exhausting and corrosive fiction. Namely, the pretence that you are not or never have been homosexual. No one gives a fourpenny shit, least of all those who have loved you most. I don't suggest for one moment that this in itself would have provided some key or enlightenment about your personality or relationships. But it would have averted much harshness, frustration, distrust and difficulty for us all. So, don't speak to me about "loyalty based on truth and on knowing each other." You have blasphemed against this principle every day of your life.

You have always made certain that your friends are split up, divided with suspicion and jealousy in the dark and that none of them should know the simplest truths or facts – let alone the revealed truth. This has made you an endless object of speculation. Flattering and useful to you, but miserable and humiliating for those who felt themselves in good faith to be your friends . . .

Your sneering, your callousness, your malingering, your sadism, your patent technique of emotional accusation and shooting in the dark places of affection are your stock in trade. And, above all, your secretiveness. You trade and build your work and life on the wealth of innocence, virtue, goodwill, forbearance, patience, kindliness and talent of your friends and those you have either abandoned or cast out. In the same way you dominate and play the bigger market of meretricious ambition, hawkers, plodding hirelings, grafters and sexual intriguers . . .

I do feel a cooling regret for I know that if you have ever been – and you have – generous, loving or loyal to anyone you have been so to me. Now and then in your own fashion. And as well as you could muster. To protect myself from your distortion of this letter or my position, I am sending a copy to Jill and also to Neil. [Neil Hartley, Richardson's right-hand man] I don't mean to place him in an invidious position. I know his loyalties and affections lie securely with you. However, I should like at least one person who is an outsider from my point of view to know actually what I have said to you. The incident is closed but not in any hysteria or railing or rebuke. It is too late for all that. It has been a clearly charted collision course and there it is. We both have other things to do.

John

38

Lost Illusions

The fatal mistake of my life.
Osborne on Jill Bennett

If there had ever been happiness and ease in Osborne's marriage to Bennett, it was gone within eighteen months. Their battles were unending as each fought for control and possession of the other in the pretence of living happily ever after.

Their wounding relationship was compared to the murderous, mutually dependent marriage of George and Martha in Edward Albee's *Who's Afraid of Virginia Woolf?*. Albee's antecedents were Engene O'Neill, who stripped away the pipe dreams of romantic illusion, and Strindberg, who scarily defined the sordid psychological power plays of marriage as "Soul-Murder". Strindberg should know: on his wedding night to his second wife, he awoke from a dream and tried to throttle her.

The toxic differences between Osborne and Bennett were already commonplace during the first year of their marriage. "I'd go into work each day and both of them had been screaming at each other half the night," Sonia McGuinness told me. "John would say, 'I can't stand any more of this.' I'd see Jill in tears. 'That fucking man,' she'd say, 'he can't even write.'"

When laid low with severe depression, Osborne wasn't able to write anything but the confessional entries in his notebooks. His increasing despair would have been hard on anyone, but the signs are that his impetuous new wife couldn't deal with it. She expected much better of him and resented his incurable retreats into the lower depths of himself.

In June 1969 – just one year into the marriage – Osborne was confiding in his notebook:

I see no future
There is no present.

No friend or friends.
My wife dislikes and despises me.

1970, January onwards:

It gets worse. I'm diminishing. J [Jill] despises me more than ever. I can't even talk to myself. I really think perhaps I do want to die.

More and more inadequate. Hostility rampant. What *do* I do? Sex impossible, only fantasy. Headaches better but feel ill. Betrayal, dislike everywhere.

Can't cry or eat. Such despair . . . I sweat too much at the far end of the bed.

Fear, always fear for my sanity, let alone anything else.

Marriage is the perfect state of hatred.
Perfect hatred is good for you.
I'm dying slowly of hatred.

McGuinness witnessed one of their physically violent fights. The nanny, visiting with his daughter Nolan from New York, called for help and she rushed from her office to find Osborne pinning Bennett down on the landing slapping her face. They dragged him off her.

"I was simply appalled," McGuinness said. "She was screaming and hysterical. He wasn't punching her, he was slapping her and she was left with a slight bruise on her face. But it was a terrible shock. He apologised but said, 'I'll kill the bitch if she carries on like this.'"

I asked if she ever saw him hit Bennett again. "No, it was just that one time – the only time I ever saw him physically violent in all the years I worked for him. She'd thrown a bottle at him, apparently. I have to say she was always throwing things. There was the glass ashtray she hurled at me when we first met. She destroyed the huge aquarium in the hall. She could be insane, Jill."

McGuinness described how Bennett wrecked the furniture at Chelsea Square in temper tantrums. She threw Osborne's jewellery away – gifts like cufflinks from Gilliatt and Rickards – and destroyed his letters. She cut the trouser legs off his suits and left his ties lopped in half. She called him a poof. She hurled all his notebooks out of the window, but that was later. (The notebooks were retrieved.) He eventually hid anything of personal value from her under a bookcase in his study.

"I never turned my back on Jill," McGuinness added. "You never knew what might happen. Anything *could* happen. I know it might seem ridiculous, but John was nervous of her."

The secretary to Bennett's first husband, Willis Hall, was Angela Marber, mother of Patrick Marber who wrote *Closer*. "I worked for a dramatist and I gave birth to one," she said proudly, and she laughed when I asked her whether she had been wary of Bennett when she worked for Hall. "We all were! Willis used to hide behind the sofa when he thought she was going to attack him."

Mrs Marber added, "I was even more scared of her mother. They were a formidable team. Jill was always horrid to me, although we became friends much later. I was young then, in my early twenties, and she imagined I was having an affair with Willis. There was no truth to it, but nothing pacified her on that score. When the marriage broke up, she said to me, 'He needs someone ordinary like you.' I don't know why John Osborne got involved with her. She was unusual and impetuous. But she was histrionic. She had to be the centre of attention. The day Willis married her at Caxton Hall, Dudley Moore called him up and said he'd got a wedding present. He played 'The Funeral March' over the phone to him on the piano."

Hall's marriage to Bennett ended after less than two years with numerous separations. Osborne's lingered on ruinously for eight years as if he no longer possessed the strength or will to begin over again. "The pestilent years of waste, frivolity and despair," he wrote bitterly to himself about the marriage. "The life that cannot be recovered."

In November 1981, he was writing in his notebook an idea for a play: "Actresses who kidnap playwrights to make them write a play for them."

Willis Hall wrote two roles for Bennett and one television drama. Osborne wrote seven (and two inconsequential TV plays). Hall's earlier plays were mostly northern working-class and Bennett's typical roles were glamorously upper-class. "You try telling that to Jill," he said to me bluntly. "She didn't want me to write a play unless there was a part in it for her. If she was working, then it was fine. But if she was unemployed and I was going to the office to write, she physically tried to stop me. She'd fight and scream, she'd throw things."

Like what? "Anything."

Hall had since been remarried for twenty-five years and his account of his unhappy time with Bennett was clear and dispassionate. "A lot of people liked Jill," he pointed out. "I think she probably made a better friend than a marriage."

John Gielgud adored her, Lindsay Anderson, too, and latterly, Ian

McKellen among others. Yet when I spoke to several people who were close to her, they described her destructive side. She was adept at finding weak spots in others and exploiting them. She encouraged confidences, but betrayed them.

She was most dangerous to herself. Hall spoke of her suicide threats. "If I was writing at the office, she'd ring and say that she'd taken a bottle of sleeping pills. There was nothing I could do but rush home in the middle of the day and check that she was all right. Sometimes she'd be sitting there drinking tea having a good laugh that she'd dragged me back. Or she could be inside the bedroom with the door locked. She wouldn't respond if I hammered on the door. So I'd break the door down and she'd be sitting up in bed reading a novel. But one time, she did take the sleeping pills and I had to call the ambulance. She was rushed to hospital. But next time, she hadn't taken the pills. And I'd break the door down again and there she was sitting up in bed. It was pretty hard stuff to cope with."

When Osborne eventually made preparations to end his marriage to her, he asked their mutual friend, the director Anthony Page, to stay close and look after her because he feared she was going to damage herself. For all her appetite for excitement and fantasy in a theatrical life, there was at Bennett's core a death wish that she dared to be fulfilled. Yet even in the worst of times Osborne rarely discussed her suicide threats with anyone, as if in some gallant truce in the unyielding wars between them there still remained a residue of tact and decency. When she died, however, he took his revenge and cruelly stripped her publicly of all illusion.

The pattern and dangerous game of Bennett's suspected suicide attempts during the marriage to Willis Hall were repeated in Osborne's, and by chance, I was an unlikely witness to one of them. Bennett, a friend of my then wife, telephoned the house from Chelsea Square one night at about 2 a.m. The worrying call itself didn't make much sense. She said she'd taken sleeping pills. Osborne was very likely at the country house in Kent. I now know that he often went there alone to get away. Bennett seemed to be calling incoherently for help. We lived nearby and tore round to her house. I called her doctor and friend, Patrick Woodcock, waking him up.

"Oh God, not again," he murmured through his sleep.

We hammered on the front door of the Osborne house for a while. Eventually, there was Jill Bennett at the door in her nightgown with a glass of champagne in hand. "What are you two doing here?" she asked cheerfully. "Come in and have some."

At which point Dr Woodcock arrived, immaculate as ever, as if he'd just been to the opera. "Leave this to me," he said firmly, and went inside with his little black bag and closed the door behind him.

He later mentioned to me that Osborne called him out quite frequently during the night to intervene in the midst of their violent rows. "You've got to come," Osborne pleaded. Dr Woodcock never saw Bennett hurt physically in any way. The bathroom adjoining the bedroom would be smashed to pieces. "The alcohol didn't help," he said. "The fights started when they were both drinking. It was awfully like *Who's Afraid of Virginia Woolf?*."

A year and a half into the marriage, at Christmas 1969, Osborne fired Sonia McGuinness without warning or even reason. The letter was delivered by his chauffeur to her home. She was seven months pregnant.

"After all those years . . ." said McGuinness, who was his loyal secretary and friend for a decade. "It didn't make sense."

But there were a number of explosive incidents like this in Osborne's life – wilful, wrong-headed decisions taken in the heat of an imagined slight or betrayal. Her dismissal made a cruel kind of sense.

McGuinness knew Osborne's handwriting better than anyone and the letter was written in a manic, abusive scrawl. She tore it up in bewilderment and hurt. It basically said that she had upset Jill Bennett and had never done her job properly. He complained about her punctuality and even her absence from work that Christmas. Yet Osborne was the one who had given her the time off. He demanded the return of the house keys immediately, ending, "The time has come to part."

She received the letter when she was at home for a week with a case of bad flu. The only other time she had missed even a day's work was when there had been a death in her family. It was a concerned Osborne who had suggested she stay home that Christmas when she felt unwell. He thought her baby was due and got the chauffeur to drive her back.

It would be five years before Sonia spoke to Osborne again and made her peace with him. Nothing was ever mentioned between them about the letter or the senseless dismissal. She wasn't the type to bear ill will, and as time passed she bore him none. She had reason to blame Bennett for what happened. But she felt that if anyone was to take responsibility, it was Osborne for being so weak.

Several months before she was fired, Bennett accused her of having an affair with Osborne. She was happily married and there was no truth to it. But the accusations continued. Osborne talked to her many times about it – smoothing things over and pacifying his wife. "He told me Jill didn't believe what she said, but she enjoyed saying it." And McGuinness soldiered on and hoped it would blow over.

In the next few months, she became pregnant with her second child. Bennett herself was now talking enthusiastically about having a child with Osborne and told her they were trying for one, too.

But she also confided to friends and McGuinness that she was either unable to have children or didn't want any. She never did have a child.

When McGuinness's pregnancy began to show, Bennett accused her of having Osborne's child. Osborne again tried to handle it, but McGuinness thought by then that when the new baby was born she might leave. Osborne wanted her to stay, however. "You could bring the baby to work with you," he told her.

Before Christmas, there was a party at the house, and McGuinness and her husband were invited. As the evening was winding down, Osborne saw her sitting alone on a sofa and asked her to dance, something they'd often done before. He liked to dance. McGuinness felt clumsily pregnant, but was happy to join him. And as he danced with her carefully, he patted her tum affectionately. Bennett saw the gesture and screamed across the room, "That's right! Look after your baby!" And hurled a glass across the room at them.

"There was an incredible kerfuffle," McGuinness said. Her husband actually calmed Bennett down. "She was pretty drunk. But she was immediately apologetic and tearful. 'What a terrible thing to do! What a monster I am.' John looked appalled and said how terribly sorry he was. He murmured to me, 'I should have thought.' And then we went home. It was a traumatic evening."

She nevertheless returned to work the following morning to find that Bennett had left a note on her typewriter. "Sonia darling – thank you for being such a help at the party. You were great and thank the staff too. I'm not in to anybody. Don't let anyone through unless it's Richard Eyre."

Three days later, McGuinness went down with flu and the concerned Osborne sent her home. A little over a week later, she was fired. When, in late January, she gave birth to a son, she received a huge bouquet of flowers from Jill Bennett.

Bennett couldn't play Annie in *The Hotel in Amsterdam*, after all, though it was the role Osborne had written for her when they first fell in love. There was a scheduling clash when *Time Present*, in which she starred, transferred to the West End as Osborne's new play opened at the Court. The excellent Judy Parfitt played the sophisticated, brittle Annie instead (and the irked Bennett reclaimed the role when the play was televised in 1971).

Despite the raves for Paul Scofield and the cast, *The Hotel in Amsterdam* received such mixed reviews when it premiered on 3 July 1968, that it took another forty years before it received a major revival in London. As the dramatist-director Nicholas Wright put it, it was so soundly forgotten as to amount to a state secret. There were those critics like John Lahr, now of the *New Yorker*, who saw in its apparent showbiz superficiality the end of Osborne as a force in theatre.

But for myself, the neglected play has always been among Osborne's most underestimated. Linked to the much lesser *Time Present* under the joint title "For the Meantime", it was both an interim work and a metaphor for greedy, aimless times. The screenwriter-hero, Laurie, and his showbiz chums bitch and gossip genially during a lost weekend in Amsterdam like heirs to the witty wastrels of Coward's *Design for Living*. Then this jolting moment transforms the hero's outwardly mundane ennui into a casual premonition of death:

"How I hate holidays. The deadly chink of ice in steaming glasses all day. Those endless, cloudless days by the pool even when it's in the blazing sun. Luxury, spoilt people. Lounging together, basting themselves with comfort, staring into pools. A swimming pool is a terrible thing to look into on a holiday. It's no past and no future. You can stare into a stream or a river or a ditch. Who wouldn't rather die in a ditch than a pool?"

Spoilt, rich Laurie is a self-portrait of Osborne at forty. If we didn't know this man, we would say that, like all writers, he needs to be loved and showered with money for doing as little as possible. But at the heart of this reckless, imperfect man is his submerged torment, the capacity to wound and be wounded. He flees boredom and fears damnation. He regrets time passing and certain lost things that can never be recovered. He places a high premium on friendship and will be unforgiving and foolish when sensing betrayal. He reviles critics. ("I work my drawers off and get written off twice a year as not fulfilling my early promise by some philistine squirt drumming up copy.") He lampoons his mother coarsely for easy laughs. ("I mean just to think of swimming about inside that repulsive thing for nine months . . .") He goes too far, obviously. He's mean and witty and pushes the *edge*. He drinks quite heavily. He enjoys showbiz camp, but needs and charms women – beautiful, strong, scary women.

Scofield, who played Laurie, eventually got to know and like Osborne, but he first intuited him through acting in his play. "I knew the quality of his writing voice," he explained. "And, as sometimes happens, speaking the words of a writer brought me close to knowing him. And I found within all the banter of the character a bitter sense of betrayal, something truly passionate, and night after night in speaking those lines I knew a deeply serious man, eloquent, unsentimental, unselfpitying and troubled. He was honestly and fearlessly articulating his loss of faith in – what? People? And I loved him for that."

In the play, three couples spend a weekend talking and drinking in a luxury hotel in Amsterdam. Led by Laurie, they've secretly fled the clutches of the powerful movie producer they're all connected to in various ways. He's known as K.L. – code for T.R. or Tony Richardson. In a scathing monologue, Osborne has given Laurie a polished version of his letter to Richardson that destroyed their friendship. He's added a curse of loneliness – for Osborne, the worst of fates, like being sent to hell.

"I simply hope tonight that you are alone – I know you won't be. But I hope, at least, you will feel alone, alone as I feel it, as we all in our time feel it, without burdening our friends. I hope the GPO telephone system is collapsed, that your chauffeur is dead and the housekeeper drunk and that there isn't one con-man, camp follower, eunuch, pimp, mercenary, or procurer of all things possible, or one globetrotting bum boy at your side to pour you a drink on this dark January evening . . ."

"On this dark January evening . . ." Even Osborne's cursed time of the New Year had been subconsciously transferred. But an Osborne play without his customary jabs and spitballs would be like a song-and-dance man without his patter. He introduced audiences to backstage showbiz patois, and theatre people have never been nuns. *The Hotel in Amsterdam* also rounds up a few of Osborne's usual suspects – among them, the perfidious French, of course; Australian nurses; airline stewardesses; homosexuals; the lower middle-classes of England (whence Osborne came and fled); and all Americans.

"Thank heavens for the charm and femininity of the English male, I say," Annie announces cheerfully.

"Well, American women certainly don't have it, poor sods," Laurie responds.

There's also Laurie's running joke and invention of "El Fag Airlines" – the airline especially for homosexuals. According to the *Oxford Dictionary of New Words*, however, the term "political correctness" only entered popular usage in 1986–87, some twenty years after *The Hotel in Amsterdam* was written. When the play was first staged, nobody gave a hoot about "being correct" and no homosexual or humourless killjoy in the audience, to my knowledge, took offence. Only the risible letters that Laurie recites from his lower middle-class relatives were criticized at the time as insulting. In fact, Osborne based them almost verbatim on letters from his own mother and various, affectionate, grasping uncles.

Raised in the age of official government censorship, Osborne wasn't about to censor himself voluntarily on any topic, pre- or post-PC. The righteous heroes of the politically correct age became a Swiftian gift to him – the gay-lib movement, the lesbian activists, "those longshore bullies with bale hooks in bras" – the militant feminists, the anti-smoking police, the do-gooding welfare workers – "God rot the *carers*" – the cheery senior citizens groups, the self-improvers and New Agers, the *types*, the herds, the prigs, the puritans and banner wavers everywhere whose formula for living would reduce life to a political slogan at the joyless cost of individualism and eccentric Englishness.

The Hotel in Amsterdam was a start. Osborne's unpoliticized homosexual friends put El Fag Airlines in the same category as his jokes about the French and Australians. The newly politicized gays of the AIDS era had more cause to take offence. But Osborne was an equal opportunity offender. In *Time Present*, Pamela asks her sister about her young lover, "Does he have a name or is he a group?" The conformist *group* was Osborne's target, not the individual.

He mocked Australians with such malicious glee, for example, that he was practically slung out of the country when he visited Australia in 1977. Yet his ex-mistress and friend, Jocelyn Rickards, was an Australian born in Melbourne. His closest friend through the Bennett years, theatre producer Helen Montagu, was born in Sydney, as was his agent for a number of years, Robin Dalton. And in 1969, Osborne was among the first public figures to acclaim that mythic bird of paradise, Dame Edna Everadge. Osborne raved amusingly about the eternal appeal of waving your gladdies at Barry Humphries. "For me, he long ago, by the simple power of his poetic instinct and genius created something that was not there before," he wrote. "That is to say, Australia."

When *The Hotel in Amsterdam* was revived in London in September 2003, at the Donmar Warehouse, Robin Lefevre's fine production with Tom Hollander as Laurie proved a great success. Drama critics almost never change their minds, and those who didn't get it the first time round didn't get it the second. But almost all the younger reviewers responded so enthusiastically it was as if they were surprised to find that the man who wrote *Look Back in Anger* wrote anything else. A new generation of theatregoers discovered Osborne forty years on and no one, incidentally, protested about El Fag Airlines. To the contrary, the tolerant, laissez-faire English seemed to be rolling in the aisles.

For myself, I was meeting again Osborne's tortured hero for the first time since Scofield played him. And as time has passed it was clearer than ever that Laurie yearns in all his banter and spleen for another chance in life, but knows that when it comes it will fail. "Don't grieve," his newly confessed love, Annie, says to him instinctively. She too senses the chance for a solution, opportunity, the salvation of love, will be lost.

"Don't grieve" – the words come from nowhere, as if Osborne had written a message to himself. A part of him would always be in mourning for his own life – grieving in the depths of his soul for some overwhelming, unconquerable primal loss.

"Then what is good?" Tennessee Williams asked rhetorically about the trappings of success, that ensnared writers like Osborne and himself. "William Saroyan wrote a great play on this theme, that purity of heart is the one success worth having. 'In the time of your life – live!' That time is short and it doesn't return again. It is slipping away while I write this and while you read it, and the monosyllable of the clock is Loss, Loss, Loss, unless you devote your heart to its opposition."

The Hotel in Amsterdam is a chamber piece about love and friendship, betrayal and loss. Beneath the gauze of its cauterized, escapist surface is the undertow of melancholy and need that seeps through all of Osborne's plays. It's about growing older and the sting of the Bitch Goddess of success.

39

The Chapter of Accidents

For the first time I thought of the mechanism of suicide.
Osborne notebook entry, 8 October 1972

On 9 May 1971, the *Sunday Times* heralded a new season of plays at the Royal Court with a photograph of the now bearded, forty-one-year-old Osborne sitting on the steps in Sloane Square with three other dramatists – David Storey, E.A.Whitehead, and a boyish, long-haired, twenty-three-year-old David Hare. You would not have a clue from the picture that the legendary playwright at its centre was in a private hell of fear that he was already a spent force in theatre.

Pinter and Stoppard were now in the ascendancy along with the new politicized playwrights like Hare and Caryl Churchill. During that 1971 season, Pinter's *Old Times* starring Vivien Merchant and Dorothy Tutin was playing at the Aldwych. Stoppard's admired *Jumpers* opened at the Old Vic the following year. Yet three Osborne plays had recently transferred from the Court to run in the West End simultaneously – a near unprecedented event. *Time Present* was at the Duke of York's, *The Hotel in Amsterdam* at the New Theatre (now the Albery), and a revival of *Look Back in Anger* joined them at the Criterion. When their producer, Oscar Lewenstein, ambled out of his office in Goodwin's Court, he could see the whole of one side of lower St Martin's Lane occupied by Osborne's plays.

West of Suez – his twelfth play – was the main attraction in the Court's new season. Set in an imaginary former British colony, its main character, the elderly novelist Wyatt Gillman, resembles a fading Evelyn Waugh who has become a spent force and a prophet opposed to change. In contrast, Hare's *Slag* – his first solo play for the radical fringe – was a contemporary satire for three actresses, partly inspired by Germaine Greer's feminism. Whitehead's *Alpha Beta* was about a crumbling modern marriage, and Storey's *The Changing Room* was a model of working-class social realism about a rugby team, with a notorious nude scene involving fifteen well-hung actors.

Hare wrote of his first meeting with Osborne during that photo shoot: "John seemed shiningly confident. He had travelled only down the King's Road [from his house in Chelsea Square], but he appeared to have come from another world to my own. I was 23. John was more expensively barbered than any man I had hitherto met and even his jacket was a work of art. I was in awe, unable to speak."

At length, they shook hands hopelessly and parted. "The silence between us was profound," Hare added touchingly. "I thought it was his job to say something. Only now do I understand it was mine."

The aspiring playwright had met the successful playwright he worshipped at school. Yet, when he came to know Osborne and even champion his work, he never ceased to be scared of him.

Hare put his strange fear down to what Joseph Heller described in *Something Happened* as "the whammy". "Heller says that when someone gives you 'the whammy' you can't speak in front of them and you begin to sweat and nothing you say makes any sense. And it's nothing to do with anything like power or personality. I always felt in front of John that I was never coherent. He gave me 'the whammy'. He was my friend in spite of the difficulty I had in being with him. I was scared of him. I spent a lot of time with him and yet I was always scared of him. I felt tested by him."

What was the test?

"Will you be as wild as I am? Will you be as wild and uncaring about what people think? That was the test."

During that same period of 1971, Osborne was in fact recording in his notebook, "Tears close to hand. That's paralysing in itself. Worried by absurdities. Who'd be my literary executor? Who'd bother? Rightly. Power without steerage. Not eaten for 4 days. Just throw it up. Squalid slime on beard and towels, face flannels. Dread the bath. Water. Even toothpaste. Mustn't go on like this . . ."

The bewildering collapse of his confidence links to the state of his corrosive marriage:

She screams in restaurants, shouts me down, wants me as a prestige office boy . . .

She hates me or is indifferent to me. No sex or admiration. I *want* to sell both houses. My *best* work is ahead of me. Even if no one wants to listen. That wouldn't matter. Everything is so ridiculous and obscene.

My days in theatre are over. I would accept that. My 17th year as a professional writer for the theatre. A birthday for me at the Royal Court! What an absurdity. I'm an embarrassment to them and myself.

In the morning, she says with scarcely any alcohol this time:
I detest her career.
I detest her as an actor.
I am a phoney "genius".
Third Rate: agreed.
Unattractive: agreed.
Sexually a non-starter: I didn't used to think so.
Wrong – the women were flattering me.

I *am* almost impotent.
"You're not even a *man*." Queer? I think she knows I'm not. I've thought about it!
They don't like me and I don't like them . . .
I've been swindled. Swindled by myself.

He blamed himself for blundering into the marriage. He was writing in sputtering rage in his 1985 notebook: "To have allowed myself to spend eight years of so contemptible and malevolent . . . to have invested such trust in a creature. I despise myself for it to the grave. The fault was mine. The inane, paltry judgment was mine."

In the wars between them during the marriage, she neutralized him. "Look at him," Bennett goaded her husband in front of others. "The poofter can't even get it up!" It passed for banter sometimes. But there are several entries in the notebooks about his waning sexual appetite when the pathologically thin-skinned Osborne was left defenceless by his wife's taunts. "Sex: The final desolation. I feel so unattractive. Never less wanted . . ." By then, he was drinking a bottle of brandy a day. "I don't think I can get it up any more," he told friends in bewildered faux jokiness.

24 June 1972

Oh yes, after talking about HG [*Hedda Gabler*] after two years for yet another four hours, JB said:
I was written out.
Disliked by all at the Court.
Always a hopeless fuck.
Even the queers don't fancy me, because my eyes are too close together.
Couldn't think *how* I earned my money!

I, the while, being like a sort of Tolworth Oscar Wilde. Why did I listen? No drink. Wanted to go to bed. Too tired – almost like a warm bath this fatuously crass abuse and invective.

She's obsessed about getting over 40. What can I do? She's attractive quite often. To me she's just a pretty scalpel . . .

His sense of unworthiness and self-abasement were the fault lines that had been running through his life since childhood when his belittling mother played on his weak spots and locked him in her embrace. "How terrible is a mother's love," he quotes Lytton Strachey in one of the notebooks. "To love so much and understand so little." Bennett triggered the same desolation provoked by his mother's mockery. Nellie Beatrice turned her humiliating put-downs into a social style just as Bennett turned their ritual battles into public performances.

Then and for the rest of his life there was no defence and there was no cure. As we've seen, he was never reconciled to his loathed and misunderstood mother. He wished her dead, but she was still alive and would not die.

"I, a middle-aged man," he wrote in his 1971 notebook, "feeling older than ever, both wishing the other far away. I sit with my wife, my mother, my daughter. With nothing to say to one another. Only emptiness and desperate twitchings of flight."

In one staggering entry, he's even contemplating suicide:

8 October 1972

The tide of events really is well out of hand. For the first time – properly – I thought of the immediate mechanism of suicide. It's a hole-in-the-corner business. I know I don't have the strength or skill to use a knife. No Roman blood to spout easily or slave to dismiss. I don't want to involve Jill – not at the wrong stage. I don't want to be vengeful. I just want it to close over my head. But how? Jill pretends to be an expert but she's not. And very practical, which I'm not. I've nothing to leave behind – except of course there'd be more money, possessions, and I should think, more opportunities for J.B. Every day brings another variant on pain . . .

Osborne's stage-managed public appearances aside, he hadn't yet rebounded from the midlife crisis that sent him into the clinic with a nervous breakdown. Three years later, he was still lost in the nightmare world of his own play, *Inadmissible Evidence*.

It's as if *Inadmissible* was an act of self-prophecy. Less and less kindliness, imagination. Brutality. Take-overs. Money, far more but less and less opportunity for the spirit of simple laughter. 1956 seems like a more or less innocent time. Greed, suspicion and disbelief. Who would have said the English people are dead. England is dead. Long live the Economic Union!

It takes 24 hours. Open gas fire in Linda's room. [Linda Drew, his new secretary.] Not ludicrous half death. I'd be discovered. Sleeping pills . . .

West of Suez opened at the Royal Court on 17 August 1971, and received mixed to tepid reviews. Even so, it transferred to the Cambridge Theatre on the strength of Ralph Richardson's performance as Wyatt, his burnt-out case stranded by changing times. Osborne was found guilty of lamenting the loss of Empire and shifting to the Right.

Wyatt Gillman is its symbol of values floundering in a celebration of Western mediocrity and junk. The play isn't about nostalgia for Empire, but fear for the destruction of language and culture. Osborne has abandoned showbiz metaphors for something bigger and more profound – a warning about the fate of modern civilization. In its essential, cataclysmic message, the now forgotten *West of Suez* was ahead of its time. It's about terrorism.

And now was the time when Osborne could easily have lost his creative nerve. The unpredictable middle years in the creative life of any dramatist are punishing enough. Playwrights don't necessarily lose their talent; they lose their audience. There are exceptions – Ibsen, still a major force in his sixties, was among them. But playwrights like Arthur Miller, Tennessee Williams, Pinter, Beckett even (though Beckett turned to plays late) are most often identified by the cluster of benchmark plays they wrote in comparatively younger days. Miller was still writing at nearly ninety, but his best work was achieved well over half a century before. Tennessee Williams's later plays could scarcely find a home. And Osborne? He was in a state of agony about his place in theatre, but there would be no surrender yet.

West of Suez was an ambitious play with big virtues and big flaws. He wrote a plum role for the other-worldly Richardson as his exhausted Prospero dispensing ironies on a Caribbean island. The atmosphere of pampered British exiles abroad decaying in post-colonial ennui is a deliberate echo of Chekhov. (There's a passing reference to Trofimov, the perpetual student of *The Cherry Orchard*.) There are also four sisters (where three is customary). One of them, the bright, cutting Frederica, unhappily married to an apparently indifferent pathologist, was played by Jill

Bennett. In their icy mutual contempt, language – words, reason, decency – has broken down.

"The play is about decaying of tongues," Osborne explained, "not just of colonial empires but of emotional empires, too." Among its serious flaws, his canvas is overcrowded. He skirts Tory nostalgia for the empty trappings and style of the old world. "The joss sticks and Burmese guns," says Evangie, one of the sisters, affectionately remembering her grandfather's study. "Saddle Oil. Back numbers of the *Times* of Natal. A Zulu grammar . . . Rawhide shields and dried python skins and brass iguanas. And the photographs . . ."

Today, it all sounds uncomfortably like a window display in Ralph Lauren. But if *West of Suez* falters, its savage message still alarms us. "In these changing times, do you still believe that words in themselves have any meaning, value or validity?" the over-earnest local journalist asks Wyatt.

The celebrated novelist wears a mask of defensive scepticism, but his response is unequivocal. "I still cling pathetically to the old bardic belief that 'words alone are certain good'."

Words gone rotten, Osborne is saying, are certain chaos. The American student who screams at Wyatt and the rest that their days are numbered is incoherent with neo-fascist rage. "Fuck", "shit" and "blood" are his verbal graffitti. ". . . bastards . . . I sit here listening to you. Having your fancy dinner and your wine from France and England. You know what I think of you? What *we* think of you? What we think of you? Fuck all your *shit* . . ."

At the play's violent close, Wyatt is senselessly killed by a group of armed islanders – today's terrorists. A moral universe has collapsed along with its culture. Osborne's ambiguous, deceptively frivolous curtain line that follows the murderous scene is his most purely Shavian. "My God – they've shot the fox." As the curtain descends, we're unexpectedly jolted back from the wrecked colonial idyll of the play to the romantic heartland of England. They've shot the fox – the leader of the pack, the hunted quarry, dying breed.

It was during the Bennett marriage that Osborne returned to what he called "the acting lark". Perhaps it was a break or diversion, and it eventually brought him surprising fame.

He had long maintained that he never took himself seriously as an actor, and few people did. But in 1968, he was playing an impressive, slightly effete, German aristocrat opposite Bennett's socialist spy in David Mercer's *The Parachute* on BBC TV. (Mercer was an old friend of Osborne's.)

In 1970, he made his film debut as Turgenev's mad romantic poet, Maidenov, lusting after Dominique Sanda in Turgenev's *First Love*. The film version was directed by Maximilian Schell – Redl in *A Patriot for Me* – and it was Schell who innocently asked him to appear in the film. He didn't know that Osborne had once been an actor.

He didn't pariculary care. "Anyone can act in films," the still handsome Schell told me. "Look at Rin Tin Tin. And he was *good*." He cast Osborne as Maidenov because he thought he looked the romantic part and his manic cameo appearance is a collector's item. Looking rakishly poetic in a black fedora, he improvised his big scene when they came across a sheep farm on location in Hungary. "I love thee!" Osborne cries, spouting mad Maidenov's poetry to the indifferent sheep. "Passion of my life! I love thee as freely as men strive for right!"

Mike Hodges, the director of *Get Carter*, had been impressed by his performance in *The Parachute* and cast him against criminal type as the classy killer, Kinnear, who runs a porn ring. Set in the underworld sleaze of villains and slags in Newcastle, *Get Carter*, starring Michael Caine, is the *film noir* that ushered in the Seventies and defined modern British gangster movies. "Sometimes I think I should just retire and piss off to the Bahamas," is Osborne's opening line as he sucks indifferently on a gold toothpick.

Hodges remembered going to meet him at Chelsea Square. "I was surprised every time I met John. He was just a very shy man, though there were also times when he could have been no one else *but* an actor. The Chelsea house was like a stage set and when I entered it I felt as if there was a fourth wall missing and I was appearing in a Terence Rattigan play with lots of champagne. Jill Bennett was there, crossing and uncrossing her legs. French actresses still do it. It was as if she wanted a role in *Get Carter* as well."

But on the first day of filming, Hodges was convinced he'd made a huge mistake. "John was playing it so quietly that I could hardly hear him," he explained. "I thought he was completely wrong for the role. But I kept bringing the camera in closer and closer to him. And then I realized that the more he underplayed it, the more sinister he became. I think he was extraordinary in it."

Osborne has just three short scenes and yet he all but steals the movie. He looks relaxed onscreen, his trim beard flecked with grey, a picture of recessive, elegant menace with unblinking eyes. Years later, when he moved to the village of Clun in Shropshire, he howled with laughter when he discovered that he was known more for *Get Carter* than anything else he did.

*

In September 1972, he was making notes for a new play, ostensibly about his marriage to Bennett, entitled *Watch It Come Down*. The title came from a sign on a demolition site: "We make it happen. You watch it come down."

But everything, it seems, was crashing around him. In November 1971, he entered a *New Statesman* competition inviting an impersonation of a play by John Osborne. He submitted a fairly typical example from his new TV play, *The Gift of Friendship* (which had just been televised, starring Alec Guinness). They didn't publish it.

In the same month he began *Watch It Come Down*, he made a notebook entry entitled, "The Chapter of Accidents". Osborne was a compulsive list-maker and what followed was a list of some thirty bad "accidents" that had lately piled up in his beleaguered life – among them, "Marriage", "No sex. Virtually", "No friendship", "Health", "Nolan", "Middle-age", "Slow Dying of old Western" (his favourite dog), "Drinking too much", "Hedda not transferring" and "Money".

His adaptation of *Hedda Gabler* for Bennett was the first Osborne play not to transfer to the West End in almost a decade. For the first time in many extravagant years, he was also concerned about debt.

October 1972

Money pours out. Nobody *pays* me. I owe £26,000 in surtax from seven years ago. My overdraft is £20,000 . . . I have lost myself to myself. "They" say they are afraid of me. Afraid of me. Of what? Of one man struggling. They think I am privileged. All the time I am being beaten up. I want the chance to work. It has receded. And I see no way out within me. I am a relic . . .

January 1973

She *can't* hurt me any more. Her attempts to devalue me, pepper me full of guilt, turn me into a fragment, a figment of what I was, am, can be. All that's over . . .

March 1973

Got attacked by JB last night. Her career or something. Too weary to listen. She put the usual *hand out* . . . Tonight to see Alan Bennett's "highly successful play". Anyway, *boffo*. Big. *He* deserves it. I'm just out of touch with public antennae.

Tomorrow is my fifth wedding anniversary. God! Agony is real. The worst is HERE.

The following apologetic note from Bennett had been left there in the pages of the notebook. A row must have been provoked by her jealousy of his former wife, Gilliatt. Osborne was most likely at the country house in Edenbridge, Kent.

". . . I have been destructive about P [Penelope Gilliatt]. I suppose to be honest I am jealous and envious although I love Nolan very much. I think you know that. But I am my own worst enemy. Please forgive me. I regret my evil temper. All I want truly is your happiness and Nolan's. I shouldn't have told you lots of things about Tearle [her first love, Godfrey Tearle] especially that he sometimes bored me. It was a mistake and a breach of confidence . . . I do love you – totally – that's why I go potty – bad excuse – not a good excuse at all. I shall think of you all day. Please ring me when I come back. PLEASE . . ."

The notebook continues with alarming entries about his failing health including a swollen liver from too much drinking, and gout.

He had suffered from spells of gout since the early 1960s. Tynan teased him about this, saying he was afflicted with Grand Old Upper-Class Theatre. But the *Punch* cartoon image of the gouty gent with a paunch and a bandaged foot resting on a stool is the myth. The reality is a high acidic content of the blood aggravated by booze and rich food. Osborne's more serious symptoms – like being unable to feel the tips of his fingers when he was in the clinic – could have been an early onset of the diabetes that eventually killed him.

9 July '73

Had a *real* scare this afternoon. Half an hour ago in fact. Was kneeling on study floor reading. Went to get up and legs paralysed up to the knee. Terrible throbbing in calves. Just managed to stagger to a stand but then couldn't walk for ten minutes . . . Still sweating with shock. That *was* it. Christ, 43 and on the way with poor Sean Kenny. [The set designer who died suddenly.] Felt so good on Saturday too. Was going to start a new play – BULLIES – tomorrow. Hope I can.

10 July '73

Still here! But feeling low, scruffy and legs painful. Saw dreadful play, *Absurd Person Singular* [by Alan Ayckbourn]. Hobbled there and sweated along with the usual Americans. Most lowering experience. Thought I was going to die there and then in the fifth row stalls . . . So out of touch with the theatre. Where, if anywhere, next?

Pressured by tax problems, he took on lucrative film work – but every project collapsed.

In 1968, he abandoned a script about Sir Charles Dilke for producer Sam Spiegel (nicknamed by him "Spiegel of Arabia"). Forgoing a fee of $200,000, Osborne cabled its director, George Cukor: "HAVE TOLD SPIEGEL WILL NOT CONTINUE WITH DILKE STOP HAVE DONE MY BEST WHICH IS CLEARLY TOO GOOD FOR HIM STOP HAVE THEREFORE SAID UNEQUIV-OCALLY TO GET ANOTHER WRITER AND JOLLY GOOD LUCK TO ALL WHO SAIL IN HER STOP."

In 1973, his script of Conrad's *The Secret Agent* for Paramount Pictures was abandoned. So, too, a lucrative assignment to write *The Hostage* for John Huston. An ersatz *Tom Jones* version of *Moll Flanders* for Sophia Loren was never made. A 1974 screenplay, *Indian Mutiny*, for Peter O'Toole didn't happen. Another abandoned script, called *Gross*, was for Albert Finney's Memorial Films and it was Osborne's original idea – a comedy about a famous artist's attempts to drop out of the spotlight into anonymous obscurity.

Its producer, Michael Medwin, happily remembered visiting Osborne at Chelsea Square on and off for a year, during which time they swapped stories over a bottle of champagne and *never* discussed the screenplay. Another abandoned film project Osborne worked on in the fallow Seventies was inspired by Michael Holroyd's life of Lytton Strachey – who became the model for the dying biographer in *Watch It Come Down*.

In a letter dated 13 July 1973 to Faber & Faber – the publishers of his plays – he responded bleakly to an enquiry about his future plans:

> I can't think of anything that might be of interest to you. I was working on a screenplay of Lytton Strachey but that seems to have fallen through. So, I suppose I shall chip away at my next play. Sorry not to be more helpful but it's all a bit uneventful at present. In fact, the horizon looks fiercely empty at present.

"We were in New York together when John turned forty," Osborne's manager, Barry Krost, remembered, "when late one night he suddenly turned to me in the street and said, 'Nobody ever wrote a great play after the age of forty.' He looked desolate."

Krost was Osborne's personal manager for a decade. A manager . . . *manages* (as opposed to more mundane agenting). A former child actor, Krost was the young Toulouse-Lautrec in John Huston's original 1952 film of *Moulin Rouge* (in which the ingénue Jill Bennett played a barmaid). He was the cockney son of a cleaning lady and a father who ended up running a café called La Roulette below a brothel in Victoria. (Michael Caine was his dad's night porter.) He went on to represent Cat Stevens, David Bailey, Angela Lansbury and Peter Finch, among many others, but when he was starting out, he was introduced to Osborne by Oscar Beuselinck with the words, "'Ere, John. I want you to meet this little poof. Great charmer."

Osborne was among his first big clients – something Krost never forgot. "That wonderfully appalling man," he said affectionately. "He was good to me." Judging by his suite of offices opposite the Beverly Wilshire Hotel in Los Angeles, where we met, this amiable charmer has prospered since he went to live in America in the mid-Seventies. Before then, he knew Osborne and Bennett closely and they socialized together. "Jill had more style than most women I've ever known," he said. "Yet on one of the first evenings I spent with her, she told me, 'Sometimes I just want to go home and take my sweeties.' Pills to kill herself, she meant. She said it often, more earnestly sometimes than others."

"Hello, you little shit," Osborne would say to Krost with a smile. "How are yew?" He remembered their carefree times together, like taking a sauna with Osborne at Chelsea Square as they drank champagne. Or the day when Tynan was having a fierce argument with John Dexter in the pub next door to the Court and Osborne jumped on the bar yelling, "Go at it, girls!" Krost was much younger than Osborne and he idolized him. "Yet John was naive in many ways," he said. "Whenever he talked about women it was as if he never understood them. He wrote brilliantly about monumental emotions, yet he ended relationships coldly. I think people hurt him and let him down, as he let himself down. But if John had been a hard man, not gentle, he would have been unbearable."

Tentatively, I asked him what he thought of the entry in an Osborne notebook that said, in effect, "Never trust a homosexual or a Jew"?

"Well, as a Jewish homosexual I signed his blank cheques," he answered, unfazed. "I wish he hadn't said it. But how much did he mean? Did he mean the terrible things he said about women I know he loved? I think John Osborne was nervous about anything that wasn't John Osborne. You're gay, you're Jewish, you're Australian, you're American, you're French, you're a *woman*. If you weren't him, you were an alien!"

"He was fond of dogs," I offered lamely. "Dogs aren't human," he replied. But one of the flaws in his novel idea was sitting opposite me. Barry Krost and Osborne got along. They were always friends.

He was there on 29 September 1972, when a madman broke into the Chelsea house and threatened to kill Osborne. It's listed as "knife hold up" in his "Chapter of Accidents". ("STARS IN KNIFE ORDEAL" was the headline the next day.) Krost was about to leave with Osborne and Bennett for an Alvin Ailey perfomance at the Coliseum when a stranger appeared and confronted them with a knife. "He thought John had sold out from the working class and wanted to kill him," Krost explained. "John was terrified and so was I. But Jill took one look at the man and said, 'Go away. I will not be late for the ballet.' And he was so amazed, he fled!"

Bennett could be wonderfully cavalier. "ACTRESS JILL IN SHOCK NUDES RUMPUS" read one headline. On 4 August 1974, the *Sunday People* reported that she had been asked to leave a London store for staring at scantily dressed girls in a changing room. "WHY I PEEP AT GIRLS – BY JILL BENNETT". "I feel that one should be interested in one's own sex," she announced. "Changing rooms in stores are interesting. You look at a girl and think, 'I've got a better bum than her' or 'She's got nice tits'. Or she may be wearing similar nicks to you . . . I am long-sighted and tend to peer at people."

There were other bizarre incidents. A death list kept by the international terrorist, Carlos Martinez – known as "The Jackal" – was found in a Bayswater flat with explosives. His assassination targets included the Sieffs of Marks & Spencer, Lord and Lady Sainsbury, and John Osborne and Jill Bennett.

There were occasions when Osborne and Bennett abused their own fame. Krost told me of the time he accompanied them to dinner at a favourite Chelsea restaurant, Provans, run by Barry Sainsbury. It was an intimate, chic little place up a flight of stairs, and they made an entrance: Bennett, dressed in Givenchy, on the arm of her renowned husband in his perfectly tailored Savile Row suit, with Krost, a bit *off*, as he described himself, in his flash Tommy Nutter suit and Mr Fish kipper tie.

"They had already been drinking for about eight hours," he said, describing their routine of champagne and cocktails from mid-morning on. The abuse between them was by now a weary ritual, and anything could happen publicly in the corrupting force of their fame. During dinner they decided to tell a long, obscene joke at the top of their voices. It went on and on in a dirty roundelay between them about cocks and cunts until they emptied the room. For the embarrassed Krost, who's no prude, they were Establishment stars behaving like boorish adolescents. It was a triumphant display of jaded lives drowning in camp malice and too much alcohol, and that night as they left the empty restaurant, Bennett slid down the steep stairs in a stupor.

Yet Krost also looked back on his days with them nostalgically, as if there had been no one else quite like this glamorous couple in reckless pursuit of illusory happiness. Before our meeting ended, he solved the mystery of another cryptic entry in Osborne's "Chapter of Accidents" – "the car crash".

Almost every Sunday, Osborne and Bennett drove to the Dulwich home of the West End producer Helen Montagu and her family for lunch. Montagu began in theatre as a casting director at the Royal Court. "On my first day, Oscar Lewenstein gave me two pieces of advice," she told me. "The first was never to be surprised at anything that goes on at the Court. The second was never to marry John Osborne under any circumstances."

Osborne was at the wheel of the Mercedes heading for lunch in Dulwich when an argument erupted with his wife. Krost was in the back seat. "There wasn't any hysteria between them," he said. "It was more a case of constant bickering." But as they approached the Wandsworth roundabout about a hundred yards away, Osborne said to Bennett, "If you say that one more time, I'm going to smash the car into the roundabout ahead."

Thus challenged, she continued goading him and he put his foot down on the accelerator.

"Murder!" the hysterical Bennett cried as Osborne sped straight for the roundabout. "Murder!"

Krost was crouched in the back praying. And the Mercedes came to a steaming halt in the middle of the island when they hit the Keep Left sign in the flower beds.

Osborne hadn't noticed that the car behind him was a police car. He was breathalysed and lost his licence for a year. Bennett sustained a fracture to her right ankle – the outcome, no doubt, of bracing herself before they ploughed into the bollard.

A newspaper photograph caught her leaving hospital with her right foot in plaster looking wan in a wheelchair. Helen Montagu received an agonized call from her when she was in St Thomas's. "John's just tried to murder me," Bennett told her. "But he didn't succeed."

Ill feeling, it's true, had been running particularly high between them shortly before the crash.

A Sense of Detachment, Osborne's latest play that premiered in 1972, was so outrageously pornographic no one at the Court would direct it. Osborne's usual director, Anthony Page, was unavailable. Various actors had also turned it down. The beloved Stanley Holloway sent Osborne's scandalous script back with a note, "Returned with disgust." One role was cast: Jill Bennett was to play the character known as the Girl. But that changed when a director, Frank Dunlop, was eventually found. Dunlop insisted on casting his own girl.

"They were all shit scared of the play at the Court," he explained. Dunlop ran the adventurous Young Vic Company and he began casting *A Sense of Detachment* from his own troupe of actors. One of them was the talented and tiny Denise Coffey who took the role destined for Bennett.

Bennett furiously took her revenge. A new play by Caryl Churchill, *Owners*, was to open at the Court's experimental Theatre Upstairs shortly before Osborne's premiered on the main stage. She accepted the leading role in *Owners*, thereby upstaging her husband. The car crash happened on the eve of Bennett's first dress rehearsal and the fractured ankle lost her the leading role.

"Pity you weren't driving Denise Coffey," she told the contrite Osborne. "Her feet wouldn't have even reached the car floor."

Meanwhile, in a sensational piece of casting, Rachel Kempson – Lady Redgrave, matriarch of the Redgrave clan – had agreed to play the sweet old lady who adores pornography and gives the audience illustrated lectures on its charms.

"Thank goodness I'm being asked to play someone who isn't a virgin," she told Frank Dunlop. During the rowdy first previews of the play, however, Peggy Ashcroft visited her backstage to talk her out of continuing in it. "Rachel, you've simply got to get out of this," Ashcroft warned her. "It's utterly disgusting."

Kempson told Dunlop afterwards, "She's only jealous."

The sophisticated ex-Etonian John Standing joined the cast in the role known as Chap, Nigel Hawthorne was the Chairman, Denise Coffey was the Girl and Rachel Kempson the Old Lady. During rehearsals, Standing took Osborne to see a Paul Raymond nude show called *Pyjama Tops* at the Whitehall. "I thought he was going to be sick, he laughed so much," he said. "The joy of it was that it was completely tasteless. For no particular reason all the girls in the show leapt into a swimming pool in their pyjama tops. And then there was the ghastliness of all these tourists in raincoats wanking in the stalls. I knew John would love it."

Osborne saw *Pyjama Tops* three times. "It's the best entertainment in London," he declared. "A hundred minutes not wasted."

A Sense of Detachment was an accident waiting to happen. When it opened at the Court on 4 December 1972, almost all the reviews were disastrous. Osborne wrote it on amphetamines – his upper of choice – and it speeds and swirls plotlessly like a racing state of mind. Dunlop shrewdly believed the freewheeling piece was like living inside Osborne's head. It was pilloried as a scatalogical indulgence whereas, in my view, it's the reverse – a morality play about a world in anarchy.

It dared to lampoon graphic pornography a generation before the onset of global Internet porn. *A Sense of Detachment* is a dreamscape about the pollution of culture and the healing power of great poetry and music. It is Blakean hymns crossed with sexual perversion. It's about the miracle of falling in love, the mystery of women, the pain of them and the redemption. It's closer to agitprop theatre than formal drama – a stream of consciousness *entertainment*, a pulpit for roundheads and cavaliers meant to provoke and outrage and raise the roof.

In its anarchic essentials, *A Sense of Detachment* is about England – about the romance of an innocent past, its debasement and finer, more beautiful things.

Osborne was courting extreme danger. He even used a plant – a boozy soccer hooligan in a box – to heckle his own play. "Load of rubbish!" "Get it off!" For good measure, he had another heckler among the audience yelling: "Couldn't agree more! Bloody awful!" "What we want is family entertainment!" "Will this *never* end?"

The trouble began when real members of the audience joined in the heckling with "Hear! Hear!" Uproar greeted courageous Rachel Kempson as a proselytizer of porn. If, today, Judi Dench played Kempson's role, the odds are there would be the same open-jawed disbelief.

"Did you ever fancy getting hold of a pretty young girl-scout and fucking her up the arsehole?" the Old Lady asks the audience charmingly as she reads from a hard porn sales catalogue. "Well, the two lucky lads in this picture story did just that . . ."

"Oh Lady Redgrave – how *could* you?" came a stunned voice from the stalls.

According to Frank Marcus of the *Sunday Telegraph* – who seemed to enjoy the show without quite saying why – the "ineffably English" Kempson read "the most explicitly-worded accounts of sexual perversions yet uttered on the London stage, thus driving a large number of shocked theatregoers to the exits".

Frank Dunlop sat in the balcony with Osborne on several occasions watching the show. They took bets with each other on how long it would take for the first person to storm out. The more protests there were, the more Osborne loved it.

At one notorious performance, the barracking grew so loud that the sixty-two-year-old Kempson leapt off the stage and attacked two men in the third row. "ACTRESS LEAPS INTO THE STALLS", ran next day's headlines. "LADY REDGRAVE SCRAPS BOO BOYS." "ACTRESS JUMPS OFF STAGE – CLOBBERS TWO MEN."

"There are times when roughhouse methods are called for," Lady Redgrave told the *Daily Telegraph* on 24 January 1973. "I just saw red." She described "two gaily dressed chaps" in the third row who were barracking her rudely throughout the performance. "I could stand it no longer," she admitted, and jumped off the stage to slap one of them and pull the hair of the other. "I hopped back on the stage and tried to calm down. I am not at all ashamed of what I did. Of course, one should not do this sort of thing. But once in a blue moon, you do."

According to John Standing, there was carnage in the theatre and he never had such fun. At the curtain call, they booed and they cheered and they threw things at the cast from the gods – a pair of old boots once, sometimes pennies from heaven.

In the cold light of day, Osborne feigned indifference to the devastating reviews and took them woundingly to heart. "This must surely be his farewell to the theatre," B.A. Young of the *Financial Times* concluded.

Who today remembers B.A. Young? But years later, Osborne was repeating his cruel, hanging judgment in various notebooks as if it were a death sentence. "This must surely be his farewell to the theatre . . ."

40

Watch It Come Down

In all this clamour, those terrible words: My God, My God, why hast
Thou forsaken me?

Osborne notebook entry, June 1973

When Osborne's young daughter, Nolan, visited London from New York,
he saw her at his former Chester Square home after prolonged negotiation
with Penelope Gilliatt. The divorce settlement had awarded Gilliatt custody
and his visits were rationed according to whim.

Even so, Nolan sometimes stayed for a week or two with her father. She
felt relaxed in Jill Bennett's carefree company and there would be jolly teas
together at Fortnum's and shopping sprees at Simpson's in Piccadilly and
along the King's Road. But when Osborne was alone with her he found
himself in the grey zone of the conscientious divorcee in strained intimacy
between near strangers. There would be the usual, tactful enquiries. "How's
Mummy keeping?" There would be talk of school and Manhattan. "Aren't
the skyscrapers tall, darling!" The wrong, well-meant gifts. (An encyclopaedia; someone's collected poetry.) The hopeful plans for an outing to
a lingering Christmas panto, meant as a treat.

Gilliatt was now a successful New Yorker film critic and Academy Award
nominee, and she accompanied Osborne to the front door at Chester Square
after he visited Nolan there one day. He walked past the sixteen-foot-high
copper doors that he noted, in his depression and defeat, had cost him a
ransom. "Goodbye then," she said to him.

"She raised her face to kiss me," he remembered, "drew back against the
porch and contemplated me. 'You've really fucked up your life, haven't
you?'"

He walked past the Royal Court, down the King's Road, and back to his
loveless marriage to Bennett and a life that had been reduced to tabloid
fodder. "It was hard not to agree with Penelope," he conceded. "There was

no escaping from it. It was an irreversible judgment, the irrefutable evidence of my visible cirrhosis of the spirit."

He wanted to shout out and for someone to hear him, "*I am not yet dead.*"

But three new plays of his would now be turned down in succession – including humiliating rejections from the Court. His audience was leaving him. The falling off had begun.

The first body blow came with the negative response to his 1972 adaptation of Shakespeare's *Coriolanus*, renamed *A Place Calling Itself Rome*. The Court rationalized that its huge cast made it impossible for them to produce. (Times had changed since extra dressing rooms were built underneath the stage for the forty-member cast of *A Patriot for Me*.) Peter Hall at the National explained that he couldn't produce it for two or three years. At the RSC, Trevor Nunn was preoccupied with his Roman season. Osborne said that he shopped his script around for over a year to a total of thirty producers and directors and was met by "iron apathy". The *Coriolanus* adaptation has never been performed.

His choice of Shakespeare's most political play was a self-projection. The play itself is liked, not loved – and in the liking comes a cold awe. It's as much about class warfare as the blood of war. Yet it outfoxes us – what do we actually feel about its proud, difficult hero who refuses to play to the gallery?

Caius Martius Coriolanus – Harold Bloom's "killing machine" who would be author of himself, the mummy's boy who is the son of a monster ("Anger's my meat: I sup upon myself"), the war leader unschooled in the oily arts of expediency, the uncompromising patrician who scorns the people. Brecht's unfinished version sees Coriolanus as a fascist. Osborne sees him as a misunderstood victim of the fickle plebs. "There is a world elsewhere!"

But, where? Osborne was a famous man without a home. Members of the public – fans! – were still sending him their plays and poems, along with earnest requests for advice and meetings. "There are passages in it which sing," the then unknown Hanif Kureishi wrote to him enthusiastically about his own novel. "Return – politely!" Osborne scrawled to his secretary on his letter. To others: "Thank him warmly." "Nice chap. But say I'm in Mexico." "Apologise about letting anyone down." "Polite rejection." "Be nice . . ."

"Can't believe it," he entered in his 1974 notebook. "Two plays written. Next: a season at Greenwich. A turn? Or no?"

Before the two new plays were staged at Greenwich, however, they were turned down everywhere like his *Coriolanus*. The rejection of his 1973 adaptation of Oscar Wilde's *The Picture of Dorian Gray* as well as a minor, low comedy, *The End of Me Old Cigar*, sent him spiralling into the worst desolation he had known.

June '73

This is becoming more of a journal than a notebook. I dare say because the raft really is beginning to drift. I think I'm starting to putrify. I'm sure I'm finished. And it will be over much sooner than I thought. I'm suddenly old, ill and too weary even to run. I just hope something really awful doesn't happen first.

Nobody wants to know. They feel *bankruptcy*. Waiting for the strike to come. *Stroke* to come? In a way, it's the logical success. The fading follow-spot. Before it snaps out. I only hope it is a snap and not a fade.

9 September '73

Suddenly, she [Jill Bennett] burst into tears and I bent down to her. Solitude. The wretchedness, the pretence, the calendar pretence of it, marked off day by day, month by month. Seven years now. Saw her off at the door. Like a wan, tripping girl. Me, shabby in soiled dressing gown, red socks covering varicose veins. Relieved, restless. 20 minutes later she rang. Reassured to hear my voice in her way. Onward . . .

4 April 1974

Can't eat. Retching blood. Even shat blood earlier in the week. During the night I was certain I was going to die. Sweat came swirling in great drops from head, hair, everywhere. I think I smell. Quite noticeably. Breath too. She told me. Trying to go out today. But don't think I can last much longer.

In all this clamour, those terrible words: My God, My God, why hast Thou forsaken me? But you have clanged down the heavens. Oh Christ, heart of my heart, providential sparrow, dead and fluttered, if you could come to my heart.

In the spring of 1974, he left his literary agent, Marjery Vosper – who had represented him since *Look Back in Anger* – and joined Robin Dalton for a fresh, new start. From long experience, Dalton understood the reason. "He left her not because she had failed him. His life had failed him. When a writer's career falters badly, the agent becomes the whipping boy or the saviour. John's career was at its lowest ebb when he came to me. He was horribly depressed, his marriage was on the rocks. His plays weren't even being staged."

In a typical pretence, a show of worldly ease, Osborne took Dalton for lunch at the Ritz when they first met. "He was shy and he was delightful," she remembered. But when they met again for dinner at her house by Lord's cricket ground, Bennett was with him and there was a dramatic change. "He scarcely said a word the entire, gruesome evening and Jill never stopped. He was like a man destroyed. She broke his balls. That's how it was." When asked if she killed him psychologically, she replied "Absolutely," and went on to confirm, "My husband was a friend of Willis Hall's when Jill was married to him and recognized the symptoms. It was exactly the same."

Yet it was Bennett – a new client of Dalton's, too – who wrote to her on 6 May 1974, encouraging her to get Osborne more work as an actor and director. "I am really writing this letter to you as an undercover agent for John Osborne as he is rather shy in asking this particular thing himself . . ."

Bennett subsequently wrote to Dalton from the South of France confiding that she wanted to end the marriage, but couldn't. "This holiday is pretty hellish between you and me. J.O. very snarly and I can do no right. Stamps all the little confidence out of me . . . The trouble is he has *no friends* and so I have to bear all his hatred (and he's good at that). I would like a little fun and encouragement. If I had the guts I'd leave. I haven't, and also economically I couldn't even afford a bedsit at the moment. I feel it's better to be miserable in comfort and hope things get better – at least the people who work for us *smile* – than be suicidal in a small room. I'm sorry to moan . . ."

Osborne's spirits lifted with news of the prestigious season of his plays at Greenwich Theatre. "But the fact is only Greenwich wanted to do them," Dalton told me candidly.

The season began promisingly in January 1975, with a revival of *The Entertainer*, directed by Osborne, with his inspired casting of Max Wall as Archie Rice. There was also the premiere of *The Picture of Dorian Gray*, directed by Clive Donner – Jocelyn Rickards's husband – with Michael Kitchen as Dorian Gray. But an exciting opportunity was missed. There had been intriguing talk of Bennett playing Dorian Gray. (Garbo once coveted the role.) Bennett as Dorian would have given the lacklustre evening a Wildean touch – an androgynous buzz.

Subtitled "A Moral Entertainment", the choppy adaptation was Osborne's third in recent, depleted times and it suggests he was running dry of his own ideas. *Hedda Gabler* was a portrait of his wife with a helping hand from Ibsen – perversely jealous, wilful Hedda, the modern woman who doesn't want sex but ownership, the suicidal narcissist who destroys three lives including her own. *Coriolanus* was his oblique, grandiose projection of himself – the once courted hero now banished, the battle-scarred warrior whose appetite for life, in Anthony Clare's ringing phrase, was sucked from his mother's milk. The adaptation of *Dorian Gray* was his grouchy Grand Guignol metaphor for the "Me Generation" of the Seventies – a shaky morality tale about the callow pre-Botoxed cult of eternal youth that worked much better in theory.

"What are the things most valued, sought after?" Osborne asked in his introduction to the published script. "Beauty, yes; youth, most certainly. Youth has become, like death, almost a taboo subject. Everyone is afraid of not merely losing it but of even admitting that such a possibility exists. Again, youth is all important, all reaching, all powerful. It is obligatory to be trim, slim, careless. The lines of age on Dorian Gray's portrait are a very modern likeness . . ."

The last Osborne play on the Greenwich bill, entitled *The End of Me Old Cigar* after a suggestive old Music Hall song, was intended as a risqué modern Restoration comedy about a brassy brothel keeper, Regine (played by Rachel Roberts) who plots to end cocksure male domination of Oppressed Women Everywhere by deviously silly means. Satire never worked for Osborne. It always brought out the juvenile in him.

"See it dangle, dingle dangle, jingle jangle in its usual petulant pendulance," goes Regine's ornery ode to the *what*? – petulant pendulance of an Alpha-male dominated world. Osborne also took boorish potshots at the young again, making him seem old and out of touch. Tynan was gratuitously insulted at peevish length. ("He has been trying to cultivate style ever since he was seen wearing lilac knickers and a top hat on Magdalen Bridge on his way to the Union reading Karl Marx in a loud falsetto.") Jill Bennett appeared in a perfunctory second act as a Mrs Isobel Sands – stylish symbol of clipped, Cowardesque sophistication in a crude world – whose plot against Man is foiled by good old-fashioned love.

The romantic Mrs Sands and a hesitant stranger visiting the brothel for an orgy in Act One conveniently fall in love like cooing doves in Act Two. The stranger thinks he can't get it up any more. "Life may be hell," is one of the more unfortunate lines, "but who can tell that unknown boredom from which no traveller returns?"

The new plays in the Greenwich season failed to ignite either the critics or the public. I remember seeing *The End of Me Old Cigar* when it opened and thinking in shock that Osborne, the hero of my own school days, had lost his way.

*

Peter Hall's diary, 27 May 1976:

> . . . to Chelsea Square for dinner with the Osbornes, just the four of us. [Hall was accompanied by his wife, Jacky.] The evening passed very pleasantly, oiled by liberal quantities of alcohol. John and Jill conduct a constant banter of war, mocking each other, usually sexually, very much like the two characters in *Watch It Come Down* – except tonight we were in comedy and not in tragedy.

Hall's decision to produce *Watch It Come Down* at the National was a boost for Osborne against all odds. It signalled he wasn't yet done. The play would be one of a series by leading English dramatists that opened the Lyttelton Theatre in the National's new home on the South Bank. *Watch It Come Down* was being presented with Pinter's *No Man's Land*, Ayckbourn's *Bedroom Farce* and *Weapons of Happiness* by Howard Brenton and directed by David Hare.

Peter Hall's diary, for 16 January:

> First reading of *Watch It Come Down* this morning. Osborne, looking curiously pink and strained, present. Bill Bryden [the director] made an incoherent speech, but it was engaging: his enthusiasm for the play bounded through like a great big puppy . . . As the actors read, they became quieter and quieter: private mumblings. I had to follow with the text. But it's a wonderful cast [Jill Bennett and Frank Finlay, among others] and I think a powerful play. The first act has vigorous sardonic humour, and the second is the one of the bleakest, most terrifying I have heard outside Strindberg.

The first act is a lacerating portrait of Osborne's marriage to Bennett. "The only life I can explore – or begin to even chart – is my own," he wrote in his 1972 notebook. In the play, Ben (Frank Finlay) is unhappily married to Sally (Jill Bennett):

SALLY: Perhaps you've never cared for the secret of getting through to other people – even little girls. Even your own tall little girl . . . Or perhaps she doesn't *like* you. Just that . . . A lot of people don't, you know.

BEN: Will you, you, will you for one minute, just stop that fucking pile of shit spewing out of your fucking mouth!

SALLY: A hit, Raymond. I say: a *palpable*!

BEN: Or you'll get my fist right in the fucking middle of it. From my puny fist even if it breaks my arm . . .

SALLY: You mustn't damage your arm . . . Can *I* have another drink?

BEN: I'm sorry.

SALLY: No, I'm *sorry*. I shouldn't have said those things. It's my fault.

BEN: I – I, well, bad time . . . But I bought you a present . . .

SALLY: Thank you. That was sweet of you. I'll open it after I've, I've had this . . .

The two of them resemble obscene versions of the bantering Blisses in Coward's *Hay Fever*, except they're the real, bilious thing. "Keep away. I'll kill her!" Ben responds when Sally smacks him in the face. "I'll kill her! She's killed *me*. She's killed everything. Long ago." The melodramatic end to Act One has them literally tearing each other to pieces. Osborne's stage direction reads: "He smashes her in the face, and they kick and tear at each other, clothes tearing and splitting. Blood and breakage. The others watch them fight . . ."

"It was just like our Sunday lunches with John and Jill," Helen Montagu told me, laughing. "If you want to know what they were like together, it's all in *Watch It Come Down*."

Her husband, a psychologist, tried to diffuse the rows during their lunches together and sometimes he succeeded. "He could see the storms coming," Montagu pointed out. He went reluctantly to see the play with her. "What was so funny is that he hates going to the theatre and only went because of John. At the end of the play, he said we should have stayed home and seen it during Sunday lunch."

But *Watch It Come Down* strives for higher ground than a cracked mirror held up to Osborne's destroyed marriage. The impulse is autobiographical, but the play is set in a near abstraction: an abandoned, countryside railway station converted into a house for refugee artists. Strictly speaking, we're not in reality. Bernard Shaw had been Osborne's ghostly nemesis since he first acted in his plays. *Watch It Come Down* is his *Heartbreak House*, a metaphor of national collapse – "this soul's prison we call England", as Shaw put it.

Peter Hall's diary, 18 February:

To the first preview of *Watch It Come Down*. I can't remember an audience more nervous. They were terrified about what was going to happen next.

Emotional terrorism runs through the play. But there's also its cultivated version of Shaw's mystical Shotover – the elderly, dying biographer, Glen, based on Lytton Strachey. "Glen is the life," declares Jo, his young platonic love. "If he goes. It all. Goes. Gone. The wit, the irony, the kindness, the struggle with himself which he never unburdened." Jo is based on Dora Carrington, the Bloomsbury bohemian loved by men and women but in love with Strachey. The barbarians are at the gates. "We've seen the future," Glen announces, *"and it doesn't work."* No haven exists from the real world on the brink, no refuge or safety. The retreat of the group of artists to the colonized countryside without a flag doesn't bring out the best in them. Rather, the blistering speeches about England's faux country idyll bring out the best in Osborne.

"Suspicion, cupidity, complacency, hostility, profiteering, small, greedy passions, tweedy romance, all that. Beef barons, pig and veal concentration camps, Bentleys and pony traps and wellies. The Country. It's the last of England for *them*, the one last, surviving colony."

The play's jaundiced view of "rural swank" is a thrilling echo of the young playwright who wrote *Look Back in Anger*:

"The town is *people* and having to *give way*. The country's not green much and rarely pleasant. Land is bad for people. The green belt of muddied, grasping, well-off peasants from public schools and merchant banks . . . *I* know what I'm talking about. With shotguns in the woods, tea and pearls, rural swank and a tub of money under the chintz four-poster. Fetes opened by local TV celebrities, restoration funds, old ducks who 'come in and do', village greens, hunting 'manners', indifferent food and pewter candlesticks, over-healthy children home for the hols, greedy Gorgon nannies, undergraduates fumbling behind bushes of floodlit lawns, dancing till dawn with Miss Sarah Crumpet-Nicely of Grasping Hall while Mummy and Daddy look on at all the young people 'having such a good time' against this nasty, brutish issue of English Country Life. No, there's not much life in the land. Fish and animals, yes; and the pigs who *own* it and *run* it."

At such truth-telling moments, *Watch It Come Down* exhilarates and the vitality of the writing takes it to the edge. It risks everything. And then it implodes. Osborne's energy gives out. The familiar themes of loss and devastation return once too often. The ugly marital fights exhaust. The end comes quickly with apocalyptic violence and death (as in *West of Suez*).

Osborne has left himself nowhere to go. It's as if he tossed a hand grenade into his own play and the rotten marriage with it.

Boos greeted the opening-night performance. (Along with counter-offensive cheers.) "Money back! Money back!" went a chant as the cast took a steely bow. Bill Bryden, its director, was sitting at the back of the dress circle with Osborne, who seemed to be enjoying the tumult. "He loved it," said Bryden, who loved the man.

Christopher Hampton recalled about the uproar: "I remember thinking about all these young writers, myself included, who wrote ostensibly shocking stuff. Yet I'd never been at a play where the audience was so provoked and angered by what was happening onstage. I admired *Watch It Come Down* enormously. But there was John, leaning nonchalantly on a wall at the back of the theatre, looking incredibly composed in the midst of his own play going disastrously wrong."

The theatre could never be a hushed temple for Osborne. He lived for a *response*. But we also know how deeply rejection wounded him. Peter Hall's diary, 20 May, notes: "John Osborne has returned from the States and found my letter about the decline in *Watch It Come Down* business, for an angry postcard arrived today saying he is dropping writing and taking up weaving."

That summer, Edward Albee signalled unusual support for a fellow playwright. Albee had just won his second Pulitzer Prize (for *Seascape*), although he too would enter the wilderness – fate's retribution on success. He had never met Osborne but felt compelled to tell him that he was "startled and intrigued by the general tone of hysteria and disdain in the press surrounding your new play at the National. Such critical reaction here in the US means that a good play has probably opened . . ."

He read *Watch It Come Down* immediately.

"My God, it's a good play!" Albee's letter went on enthusiastically. "Anger *and* disgust: hot and cold together. I'm sorry I missed seeing the production . . . You've been writing plays for a long while. A *Sense of Detachment* wasn't a bad play either!"

He signed off: "One playwright writing another in this manner might not be good form but . . . What the hell. Best wishes, Edward Albee."

Osborne responded thanking him warmly for his "kindly, charitable act". "Life here is quite bloody – almost literally," he wrote. "Hedged in by malice, vindictiveness and a passion to wound . . . There is so much hatred in the air . . . Captain Hall steering his *Titanic* straight for the ice."

He ended by inviting Albee to visit him in England, signing off wearily, "Onward, I suppose."

Osborne's future looked perilous. "I'm finished," he wrote in his note-book. "My days in theatre are numbered." He had, as Albee said, been writing for a long while.

The will to write kept him alive. The state of his loveless marriage was destroying him. "Too much bile has gone into the stream," he wrote in his 1973 notebook. "Too much waste and filth and poison."

There was no insult Osborne and Bennett hadn't exchanged, no row they hadn't had. They were like Jorge Luis Borges's two bald men fighting over a comb. There was nothing left.

Bennett was now telling friends that the roles he wrote for her weren't big enough or good enough.

> J.B. complaining more and more. She slept almost all of Sunday. I made some aching desultory efforts. No avail . . . I see she's leaving notes for the secretary to read when she comes in first thing in the morning again: "I can't stand this. No sex. No love. No affection. Death is the only way out etc."

At Chelsea Square, he frequently locked himself in his study on the top floor for much of the day. During social gatherings at the house, he would sit sullenly alone unable to face anyone. "Everybody came," as Alice B. Toklas once said, "and nobody made any difference." There would be several of his wife's camp followers and friends from the ballet world like Donald McLeary (ballet master of the Royal Ballet). It couldn't have helped much that Osborne defined ballet as "poof's football".

During rehearsals of *Watch It Come Down*, the cast provided some new blood at the house after the show. "The poof's footballers were all in one room," Bill Bryden pointed out, "and *we* were in another." Helen Dawson was another new guest at the house. She had recently left the *Observer* and was marking time at the National where she edited a few programmes for them. One was for *Watch It Come Down*.

Dawson already knew Bennett through their mutual friend, theatre producer Helen Montagu. The three of them met occasionally at San Frediano's for lunch. Barry Krost remembered Bennett saying when she was planning a dinner party, "Let's have Helen Dawson along – she's no trouble."

When his wife was in repertory in *Watch It Come Down*, Osborne usually fled to Christmas Place, his country house in Kent. The notebooks tell us he was drinking heavily. "Too much to drink." "Drinking too much." "I could drink myself to death, if I'm not doing so already . . ." His daily intake was a bottle of vodka, a bottle or two of wine, champagne on tap, along with various amphetamines, codeine and sleeping pills. He had lost a great deal of weight, his health had seriously deteriorated. All the signs were that he was destroying himself.

He lived in hiding in the country house. A live-in couple looked after the property as housekeeper and gardener. But there were no guests. The Edenbridge locals never saw him in the village or even knew that he was at the house. He was sometimes glimpsed in the private lane outside, unkempt as a recluse. In the past, Bennett had been spotted riding her horse on the South Downs. The local schoolteacher who lived at the top of the lane had seen Osborne walking with her but they were arguing furiously. Bennett rarely went with him now and Christmas Place itself wasn't to her liking. She called it "The Abortion Clinic". Osborne loved the place as his only sanctuary.

"I'm suddenly old, ill and too weary even to run . . ." He was in a state of near collapse, spinning in Bennett's emasculating vortex unable to summon the strength to make a final break. Her letters and telegrams to Edenbridge plead with him to answer the phone and meet her: "I have given you air – as you asked for – haven't come down and smashed up the joint – couldn't – too tired of it all. I just want to see you and talk to you . . . will you ring me? Or me you? Or what? It's very bleak here without you . . ."

On 8 June 1976, Bennett's mother wrote to Osborne and implied the danger of her daughter's suicide: "My dear John, I may be an interfering old Mother-in-Law. Just treat me as an old bag who is very fond of you and who loves Jill dearly. I cannot bear to see the distress you are both in. It's the first time she has confided in me and she blames herself in many ways, but nothing can be helped till you meet . . . You know her temperament and how difficult it is for her to keep calm. She is calm – dangerously so . . ."

On 21 June, Bennett was in her dressing room changing into her costume for the evening perfomance of *Watch It Come Down* when Michael Halifax, the National's company administrator, popped in to see her half an hour before curtain up. This was the courtly man who, twenty years before, had been the Court's stage manager who found the furniture for *Look Back in Anger* in junk shops. He usually visited all the actors backstage before a show.

He found Bennett in a terrible state, crying bitterly as she dressed to go onstage. "John had just phoned to tell her he was leaving her," Halifax explained. "He'd told her before the performance of his own play."

In her shock, Bennett warned Osborne she would be driving to Edenbridge immediately after the performance. "I shouldn't," he replied, informing her that he was with Helen Dawson.

41

A Better Class of Person

> I wanted to make him happy.
> Helen Osborne, October 1998

And so our story comes full circle as Helen Dawson – the only wife to take Osborne's name – gave him back his life.

She loved him pure and simple, without question or doubt, for the rest of their lives together. This steadfast, modest woman wasn't the type to make claims for herself. According to Helen Montagu – Bennett's closest friend at the time – she offered Osborne "deep, deep peace" after the years of turmoil and waste. Whether he ever found inner peace is the subject of these remaining chapters, but that he discovered the pleasure of living again, I am certain.

Xmas, 1978

My darling,
You've made this place the happiest thing I've ever known. Do believe me. I've never known such simple delight and honest pleasure *every* day.

Thank you for the *very* best years of my life. [Next year] will be more than all right. I'll see to it. I promise.

Your loving John

Osborne first met her when she was arts editor of the *Observer*. Penelope Gilliatt introduced them casually at the theatre one evening. The three of them had an occasional drink together during intervals of various shows, including Osborne's. She was already part of the London scene – a friend of the Mortimers and a long-time friend of Eileen Atkins since their twenties. Before she and Osborne grew close, she was a guest for summers at Nid de Duc, Tony Richardson's estate in the South of France. It was Helen who helped reconcile Osborne with Richardson after their bitter falling out over *The Charge of the Light Brigade*.

She was the only one of Osborne's wives who wanted to live anonymously beyond the public gaze. It was their relaxed sense of fun in each other's company that characterized them. "Such laughs and pleasure," she would say of a day at the races with him, an outing to Brighton, a good book. True, he called her "WOW" – short for "Washout Wife". But she was the one who confidently invented the anti-feminist Washout Wives Club, and formed it with Penny Mortimer. The exclusive WOW club for the wives of playwrights met for lunches and its founder members included Christopher Hampton's wife, Laura, and the wife of Peter Nichols, Thelma. Dr Miriam Stoppard, then wife of Tom, wasn't allowed to join because she actually *worked*. Similarly Maureen Lipman, wife of another playwright, Jack Rosenthal. Dusty Wesker wanted to join, but Arnold wouldn't let her.

Helen Dawson was Osborne's fierce protector and kindred spirit, and when they met at those Chelsea Square gatherings where he felt displaced and isolated, he gravitated toward her. "We never stopped *yacking*," she told me happily. "It was the most extraordinary thing. From the moment we got together we never stopped talking to each other."

They shared a drinker's conviviality. She could keep up with the best of them, though she weaned him off the hard stuff (the bottle of vodka a day). The marriage to Bennett had left him like a recovering addict. "Physically, he was just in a terrible, terrible state," she said. "He believed he had no friends. I knew that people were very fond of him, but it made no difference. He'd stopped *eating*. He thought his talent had gone."

"God, I'm hungry," Osborne announced to his own surprise one day at her flat in Dorset Square, and his recovery slowly began.

Also known to him as "The Geordie Tyke", she was born in Gosforth, Newcastle, the only child of an accountant. (Her mother died young.) She attended Hunmanby Hall, the Methodist boarding school in York. "Bet you didn't know *that*," she said to me in her self-deprecating way. When she was sixteen, she won first prize in the school's Literary and Debating Society and was offered the choice of a book. Her choice was the published version of *Look Back in Anger*, which she presented to Osborne on their wedding day. It's inscribed: "And back to you, on June 2 1978. With *all* my love, ever and ever. Helen."

She read history at Newcastle University, then took a year's jaunt in America studying American politics at prestigious Brown University in Providence, Rhode Island, and joined the *Observer* soon after. As an editor, she was known for her supportive rigour and intelligence. Osborne, she said, gave her confidence in herself and calmed her habitual anxiety. They rooted for each other. She was the one who got him writing again by encouraging him to write *A Better Class of Person*.

She had two long-term relationships before Osborne, not counting what she called "twiddles in between". She was thirty-seven and he was forty-eight when they married and the tentative progression of their affair was at first between two orphans of the storm. Theirs was a romantic love and, as it deepened, he told her that he intended to live permanently in the country one day soon and asked if she would wait to join him.

"He was asking me to trust him and I trusted him completely," she said proudly. "John had his own timetable. I never doubted him for a second."

They went on meeting in secret for another four or five months until, on 14 June 1976, he left Chelsea Square to live in Edenbridge for good.

But the call didn't come. Bennett had unexpectedly joined him in the country.

Six days later, on 20 June, she returned to London to continue in repertory in *Watch It Come Down* at the National.

That night, Osborne called Helen at her London flat with the train times to Kent.

Her diary has an asterisk by the 21st of June with the single entry, "To Edenbridge."

"It Takes Guts to Survive Rejection When You're in the Public Eye" – interview with Jill Bennett by Catherine Stott, *Cosmopolitan*, June 1977. "I've got a terrible tongue and I say very wounding things," Bennett confessed. "And now I've got no one to wound. You miss that. I'm very violent in my affections. I say these dreadful things knowing I can always make it up. I'm very careful with people who mean nothing to me . . ."

Bennett never met Helen again after her husband left her, though there was a tense scene in Langan's restaurant when they studiously avoided each other at separate tables. Peter Langan was reeling around his own restaurant as usual and weaved his way toward Bennett's table. "Osborne's met a better woman than you!" he told her. (She rose above it.)

Bennett's public front was generally stoic and she rarely mentioned Osborne's name intimately again. She referred to him as "Mr Osborne" or "John Osborne" and sent him a blue shirt he'd left behind with the message, "I'd like the contents of this shirt back some time." She announced that her "best friend" had run off with her husband, or more wittily, "an usherette" stole him away. She said later that, "John's gone a bit potty".

He in turn announced that he was free at last to eat onions again, and began calling Bennett Adolf Hitler. He sent letters and cards addressed to "Mrs Adolf Hitler, Pouffs' Palace, 30 Chelsea Square." (They were delivered.)

JOHN OSBORNE

He also formed a branch of Alcoholics Anonymous named Adolf's Anonymous with Willis Hall. Anyone tempted by the sudden urge to marry Jill Bennett could ring the organization at any time of the day or night and be talked out of it. He wrote to ex-mistress Rickards, now back in the fold: "Dearest Jocelyn, Adolf having last days in the bunker. Daily threats of coming down here [to Edenbridge] with thugs to beat us both up and disfigure Helen for life . . . The Head Usherette at the National Theatre sends her love. As I do."

In fact, Bennett never went to the country house again, though for a time she refused to accept that Osborne had left her. "I need to see you. It won't be ugly. No war of nerves," went her pleading letters to him. "I am very lonely. Please answer." "I am your Real Friend. Be mine." "Please talk to me on the phone. I cannot bear it . . ."

He returned once to Chelsea Square to pick up a few belongings. "Dearest," she wrote to him immediately. "It was lovely to see you, admit it. Quite larky in patches. I think of you all the time. Please miss me. My loving thoughts . . ."

When the divorce proceedings began, she sent him this dignified peace offering on 19 May 1977: "I am glad you are happy. I know now you were right to leave me – we are better apart. But could we still have some sort of affection? It should be possible. I shall always have affection for you – and I can be a good friend. Bad lover no doubt, as you once so rightly said. Don't be angry at hearing from me. Let's have no more pain and think kindly toward each other. I do wish you well. Fondest thoughts. Please answer if you can."

He telegrammed her back on 6 June: "JUST RETURNED. THANKS FOR YOUR NOTE. I AGREE WITH YOU ENTIRELY. JOHN."

But the truce didn't last and the wars went on. Another of Bennett's letters to him mentioned a *Guardian* letter in which Osborne referred to himself self-mockingly as an "ex-playwright" and it triggered the following devastating response from him. His raw emotion and fury reveal his true state of mind in the aftermath of the ruinous marriage. The stinging reference to the calumny of his own "trade" is the outcome of Peter Hall taking off *Watch It Come Down* after it failed at the box office.

Christmas Place, Marsh Green
Nr Edenbridge Kent
[July 1977]

Dear Jill,
As to your concerned little note of the 22nd: I should have learned

at this stage of my life what indeed a pliant weapon is irony when stupid people are at the other end of it. No, I am *not* an ex-playwright. Or ex anything else. I am also the best, as you truthfully point out. However, I expect no favours. Certainly no kind words from anyone and you above all. I have done without love, affection – even the merest regard in your case – for many years. I can sustain *that* all right. That goes for the frequent calumny and treachery of my own trade. It has always been so and I expect nothing else. As in my profession, I expect no favours or grace or charity – from *you* least of all.

In other words, to hell with your mock kind words. They stink of bad intention. Go on as you have done. Plot and giggle with that little suburban friend of yours from Stanmore [his secretary, Linda Singer, now Bennett's confidante]. You may have found your exact level. Get all the money I have sweated for since I was 15. Get the lot. You probably will. You've never *worked*. Not as I have, not as I *know*. I carry a knife for you and all your kind. The ones like you that are all crafty ruthlessness and unyielding ambition. Yes, there is an eighth deadly sin, and it is AMBITION. But, most of all, there is CRUELTY. And that *you* have in abundance.

But – and it's a good one – you cannot hurt *me*. I have taken too much from better ones even than you. That's what people like you fail to understand. When the bell rings, I not only always *come out*, I'm the *first out*. Fighting. And I always shall be. So: spare me your sympathy. I don't need it. Yours or anyone's. One is merely alone. That is all simple. In the meantime, you blaspheme against all affection and memory.

The neutral, unfeeling jargon of divorce had been literally duplicated in *Inadmissible Evidence* as an Orwellian nightmare. (Bill Maitland is a divorce lawyer.) And now the bitterly contested divorce between Nora Noel Jill Osborne (Bennett) and John James Osborne mirrored the convoluted lawyerspeak in the play.

"WHEREAS –

"There has arisen other disputes and differences between the parties which they have agreed to resolve in the manner hereinafter appearing and upon the terms hereof: NOW THIS DEED WITNESSETH as follows . . .

"To fully and effectually indemnify Miss Bennett (and her estate personal representatives and successors in title) from and against all tax and other liabilities of whatsoever nature . . .

"Mr Osborne is presently indebted to Miss Bennett in the sum of . . ."

But in the midst of all the fine print, there was a crucial proposal in the

Bennett Deed of Indemnity against Osborne that would haunt him for years:

"Mr Osborne hereby warrants as follows: To refrain from making direct or indirect reference in any interview, broadcast, publication or literary works to Miss Bennett without first submitting a draft of the reference to Miss Bennett . . ."

She was after a gagging order. If Osborne agreed to it and wrote, for example, his autobiography, he would be compelled to submit it to Bennett for her prior approval or risk substantial damages and jail.

The divorce proceedings themselves were hostile. Bennett's sworn testimony, naming Helen Dawson as Co-Respondent, accused Osborne of violence, uncontrollable temper, drinking and physical assault. He retaliated by accusing her of exactly the same things. She claimed that he heckled her during a performance of Terence Rattigan's *Separate Tables*, in which she played a leading role at the Apollo Theatre, and he denied it saying that Rattigan was a dear friend and colleague.

There's no question that he ridiculed her both publicly and privately. Bennett's sworn testimony that he killed her dog, however, strikes us as hard to believe. It would have been easier for him to kill a human being. Osborne had been a dog lover since childhood when he had to make do with a toy terrier on wheels. What actually happened with Bennett's dog was that it had been sick for a long time and had to be put down by the local vet in Edenbridge. Bennett knew all about it, and Osborne had the vet's report to prove it.

He wrote brilliantly on loving dogs, incidentally, in one of his last *Spectator* columns. "For a child to take a dog into its life is a perfect form of moral and emotional instruction. It will initiate him into containing the power of the pack, the necessities of those who demand you to lead as well as love them, and instil more practical wisdom about selflessness, procreation and death than schools or even parents. The first few bars of the 'Enigma Variations' were inspired not by organs and cathedrals but by Elgar's great bulldog, Dan, falling down a steep bank of the River Wye, his paddling upstream to find a landing place (bars two and three) and his rejoicing bark on reaching dry land (second half of bar five). The organist at Hereford Cathedral had suggested, 'Set that to music.' 'I did', wrote Elgar. 'Here it is.' In the autograph sketch of 'Variations', he inscribed the one word, 'Dan' . . ."

There was a serious setback for Osborne during the divorce. Bennett testified that she lived in fear he would return to the house in Chelsea Square and assault her. Her friend, Mrs Linda Singer – the secretary Osborne hired to replace Sonia McGuinness – confirmed that she herself had been called "a fucking little turd" over the phone and was threatened by Osborne that unless she returned his typewriter he would "come up there and smash the living daylights out of you". Mrs Singer also claimed that she received heavy breathing calls. "I do not know that these came from the Respondent but I suspect they did . . ."

Bennett and the secretary won a restraining order "enjoining" Osborne from "assaulting, molesting, or communicating with either of them". He was warned by his own solicitors that if he breached the court order he could be committed to prison for contempt.

But the abusive letters and cards to Bennett continued. He sent her this crude, handwritten letter – a mock party invitation – during the divorce:

> The Abortion Clinic,
> Christmas Place
> Sept 6 1977

You are cordially invited to the 46th Birthday Party of Adolf Bennett. She will be weeping for herself and tears will be streaming down her 46-year-old face. She is quite frigid so do not approach too near. It will be given at the Pouff's Palace, 30 Chelsea Square. Usherettes will be in attendance, including the Famous Evil Witch of Stanmore [former secretary, Mrs Singer]. Dancing and entertainment by members of the Royal Ballet or any old queen trolling down the King's Road. This will form the nucleus of a National Theatre production performed on the terraces of its delectable building . . . Keep on bashing, dear . . .

He was already risking jail by breaking the restraining order against him. As for the divorce itself and Bennett's financial settlement, Osborne was perceived as the guilty party who "deserted' the happy home. He subsequently claimed that she took him to the cleaners. But he said the same about Gilliatt after their more amicable divorce. (Legally, Gilliatt was entitled to a big chunk of Osborne's then considerable fortune. She settled for the house in Chester Square in trust for their daughter and reasonable child maintenance – waiving all financial rights in her favour.) The despairing Oscar Beuselinck even informed him that as a leading playwright he made a lousy lawyer – and more to the point, failed to appreciate how lucky he was. "Leave this to me, son," Beuselinck always told him, with good reason.

The outcome of the Bennett divorce was that they shared the proceeds from the sale of the Chelsea Square house – enabling her to buy another house in Britten Street – and she quite generously waived certain financial claims. The sticking point in the divorce, however, was that she had a legal claim to a share in the country house – where Osborne now proposed to live with Helen Dawson.

The Edenbridge house was crucial to him. He had burned through his money during the Bennett years and now had tax problems. On the other hand, she remained obsessed with what he might now reveal about her. Beuselinck therefore used the proposed gagging order as leverage over the fate of the country house. The laws of libel in any case prevented Osborne from defaming Bennett. He signed the order and kept the house.

But he rued the day. The man who defied centuries of government censorship lived by Job, 7:11, "I will not refrain my mouth, I will speak in the anguish of my spirit, I will complain in the bitterness of my soul." And it's why, years later, when Bennett died suddenly just as part two of his autobiography was going to press, he added an unforgiving chapter damning her to hell. He was free to speak out.

Or, as Oscar Beuselinck wryly announced whenever an Osborne divorce came through, "You are now free to re-marry."

The sea change in Osborne's life is best illustrated by the entries in Helen Dawson's diary before they were married. There's a new atmosphere of opening the locked doors at reclusive Christmas Place, of carefree day trips and treats as if Osborne had emerged with her blinking into the country light.

"Mid-September: Friends begin coming to house. Exploring in the Alvis [which had been rotting in a barn] – fish and chips in The Seagull at Hastings, theatre in Eastbourne. *The Student Prince*. Brighton, Rye, Bognor Regis, country pubs . . . To London for first time. Thanksgiving lunch at Neil Hartley's [Tony Richardson's right-hand man]. To the Mortimers for weekend in the country. Their daughter Emily says to John, 'You're like Henry VIII, aren't you?'

"November, Edenbridge: JO to Evensong. *Look Back* on TV. Riding. Suppers at Chiddingstone. Racing at Lingfield. Bonfire night.

"December: Removal from Chelsea Square. Books. Shelves up; shelves fall down. 'Oh dear,' says Mr Buffin. 'I like to do a nice job.' Buying furniture. Tunbridge Wells. Brighton. J.O. buys me clothes.

"Christmas Day: Walk with Luther in thick forest and sunshine. To Robin Dalton's for turkey. Ben Travers there. Angela Rippon's legs on 'Morecambe and Wise'. Home to watch 'Yankee Doodle Dandy'. Perfect."

There was little stamp of Jill Bennett on the Edenbridge house except for mirrors surrounded by bright bulbs and a peculiar bathroom on the top floor with a bright orange carpet and a deep purple ceiling. Under protest from his London accountants, Osborne celebrated his new life by installing an expensive, glassed-in swimming pool in the grounds. (He borrowed the money to build it from the obliging local bank manager, a fan of his plays.) He bought Helen an MG, and then a pragmatic Morris Traveller. The Alvis was reaching vintage status. The Bentley and Mercedes coupé were gone.

He immediately gave booze a rest. A black dot in his notebooks signalled the day he went on the wagon, an x marked the day he fell off. (There could be weeks between.) Musical notes meant his excited anticipation of a trip to Manhattan. In their first months together they took a slow boat to Cape Town, the Orient Express to Venice, as well as travels to Bangkok, Singapore, Barbados, Tenerife and Nice.

A photograph from the time reveals a fattened up Osborne, his beard flecked with grey, looking relaxed in a Royal Court T-shirt and jeans. He's holding up a startled labrador puppy for the camera – a new addition, Max from Harrods, named after Max Miller. There was also Max's sister, Minnie, and Lulu, a boxer, as well as two hacks to ride, Charky and Annabel, and two donkeys, Jenkins and Alice, from a RSPCA rescue.

Ye Olde High Street in Edenbridge still looks as if Miss Marple might suddenly appear bustling along it solving crimes. There are five pubs along the High today: the King and Queen, the Old Crown, the Old Eden Inn, the Star Inn and the White Horse. Norene Thomas, the daughter of a firefighter, was a barmaid at the Old Crown when she first met Osborne and became a friend. He helped to finance a dog salon she opened in the town named Hair of the Dog.

She told me, "I think we all knew that John lived somewhere in Edenbridge, but we never saw him. He was convinced that he wasn't welcome in the village so he kept away. For all his talent, he was very easily squashed. Then one day, he came into the Crown with Helen and at first you could see that he felt uncomfortable, like a fish out of water. He was a very diffident man, anyway. I think she nagged him a bit to come into town. She was magic, Helen. But it didn't take him long to feel relaxed with us because everybody was ever so pleased to see him. It was a strange phenomenon. We knew he was a famous man, but he seemed so nice."

He was now seen in town shopping for groceries each week – a diverting ritual of unknown domesticity for him. Helen was petite in her Beatles cap and he walked with his arm protectively round her carrying a wicker basket and a shopping list he'd compiled to compare the price of cucumbers like an old maid. Before driving home to Christmas Place, they would stop in one of the pubs along the High for a beer and end up at the clubby Old

Crown. The Crown was run by an eccentric landlord whose company Osborne enjoyed.

"Henry loved John, and John loved Henry," Norene Thomas explained amusingly. "He must have been the rudest landlord in Kent. He had all the tact and diplomacy of a leg iron. But he was a very kind man. He was lovely. He charged much less for a double than two singles. You always knew when Henry was drunk because his trousers fell down."

Osborne's first wife, Pamela Lane, came to stay – breaking the ice with the past. Penelope Gilliatt also stayed, lugging books and bottles of gin with her in an overnight bag. The guest list at weekend lunches included the Oliviers, Michael Gambon, Eileen Atkins and husband Bill, *Observer* friends like travel writer Edward Mace, National Theatre director Bill Bryden and his wife, and another old friend of Osborne's, Royal Court director Robert Kydd with his wife Jenny Sieff. "It's a good memory I have of being with them," Sieff told me, looking through an old photo album of visits to Christmas Place. "It was always very relaxed and fun. We'd sit in the kitchen with the dogs and chat and gossip and eat spaghetti and drink too much. They were lovely together."

Osborne began work on what would be the bestselling, first volume of his autobiography entitled, ironically, *A Better Class of Person*. Helen edited it, and as she read each new chapter in her own study he lurked outside the door, listening.

"What page are you on!" he would cry. "Why haven't you laughed yet?" He aimed for 9,000 words a week. (It took him three years.) When they sailed to Cape Town on the *SA Vaal*, he wrote two minor TV plays on board as if warming up for bigger things. But one of them, *Try a Little Tenderness*, about a rock festival that turns a country village into a battlefield, has never been performed. The second, *You're Not Watching Me, Mummy*, was more successful. It was about the desperate relationship of a narcissistic stage actress, Jemima, and her campy dresser, Leslie. Peter Sallis played the devoted dresser, and Anna Massey gave a perfect impersonation of Jill Bennett.

On 12 April 1976, Osborne sent a rare apology to a drama critic, Harold Hobson, who had just retired. "I once sent you a rather churlish, ill-mannered letter. I have regretted doing so ever since. This is merely to say so and also that you will be sorely missed by many of us in this mad profession."

On 17 October 1977, a small advertisement appeared in *The Times* enlisting recruits to the newly founded British Playwrights' Mafia (motto: "With Pen and Sword")led by Lt. Col. John Osborne, c/o The Loyal BPM (Yeo.) Edenbridge, Kent.

Announcing a fatwa on all drama critics, the relaxed Osborne, indulging his silly streak, was the self-appointed Colonel of the 1st Battalion assisted by Corporal Charles Wood 225. (They were Wood's real army number and rank from his days as a professional soldier.) There was even a club tie that Osborne designed – a quill pen crossed with a bloody dagger. The Playwrights' Mafia lark consisted of insulting critics via anonymous seaside postcards. Sheridan Morley was sent the severe warning, "Fatty Morley – Watch out on dark nights." Bernard Levin was threatened with being pushed under a train. Irving Wardle received a threat of physical violence that was signed by the playwright Alun Owen in Osborne's handwriting. Benedict Nightingale got a woozy warning telling him it would be better for his health if he avoided downtown Chichester. A bewildered Francis King of the *Sunday Telegraph* received two cards calling him a cunt. When he got the second missive, he politely wrote back to Osborne, "I really do think you should seek out some medical advice . . ."

On 2 June 1978, John Osborne and Helen Dawson were married at Tunbridge Wells Register Office, having arrived for the ceremony in the van of the local fishmonger named Dissington. The Dissingtons were new friends, and they cheerfully offered the bride and groom a lift. The best man was Richard Findlater – Helen's oldest friend from their days together on the *Observer* and the former *Tribune* drama critic who long ago had encouraged the unknown Osborne to keep writing his plays.

The small wedding party included the Mortimers, the Dissingtons, Robert Kydd and his wife Jenny, and Brian Walden (father of Osborne's godson, Ben). The cub reporter on the Tunbridge Wells wedding beat missed a scoop. He didn't recognize Osborne. But, seeing a middle-aged man with a beard, he asked him if he had been married before.

"Yes," he replied. "Four times." Where was he going on honeymoon? "Can't afford one!" And off they all went for a jolly lobster and champagne lunch in the garden of Christmas Place. (Fish by Dissington.) And down to the Chinese in town in the evening.

42

Country Matters

I just want simple, familiar, English comforts.
Osborne letter to a friend, 1980

In a very suprising turn of events, Osborne's daughter, Nolan, arrived from New York only two weeks after the marriage, to live in Edenbridge for good. She was now thirteen years old. Yet her father scarcely knew her and in the years of their long separation and dutiful visits he thought of her with a mixture of romanticism and guilt. Soon after his divorce from Gilliatt, he argued for her return to England because he'd read alarming reports that New York was violently unsafe. Later, he tried blaming the US educational system and wanted her to attend an English boarding school. But Nolan's abrupt return was for different and disturbing reasons.

Perhaps it was Gilliatt's neurotic drive for perfection that caused her descent into drugs and alcoholism or the critical disappointment in her novels that escalated it. She was cared for by the kindly Vincent Canby, film critic of the *New York Times*, who helped raise Nolan. But since the end of her three-year affair with Mike Nichols, her drink problem and irrational behaviour had escalated to the point where she was beyond the help of her friends. Gilliatt was no longer capable of looking after her daughter.

A dramatic change in her was evident when she first visited Edenbridge, though she could be adept at disguising her true condition when it came to work. She still wrote for the *New Yorker*, and it's ironic that two of the London *Observer's* brightest stars – Gilliatt in Manhattan and Tynan dying of emphysema in Santa Monica – were carried through their troubled, declining years by William Shawn, the legendary editor of the *New Yorker*.

There's evidence to suggest that Gilliatt never stopped loving Osborne. Yet she also resented him. On 14 January 1980, the *New Yorker* innocently published her thinly-veiled message to him written in the form of a little play entitled *In Trust*. It's clearly about the upbringing of Nolan – or "Kate", as she's named in the story – and the grand Chester Square house in Belgravia that was left in trust for her. Osborne is the man described as the "quitter father".

When the piece was published, Nolan had been living with her father for two years. Aware of the magazine's hallowed writing style, he fired off a rude response to the editor of the *New Yorker* with a copy to Gilliatt.

18 March 1980
Edenbridge

Dear Mr Shawn,

Have you lost your bleeding marbles, you poor old cock? I fear so, publishing P. Gilliatt's headlong, burbling fantasies about our daughter Nolan (Kate) and her own loot, accumulated by *my* Almighty sweat . . . Your poor bloody readers must have been rubbing their mincers. (ED note: Mince pies: eyes. Cockney rhyming slang). Are you *all* feeling unwell over there, we ask ourselves? Or is the *New Yorker*, like the famed Oozlem bird that flew in ever diminishing circles, about to disappear up its once glossy sphincter?

Whatever is the cause, we hope it gets better soon.

Yours Sincerely,
John Osborne
("Quitter Father" – for it is He.)

A concerned Shawn responded with typical courtesy explaining that it simply hadn't occurred to him that Gilliatt's contribution was autobiographical. "At any rate, I am distressed that this story caused you pain and embarrassment. I am truly sorry. With admiration and best wishes . . ."

There were concerns for Nolan's safety when she lived with her mother in Manhattan. She was seen with friends in Central Park after dark (a notoriously dangerous place in the Seventies). Neighbours in her West Side apartment building took her in one night after Gilliatt had locked her out. The drinking problems sparked violent mood swings and furies. There was frequently no food in the house. The neglected Nolan was left to fend for herself.

Before she arrived in the Kent countryside that summer, she was privately tutored at home in Manhattan by the nanny, Christine Stotesbury, and subsquently attended Brearley, the exclusive private school in the city, for two years. It was Brearley's head of middle school, Mrs Elizabeth M. Lee, who telephoned Osborne to tell him that it was no longer safe for Nolan to live with her mother.

The nanny had meanwhile become the surrogate mother. But Nanny Stotesbury – who confirmed all this for me, as Nolan would when we met – felt compelled to leave after another abusive confrontation with Gilliatt. "Nolan had a very strange upbringing at the best of times," she told me. "As a child, she was never allowed to play with dolls that weren't beautifully designed. She was never allowed to read a book that Penelope didn't think was educational or uplifting. She was never allowed a comic."

It was the nanny and Gilliatt's West Side neighbours who initially alerted Brearley's headmistress, Evelyn Halpert. She told me about Osborne's response to the school's urgent phone call: "He couldn't have been more concerned or more thrilled to have Nolan back with him, and we couldn't have been more surprised." Mrs Halpert's surprise was the outcome of Osborne's turbulent reputation following him to New York via his plays.

Gilliatt made no objection to her daughter's return to England (though Nolan was legally under her care and control). "Oh Banksie," she wrote to Osborne with such sadness about her troubles. "What a lot of brutish and idly constituted lives . . ."

So the newly married Osbornes welcomed home the shy, subdued prodigal daughter with the light American accent, and enrolled her at St Michael's private school in nearby Limpsfield where she made new friends. She was back with the father she had scarcely known since childhood, and though he knew nothing about raising children, he wanted this moment. His new wife was glad for him and would always be welcoming. For a time all seemed well.

After the civil wedding in Tunbridge Wells, Osborne's marriage to Helen had been formally blessed in Edenbridge parish church by a new friend to them both, Canon Richard Mason, and Nolan would be confirmed at Easter in the same historic church. For Osborne's critics, the transformation of the former rebel into a practising Christian was only further proof of his decline, as if faith must be wet and Christianity in Kent blimpish. He was aware of a certain irony. In one of his gossipy letters to ex-mistress Rickards, he wrote en passant, "God, I'm getting (a) more chauvinistic (b) High Tory (c) Anglican (d) predictable and boring. The funny thing is I don't *feel* any older . . ."

Another of his letters mentioned Nolan's confirmation day. "The Vicar came to dinner with some of the choir, who left at about 4 a.m. We're going to the church dinner dance at Hever Castle on Friday. Big deal this one – 200 drunken *v* randy communicants. As you may have guessed, I have rather taken to God recently . . ."

The most surprising *Spectator* column Osborne wrote in a decade of unpredictable columns was his first. "About ten years ago," his opening line announced on 22 December 1984, "I resumed regular church-going after a long lapse."

The lapse had so far lasted all his life. God, on the other hand, like Osborne's enduring sense of guilt and sin and strange foreboding fears, had always been present. He believed words were closest to God. Fifteen years before he went to live in Kent, he depicted an ecstatic Martin Luther racked by spiritual hunger and penitence as if theatre itself were an act of communion.

The turning point came when his life hung precariously in the balance during the tormented days alone in Edenbridge. Osborne in crisis reached out to God and formal prayer as T.S. Eliot turned to Christianity for significance and meaning in his own waste land. Even damnation, Eliot maintained, might be a form of salvation from the eternal pain and ennui of being alive.

Osborne's *Spectator* column went on to say amusingly, "There are times when I feel God needs protecting from the likes of me. He doesn't deserve it, nor bringing Him into the house on the wintry boots of a lone visit to Evensong. Even now, my present, devout Geordie companion snaps at me each Sunday morning around noon: 'Are you talking to God this evening or not?' If I am locked in the passages of some hardy gloom. I say no."

In his eccentric, worshipful way, Osborne didn't like to trouble God with his depressions. He didn't want to waste His time. So he went to church when he had something interesting or jolly to offer, preferring the reflective solace of Evensong to "the hi-de-hi squalling family service at 9.30 hours that is as unassailable as pub lager".

Canon Mason often visited the Osbornes at Christmas Place, for he had come to enjoy the company of the man who ventured one day into his church. Helen would leave them to talk for hours into the night as if in learned holy disputes. On one unspoken level, Osborne's need for faith opened the door to his ultimate father figure. The wellspring of his belief was informed by liturgy, however, not dogma – the numinous prose of the Thomas Cranmer Prayer Book together with Orwell's treasured language of England, the King James Bible.

Osborne had made the connection between his innate love of the English language and the unifying continuity of Anglican worship. Repeated obsessively in all his private notebooks from then on was the mantra, "To Serve is Perfect Freedom" – the prayer from the Second Collect.

He had a brave new cause: the historic masterpieces of the Anglican

Church versus the Alternative Prayer Book's modernized, lumpen liturgy. The sticker in the back of his car now proclaimed: "Support the Book of Common Prayer!" He read the lesson at Edenbridge church. He opened his gardens in aid of restoring the church roof. He railed against the pieties of born-again populism, ungodly, blustering social workers and the theological vandalism of trendy vicars. He fired off harrumphing letters to *The Times* and *Telegraph* like "Outraged of Tunbridge Wells". He quoted Auden on rewriting the King James Bible in the name of dumbed-down accessibility: "Why spit on your luck?"

On Christmas Eve, Canon Mason sometimes joined the Osbornes for supper at the house and they would go with him to midnight mass. This understanding, exceptional man said of Osborne's return to the fold that his concern to preserve the legacy and beauty of the Anglican Church seemed to him to possess the deeper concern "of one to whom God was a reality, a Being who was drawing John's inmost self back to its home and origin. His spirituality seemed to be quintessentially English, restrained, measured, devoid of 'enthusiasm' and drawing for its sustenance on the great writings and prayers of the Christian tradition. If some of his own dramatic writings appear to be somewhat at variance with such a view, I for one would be happy to stand by it, believing that in so complex a character it was not too far from some his deepest roots."

Soon after *A Better Class of Person* was published in 1981 and provoked a public storm over Osborne's uncharitable loathing of his mum, he was interviewed on *Desert Island Discs* on BBC Radio 4. The reassuring Roy Plomley said to him chattily between choosing his favourite music, "You made quite a bitter attack on your mother, John, for what you consider the inadequacies of your upbringing?"

Osborne was relaxed and took it in his stride. "I don't think it was a bitter attack. It's simply a record of my feelings, really, at the time. I haven't gilded it at all in any particular way."

"Has she commented on the book?" Plomley enquired.

"Oh, no. She wouldn't read it, anyway."

Although it isn't known whether Nellie Beatrice did read it, Osborne had long since stopped speaking to her. It might be asked of his treatment of his mother, as was asked sanctimoniously of Evelyn Waugh: "How could you, as a church-going Christian, be so unkind?" To which Waugh replied, "Imagine how much worse I would be if I weren't a Christian . . ."

"What did you wish to be as a youngster?" Plomley asked.

"A newspaper editor, opera singer or a priest," he replied.

The first record he ever bought as a schoolboy, we learn, was by Fats Waller. The second was Handel – "The Arrival of the Queen Sheba" from *Solomon* – with Sir Thomas Beecham conducting on the old dark blue Columbia label. Osborne's adored father, Thomas Godfrey, was a music lover. One of the favourite recordings his son played repeatedly at home was Paul Robeson's melancholy song of yearning, "Just a Wearying For You." Robeson, he told Plomley, was a Blakean figure of goodness and the lament made him think of the father he had missed all his life.

Adagio from Elgar's Cello Concerto, composed in the Edwardian twilight, was another choice. "It's so unbearably moving about a time I never knew," he said. Jimmy Porter's favourite composer, Vaughan Williams, was Osborne's favourite, too. *The Lark Ascending* was his choice for its soothing calm. He said that listening to Vaughan Williams's music on a desert island, he could imagine himself looking up at the sky and thinking he was living in the Kentish countryside, and he would remember England.

And the one book Osborne would take with him apart from Shakespeare and the Bible? He named *Holy Living and Holy Dying* by the seventeenth-century divine, Jeremy Taylor. A schoolmaster long ago had introduced it to him.

Plomley delicately brought up the absence of a new Osborne play. "The rate of playwriting has slowed up, John?"

"Well, as far as playwriting, that's true. I've spent three years on that book of mine [*A Better Class of Person*]." There were still lots of plays in him, he added reassuringly. "When to put the horse in the race, you know. It's there."

But was it? Six years had elapsed since his last play, *Watch It Come Down*, and there were no signs that he was at work on a new one. His sporadic notebooks of the period offer little clue. The letter "P" signalled an idea for a play and one isolated entry in particular caught my attention:

"P – THE BIOGRAPHER. The Outsider's view of the 'Great Man'. The Biographer/Critic versus The Wife ('He wasn't like that . . .')."

Helen told me that he had in mind a new version of *The Beggar's Opera*, as well as a play about Falstaff. He was thinking about a play with music about friendship based on Elgar's *Enigma Variations*. He long ago had an ambitious idea for an epic drama about the Third Reich, and for many years, he also talked of a play about Judas. "I know all about betrayal," he wrote to the director Bill Bryden, who functioned as an intermediary between Osborne and the National. But none of these ideas got written.

At least his now classic plays were being *revived* – the consolation prize of the middle-aged dramatist. In 1978, Osborne directed his own revival of *Inadmissible Evidence* at the Court and it was superior to the 1964 original with the older Nicol Williamson now the right age for Bill Maitland. The programme for the admired new production was unique in its defensive way. It quoted from no less than twenty scathing reviews of Osborne's plays. "This must surely be his farewell to theatre . . ."

In 1980, *Look Back* was revived in New York with Malcolm McDowell as Jimmy. In 1981, another production of *Inadmissible* with Nicol Williamson also opened in New York. (During its 1965 US tour, its all-powerful producer, David Merrick – "roaring around like a war lord", according to Osborne – had fired the director Anthony Page in Philadelphia for refusing to make cuts in the script without Osborne's permission, and the enraged Williamson took a swing at Merrick outside the stage door, knocking him into a dustbin. Page was eventually reinstated and emissaries were urgently dispatched to the airport to stop Williamson catching a plane home after Merrick announced he would never work again in any medium in the world.)

Williamson was back in New York in 1983 playing Archie Rice. That same year, Alan Bates played Redl in a successful revival of *A Patriot for Me* at the Chichester Festival Theatre. The Chichester production transferred to Los Angeles where Osborne was reconciled with Tony Richardson as if nothing had happened between them. He and Helen were Richardson's guests in the West Hollywood mansion he'd bought from porn star Linda Lovelace down the road from Liberace's place. It had a mosaic swimming pool, a well-used tennis court, and a moody macaw that could squawk, "Have a nice day! Have a nice day!" But only when it felt like.

"Stare dozily out of the window at the mist on the lake by the house, the tall trees and fields that surround us on all sides," Osborne wrote about a typical, lazy Sunday at home in Edenbridge. "It looks like an H.M. Tennant set for *The Seagull* . . . Glass of champagne in bed. ('What do you *do* all day long down there? When are you going to come up to London?') Haven't had a sleeping pill for six months. Doze off, dreaming of all those foreign royalties coming in from Germany, France, Denmark, Sweden, Italy, Spain, Poland, Australia and so on. J Porter still slogs on and all the other plays as well. If I depended on the loyalty and taste of the British public I should be destitute without any doubt. My next piece will be one about Judas Iscariot . . ."

If he wasn't writing plays in Kent, he was enjoying the escapist country camp of village fêtes and church hops instead. Each day, his wife was busy doing the school run with Nolan and helping with the homework, while he was after "simple, familiar, English comforts" following "the years of pestilence" with Jill Bennett. Billed as a "Special Guest", he opened the parish fête: "Cream teas at 4.30 p.m. Followed by Punch and Judy Show. Drawing of raffles. (To be held in Church House if wet.)" He lit the Edenbridge bonfire on Bonfire Night – an honour previously bestowed on Winston Churchill and another local celeb, the fearless "First Lady of Fleet Street", Jean Rook.

"All that lovely lolly," he liked to say about his royalties apparently flowing in annually from around the world. But the truth was that he was heading towards bankruptcy. He was spending more than he earned, and the big money in his Woodfall Films accounts had been run down over the years. There were serious tax problems. But there *was* money – there always had been money – and he didn't care enough to worry about the details. Even mundane household bills were sent directly to his international firm of accountants, Touche Ross, which is like hiring a top lawyer to pay a parking fine. He had never troubled to read his bank statements. His daughter went to an expensive private school. His wife was as much in the dark about the real state of his finances as he was, but she had no reason to assume there was a problem.

In 1981, three years after they married, he bought a west Cornwall cottage on a whim. They'd taken the Paddington train to Cornwall for a weekend away and ended up falling for a tiny seaside cottage in Portscatho. He joined the Portscatho Social Club for a pound a year to play leisurely games of snooker with the locals (and listed the club along with the Garrick in his *Who's Who* entry).

In a revealing May 1983 notebook doodle, he idly listed the different people in his life who lived in Portscatho, Edenbridge and London.

"London: Solicitors; accountants; 'actors'; producers; directors; 'writers'; lawyers; agents."

"Portscatho: Postmistress; retired schoolmasters; assorted lesbians; Group Captain; fisherman; social club manager; pub owner."

"Edenbridge: 4 vicars; 2 pub landlords; 2 electricians, ex-RAF, Navy; one drayman; diverse barmaids; florist; newsagent (lad); bookseller; our bank manager; one dog clipper; two farmers; one member Royal Household; one romantic novelist; two water board officials; several church workers; one builder; Indian restaurant; one vet."

On 28 May 1981, Eafor Ali and his business partner, Abdul Mumaim, opened the Quality Tandoori Restaurant on Edenbridge High Street, and it was Mr Ali who told me when I dropped in unexpectedly that Osborne had been his guest of honour on the first night. "Before we opened the restaurant we asked the local people who was a well-known person in the public eye and we were kindly recommended Mr John Osborne, the playwright."

Osborne subsequently went to his Indian restaurant once a week and had a big champagne and vindaloo birthday party there with balloons. How did he strike Mr Ali? "A very nice man, very polite, very presentable. When he came in to eat with friends, he would pay for them all as well. Sometimes I had to make him wait for a table but he didn't mind. He went to the pub and had a drink and then he came back. He always chatted to me whenever we met here or in the street. I've missed him since he died. He signed the Visitor's Book. Look –"

"The best and always better – John and Helen Osborne, 21.8.82."

"Did you go to his big summer parties," I asked.

"I did. I was surprised to be asked. But John invited me and said, 'Ali, come to my party with your wife and children and your cats and dogs.'"

He explained good-naturedly that he went with his wife and four of his children. "You could drink champagne or Coke at these wonderful parties, you could swim in his pool, or you could read the books on his shelves. But one thing was amazing. There were so many famous people there, they were from the TV screens and film, they were great actors and actresses, and you thought, 'What is their name? What *is* their name?' And then you looked again and you remembered who they were."

What would Mr Ali say if I told him some people didn't like John Osborne? "I would say *mittha baddi*," he replied. "It isn't true."

It was true for some – like the elderly schoolmistress who lived at the top of Osborne's lane and honked her car horn to irritate him whenever she drove past his property. Sir Simon and Lady Bland were his neighbours a mile down the lane and they had mixed feelings about him, too. They now lived just off the High Street and the framed, signed photographs of royalty in their drawing room reminded me that Sir Simon was the member of the Royal Household listed by Osborne among the Edenbridge people he knew. He was Private Secretary for some thirty years to the old Duke of Gloucestershire, younger brother of King George VI.

Like Mr Ali, he and his wife, Lady Olivia Bland, a military historian of Scots landed gentry descent, socialized with Osborne and went to all the summer garden parties.

Even so, Lady Bland began by saying, "I was terrified of him."

"I found him challenging and rather good value as a neighbour," said Sir Simon. "But he was totally immoral. Having read his book that he gave us [A Better Class of Person], one realizes he was a bit of a horror. Perhaps immoral is the wrong word. He largely took the mickey."

"I think immoral is the right word," taciturn Lady Bland insisted. "I thought he was cruel. He was dismissive. He had a very sneering way with him."

Their copy of *A Better Class of Person* was inscribed, "To Simon and Olivia and all chez Bland, most neighbourly regards, John (what wrote it), August 31st 1981."

"Doesn't sound *too* intimidating," I suggested to Lady Bland.

"He always made me feel frightfully stupid," she continued. "He was a terrible intellectual snob. Once, when we went for lunch, the Oliviers were there. Just them and us. That was intimidating in itself."

"There were undercurrents at the lunch," her husband explained, anxious to be fair. "I don't think John cared too much for Joan Plowright."

Lady Bland was unmoved. Osborne, it was clear, had unnerved her, needling and teasing her in a distant echo of the Jimmy Porter class wars. He instinctively identified more with her old school husband, a former colonel like decent Colonel Redfern in *Look Back*. Still, I ought to have resisted saying to Lady Bland, "Did you go to Osborne's champagne parties chained to his ankle?" It was getting rough. "I accepted lots of his hospitality," she answered evenly. "It wasn't that I didn't like him. I was frightened of him."

"Like a number of people, I don't think you knew where you quite stood with him," Sir Simon commented diplomatically. (They had been married for forty-four years.) "And I don't think you laughed at his jokes."

"He made me feel stupid," she insisted. "I liked Helen."

Their friend, Mrs Gregg, who knew Osborne socially from the winning combination of the pub and the church, was present, too. "He could make you feel small at times," she chimed in. "I used to sit there and think to myself, 'Don't make me think I'm a nonentity. I know you're a good playwright.' Which he was. You can't deny him that. He used to come to Evensong half-cut in his cape. He'd had one or two over the top."

But Mrs Gregg also pointed out that when she had a family problem one Christmas, she stayed with the Osbornes. "He was an awkward devil at times, but a very kind man. He'd got his likes and dislikes, just like us all."

In spite of his reservations, Sir Simon seemed quite fond of him. "He was very hospitable in his own way," he concluded. "If only he could have *relaxed*. Taken life more as it comes." He said gently to his wife, "But we got to know him better. Even you did, sweetie. A lot of people who live round here I wouldn't know them from Adam. But it would have been a pity if John Osborne had lived in Edenbridge and we hadn't realized it."

Lady Bland had nothing more to say.

Osborne's closest friends in Edenbridge were his neighbours, the successful romantic novelist Pat Clark, and her long-time partner, Mel. Pat Clark was otherwise known as Claire Lorrimer whose first historical novel, *The Chatelaine*, sold three million copies in America alone. "I just struck lucky," she said to me.

The author of ten other historic sagas and seventy light romantic novels, she cheerfully remembered, "John would come for lunch and say, 'Well, Pat – how many books have you written this week?'"

She didn't mind him teasing her at all. She always enjoyed his unpredictable company. But that wasn't how this remarkable woman felt when they first met. She and her amiable partner, Mel Hack, a self-made millionaire in the car business, had just moved in down the lane when Osborne came strolling by with Helen and saw her pottering about the garden. She invited them in and as the four of them enjoyed a welcoming drink, Osborne suddenly told her manically to fuck off.

"He came out with this appalling abuse for absolutely no reason," she explained. "I said to Mel later, If this is what our new neighbours are like, heaven help us. I didn't want that man in our house ever again."

"I enjoyed it," Mel added unexpectedly. "I was born in the north of England and it was right up my street in a way. He was testing us via shock tactics."

"I think it was more than that," she said. "There were two Johns."

The following morning, Osborne came down the lane again and apologized abjectly to them both. "That was John! He could be the nicest person you could ever meet or the rudest."

"But just imagine what a bloody awful life it would be if everyone was happy," said Mel.

After the apology, they all became surprising, close friends, and met regularly each week. "Life was different when John was around," said Pat. "He would come up and put his arm around you and give you a kiss."

"Including me," said Mel happily.

"He never talked about his writing, though. He was teasing me once about writing millions of words and I said to him, 'John, if I could swap a million of my words for even one of the speeches in your plays I should be really proud.'"

What did he say?

"He looked astonished and thought I was kidding him. I meant it. I said, 'I'm serious, John.' But I don't think he had any confidence left."

The summer parties they all went to were Osborne's renowned Cranmer Balls in the grounds of his home. Nolan was included on the coveted invites:

JOHN, HELEN and NOLAN OSBORNE
invite you to
CRANMER'S ANNUAL SUMMER BALL
Poolside 1662
July XXII (22nd) 12.30 onwards

Horrid Kiddies, Teenagers,	Dancing to
Aussies, Guardian Readers	The Colin Welland
Feminists on lead only.	British Fatwarmers
Large dogs welcome.	Outside If Wet.

There were some 300 guests each year, with marquee tents in the gardens, picnics by the lake, and limitless champagne. "One of the clearest images I have of John is at one of his summer parties," Melvyn Bragg remembered. "The jazz band playing in the garden, kids yelling round the lawns, scores and scores of friends, neighbours, acquaintances swirling about the open house at Edenbridge and the host himself in a white suit, having taken a drop or even two, sitting alone on a bench, smiling gently at the amiable havoc . . ."

In the tradition of village fêtes, prizes were awarded for the "Most Elegant Couple". (5th Prize: Evening with Helen Osborne. 6th Prize: Two evenings with Helen Osborne.)

The theatre crowd from London arrived by train and car for the big day – among them, Alan Bates and his sons, Ralph Richardson and his wife, Mu, the Oliviers, Harold Pinter and Antonia Fraser, the Fox brothers (Edward and Robert), Maggie Smith and family, Christopher Hampton and his family, Eileen Atkins and Bill, Peter Nichols and Thelma, Peter Bowles, Natasha Richardson, Michael Gambon, David Hare, Denholm Elliot, Glenda Jackson, the Weskers, the Mortimers. Lord Snowdon was there with his son. And there was artist Patrick Procktor, Janet Street-Porter and George and Diana Melly. And wasn't that the red-headed temptress, Edna O'Brien, having a little smooch with Osborne behind a tent pole?

"What is their name? What *is* their name?" Mr Ali thought as he was introduced to Edward Fox and a convulsed Olivier swapped risqué jokes with Edenbridge's sometime barmaid and poodle parlour owner, Norene Thomas. "John was never a *snob*," she said emphatically. "He was like a kiddie in a toy shop."

"Who are all these people?" a puzzled theatre grandee wanted to know, surveying the strangers in their midst. They were the locals. "Everybody was invited," said Jenny Forbes, the Osbornes' housekeeper for four years. "He'd just say bring your nearest and dearest, and half Edenbridge and Marsh Green would turn up. I still miss John. When I'd finished work for the morning at the house, we'd have a gin and tonic with Helen or he would come in with the old champers. I used to get in my little car afterward and say, 'Take me home.'"

The local electrician, John Diplock – Osborne nicknamed him "The Lamp Lighter" – went to the parties with his wife and three children. "A fun time that was! Not 'alf. It didn't matter what you did in life, he would ask you. It was unbelievable, really. Some of these actors are a bit snobby, aren't they? Even some of the writers are a bit snobby. But John wasn't. He came to my daughter's wedding."

It's been said that Osborne played Lord of the Manor in Edenbridge. But local people like the Diplocks were his real friends. They went on holiday together – a doomed, comic canal trip with Nolan in narrowboats up the Severn. (Osborne, dressed in shorts and Union Jack socks, checked into a Stratford-upon-Avon hotel for the night when his boat broke down.) The Diplocks, and others, were loaned the Portscatho cottage for holidays. Mrs Gregg was invited to stay at Christmas Place when she had family trouble. Similarly, housekeeper Jenny Forbes, who stayed for New Year when her father died. Norene Thomas and several others visited Clun when the Osbornes moved to Shropshire. The friendships were real and lasting.

So were the old animosities. Party guests roaming through the open house could see cut-out newspaper photos of Jill Bennett pinned to the kitchen cabinets with a moustache drawn on her and the caption, "*Achtung!*"

It was perverse therapy for Osborne and public pillory for her. He was still defying the court orders against him by continuing to send abusive postcards to Bennett (while denying they were from him). One was sent with a fake turd that could be ordered from *Private Eye*, along with the message, "Someone somewhere thinks you are a shit."

Oscar Beuselinck wrote to Osborne on 8 December 1980, warning him about the legal consequences:

My dear John,
You are my friend and client and therefore your interests are paramount. Consequently I must warn you, quite seriously, that you are likely to end up in prison . . .
I am far too fond of you that you should let this canker in your system

continue to fester and I beseech you to forget all about Jill and get on with your life.

It was John Diplock who told me how Osborne fired off his postcards instantly to one and all. When he was working in the house, he saw him reading all his mail and the newspapers in bed. "And then all of a sudden, you'd hear the door bang and he'd be running down the stairs and into his study. He kept a pile of old seaside postcards on the desk, and he'd write something quickly on one, put a stamp on, and fly straight out of the front door in his pyjamas and mail it off in the postbox on the other side of the road."

He was the human equivalent of "Send Now". Osborne was incapable of "Send Later" – a pause, self-censorship, *delete*.

43

What Happened to Nolan

I put it to you that we dispense with the absurd charade that you regard
this as your home.

Osborne letter to his daughter, 5 January 1982

Nolan Osborne never spoke to her father again after the day he cast her
out of the house in convulsive fury like a mad Lear. She was then just about
to turn seventeen years old.

When I met her at her country home on the borders of East Sussex, she
was thirty-four and happily married with two young children. She resembled her mother, without the fiery red hair – an attractive and assured
young woman with a firm handshake, who laughed easily, and smoked a
lot. Her mild American accent from her upbringing in New York had
become slightly posh and middle-class. If she resembled her father at all it
was around the eyes that took your measure with a steady gaze.

The man she long ago regarded as her substitute father, sixty-four-year-
old Rev. Guy Bennett of St Mary's in Oxted, Surrey, sat in on our lengthy
meeting. He was the one who took her in when she was seventeen. Nolan
had been close to Bennett's own daughter since their schooldays and when
Osborne abandoned her, she went to live as one of the family at the rectory.

I was surprised that Bennett would need to be present at our meeting,
but it was a condition of my seeing Nolan. "I know this makes me sound
like a security guard," he explained. "But having tried to defend her interests in the past, she says she'd be happier with me present."

Perhaps her caution was understandable. She had consistently declined
all requests for interviews in the past, particularly when Osborne died in
1994 and the tabloids stalked her and photographed the children. She also
refused significant offers to tell all. When she lived with Osborne in
Edenbridge, he could get so enraged at her that he took the precaution of
removing his big signet ring in case he hit her. (He never did.) He sniped

at her publicly, calling her "insolently smug", "devotedly suburban", "a very cold creature". He dropped her from his *Who's Who* biography as if she didn't exist. But she had steadfastly kept her counsel over the years, and never responded before.

Even so, the rector's concern seemed over-protective. My written requests to meet Nolan had to be submitted through him, and were initially rejected by him. Then he suggested that I could submit questions via him, to which she would respond. At length, it was agreed that we could meet at her delightful seventeenth-century farmhouse close to the village of Ashers Wood. The grey-haired rector met me at the station and drove me there as if to a secret destination.

Just as I arrived, Nolan's husband, Simon Parker, a financial consultant, was giving her a reassuring hug in the hallway. When they married thirteen years ago, she was given away by Rev. Guy Bennett. She was twenty-two and Simon was two years older. "It didn't seem too young to marry at the time," she told me, and laughed. "It does now." She added that their wedding was the first her husband had ever been to.

Photographs of their children were displayed in the sitting room – nine-year-old, carrot-topped Joshua and his younger sister, Anna. They were Osborne's grandchildren, though he never acknowledged their existence. A framed photograph of Jill Bennett stood on an empty bookshelf in the room like a ghostly theatre prop. But Nolan was fond of her (and her former stepmother remembered her in her will). She recalled little about visiting her father from New York as a child. She could picture the Chelsea house very well, all the dogs, and spending a lot of time in the kitchen with the staff – the cook, the cleaner and the chauffeur.

She could just about remember an image of her grandmother, Nellie Beatrice (who died in 1983). She was watching wrestling on the telly with her cats on her lap.

She still kept in touch with her father figure in New York, film critic Vincent Canby, who helped raise her for seven years. "Noelie's a very bright and lovely person," Canby told me affectionately. "She's very important in my life." But when I asked this kind-hearted man about Osborne, he replied, "I've nothing to say about the bastard."

Nolan herself was clear, unsentimental and unforgiving about her father. In fact, throughout our meeting, she never referred to him as her father. (In the same circular way, he could never bring himself to call Nellie Beatrice "mother".) The alcoholic Gilliatt was "Mom" to Nolan, but Osborne was "he" or "him".

The man she called "Dad" was the rector sitting quietly in the armchair opposite us in the sitting room. He referred to Nolan as his daughter. Her two children called him "Papa".

Nolan's former nanny and substitute mother, Christine Stotesbury, now lived in Kent with her husband and had remained a close friend. She still saw the Osbornes from time to time, hoping for a reconciliation between father and daughter until her position became impossible. In January 1990, she told Osborne by letter that he had become a grandfather. He responded that he refused to be. (Notebook entry: "How grisly grandparents are – all that slobbering pride".)

"I have no intention of becoming a grandfather," he wrote back to Stotesbury, adding about his estranged daughter, "I don't know her married name, if indeed she is married, address or anything about her. However, I seriously doubt that she could be a blood relative of mine and have thought so for a long time. She bears no resemblance to me whatsoever."

Did ever a daughter deserve such a fate? Did ever a father? After he cast Nolan out, they never met or spoke to each other again for the rest of his life. In effect, they disowned each other. But when she was twenty-three and working in London, they literally bumped into each other in the street. By then, she was married and working at a publishing house opposite the Garrick Club. It was quite late, the end of the working day, and pouring with rain.

She told me, "I ran out the door putting up my umbrella, and I knocked into this man and said, 'Oh excuse me.' He didn't move, and I looked up and it was him. Then he looked at me and he just walked off in a different direction."

She was certain he recognized her? "I'm sure he knew it was me."

She related the story without emotion. Did it upset her at the time, perhaps?

"No, it didn't upset me. I just thought, how bloody obstinate. Why didn't he just move out of the way?"

There's no doubt that Osborne welcomed Nolan enthusiastically when she first came to live in Edenbridge. If anything, he and Helen spoilt her. They gave her generous pocket money and bought her lots of new clothes. Christmas Place had its own stables. She had a pony to ride like a typical English country girl. Her schoolfriends were invited to stay at the house. She seemed happy and even told Stotesbury that after the traumas with her mother in New York it was like living in a dream. Then it all went dramatically wrong.

It would be laughable had it not ended so badly. In the four roller-coaster years that Nolan lived with her father – from the age of thirteen to seven-teen – he simply couldn't grasp what every despairing parent knows and dreads: adolescents find parents a total embarrassment. Helen tried to keep the peace between them (and was still well liked by Nolan). "John wanted to awaken in her the best that life could offer," she explained. "But the reason he couldn't sympathize with her was because he'd never been a teenager."

It was true. Osborne claimed there were no teenagers when he was growing up, only failed adults. Besides, his younger self actually enjoyed the company of his adult relatives and he thought his daughter would feel the same way about him.

"It was more difficult because I never grew up with him," Nolan said. "He couldn't understand why I'd prefer to spend an evening in Oxted with a bunch of my friends than go to the opera. I was thirteen or fourteen years old and he was flabbergasted when Laurence Olivier came to dinner and I didn't want to stay up till the early hours talking to him. He couldn't accept that I'd rather have met Mel Gibson."

Then there was the trip to introduce Nolan to the splendours of Venice. "But a Bond movie was being made there at the time," Helen remembered, "and all Nolan wanted to do was meet Roger Moore! Well, why not? It made me laugh."

They *tried*. On another occasion, they went to London for Nolan's birthday treat to see an Elvis show at the Victoria Palace. Right idea, wrong era. "There were all these ancient Elvis lookalikes in the audience and we found it so funny we loved it," Helen said. "But Nolan was bored to tears. She thought we were mad. She was right."

Ex-nanny Stotesbury told me that one of the flashpoints was that Osborne read about himself in Nolan's diary. When he discussed it with Stotesbury, he complained indignantly, "How can you defend Nolan when she's written all these terrible things?"

"I told him first of all that I thought far less of him for reading her private diary than I did for her writing it."

"All very well," he insisted, "but you should see what she's written about *you*."

"Whatever it is," the formidable Stotesbury insisted, "it won't affect how I feel about her."

"She called you a fat old cow," said Osborne.

"Well, I *am* a fat old cow!" she replied. "If you're fifteen years old and you're with someone who doesn't want you to smoke – that's a fat old cow who won't let you get away with it. I'd rather Nolan got it out of her system in her diary than stayed away from me."

But Osborne couldn't be persuaded.

Nolan was a mild rebel compared to your average teenage werewolf. She didn't drop acid or return home with a green Mohican hairdo and a ring through her nose. She smoked, and in a big domestic drama she denied nicking money from the housekeeper to pay for cigarettes. One traumatic day, she accidentally set fire to her bedroom, but all was well in the end. Helen often covered for her. She talked forever on the phone as adolescents do (and was given her own phone line). She slept late, flopped around the place and found backwater Edenbridge a bore. She had a crush on a schoolboy who was unsurprisingly loathed by Osborne. They hung around together at nearby Oxted where Rev. Guy Bennett, rector of St Mary's, lived.

Bennett's daughter was the same age as Nolan and they both went to St Michael's School. They subsequently called themselves "sisters". Each day, Nolan was driven from home to Edenbridge station to commute by train to Oxted, and then she walked to St Michael's twenty minutes away. The rectory was close by the station and Bennett was soon running both girls to school. He gave Nolan a door key and she sometimes stayed the night with her friends. She would come to spend more and more time there until it became her second home.

In one unexpected way, the Rev. Guy Bennett had far more in common with Osborne than Nolan did. He was stagestruck. For many years, he had been a voluntary chaplain who visited theatres on behalf of the Actors' Church Union. He was chaplain to the London Palladium and was always welcomed backstage, he told me, except by Bing Crosby. "I'm not in the league of the Royal National Theatre," he acknowledged. "I'm more at the other end of the spectrum. The Palladium. The West End theatre. The Grand Order of Water Rats. Sadly, I do a lot of comedians' funerals. But a showbiz funeral is quite different from any other funeral. It's more a celebration of life."

"Have you done any comedian's funeral we might know?" I enquired.

"I did Michael Bentine's. There's the other side of it as well. I took Roy Hudd's wedding. I've done charity concerts at a little amateur theatre down here with Ronnie Corbett. I was chaplain to the Phoenix Theatre in the West End when Jill Bennett was starring in a play called *West of Suez*. I actually met John there once, but he wouldn't have remembered. I suppose I became a bit of a shoulder for Jill to cry on. In fact, I eventually did her funeral at Putney crematorium."

The rector and his then wife were entertained by the Osbornes at Christmas Place during Nolan's time there and they went to the summer garden parties. "He was very much Lord of the Manor down there," he offered. "A better class of person. My only explanation of what went wrong was that Nolan didn't really fit his bill."

The daughter Osborne idealized as a child had grown into an adolescent who rejected his world. Thin-skinned at the best of times and a man to whom rejection was a mortal wound, he wept with frustration and disappointment at the gulf with his only child. The disinterested, teenage Nolan wasn't the daughter he imagined. But, more dangerously, she became the symbol of every woman who couldn't be the woman he wanted.

"I didn't think I'd come to sire a child who is a stony image of Penelope *and* MY MOTHER," he wrote in 1980 to his confidante and ex-mistress, Rickards.

His notebook entries about Nolan reveal a shocking change in heart.

28 July 1973

Nolan [then eight years old] comes in ten days. I am in such a dual frenzy inwardly. I'd like to get to know her but I doubt if it's possible.

1980 [Edenbridge]

Nolan: I'm afraid she's an ugly duckling who will turn into an unlovely petulant duck.

30 April 1983

Nolan: a mole of nature.

24 Feb 1987

Nolan's birthday. God rot her. 22 pinched little years.

Yet at first he blamed himself for what went wrong between them. "I gave Nolan the most awful bollocking about her attitude to me/the world," he wrote when she first arrived in Edenbridge. "Endless middle-aged cant and, my goodness, I regretted it." But he was soon belittling her even in front of his embarrassed friends. He wrote to Rickards: "I'm afraid Nolan will be sorry when she's grown up. She's Miss V. Average. Conformist, conservative, most appalling taste in just about *everything* . . . So long as she's healthy, as they say."

Osborne mocked her apparent ordinariness in the same way that his loathed mother had crushed him publicly as a child by mocking him. It was all he knew about parenting. "You ought to ease up a bit on her, John," neighbourly Mel Hack advised him gently on more than one occasion. Others did the same. But he couldn't ease up – least of all could he censor himself when he reached for his pen. He was a man incapable of repressing anything. "Speak what you feel," was Osborne's byword, "not what you ought to say."

"Did he ever tell you that you looked lovely?" I asked Nolan. "Did he ever say, 'I love you'?"

"Not that I remember," she answered.

Nor did he discuss the problems between them personally, and Nolan couldn't risk it. (Helen was her sympathetic ear.) She avoided confrontation. "I wasn't going to get involved in a big argument with him because I knew he would always win. It was the same with my mother's outbursts. It was just easier to let things ride. I could have quite easily stood up and told him, 'All my friends are like this. It doesn't make me a bad person.' I knew it wasn't worth it."

Rather than confront a crisis personally, Osborne left letters and notes in the house for Nolan to read instead. The following extract from an eight-page rant was written to her when she was still fifteen. Osborne had been awoken by the driver of the hire car who had come to fetch her for school. She was still sound asleep upstairs. So was his wife. It was December – the dangerous time of the year. The enraged father sat down in his study to write to his daughter.

Christmas Place
December 16th 1980

My dear Nolan,

I want you to *think on this*: This note may seem an intemperate reaction to a petty incident (indeed it is) but small incidents create political catastrophes and the reason I am so angry (it's as well you're not here or I might knock you across the garden) is that it is yet another depressing example of your monumental selfishness.

People tell me repeatedly that it is the flaw of your age group. That may be and, if so, it is very sad indeed. I find it hard to believe that an entire generation can be so consumed with ignorance and self-regard.

What I do believe is that *you* are almost uniquely cold-hearted. That, far from being the result of a troubled inner life (clearly, you have no inner life whatever, just a commonplace hole in the air, composed of idiotic quarrels, feuds and top of the fucking pops) or a difficult upbringing, it is from your own appalling nature, which I commonly assume is your Mother's principal, almost only, gift to you. It's become clear to me that I should have left you in New York.

So it cruelly and unstoppably goes. He went on to compare her to a selfish lodger in the house (and peculiarly, to stiff-necked, "cold-hearted" Jews). He could not edit himself. He even interrupted the letter with the thought, "I need a cup of tea." Then he suggested that Nolan might live away from home in the New Year. "The present situation is unrewarding for you, irksome for me and provides almost total lack of mutual pleasure . . . I can't put up with the present arrangement. Mrs Thatcher may be called the Iron Maiden but at least I don't have to have her in my house. Oh, and apologise to Alan [the driver] with some sort of ill-becoming grace, and remember that you owe me 2 pounds 40 pence."

The letter ended, "I made some sort of reputation writing embittered letters like this, but this one I do mean, I really do. So I will sign myself, Your most fatigued and fed-up Father, John Osborne."

Fed-Up Father *and* Famous Writer! The letter is all about him. But its spontaneous abuse is mild compared to the considered, devastating letter he wrote casting out Nolan one year later.

At sixteen, she left St Michael's and went to d'Overboeck's Tutorial College in Oxford to cram for A levels and university. "Nolan has a good mind," her November 1981 report from d'Overboeck's read when she returned home for Christmas. "She is well balanced. She is pretty and full of charm, and bubbling with life. She was obviously born under a happy star. Lucky girl!"

Though Nolan told me that she remembered nothing went specifically wrong that Christmas, she apparently spent a good deal of time with her boyfriend and their group in Oxted. Back in Edenbridge, she overslept on Christmas morning as Osborne stewed with Helen, the unwrapped gifts on hold under the tree.

She returned to Oxford and d'Overboeck's early in the New Year. She was now almost seventeen years old.

Christmas Place,
5 January 1982

My dear Nolan,
Since you left on Sunday, I've been giving long and overdue thought to your concerted behaviour and attitudes, not only during the past short holiday but over the past three and a half years.

As a result I have decided upon two things:

1. That you should find some other place to live.
2. That there is no point in your continuing studies in d'Overboeck's. Your token interest in anything academic, whether it be Art, Literature,

Painting, Music or anything else for that matter makes the whole exercise a total waste of time, skill and effort of others, to say nothing of the unbearable financial burden on myself. The life of the imagination is not something you will strive for.

So much for the broad decision. You made it patently, indeed painfully clear, that your snatched visits here at Christmas gave you no pleasure at all – only boredom and vexation. The insolent indifference and open cupidity of the grasping ingrate you undoubtedly are was palpable to all – not merely myself. If you should ever bring yourself to read KING LEAR without coaxing, look up the very First Act: "How sharper than a serpent's tooth it is to have a thankless child."

I put it to you that we dispense with the absurd charade that you regard this as your home. It is a place you have never liked nor its occupants, whom you regard with contempt or indifference. This does not only include myself and Helen but my many friends. These are people for whom I have great regard and lasting affection and I will no longer tolerate their being objects of your mindless ennui. There is not one of them who is not worth a dozen low lifes like you.

Helen and I work hard – and gladly – to make a full and enjoyable life for us all here. Not difficult but it requires energy, goodwill and some imagination. Over the past three years you have made it brutally clear that you care for none of it. So be it. Go your own way. But do stop feigning affection, loyalty or allegiance to anyone – at least in this house.

Your heart – such as that is – is irretrievably elsewhere, a place without spirit, imagination or honour.

I have made no secret of my detestation of your odious companion. I know that the only reason you spend even a few reluctant hours here is so you can cadge more money from me in order to pursue this squalid and ludicrous shopgirl's liaison with him and his drunken dreary friends . . .

Never did a mother deserve such a daughter. Such sublime selfishness must have its match! Less art more meat. I will not continue to be treated in this way by someone as criminally commonplace as yourself.

Helen, not only in the past weeks, works like a dog to make life interesting and agreeable to you. So do others. And for what? To sum up:

Don't bother to come here. A life of banality, safety, mediocrity and meanness of spirit is what you are set on. You have never asked for my confidence. Don't ask for it now. Above all, don't unerestimate my resolve or anger. I see you lying, cheating, dissembling, stealing daily. It is not a spectacle I wish to watch any longer.

He then told her that he was withdrawing her formally from school and would pay no further fees. He informed her Oxford landlady, and he closed her bank account.

> In the meantime, I suggest that you make arrangements about getting some suitable accommodation either with friends temporarily or in lodgings or an hotel when you may start looking for a job. You may, of course, send the bills, providing they are reasonable, to me.
> I have told Phyllis [the housekeeper] to pick up your books, clothes, records etc. They will be stored in the stable until the time when you are able to pick them up . . .
> What a pity for us all that you didn't remain at Brearley. I only took you in because Mrs Lee [the head of middle school] begged me to – because you were being criminally neglected. Perhaps you could persuade your Mother to take you back . . .
> Happy 1982. This is where the long road really starts – On Your Own.

The wonder is that she ever recovered from it. But breathtaking abuse like that had been the chilling norm in Nolan's life long before she returned to England. Her survival instinct was already strong and it saved her.

"I probably wouldn't have survived if it hadn't been for the three years I spent alone with my mother in New York," she told me. When her protective nanny left, she learned to cope alone with her alcoholic mother's mad mood swings and neglect. Nolan was on her own long before her father abandoned her.

She was also hardened to his insults. "I had the ability to protect myself, to be cold, really. Even when I received the letter throwing me out I just got on my bike and went round to my best friend's house in Oxford to tell her about it. I knew I had friends who thought enough of me to put a roof over my head. I knew that Guy [the rector] and Sally [his daughter] would say I could stay with them, if only temporarily. I didn't have to ask."

There was no question of her returning to live with her mother. On a visit to England, Gilliatt had turned up drunk at Nolan's old school, St Michael's. On another occasion, Nolan was in London with her friend, Sally, when they made an unexpected visit to see her mother at the house in Chester Square that Osborne had left in trust for her. Gilliatt stayed there when she was in London. There was no reply from the house, but the front door was unlocked. They entered to find the dusty interiors frozen in time like the faded mansion in *Sunset Boulevard*. Gilliatt had left the place untouched since she lived there with Osborne. The two girls ventured upstairs to the master bedroom where Nolan found her disturbed mother lying naked on the bed. Screaming at her blurred visitors, she threw them out.

The Rev. Guy Bennett collected Nolan's belongings from Edenbridge. He had told me in a separate interview how worried he had been about the reception he might receive. "As I approached the house I thought to myself, what happens if John says, 'How dare you? I want my daughter back.' I knew Nolan didn't want to go back. At sixteen, she could legally live where she liked. On the other hand, if a parent wants their child back it could be painted as child snatching."

But according to Bennett, their meeting turned out like a bizarre social occasion. They had a civilized drink together for twenty minutes or so. Nothing was really said. "It was almost as if Nolan were coming to stay the weekend," he remembered. Osborne even helped him carry Nolan's belongings to the car.

Did Osborne fully grasp what was happening? Bennett was sure he did. But one small incident he told me about the visit disturbed me. "We to'd and fro'd carrying the stuff out," he said, "and the only thing I can remember is seeing this box with Nolan's teddies or dolls. It was one of those illogical, emotional things, thinking, he's not going to touch those, and grabbing them and taking them myself. It was a sort of possessiveness, I suppose."

And then he remembered driving away from Christmas Place with tears streaming down his face.

Osborne subsequently wrote the rector two letters vilifying him and blaming him for abducting his daughter. "The ungodly abductor," he called him. "But what do you say to your friends when you've just thrown your daughter out?" Bennett rationalized when we discussed it. "You need some explanation. He was obviously very peeved that she hadn't fallen on her face and disappeared into Soho."

"Did you ever consider reconciling with your father?" I asked Nolan.

"It never occurred to me," she replied. "Not for a second."

"Nor did it occur to him," Bennett added from across the sitting room.

But according to Helen, a contrite Osborne asked their friend, the late Richard Mason, Archdeacon of Edenbridge, to intervene with the rector in Oxted and effect a reconciliation. Bennett had no memory of Mason coming to see him, however, and Nolan flared for the only time. "That's ridiculous," she said. "It's just weak. They're big children those two, aren't they? You don't expect another grown adult to fight your battles for you. If he thought he was wrong or he'd made a mistake, he was old enough and he was ugly enough to do it himself. I wouldn't expect someone else to intervene between me and my child."

"The logical thing is, father and daughter ought to be re-united," the rector added. "But the priestly thing is what is best for the people concerned, and I was concerned for Nolan's welfare."

As our meeting ended, I asked Nolan why she had kept the name Osborne until she married. But there was nothing to read into it, she said. "It was a legal hassle to change my name and I knew in all other senses I was part of the family." The rector had offered to adopt her, too – but again, she said she hadn't felt the need.

When Nolan left her tutorial college to live with the Bennetts, she attended the local Reigate College and took a quick secretarial course. She then worked happily in the production department of the London children's publisher, Usborne's – the only time she wished she'd changed her name. People thought she was an Usborne.

With her marriage to Simon Parker, she gave up work to become a housewife and raise her children. And life worked out well for her, she told me. She had no talk-show tears to shed about the past. "It was a very long time ago," she said. "Another part of my life."

When she heard about Osborne's death on Christmas Eve 1994, she didn't feel upset. The chapter was closed. "I just felt bad for Helen," she said.

Did she know any of her father's plays? I wondered. He had taken her with him to see *The Entertainer, West of Suez* with Jill Bennett, and *Inadmissible Evidence*. But she was too young to appreciate them.

I mentioned that *Inadmissible Evidence* had been written just before she was born and that it turned out to be a play of amazing clairvoyancy. For everything in it later happened in her father's life – including the middle-aged hero abandoning his seventeen-year-old daughter.

The affecting monologue of Bill Maitland as he confronts his teenage daughter is a marathon of yearning and fury that's four pages in length. She's named Jane and described as "cool, distressed, scared". Her father tells her in effect, "I can't connect to you, I don't understand your taste or your generation. I don't know your thoughts, I don't understand anything about you."

"Do you want to get rid of me?" he demands as she grows increasingly frightened. "Do *you*? Um? Because I want to get rid of you . . . Oh, I know it's none of your fault . . . that when I see you I cause you little else but distaste and distress, or, at least, your own vintage, swinging indifference. But nothing, certainly not your swinging distaste, can match what I feel for you. Or any of those who are more and more like you. Oh, I read about you, I see you in the streets, I hear what you say, the sounds you make, the few jokes you make, the wounds you inflict without even longing to hurt; there is no lather or fear in you, all cool, dreamy, young, cool and not a proper blemish, forthright, unimpressed, contemptuous . . . I don't know what you have to do with me at all, and soon you won't, you'll go out of that door and I'll not see you again."

I showed Nolan the rest of the speech from the play and she seemed interested enough to read it silently with me. Osborne's imagined howl of paranoid contempt and need from the father to the frightened daughter ends in a kind of blessing. "God said, He said be fruitful and multiply and replenish the earth. And *subdue* it. It seems to me, Jane, little Jane, you don't look little any longer, you are on your way at last, all, to doing all four of them. For the first time. Go on now."

"They elude each other," goes the bleak stage direction, and the daughter leaves without a word, just as Nolan had nothing to add, for there was nothing more that could be said.

So our meeting ended. But four months later, I received the most shocking news. The Rev. Guy Bennett of St Mary's Parish Church, Oxted, had pleaded guilty at the Old Bailey on 28 May 1999, of indecently assaulting three eleven-year-old girls between 1976 and 1988. Now adult, they were all his former pupils at St Mary's School, where he taught, and had come forward after hearing of another sexual allegation against him.

Bennett at first denied the charges. Suspended from St Mary's after his subsequent arrest, he had since retired. Two character witnesses were put on the stand at the Old Bailey who gave evidence on his behalf. One was Nolan Parker who told the court she had lived with his family between the ages of fifteen and twenty and that he had been a "steady rock" in her life – "the most caring and unselfish person I have ever met".

Bennett bowed his head as Judge Giles Forrester sentenced him to nine months in jail and ordered that his name remain on the Sexual Offenders Register for ten years. Nolan Parker burst into tears as the sentence was announced.

44

En Route to Shropshire

I prayed for us both in the midst of all we are leaving.
Osborne notebook entry, 17 November 1986

On 7 April 1985, Osborne fell seriously ill, as if cursed. Several house guests were staying at Christmas Place for the weekend, but he was unable to join them. He was confined to bed and was throwing up blood. The following day, a Sunday, he drifted into unconsciousness.

Osborne's doctor, Patrick Woodcock, lived in London and for an alarming time there was no medical help. Urgent messages were left at the surgery of a local doctor in Edenbridge, but there was no response. In her panic, Helen Osborne had neglected to leave their ex-directory phone number. As his condition grew worse, she became terrified and dialled 999 for an ambulance.

He was carried out of the house on a stretcher shortly after nine o'clock that evening and sped to the Kent and Sussex Hospital in Tunbridge Wells where he was checked into intensive care in a coma. His stunned wife was informed that it was unlikely he would recover.

He lay in a coma for three days before he rallied and squeezed her hand, remaining a further ten days in intensive care before he returned home on 26 April.

The man who saved his life, consultant physician D.S.J. Maw, opened a bottle of champagne in Osborne's memory when we met at his home in Tunbridge Wells. "I think bubbly would be in order, don't you?" he suggested.

There was a quiet, calm authority about this man who was raised in Bath, the son of a schoolmaster. He understood Osborne's fierce resistance to hospitals and moralizing doctors. Maw's wayward patient had feared the medical profession all his life – ever since his sickly childhood with suspected tuberculosis had left him trailing reluctantly after his mother's hand into bleak Victorian hospitals.

A grateful Osborne sent him a case of claret when he returned home. "To your health – and saving mine!" went his breezy message.

Maw, a specialist in diabetes and endocrinology, gave me an important insight into what had gone wrong with Osborne's health, and Helen filled in the rest.

Osborne had been a diabetic for at least four years before the 1985 crisis – and possibly, I discovered, for much longer. On 19 June 1970, Jill Bennett gave him six bottles of low-sugar John Harvey of Bristol "Wines for Diabetics". But when I mentioned it to Dr Woodcock, he interpreted it as a bad joke. (The wine, he maintained, is all but undrinkable.)

A decade later, on 2 May 1981 during the telecast of an interview with Bernard Levin, Osborne could be seen licking his lips repeatedly – a dry mouth, obvious symptom of diabetes. It would be another year before he sought medical help, however.

He saw Dr Kenneth Marsh of King's College Hospital on 10 June 1982. "Your blood tests showed that you are drinking far too much alcohol," the medical report reads, "and, very much more significant, your blood sugar at 14.8 is twice the limit of the normal . . . I would urge you to stop drinking all alcohol for the moment."

Diabetes is caused by fluctuating sugar levels in the blood and seriously aggravated by high alcoholic intake. (Champagne is particularly high in sugar.) Dr Marsh's medical report also made reference to pain and numbness in Osborne's feet, a cardiac murmur from his childhood rheumatic fever, and the necessity of immediate treatment for diabetes. He also advised him to stop smoking. "All this sounds thoroughly mean to a chap," Dr Marsh concluded, "but really I am sure you will understand that in the long run it will be worthwhile."

But he never did think it would be worthwhile. "What's the use of living to be a hundred if you can't drink and smoke?" he asked toward the end of his life.

He visited a Harley Street specialist in diabetes on 9 August 1982. Dr Oakley prescribed pills and diet. "I'm lucky," he informed the Osbornes. "None of my patients die of diabetes . . ."

There's no evidence that Osborne went on a special diet, however. In any event, the pill treatment didn't work.

"One of the things about John that amazed me," Maw told me in Tunbridge Wells, "was that he was a totally different character to the one I'd read about. There were no scenes, no fiery temperament. He discussed his medical problems with me very sensibly. The only time I saw anger come into his eyes was when we talked about the state of theatre."

But when he was released from hospital, he made his own sleuthing enquiries into the cause of his sudden collapse and came up with the bizarre theory that rats' piss in his swimming pool had been to blame. If the theory were true, he was off the hook! Rats had been seen in the stables a few yards from the swampy pool where he swam at a leisurely pace each evening, music speakers blaring.

Maw explained, "One of his blood tests revealed evidence of an infection you can get from rats that causes Weil's disease or leptospirosis. I didn't think it was the answer to his health problems."

Diabetes is a life-threatening condition and Osborne had additional complications. His coma was the outcome of his liver collapsing. His battered liver had in turn been aggravated by diabetes and years of heavy drinking. The textbook solution is to take twice-daily injections of insulin to ensure the sugar levels in the blood are normal and to give up alcohol.

Osborne took self-administered insulin and blood tests for the rest of his life, but Maw knew from their discussions that alcohol was a pleasure he couldn't refuse.

There were doctors in Osborne's life who turned him away as an incurable alcoholic and refused to treat him. But the compassionate Maw looked on the problem differently. He pointed out that Osborne was prepared to stop drinking for as long as it took to get over a crisis. In fact, he went on the wagon for almost six months after the first scare in 1985 (smoking hash to help him through). Medically, his liver recovered, though not completely.

"I've no doubt that the rest of John's life would have seemed like an eternity if he'd never been able to look forward to a drink," Maw said. He therefore recommended that he kept strictly to one or two glasses of wine three times a week, no spirits. It was like asking him to give up life.

But for a while, Osborne did keep conscientiously to his new spartan regime. On 18 October 1985, he wrote to Maw from holiday in Beaulieu-sur-Mer in the South of France that he had just enjoyed his "first glass of holy nectar".

It was a supreme irony of Osborne's emergency hospitalization in Tunbridge Wells that a TV film he'd recently written, entitled *God Rot Tunbridge Wells!*, was televised the evening before he fell ill.

The film celebrated the 300th anniversary of Handel's birth and Osborne based its opening scene on a true incident. At the end his life, Handel attended a performance of *Messiah* on 6 April 1759, given by the Tunbridge Wells Ladies' Music Circle. But the performance was so bad that he walked out, took to his bed and died a week later.

Osborne's script was filmed by Tony Palmer with the elderly, volcanic Trevor Howard in an unlikely – and extraordinary – performance as Handel. Osborne subsequently made light of his coincidental illness, maintaining that he had been struck down by mediocre critics and the revenge of the Tunbridge Wells Ladies. The Kafka-esque nightmare of his hospitalization dawned on him as he regained drowsy consciousness and looked up to see a pretty nurse asking him, "Do you know where you are?"

"New York," he replied.

"You're in Tunbridge Wells!" she yelled back, urging life back into him.

"As it was in the beginning, is now and ever shall be, world without end, even in Tunbridge Wells!" Trevor Howard's near blind Handel rages in his nightgown against the dying light like a mad ghost with a drinker's nose. "The shame, the shame of it!"

Osborne's script is an unexpected gem – the best thing he'd written in years. He connected to the bitter furies of that born complainer, Handel, but his achievement was to root his lean script thrillingly in the language of the King James Bible. "Great music helped John to lay his demons to rest," said Tony Palmer, who came to know Osborne well. "The music he loved was deeply related to his emotional centre and romanticism. His inspired use of biblical language gave the script its honest force and rigour."

But seeing the 1985 film today is unsettling when we remember Osborne's intuitive flair for dramatic clairvoyancy. His palsied, unfashionable hero is a portrait of an angry, dying man looking back. "Oh scraps of memory, scraps of memory!" Handel cries out deliriously. "Yeh, the caprice of fashion, the blot of bankruptcy, insolvency and ill health, surgery without relief or much hope, the whims of brokers and pit goers, theatre managers and the despair of foundlings . . . Damn your iambics – all of you! . . . I have accepted faith and denied myself certainty. Arise – shine, for thy light has come!"

There was still no evidence of a new stage play. "It's all in here!" Osborne would say to his wife as he tapped a notebook. But it had now been nine years since *Watch It Come Down*.

"Are you writing anything these days?" went one of his reverberating, nagging notebook entries. "ARE YOU WRITING ANYTHING? MY FUCKING EPITAPH."

He was writing diverting one-liners in the notebooks instead: "Stoppard: the thinking man's laxative." "Insulting Americans – is it *possible*?" "If I have offended, you have."

Or scribbling random thoughts: "Women you fucked but no longer do.

Their attitude to you: Faint collusion, like a bus conductress who remembers letting you off without paying the fare."

Or indulging in his taste for limericks – idle, dirty doodles in the night:

> And with anal dilation
> Appalling the nation
> A sensitive writer of Arden
> Sucked thespians off in his garden
> Said I can't get enough
> Of this heavenly stuff
> Begging your Thatcherite pardon

But the longer Osborne was unable to write a play, the more agonized he became. "No friendship in the theatre," he wrote miserably in his notebook. "THE LOST YEARS: 1965–1985. What happened?" "Blue and gold passport – no profession. Gone."

Dominic Lawson, former editor of the *Spectator*, recalled meeting Osborne at the Savoy for lunch to persuade him to contribute a weekly column. It should have been easy for Osborne to write, but Lawson told me, "He revealed an amazing lack of self-confidence. I was in awe of him and yet he seemed grateful even to be remembered."

Osborne made this notebook entry shortly after the move to Shrophire, on 24 November 1986: "These odd bits of journalism, which require a professionalism and facility that come hard to me, at least reassure me a little that my faltering nerve hasn't completely burnt out."

He spoke about his place in the theatre as if he'd become an abandoned relic. And yet, at a pivotal moment when a renaissance in his fallow career was possible, his self-destructive streak sabotaged a major revival of *The Entertainer* at the National Theatre.

In July 1985, Peter Hall announced the new production starring Alan Bates as Archie Rice and Joan Plowright as Archie's gin-sodden wife, Phoebe. There was an additional frisson in the casting: Plowright had met Olivier during the original 1957 Court production when she played Archie's daughter, and Bates had played Archie's son in the original film. The director was to be Ronald Eyre who staged the acclaimed 1983 revival of *A Patriot for Me* at Chichester with Alan Bates as Redl. All was set for Osborne's return to favour with a potentially exciting revival of *The Entertainer*, along with the powerful backing of the National and the likelihood of a West End transfer.

But Osborne had harboured a pathological dislike of Joan Plowright since she took Mary Ure's side in the marital wars and subsequently replaced

Vivien Leigh in the affections of his hero, Olivier. "Scunthorpe's own," he called her. Even so, the Osbornes were guests at the Oliviers' country house in West Sussex, and the Oliviers in turn spent occasional weekends in Kent and later in Shropshire. "Separate bedrooms, dearheart," Olivier informed Osborne in advance.

According to Helen, he opposed Plowright in *The Entertainer* for two reasons. He thought she would sentimentalize the role of Phoebe (who was partly based on his hated mother) and, most damaging to his pride, he claimed that he hadn't been consulted in the decision to cast her.

Dramatists of stature are traditionally consulted about casting major roles. But Peter Hall insisted Osborne *had* been consulted during a meeting with him at the National and that he expressed no reservations about Plowright whatsoever. Hall wasn't, in any case, about to inform his star actress – and Olivier's wife – that she was being replaced. Osborne stubbornly wouldn't change his mind. And when he refused to back down, the production was cancelled.

"This is madness," I argued with Helen when she told me all this. She seemed surprised. Though I'm not the most pragmatic of men, I rationalized, "Let's say there was a misunderstanding with Hall. A great deal was at stake. It's the perfect time for a major Osborne revival. There are worse fates than having Joan Plowright in your play. Why not compromise?"

"I don't think John knew how to spell the word," she replied.

"But the result is that people believed he was impossible to work with," I pointed out. "In the end, he isolated and marginalized himself."

"I think John would have said it was a price worth paying," she insisted, and I had no doubt that she was speaking accurately for him. "If that was the way theatre was going, so be it. He believed Plowright was wrong for the role he created. If you give in to them, you're giving in to *their* standards. If you compromise with them, they win."

Another factor in the story was Peter Hall – *them* – the man Osborne publicly lampooned after he closed *Watch It Come Down* when the box office failed. Osborne criticized Hall's published diaries for their "numbing record of banal ambition, official evasiveness and individual cupidity", and nicknamed him Fu Manchu.

"John was one of the nicest people I've ever known," Sir Peter said when we met. "I really do think of him with great fondness."

"People won't believe you," I said.

"I don't care a fuck whether they do or not. He was a mortal man," he pointed out firmly (and calmly). "He was a dangerous man, a silly man, a paranoid man, and a man with enormous warmth and wit. He was a charmer, a sweetheart, and he really was lovely to spend time with. He was also a bastard and a liar and a shit."

"Not a liar, surely," I suggested.

"He lied completely about *The Entertainer*, there's no question about it. On my father's grave, I swear he sat in my office opposite me and agreed Joan Plowright would be wonderful. So he was a liar. I think he had an opportunity to hurt her and he couldn't resist it. I don't think we've had a writer who has been better at invective since Swift. But his gift went to his head. When he had a pen in his hand it was like giving a kid a machine gun. That was John. He declared war on critics, he declared war on Englishness, he declared war on theatre. He hated everybody, I think, at a certain point, in a certain way."

"He regularly attacked you," I reminded him.

"I was one among many. I didn't take it terribly seriously. Of course you hate it when it happens. But if John had written a wonderful play and given it to me I would have produced it in spite of his hostility to me. In many respects he was a fool out of control. He used to get his rocks off by having huge crises. If he could see a good one, he would pursue it with a kind of mania even if it hurt him. The only person who was hurt by *The Entertainer* business was finally him, because we didn't do it."

The move from Kent to Shropshire had been discussed for two years. Yet Osborne had first searched for a home on the Welsh border some twenty-five years before he left Edenbridge. He was now almost fifty-eight. Shropshire was the closest he could get to the distant land of his father without leaving England.

The untranslatable Welsh word *hiraeth* suggests an unspecified, melancholic yearning for your true home, for your soul. Jan Morris said that a lyric pathos is part of it and was made narcotic for her at a time when she felt "the allure of lost consequence and faded power is seducing me, the passing of time, the passing of friends . . ."

Osborne's choice of Shropshire was connected romantically to *hiraeth*, but the specific reasons to move away from Kent in the first place were far more prosaic.

He claimed that the four-acre lake in his grounds had become a handy marker for planes circling to land at newly expanding Gatwick airport. The likelihood is that the marker was, in fact, nearby Marsh Green, but it made no difference to him. "The curlews, who also lived in a nice place along the River Eden, had vanished," said Helen. "It was time for us to go, too."

Osborne had a lifelong phobia about noise – planes, Hoovers, church bells, birds, washing machines, *noise*. He put up a notice in the lane outside the Edenbridge home: "Lorries bugger off." In 1968, when he lived in Chelsea, he wrote to his MP and the Noise Abatement Society complaining about low-flying jets. "Last night, I counted 42 between 7.15 and 9.15 . . ."

Now, as planeloads of eager tourists stacked to land at Gatwick, he was complaining that he could see the whites of the pilot's eyes. According to Helen, he counted the seconds obsessively between each engine's roar.

But there was another, more private, reason for the move from Kent. Osborne had finally woken up to the fact that he was all but broke. The sale of his considerable property in Edenbridge would raise funds to pay off his debts.

He wrongly blamed his accountants, Touche Ross, for his financial mess (and threatened a lawsuit). He complained to friends about his "abiding, dumb trust" in financial advisers over the years. He even suspected the motives of his long-time lawyer, Oscar Beuselinck, most loyal of them all. But he had always lived on the grandest, magical scale. Even when the unforgiving Inland Revenue was closing in on him, he was still throwing his carefree summer parties for hundreds of people and holidaying in the South of France.

Where had the millions gone from *Tom Jones*? Until he realized he was broke, Osborne had never even read a financial statement from his own company, Woodfall Films. In his naivety, he assumed the money would simply never run out. In that unworldly sense, he was as disinterested in the boring details of finance as the spendthrift Tony Richardson.

In February 1984, Beuselinck was asked by Osborne's agent to look into the tangled web of the Woodfall partnership and find out what had happened to the money. Osborne himself personally financed Woodfall's early films – including *The Entertainer* – from the profits of his plays. The international success of *Tom Jones* meant they were later "flooded with money". But Beuselinck presents a picture of waste and carelessness. To his amazement, Woodfall (a small film company) owned five Rolls Royces. But who actually drove them was a mystery.

Some of Osborne's money wasn't strictly kosher. With sweaty palms, he used to visit a bank in Fenchurch Street where he kept a cash account. The cash was couriered to London via Switzerland, and had long since run dry. When he and Richardson were business partners, the pattern of spending appears to be that they independently took chunks of money out of the joint Woodfall account whenever they needed it, and neither of them cared how much either of them spent. Osborne burned through his fortune from *Tom Jones* by spending it freely on his wives and grand houses. Richardson lived well, but used up his vast *Tom Jones* profits as cross-collateral for his own films.

Crucially, Osborne never considered leaving England for tax purposes. The fortune he once enjoyed was taxed to the hilt. During the Harold Wilson years, taxation of the super rich averaged 85 per cent and climbed as high as 95 per cent. Hence the cynical Beatles song, "Taxman": "Should five per cent appear too small/Be thankful I don't take it all . . ."

As Osborne now prepared to leave Kent for Shropshire, he was in a state of bewildered disbelief. In September 1986, his known tax arrears were £98,938. His overdraft at Barclays Bank was £100,000. He also owed the accountants he was suing a further £33,223.

The vagaries of a writer's income meant that his earnings varied from year to year. But his income had seriously diminished since the golden days. In 1987, he would make only £25,000 – his worst year in thirty years. He still had another source of income from Woodfall's now vintage films like *A Taste of Honey* and *Saturday Night and Sunday Morning*, but their annual profits had lately dwindled to little or nothing.

There was money to come from Faber & Faber for the second part of his autobiography, *Almost a Gentleman* (originally subtitled *The Downhill Struggle*). But it would take him nine years to deliver. His TV version of *A Better Class of Person* was shown on ITV on 13 July 1985, and raised some revenue. There was still some £50,000 left in his own company, John Osborne Plays Ltd., but those savings would go toward settling debts. The *Spectator* column earned him a token amount (£125 a column). Without a successful new play there was no hope of generating real income. But his artistic capital appeared to be spent, too.

Against that bleak picture, Osborne's earnings from the worldwide rights to his plays usually averaged £50,000 a year and sometimes twice as much. The reason for his financial mess was simple: he spent far more than he earned. He saw it as his *right*. "First class all the way, skipper!" as his father had told him. His new accountant in Shropshire, Peter Forrester of Moore Stephens, would help him considerably, but even he was floored when Osborne announced to him in all seriousness that he didn't believe in paying tax. "John saw artists as outside the club," Forrester told me, and began to laugh. He was fond of him. "My job was to sweep up behind. Whenever I advised him about not spending money, he spent it just the same."

*

On 2 June 1986, Osborne wrote this note to his wife on their wedding anniversary.

Ten years, my darling Helen. If only they'd been twice as many. But what a gift! Unlooked for and so wanted. Thank you for every one of them, every minute of them. You are *there*, my heart forever. Always, past and future, my love. John.

And on 17 November 1986, he made this notebook entry on the eve of their departure for Shropshire:

Leaving Christmas Place – six days to go. Dear Helen wept and wept tonight. I have never loved her more or felt so thankful. She is the reality of the life I love each day. Her courage shines. She reminded me of Adolf's horrible dismissal of this house, The Abortion Clinic she called it. God rot her. Will the new home be alright, Helen asked. It will, I feel sure of it, though the task suddenly seems tremendous. Like every-thing else, it will have to be *lived* for a while. I cannot bear the thought of Helen looking wrecked and rather frightened. There is so much yet to *bear*, but we must plunge on into it. I prayed for us both in the midst of all we are leaving.

When the couple who bought Christmas Place moved in with their chil-dren, they had the four-acre lake dredged because it was heavily silted. Buried in the banks, they found scores and scores of empty champagne bottles.

45

Strindberg's Man in England

I can do anything here! I'm just starting.
Osborne, first days in Shropshire

The 1812 manor house in Clun, Shropshire, was found on the wary recommendation of playwright Peter Nichols. Nichols and his family lived at that time in the nearby rectory at Hopesay, and learning of Osborne's interest in moving to the area he mentioned a twenty-room house named The Hurst that was for sale.

The two playwrights had known each other since they were struggling actors together at Frinton-on-Sea Summer Theatre in the early Fifties. After Nichols became a successful dramatist with A Day in the Death of Joe Egg, Osborne sent him opening-night telegrams for years saying, "Good luck to all from Frinton!" But they were never close.

"We went to live in Shropshire to escape theatre people," Nichols explained to me a tad sourly. "I was very fond of John in many ways and in others I disliked him intensely and found him patronizing. There was always a side of him that meant you either became one of his court or one of his staff."

Which was Nichols? "I was more in the position of an attendant lord," he replied, brightening. "I was good enough to swell a scene a two . . . The other thing was that I couldn't afford to live the way John did. He thought getting into debt was a sign of nobility."

"Nichols lives well," Osborne recorded loftily in his 1985 notebook, "but always in the shadow of penury . . ."

"When we recommended they look at the house in Clun I didn't think he would actually decide to live in Shropshire," Nichols went on. "I said to Thelma, 'We're quite safe.'"

As the Osbornes drove through the slumbering Clun Valley – Housman's "quietest place under the sun" – and glimpsed from the road by the river the chimneys of the Brontë-esque house on the hill, they both thought, "Please, let that be it."

"And, praise be, it was," said Helen.

Nichols and his wife of some forty years, Thelma, were waiting afterwards to meet them in a local pub. "Wasn't any good?" he asked hopefully when they arrived.

"Oh, yes," Osborne replied, ordering champagne for all. "We bought it."

They bought The Hurst impulsively without bothering about a survey. Yet the place with its thirty acres and various tumbledown outbuildings had obviously been neglected. Helen remembered that the previous owners had done a midnight flit, even leaving their supper dishes in the sink. "Steak and kidney pie, by the look of it," she observed. "There was much to be done."

The roof was collapsing. The chimneys were crumbling. There were sagging floors and there were plumbing problems. The cost of several months' renovation work ate into the profit from the sale of the home in Edenbridge that was meant to pay off the debts.

By the first snowy December, when they lit a fire in the study and dead crows came tumbling down the chimney, Helen was sobbing herself to sleep. What had been so bad about a few jets heading for Gatwick? she wondered.

Then she was awoken in the middle of the night by banging on the walls. It was Osborne hanging pictures. On the first landing by the main guest room, he hung a framed poster of Jill Bennett in *Time Present*. As you ascended the stairs, she was staring at you. Next to it was hung a photograph of a small child with the printed caption "Our Baby."

"Soon be alright," he reassured his wife. "You'll see. Best thing we've ever done. Marvellous!" *Don Giovanni* rose to the rafters. "I can do anything here!" Osborne declared. "I'm just starting."

He wrote to his confidante, Jocelyn Rickards, "It's superb up here in spite of all the mayhem and chaos. I still can't get over the triumphant inspiration of coming here. Not for 'the final years' but as a new outburst of energy."

When the bank statements came in, Helen said that Osborne declared, "I may be the poorest playwright in England, but I've got the best view!" She believed that Shropshire became a succour and blessed plot of England for him. "At dawn you could watch the mist clearing over Clee Hill, the highest point east until the Urals," she wrote. "The rain may pelt at you as though the Furies are having a bad day or the sun dapple over the pond as the trout leap and the ducklings scatter. And, at night, when the last owl is silent, there is sometimes such a deep peace that I don't quite know what it means."

It was assumed in London theatre circles that Osborne stopped writing plays in Shropshire. His life had slowed down since the heavily social years in Edenbridge. Apart from the Nichols family in Hopesay, the Osbornes saw the political journalist Anthony Howard and his wife Carol, who lived in nearby Ludlow, and latterly Mrs Thatcher's gregarious arts minister, the Earl of Gowrie – known as Grey – and his wife, Neitie, who kept a farmhouse near Welshpool just over the border in Wales. But fewer friends visited from London (almost a four-hour train ride away) and illness had taken a toll on Osborne. Visiting his agent in London, he was shocked to hear a young man up a ladder on a building site call out to him, "Got the time, grandpa?"

He had seemed young even in middle age but now his age was showing. The impression that he had cut himself off from contemporary theatre was fostered by sightings of him on visits to "town" dressed like a showbiz Edwardian gent in full countryman regalia.

When 12 December 1989 approached, Jonathan Miller interviewed him for BBC TV to celebrate his sixtieth birthday. Though Miller's debut in theatre was as the director of Osborne's early incest and knicker play, *Under Plain Cover*, and his memory of the experience was a happy one, the two men had nothing in common and the interview did not go well.

Miller explained to me, "By that time he'd become a weirdly dandified curmudgeon and clearly resented being interviewed by what he regarded as a spoilt, nannified Hampstead Lefty. He was ornamentally dressed as an Edwardian fop, with quadruple vented hacking jacket and an elaborately flowing cravat. The interview was conducted, at his choice, in the billiard room of the Garrick. He sat in a large leather armchair with an ice bucket filled with two bottles of some absurdly grand champagne. When I asked him about his 'drift' to the Right he growled that he thought this was supposed to be a 'birthday' interview and terminated the affair with, 'Many happy fucking returns.' I never saw him again."

On trips to London with his wife, Osborne sipped champagne steadily during the long train journey from Clun and stayed at the quite grand Cadogan Hotel in Chelsea, or "Oscar's gaff", as he called it. He wasn't yet cutting down on his spending (or the champagne). In London, they would see old friends, shop, and go to the theatre in anticipation and dread. He usually travelled alone from Clun for what he called his "Boy's Own" outing – the monthly lunch at the Garrick of the 1400 Club. The inner sanctum was originally founded because the Garrick's dining rooms closed too early for some. The 1400 Club therefore gathers at 2 p.m. in a private room for an extravagantly long lunch with very carefully chosen wines, and ends about tea time.

It is for people with time on their hands. The acknowledged star members were Kingsley Amis and Osborne – but these two icons of their time refused to speak to each other except through third parties. (Nobody knew the reason, though Amis hated all theatre post-Ibsen.) Acting as host of the boyish, joshing lunch when I attended as a guest was Sir Kenneth Bradshaw, Clerk of the House of Commons – the man who had paid for Osborne's consoling drinks at the Jacaranda nightclub with Peregrine Worsthorne after the mixed opening-night reception of *Look Back in Anger* in 1956. Among Osborne's other 1400 Club friends were a publisher, an obituarist and former drama critic, an historian, a sometime actor, Nordist and dramatist, a BBC diplomatic correspondent, a theatre manager and a librarian. "A broad church," it was explained. "John never minded the old duffers of the Garrick. Happens to us all . . ."

On 20 June 1987, Osborne was diagnosed with a life-threatening twisted hernia. Once again, he hadn't registered with a local doctor. At length, the surgery of Dr Jill Gray was contacted and an ambulance rushed him in agony to be operated on at Nuffield Hospital in Shewsbury. He would come to name it "The Nuffield Hilton".

"Emergencies were John's specialty," Dr Gray told me in her light Edinburgh accent. "I never attended him for anything less than an emergency! That was his style. He distrusted doctors so much he delayed calling them until it was almost too late."

He was fortunate to have this remarkable woman for his doctor. The idealistic Dr Gray refused to treat private patients, for the ailing are created equal. When Osborne first became her patient, she was a young woman in her twenties with red hair, and in time he did come to trust her in a hopeful, mildly flirtatious way. When he was laid low with severe depression, she was the only visitor he would see.

Osborne's specialist in Tunbridge Wells had now become a friend of the Osbornes and when he and his wife stayed at The Hurst from time to time, his social visits were also a discreet way of keeping an eye on his former patient. He gave Osborne check-ups and blood tests at the house and sent the results to Dr Gray. Both doctors agreed that it was pointless trying to lecture him about his drinking.

"He delighted in telling me all the things he hoped would shock me,"

Dr Gray remembered. "How much champagne he drank and the cigars he smoked. He may even have made it seem worse than it was. I liked John a lot. For one thing, I admired him because I admired his plays. He was courteous, he was almost a gentleman. I didn't make any attempt to boss him around or tell him how to live his life, but it was my responsibility to explain the score to him. I told him when I first treated him, 'I'm your GP. I'm not your nanny. If you carry on the way you are, you'll have a short life.' I didn't know by how many years, but with uncontrolled diabetes his life would be shortened. There's no question about it."

How did he react?

"He just grinned."

The diabetic needs a watchful, sober, well-ordered life – the sort of life Osborne couldn't accept. One serious danger of diabetes is hypoglycaemia – a hypo attack caused by a sugar inbalance that leads to coma. There's also chronic hypoglycaemia that can cause violent mood swings and irrational behaviour. An immediate glucose tablet induces rapid recovery from a hypo. The dramatic alternative is intravenous glucose. Unless properly treated, however, the hypo will be fatal.

Osborne would sometimes forget to take his insulin injections. There was also the Christmas when he accidentally doubled his insulin dose and almost died. There were other times when he forgot to carry glucose with him on his long walks with the dogs in the surrounding Clun hills. He had nine lives when it came to hypoglycaemic attacks and he made light of the obvious dangers. On 27 September 1989, he sent a postcard to Dr Maw with whom he corresponded frequently:

A particularly malign piece of treachery came through the post last week. I stormed several hundred feet up the Shropshire hills and after about an hour or so, realized I'd forgotten my "fix". No glucose or cucumber sandwiches either. Was aroused by a rather attractive girl on a pony who found me stretched out in her path. I blundered about like Captain Oates looking for a Happy Chef. The dogs were v. upset. Took me two and a half hours to get home. Helen, like a Welsh miner's wife waiting at the pithead in a 30's movie . . .

Both doctors prescribed low doses of codeine for his continual, thudding headaches. (His requests for amphetamines were refused.) His notebook reveals that the twisted hernia, though unrelated to his diabetes, shocked him into giving up drink for twenty-two days. Another entry shows him on the wagon for a further fifty-eight days. Released from Nuffield Hospital on 27 June 1987, he later recuperated in Venice at the Danieli with Helen.

As with his illness, Osborne simply refused to face reality about his debts. It would be another eighteen months before his brave new accountant, Peter Forrester, took charge. "It was basically terrifying," Forrester said. "There was no money left to pay for anything."

Yet, throughout all the anxiety and upheaval, Osborne had begun work at last on a new play, he was still battling to complete the second volume of his autobiography, and the National Theatre, now led by Richard Eyre, had commissioned him to write a new adaptation of Strindberg's ferocious portrait of a marriage, The Father. It was good casting. Osborne, like the thrice-married Strindberg, knew all about women who drive men mad.

His new generation director of The Father was David Leveaux, who visited him in Shropshire. "There I am," Osborne observed about himself on 6 August 1988, "closeted with some fucking 26 year-old director who thinks he knows more about writing than I do."

But from the Leveaux's point of view, their meeting couldn't have gone better. He arrived at the house in awe of Osborne's intimidating myth and felt relieved when he turned out to be so welcoming. "He was genial, encouraging and very cooperative," he explained. "And when in Rome . . ." He meant joining Osborne in a morning bottle of champagne.

Leveaux had heard that he would be impossible to work with, and that he was blocked and even written out. "But he was imaginatively excited by Strindberg," he said. "He conveyed exhilaration at working at the National again – a sense of joy knocking on a locked door. He was great to work with on the script, open to suggestions and highly focused. But the main thing I felt about him was that he possessed an undeclared state of grief. I sensed it immediately. He shared Strindberg's specific quality of mourning an irretrievable loss."

It was why Osborne's spare and disciplined adaptation of The Father turned out so well, even brilliantly. He connected with Strindberg's damaged soul rather than with the obvious misogyny. He identified with him thoroughly. In the introduction to his published script of The Father, Osborne wrote, "I had never felt such proprietary instincts for the work of another playwright, and I was determined that if anyone were to become the keeper of that unpredictable flame, the task should be recklessly entrusted to me. I was Strindberg's Man in England. He had been done such disservice in his own land and time after, I hoped that I could make some petty reparation for his sufferings, vilification and enduring exile."

Leveaux's long day at The Hurst ended with an image of Osborne standing alone in the middle of his sitting room at about 1.30 a.m. holding up a glass of champagne as he listened in rapture to Mozart. The following morning, Leveaux returned to London to work on the production while his dramatist went off to open the Clun Carnival and judge a dog show.

Osborne went to rehearsals of *The Father* intermittently, and Leveaux remembered him conceding the territory to him and the actors in the rehearsal room where he was "very helpful, supportive and quiet". And then it all blew up.

Attending an early preview of *The Father* at the National's Cottesloe Theatre, Osborne walked out after half an hour. In effect, he walked out of his own show. He subsequently wrote to Leveaux and Richard Eyre disowning the entire production. He was alone when he saw the performance and he made no scene or fuss. But he had had too much to drink and as he weaved his way out of the intimate theatre, he was actually heading straight for the stage. An usher spotted him and quickly guided him to the exit.

Before the preview that night, Leveaux had met Osborne backstage in the green room. "He was in full flight about the great actors of yesteryear and what it had been like at the Court," he recalled. "John had obviously had a fair amount to drink, but he kept slagging off anything in the theatre that didn't happen in his day. Nothing was good enough."

In my day, in my day . . . Osborne had become a cracked reflection of the very thing he loathed – a green room bore. The production of *The Father* received quite positive reviews. He didn't attend the opening night.

When he heard the news of Jill Bennett's suicide on 6 October 1990, he read all the glowing obits about her and reached for his pen.

"Nora Noel Jill Bennett committed suicide yesterday," he began. "Except, of course, that she didn't, merely perpetrating a final common little deceit under the delusion that it was an expression of 'style', rather than the coarse posturing of an overheated housemaid . . ."

The second volume of his autobiography, *Almost a Gentleman*, was just about to go to press. It had recently been completed after nine, difficult years and he sent in the last hundred pages in patchy instalments to Robert McCrum, his editor at Faber & Faber. Volume 2 originally went from 1955 to 1966 – ending before the marriage to Bennett.

With her death, however, the restraining order on Osborne from their bitter divorce no longer applied. He was free to write about her.

McCrum, then editor-in-chief at Faber (and now literary editor of the *Observer*), was on a break away from the office when Osborne inserted his lacerating chapter about Jill Bennett into the proofs. At liberty to write about their marriage as he saw it, he rejoiced in her death, vindictively ridiculing every conceivable thing about her – including her talent and age, her toilet habits, her so-called frigidity and malign avarice, her staged suicide gone "tragically" wrong, and her ultimate contempt for all her gay friends "clamouring for AIDS charities". Bennett had left almost her entire estate of half a million pounds to the Battersea Dogs Home.

"Everything about her life had been a pernicious confection, a sham," he concluded. "I have only one regret now in this matter of Adolf. It is simply that I was unable to look down upon her open coffin and, like that bird in the Book of Tobit, drop a good, large mess in her eye."

When McCrum returned to the office, he learned what had happened as the presses were rolling. He read the scandalous chapter that Osborne sent over at the last minute and rang him immediately in Shropshire. McCrum loved Osborne and looked on him as a singular hero. But he found the Bennett diatribe shocking.

"I thought it was gratuitously cruel and tasteless and even silly," he told me. "It showed a side of John that was characteristically honest, but also chararacteristically self-destructive. I thought it would do him great harm."

Osborne very rarely came to the phone, and he didn't this time. McCrum spoke to his wife. "Well, you know John," she told him from Clun. "It's what he wants to say."

There was also the suspicion that Osborne was aware that what he wanted to say would create a blaze of publicity. The following morning, McCrum spoke to Helen a second time, arguing for withdrawal, but there would be no surrender.

"It was his book," McCrum explained philosophically, and so the chapter about Bennett stayed in *Almost a Gentleman* to subsequent uproar.

De mortuis nil nisi bonum. But the censored Osborne who was now free to speak his furious mind was not concerned with insipid propriety or "hurt". It takes mad courage not to give a damn what people think. The unforgiving Osborne who complained bitterly in his 1985 notebook that "People are afraid to hate anything" demanded the right and freedom to hate until, like Hazlitt, he came to hate himself.

It was truthfully said that no one despised Osborne more than himself. But his late wife surely didn't deserve his passing, cruel revenge. After all, he had loved her once.

Let be.

46
Déjàvu

Anger is not about . . . It is mourning the unknown,
the loss of what went before without you, it's a love
another time but not this might have sprung on you . . .

Jimmy Porter, *Déjàvu*

The play that Osborne had at last begun to write was a sequel to *Look Back in Anger*. He was coming full circle. He was preparing to say farewell.

As with *Look Back*'s original title page, the new manuscript tried out various titles: *Déjàvu*, or *Everybody Loves You When You're Down and Out*; *Who Would You Rather Sleep With*; *Grey Haired Youth*; and *A Play (or Caprice)*.

He chose *Déjàvu* with its slurry, deliberately misspelt title as if memory itself were a blur. Revisiting Jimmy Porter some thirty years on, Osborne now described him as "a gray haired man of indeterminate age, casually and expensively dressed . . ." Apparently bourgeois, he lives in a grand country house and drinks endless bottles of wine known as Nicaraguan '89. "J.P. is a comic character," Osborne continued. "He generates energy but, also like, say, Malvolio or Falstaff, an inescapable melancholy . . . The core of his personality is best expressed, not only theatrically but truthfully, by a *mild* delivery."

But the ageing Jimmy Porter isn't mild and the man who wrenched *Déjàvu* out of himself was prepared to go down in flames. "J.P." is "J.O." The one is as real as the other, the inventor has become the invention. They both remain unchanged in the furious essentials waging war on the glib pieties of England as if its levelling political correctness had coerced them into one last stand. *Déjàvu* announces "No surrender!" "Good taste" need not apply. It's a howl of scattershot protest against the rule of mediocrity.

Jimmy Porter's oldest friend and foil, Cliff, has returned. (He works for the BBC and sent his children to trendy Bedales School.) Alison is still ironing J.P.'s shirts as the curtain rises – but *this* Alison is his daughter and she loathes him. "No wonder he prefers dogs to people," she announces at one point. "He came into this world bitching and he'll go out the same way. Unloved . . ."

"Teddy's quite fond of him," Cliff responds loyally.

One of *Look Back*'s maligned teddy bears is now propped up in *Déjàvu*'s country kitchen like a separate, watchful character – a scruffy dumb show, an ironic reference point. "Teddy has low self-esteem," Osborne recorded in his 1986 notebook, "grew up without a role model in an unconstructed environment. He is a dangerous sexist, has racist inclinations, and yet he appears to be helpless. Counselling is denied him because he belongs to a minority group. Teddy does not wish to be a stereotype."

"I am Concern," went another of the notebook entries that would be polished for the final script. "I am Compassion, I am Care and Counselling, I am a Report, a Survey, I am History in the unmaking, I am relevant to modern need, the unscheduled delay, industrial action, I am new attitudes and ideas, I am Victim, I am Yoof. I am Today's Society."

Osborne plotted *Déjàvu* through 1987, and, in his unusual case, plotting – or mapping out – a new play meant meticulously numbering hundreds of ideas and phrases until entire notebooks were crammed with them and he was ready to write the script.

9 December 1988, notebook: *Déjàvu est commencé.*
30 January 1989: Act One *Déjàvu* finished.
10 April: Play finished.

But there was no celebration or relief in the finishing. Osborne wrote *Déjàvu* in the midst of churning anxiety over his failing health and the shadow of the tax inspector hovering in the wings. "Overnight Inland Revenue disaster," he recorded on 20 March 1989. "Helen tired, tired, tired, tired. Health deteriorating quite alarmingly. No long walks in the hills since before my birthday. No energy. *Struggling* to finish last few pages of the play. Can't *raise* anything. It doesn't augur well. But I have to get it off."

He sent the three-act *Déjàvu* to Richard Eyre, the National Theatre's artistic director. Eyre had shrewdly got Osborne writing again by commissioning the Strindberg adaptation (and had greatly admired it). There was no ill feeling between them over the production of *The Father*.

On 23 April 1989 he wrote to Osborne:

Dear John,
I am sorry not to have responded sooner to your play. I can't remember

ever looking forward to receiving any play more than yours, and my disappointment is perhaps partly due to my exaggeratedly high expectations . . .

It's presumptuous to suggest it but I thought that the play would be wonderfully effective as a monologue performed prior to a performance of LOOK BACK IN ANGER. Both the old and the new J.P. speak very powerfully for their respective generations. I'm sure this suggestion adds insult to injury, and I'm just as sure that to respond to DEJAVU with anything less than great enthusiasm seems at best churlish and at worst very hurtful. I'm sorry; I do admire your work enormously.

If you felt there would be any point meeting to talk about the play I'd be very happy to do so.

Best wishes,
Richard.

Osborne did not respond.

He had already sent *Déjàvu* to Robert Fox, one of the leading independent producers in London. Fox had immediately offered to stage it.

"I thought it was a fabulous play," he explained. "It was about an hour and a quarter too long, but it made me howl with laughter. It didn't have to be a *great* play. I didn't think it was. But what else was the National or anyone else producing at the time that was better? I thought it was fun and it was saying things about England that needed to be said."

Fox had always got along with Osborne across the generational divide, sharing his appetite for irreverence. They'd known each other well since he worked as a twenty-year-old assistant director at the Royal Court on the uproarious *A Sense of Detachment* when Rachel Kempson leapt into the stalls to beat up two hecklers. Osborne sent him a note on the opening night saying, "I couldn't have done it without you."

Aware of *Déjàvu*'s publicity value as the sequel to *Look Back in Anger*, Fox had a brainwave. He wanted Tony Richardson – *Look Back*'s original director – to come back from America to direct it. When Osborne was told of the idea, he was pleased and amazed, and responded defensively that Richardson wouldn't do it.

But Fox had some influence: he was soon to marry Richardson's daughter, Natasha. He mentioned *Déjàvu* casually to his future father-in-law during one of his occasional visits to London. "I don't suppose it's any good," Richardson said.

He read the script that night and telephoned Osborne in Shropshire to tell him, "I think you've written the best play since *Look Back in Anger*."

Fox then sent the script to the Royal Court (where he was a member of the board). He believed that if *Look Back* II were launched at the Court with Richardson directing, it would be a sensation.

But the Court's long-time artistic director, Max Stafford-Clark, unceremoniously turned it down.

"Hasn't he got *any* entrepreneurial flair?" Richardson groaned when he heard the decision.

I asked Stafford-Clark whether the Court had a moral responsibility to produce the play, if only because without Osborne there wouldn't have been a Court. Furthermore, Richardson had been George Devine's first co-director. They were both, in other words, the Court's founding fathers. Where was the respect due them?

Stafford-Clark argued, however, that his artistic policy from the beginning of his fourteen-year tenure had been to break with the crushing weight of the Royal Court's past. Having nothing in common with the Stafford-Clark era, Osborne had contemptuously renamed the Court "Ron and Les", nicknamed its artistic director "Pol Pot" and continually mocked his choice of socially conscious dramas (feminist, Irish and gay). "I'd rather watch *Crossroads*," he told the *Sunday Times*.

Stafford-Clark insisted that *Déjàvu* was judged on its merits, even so. "Other people read it who weren't as involved as I was and they couldn't respond to it. They found it dated," he pointed out. One of them was the incoming artistic director of the Court, Stephen Daldry.

Daldry, who wasn't born when *Look Back in Anger* first opened, was then at the start of his successful career. At the time, he was often compared to a young Tony Richardson.

He met Osborne only once. Osborne was elderly by then and he made a point of going over to him in the Ivy restaurant to shake his hand. But when Daldry read *Déjàvu*, he asked himself, "If I blanked out John Osborne's name and put someone else's on it, would this be a play that I would want to see? The answer was a reluctant, no. But if they'd ditched the play and got John Osborne onstage at the Court to act it as a monologue, you would have packed the place out. He would have found a new audience. He would have reinvented himself."

This is the way Osborne's world would end – not with a play, but a cabaret. A rogue *act*, a circus sideshow, a curmudgeonly "turn" – See the Original Angry Young Man while you can!! *Alive and in Person!!* (with songs). Yet Daldry's idea of a *Déjàvu* monologue performed by Osborne coincided with Richard Eyre's proposal for the National.

"Well, what did you *expect*?" Osborne said, mimicking Richardson's ritual response when it came to any setback in life. But the Court wasn't crucial to their plans. Fox now intended to open *Déjàvu* directly in the West End and Alan Bates had agreed to play the lead. In another theatrical coup, Bates – the orginal Cliff in *Look Back* – would be returning to play Jimmy Porter.

To Fox's disbelief, however, Osborne told him Bates was wrong for the role. The first cracks in their partnership had begun. Whenever Fox and Richardson argued for Bates, Osborne insisted that he would have to audition for the part. "I thought it was fucking ridiculous," said Fox. "He knew what Alan Bates could do. There was no way I was going to ask him to audition and no way he would."

On 25 June 1989, Osborne entered Nuffield Hospital for elective surgery to his damaged hernia. He wrote a little play as he recuperated there (and sent it off to various friends):

NURSE: Everyone here tells me you're very famous.
J.O: Oh no – not at all.
NURSE: I didn't think you were . . .

He had now developed a diabetic complication known as peripheral neuropathy – an incurable abnormality of the nervous system that numbs feeling in the hands and feet. A bigger concern, for the moment, was the disruption to his shaky health caused by sleepless anxiety over the fate of *Déjàvu*. Weeks now went by when he was living day for night. The irregular hours – "the terror of the small hours", he called it – were disastrous for the control of his diabetes.

He needed regular medical care and diet, but he was still awake at dawn scribbling in his notebook to get through the night. October 1989: "Last night I really thought it was d-e-a-th flapping its little wings against my upturned face on the drawing-room floor. Couldn't get up, find my way to the kitchen. Squalid, helpless, and above all, yes, alone. No one."

Helen was now waking up in the middle of night to make certain he'd taken his insulin. Their loving relationship was so close that on two different occasions when he had a hypo attack during sleep, she woke up instantly each time and saved his life.

Even in calmer periods, there always remained the danger that he would drowsily forget to take the insulin as if refusing to let illness rule him. In early October 1990, he collapsed during lunch with Robert Fox at San Lorenzo, the fashionable restaurant close to Fox's offices in Beauchamp Place. He had been drinking quite a bit, but Fox realized this was serious and in the panic he called an ambulance. But when the paramedics arrived, Osborne recovered and violently threw them off him. He stormed out of the restaurant and ran down Beauchamp Place.

Fox remembered vividly, "I rushed after him and grabbed him, saying, 'Come on, John, you should go to hospital.' But he flung me against the wall with the strength of a mad bull and off he went again. I chased after him and he shouted, 'I'm not going to hospital – they'll fucking kill me if they get me in there. I've just made a mistake. I'm a silly bugger.' He went back to his hotel and he was fine. He took his insulin."

"He was amazing," Helen said to me touchingly one day. "He never stopped fighting. Fighting the world, fighting life, fighting death at the end."

In August 1989, a successful revival of Look Back at the Lyric, directed by Judi Dench and starring Kenneth Branagh and Emma Thompson, brought welcome financial relief. But by the end of 1990, Osborne's tax debt alone had grown with interest charges to £152,000 and there was no money to pay it off.

The treadmill of anxiety over his debts only further endangered the state of his health. His new accountant, Peter Forrester, would refinance the mortgage on The Hurst and negotiate a reduction of the crippling back tax owed to the Inland Revenue. Helen took dutiful charge of the everyday accounts, itemizing every penny spent (except for essential treats). But, unless Osborne's income increased miraculously in the near future, the battle to pay off the loans and overdrafts and keep afloat was bound to fail.

Then in early January 1990, Albert Finney informed him by letter that he was taking legal action against Woodfall Films for royalties still owed from Tom Jones. The total sum owed jointly by Osborne and Richardson was in the region of £75,000. Finney's letter explained that he was writing "for old times' sake" and ended, "Hope you are busy, well and heading towards the year 2000 in good heart."

Osborne had no knowledge of the debt, just as he had been ignorant of his own dwindling money in the Woodfall account. He didn't dispute Finney's legal rights, though Richardson was outraged. "He's had far too much money already!" he protested, indignantly claiming that it was Woodfall's generosity with shares in the profits of Tom Jones which had made Finney a millionaire.

The penniless Osborne now had to find £32,000 to avoid his lawsuit. Approached by a mutual friend to forgive the debt, Finney refused. In a letter to me, he denied there was any ill feeling. Perhaps he didn't receive the note to him that was headed, "With the compliments of John Osborne" and that went on to say, "I only hope one of your fucking racehorses tramples you to death."

It was inevitable that Osborne would fight again with Tony Richardson, for their feuds went with their brotherhood. "Dear Tony," he wrote on 7 October 1989, needled that Richardson had returned to Los Angeles to make a minor TV film. "I know that my little theatre piece is only a pit-stop in the Grand Prix of your career . . ."

Richardson was so convulsed with laughter when he read that line, he loved his old adversarial friend more. "Do you know what Johnny has said about me *now?*" he told Fox, delightedly repeating the "pit-stop" joke. But Richardson was no longer the power he had once been and he was ailing, too.

Osborne's letter to him ended dispiritingly, "Six months ago, I felt, quite absurdly, that I might have done the best thing in my life. No more of that, my lord. No more of that . . ."

Three days later, still stewing in Shropshire, he wrote to Fox: "What astounds me is that I could ever have been so DUMB as to be gulled into accepting that T.R.'s intentions might be honourable. I am v. angry with myself. By now we could have been in Brighton or Newcastle with six weeks to go before opening . . . I hope you will pass on my regard for T.R.: an irredeemably treacherous, prevaricating, contemptuous Shipley cunt/fag. On with the dance . . ."

As the end of the year approached, Fox reluctantly withdrew from *Déjàvu*. Osborne was not only insisting that Alan Bates audition for the lead, he wanted practically every other actor on his own "A" list to audition for him, too – including Derek Jacobi, Alan Rickman, Michael Gambon, Tom Courtenay and Anthony Hopkins. Among the star actors he'd also listed bewildering, irrational choices (the comedian Dave Allen was one).

Fox decided his friendship with Osborne was worth more than the escalating insanity over the play. "The writing was on the wall," he explained, and with his departure, Richardson and Bates eventually dropped out, too. "In the end, John just didn't trust anyone," Fox added regretfully. "He didn't trust Tony. He didn't trust me. He didn't trust Alan Bates. I thought he was blowing it deliberately in some self-sabotaging way. I'd known John almost all my life. I loved him. He was a friend of my dad's [the super-agent Robin Fox]. We kept our friendship."

In his notebook on 23 October 1989 Osborne wrote: "No one wants to do my play. Everyone knows in London that it has been turned down."

This subsequent letter to *The Times* on 18 April 1991, complaining that star actors weren't even troubling to read his script was an unprecedented public protest from a leading playwright:

> Sir – Exactly two years ago this week I finished a new stage play. Since then I have discovered that it is almost impossible to persuade star actors even to *read* a manuscript. Should they do so, passionate avowals of loyal commitment are reneged upon abruptly and without explanation . . . Old acquaintances and former colleagues, grown bullish in the lush pastures of film and television, disregard a personal postcard and loftily refer you to their agents . . .

But his public protest had been provoked less by egotistical star actors than the blow to his pride at failing to get *Déjàvu* produced. His wounded sense of rejection reduced him to abject despair at what his life had come to.

On 5 August 1991 he noted: "Twenty-eight days without a drink. Difficult beyond words at times . . . I am dissatisfied only with the tangible details of my life. Having to beg. Asking for work. Unable to do or go where I like. I'm not much better off than I was when I was 27. Then at least I had a future. What have I now? I can surprise and delight no one. Growing *old* is loathsome. I feel ignored. Nothing that has *been* counts for anything. I am dispossessed. How I *hate* this age I am trapped in. I'm a mere bystander. No one catches my eye. My head bursts as it did fifty years ago. I disintegrate. 28 days: I feel no better, no stronger. Only robbed of my life. How can I begin again? I can't."

There was no evidence, however, that any actor had actually turned down *Déjàvu* as he complained in *The Times* – except for one bizarre example. On 18 October 1990, Osborne had met Barry Humphries for lunch at the Savoy to tell him he was the only one who could play Jimmy Porter in *Déjàvu*.

"I must have been mad," he wrote afterwards in his notebook. Humphries thought so, too.

Indelibly associated with his own mythic invention, Dame Edna Everage, Humphries told me that he was astonished to be asked. Worse: he read *Déjàvu* and found it "as long as three plays, alienating in its rage, with a few too many Aunt Sallies and worryingly unactable. I got out of it as best I could."

Fox's option to produce the play had meanwhile passed to another of Osborne's oldest friends, Helen Montagu, now managing director of H.M. Tennant (Binkie Beaumont's former West End empire). Montagu threw down an ace: Peter O'Toole wanted to play Jimmy Porter.

Whereas Bates would have brought empathy and charm to the exceptionally demanding role, O'Toole promised the excitement and danger of a bravura performance. He had recently enjoyed a West End success in Keith Waterhouse's *Jeffrey Bernard is Unwell* (and surely couldn't have known that Osborne had seen it and left at the interval). "It feels like old times," O'Toole wrote to him enthusiastically on 25 April 1991. "We could stir up a hell of a fuss."

Though Osborne never identified with "hellraisers" like the capricious, gifted Peter O'Toole, he always maintained that the best Jimmy Porter he ever saw was the twenty-three-year-old O'Toole just out of RADA in a 1957 *Look Back* at the Bristol Old Vic. Now almost sixty, the veteran actor was writing warm postcards to Osborne addressed to: "T. Bear Esq, Clun, Shropshire" and calling him, "Esteemed Author".

O'Toole made a pilgrimage to Clun in July to discuss the play. "I *do* feel terrific," Osborne wrote excitedly to Jonathan Maw. "Looks as if Sir Peter O'T. is *on*. So: will send you two good seats on the day . . ."

There was no director, however. Osborne had opposed O'Toole's personal choice of an elderly, compliant stooge and approached Lindsay Anderson instead. But Anderson complained that he could never get a response from O'Toole, who always seemed to be too busy playing cricket. Another Court veteran, Stuart Burge, would briefly become the director of choice. But the real battleground was over Osborne's refusal to cut the play.

O'Toole, like Alan Bates before him, believed the three-act *Déjàvu* was too long. Everyone who had read the script agreed. Osborne's big, sprawling plays were always lengthy, and he reasoned stubbornly that *Déjàvu* was no different to *Look Back*'s original running time. But, making his own careful reading, O'Toole clocked the time of the play at exactly four hours and eight minutes with two fifteen-minute intervals.

He pointed out amusingly to Osborne that he had lapsed into a coma during *Long Day's Journey into Night*, as well as other theatre marathons, including the last third of his own performance of the uncut *Hamlet*.

Osborne argued back that if *Déjàvu* needed to be cut, he would decide what would go during rehearsals. But, by then, from O'Toole's point of view, it would be too late.

"Sing it, hum it, shout it, speak it, rapidly recitative it, exit and entrance it on golf carts or bumper cars," he told Osborne, "when Act II of DEJAVU is uttered out loud it lasts for approximately 1 hour 45 minutes. That is 5 minutes less than the entire playing time of *Jeffrey Bernard is Unwell*."

Osborne did then promise that cuts would be made, and a pre-West End run of *Déjàvu*, starring O'Toole, was announced to open in mid-November at the Liverpool Playhouse.

On 2 October, Osborne wrote ominously in his notebook, "O'Toole a tiring sprinter, a flyweight. Not, certainly, a *stayer*. Three rounds of huff and puff, but 15 – he couldn't go the full *fifteen*."

In bravado contrast, he noted about himself: "I am not a Flat racer, although I *can* sprint. But I don't reach my peak easily for early retirement and critical stud. I am a stayer. I revel in the mud and danger and certainties of breakages. I am the Desert Orchid of literature, except that, instead of inciting adulation, I weigh in to the enclosure for dismay, bafflement and dislike."

Shortly before rehearsals of *Déjàvu* were due to begin, he cut some forty-five minutes from the script. But O'Toole found the changes unsatisfactory, rowed bitterly with Osborne and abruptly left the production.

Déjàvu's producer, Helen Montagu, was unable to cast a star actor to replace him in time for the Liverpool opening, and the production was postponed indefinitely. Osborne began to name O'Toole "Gloria O'Swanson". Montagu subsequently bowed out of *Déjàvu*.

On 14 November 1991, a devastated Osborne came downstairs from the library at The Hurst and wept inconsolably with Helen. Listening to the news on the radio, he'd learned that Tony Richardson had died of AIDS in Los Angeles.

It took three long years of frustration and craziness before *Déjàvu* was at last produced.

After the O'Toole fiasco, Osborne faxed the wealthy West End impresario Bill Kenwright, on 14 February 1992. Among Kenwright's popular hits was *Blood Brothers* (which Osborne had seen and left after six minutes, a personal record). He also ran the Liverpool Playhouse as well as Everton Football Club. "I don't suppose the following proposition will have much appeal," Osborne's fax began. "However, here goes."

> I now have two leading actors – not stars, but two fine actors I've worked with before. I've had enough of stars. My belief now is that the play must be the 'star' (The published version sold out in five days last month and is reprinting . . .) I also have a director and am all ready to go. Would you consider taking over the production and presenting it yourself? I'd be grateful for a speedy response.
>
> Best wishes,
> Yours sincerely,
> John Osborne

Kenwright admired *Déjàvu* and wanted to help. He agreed to produce the play at the Thorndike, Leatherhead (he owned the theatre) and then transfer the production to the West End.

The two leading actors Osborne had already cast were the urbane John Standing as Jimmy Porter and T.P. McKenna as Cliff. His choice of director was Tony Palmer, who had never directed a play before.

Palmer was well known for his opera work and film biographies (among them, the Handel film for television that Osborne scripted). He had once been a music critic for the *Observer* where he was edited by Helen Dawson. Osborne trusted Palmer in an untrustworthy world. In a notebook entry from 1989, he compiled a list of all the people he thought had consistently betrayed him. The list ran to twenty-two – including ex-wives, Faber & Faber, the Royal Court, the National Theatre, the Press, lawyers, accountants, his mother and Albert Finney.

Osborne had promised John Standing that he would cut *Déjàvu* by a minimum of one hour. But when Standing came to read the script he timed it at over four hours, like O'Toole. After the first informal read-through, the cast went out to dinner in Notting Hill Gate with Osborne and Palmer. Rehearsals were to start the following morning. It was a jolly evening until the issue of the cuts arose.

Palmer remembered Standing saying to Osborne as the wine flowed, "'Dear John, we're going to have to cut the play.' There was a very long silence until he replied, 'Are you telling me that after forty years of writing plays, I don't know what works on the stage?' A lot of shouting followed and Standing finally got up from the table and very politely said goodnight."

The following morning, Standing and T.P. McKenna withdrew from *Déjàvu*.

Media gossip about the stillborn production was by then damagingly commonplace. Three Jimmy Porters had so far dropped out. Apart from the humiliating rejections by the Court and the National, Osborne was on his fourth West End producer and his fifth or sixth director.

Déjàvu was quickly re-cast, however. Peter Egan was to play Jimmy Porter and Gareth Thomas was Cliff. Alison Johnston was cast as Jimmy's daughter, and Eve Matheson played her best friend Helena. Rehearsals went smoothly. Osborne cut the script down to a manageable two and a half hours.

The first performance of *Déjàvu* took place at the Thorndike Theatre on 8 May 1992, though it had been scheduled to open three days later. Director Tony Palmer brought the opening forward to coincide sentimentally with the mythical date of 8 May when the original *Look Back* had opened at the Royal Court thirty-six years before.

Because of the change, the house manager intended to go onstage to welcome everyone and explain that if an actor appeared with the script during the last scene, not to worry. The rehearsal time had been cut a little short, but they wanted to perform the show because of the significance of 8 May.

But when he strode onstage, he announced something very different.

"Ladies and gentleman," the house manager began. "Tonight is an extremely emotional and important occasion for all of us. *Déjàvu* is John Osborne's first play in some time and we're very proud to be performing it. What's more, Mr Osborne is sitting over there in the audience with us tonight."

And everyone stood up and applauded him! Nothing like it had ever happened to him before. He was overcome.

"Why is everyone being so nice to me?" he asked afterward.

Perhaps it was fated that the one element nobody could have anticipated for *Déjàvu*'s West End opening in June was a sweltering heatwave. The summer of '92 was the hottest for years with disastrous consequences for every show at the box office.

Producer Kenwright is a natural enthusiast, but he acknowledged that *Déjàvu* opened at the worst time he could remember for West End theatre. There were other potential difficulties: Peter Egan was a well-respected choice as Jimmy Porter, but not a marquee name and the Comedy Theatre in Panton Street, with its narrow auditorium and awkward sightlines, isn't a leading West End theatre. Expectations for Osborne's first play in sixteen years were inevitably too high. But the unforeseen, freakish heatwave had become the issue.

Even hit shows were playing to miserable 20 per cent houses. Nobody else was contemplating openings during that sweltering summer, but Kenwright rationalized optimistically that it handed them an opportunity. The show would receive major coverage. *Déjàvu* had the field to itself.

It had been many years since first nighters in the West End had seen Osborne and some were shocked at the changes in him on *Déjàvu*'s opening night. He had become frail and elderly in the intervening years and was leaning heavily on a cane, though his spirits were buoyant.

"Thank you once again for your faith in the piece and all you've done," he wrote affectionately to Kenwright during rehearsals. "I'm on red alert when needed, teeth in place and Semtex in my handbag. Love from us both, John."

"All love and luck for tonight," went the ritual opening-night notes to the nervous playwright who had returned from the wilderness. "Wishing greatest success." "Welcome back, dearest John." "All our fondest love . . ."

Déjàvu opened at the Comedy Theatre on 8 June 1992, and closed after a run of only seven weeks on 1 August. There were newspaper reports that as early as the second night, the theatre was at best half full. A month into the run, the production was already fighting closure. By the end, the balcony had been sealed off and its ticket holders ushered into the empty seats in the stalls.

On the final page of the script of *Déjàvu*, there's an extraordinary stage direction – the last words Osborne wrote in a play – that in its defeatist irony deserves to go down as a footnote in theatre history along with "Exit, pursued by bear". As the curtain descends, Jimmy Porter exits with an operatic flourish, an exultant wave, a proud, defiant, final farewell, to the strains of Mozart's Champagne Aria. But, concerned about the audience booing, Osborne's stage direction advises, "In the unlikely event of audience dissent at the end of the performance, the loud playing of martial music can be effective." He suggested "Molonello" played by the Grenadier Guards, the quick march "St Patrick's Day" or the "Radetszky".

But there were no boos to drown out at the curtain call of *Déjàvu*. The cast was often greeted by cheers and many of the major reviews had been supportive. Though this had been Tony Palmer's debut as a theatre director, no one faulted the production, and if Peter Egan was seen by some as too pleasantly lacking in Porter's unflinching bile, his achievement was memorable. Osborne acknowledged it more than anyone, writing to him after the closure:

My dear Peter,
I do want you to know how affected I have been by what has emerged from our too brief collaboration. Your "performance" has been indeed magnificent in every way, as much "off" as on. You made the play work as much as I could ever have hoped. In some way, your impeccable behaviour has made the outcome almost more difficult to bear. After over forty years, I am still stage struck and you have fortified that contract, however foolish it may be and inspite of present desolations, where I see no future for the likes of myself. I did try to perpetuate "language" and theatricality. You miraculously made it *work* and brought it to thrilling life. I can only tell you that for my part you rate among the very best.
God bless you, my dear friend.

Perhaps the ill-fated heatwave was decisive in *Déjàvu's* failure, but to be sure, the play's weaknesses were blatant enough. It flayed and it exhausted. It was an act of nostalgia for its younger self, but its quartet of characters now spoke with only one voice – Osborne's. It was self-justifying and self-lacerating. "Finally," Jimmy Porter announces at the close, "I still am, after thirty years, a churlish, grating note, a spokesman for no one but myself; with deadening effect, cruelly abusive, unable to be coherent about my despair . . ." For some of us, the play was a heroic gesture in spite of its flaws, but the bigger truth was unpalatable. The sixty-two-year-old Osborne no longer had an audience.

If only he could have made the giant leap to create a new one. If I were granted one wish for him, it would be that he had resisted going back in time with *Déjàvu* and ventured instead into those timeless places of the anguished heart and soul where Strindberg found a fantastic second life in his late expressionist dream plays. "It is pitiful to be human!" they cry out. The seeds were there for the ageing Osborne in the swirling nightmare dreamscapes of *Inadmissible Evidence* and in the religious ecstasy of *Luther*. "Oh, Christ, heart of my heart, providential sparrow, dead and fluttered, if you could come to my heart!" The kingdom of the unearthly and the mad were there in the darkest passages of his private notebooks.

But his cause was always the triumphant domain of the English language where words alone are certain good and man grapples with defeat and sadness. *Déjàvu* is all but forgotton today (it has never been revived). Yet its distinctive stage poetry and passion still resonate and the flashes of lightning electrify.

In an important *Times* feature during its run, the *Times* drama critic Benedict Nightingale argued forcefully that the theatre's verbal vitality had been watered down by England's conforming cloth-eared playwrights, but that Osborne's tirades were airborne with exhilarating energy. He placed the singular power of his burning rhetoric in the league of natural poets like O'Casey, Thomas, Behan, Pinter and Mamet. The blaze and versatility of the English tongue still shocks and stirs the blood in this passage from *Déjàvu* as Jimmy Porter refuses to go quietly:

If I am propped up on state pillows, being catheterized and patronized by some hell's angel of check-out mercy, young Nurse Noylene, I shall rise like some last-gasp Lazarus of a bygone smoke-filled civilization; I shall rise from my bed of unheeding profligacy and if any frowning gauleiter breathes their concern or care over my fetid and exhausted form, or any smarmy dietician dares lay her menu of lower-middle-class mush, asking old Mr Porter what putrid filth he'd like to pass through his National Health dentures for his dinner at noon – if anyone, any of those creeping refuse collectors, should refer to me as a senior citizen, they will get one last almighty smack in their sanitized fucking mouth.

47
The End

Sorry
Osborne, Christmas Eve, 1994

One month after the closure of *Déjàvu*, Osborne wrote to his literary agent acknowledging that his life in theatre was over.

> I have come to the conclusion which should surely have been self-evident ages ago . . . If Helen and I are going to avoid the gutter, I must face the fact that I shall simply have to take on ANY OLD WORK that I'm lucky enough to get. That it "should come to this" after 40 years of grime and sweat is bitterly hard to accept, but I do. I have no alternative. Whatever "creative" days I may have once assumed are clearly over.

Osborne had known from the beginning that the British have an unusual talent for a maiming with indifference. According to his old friend, Jocelyn Rickards, *Déjàvu*'s reception destroyed him. "I've half a dozen plays in front of me and *still* the fugitive energy and spirit to embark on them. But what's the point? No one wants them," he wrote to her bitterly. "After 16 years – Welcome back J O! . . . The theatre is *closed*."

The fate of the *Déjàvu* production meant that his financial problems were unsolvable. "Not much coming in lately," he'd say with obvious irony. The situation was desperate. Local tradesmen – the coal and wine merchants – were cutting off his credit and the gossip spread through Clun. A determined tax inspector he nicknamed Lucrezia Borgia was pursuing him for thousands in back taxes he couldn't pay. His cheques were bouncing. Sleepless with anxiety, he was terrified the bank would foreclose on his heavily mortgaged house.

His accountant, Peter Forrester, told me, "There was no way he could reduce his standard of living because there was basically nothing left to reduce." He was compelled to live frugally, but he could still lapse like a tempted shopaholic. Visiting London, he'd go to Turnbull & Asser and buy an expensive gift for his wife on his credit card. Though The Hurst was costly to run, Forrester explained that the rambling house was his best asset. (Loans were raised on its equity.) The house would be sold only as a last resort. The Cornwall cottage was gone. The shares in Woodfall Films had been sold for a low £25,000 and a small pension that would pass to Helen for as long as she lived. His overdraft still stood at £150,000.

He was even considering the drastic solution of selling off the copyrights in his plays as well as the contents of the house (among the valuables were a Frink sculpture, a Gwen John painting, his glittering Oscar statuette, and perhaps the Rosoman paintings for *A Patriot for Me*). Robert McCrum, Osborne's editor at Faber & Faber, was alarmed and upset to receive what amounted to a begging letter from him. "Apart from being unable to find the money, literally to be able to eat," Osborne wrote to him on 23 October 1992, "I can just about raise the fare to London."

The letter went on:

All the artefacts of my life are built into this house. If I were forced to give it up at this stage, the disruption would be so complete I honestly don't see how I could start again. It isn't just a matter of possessions. It's my life. Your firm has been my publishers for over 35 years. I simply beg you to consider some way of helping me to continue working without this burden of uncertainty and disruption. I don't know what I'm suggesting. I suppose an investment in my present and future career . . .

McCrum pleaded at a board meeting with Matthew Evans, managing director of Faber & Faber, that Osborne should be rescued. Evans suggested they first establish for themselves how bad his finances were. But when McCrum and the Faber accountant, Peter Dubuisson, visited Osborne at The Hurst, he appeared to be on top form and served them champagne all afternoon.

"It wasn't a great way to impress an accountant that you're broke," McCrum told me, beginning to laugh. But the day turned miserable when Osborne itemized all his debts for Debuisson, who concluded they were so serious that Faber could never justify paying them off.

David Hare, Robert Fox and McCrum subsequently met Osborne and his wife at the Cadogan Hotel to suggest various schemes to help him. This was the summit meeting of the do-gooders and the humiliated playwright that went disastrously wrong. "CUNTS!" Osborne scribbled shakily that night in his notebook next to their names.

Scrambling round for quick, lucrative work, he forlornly asked his literary agent to try to get him lecture tours in America. "Helen thinks it would kill me – quite literally – but I think it would be as good a way to go as any . . ." Nothing came of it, however – nor from his attempts to sell his archives and manuscripts to an American university on the advice of Stephen Spender. He contacted his former manager in Hollywood, Barry Krost, for the first time in fifteen years: "You were always bristling with good humour (I was going to say 'GAITY') and energy. There's not much of it around here. Things have been pretty dismal for the past 3 years or so – financially at least . . . I could sorely do with a nice, lucrative part in a film to keep the Inland Revenue from banging at the door. Also available for 'Special Weeks', Pantomime, Demon King etc."

He was signing his name "John Osborne, ex-playwright", or "Yesterday's Man", and scanning the Situations Vacant columns with self-lacerating humour. "Fully experienced person required by net curtain company," he read aloud to his worried wife one night, and asked her, "Do you think they'll take me?"

In his despair, he reminds us uncomfortably of clapped-out old Willie in Beckett's *Happy Days* whose watery eye is brightened by advertisements reading "Opening for smart youth." On insomniac nights, Osborne whiled away the time watching *Job Finder* on the telly and made earnest notes of golden opportunities. "Marketing Officer. Salary up to £11,244. You will need good all round communication skills . . ."

He received a rare accolade when The Writers' Guild of Great Britain unexpectedly presented him with its Lifetime Achievement Award. The gala dinner was held at the Dorchester Hotel on 27 September 1992. But when the President of the Guild, dramatist Alan Plater, first wrote informing him of the prestigious award, he received a letter back turning it down.

25.7.92

Dear Alan,
Please forgive this tardy response to your letter. I'm in some confusion at the moment. I don't mean to seem churlish, but my life work seems to represent *absolutely no* ACHIEVEMENT at all, whatever. At present, it seems to add up to TOTAL FAILURE. I've no audience, public or future . . . anyway, thank you for your very kindly letter.

But Plater, a working-class Geordie who was among the generation of playwrights who saw Osborne as a hero, persisted. "There's only one bastard in the business who can write like that," he said to his wife after seeing

Déjàvu. Osborne responded positively to his appeal to accept the award. "I'm constantly astonished by the generosity of fellow scribblers," he replied, typically naming two exceptions (Steven Berkoff and Snoo Wilson).

On the big night, Robert McCrum met Osborne and Helen at the Cadogan Hotel to accompany them to the awards ceremony. Dressed in his dapper dinner jacket, Osborne was already sipping champagne. When they left for the Dorchester, McCrum felt him leaning heavily on his arm.

"You realize if you ask the Osbornes to anything, you're inviting trouble?" Helen teased Plater during the long dinner.

"Of course," he replied. "Why do you think we asked you?"

Plater and his wife, Shirley, were shocked at how frail and grey Osborne appeared. They hadn't seen him for many years.

The Writers' Guild dinner – chaired that year by Ned Sherrin – has never been a sober occasion. Plater explained that it has something to do with lonely writers being let out of the house. "They don't behave by *the rules*," he said approvingly. No TV cameras are allowed into the Guild awards ceremony, but the print media attends and Osborne had drawn the biggest contingent of reporters the event had ever known. His Lifetime Achievement Award came last, however, and for over three hours some thirty other awards – many of them for TV shows – were presented. (Best original drama: *Inspector Morse*. Best TV film screenplay: *Truly, Madly, Deeply*. Best play or film: *Memento Mori*.) As the evening wore on, his mood couldn't have been helped by the toast to the Guild from Michael Grade, head of Channel 4, that was greeted mostly in silence. Grade, who seemed to assume he was addressing a gathering of TV people, offered a vision of the future in which the role of the writer would be downgraded in favour of writing by committee.

At long last, Alan Plater introduced Osborne. "This is the Designated Big Moment Award," his rousing speech began. He spoke of the day when he first saw Osborne's *Look Back in Anger* and of all the great plays that he had written since:

"We honour him tonight because he's told the truth, whatever the cost. Because he was the first dramatist in our time to reclaim the English theatre for passion and creative dissent. Because, to paraphrase Shakespeare, he is not only a writer himself, but the cause of writing in others – sometimes with dire consequences but that's not his fault. Finally because he has never pandered to his audiences – has never crawled, grovelled or otherwise played to the gallery. He has not asked for this prize or for our applause. That doubles the value of both and, I hope, of this award. So, your applause, please, for the lifetime achievement of John Osborne."

But as Osborne rose from the top table to make his way across the ball-room to the dais, he wobbled unsteadily on his feet and didn't seem to know where he was. Watching from nearby, the horrified McCrum closed his eyes and thought to himself, "This is the end."

"Apparently tired and emotional, Mr Osborne took two steps forward and one step back," the *Daily Express* reported in its big story the following morning. *The Evening Standard*'s headline read, "MUMBLINGS OF AN ANGRY OLD MAN": "The 63-year-old playwright had to be helped to the podium where he mumbled incoherently about Congreve and various apparently unconnected subjects before finally managing a complete sentence and announcing: 'This is a horrible profession which has never been held in such contempt, it is awful.'"

The few notes he scribbled for the speech during the endless dinner reveal at least that he promised a graceful conclusion: "Final: GRATITUDE & PRIDE. RESPECT & GOODWILL." But he never reached that point. His eyes were scarcely open. For four or five agonizing minutes, he was struggling to get the words out. The playwright who believed that language comes as a gift from God had been rendered speechless.

People began to boo him. "Get off!" barrackers shouted. At length, the TV comedy writer Barry Took strode across the room in front of him and said loudly, "I'm going to have a pee."

Alan Bleasdale – of *G.B.H.* and the finest writer in television since Dennis Potter – turned furiously on the hecklers. "Shame on you!" he protested. "We're talking about one of the greatest writers of the twentieth century." Along with writer Lynda La Plante and producer Linda Agran, he then rushed to the podium to help the disorientated Osborne. Alan Rickman was another who joined them. Photographs show their faces creased with concern as they took his arm and guided him back to his seat.

Bleasdale alone sensed something terrible was wrong. "He's dying," he said to Plater afterwards.

Dr Jill Gray in Shropshire was angry when she read the newspaper reports the next day. She knew instantly that Osborne hadn't been drunk. The symptoms of a diabetic hypoglaecemic attack are exactly the same. Osborne had forgotten to take his insulin. He was having a hypo, drifting into a coma in front of everyone.

Helen blamed herself. In the excitement of the day, she had neglected to remind Osborne to bring his insulin. But once back at his table, he ate a little and drank some Lucozade, and he recovered. And as he did so, many of the writers in the room began to surge round him. They stood in line to shake his hand.

Dr Gray sensed that everything was going downhill for her patient from the beginning of the New Year. He had twice collapsed on walks in the Shrophire hills. Helen hurried to the rescue when the dogs returned home without him.

His eyesight was suddenly failing – a consequence of diabetes – and he was wearing dark glasses. Though the problem grew no worse, Osborne was terrified that he would go blind. His father had gone blind overnight when he appeared to his horrified ten-year-old son stumbling at the top of the staircase like a vision of a naked Christ.

At the same time, Osborne was humiliatingly losing his teeth – the AYM defanged. "Well," said his Harley Street dentist, attempting a joke as he examined him in the chair. "You were never at a loss for words before." Osborne nicknamed him "The Dental Nazi" and exaggerated his bills to amounts as high as £45,000. The painful treatments – continued in Shrewsbury with a sympathetic man he called "The Schindler of Dentists" – were prolonged and complicated by his diabetes. The bills amounted, in fact, to £18,000. Perhaps he hoped for a sudden windfall from his foreign royalties, but he couldn't pay any of it. Threatened with legal action, he appealed to the Royal Literary Fund, a charity for impecunious authors subsidized by the estate of A.A. Milne. "Definitions of poverty are rather subjective," Osborne pleaded with Fiona M. Clark, the secretary of the Fund, in what amounted to another begging letter. "I had seven years in a garret starving in my twenties, but at the age of 63, pensionless, toothless and maybe eyeless, energy and hope have receded considerably."

He was partially bailed out by a grant of £6,700.

In a panic manoeuvre, the original, handwritten manuscript of *Look Back in Anger* was put up for auction at Sotheby's on 26 April 1993, but it failed to reach its reserve price of £40,000. The highest bid was half that – an unmistakable sign of how low his reputation had sunk.

The failure at auction let in the Harry Ransom Research Center of the University of Texas – the world's leading collector of authors' manuscripts. The Center's president, Tom Staley, had been waiting in the wings for the right opportunity. He purchased the manuscript in May 1993, together with extensive notes and diaries, for a comparatively low $50,000 (or about £20,000). It all went to the Inland Revenue.

Dr Gray's visits to The Hurst increased during the year. "He was losing heart. 'I can't do it any more,' he told me. 'I've lost it.'"

How was Helen coping, I asked her. "He was her life. She just loved him, and my impression was that he adored her. It was a very strong, loving relationship. There was lots of banter between them. I don't think either of them could live without the other. She coped wonderfully with John, but sometimes she was brought close to breaking point. She would never let you know, though."

They had their difficult times, no doubt. "I should have married a lorry driver," Helen complained to a friend one day when Osborne was being impossible. But such times were rare and everyone I spoke to has confirmed they loved each other till the end. She was the only one of his wives he would never say – or hear – a word against. When the possessive Rickards patronized her during an interview in the *Mail*, Osborne all but ended their long friendship. "Your patent scorn for the way she has sustained and comforted me – indeed, saved my life – is inexcusable," he wrote to her. When Rickards subsequently fell ill, however, their friendship was renewed.

"But for Helen . . ." he wrote darkly to his first father figure, Arnold Running, renewing contact with the Canadian-born journalist who had hired him almost half a century before as a cub reporter on *Gas World*. But the loving, older man who remained so proud of him grew worried.

22 June '93

Dear John,
Your letter was distressing to read . . . For Godsake don't get depressed, don't lose faith. Remember how you fought and won recognition.

On 9 May 1993, the body of Penelope Gilliatt was found in her west London flat by her sister, Angela Conner. She had recently returned from New York to live in London and died suddenly, age sixty-one, in Bayswater. Reading the news of Gilliatt's death in the *Guardian*, the shaken Osborne wrote a strange protest to its drama critic, Michael Billington.

21.6.93

Someone has just sent me – with most unkindly intent – a cutting from the GUARDIAN reporting the inquest on Penelope. "Writer's Death due to Alcoholism". I wouldn't believe that anyone could have been so cruel as to have printed this. She was driven by absurd ambition and then into a kind of madness and a form of malignity. But she was not wicked. Anyway, she didn't deserve this peculiar reportage. I don't think anyone else used it. Only a few hundred people had heard of her. Such cruelty is the preserve of liberals.

Angela Conner invited him to the funeral, but he didn't attend. Nolan was among the small gathering. The grand house in Chester Square Gilliatt once shared with Osborne was inherited by Nolan, who sold it.

On 22 March 1993, the director Di Trevis made a pilgrimage to Clun on behalf of the National Theatre. She was to stage the first major revival of *Inadmissible Evidence* in fifteen years – since Osborne had directed his own acclaimed production with Nicol Williamson – and as she made the long drive from London to meet him at The Hurst, she had her doubts and fears.

Though she was an established director (who would become well known for her productions of Harold Pinter), she felt that she was auditioning for Osborne in some way. Perhaps he was expecting a rabid feminist chewing tobacco, she thought to herself. Radical feminists had already lobbied her not to touch the apparently misogynist play (though she saw it as the reverse – a play that revolved around the disappointed hero's passion for women). She had also received a weird warning from an American society of fetishistic witches known as the Daughters of Eve who had already put what they called a Zuni curse on Osborne – as well as Pinter and Ted Hughes – for "fatal damage" to Jill Bennett, Vivien Merchant and Sylvia Plath, respectively. "WOMAN who assists in realizing the fantasies of Pinter/Osborne/Hughes in any medium," went the Zuni curse on Trevis, "is in complicity with them and their crime."

"Why am I getting myself into this?" she brooded on the drive to The Hurst. Her theatre friends had already warned her how difficult Osborne could be.

"He turned out to be completely charming," Trevis told me. "But what was so extraordinary, *he* seemed nervous of me." And she was surprised, too, that he didn't appear keen on discussing the play. But there was nothing unusual about that. Osborne avoided dutiful research. "Why don't you put your notebook away?" he said to David Hare one day at the races, "and enjoy the day?"

"He was bright and bitchy and he gossipped about the old days at the Court," said Trevis, He had already approved her choice of Trevor Eve in the Herculean role of Bill Maitland (though the actor was an unknown quantity to him, apart from his television work). He had also written to Richard Eyre at the National Theatre enthusiastically endorsing the new production. Though Eyre had rejected *Déjàvu*, there was no apparent ill feeling between them. Trevis returned to London with the impression that Osborne felt neglected, however, and she arranged a welcoming champagne lunch for him at the National with the artistic director and her lead actor. The *Inadmissible Evidence* production would be Osborne's last hurrah.

On 4 May, he attended the rehearsals for the first and last time. Accounts differ about exactly what took place. The disastrous outcome was that Osborne was left in tears, effectively banned from future rehearsals of his own play.

More than a decade later, Trevis was still upset by the memory of that day she described as heartbreaking. She had buried the details, but recalled how it went badly wrong. "I've got John Osborne in the room and he is not happy," she remembered. "A terrible atmosphere was coming from him after only a few minutes." His disapproving mood paralysed the rehearsal. Trevor Eve was running through the last scene of the play for the first time. The rest of the cast were present. Trevis eventually halted the rehearsal. "Anything to say, John?" she asked the unhappy playwright. According to her version, an extraordinary outburst followed. Against all theatre protocol, Osborne openly dismissed Eve's performance. "He was angry and his disdain poured out of him," Trevis said. A shouting match followed with the defensive Eve arguing back. "He wasn't going to be walked over," she added. The rest of the cast were embarrassed. They had all been in awe of Osborne when he quietly entered the room leaning on his walking stick.

Eve stormed out, and the director followed him. "My loyalty was to the actor. He's the one *doing* it."

Osborne was left to find his way out of the maze of backstage corridors at the National, and returned to the Cadogan Hotel where he broke down in tears.

The incident was widely reported in the press, fuelling the myth of Osborne as the troublemaker whom no one could work with. But two newspaper interviews that Trevor Eve gave soon afterwards tell a very different story. "Unfortunately we were working on a scene we hadn't looked at since the first read-through and we were improvising," he told the arts section of the London *Evening Standard* a week before the opening night. "He couldn't understand the process of how Di and I wanted to work the scene. There was no shouting or harsh words." He also told *Time Out*: "He came in for about two minutes and it was really quite an amicable exchange. Do you know him? You can imagine him sitting there, can't you . . . ?" But Trevis had telephoned The Hurst and informed Helen that it would be better if Osborne didn't attend rehearsals again.

In both interviews, Eve claimed that Tony Richardson had earlier also banned Osborne from rehearsals. But that never happened. And, had it happened, it would have been against all entrenched policy of George Devine's Court where the playwright was regarded as king. Osborne's unusual practice throughout his working life was, in fact, to visit rehearsals only occasionally to offer advice, like constitutional monarchs, when asked. Every other Osborne director I've spoken to – including Bill Bryden (*Watch It Come Down*), David Leveaux (*The Father*), Clive Donner (*The Picture of Dorian Gray*), Max Stafford-Clark (*The End of Me Old Cigar*), Frank Dunlop (*A Sense of Detachment*), and Anthony Page (the original director of *Inadmissible Evidence* as well as five other Osborne premieres) – pointed out how supportive Osborne always was in rehearsal.

Page confirmed, "He came into rehearsals only when he felt he could be helpful. He was amazingly easy to work with and got enormous pleasure from seeing the work develop. He never pushed to be in there 'overlooking' everything. He gave very specific notes, sometimes typewritten. He hated glumness, over-intense, earnest theorizing, and he loved fun, improvised daring, leaps of courage, and the camaraderie of actors."

It's an unattractive myth that Osborne was impossible to work with. As a former actor himself, he understood the rehearsal process better than most playwrights and conceded the territory to the actors and director. The truth of what happened during the Di Trevis rehearsal is almost certainly closer to her observation that three vulnerable people were in the rehearsal room that day. The volatile leading man longing for approval, his anxious director, and the intimidating, legendary playwright.

The National's artistic director, Richard Eyre, stood by his production team. Osborne defended himself privately in a letter to him on 2 June. "I have always been consulted, done what I could to help, and no one has ever opposed, let alone ignored my judgement," he said about his rehearsal experience that went back forty-five years. "I shouldn't have to *ask* if I may attend rehearsals of my own play. As you know, it's my right. It shouldn't need saying. None of it should. This is no way to run a chip shop . . ."

He didn't attend the opening night on 17 June. It made no difference to him that the production was generally well received or that the public was reminded of another time, a brave new time, when he was at his height. He had just learned that a BBC TV production of *The Entertainer* starring Michael Gambon had dropped all the original songs without informing him. Cut *The Entertainer*'s Music Hall numbers and you cut out its heart. When Osborne protested, he received no response.

The bitterly disappointed playwright believed there was no place left for the likes of him. The *Inadmissible* experience convinced him that he'd been driven out of the theatre in the unwinnable war against mediocrity. "This will certainly be the last presentation of my work in London during my lifetime," he wrote to the sorrowful Richard Eyre, "and it is a melancholy way to say farewell to one's profession. I still had fugitive hopes for it – a humiliating and bitter way not even to bow out. Everyone can go on acting in other plays, directing plays or running theatres, but my options have run out."

Notebook entry, 1993: "What can I *do*? How can we stay here? No future, 63, and nothing. Debt. No pension. No home for me in the theatre, anyway. How much more can Helen take? Dear God. I don't know what to do. What *can* I do? A play? Don't make me laugh."

He marvelled at the irony that the only people left who seemed to respect his writing were journalists. He kept working on his well-regarded columns and book reviews for the *Spectator*, as well as flogging himself through illness to undertake lucrative hack work for the *Mail on Sunday* ("think pieces" on the blight of tourism and the new Brighton). On good, self-boosting days, he identified with renowned writers from previous centuries who delighted in journalism – Johnson, Hazlitt, Dickens, Thackeray, Kipling, James, Shaw, Arnold Bennett. On bad days, as he wrote to Rickards, "That's how you end up – a fucking journalist."

In a pre-emptive strike against his own obituaries, his *Spectator* columns began mentioning the punishing world of theatre with its caprice of cruel fashion and short working lives of playwrights. (Wilde had three years, Sheridan four, Congreve seven.) "We theatre scribblers average about a dozen years or so," he wrote, and concluded with the thought that this was his forty-fifth year in what Pinero described as "this rotten profession" in *Trelawny of the Wells*.

There were times, though, when he no longer had enough strength left to write. "Last week I had to give in once again and send for the doctor," goes the opening line to a draft for another *Spectator* column. But in a determined effort to get it started, the man who once wrote entire plays with scarcely a correction, has written the same line six times as if choking into life like an exhausted engine.

On 25 August 1993, he visited Stratford-upon-Avon to see one of his oldest chums, the newly knighted Robert Stephens, play King Lear. Stephens was ailing, too, and this would be one of his last appearances on the stage. After the performance, they dined together with friends and were last seen arm-in-arm in the street, drunk as lords, singing Marlene Dietrich's "Falling in Love Again."

The following month, Dr Gray was called urgently to the house again. Osborne had grown alarmingly weak with acute anaemia. His blood count had dropped to about one-third of normal. She admitted him, suffering from a duodenal ulcer, to Nuffield Hospital for blood transfusions.

"Get me out of this fucking place, please," he said to one the nurses.

Little had been seen of him in Clun village for more than a year. He usually walked to the nearby church for the early morning service but was no longer glimpsed shopping in the village street or having a drink at the pub. But on Guy Fawkes Night, there was always a gathering in the grounds of The Hurst where Andrew, who looked after the property, built a big bonfire on the hill and everyone they knew from the village came.

Few people stayed at the house now, except for Osborne's godson, the actor Ben Walden, who went frequently. Ben had worshipped Osborne since childhood. He looked on him and Helen as his surrogate parents and perhaps the enthusiastic boy reminded Osborne of himself when he was on the threshold of a life in theatre. "How are you, sweetheart?" he would say to him, his eyes lighting up whenever he came into the room.

Ben was glad to stay up half the night listening to his stories. "I think John felt that people who went to bed early had given up on life," he told me. "He was a child in many ways. He wanted you to talk and talk and talk and drink lots of champagne and *collapse*." One day, Helen asked him what on earth the two of them had talked about till dawn. "Shakespeare, God, Olivier and Jimmy Cagney," he replied.

And there were the quiet, occasional pub lunches and suppers in Ludlow with friends like the Gowries who lived across the border in Wales. "We talked about everything, including my shoes," said Grey Gowrie's wife Neitie. "I knew all the rumours about John, but I loved his company. One summer, a middle-aged lady from the shires came up to our table and asked for his autograph. She seemed such an unlikely fan, yet she gave the impression that she was in the presence of God. He was amazed. He gave her his autograph and looked *extremely* pleased. But when we knew him in the last four years of his life, I had the feeling of tragedy. He seemed a tragic figure because there was no consolation in him."

Dr Gray was called out by Helen to visit him on Christmas Day 1993 – the dangerous time of the year for him. "We had a couple of burnt turkeys at home because of John," she told me gently. As the New Year approached, he lay in his darkened bedroom unable to function. "He always tried to rally when I saw him and have a few digs at the medical profession. I mostly listened to him talk. He said his family life had been non-existent as a child and he told me about the grim Christmases they had and his hatred of his mother. There were so many people in his life that he still felt burning anger toward."

Unknown to Osborne, Arnold Wesker had begun lobbying his MP to propose him for a knighthood. But Osborne was among the first public figures – with Malcom Muggeridge and John Grigg, the former Lord Altringham – who dared to attack royalty in the 1950s. Royalty does not forget. He was never offered a knighthood (or any official honour).

"I wonder if he would have accepted one?" Harold Pinter – who refused a knighthood – asked. "He was an extremely independent and unpredictable man. He might have said yes, or he might have said no."

Pinter's question took me by surprise. I had assumed a knighthood would have pleased a patriot for us, even one without clean hands. "There is nothing more palpable than a lifetime's disavowal of honour in your own country," Osborne wrote in his notebook of October 1993. But Pinter regarded him as a renegade. "I don't think he obeyed any rules," he said. "He was a wonderfully fiery spirit who certainly didn't bow down to authority. He did what he liked."

The two playwrights were often considered competitors, particularly in younger days. But Pinter told me he never forgot that when an early, idio-syncratic radio play of his entitled A Slight Ache was staged at the Arts Theatre in 1961, Osborne saw it and sent him a note congratulating him. He was still a struggling writer and he was astonished to hear from the famous playwright, whose own play, Epitaph for George Dillon, he under-studied as an actor.

They subsequently became friends and enjoyed each other's occasional company. They both had an embarrassing knack for saying the wrong thing. "The choices you make sometimes go down the plug hole," Pinter explained in his precise way. "I took to John every time I met him. He was a much warmer chap than me and naturally very funny. He made me laugh. The great thing about John Osborne was that he was a piss-taker. He just liked to take the piss out of everybody, including himself. We were apparently on opposite sides of the political fence, but I think he assumed the posture which amused him of being the right-wing squire. He would say to me, 'Hello, you old lefty cocksucker!' And I would say, 'A superb definition! Absolutely right. Let me shake your hand.'"

On 2 June 1994, a Garrick Club bus took its members who were racing enthusiasts on their annual outing to the Derby and the Osbornes were as usual there. But after wandering off to place his first bet, Osborne disappeared. They couldn't find him all afternoon and Helen frantically called the police.

He turned up that evening at the Cadogan Hotel after hitching a ride back to London with another bus outing. At some point, after placing the bet, he had a hypo attack and passed out in a field. That he woke up at all was considered near miraculous.

His health deteriorated rapidly during the last six months of his life. Contracted to write a TV script for Tony Palmer that celebrated the tercentenary of Purcell's birth, he felt too exhausted to make any progress and had to abandon it.

He sent a postcard to David Hare which said: "I look out on the blue, remembered hills and they are saying to me, 'Oh bugger off!'"

On 23 June, at lunch with Alec Guinness at Cecconi's in London he had such a serious nosebleed that he was rushed to St Thomas's Hospital where the crisis eventually subsided. Guinness rang the hospital every half hour to make certain he was all right.

There had been another emergency nosebleed earlier in the year when an ambulance was called to the house, but he adamantly refused to get in it. Dr Gray argued with him for half an hour. "It was like getting a frightened racehorse into a boxcar," she said. "But he absolutely wouldn't do it. It was the only time I felt completely defeated by him."

By September, his physical decline had left him painfully gaunt as he developed a condition called ascites: his liver was reaching the end of its lifespan. He was even finding it difficult to walk. A serious danger of uncontrolled diabetes is the development of ulcers on the feet that can lead to amputation. The circulation to his legs was blocked. Fearing that he was developing gangrene, a desperate Dr Gray called in a consultant physician.

Osborne refused at first to go into hospital. "I remember just hanging onto him in the night," said Helen, "and pleading with him, 'Let's not give in. Let's see how they can help you'."

He entered Nuffield Hospital the following morning ostensibly for treatment to his right foot. It was the day before his sixty-fifth birthday, 12 December 1994.

He took with him *Holy Living and Holy Dying* by the seventeenth-century divine, Jeremy Taylor, in which he had marked this passage:

> If your case be brought to the last extremity and that you are at the pit's brink, even the very margin of the grave, yet then despair not. At least, put it off a little longer, and remember that whatsoever final accident takes away all hope from you, if you stay a little longer and in the

meanwhile bear it sweetly, it will also take all despair too. For when you enter the regions of death, you feel rest from all your labours and your fears.

Five days later, his foot had healed. "I thought, this is incredible! It's going to be all right," said Helen. "Everyone had told me it would never happen, and he was recovering."

But as one danger passed, his liver and kidneys were failing completely. She moved into his hospital room on 19 December and slept there on a cot. The weather was cold and icy and Helen told him the roads were too dangerous to drive home.

He began to drift in and out of consciousness as she kept vigil. "Can I go now?" he said to her one day. They smiled wanly. It was a private joke between them. Whenever they went to the theatre, sooner or later he always whispered, "Can I go now?"

His last word was, "Sorry."

Sorry he wasn't going to make it. Sorry he was leaving her.

He died in her arms at 10.10 p.m. on Christmas Eve.

Epilogue and The Search for Faith

Lift your eyes
Where the roads dip and where the roads rise
Seek only there
Where the grey light meets the green air
The hermit's chapel, the pilgrim's prayer.

T.S. Eliot, "Usk"

The official cause of John Osborne's death was heart failure, secondary to liver and kidney failure. His diabetes was a decisive, complicating factor. When Helen gathered together his possessions in Nuffield Hospital, she found the words "I have sinned" scribbled shakily on a cigarette pack – the last words he wrote.

She also found a prophetic note on which he'd written these three dates and nothing more – 4 December, which was the day he wrote the note, his birthday, 12 December, and 24 December, the day he died.

As Helen returned home to The Hurst, she saw various couples leaving the hospital car park to spend Christmas and the rest of their lives together and she felt the grip of envy. "There are no road maps in this blasted landscape," she wrote seven years later, "there are no guidelines for grief, parameters to loss."

The glowing obituaries of her husband went unread by her, she said, for there could be no consolation. "Physically I felt as though I had been in a multiple car smash. My body was broken. There was no rest, even in the refuge of our double bed where the other side – his side – was still feral in my imagination. I was brutally aware of how colourful, resonant and invigorating the most humdrum events of a shared life had been – the post, the papers, cheese on toast, the dopiest of repeated jokes, bugbears, tunes . . . I quaked at the desert future, a diary without dates: survival seemed impossible without the daily solaces of security and surprise and the counsel of the one person who always rooted for you, no matter your frailties."

And when time had passed, and the bruises became barely visible, she said that she probably looked as "normal" as she ever would, but still awoke in the night just the other side of tears to cry out in the empty house, "Where are you?"

The funeral took place at 2 p.m. on New Year's Day 1995, at St George's Parish Church in Clun. It was attended by the close-knit community of the valley, and friends came from London and others from nearby. When the formal service ended, a trumpeter sounded the Last Post and the burial took place as snow fell.

Though the National Theatre sent a wreath to the graveside, there were no flowers from the Royal Court, no words of tribute were spoken on behalf of the theatre that he helped found, no attention paid.

Osborne's last *Spectator* column in the 1994 Christmas double issue was written by his wife. The front cover was a pastiche of an old-fashioned theatrical billboard with "The One and Only John Osborne and his Diary" taking top billing over his co-stars, William Boyd, Muriel Spark and Auberon Waugh. But when the cover went to press, the desperately ill Osborne entered Nuffield Hospital unable to write his column. Helen saved the day by cobbling it together from his jottings.

"I am haunted by thoughts of the things I will never do again," is the line that we remember.

The posthumous column raises a question: How much more of Osborne's work may have been written by his wife? Her fingerprints are all over *Almost a Gentleman*, the second volume of his autobiography that he had difficulty completing, and I suspect that she contributed to his essay on Strindberg's *The Father* that prefaces the published script for Faber & Faber. She swore to me, however, that she wrote only two other Osborne articles that appeared under his name when he was too ill to write them himself. One was a piece for the *Evening Standard* on Gore Vidal, the other a long, learned review of Ingmar Bergman's autobiography, *The Magic Lantern*, for the *New York Review of Books*.

England, My England, Tony Palmer's TV film celebrating the tercentenary of Henry Purcell was dedicated to Osborne's memory and broadcast on Channel 4 on Christmas Day 1995. Though Osborne was also credited with co-writing the script with Charles Wood, his contribution amounted to little before illness forced him to abandon the project. Wood wrote the script as a tribute to his old friend, keeping Osborne's original concept of two time zones embodying the same spirit across the centuries. Simon

Callow played the dual roles of King Charles in the seventeenth century and a young actor-dramatist in the twentieth who was modelled on a young actor-dramatist named Osborne. He had just signed on to appear in the film when Osborne died. "I went into shock," he remembered. "It was well enough known that he was unwell, in and out of hospital, but one had somehow expected him to be there, in whatever state of repair, for the rest of one's life."

The actor couldn't have failed to notice, even so, that as time went on Osborne had taken aim at one too many of the usual suspects, including Simon Callow. "His later occasional journalism in the *Spectator*, for instance, was spellbinding," Callow added graciously, "all the more so since one invariably fell into one of the many categories upon which he vented his spleen – queers, modern actors, people who thought they could write, Labour voters – the list was unending. It never crossed my mind for one moment that he should be stopped, or taken to court or anything of the sort, because for every custard pie that winged its way into my face, or those of friends, there was a soaring phrase or chiselled epigram that came from a heart of goodness and deep understanding."

Osborne had left behind a letter dated 18 July 1984: "To be opened immediately on my death".

"It's a bright summer Edenbridge day," he began cheerfully. "So here are some requests for my funeral/memorial." But if the requests had been granted, both services would have lasted about six hours each. "Cuts, cuts, cuts!" he added in an ironic note.

The crowded memorial service took place in London on 2 June 1995, at St Giles-in-the-Fields. "It is impossible to speak of John without using the word 'England'," David Hare said in his address. "He had in some sense made the word his own." Hare continued in the uncompromising spirit of the man he was eulogizing. "John Osborne devoted his life to trying to forge some sort of connection between the acuteness of his mind and the exceptional power of his heart. 'To be tentative was beyond me,' he said. 'It usually is.' That is why this Christian leaves behind him friends and enemies, detractors and admirers. A lifelong scourge of prigs and puritans, whether of the Right or the Left, he took no hostages, expecting from other people the same unyielding, unflinching commitment to their own view of the truth which he took for granted in his own. Of all British playwrights of the twentieth century he is the one who risked most. And, risking most, frequently offered the most rewards."

Osborne's favourite music was played during the service between the solemn prayers and hymns, and there were several readings – Shakespeare, Bunyan, Housman – by leading actors on best behaviour. At one delightfully unexpected point, Michael Ball sang "If You Were the Only Girl in the World" and everyone joined in the lilting old Music Hall favourite, humming and singing along to it sadly.

> Nothing else would matter in the world today
> We could go on loving in the same old way
> If you were the only girl in the world
> And I were the only boy . . .

Then we drifted off to the Garrick Club for the wake and a glass of plonk. But though the memorial service had been correct in every way, it caused uproar in the press and Osborne would make headline news from beyond the grave. The trouble was caused by a notice that had been posted on the gate of the church before the service began:

> The undermentioned will NOT be admitted:
> Fu Manchu
> Albert Finney
> Nicholas de Jongh
> The Bard of Hay-on-Wye.

The list of the banned had been compiled as a schoolboy prank in loving memory of Osborne by the Memorial Committee (which included Helen Osborne, Melvyn Bragg, Dominic Lawson and Robert Fox). The following day, righteous newspaper articles and think-pieces condemned the ban from the church service as un-Christian. Whereupon the Earl of Gowrie responded in a letter to *The Times* asking, "Who says the Almighty has no sense of humour?"

Fu Manchu, everyone knew, was Sir Peter Hall. The mysterious Bard of Hay-on-Wye was Arnold Wesker (who lived close to Hay-on-Wye). Wesker found himself banned because his *Guardian* tribute to Osborne, though well intentioned, had misfired. He seemed to have claimed disapprovingly that Osborne had been drunk at a Buckingham Palace party hosted by the Queen.

Representing a cross-section of British life, the informal evening at the palace for 800 guests on 20 June 1994 was the last public event that Osborne attended. He had been surprised and flattered to be asked. He was equally surprised to meet three other playwrights there: Wesker, Hare and Pinter. "They were just as startled to see me, and each other," he wrote. "Each was unnerved to discover that he wasn't the only dramatist present and that his cover, consequently, had been blown." Harold Pinter and Antonia Fraser spent some time in Osborne's company as they sipped champagne and the band of the Irish Guards played selections from *Oliver!* When they read Wesker's account of the party, they wrote a joint letter to the *Guardian* in protest.

"Osborne didn't appear to be in the least bit drunk, nor did we hear him utter obscenities," they reported steadfastly. "We found him wry, detached, amused and amusing. Of course he's no longer able to comment on the company he kept . . ."

Others who were there sided with the Pinters – among them, the Gowries, Hare and his wife, Nicole Farhi, and Paul Johnson who remembered a furious argument erupting at the palace when Wesker complained bitterly to Pinter about the evening he gratuitously insulted a friend of his as the biggest bore in Christendom. According to Johnson, Osborne benevolently tried to come between them by threatening to have them both thrown to the corgis.

The hapless Wesker, who last saw Osborne tap-dancing for him in the street after they left the palace, apologized publicly for his *Guardian* gaffe. He later made a lonely pilgrimage to Clun to lay flowers on the grave.

Osborne's entire estate was left to Helen. But with it came his debts that now totalled £377,000. These were eased a little when his archives and private papers were sold posthumously in April 1995, to the Harry Ransom Humanities Research Center in Austin, Texas (which bought the original manuscript of *Look Back in Anger*). Osborne's initial asking price had been an unrealistic $950,000. "This is my *life*," he kept telling its president, Thomas F. Staley.

Staley met him half a dozen times before he died, enjoying his company and negotiating the price. "We got along well," he told me. "He was forthcoming about needing the money, and another side of him gave me the impression that he didn't give a damn whether we bought his archives or not. His price was ridiculously inflated." The Osborne archives were ultimately sold for just over $200,000, which paid off a substantial part of the tax debt of £177,000.

"Hang on to the house if you possibly can," Osborne had said to his wife, who wanted to remain there somehow. The house was saved with the discreet help of the Earl of Gowrie (who had been Mrs Thatcher's Minister of the Arts). Supported by more than £1 million in lottery money, The Arvon Foundation – the country's most influential literary foundation – bought The Hurst in July 1998, to convert it into one of its rural retreats for writers. The £200,000 mortgage on the house was thus paid off and Helen continued living in the main wing of The Hurst rent-free for the rest of her life.

Initially hesitant about the Arvon project, she warmed to the idea and found that she enjoyed the unexpected company. Osborne might have been spinning in his grave at the notion of earnest writing courses being taught in his home (or anywhere). But the late Poet Laureate Ted Hughes, an inspiration behind Arvon, had also sold his Yorkshire millhouse to the foundation. The newly named John Osborne Arvon Centre was formally opened at The Hurst on 28 March 2003, by two good friends of the Osbornes, the Earl of Gowrie and Dame Maggie Smith. The first guest teacher was director William Gaskill, successor to George Devine at the Royal Court.

Meanwhile, I was continuing an obsessive search. Towards the end of his life, Osborne had begun to talk about his sister, Faith, who died of tuberculosis when he was two years old. Perhaps it's understandable that he would mention her as he lay dying. Yet he admitted in his autobiography that he couldn't recall anything about her. All he really knew about Faith was that she was the beatified member of his family who died tragically young.

"She was spoken of as an exquisite prodigy," he had written, "but she exists to me only as a description of the last moments of her life, and my mother and father walking down the steps of Westminster Hospital afterward with Big Ben chiming as they did so."

What date did she die? The constellation of deaths in Osborne's life around Christmas – including his own – is uncanny. As we've seen, his immobilizing depressions affected him with the approach of each New Year and were almost certainly triggered by the anniversary of his father's death in January. Three years before Osborne died, he planted a cherry tree in his father's memory in the garden of The Hurst. He toasted the flowering tree with Helen, "To Dad!"

But what, I wondered, if the cause of his depressions wasn't the death of his beloved father, or the baleful influence of the mother he blamed for his father's death? Suppose there was another cause that was buried so deep within him that he could never grasp it?

He gave no date for his sister's death. My starting point was the hunch that she died at Christmas as a New Year approached. It should have been a simple matter to find the date. And yet everything that followed conspired against its discovery as if Faith Osborne had never existed.

The death certificate should have been registered at the Family Records

Centre in London – but no record of her death could be found there. If, as Osborne remembered, Faith died when he was two years old, the year would have been 1931 or 1932. I broadened the search from 1930 to 1935. A further search at the General Register Office in Southport failed, as did another via a computer service. The archive of death certificates at Westminster Hospital where Faith died no longer survived.

Osborne wrote that she was buried in the cemetery off the Fulham Palace Road on the long road to Putney Bridge. "It stretches as far as Fulham Broadway," he wrote, "where my mother would walk past my sister's grave . . ." But when I visited the cemetery, I was thwarted again. At some stage in the last seventy years, the burial records had been moved to Fulham Town Hall. But no record of Faith was to be found there. It was most likely lost in the transfer, I was told.

I walked for hours by every headstone in the cemetery looking for the grave. I found one marked "Osbourne" – but that was all. It's possible that Faith's headstone had been laid flat and was now covered by grass. But she was nowhere to be found.

I spoke to Helen about my visit to the cemetery. "I could have saved you the trouble," she said. "John went there more than once and he couldn't find her either."

But why had he gone in search of his sister's grave? Why more than once? Osborne was middle-aged when he was still looking for Faith, searching for some unfathomable link, some explanation, a sign from beyond the grave. Helen had seen a photograph of her as a baby and I had easily found her birth certificate. Faith was born on 24 April 1928. She did exist.

There was nothing more I could do, though I continued scanning the plays and notebooks for a clue. The 1985 notebook entry in which Osborne spoke of an "original theft" in his life as if it were an original sin struck me forcibly again as a mysterious key. "I was born with a sense of loss," he wrote without explanation or warning, "a feeling of things withheld and banished. This initial deprivation of inheritance, this original theft abided . . ."

Then, much later, an extraordinary coincidence occurred. An old friend and former *Observer* colleague, Anthony Sampson, died and in March 2005 I travelled to London to attend his memorial service at St Martin-in-the-Fields, opposite Trafalgar Square. When I was looking round the church after the service, I realized this was the church where Faith Osborne had been christened. It was the only detail about her that Osborne knew – part of family folklore. She was christened by the Reverend Richard Sheppard in St Martin-in-the-Fields.

I had one more day in London before returning to New York. Taking the coincidence as an omen, I decided to search again for Faith's death certificate at the Family Records Office in Islington. This time, I spread the years from her birth in 1928 to 1935. But when I looked through the big index volumes where births and deaths are entered in ink like a roll call of England, she was still nowhere to be found. There was just a chance of a misspelling of the surname "Osborne". But, even among the "Osborns" and "Osbournes", she didn't exist.

In my disappointment, I asked an assistant if there was anywhere else the death certificate might conceivably be found? She shook her head at first, but asked me where Faith had died. When I told her Westminster Hospital and the approximate year, she explained there was a slender chance that the death certificate might still be in the archives at Westminster Register Office.

I hurried there. "You can look yourself, if you like," a young official said to me behind the reception at Births, Marriages and Deaths. He didn't have time to search through the piles of registers himself. Nor did he hold out any hope. The boundaries of the old district maps – Holborn, Victoria, Fulham and so on – had changed over the years and the dusty index volumes on the shelves didn't seem to be in any order. As I searched among them, I realized it was hopeless.

"If she is not here, she is nowhere," the registrar said firmly when I told him my story. He possessed the stern authority of a sergeant major and pulled down a new pile of indexes at random from a top shelf saying it was down to luck whether we found her. The first volume in his pile was marked 1930, Volume 16. Faith Osborne was entered last in the "O" section, reference number 75.

The index number could now be matched with the death certificate on file in the archival cellars. It would take two hours: "There are other people before you, you know." I whiled away the time in Marylebone and then returned.

"Found her, did you?" said the young man behind the counter, grinning. I paid £25 for the certificate that he handed me in an envelope and sat on a bench to open it, trying to keep calm. Faith's death was suddenly very real to me as I held the certificate in my hand. I had to squint to read the faded, scrawled handwriting of the registrar. And then I saw that she hadn't died at Christmas.

For a moment, I felt like the man who had gambled everything on the wrong throw of the dice. Faith Osborne died in Westminster Hospital on 12 March 1930. But as I peered again at the document I realized that the date of her death wasn't the point. It was the year that mattered. The false trail had led to a much bigger discovery. Osborne's sister lived for only twenty-two months. And she died just three months after his birth. It's why he couldn't remember anything about her. The significance of Faith's death is in its proximity to his birth. She was dying as he was born.

"I was born with a sense of loss," he had written in the notebook. The genesis of that "original theft" and "initial deprivation of inheritance", which he intuited but could never understand, was there in his sister's death. Osborne was born at Christmas time into a world of profound sadness where a baby girl was dying. The cause of Faith's death is given on the certificate as "milinary tuberculosis". She would have suffered terribly from lesions all over her body as she died in a hospital isolation ward. Her grieving mother beatified her first child. Her father was himself infected with TB.

Osborne wrote that he first came to know the terror of death at ten years old when his father died. But he had known it since birth. It was his own birth and survival that Osborne was mourning in darkened rooms with each approaching New Year, for with his birth came Faith's death and the never healed wound of that loss.

Helen lived on at The Hurst for nine years, and during that time she put her husband's estate in order and returned to journalism, writing admired book reviews for the *Spectator* and *Sunday Telegraph*. "The fee for this article," she wrote to one editor, "is going to the Helen Osborne Survival Fund."

And survive she did, in her way. "I can scarcely believe that I am still here," she wrote, "flailing maybe but less obviously feeble. I have tried to do my best for my husband's memory and especially for his work. Sometimes I have let him down lamentably. I have tried to stay true to his enthusiasms, to watch the world as warily as he did, and to cock a snook at humbug at all times."

She went on as if speaking directly to him, "Sometimes, like a child demanding reassurance, I imagine you as a constant star keeping watch over me above the oak tree. Occasionally, I feel I glimpse you in the garden, or hear your footfall on the stair, a laugh behind a half-open door. And very, very rarely your arm is on my shoulder. I could almost swear it."

In time, she ventured out to visit friends or went to the seasonal races at nearby Ludlow for a flutter on a favoured outsider to romp home. She doted on "the boys" (the two labradors and the Springer spaniel). She drank too much, but never enough. She kept in touch with London theatre and stayed with Maggie Smith. She travelled to Tuscany to holiday with the

Mortimers, and came to New York for an important American production of *Look Back in Anger* that was so confused she forgave them. "That's the first time I've heard Jimmy Porter with an upper-class accent," she said to me, smiling over a glass of gin.

When I last spoke to her it was another Christmas, and she calmly told me that she had been quite ill. Yet she made me laugh, and we arranged to talk again in the New Year. She died, aged sixty-four, in Nuffield Hospital on 12 January 2004, and was buried next to her husband in the country churchyard twelve days later.

As I drove away from the reception at The Hurst after the funeral that day I looked back at the house knowing I would never visit it again. A time had come to an end, and with it was buried a generation. And yet on the long journey home through blue and grey light when I was lost in thought about John and Helen Osborne, it seemed to me the saving grace of Osborne's life of unruly passion and torment was that great playwrights achieve the miraculous. Only a great playwright creates people who have never existed before. In becoming bigger than their creator, they are immortal. And I took comfort that Jimmy Porter, Archie Rice, Bill Maitland and others we have come to know are alive in time and space and light.

Good evening, ladies and gentlemen – Archie Rice is the name. Archie Rice. Mrs Rice's favourite boy. We're going to entertain you for the next two and a half hours and you've really had it now. All exit doors locked.

Oh heavens, how I long for a little ordinary enthusiasm. Just enthusiasm, that's all. I want to hear a warm, thrilling voice cry out Hallelujah! Hallelujah! I'm alive!

Well, I 'ave a go, lady, don't I? I 'ave a go. You think I am, don't you? Well, I'm not. But *he* is!

I said: have you ever watched someone die . . . ? For twelve months, I watched my father dying – when I was ten years old. He'd come back from the war in Spain, you see. And certain god-fearing gentlemen there had made a mess of him, he didn't have long to live. Everyone knew it – even I knew it. But you see, I was the only one who cared.

I'm just a guy called Paul Slickey

And the job that I do's pretty tricky . . .

Writers are born to be reviled.

No they're not. They sit in judgement on themselves all the time without calling in outside help. They need to be loved and cared for and given money . . .

I've never had any patience with all your mortifications. All these trials and tribulations you go through. They're meat and drink to you.

I lost the body of a child, a child's body, the eyes of a child; and at the first sound of my own childish voice, I lost the body of a child; and I was afraid, and I went back to find it. But I'm still afraid, I'm afraid, and there's no end of it.

Seems to me there are three ways out of despair. One is faith in Christ, the second is to become enraged at the world and make its nose bleed for it, and the third is the love a good woman . . .

"What's he *angry* about?" they used to ask. Anger is not *about* . . . It is mourning the unknown, the loss of what went before you, it's the love another time but not this might have sprung on you, and the greatest loss of all, the deprivation of what, even as a child, seemed to be irrevocably your own, your country, your birthplace, that, at least, is as tangible as death.

There's a bloke at the side here with a hook, you know that, don't you? He is, he's standing there. I can see him. Must be the income tax man. Life's funny, though, isn't it? It is – life's funny . . . You think I'm gone, don't you? Go on, say it, you think I'm gone. You think I'm gone, don't you? Well, I am. What's the matter, you feeling cold up there? Before I do go, ladies and gentlemen, I should just like to tell you a story, a little story. This story is about a man, just a little, ordinary man, like you and me, and one day he woke up and found himself in paradise . . .

Let me know where you're working tomorrow night – and I'll come and see *you*.

Notes and Sources

My principal sources throughout the biography were the personal interviews I conducted with many people who knew Osborne, as well as the John Osborne archives and papers at the Harry Ransom Humanities Research Center (HRHRC) in Austin, Texas, his two autobiographies, *A Better Class of Person* (Faber & Faber, 1981) and *Almost a Gentleman* (1991), and his private notebooks.

The notebooks, formerly kept by Osborne's widow Helen Osborne with some of his papers in their Shropshire home, are currently under the care of the Arvon Foundation in London. The bulk of the Osborne archive remains in Austin, Texas.

The quotations from Osborne's notebooks and letters throughout the text have been edited for length. Though this is the authorized biography, no conditions were made by the literary executor, Helen Osborne, save for her wish to correct factual errors. Upon her death, Osborne's literary estate passed to the Arvon Foundation and the same freedom in writing the book was continued. All quotations from Osborne's published and unpublished writings are reproduced by kind permission of the executors of the Estate of John Osborne on behalf of the Estate and his publishers Faber & Faber.

Chapter 1: The Hurst

This was the first of my visits to The Hurst, the Osborne home in Shropshire, and I stayed there on five subsequent occasions researching the book and interviewing Helen Osborne. My interviews and informal conversations with her continued until her death on 12 January 2004.

The director Lindsay Anderson was known as "The Singing Nun" because he liked to chant hymns in Latin during a crisis. His *Spectator* review of *Almost a Gentleman* ("Court in the act", 9 November 1991) described Osborne as a performer as much as a writer. Anderson, a close friend of Osborne's ex-wife Jill Bennett, also protested about his "venom" toward her in the autobiography.

I was first told by theatre producer Robert Fox about the emergency meeting among Osborne's friends to solve his financial crisis. The three others who were present, Helen Osborne, David Hare and Robert McCrum, confirmed what took place. Osborne's ex-mistress, Jocelyn Rickards, was also alarmed to learn about the perilous state of his finances and offered him money that was refused (correspondence between Rickards and Osborne, HRHRC).

"Oh blimey – not *you* again!" The story of the stage carpenter's ritual greeting to Osborne on tour in Brighton is related in *Almost a Gentleman*. Robert Fox learned from Tony Richardson that the fridge in the flat once shared with Osborne was full of Dom Perignon and oranges. Richardson was briefly Fox's father-in-law via his marriage to Natasha Richardson. Fridge in Osborne–Jill Bennett bedroom stocked with champagne (and caviar for midnight snacks) – "Why Jill Bennett Has Fridge in Her Bedroom", 15 July 1973, *Sunday Express*. According to Osborne's business manager Barry Krost, Osborne always referred to champagne as "some", e.g., "I think we'll have some."

Mike Hodges, who directed Osborne in the seminal 1970s British gangster film noir *Get Carter*, described to me the summer day he was greeted by Osborne in a boater and pinstriped blazer like something out of a touring production of *The Boyfriend*. The deckchair colours of his summery outfits were usual. Osborne's description of Nicol Williamson as a "delinquent cherub" is from *Almost a Gentleman*. The various nicknames of Osborne's wives and mistress are evident from his correspondence with them (HRHRC). The description of Osborne's performance of Hamlet, together with his mother's lacklustre response, are from *A Better Class of Person*.

The inscription on Osborne's tombstone: "Playwright Actor and Friend". Helen Osborne told me that when they were visiting Bath toward the end of her husband's life, he was impressed by a plaque that paid tribute to John Christopher Smith as "secretary and friend to Handel". The man who imagined enemies everywhere turned to his wife and exclaimed, "How wonderful to be described as a friend!"

Chapter 2: A Patriot For Us

The principal source for this chapter was Helen Osborne together with personal interviews with John Mortimer, Brian Cox, Willis Hall and the manager of The Hurst estate, Andrew Williams. Osborne gave Williams land in the grounds of The Hurst on which he built his own house.

The entries in the notebooks were made in exercise books and Reporter's Pads. Osborne scribbled notes spontaneously on anything to hand – matchbooks, napkins, cigarette packs, bits of paper. But individual notebook entries were frequently undated. The year of each notebook doesn't always indicate the same year that an entry was made. As I learned to decipher Osborne's near-illegible handwriting, various clues led me to the approximate dates of the undated notes.

"Not necolatry but pleasant comfort." On the eve of Osborne's memorial service in London, Helen Osborne wrote a moving column in the *Spectator* (3 June 1995): "My own death has lost any residual fear, John's shirts, his ties, his suits – the wardrobe of an occasional dandy – are where he left them. His pens, pipes, specs are within easy reach; not necolatry but pleasant comfort."

"'Little' was a belittling word in Osborne's vocabulary . . ." In Alan Carter's literary biography *John Osborne* (Oliver & Boyd, 1969), the erudite author points out the influence of Noel Coward on Osborne's plays "bearing in mind the dismissive use of 'little'" – as in "nasty little" or "sordid little". According to Mr Carter, the use of the word "little" occurs 353 times in Osborne's plays (but only up to *The Hotel in Amsterdam*).

The bulging cuttings books were stored in the attic of The Hurst along with various documents and editions of the plays. When Osborne's daughter Nolan left New York and first went to live with her father in Kent in June 1978, she collected newspaper cuttings about him. Osborne's 7 July 1968 *Observer* interview was with Kenneth Tynan. The reference to Violet Bonham Carter's 1961 meeting with Osborne is from *Daring to Hope: The Diaries and Letters of Violet Bonham Carter, 1946–1969* (ed. Pottle, Mark, Weidenfeld & Nicolson, 2000).

Chapter 3: Mother and Son

The major source for Osborne's relationship with both his parents was Osborne himself in the account of his early years, *A Better Class of Person*. In addition to his memoirs, notebooks and papers, principal sources for this chapter also include the letters of Osborne's mother and personal interviews with Helen Osborne, Lady Elizabeth Cavendish, Jocelyn Rickards and Osborne's former secretary, Sonia McGuinness.

The marriage certificate of Osborne's parents is dated 4 June 1929, and lists Tom Godfrey Osborne's profession as "Advertising Copy Writer and Artist". Osborne's mother, the daughter of a publican, was born in a pub named the Bramcote Arms. (documents in HRHRC). The Osborne article for the *Sunday Times* was rejected by the editor, Andrew Neil. (Osborne correspondence demanding to be paid, HRHRC).

We have several sources to confirm that Osborne supported his mother financially from his first success to her death – among them, the family correspondence in HRHRC, and Osborne's first employer, Arnold Running. Lady Elizabeth Cavendish was one among a number of witnesses who confirmed how well he looked after her. Osborne's doctor, Patrick Woodcock, regularly visited her at his son's request. The mother herself confirmed in the 1960 *Empire News* interview that her son gave her everything she needed.

The witness to Osborne's murderous shove of his mother down the staircase back-stage at the Royal Court was his manager Barry Krost, who was standing behind Osborne at the time. The date of the notebook reference to "the disease" that was the genetic curse of his mother is November 1955. The source for "I've spent a life-time trying to escape this place" was Jocelyn Rickards who was in the car with Osborne travelling along the Fulham Palace Road. Osborne told his wife Helen that his protec-tive father would say during domestic rows with his mother, "Leave the boy alone."

Osborne wrote in *A Better Class of Person* that ex-wife Jill Bennett described him as a "Welsh Fulham upstart". The *Empire News* interview with his mother was found in the 1960s cuttings book at The Hurst.

The various people who met his mother and offered a general impression of her were Lady Elizabeth Cavendish, Angela Conner (sister of third wife Penelope Gilliatt), director Anthony Page, business manager Barry Krost, secretary Sonia McGuinness and Osborne's driver Jimmy Gardner who chauffeured his mother around on shopping days.

I have found no reliable evidence that his mother complained to anyone about Osborne's public caricature of her. Sonia McGuinness, who spent time looking after her, told me that she responded to the fuss with "It was just John". McGuinness, who was secretary to Osborne when he married Gilliatt and then Bennett, was the source that they both irritated him by calling his mother "Mum". She also related how Osborne's mother said, "Mary's got the cream," when Ure married him after the success of *Look Back in Anger*.

There are 34 letters from mother to son in HRHRC. Usually undated, they were written between July 1963 and the early seventies. Osborne's polemic about his mother, entitled "Wrath", appears never to have been published. The original essay is in the Texas archives. The description of Osborne's "tough, sly old Cockney" grandmother was extracted from his 1957 essay "They Call It Cricket" (*Declaration*, ed. Tom Maschler, MacGibbon & Kee). It was sometimes assumed that next to nothing was known about Osborne's family until his 1981 autobiography. In fact, he was writing and talking about his lower-middle-class roots from the beginning of his first success. *The Entertainer* is the play most closely based on his own family.

Chapter 4: Every Day is Mother's Day to Me

I drew on several more of his mother's letters to her son for this chapter, as well as Osborne's notebook entries about her and personal interviews with his wife and Eileen Atkins. The film of *A Better Class of Person*, in which Atkins appeared as Osborne's mother and Alan Howard played his father, was first televised by Thames TV in June 1985, produced and directed by Frank Cvitanovich. There is an implication in the many rented rooms the mother lived in with her son that bartending was either an itinerent job for her or she was fleeing the bailiffs. Osborne suggests the latter when he lists all the unpaid bills. The one existing photograph of mother and son I've found was in a box kept in the attic at The Hurst. A photograph of the father was on the wall of the landing leading to Osborne's study.

It is often assumed that Tony Richardson was the driving force behind Woodfall Films. Osborne was an active partner commissioning new scripts, however. He loved films, but disliked writing them.

David Hare related to me that Osborne said that his mother told him the only play of his she liked was *A Taste of Honey*, written by Shelagh Delaney.

Chapter 5: Father and Son

The major sources of this chapter were Osborne's memoirs and private notebooks, together with a personal interview with his only close surviving relative, cousin Tony Porter. Helen Osborne was the principal witness to Osborne's severe depressions, and D.S.J. Maw, the diabetic specialist who saved Osborne's life in 1985, confirmed that Osborne resisted all forms of psychotherapy.

William Styron, *Darkness Visible: A Memoir of Madness* (Vintage Books, 1992).

The vignette about his father's side of the family was extracted from Osborne's *Declaration* essay. An edited manuscript of his BBC TV interview with John Freeman in the *Face to Face* series can be found in *The Playwrights Speak* (ed. Walter Wager, intro. John Russell Taylor, Longman, 1967).

It was the light Welsh accent of Sonia McGuinness's father that reminded Osborne of the essence of his own father.

Chapter 6: The Naked Christ

Susan Sontag, *Illness as Metaphor* (Farrar, Straus and Giroux, 1978).

The leading American doctor who caught TB and explained its stigma for me wished to remain anonymous. The portrait of the father has been expanded from Osborne's memoirs to include extracts from his detailed essay "My Father", first published by the *Sunday Telegraph*, 13 January 1963 (republished in Osborne's *Collected Prose*, *Damn You, England*, Faber & Faber, 1994). The twelve-year-old Osborne submitted his own short stories to the writing institute as well as his father's. He gave up when he found the iron-clad lessons "as intimidating as the rules laid down in *Scouting For Boys*". The narrative of his father's decline and death during the family's evacuation to Ventor in the Isle of Wight has been reconstructed from Osborne's first autobiography, the essay "My Father" and Osborne's film adaptation of the autobiography, also entitled *A Better Class of Person* (Faber & Faber, 1985).

"Those hours after he died, when I was dragged back from the corpse . . ." is from the 1953 notebook in HRHRC.

The only surviving letter from his father, 31 December 1939, is also in the Texas archives.

Chapter 7: Why Ozzy was Expelled from School

I drew heavily on Osborne's account of his boarding school days in *A Better Class of Person* for this section. The school wasn't named St Michael's, however. It was Belmont College. Osborne changed the name for legal reasons (calling it St Michael's after his daughter's school in Kent).

The letter from his fellow pupil reminding him that he was known as "Ozzy" is dated 9 December 1981 (HRHRC). The letter from Osborne's classmate to the *Sunday People*, 20 October 1957, was found in the scrapbooks at The Hurst. Osborne's school reports, *Sunday Express*, 4 October 1957. Osborne's steadfast version of hitting his headmaster was taken from his memoirs and the *Sunday Express* interview.

Chapter 8: The First Father Figure

The essential information for this chapter was provided by my personal interview with Osborne's first employer Arnold Running, together with his wife. The Osborne letters were provided by Running.

The quotation about Devine's response to his white hair and pipe is from William Gaskill, *A Sense of Direction: Life at the Royal Court* (Faber & Faber, 1988). Vivien Leigh's response to Devine's "fucking awful pipe" is from *A Better Class of Person*.

Chapter 9: The Apprentice Actor in Search of a Home

Osborne's autobiographical account of his route into repertory theatre has been informed by the unedited 941-page original manuscript of *A Better Class of Person* (HRHRC). Alan Bennett in an essay on Kafka wrote of discovering a word – *paralipomena* – for the best thoughts and jokes that had been edited out of his work for various reasons, but which he cannily used elsewhere as afterthoughts. In such a way, I have occasionally used extracts from Osborne's unedited manuscript. The description of his first meeting with Michael Hamilton of Barry O'Brien Management is an example. The same meeting was also repeated in Osborne's unproduced film script about his repertory days, provisionally entitled *No Fancy Salaries, No Queer Folk* or *An Actor's Life for Me* (HRHRC).

Osborne's 1948 pocket diary was kept at The Hurst. Another source for this chapter was a personal interview with Charles Wood. Kate Dunn's *Exit Through the Fireplace: The Great Days of Rep* (John Murray, 1998) is an invaluable account of a vanished era. Dunn also offers an important insight into the style of the traditional "Loamshire Play" by observing that the most popular stage sets of the period were a drawing room with French windows (and a piano, if required).

I owe my knowledge of the existence of Osborne's letter in the March 1952 *New Statesman* to Robert Hewison's *In Anger: British Culture in the Cold War, 1945–60* (Weidenfeld & Nicolson, 1981).

Chapter 10: What is Truth and What is Fable?

Kenneth Tynan review of Osborne's appearance in Nigel Denis's *Cards of Identity*, May 1956, is in *Curtains: Selections from the Drama Criticism and Related Writings* (Atheneum, 1961).

Osborne took a critical look at his own acting in his essay "That Awful Museum" (*Twentieth Century*, February 1961). Other opinions of Osborne the actor come from my interviews with the following who appeared onstage with him: Alan Bennett, Nigel Davenport, Frank Middlemass, Michael Blakemore and Peter Nichols.

The original 1950 notepaper of the Saga Repertory Company was found among the Osborne–Creighton letters (HRHRC). Michael Billington, *The Life and Work of Harold Pinter* (Faber & Faber, 1996). Osborne and Pinter learned their trade in provincial reps while they were both married to actresses (Pamela Lane, Vivien Merchant).

Osborne on Somerset Maugham: Introduction to *Look Back in Anger, Collected Plays*, Vol.I (Faber & Faber, 1993). Osborne letter critiquing Michael Billington's high opinion of G.B. Shaw, *Guardian*, 23 June 1977.

Chapter 11: Aunt Edna's Knitting Needles

The Arthur Miller quotations are from a personal interview as well as his autobiography *Timebends: A Life* (Penguin Books, 1995). Other books consulted for this chapter were Joan Littlewood, *Joan's Book: Joan Littlewood's Peculiar History as She*

Tells It (Minerva, 1995), Jonathan Croall, *Gielgud: A Theatrical Life, 1904–2000* (Continuum, 2001), Peter Brook, *The Empty Space* (Penguin Books, 1990), Dan Reballato, *1956 and All That: The Making of Modern British Drama* (Routledge, 1999), Peter Ackroyd, *T.S. Eliot: A Life* (Simon & Schuster, 1984). Michael Holroyd, *Bernard Shaw: The One-Volume Definitive Edition* (Vintage, 1997).

The 1952 Hobson quotation is from his essay "London Survey" reprinted in a fuller version in Dominic Shellard's *Harold Hobson: Witness and Judge* (Keele University Press, 1995). The 1954 Tynan quotation from "West End Apathy" reprinted in full in *A View of the English Stage* (Davis-Poynter, 1975).

The case for Aunt Edna: *The Collected Plays of Terence Rattigan*, Preface to Vol.11 (1953). The case for *Hobson's Choice*: Richard Eyre and Nicholas Wright, *Changing Stages: A View of British Theatre in the Twentieth Century* (Bloomsbury, 2000). In addition to Osborne's memoirs and notebooks, I drew on two of his essays: "The Revolutionary Moment" (*Tribune*, 27 March 1959) and "The Fifties" (*Daily Express*, 2 December 1959), both reprinted in *Damn You, England: Collected Prose*.

Chapter 12: The Apprentice Playwright in Search of an Audience

Osborne letters to Richard Findlater and the original manuscript of *The Great Bear* or *Minette* (HRHRC). I owe additional knowledge about the fate of *Personal Enemy* to Martin Banham, *Osborne* (Writers and Critics Series, Oliver & Boyd, 1969). The full version of Patrick Desmond's description of his visit to the Lord Chamberlain can be found in Richard Findlater, *Banned! A Review of Theatrical Censorship in Britain* (MacGibbon & Kee, 1967). Findlater is my principal source for background on the history of the Lord Chamberlain's office. Additional material: Dominic Shellard, *British Theatre Since the War* (Yale University Press, 1999).

Epitaph for George Dillon (Faber & Faber, 1958). The full portrait of Helen Henderson, the model for Ruth in the play, was extracted from Osborne's unedited manuscript of *A Better Class of Person* (HRHRC).

According to William Gaskill, the director of *Epitaph for George Dillon*, the show reopened at a different Broadway theatre soon after it flopped. The unprecedented reopening came about because Marlene Dietrich and her friends Noel Coward and Tennessee Williams petitioned producer David Merrick to keep the play running. Moss Hart and William Inge joined them. It didn't do any good.

Chapter 13: First Love, First Marriage

The primary source for this chapter was the first of two long interviews with Pamela Lane and the script of *Look Back in Anger*. Further interviews were conducted with Alan Bates, Frank Middlemass and Lynne Reid Banks.

Osborne told his wife Helen that the model for the Welshman Cliff in *Look Back in Anger* was, in fact, the Welsh actor John Rees (whom he knew at Derby). The Lane–Osborne letters are in HRHRC. So, too, are the Osborne–Creighton letters.

Chapter 14: First Divorce

This chapter draws mostly on the personal interviews with Lane and extensive quotations from the Lane–Osborne letters. Osborne's essay on Tennessee Williams, "Sex and Failure", was a review of Williams's published plays (*Observer*, 20 January 1957). "To be as vehement as he is . . ." is from the introduction to *Look Back in Anger*. The 1955 Pocket Diary is in HRHRC.

The Osborne–Lane divorce, 9 April 1957, cited the actor John Rees as co-respondent. The innocent Rees agreed to be named in order to facilitate the divorce.

Chapter 15: A Subject of Scandal and Concern

Osborne's sexuality was discussed in interviews I conducted with his alleged lover Anthony Creighton, as well as with Osborne's two surviving wives Helen Osborne and Pamela Lane, former mistress Jocelyn Rickards, substitute parents Arnold and Pam Running, former flatmate Frank Middlemass, director William Gaskill and business manager Barry Krost. I also interviewed Angela Fox for this chapter and Osborne's literary agent Gordon Dickerson.

"John Osborne's Secret Gay Love", by Nicholas de Jongh (*Evening Standard*, 24 June 1995). "The Osborne Deception" by Nicholas de Jongh (*Evening Standard*, 29 December 1994). The description of Gaskill's first meeting with Osborne and Creighton is from *A Sense of Direction: Life at the Royal Court*. I have also quoted from Tony Richardson, *The Long Distance Runner: A Memoir* (Faber & Faber, 1993). John M. East's *Max Miller: The Cheeky Chappie* (Robson Books, 1983) is the definitive work on Osborne's Music Hall hero. The Cynthia Ozack essay on biographical revelation and sexual secrets was published by the *New Republic* ("The Selfishness of Art", 10 May 1999).

Creighton also collaborated with Bernard Miller on a play, *Tomorrow with Pictures*. He died in London, aged 82, 22 March 2005.

Chapter 16: The Father Reclaims the Son

Irving Wardle's 1978 *The Theatres of George Devine* (Jonathan Cape) still remains the authoritative book on Devine. I am indebted to it in this chapter and elsewhere. I was also informed about Devine and his era by personal interviews with first-generation Royal Court directors William Gaskill and Anthony Page, first resident set designer and Devine's lover Jocelyn Herbert, the Court's first literary manager Donald Howarth, first stage manager Michael Halifax, first box-office manager Marie Shine, associate directors Peter Gill, Nicholas Wright and Bill Bryden, Devine's resident adviser George Goetschius and Arnold Wesker.

Additional reading includes *At the Royal Court: 25 Years of the English Stage Company* (ed. Richard Findlater, Amber Lane Press, 1981), Osborne's review of Wardle, *The Theatres of George Devine* (*Observer*, 28 May 1978) and his essay "On The Writer's Side" (from *At the Royal Court*), Lindsay Anderson's "Get Out and Push!" (*Declaration*, 1957), John Dexter, *The Honourable Beast: A Posthumous*

Autobiography (Nick Hern Books, 1993), *Kicking Against the Pricks : The Memoirs of Oscar Lewenstein* (Forward by Keith Waterhouse, Nick Hern Books, 1994), *Changing Stages* by Richard Eyre and Nicholas Wright, *Inside the Royal Court Theatre, 1956–1981; Artists Talk* (ed. Gresdna A. Doty and Billy J. Harbim, Louisiana State University Press, 1990), and Philip Roberts *The Royal Court Theatre and the Modern Stage* (Cambridge Studies in Modern Theatre, Cambridge University Press, 1999).

The story of how Devine first came to meet Osborne was reconstructed from six sources: my personal interviews with Jocelyn Herbert and George Goetschius; the Osborne memoirs; the extract from Devine's abandoned autobiography published in the *Sunday Telegraph*, 23 January 1966; and the memoirs of Tony Richardson and William Gaskill.

Estimates vary about the number of play manuscripts submitted to the Royal Court for its first season. Findlater said it was between 675 and 750, and Wardle 750.

Sophie and George Devine were married in 1940. Sophie Devine, her sister Margaret ("Percy") Harris and Elizabeth Montgomery were the design firm known as Motley that became established when Sir John Gielgud hired them to design his 1932 *Romeo and Juliet*. Devine's 1945 letter from Burma to Edith Evans is in HRHRC. Osborne disliked groups and improvisatory experiments: He never attended the Writers' Group meetings at 7 Lower Mall. The source for the Herman Melville quotation was Melville biographer Hershel Parker. The source for Devine's "He's going to be a dramatist worth watching" was his friend John Goodwin. Jocelyn Herbert provided me with the key surviving letter from Devine to Osborne, 11 May 1956, as well as other letters from Osborne. More of Devine's notes and cards to Osborne are in HRHRC.

Chapter 17: Proceed to Texas

The chapter is based on my archival researches in Austin, Texas, as well as the Osborne notebooks for *Look Back in Anger* in the research centre. A guide to the various collections in HRHRC is published by the University of Texas at Austin. The Library Chronicle is a record of the Center's theatre archives from 1956 to 1996.

I am indebted to William P. Germano, scholar and former vice-president at Routledge, for informing me about Francis Bacon's *"looke back vpon Anger"*, revised *Essays* (1625 edition, Oxford University Press). List of phrases like "AYM" that define the century, *Times* compilation from *Collins English Dictionaries* (November 1997). "I hate all this pharisaical twittering . . .", Kingsley Amis quoted by Tom Maschler in his introduction to *Declaration*. Artie Shaw on jazz is from Whitley Balliett ("Louis, Miles and the Duke", *New Yorker*, 25 December 2000 & 1 January 2001). Peter Hall quoting Devine on Osborne, personal interview with Hall.

Chapter 18: Critics

All dates and locations of Osborne premieres throughout the book – excluding *Déjàvu* – are from *File on Osborne* (compiled by Malcome Page, general editor Simon Trussler, Methuen, 1988). I was informed by the opinions of the drama critics quoted in the

File, as well as by the work of other leading critics. Unless otherwise stated, however, the views of Osborne's plays are my own.

The first negative reviews of the premiere of *Look Back in Anger* appear to have become more positive with the passage of time. In the 1982 reprint of the *Look Back in Anger Casebook* (Macmillan Press), its editor John Russell Taylor claimed that "the reception of the play, or at any rate of the playwright, was almost uniformly favourable". If that had been the case, Osborne wouldn't have been discouraged. Nor would the play have faced possible closure within its first week – and, with it, the end of the newly founded Royal Court.

The day after *Look Back* opened, Peter Hall was producing *Love's Labour's Lost*, his first production for the RSC, and had lunch in Stratford with its director Glen Byam Shaw (an old friend of Devine) and designer Margaret Harris (sister of Sophie Devine). Shaw and Harris were convinced the Royal Court wouldn't survive the first disastrous reviews of *Look Back*. Interviewed by Ian Hamilton in 1986, Osborne remembered the reviews as mostly "depressing", "carping" and "dismissive", and said of the opening night, "It just seemed a rather dull disappointing evening." ("Still Angry After All These Years", *Bookmark*, BBC2, 10 April 1986). Tynan recalled on *Bookmark* that he left the theatre "serenely glowing, surrounded by disgruntled middle-aged faces."

All reviews of the first-night performance of *Look Back in Anger* are reprinted in *Casebook*. The production opened in New York, 10 October 1956. The response of the leading US critics – among them, Brooks Atkinson, Walter Kerr and Mary McCarthy – were generally favourable. Osborne received the New York Critics Best Play Award.

In October 1998, the Royal National Theatre invited over 800 playwrights, directors, actors and arts critics to choose the century's most important plays. *Look Back in Anger* came fourth out of 377 works (ahead of *Long Day's Journey into Night* and *Private Lives*, but behind *A Streetcar Named Desire*, *Death of a Salesman* and *Waiting for Godot*.)

Osborne was briefly a professional theatre critic. He was the guest reviewer for one column – it was scheduled for two – in the *Sunday Telegraph*. Describing himself as "no scab and no critic either, thank God", he dismissed two Margaret Duras plays at the Cochrane Theatre as "unspeakably French". ("On Critics and Criticism", *Sunday Telegraph*, 28 August 1966).

Personal interviews for this chapter were with Peter Hall and Michael Halifax. Peregrine Worsthorne's account of meeting Osborne at the Jacaranda nightclub, *Sunday Telegraph*, 1 January 1995 ("Playwright We Still Miscast After 40 Years"). Kenneth Bradshaw – who became Sir Kenneth, Clerk of the House of Commons – was also at the Jacaranda that night and confirmed buying drinks for the broke and disconsolate Osborne. Mary McCarthy's essay on the *Hamlet* within *Look Back in Anger* was first published in *Harper's Bazaar*, April 1958 (reprinted in Mary McCarthy, *Sights and Spectacles, 1937–1958*, Heinemann, 1959).

The upturn at the Royal Court box office for *Look Back* was caused firstly by the 16 October eighteen-minute extract on BBC TV, and then by Granada TV's transmission of the entire play on 28 November. "You knew that something was happening . . ."

Keith Waterhouse, "Hidden gentleness of a man who loved to feud", *Daily Mail*, 27 December, 1994.

Chapter 19: Context is All

Principal sources for this chapter were my interviews with Alan Plater, Anthony Page, William Gaskill, Lord Harewood, Peter Gill, Ian McKellen, Alan Bates, Christopher Hampton, David Hare and Angela Fox.

I am particularly grateful to Robert Hewison's cultural history of the period, *In Anger: British Culture in the Cold War, 1945–60*, and to "The Politics of Vital Theatre", Chapter One of Dan Rebellato's *1956 and All That*. Additional reading for this chapter and others includes Brian Moynahan, *The British Century: A Photographic History of the Last Hundred Years* (Weidenfeld & Nicolson, 1997), Peter Vansittart, *In the Fifties* (John Murray, 1995), Anthony Sampson, *Harold Macmillan: A Study in Ambiguity* (Allen Lane, 1967), *The Noel Coward Diaries* (ed. Graham Payn and Sheridan Morley, Weidenfeld & Nicolson, 1982). *The Cambridge Illustrated History of British Theatre* (ed. Simon Trussler, Cambridge University Press, 1994), George Jean Nathan, *The Theatre of the Fifties* (Alfred A. Knopf, 1953), Simon Trussler, *The Plays of John Osborne: An Assessment of the Work of the Most Important English Dramatist of Our Time* (Panther Books, 1971), Martin Esslin, *Anger and After* (Methuen, 1962), Ronald Hayman, *John Osborne* (2nd edn, Heinemann, 1969), Luc Gilleman, *John Osborne, Vituperative Artist: A Reading of his Life and Work* (Studies in Modern Drama, Vol. 13, Routledge, 2001).

Also, John Lahr, ed., *The Diaries of Kenneth Tynan* (Bloomsbury, 2001). Harold Clurman, *The Fervent Years: The Story of the Group Theatre and the Thirties* (Dennis Dobson, 1946). Peter Kellner, *It Wasn't All Right, Jack* (*Sunday Times* cover story, 4 April 1993).

It remains a curious social irony that the Royal Court's Oxford-educated Lindsay Anderson and Anthony Page were both cradled in the British Empire. The sons of army men, they were born in the same military hospital in Bangalore, India, and raised by *ayahs*, or nannies.

The John Gielgud quotation is from Jonathan Croall, *Gielgud: A Theatrical Life*. The Noel Coward quotation is from *The Noel Coward Diaries*. The report of the Devine–Rattigan conversation is from Irving Wardle, *The Theatres of George Devine*, as is the source for the Devine quotation. The Royal Court "born in the ashes of the old literary theatre" is from Tony Richardson, *The Long Distance Runner: A Memoir*. The Paul Barker quotation about the "gin, hot bath and abortion" axis is from the *Times Literary Supplement*, 11 January 2002. "Don't tell anybody . . .", Angela Fox, wife of agent Robin Fox, an early board member of the Royal Court. The original *Look Back in Anger* programme advertising afternoon tea is in HRHRC. The BBC TV listings of 8 May 1956 are on *The Times* microfilm at the New York Public Library.

Shelagh Delaney said that she wrote *A Taste of Honey* in response to Rattigan's portrayal of homosexuality in his 1958 *Variations on a Theme*. The principal source of information about Joan Littlewood was her autobiography, together with a personal interview with one of her original troupe, Victor Spinetti, and Benedict Nightingale's obituary of Littlewood in the *New York Times* (24 September 2002). Osborne book review of *The Letters of Brendan Behan* (ed. E.H. Mikhail, Macmillan, 1992), *Sunday Telegraph*, 2 February 1992. ". . . about as angry as Mrs Dale's Diary" – Joan Littlewood memoirs. "The judgment and timing of a first-rate hangman cannot be acquired . . ." Albert Pierpoint, *Daily Telegraph Book of Obituaries* (ed. Hugh Massingberd, Pan Books, 1995). Graham Greene told me the story about the national anthem and north country strip clubs (Greene profile, "On the Dangerous Edge", *Observer Magazine*, 7 December 1975).

David Hare was the source for Osborne on Beckett. ". . . A formal, rather old-fashioned play", Osborne introduction to *Look Back in Anger, Collected Plays*, Vol. 1. "I want to make people feel . . ." Osborne essay "They Call It Cricket". Fuller quotations from the 1966 Osborne Symposium at the Court can be found in the *Look Back in Anger Casebook*. David Hare on *Look Back in Anger* is from his inaugural Osborne lecture, Hay-on-Wye Literary Festival, June 2002. ". . . it was a copy of John Osborne, really", personal interview with Christopher Hampton. The Kenneth MacMillan letter to Osborne, 4 October 1992, is in HRHRC.

Chapter 20: Three Prize Victims

The Times interview with Terence Rattigan, Sheridan Morley, 9 May 1977. Willis Hall was my source for J.B. Priestley's "I was angry before you buggers were born!" Mark Ravenhill, *New York Times*, 18 November 1999 ("Looking Back Warily on a Heterosexual Play"). The D.H. Lawrence quotation is from Richard Eyre and Nicholas Wright, *Changing Stages*. "God help us . . .", Arnold Wesker interview, *Guardian*, 18 November 1999 ("Angry Young Men Under Fire from Gay Writer").

In addition to Osborne's opinion of Noel Coward in his memoirs and letters, I have drawn on his book reviews of *The Noel Coward Diaries* (*New York Times Book Review*, 3 October 1982) and of Clive Fisher, *Noel Coward, Spectator*, 2 May 1992. The Coward quotation on Beckett is from my interview with Coward ("Noel Coward at 70", *Observer*, 14 December 1969). The Coward–Osborne telegram is in HRHRC. So, too, the Osborne–Coward letters. "Never, never trust a woman . . ." is from Osborne's unedited manuscript of *A Better Class of Person*. Osborne repeated the Coward conversation with variations in his published memoirs and interviews.

The view that Coward was an apostle of superficiality can be contradicted by *The Vortex*, his early 1924 play about drug addiction and closeted homosexuality. Sheridan Morley pointed out in the *Spectator* ("Coward's Courage", 16 May 1992) that *The Vortex* was first described as "dustbin drama" by Gerald du Maurier – virtually the same term that Coward used to attack the new drama at the Royal Court.

Osborne's 1993 letter to Michael Billington about the personal impact of *The Deep Blue Sea* was provided by Billington. The 1959 notebook and the Rattigan–Osborne letters are in the HRHRC.

The Donald McCullin photograph of the British Playwrights' Mafia and accompanying Osborne article, "The Theatre Critics" by John Osborne, *Sunday Times Magazine*, 18 October 1977. But there never was a meeting of the British Playwrights

Mafia, as Osborne claimed. He solicited the views of all the "members" by mail and published their response as if reporting a historic meeting (correspondence, HRHRC).

The Hilary Spurling quote on Rodney Ackland is from her essay in the programme of the National Theatre's 1995 revival of *Absolute Hell* ("The Strange Case of the Invisible Playwright").

Chapter 21: Success

The principal sources for this chapter were my interviews with Paul Scofield, Charles Wood, Tarn Bassett, Jimmy Gardner, Peter Brook, John French and Noel Davies. Mary Ure's letters to Osborne (HRHRC). Quotations from Christopher Isherwood *Diaries Volume One: 1939–1960* (ed. Katherine Bucknell, HarperCollins, 1996). The Rachel Powell quotation is from her letter to the *Observer*, 3 November 1991, protesting Osborne's critical view of Ure in the paper's serialization of *A Better Class of Person*. Other UK newspaper quotations are from the Osborne scrapbooks at The Hurst and HRHRC. Michael Halifax informed me about Osborne's customized AYM number plates on his first car. Osborne claimed defensively the car dealer who sold him the car put them on without his knowledge.

Tynan on Osborne's wealth: "The Angry Young Movement" (*Curtains*). The Osborne–Creighton letters (HRHRC). Sonia McGuinness told me of Osborne's secret money box behind his bookcase. "John Eastbourne, the Hungry Young Man", David Nathan, of *Hancock* (1st edn, William Kimber, 1969). Osborne ended his vegetarianism in a "repudiating orgy of farewell", from the unedited manuscript of his memoirs (HRHRC). Frank Rich obituary of Merrick, *New York Times*, 27 April 2000 ("David Merrick, 88, Showman Who Rules Broadway, Dies").

"Now that's the kind of woman you and I could never get near . . .", *A Better Class of Person*. The Osborne *Evening Standard* interview was dated 19 December 1959. Osborne's portrait of Oscar Beuselinck and his raunchy side were supplemented by a personal interview with Barry Krost, the *Guardian* obituary of Beuselinck, 30 July 1997 ("The Oscar goes to . . .") and the *Daily Telegraph* obituary "Oscar Beuselinck", 30 July. Osborne, the bar lady's son, occasionally referred to staff as "servents" in legal correspondence and could be insulting towards Beuselinck. "Try to be less impertinent and more efficient and remember you are highly dispensable if not indeed downright liability", telegram to Beuselinck (date unclear, HRHRC). Osborne's 1959 notebook is in HRHRC.

Chapter 22: A Typical Night on Montana Street

The night in question was reconstructed from the different perspectives of Osborne's memoirs, the Christopher Isherwood diaries, Tony Richardson's autobiography and Joan Plowright's *And That's Not All: The Memoirs of Joan Plowright* (Weidenfeld & Nicolson, 2001).

Osborne's 1962 notebook was kept at The Hurst. "Their intimate times together were planned laboriously in advance" – substantiated by Ure's letters to Osborne in the HRHRC and by my interview with Tarn Bassett. The Francine Brandt letters are in HRHRC. Sources for Richardson's overcrowded house parties – Osborne and my interview with John Mortimer. The Isherwood–Osborne correspondence is in HRHRC. So, too, Osborne's love letter to Jocelyn Rickards. The source for Brandt, the "model" and "current mistress", is the Plowright autobiography, as is ". . . dubbed 'The Girl Guide' for her trouble . . ."

". . . began to moan with delight rolling on the floor" – personal interview with Robert Shaw's former agent John French. Ure's increasing psychological problems were also described in French's biography of Shaw, *The Price of Success* (Random House, 1999). The observations about Ure's Ophelia in the Scofield *Hamlet* are from my interview with Peter Brook. Helen Osborne coincidentally interviewed Mary Ure for the *Observer*. The troubled Ure was unable to cope, however, and only a photograph of her was published. She died on 3 April 1975, aged forty-two, from an accidental overdose of alcohol and barbituarates hours after opening in a new West End play, *The Exorcist*.

Chapter 23: Take My Wife – Puhleeze!

The Entertainer (Faber & Faber, 1957). The role Arthur Miller played in Olivier's first meeting with Osborne is described in Laurence Olivier, *Confessions of an Actor* (Weidenfeld & Nicolson, 1982), as well as in Osborne's *Almost a Gentleman* and Miller's *Timebends*. Osborne's review of *Timebends*, 5 December 1987, *Spectator* (reprinted in *Damn You, England*). Both Osborne and Richardson related in their autobiographies that Olivier originally wanted Vivien Leigh to play the role of Archie Rice's elderly gin-sodden wife. During a meeting in the Oliviers' suite at the Connaught Hotel, Richardson tactfully explained that she was much too beautiful for the role and Olivier astonished him by suggesting she could play her in a rubber mask. "Rubber masks! Oh, my dear God," Richardson exclaimed afterwards.

"It's just a travesty on England . . ." is from *Timebends*. Anthony Holden, author of *Laurence Olivier: A Biography*, informed me that, years before *The Entertainer*, Olivier played a failed comic named "Larry Oliver" as a party trick for friends. Source for Olivier's "all that anti-Queen shit . . .", Richardson autobiogaphy. Lord Harewood told me his account of the Royal Court council rejecting both the production of *The Entertainer* and Olivier. Oscar Lewenstein gave his own version in his autobiography. "You must be balmy . . .", Elaine Blond quoted by Richard Findlater in *At the Royal Court*.

I owe my knowledge of Peter Barnes's 1978 *Laughter* and its grotesque metaphor of comedy to Christopher Innes, *Modern British Drama*. Osborne interview with Melvyn Bragg, *Observer*, 8 June 1986. Osborne letter about Brecht, *Sunday Times*, 30 September 1956. Devine letter to Brecht about Osborne, HRHRC. Osborne article on Music Hall, *Observer*, 20 April 1975 ("On the Halls", reprinted in *Damn You, England*). I interviewed Keith Waterhouse about Osborne and Music Hall. "He once had a waiter in such stitches . . ." is from Waterhouse, *Daily Mail*, 22 December 1994. Osborne on Sid Field, *Spectator*, 21 May 1994. Philip Larkin's Music Hall metaphor is from the introduction to his *Collected Poems* (Farrar, Straus and Giroux, 1989). The source for Osborne on James Cagney was a personal interview with Ben Walden. Tynan on Max Wall, *The Diaries of Kenneth Tynan* (ed. John Lahr). My profile of Ken Dodd was published in the *Observer Magazine*, 14 November 1966.

"D'you give in? . . ." – Eric Shorter provided me with Osborne's 7 July 1993 letter to him about Ken Dodd. The David Hare quotation, from his Arvon lecture at the Hay-on-Wye Festival. Peter Bowles on Osborne is quoted from Tony Palmer's film documentary on Osborne, Channel 4, May 2006. "No English playwright has put the English language on the line like this . . .", Nicholas Wright, *Ninety-Nine Plays* (Methuen, 1992). The Al Alvarez quotation about Beckett is from Eric Bentley, *The Theatre of Commitment and Other Essays on Drama in our Society* (Methuen & Co., 1968). Mary McCarthy on *The Entertainer*, "A New Word", McCarthy collected essays, *Sights and Spectacles*.

John Fisher's *Funny Way to be a Hero* (Frederick Muller, 1973) was among the books about music hall on Osborne's library shelves at The Hurst. Fisher's book is the jewel in the crown and it informed this chapter together with other expert opinion on the halls and variety such as Roger Wilmut, *Kindly Leave The Stage! The Story of Variety from 1919–1960* (Methuen, 1985), *The Book of Comic and Dramatic Monologues* (compiled and edited by Michael Marshall, Elm Tree Books/Hamish Hamilton, 1981), Roy Hudd with Phil Hiddin, *Cavalcade of Variety Acts: A Who Was Who of Light Entertainment 1945–60* (Robson Books, 1988), *Roy Hudd's Book of Music-Hall, Variety and Showbiz Anecdotes* (Robson Books, 1993), and *American Vaudeville As Seen By Its Contemporaries* (edited and with a commentary by Charles W. Stein, Alfred A. Knopf, 1984).

Chapter 24: Good, Brave Causes

My interviews for this chapter included Michael Foot, Al Alvarez, Keith Waterhouse and Eric Bentley. My view of Osborne's politics is based on several of his essays and letters to the press: "A Writer in his Age", *London Magazine*, 1957; "Fighting Talk", *Reynolds News*, 17 February 1957; "The Socialist Once Angry", letter to the *Daily Herald*, 14 March 1962; "Market Swindlers", *Tribune*, 12 October 1967; "Supporting the Cause", *Encounter*, September 1967; "Voting Pattern", *Observer*, 6 October 1974; a feature on the Common Market for the *Daily Mail*, 2 June 1975; and "A Working Man", *The Times*, 23 January 1973.

Osborne was raised on a weekly fix of the *Tribune* and *New Statesman* – my interview with Arnold Running, the Osborne–Creighton letters. The John Wells quotation was from "Music music music", *Spectator*, 12 July 1968. "Look at that human garbage", interview with Barry Krost. Osborne's essay on Swift is in HRHRC. Osborne on "feeling", "They Call It Cricket" (*Declaration*). Osborne on Williams, *Observer*, 20 January 1957. Hobson on *Look Back*, Harold Hobson, *Theatre in Britain, 1920–1983* (Phaidon Press Limited, 1984). Osborne, "My Moscow", *Sunday Times*, 4 and 11 August 1957. "This Bus Does Not Sing", interview with Keith Waterhouse.

The section on political plays was informed by interviews with Eric Bentley and by Bentley's "The Pro and Con of Political Theatre", *The Theatre of Commitment*

(Methuen 1967). John Peter on Osborne, *Sunday Times*, 13 August 1989 and
1 January 1995. Richard Eyre, *Utopia & Other Places* (Vintage, 1994). Peregrine
Worsthorne, "The Angry Young Man at Sixty", Profile, *Sunday Telegraph*, 10
December 1989. Anthony Sampson on *Look Back* in "Home Thoughts", *Independent
Magazine*, 26 August 1989. Osborne on architecture – his letters to the *Daily Telegraph*,
13 and 19 August 1964.

Chapter 25: Damn You, England

"Letter to my Fellow Countrymen", *Tribune*, 18 August 1961 (reprinted in Osborne
Casebook). "The very worst it could do . . .", Archbishop of Canterbury quotation
on the H-Bomb from Peter Vansittart, *In the Fifties*. The letters to *Tribune* for and
against Osborne were read in the *Tribune* library. "Well, this is a rum do . . .", inter-
view Sonia McGuinness. Osborne gave his scrawled, original draft for his "letter of
hate" to George Devine as a souvenir. (It was shown to me by Jocelyn Herbert.)
"Are these oranges from South Africa?", interview Barry Krost. My account of the
CND marches was supplemented by *In the Fifties*, William Gaskill's autobiography,
Robert Hewison's *In Anger* and George Goetschius's essay "The Royal Court in its
Social Context" provided by the author. "May God gag all actresses forever", Osborne,
Encounter, September 1967.

Osborne at the 17 September 1961 rally in Trafalgar Square is based on his account
in *Almost a Gentlement*, his *Encounter* essay and my interview with Doris Lessing.
Frank Kermode on Lessing, *Times Literary Supplement*, 14 September 1997. Lessing
wrote three plays (*Each his Own Wilderness*, *Play With a Tiger* and an adaptation of
The Storm) and guested for Tynan as the *Observer* drama critic for six weeks. Doris
Lessing, *Walking in the Shade: Volume Two of my Autobiography, 1949–1962*
(HarperCollins, 1994).

Chapter 26: The Biggest Floperoo Ever

The World of Paul Slickey (Faber & Faber, 1959).The Machievellian plot by Emile
Littler, producer of *Slickey*, to get his own show banned by the censor was revealed
in the files of the Lord Chamberlain in the British Library. The account of the *Slickey*
disaster is based on Osborne's supplemented by a personal interview with Jocelyn
Rickards. In a letter to the *Observer*, 3 November 1991, Adrienne Corri, one of the
stars of the show, remembered, "Miss Ure's pain and misery when Mr Osborne publicly
paraded his liaison with Miss Rickards in front of the cast during the rehearsals of
Slickey" and that "Mr Osborne sat off-stage weeping, while we, the cast, took the
boos of the audience on the first night . . ."

Coward quote on his own distastrous *Sirocco* – *Observer* interview with myself.
Osborne on *Slickey's* critics – *New York Times*, 8 May 1959 (quoted in *File on Osborne*).
Osborne's own collection of *Slickey's* negative first-night reviews, "A Night to
Remember", published in *A Night at the Theatre* (ed. Ronald Harwood Methuen,
1982).

Chapter 27: Runaway Lovers

The principal source of this chapter was Osborne's mistress, Jocelyn Rickards. Rickards provided me with all Osborne's letters to her (now in HRHRC). I also interviewed her husband Clive Donner, Sonia McGuinness and Zoe Caldwell. ". . . an outstanding capacity for friendship", Graham Greene quoted from Rickards, *The Painted Banquet: My Life and Loves* (Weidenfeld & Nicolson, 1987). Vanessa Redgrave on Penelope Gilliatt, *Vanessa Redgrave: An Autobiography* (Random House, 1994).

Chapter 28: Another Perfect House Party

The South of France house party was reconstructed from five sources: my interviews with three of the guests, Jocelyn Rickards, Don Bachardy and Jocelyn Herbert, together with Osborne's account in *Almost a Gentleman* and the letters of Osborne and Gilliatt. Angela Conner – Gilliatt's sister – provided me with most of the Osborne–Gilliatt letters quoted here and in later chapters. The rest of their correspondence is in HRHRC.

Richardson's distinctive voice and accent were widely impersonated. Osborne mimicked him making pronouncements like, "Well, *I* didn't invite them all, did you, Johnny?" His favourite was Richardson's, "Well, what did you *expect?*" The Christopher Isherwood quotations are from the forthcoming volume of his *Diaries* (to be published by Random House).

Chapter 29: The Case of Osborne's Son

The major sources for this chapter were the divorce documents and legal correspondence in HRHRC, Osborne's account of events in *Almost a Gentleman*, and personal interviews with John French, Jocelyn Rickards, Donald Howarth, Tarn Bassett, Helen Osborne and Noel Davis.

Chapter 30: Spritual Longing

Luther (Faber & Faber, 1961). Osborne on his source for *Luther* in *John Obsborne: A Casebook* (Casebook Series, Macmillan). Tynan review of *Luther*, *Observer*, 9 July 1961 (republished in *A View of the English Stage*). Hobson review of *Luther*, *Sunday Times*, 30 July 1961. A compromised Osborne asked for Penelope Gilliatt's quotation from her rave review of *Luther* in *Queen Magazine* to be removed from the marquee over the entrance to the Phoenix Theatre (19 October 1961, letter to his lawyer, HRHRC). Alan Bates on Osborne – my interview with Bates. *A Subject of Scandal and Concern* (Faber & Faber, 1961). Also, Osborne's satirical 1960 "The Epistle to the Philistines", published in *Look Back in Anger* Casebook Series. Dr Eric H. Erikson, *Young Man Luther, A Study in Psychoanalysis and History* (W.W. Norton, 1958).

Chapter 31: Third Marriage

The personal interviews for this chapter were with Angela Conner, Doug Hayward, Lady Elizabeth Cavendish, David Astor, Michael Davie. Anthony Sampson, Sonia McGuinness and Helen Osborne. The quotations from Ben Sonnenberg, Lord Snowdon and Kathleen Tynan are from the obituaries of Gilliatt in the *Independent* and *Guardian*. "Penelope always greets you as if you had suffered a grievous loss", Osborne, *Almost a Gentleman*, though the original source was Terence Kilmartin of the *Observer*. "Damn you, Osborne" placards and interviews with Hellingly protestors, *Sussex Express & County Herald*, 29 September 1961, scrapbook at The Hurst. William Hardcastle private letter to editor of the *Daily Mail*, 26 September 1961 (HRHRC).

The Blood of the Bamburgs, published with *Under Plain Cover*, under joint title *Plays for England* (Faber & Faber, 1963). Censors' reports, Lord Chamberlain archives, British Library. Re: the 'knicker play': in the Osborne archives in Texas is a long, lingering advertisement for best-quality girls' school bloomers. "How I wish *I* had written this superb piece of prose!" Osborne has written in its margin. The gross profits of *Tom Jones* of $244.7 million, taking into account ticket-price inflation as of 23 January 2002, is from Boxofficereport.com. The equivalent gross profit of the 1963 *Lawrence of Arabia* is $287.7 million. *Tom Jones* film script (Faber & Faber, 1964). Osborne and Gilliatt wrote *Panic Stations* together – an original Woodfall Rank comedy that was never produced (outline in HRHRC). Osborne's bills and receipts, ibid. Devine–Osborne correspondence, ibid. "Johnny will be forever", personal interview Sonia McGuinness.

Chapter 32: Inadmissible Evidence

Inadmissible Evidence (Faber & Faber, 1965). "His own accuser . . .", Walter Kerr, *New York Herald Tribune*, October 1965. Robert Brustein on *Inadmissible* from *The Third Theatre* (Cape, 1970), quoted in *File on Osborne*. ". . . the foul rag and bone of the heart", from Yeats poem, "The Circus Animals' Desertion". *Inadmissible* and Nicol Williamson audition, my interview with director Anthony Page. Williamson on Williamson, Tony Palmer 2006 TV documentary on Osborne. Gilliatt letter to Osborne about *Inadmissible* (HRHRC). Pamela Lane confirmed that when she was at Bromley Rep she was offered the role of the lover Helena in *Look Back*, but wasn't thought suitable for the role of Jimmy Porter's wife. Osborne's working methods, interview Sonia McGuinness. His notes to McGuinness were in her possession. The 1972 and 1993 notebooks were at The Hurst. Christine Stotesbury on Osborne, Gilliatt and the newly born Nolan, personal interview with Stotesbury.

Chapter 33: A Patriot For Me

A Patriot for Me (Faber & Faber, 1966). "Notes for a New Play" (HRHRC). James Fenton, "A Patriot's Last Refuge", *Sunday Times*, 1983. ". . . high Hapsburg queerdom", Ronald Bryden, *The Unfinished Hero* (Faber & Faber, 1983), quoted in *File on Osborne*.

"Why did Osborne do this?" Mary McCarthy, *Observer*, 4 July 1965. Kenneth Tynan, "Missing Osborne's Point", letter to *Observer*, 18 July 1965.

Additional reading for this chapter included Osborne's evidence before the Joint Committee on Censorship of the Theatre, 29 November 1966 (documents in HRHRC). Richard Findlater, *Theatrical Censorship in Britain*. Nicholas de Jongh, *Politics, Prudery and Perversions – The Censoring of the English Stage, 1901–1968* (Methuen, 2001). Luc Gilleman, *John Osborne, Vituperative Artist*. Interview with Peter Gill, director of 1995 RSC revival of *Patriot*, 17 October 1995, *Daily Telegraph*. All quotations from censors and correspondence with Lord Chamberlain's office, Lord Chamberlain archives, British Library. Olivier was one of the theatre grandees who visited Lord Cobbold to plead the case of *Patriot*.

"I am getting out just in time . . .", Wardle biography of Devine. Osborne's share of *Patriot* production costs was £7,500. I am indebted to Michael Feingold of the *Village Voice* for his information on the history of gay theatre in New York. The insights into casting A *Patriot for Me* were provided by the Wardle biography, *Robert Stephens, Knight Errant – Memoirs of a Vagabond Actor* (Hodder & Stoughton, 1995), together with personal interviews with Anthony Page, Jocelyn Herbert, Peter Gill and Edward Fox. Paul Newman turned down the role of Redl, Newman letter to Osborne (HRHRC). Before the New York transfer of *Patriot*, Osborne threatened the all-powerful David Merrick with forgetting the whole enterprise if he interfered with the production. "As I think I've told you before, neither my reputation nor my livelihood depends upon Broadway. Thank the good Lord." (8 March 1966 letter to Merrick, HRHRC).

The *coup de grâce* to the Lord Chamberlain's office was finally delivered by Edward Bond's 1965 *Saved*. "And art made tongue-tied by authority . . ." Sonnet LXVI. Gilliatt's telegram to Jill Bennett (HRHRC). Bennett's recurring dream, interview with Nicholas Wright. Other sources on Bennett for this chapter included personal interviews with Patrick Procktor, Sonia McGuinness, Jocelyn Rickards, Pamela Lane, Angela Conner and John Copley.

Chapter 34: The Death of George Devine

How Osborne learned of Devine's death is from his own account in *Almost a Gentleman*. Other sources include my interview with Jocelyn Herbert, the last letters of Devine to Osborne (provided by Herbert), Osborne's letter to Herbert (ibid.), and Osborne's tribute to Devine, *Observer*, 23 January 1966. The full text of his curtain speech on the last night of A *Patriot for Me* is in HRHRC. According to Irving Wardle, Osborne, Gilliatt and Joan Plowright kept a round-the-clock vigil by Devine's bedside with Herbert. Tony Richardson interrupted filming of *Mademoiselle* in France to join them. All Devine's medical expenses were paid by Osborne and Richardson.

On the death of Devine, Nellie Beatrice compared Osborne's father to Devine in an undated letter to Gilliatt: "He was so much like Daddy . . . so I shall be going through just as much pain (believe me)." The Royal Court's first box-office lady, interview with Marie Shine. William Gaskill related how Devine's funeral at the Golders Green Crematorium was a tense occasion "because Sophie, George's wife, and Jocelyn, his mistress, were both there and we felt that where we sat in the chapel was a declaration of our loyalties".

Chapter 35: Breakdown

Osborne's 1966 private notebook with his scattered notes made at the clinic was a major source for this chapter (the notebook is in HRHRC), as was my interview with his doctor Patrick Woodcock. The notes in the clinic are dated 21 September 1966, to the last entry on 5 October. My interviews with his visitors in the clinic were with Jocelyn Herbert, Anthony Page, Sonia McGuinness and Jocelyn Rickards. "Send sticky buns . . ." letter in HRHRC. Jill Bennett–Osborne correspondence (ibid.). Gilliatt letters to Osborne in clinic (ibid.). An insomniac, Osborne purchased sleep conditioning tapes on 5 April 1965 (documents in HRHRC). Dinner with the upset Osborne, personal interview with Leonard Rosoman. Peggy Ramsey's "John Osborne slept here" – told to me by Christopher Hampton. William Hickey announcement, 8 July 1966, scrapbooks at The Hurst.

A Bond Honoured (Faber & Faber, 1966). Background on how the English translation of the play was discovered by Tynan at the National Theatre, interview with Eric Bentley. A full account is to be found in Arnold P. Hinchcliffe, *John Osborne*. "John Osborne's Perfect Hero", Ronald Bryden, *Observer*, 12 June 1966, extracted from *File on Osborne*. 9 June telegram to *The Times* and seven national critics with their responses, HRHRC. Osborne paid £250 for writing *A Bond Honoured*, "On Critics and Criticism", *Sunday Telegraph*, 28 August 1966.

Description of backstage scenes at the Old Vic Devine gala, Robert Stephens memoir together with personal interviews with Helen Montagu, Angela Conner and Jocelyn Herbert. "Strong character, weak temperament", personal interview with Anthony Page. When Gilliatt lived with Mike Nichols in New York, Osborne sent his ex-wife a doll with all its hair shaved off that was ostensibly meant for his daughter. Nichols has alopecia. Osborne's friendship with Herbert subsequently cooled when she advised him not to leave Gilliatt. "Do please count to ten . . ." (Herbert letters to Osborne in her possession).

Chapter 36: The Real Thing

Time Present, published with *The Hotel in Amsterdam* (Faber & Faber, 1966). Among Jill Bennett's close friends I interviewed about her were Helen Montagu, Dr Patrick Woodcock, Barry Krost, Anthony Page, Patrick Procktor and Ian McKellen. Others I interviewed who knew her included her ex-husband Willis Hall, Angela Marber, Paul Scofield, Tarn Bassett, David Kernan, Jocelyn Rickards, Pamela Lane, John and Suzanne Goodwin, John Copley, Michael Blakemore, Richard Eyre, Robert Fox, Edward Fox, Sonia McGuinness, John Standing, Valerie Newman, Angela Conner, Nicholas Wright and Peter Eyre.

"John Osborne has grown a moustache . . ." *Observer*, 6 August 1967. "I've Met My Match At Last", Bennett interview, *Daily Mail* 23 September 1967. "Why Jill Bennett Has a Fridge In Her Bedroom", *Sunday Express* 15 July 1973. "Jill Bennett

On Being An Actress, Talking to John Heilpern", *Observer*, 2 September 1973. "Thus do the angry young men . . ." Martin Esslin "Anger Twelve Years On", *Plays and Players*, July 1968, quoted from *File on Osborne*. "Never marry an actress . . ." personal interview with Christopher Hampton. "Such sad words . . ." interview with Paul Scofield. Bennett–Osborne correspondence, HRHRC. Jill Bennett, *Godfrey: A Special Time Remembered* (Hodder & Stoughton, 1983).

Chapter 37: My Dear Tony

Osborne–Richardson letters, HRHRC. The differing version of events is from their autobiographies. "Case Reviewed" by Christopher Mulroony (www.paramater magazine.org/Osborne.him) was helpful background on the plagiarism lawsuit, with extracts from Charles Wood's account, "Into the Valley", *Sight and Sound*, 1992. "Blue skies and buggery . . .", Osborne notebook. "I am here at your bidding . . .", my interview with Neil Hartley for "The Making of Charge of the Light Brigade", *Observer Magazine*, April 1968. "They have to keep paying you for the drafts", personal interview Charles Wood. One of the very few plays Osborne directed was Wood's *Meals on Wheels* for the Royal Court, 30 June 1965.

Chapter 38: Lost Illusions

Personal interviews for this chapter were with Willis Hall, Angela Marber, Dr Patrick Woodcock and Sonia McGuinness, together with Scofield, McKellen and Page. "Fear, always fear for my sanity . . ." is from the 1972 notebook in HRHRC. According to McGuinness, Jill Bennett also cut the lining out of Oscar Beuselinck's overcoat during a Christmas party at Chelsea Square. During his rows with Bennett, Osborne deposited his manuscripts with his bank during the summer of 1974 because of "JB's Hedda Gabler proclivities" (legal correspondence, HRHRC). "I knew the quality of his writing voice . . .", interview with Scofield. Osborne tribute to Barry Humphries, 13 October 1969 (original copy in HRHRC). Tennessee Williams, *The Catastrophe of Success* (New Directions, 1999).

Chapter 39: The Chapter of Accidents

Personal interviews for this chapter were with David Hare, Maximilian Schell, Mike Hodges, John Standing, Nicholas Wright, Frank Dunlop, Helen Montagu and Barry Krost. *Sunday Times* picture of Osborne with Hare, Storey and Whitehead, 9 May 1971. "John seemed shiningly confident . . .", from Hare's Arvon lecture. ". . . the whammy . . .", interview with Hare. *West of Suez* (Faber & Faber, 1971). "The play is about the decaying of tongues . . ." Osborne, *Evening Standard*, 30 July 1971, quoted in *File on Osborne*. It also links with Osborne's 1974 TV play *The Gift of Friendship* whose hero is an elderly dying writer played by Alec Guinness.

Gary O'Connor reports in his biography of Ralph Richardson (*The Actor's Life*, Applause Theatre Books) that Richardson cut the lengthy *West of Suez* himself during performances by deliberately missing out entire passages of the script and ploughing on, regardless. When Osborne went backstage to have a word with him about it, the eccentric Richardson pre-empted him by saying he must be getting senile.

Osborne claimed that Helen Dawson gave *West of Suez* its only positive review. ("This is a brave and loving play", *Observer*, 22 August 1971). But Hobson's was favourable (*Sunday Times*, 10 October 1971) and Billington's in the *Guardian*, 7 October 1971 (republished in Michael Billington *One Night Stands – A Critic's View of Modern British Theatre*, Nick Hern Books, 1993).

David Mercer's *The Parachute*, BBC TV, 21 January 1968. *First Love*, directed by Maximilian Schell, was nominated for an Academy Award for its director. "Anyone can act in films . . .", personal interview with Schell. "I was surprised every time I met John . . .", personal interview with Mike Hodges. "I have been destructive . . .", Bennett letter found in Osborne's 1972 notebook at The Hurst. "Spiegel of Arabia" letters in HRHRC. Osborne 27 August 1968 cable to Cukor, ibid. Michael Medwin on *Gross*, ibid and his *Guardian* tribute on Osborne's death. "Grand Old Upper–Class Theatre", Tynan on Osborne's gout, letter in HRHRC. Osborne letter to Faber & Faber, 13 July 1973, ibid. Barry Krost on life with Osborne and Bennett, personal interview. "John's just tried to murder to me . . .", source Helen Montagu. "Why I Peep At Girls", Bennett, *Sunday People*, 4 August 1974. Sunday lunch with the Osbornes, personal interview Helen Montagu. The "murder" incident – my interview with Barry Krost.

A Sense of Detachment (Faber & Faber, 1973). About the production – personal interviews with director Frank Dunlop and John Standing. "Pity you weren't driving Denise Coffey . . .", interview Nicholas Wright. "Returned with disgust", Nicholas Wright. "My favourite play is *Pyjama Tops* . . .", Osborne interview with Mark Amory, *Sunday Times*, 24 November 1974. "There are times when roughhouse methods are called for . . . .", Rachel Kempson, *Daily Telegraph*, 24 January 1973.

Barry Krost's tolerance of Osborne's apparent anti-Semitism and homophobia is more typical of his friends than his critics. When I asked another gay friend of Osborne's, Donald Howarth, whether he ever said anything to him about his anti-gay remarks, he put his hand jokily on his hip and replied, "Well, that would have been very *queenie* of me, wouldn't it?"

Osborne goaded and attacked all politicized groups – from militant feminists and righteous banner-waving CND marchers, to well-meaning New Age vicars and the gay lib movement. (Ian McKellen was therefore described as "beaming his homosexuality from every lighthouse".) There are a number of examples of Osborne's homophobia and anti-Semitism in the notebooks. Among them: "Never work for a poof or a Jew" (1971). "That twisting, humiliating squalid agent. Jewish Facist. Cold, brainy" (1971). "So miss the queens. Always. Memo: Never try to make a *friend* of a homosexual. If he can't really participate in your humiliation or despair, he knows he can't destroy you" (1972). "Shifty Jewish bastard," he wrote to Creighton in the 1950s about a literary agent.

Such offensive remarks are unacceptable, and Osborne used them as a social style, particularly in the needling public malice he shared with Jill Bennett. But it is important to point out that neither the notebooks nor the books are rife with them. Unlike the virulent biases of T.S. Eliot, or Philip Larkin and Kingsley Amis, Osborne's weren't central to him. In younger days, he publicly supported homosexual artists (the director John Dexter, among them). And where it mattered most – in his plays – the characteristic message isn't one of intolerance. In A Patriot for Me, he made his sympathetic version of the homosexual Colonel Redl a Jew – turning him into a metaphor of the ultimate persecuted outsider – although the real Redl wasn't a Jew. In Luther, he ignored the anti-Semitism of the founder of Protestantism who compared Jews to a "brood of vipers" and wrote the 1543 "The Jews and Their Lies". It is often overlooked, too, that in Inadmissible Evidence the frightened character named Maples is a sympathetic portrait of a hunted-down homosexual.

Chapter 40: Watch It Come Down

Personal interviews for this chapter were with Robin Dalton, Clive Donner, Bill Bryden, Christopher Hampton, Michael Halifax and Helen Osborne. Apart from the Belgravia house Osborne left in trust for his daughter, he paid her school fees and child maintenance. The story of his meeting with Gilliatt at Chester Square is from the final chapter of Almost a Gentleman. Osborne's unperformed A Place Calling Itself Rome, adaptation of Shakespeare's Corialonus (Faber & Faber, 1973). Harold Bloom's "killing machine", Shakespeare: The Invention of the Human (Riverhead Books, 1998).

The End of Me Old Cigar opened in Greenwich on 16 January 1975 (Faber & Faber, 1975). The Picture of Dorian Gray opened in Greenwich on 13 February 1975 (Faber & Faber, 1973). Robin Dalton told me about the talk of casting Jill Bennett as Dorian Gray. "He left her not because she has failed him . . .", personal interview with Dalton. Dalton also provided Bennett's letters to her. Watch It Come Down (Faber & Faber, 1975). Peter Hall's Diaries (ed. John Goodwin, Hamish Hamilton, 1983). Osborne's dislike of Joan Plowright might have escalated for unexpected reasons. According to Helen Osborne, Olivier, admiring the Osborne dogs during a visit to Kent, told her husband that he had always wanted a white Alsatian. Osborne sent him a gift of a white Alsatian puppy and Plowright refused to let him have it. Plowright denied the story in her memoirs, saying the decision was left to Olivier. John Mortimer told me, however, that when Olivier first saw the Alsatian he stepped back in alarm and fell into his swimming pool.

Hanif Kureishi letter to Osborne, 3 January 1975 (HRHRC). "J.B. complaining more and more", 1973 notebook. Edward Albee letter to Osborne, 10 August 1976 (HRHRC). Osborne's response to Albee, 22 August 1976 (ibid, and quoted in Mel Gussow, Edward Albee, A Singular Journey, Applause Books, 2001). "Too much bile in the stream", Osborne notebook, 8 March 1973.

Chapter 41: A Better Class of Person

Principal interviews for this chapter were with Helen Osborne, together with Helen Montagu, Norene Thomas and Jennifer Johnson. ". . . deep, deep peace" – Mrs Patrick Campbell's "hurlyburly of the chaise longue compared to the deep, deep peace of the double bed". The Osborne letters to his wife were kept at The Hurst. So, too, her inscribed copy of Look Back in Anger. "It Takes Guts to Survive

When You're in the Public Eye", Jill Bennett interview, *Cosmopolitan*, June 1977.
"Osborne's met a better woman than you!", Helen Osborne. "Adolf's
Anonymous", Willis Hall. Osborne letter to Jocelyn Rickards, 7 May 1994, now
in HRHRC. Osborne on dogs, *Spectator*, 7 May 1994. Bennett–Osborne correspondence, the divorce documents, testimony and rulings, HRHRC. Gilliatt eventually
waived Osborne's £1,000 a year maintenance for Nolan. The trustees for the
Belgravia house left in trust for Nolan were Sir Hugh Casson and Jocelyn Herbert.
Legally, Osborne was entitled to see his daughter six weeks a year. Beuselinck letter
to Osborne, 14 July 1970, "I may be a philistine in these matters [art, theatre], but
boy – you're a philistine in the law."

Helen Osborne provided me with her diary of the first weeks in Kent. "I think
we all knew that John lived somewhere in Edenbridge . . .", personal interview
Norene Thomas. "It's a good memory I have of being with them . . .", Jennifer
Johnson. Osborne, 12 April 1976 apology to Harold Hobson, letters HRHRC.
Osborne's postcard warning "Fatty Morley – Watch out on dark nights" was kindly
provided to me by Sheridan Morley. The story of Benedict Nightingale's woozy
Playwright Mafia warning, personal correspondence with Nightingale. David Nathan
told me of Osborne's postcard threat to Wardle and Levin. Nathan maintained that
at a meeting of the Drama Critics Circle, those who didn't receive a threat felt left
out. Francis King's response to Osborne calling him a cunt, letters in HRHRC.
Charles Wood listed the British Playwright Mafia as his club in *Who's Who*. Its
modern equivalent is "The Monsters", a loosely based association formed by a group
of new British playwrights to assassinate elderly critics on opening nights.

Chapter 42: Country Matters

"I just want simple, familiar, English comforts" – letter to Jocelyn Rickards. Principal
sources for this chapter were the personal interviews with Helen Osborne, Christine
Stotesbury, Evelyn Halpert, Elizabeth M. Lee, Eafor Ali, Sir Simon and Lady Bland,
Pam Gregg, Pat Clark (aka Claire Lorrimer) and Mel Hack, Jenny Forbes, Mr and
Mrs John Diplock. Osborne letters to his lawyer on violence in New York and the
US educational system, 3 February 1969 and 4 May 1971, HRHRC. John Gale, "the
Green Line Belt", *Observer*, 11 January 1970.

In early March 1978, Osborne pleaded guilty to harassing the live-in couple who
looked after his house in Edenbridge. He had cut off their electricity when they
refused to leave and was fined £40. "What a lot of brutish idly constituted lives . . ."
Gilliatt letter to Osborne, HRHRC. "God, I'm getting (a) more chauvinistic . . ."
4 February 1980 letter to Rickards, ibid. Osborne on his religious "conversion",
Spectator, 22 December 1984. Additional reading: letters to *The Times* opposing
Alternative Service Book, 17 November 1979, 20 June 1980, and 25 November
1980. "The Book of Common Prayer", *The Oldie*, 11 December 1992 (reprinted in
Damn You, England). Canon R.J. Mason letter of 29 January 1982 to Osborne,
HRHRC. ". . . one to whom God was a reality . . .", quotation from Canon Mason
letter to Peter Whitebrook, 6 November 1996.

A transcription of Osborne's 27 February 1982 *Desert Island Discs* was made from the tape at The Hurst. "The Biographer/Critic versus The Wife", 1983 notebook at The Hurst. The source of the David Merrick–Nicol Williamson incident was Anthony Page. "Stare dozily out of the window", from "Months in the Country", original article in HRHRC. Osborne's link with Cornwall was John Betjeman. The beloved Betjeman shared with Osborne an insular sentimentality about England. He was also a champagne-drinking depressive who identified so closely with Osborne's Bill Maitland that he signed an enthusiastic letter to the playwright about *Inadmissible Evidence*, "Bill Maitland-Betjeman".

Typical Cranmer Summer Ball invites were shown to me by Charles Wood and Peter Nichols. "Melvyn Bragg Meets John Osborne", *Observer*, 8 June 1986. "Someone somewhere thinks you are a shit . . .", legal correspondence (HRHRC). Beuselinck warning to Osborne, 8 December 1980 (ibid.). In a 30 March 1980 letter to his former secretary Sonia McGuinness. Osborne asked her to send Bennett an abusive telegram anonymously while he was abroad on vacation "or I'll get carted off to jail". Bennett was opening at the Royal Court as Gertrude in *Hamlet*. "NOW AT YOUR AGE THE HEYDAY IN THE BLOOD IS TAME. That should give her a mild heart attack."

Chapter 43: What Happened to Nolan

The basis for the chapter was my interview with Osborne's daughter, Nolan Parker. I separately interviewed her surrogate father, the Reverend Guy Bennett. According to Bennett, Osborne refused to return his daughter's diary hinting that he intended to use it for his memoirs. Nolan's friend and former nanny Christine Stotesbury was another source for this chapter. I also interviewed Helen Osborne for her point of view as well as several members of the Edenbridge community.

The school reports are in HRHRC. ". . . insolently smug . . . devotedly suburban", Osborne on Nolan, interview with Lynn Barber, *Independent on Sunday*, 2 February 1992. "Daughter Spurned by Angry Old Man", Mary Corbett, *Daily Express*, 4 May 1992. Bennett provided me with one of Osborne's personal letters to him. All other correspondence in this chapter is in HRHRC. The Old Bailey trial on 28 May 1999 was attended on my behalf by Paula Hogben. "Former vicar is jailed for assaults", *Daily Telegraph*, 29 May 1999.

Chapter 44: En Route to Shropshire

Personal interviews for this chapter were with consultant physician D.S.J. Maw, Dr Jill Gray, Peter Hall, Dominic Lawson, Peter Forrester, Tony Palmer and Helen Osborne. "To your health . . .", all Osborne–Maw correspondence provided by Maw. "Wines for Diabetic", HRHRC. Dr Marsh's 10 June 1982 medical report, ibid. Bernard Levin TV interview with Osborne, 2 May 1981. "What's the use of living . . .", told to me by Helen Osborne. ". . . first glass of holy nectar . . .", 18 October 1985, HRHRC. *God Rot Tunbridge Wells!*, Channel 4, 6 April 1985.

Fourteen-page script of *God Rot Tunbridge Wells!* published with TV script of *A Better Class of Person* (Faber & Faber, 1985). "Do you know where you are? . . ." *Spectator*, 13 July 1985. The Osborne playlet written in Nuffield Hospital was sent to Charles Wood among others. "It's all in here! . . ." Helen Osborne. Osborne review of Peter Hall *Diaries, Sunday Times*, 23 September 1983. ". . . the allure of lost consequence . . .", Jan Morris, *Trieste and the Meaning of Nowhere* (Simon & Schuster, 2001). Osborne letter to his MP, 27 September 1968, (HRHRC). Osborne also subscribed to the Chelsea and Kensington Committee on Aircraft Noise.

His agent at this time was Kenneth Ewing of Fraser and Dunlop. (Robin Dalton had become an independent film producer). The Beuselinck letter looking into the finances of Woodfall Films was provided by Gordon Dickerson. Osborne's tax debts and earnings, documents provided by Peter Forrester of Moore Stephens. 2 June 1986 note to Helen Osborne and the 1986 notebook were kept at The Hurst. Empty champagne bottles in lake, personal interview with the new owners of Christmas Place.

Chapter 45: Strindberg's Man in England

Interviews for this chapter were with Peter and Thelma Nichols, Jonathan Miller, Sir Kenneth Bradshaw and members of the Garrick 1400 Club, Dr Jill Gray, Peter Forerester, David Leveaux and Robert McCrum. Helen Osborne on The Hurst – from personal interview, together with article for the Arvon Foundation provided by her. ". . . Not for 'the final years' . . .", 9 November 1987 letter to Rickards. "We're quite safe . . .", interview Peter Nichols. ". . . a weirdly dandified curmudgeon . . .", Jonathan Miller. A big sixtieth birthday party for Osborne at the Garrick was belatedly cancelled because he was too depressed to attend. "Got the time, grandpa?", Helen Osborne. "A broad church . . .", member of the 1400 Club. "Emergencies were John's specialty . . .", interview Dr Gray. 27 September 1989 postcard provided by D.S.J. Maw. "He was genial . . .", interview David Leveaux. *The Father* adaptation (Faber & Faber, 1989). An Osborne letter to Jocelyn Rickards on 23 October 1990, now in HRHRC, contains a near hysterical rant about Bennett. Jill Bennett's will that left her entire estate to the dog home was contested when a later, unsigned will was discovered. A financial settlement was made by Bennett's solicitors with her assistant, Linda Drew, among other beneficiaries.

During Leveaux's weekend visit to The Hurst, Osborne rowed with his agent Kenneth Ewing and Gordon Dickerson became his literary manager. "Do let us end our miserable association *at once* . . .", letter to Ewing, 24 December 1991 (HRHRC). He also fell out with Peter Nichols for not paying a dinner bill as promised. "I have never encountered such surly, churlish and, frankly, common, yes, common behaviour in my life – well not from someone I regard as a friend," Osborne wrote to Nichols on 8 August 1988, and went on to insult his son whose "knuckles brush the floor" at the first sound of the "rattling stick in the champagne bucket". It was the end of a beautiful friendship.

However, Nichols later wrote to Osborne from his new home in London to say that, despite their differences, he had greatly enjoyed a revival of *Look Back in Anger*. "Without your lead," he added, "most of us would never have written anything at all." Osborne replied on 16 August 1989, thanking Nichols for his generous response – "It's one's peers' opinions that count" – and then went on to repeat his side of their year-old dispute for the next three and half pages.

Chapter 46: Déjàvu

Principal sources for this chapter were Robert Fox, Richard Eyre, Max Stafford-Clark, Stephen Daldry, Barry Humphries, Helen Montagu and John Standing. *Déjàvu* (Faber & Faber, 1992). The alternative title, *Who Would You Rather Sleep With*, was from a party game played by Osborne and Tony Richardson in which guests choose who they would rather sleep with – George Bush, say, or Mrs Bush? Elton John or Ben Elton?

An Osborne letter in *The Times* of 26 December 1991, lamenting the demise of his favourite Turkish cigarettes because of an EC diktat, is one of his wittiest protests againt Europeanism. He subsequently received consoling supplies of raffish Turkish cigarettes from sympathetic smokers in many countries, including Turkey. "*Civic Britannicus sum* no longer," he wrote in gratitude to *The Times*, "but I may at least puff delicious, poisonous clouds of vaporous contempt into rings, proclaiming God rot the powers of Brussels and Westminster – and to hell with Burgandy" (correspondence and *Times* editorial, HRHRC).

The entire Osborne–Richard Eyre correspondence was provided by Eyre. Many of their letters are in HRHRC. The Osborne–Robert Fox correspondence was provided by Fox. Osborne was elected a member of the Garrick Club in 1970, proposed by Marius Goring and seconded by J.P.W. Lambert. Osborne often left a show at the interval (or before) apparently oblivious to people's feelings. (But Keith Waterhouse, for one, didn't seem to mind when Osborne left *Jeffrey Bernard is Unwell*.) "I don't suppose it's any good . . ." and "Hasn't he got *any* entrepreneurial flair . . .", Robert Fox. "Ron and Les" were invented by Osborne to personify the Royal Court. Max Stafford-Clark drives a vintage Bentley. "Isn't that a little too John Osborne?" his neighbour Michael Frayn said to him when he saw it.

"He met Osborne only once . . .", interview Stephen Daldry. The Osborne playlet written in Nuffield Hospital, HRHRC. Osborne's hypo attacks in the night, Helen Osborne. "Come on, John, you should go to hospital . . .", interview Robert Fox. Albert Finney letter to Osborne, 3 January 1990, with his response attached, HRHRC. Finney's letter to me saying that any ill feeling was "all my eye and Betty Martin", 27 August 1999. Osborne letter to *The Times*, 18 April 1991. (Osborne mistakenly claimed to have worked with Gielgud in the letter.) Barry Humphries lunch with Osborne, 18 October 1990. O'Toole correspondence, HRHRC. "I am the Desert Orchid . . .", Osborne notebook, 15 November 1991. Postcard to D.S.J. Maw provided by Maw. Lindsay Anderson letter to Osborne, HRHRC. Osborne talked of writing a TV biography of Vivien Leigh during this period, but he didn't write it. Tony Richardson returned to Los Angeles to direct a TV film version of *Phantom of the Opera* (not the musical). The day Osborne heard of Richardson's death, interview with Helen Osborne.

On 2 February 1992, Osborne told the *Independent on Sunday* that his failure to get *Déjàvu* on was "like having a dead baby inside you". 14 February 1992 Osborne fax to Bill Kenright, HRHRC. "Dear John, we're going to have to cut the play . . .", Tony Palmer. Semtex letter to Kenright, 20 May 1992, HRHRC. Osborne cut 45-minutes from *Déjàvu* – *Independent*, 14 November 1991. Audience attendance at *Déjàvu*, Sheila Stowell essay, John Osborne *Casebook*. Half-full houses, *Scotsman*, 13

June 1992. Fighting closure, *Standard*, 3 July 1992. Letter to Peter Egan, HRHRC. "Exit poetry, stage left", Benedict Nightingale, *The Times*, 24 June 1992.

Michael Holroyd, Bernard Shaw's great biographer, and his wife Margaret Drabble visited Osborne at The Hurst on 21 November 1992. Drabble wanted to know his recollections of Angus Wilson and, though they arrived very late for the meeting, both decribed him to me as "unexpectedly warm and welcoming". Drabble found the sprawling Hurst "a strange version of the dream of an English country life", however. Holroyd, knowing of Osborne's intense dislike of Shaw, was "very apprehensive" when he learned that he was reviewing his biography for the *Spectator*. In fact, Osborne's review was positive. (Michael Holroyd, *Bernard Shaw: Volume 1: The Search for Love*, *Spectator*, 24 September 1988). "I think he was touched by the bleakness of his early years," Holroyd rightly surmised, "– his poverty, the unhappy relations with his mother, the struggle to get his work on the stage – not much of which he had known earlier on."

Chapter 47: The End

Principal interviews for this chapter were with Harold Pinter, Neitie Gowrie, Ben Walden, Dr Jill Gray, Alan and Shirley Plater, Di Trevis and Helen Osborne, together with Peter Forrester, Robert McCrum, Thomas H. Staley, Gordon Dickerson, Richard Eyre, Anthony Page and Alan Rickman.

Letter to his agent Gordon Dickerson, 3 September 1992, HRHRC. Rickards letter, ibid. "Helen thinks it would kill me . . .", also from 3 September letter to Dickerson. "I can just about raise the fare to London . . .", 23 October 1992 letter to McCrum, ibid. Background to Osborne's finances, interview with Peter Forrester. "You were always bristling with good humour . . .", Osborne 21 July 1993 card to Barry Krost provided by Krost. "Do you think they'll take me? . . .", Helen Osborne. Writers' Guild Awards, 27 September 1992. Osborne–Alan Plater correspondence provided by Plater. "There's only one bastard . . .", interview with Plater. I also interviewed Alan Rickman about Osborne's speech and its rough reception. Osborne's notes of his speech provided by Plater. "Mumblings of an Angry Old Man", *Evening Standard*, 28 September 1992. "The Shock of the Old", Mr Pepys, *Evening Standard*, 29 September 1992. "Lurch Back in Anger", *Daily Star*, 29 September 1992. "The Day John Osborne Sang . . ." *Daily Express*, 29 September 1992. "Still Angry After All These Years", *Today*, 29 September 1992. "John Looks Blank in Anger", *Daily Mirror*, 29 September 1992.

Letter from Royal Literary Fund, 10 December 1992, with draft of Osborne's appeal, HRHRC. In addition to Osborne's physical decline, he was having difficulty hearing. Information about the purchase of the Osborne archive, interview with Thomas H. Staley. "Your patent scorn", Osborne letter to Rickards, HRHRC. Osborne–Arnold Running correspondence provided by Running. Letter to Michael Billington, 21 June 1993, provided by Billington, Osborne also wrote to fellow Garrick Club member and former drama critic Eric Shorter about Gilliatt's death: "Her death was such a shock to me, although I knew it was imminent for so long. We had a few joyful years together before ambition overwhelmed her, turned into madness . . . But she was not wicked, and didn't deserve this spitting on her grave . . .", 7 July 1993 letter provided by Shorter.

"Daughters of Eve" literature in HRHRC Account of the *Inadmissible Evidence* rehearsal, interview with director Di Trevis. Osborne–Richard Eyre correspondence, HRHRC and provided by Eyre. "All About Eve" *Time Out*, 16 June 1993. "The truth about me and Johnny O", Trevor Eve interview with Michael Owen, *Evening Standard*, 19 June 1993. Michael Gambon *Entertainer* broadcast 7 December 1993. Osborne on the brief lives of playwrights, 3 June 1992, *Spectator*. "That's how you end up – a fucking journalist . . .", letter to Rickards, 7 December 1993. ". . . Lifetime's disavowal of honour in your own country . . .", notebook, 28 October 1993. The note was made by Osborne en route to Italy to receive an award named Il Rosone d'Oro. (He fell ill during the trip.) Osborne also received the 1992 J.R. Ackerley Prize for Autobiography (19 March 1992 letter from International PEN, HRHRC). "Get me out of this fucking place . . .", Osborne relating his hospitalization to his specialist D.S.J. Maw, 11 December 1993 letter provided by Maw. "Last week I had to give in once again and send for the doctor . . .", Osborne notebook.

Epilogue

Dr Gray provided the official cause of Osborne's death. Osborne kept two 1994 pocket diaries. In his *Spectator* diary, among other entries, he underlined 24 and 25 December, and entered in capital letters "Xmas Day". In his Smythson diary, however, he made only one entry for the week of the 19 December: "Christmas Eve" – the day he died.

"There are no road maps in this blasted landscape . . .", Helen Osborne, *Sunday Telegraph*, 29 June 2003. "The One and Only John Osborne and his Diary", posthumous column, *Spectator*, Christmas double issue, 1994. Simon Callow on Osborne, "A Patriot Revealed", *Sunday Times*, 24 December 1995. Letter left by Osborne to be opened on his death, 18 July 1984, kept at The Hurst. Hare's memorial address republished in Osborne *Casebook*. Gowrie's letter to *The Times*, 9 June 1995. Osborne's night out at the palace, 20 June 1994, reported in his *Spectator* column, 3 December 1994.

Arnold Wesker *Guardian* article, "An Entertainer's Farewell", 11 January 1995. Pinter–Fraser protest letter to *Guardian*, 13 January 1995. Helen Osborne letter also published in *Guardian* that day pointing out that her husband was "already gravely ill, until death as it turns out" and accusing Wesker of being a humourless bore. Paul Johnson's observations, *Spectator*, 3 December 1994. Wesker's pilgrimage to Osborne's graveside, personal interview with Wesker.

Accountant Peter Forrester negotiated Osborne's outstanding tax debt down to £98,000. "This is my *life* . . .", Osborne quoted by Thomas F. Staley, President HRHRC. "She was spoken of as an exquisite prodigy . . .", Osborne on sister Faith, *A Better Class of Person*. "To Dad!", Helen Osborne. Osborne on Fulham cemetery, *A Better Class of Person*. "I can scarcely believe that I am still here . . .", *Sunday Telegraph*, 29 June 2003. Helen Osborne died of cancer on 12 January 2004, and is buried next to her husband in St George's Parish Church, Clun, Shropshire.

The final quotations on pp. 484–5 are from *The Entertainer*, *Look Back in Anger*, *The World of Paul Slickey*, *The Hotel in Amsterdam*, *Luther*, *Déjàvu* (Faber & Faber).

Index

Absolute Hell/The Pink Room (Ackland) 193–5
Absurd Person Singular (Ayckbourn) 370
Ackerley, J. R.: *Prisoners of War* 308
Ackland, Rodney 190, 308; *The Pink Room/Absolute Hell* 193–5
Addison, John 263
Agate, James 137
Agran, Linda 464
Albee, Edward: encouragement 386; *Who's Afraid of Virginia Woolf?* 233
Albery, Donald 166, 251
Ali, Adfor 407–8, 411
Almost a Gentleman (Osborne) xiii, xv, 1–2, 435; dedication 10; Helen Osborne and 476; reaction to Jill Bennett's suicide 443–4
Alpha Beta (Whitehead) 362
Alvarez, Al 226, 231
Amis, Kingsley 164–5, 166, 440; *Lucky Jim* 179, 180; politics 228
Anderson, Lindsay 2, 164, 237, 453; CND and 243, 244; and Jill Bennett 354; Moscow production 232; New Wave cinema 180–1
Angels in America (Kushner) 233
Anouilh, Jean: *Becket* 281; *Time Remembered* 197
Arden, John 185, 190, 244
Armstrong-Jones, Anthony (Lord Snowdon) 249, 285, 287, 291, 411
Arvon Foundation: The Hurst and 480
Ashcroft, Peggy 94, 152, 157, 217, 327, 375
Aspey, Robert: *The Panther's Feast* 303
Astor, David 285–6
Atkins, Eileen 38–9, 389, 398; *Exit Through the Fireplace* 83
Attlee, Clement 236
August for the People (Dennis) 266
Ayckbourn, Alan: *Absurd Person Singular* 370
Ayer, A. J. 256, 300

Bacharach, Don 198, 263, 268
Bacon, Francis 164
Baker, Hylda 220–1
Ball, Michael 478
Banbury, Frith 187, 194
Banks, Lynne Reid 117–18, 119–20
Barber, John 170
Barber, Lynn 19

Barnes, Peter: *Laughter* 217
Barnstone, William 325
Barrie, J. M. 219
Barstow, Stan: *A Kind of Loving* 181
Bart, Lionel 183
Bassett, Tarn 197, 207–8, 209, 273; on Jill Bennett 336–7
Bates, Alan 86, 175, 181, 279, 307, 411; *Déjàvu* and 449, 451; in *The Entertainer* 431–2; in *Look Back in Anger* 115
Beaton, Cecil 201, 252
Beaumont, Hugh (Binkie) 93–4, 191, 194, 197
Becket (Anouilh) 281
Beckett, Samuel 98, 157, 162; Coward dismisses 191; *Endgame* 184, 226; politics 233; *Waiting for Godot* 183–4; *Worstward Ho* 159
Beecham, Sir Thomas 405
Behan, Brendan: *The Quare Fellow* 183
Bell, Mary Haley: *Duet for Two Hands* 20
Bell, Norman 239, 240
Belmont College, Devon 64–8
Benn Brothers publications 70–4, 80
Bennett, Alan 287, 369; on Osborne as actor 87
Bennett, Arnold 58
Bennett, Billy "Almost a Gentleman" 2
Bennett, Jill (fourth wife): acting career 79, 342–3, 371; *The End of Me Old Cigar* 382; Guy Bennett and 418; *A Patriot for Me* 312–13, 327; *Time Present* 234; *Watch It Come Down* 383–8; *West of Suez* 366–7, 418; character of 36, 312–13, 336–7; angling for role 368; deception of 314–15; Lessing on 248; pills 372; suicide 17, 339; threats of suicide 355, 388; relationship with Osborne 4, 8, 363–5, 369–70, 380–1; affair with 192, 322–5; car crash 374, 375; fictional portrait of marriage 383–4; fridge in the bedroom 3; gagging order 394, 396; and Godfrey Tearle 344–5; happier days 337–42; at knife-point 372–3; nickname 10; Nolan and 415; Osborne's abusive letters to 412–13; Osborne's breakdown 330, 331; and Osborne's family 25, 26; Osborne's reaction to suicide 443–4; physical violence 353, 394; public squabbles 373–4; sacks Sonia 356–7; separation and divorce 381, 388, 391–6; unhappy days 352–7; wedding 334–5; witches avenge 467

Bennett, Rev. Guy 418–19, 426; Nolan and 414–15, 418, 423, 424
Bentine, Michael 418
Bentley, Eric 233, 325
Berger, John 243
Bergman, Ingmar: *The Magic Lantern* 476
Berkoff, Steven 463
Bernstein, Leonard 291
Bessborough, Earl of 178
The Best People (Grey and Hopewood) 187
Betjeman, John 16, 22, 69, 290, 291
A Better Class of Person (Osborne) xiii, xiv–xv, 435; dedication 10; Helen's encouragement 390, 398; neighbours worried by 408–9; on Osborne's mother 38–9; portrayal of mother 21–3, 26, 404; on repertory days 92; television production 38–9
Beuselinck, Oscar (Osborne's lawyer) 204, 263, 295; best man 274; and censorship of *The World of Paul Slickey* 253–4; CND and 244; introduces Krost 372; and Osborne's finances 434; on *Tom Jones* 289
Billington, Michael 90, 186, 192, 466
Billy Liar (film) 181
Birmingham Repertory Theatre 83
Blacksell, J. E. 177
Blakemore, Michael 88, 343
Bland, Sir Simon and Lady Olivia 408–9
Bleasdale, Alan 464
Blithe Spirit (Coward) 80, 190
Blond, Elaine 216
Blond, Neville 177–8
The Blood of the Bambergs (Osborne) 205, 287
Bloom, Harold 379
Bogarde, Dirk 309
Bolt, Robert 187–8; *A Man for All Seasons* 281
Bond, Edward 154
A Bond Honoured (de Vega): Osborne's adaptation 325–6
Bonham Carter, Violet 19
Bora, Katharina von 281
Bourdet, Edouard: *The Captive* 309
Bowles, Peter 225, 411
Boyd, William 476
The Boy Friend (Wilson) 250
Bracken, Brendan 201
Bradshaw, Sir Kenneth 169, 440
Bragg, Melvyn 411, 478
Braine, John 240; *Room at the Top* 180, 181
Branagh, Kenneth 450
Brando, Marlon 310–11
Brandt, Francine 203–4, 208–11, 274
Brecht, Bertolt 157, 182, 281; *Galileo* 217; *The Good Woman of Szechuan* 217; *Mother Courage* 217, 233; theory of theatre 217–18
Brenton, Howard 185, 233
Brideshead Revisited (Waugh) 180
Brief Encounter (film) 181
Brighouse, Harold: *Hobson's Choice* 100–1
British Theatre Since the War (Shellard) 106
Britten, Benjamin 177

Brook, Peter 185, 197; *The Empty Space* 94; on Mary Ure 212
The Browning Version (Rattigan) 97
Brustein, Robert 296
Bryden, Bill 194, 398, 469; directs *Watch It Come Down* 383, 386
Buffen, Joan 31
Bulmer, Angela Conner *see* Conner, Angela
Burge, Stuart 453
Burns, Robert 58
Burton, Richard 175, 201, 310; *A Subject of Scandal and Concern* 279
Burton, Sybil 201
Byng, Douglas 219

Cagney, James: *Yankee Doodle Dandy* 221
Caine, Michael 290, 371–2
Calder, John (publisher) 244
Callow, Simon 476–7
Cameron, James 243
camp, showbiz 81–2
Campaign for Nuclear Disarmament (CND) 242–6, 266
Canby, Vincent 400, 415
The Captive (Bourdet) 309
Cardiff, Jack 197
Cards of Identity (Dennis) 86
Carrington, Dora 385
Casson, Sir Hugh 251, 291
Cavendish, Lady Elizabeth 290, 291–2; on Nellie Beatrice Osborne 22–3
censorship 85, 101, 287; homosexuality in plays 308–10; *Lady Chatterley's Lover* 108; Lord Chamberlain's duties 107–8; *A Patriot for Me* 36, 307–8, 310; *Personal Enemy* 106–8; *The World of Paul Slickey* 252–4
The Changeling (Middleton) 259
The Changing Room (Storey) 362–3
The Charge of the Light Brigade (film) 301, 340, 389; Richardson and Osborne fall out over 344–51
Chekhov, Anton 233; *The Cherry Orchard* 366
Chelsea Square house 391, 392, 394–6, 397
The Cherry Orchard (Chekhov) 366
Chichester Festival Theatre 406, 431
Christie, Agatha: *The Mousetrap* 309; *Ten Little Niggers/And Then There Were None* 89
Christie, Julie 181
Churchill, Caryl 185, 189, 233, 362; *Owners* 375
cinema: British New Wave 180–1
Clare, Anthony 382
Clark, Fiona M. 465
Clark, Pat (Claire Lorrimer) 410
Classic Stage Company 188–9
Clayton, Jack 181
Clore, Charles 249
Closer (Marber) 189, 233
Clun, Shropshire *see* The Hurst
The Cocktail Party (Eliot) 101
Coffey, Denise 375
Collins, Canon John 243

Index

The Comedians (Griffiths) 217
Comedy Theatre: *Déjàvu* 457
Congreve, William 100
Connolly, Cyril 256
Conner, Angela (Bulmer) 23, 143, 284, 285, 288; consoles sister 323; on Jill Bennett 314; Penelope's death and 466–7
Conner, Penelope *see* Gilliatt, Penelope
Connery, Sean 251
Conrad, Joseph: *The Secret Agent* 371
Cooper, William: *Scenes from Provincial Life* 180
Copeau, Jacques 157
Copley, John 291, 314–15
Corbett, Harry H. 182
Corbett, Ronnie 418
Coriolanus (Shakespeare): Osborne's adaptation 379, 381–2
Corri, Adrienne 252
Cottesloe Theatre: *The Father* 443
Courtenay, Tom 181; *Loneliness of the Long Distance Runner* 175
Coward, Noel 18, 94, 188, 327; appalled by *Slickey* 252; context of 96–7; *Diaries* reviewed 190; image of 82; on new drama 176, 190–1; on Osborne's wives 187; plays of: *Blithe Spirit* 80, 190; *Brief Encounter* 181; *Design for Living* 358; *Hay Fever* 190; *Nude with a Violin* 101; *Private Lives* 96, 101; *Relative Values* 88, 101; *Sirocco* 252; queer percentages 135–6; Ravenhill on 190
Cox, Brian 19
Cranko, John 101
Cranmer, Thomas 7
Creighton, Anthony 38; "Cliff" and 124; *Epitaph for George Dillon* (with Osborne) 103, 108–10, 139, 143, 147; failed production company 90; information about drag 304; later years 148–50; Mary Ure wedding 197; "Tony's Mum" 146; nature of friendship with Osborne 133–50; Pamela and John move in with 124; production company with Osborne 124–5; and Rattigan 90
The Cripple of Inishman (McDonagh) 189
Crosby, Bing 418
The Crucible (Miller) 176, 213
Cry for Love (Osborne) *see* **The Devil Inside**
Cuckoo in the Nest (Travers) 87
Cukor, George 371

Daldry, Stephen 448–9
Dalton, Robin 360, 380–1
Dance of Death (Strindberg) 132
Darkness Visible (Styron) 44
Darling, Sheelagh (née Glover) 64
Davenport, Nigel 87
Davies, W. H. 58
Davis, Noel 273–4
Dawson, Helen (later Osborne, fifth wife): career of: arts editor 11; Gilliatt and 285; *Vera* 9; on Creighton 139; last years of 4, 483–4, 484; life before Osborne 390–2; relationship with Osborne 389–90, 466; Gilliatt's unhappiness

323; hands over notebooks xiii–xiv; health alerts 449; help with last writings 476; last days together 473–4; life in Edenbridge 396–9, 406–13; on life with Osborne 7–12; on Nellie Beatrice 39–40; Nolan and 417, 420, 422, 425; Osborne leaves Bennett for 388; on Osborne's father 62–3; on sale of Edenbridge house 433; visits Osborne and Bennett 387; wedding 399, 402
Day Lewis, Cecil 243
De Jongh, Nicholas 138–9, 144–6, 478
Dearden, Basil: *Victim* 309
Death of a Salesman (Miller) 233
The Deep Blue Sea (Rattigan) 97, 192
Déjàvu (Osborne) 166; Daldry sees as monologue 448–9; Eyre rejects 446–7; Kenwright's production 454–9; kitchen setting 7–8; Montagu attempts 452–4; plot and characters 445–6; Richardson and 451–2
Delaney, Shelagh 183, 244; *A Taste of Honey* 175, 181–2, 308
Delyanoff, Countess Sophia 305
Dench, Judi 83, 342, 450
Dennis, Nigel 164; *August for the People* 266; *Cards of Identity* 86
Desert Island Discs 404–5
Design for Living (Coward) 358
Desmond, Patrick 104, 107, 108, 133
The Devil Inside (Osborne): first production and revival 105; starts as *Resting Deep* 104
Devine, George 86; character of 151–3; CND and 243; death of 317–21; defends *Look Back* 176; friendship with Osborne: attends wedding 197; continued friendship 291; as father figure 69, 73; French holiday 262–3; Osborne's photo of 6–7; Richardson house parties 210; ill-health 311, 316–17; Jocelyn Herbert and 153–5; in *Luther* 281; onstage 158–9; on Osborne's method 166; Oxbridge 174; on Rattigan 192; Royal Court and: accepts *Look Back in Anger* 110, 152, 153–6; nervous breakdown 266; hopes for *Luther* 276–7; Miller with Olivier 213; Osborne's fame 199; *A Patriot for Me* 311–12; playwrights in rehearsal 469; reception of *Look Back* 170; rejects *The World of Paul Slickey* 251; turns down *Epitaph for George Dillon* 109–10; *Tom Jones* 268, 289; Wardle and 326
Devine (George) Award 326–7
Devine, Sophie 153, 320
Devlin, Polly 19
Dexter, John 175, 243, 287, 325
Dickens, Charles 58; *Nicholas Nickleby* 53
Dickerson, Gordon 139
Dietrich, Marlene 202, 470
Dilke, Sir Charles 371
Diplock, John 412, 413
Dissington, Mr and Mrs 399
Dodd, Ken 223–3
Donner, Clive 257, 381, 469
Douglas-Home, William 96; *The Reluctant Debutante* 89

The Drag (West) 309
Drew, Linda 339, 366
Dubuisson, Peter 461
Duet for Two Hands (Bell) 20
Duff, Charles: The Lost Summer 187
Duke of York Theatre: Time Present 362
Duncan, Ronald 176–7, 216
Duncannon, Viscount 178
Dunlop, Frank 469; directs A Sense of Detachment 374–6
Dunwoody, Gwyneth 14

East, John M. 137
Edel, Leon 44
Eden, Anthony 178–9
Edenbridge, Kent 7, 338–9, 388; after Jill 396; life in the community of 406–13; life with Helen 396–9; sold to pay debts 433–6
Edgar, David 233
Education Act (1944) 175
Egan, Peter: in Déjàvu 455–7
Elgar, Edward 405
Eliot, T. S. 105, 134, 162, 188; The Cocktail Party 101; The Family Reunion 101; Music Hall and 220; "Usk" 475; The Waste Land 44; West End plays 96
Elliott, Denholm 411
The Empty Space (Brook) 94
The End of Me Old Cigar (Osborne) 220, 250, 380, 382
Endgame (Beckett) 184, 226
Enemy of the People (Ibsen) 294
England, My England (television) 476–7
English Stage Company 177, 186, 216
The Entertainer (Osborne) 278; actors in 88; Archie's fears 223–7; being normal 17; conception of 214; Coward detests 190–1; dedicated to Creighton 134; Devine and 327; family influence 30; Music Hall and 5–6, 218–21; Olivier and 75, 213–16; parting shot 12; politics of 215–16; revivals 381, 431–3; without the songs 469
Entertaining Mr Sloane (Orton) 308
Epitaph for George Dillon (Osborne and Creighton) 80, 86, 92, 103, 147, 179, 278; Gaskill directs 143; Broadway premiere 136, 202; on radio 139; Stella and 104; turned down 108–10
Erikson, Erik H.: Young Man Luther 280
Esdaile, Alfred 177
Esslin, Martin 335; Plays and Players 326
European Economic Community 229
Evans, (Dame) Edith 94, 157, 289
Evans, Matthew 461
Eve, Trevor 467–8
Exit Through the Fireplace (Atkins) 83
Eyen, Tom 309
Eyre, Richard 235, 431, 469, 470; NT produces Inadmissible Evidence 467–8; rejects Déjàvu 446

The Family Reunion (Eliot) 101

Farhi, Nicole 479
The Father (Strindberg) 235, 476; Osborne's adaptation 442–3
Fearon, George 164
Fenton, James: on A Patriot for Me 304, 306
Field, Sid 221
Fiennes, Joseph 109
Finch, Peter 297
Findlater, Richard 103, 318, 399
Finlay, Frank: in Watch It Come Down 383–8
Finney, Albert 83, 93, 371, 478; Luther 91, 175, 277, 327; Saturday Night and Sunday Morning 181; sues Woodfall 450, 455; Tom Jones 289
First Love (Turgenev) 368
Fisher, Archbishop Geoffrey 239
Foot, Michael 231, 241–2, 243
Forbes, Jenny 412
Forrester, Judge Giles 426
Forrester, Peter 435, 442, 450, 460–1
Forster, E. M. 41
The Four Feathers (film) 34
Fox, Angela 135
Fox, Edward 311, 411
Fox, Robert 3, 411, 461, 478; accepts Déjàvu 447–9; withdraws from Déjàvu 451
Fraser, (Lady) Antonia 411, 479
Frayn, Michael 233
Freeman, C. T. 286
French, John 212, 271, 275
French Without Tears (Rattigan) 96
Freud, Lucien 256
Friel, Brian 162
Frink, Elisabeth 6
Fry, Christopher 96, 188; Venus Observed 214
Fry, Stephen 96–7
The Fugitives (Galsworthy) 187

Gaitskell, Hugh 236, 240, 242
Gale, John 339
Galileo (Brecht): Luther and 217
Galsworthy, John: The Fugitives 187
Gambon, Michael 83, 398, 411; The Entertainer 469
Gardiner, Lord 308
Gardner, Jimmy 204–6, 259
Garrick 1400 Club 439–40
Garrick Club 472–3, 478
Gas World (journal) 70–1, 199
Gaskill, William 134, 142–3, 175, 337; John Osborne Arvon Centre 480; politics 237; and The World of Paul Slickey 251
Gaycroft School of Music, Dancing, Speech, Elocution and Drama 79, 81
Genet, Jean 147, 157, 310
Get Carter (film) 368
Gielgud, John 94, 101, 157, 252, 354; Old Times 362; worried by Osborne 176
The Gift of Friendship (Osborne, TV drama) 369
Gill, Peter 100, 154–5, 194, 311
Gilliatt, Dr Roger 260–1, 263, 274
Gilliatt, Penelope (née Conner, third wife):

affair with Osborne 140, 142, 260, 265, 267–8, 269, 274; after Osborne 378, 400–2; Bennett and 314–15, 370; career of 4, 284–6; devotion to work 298–9, 315, 324; Helen Dawson on 11; interviews Osborne 199; reviews of Osborne 285; script for *Sunday, Bloody Sunday* 309; character of Constance 334; death of 466–7; distressed 327–8; divorce 192, 322–5, 329, 337, 395; introduces Helen 389; Lessing on 248; letters to and from France 263–6; married life 274, 283–4, 289–93, 297–9, 314; motherhood 258, 292, 300–1, 301, 423–4; nicknames 10, 143; Osborne's breakdown 330, 331–2; on Osborne's drinking 3; and Osborne's mother 23, 26; red hair 114; Richardson and 264; drug overdose 328; visits John and Helen 398; wedding 286

Gilpin, Sally 318

Glenconner, Lord 262

God Rot Tunbridge Wells! (Osborne, TV drama) 429–30

Godfrey: A Special Time Remembered (Bennett) 344

Goetschius, George 155–6, 161, 251, 280

Golden (John) Theatre 202

The Good Woman of Szechuan (Brecht) 217

Goodman, Lord 308

Goodwin, John 344

Goodwin, Suzanne: *Godfrey: A Special Time Remembered* 344

Gordon, Lyndall 134

Gordon-Maclean, Major Colin de Vere 267

Gowrie, Earl of (Grey) and Neitie 439, 471, 478, 479; Arvon Foundation and The Hurst 280, 479

Grade, Michael 463

Granger, Derek 170

Grant, Cary 222

Gray, Dr Jill 440–1, 464, 471, 473

The Great Bear/Minette (Osborne) 105–6, 124

Greene, Graham 162, 178, 255, 256, 262

Grey, David: *The Best People* (with Hopwood) 187

Griffiths, Trevor 233; *The Comedians* 217

Grigg, John 472

Gross (film) 371

Grove family (maternal relations) 25, 29–30, 33; *The Entertainer* and 223; religion and 277–8; Uncle Jack 30, 126, 130

Guinness, Alec 327, 473

Guthrie, Sir Tyrone 94

Gwatkin, Brigadier Sir Norman 253, 287

Hack, Mel 410, 419

Haigh, Kenneth 175, 203, 327

Halifax, Michael 172

Hall, Peter 183, 187, 379, 478; *A Midsummer Night's Dream* 255; plans to revive *The Entertainer* 431–2; produces *Watch It Come Down* 383–8, 392

Hall, Stuart 237

Hall, Willis 241, 337; Adolf's Anonymous 392;

marriage to Bennett 354–5; remembers Osborne 19–20; symptoms of marriage 381

Halpert, Evelyn 401–2

Hamilton, Michael 81, 82

Hamlet (Shakespeare) 212

Hampton, Christopher 186, 194, 337, 411

Hampton, Laura 390

Handel, G. F. 405; Tunbridge Wells and 429–30

The Hands of Orlac (film) 20

Hardcastle, William 286

Hare, David 3, 185, 189, 223, 233, 411, 467, 478–9; money schemes 461; Osborne's memorial service 477; *Slag* 362; "whammied" by Osborne 363

Harewood, Lord 172, 177; appeals to censors 308; fights for *The Entertainer* 216

Harmsworth, Bubbles (Lady) 252

Harris, Frank xiv

Harris, Percy 232

Harris, Richard 181

Harris, Rosemary 83

Harrison, Rex 80–1, 266

Hartley, Neil 350, 396

Harvey, Laurence 181; *Charge of the Light Brigade* 347

Harwood, Ronald 252

Hawkes, Jacquetta 243

Hawthorne, Nigel 375

Hay Fever (Coward) 190

Hayward, Doug 4, 290–1

Hazlitt, William 91

Heap, J. F. 239, 240

Heartbreak House (Shaw) 91

Hebbel, Friedrich 233

Hedda Gabler (Ibsen) 343, 369, 381

Heffer, Mr (teacher) 64–7

Heidegger, Martin 32

Heller, Joseph 363

Hellman, Lillian 310

Helpmann, Robert 210

Henderson, Helen 110–12

Herbert, Jocelyn 153–4, 160, 291; attends wedding 197; Devine's funeral and 320; French holiday 262–3; with Gilliatt in distress 327; Osborne's breakdown 332; on *A Patriot for Me* 311; Richardson house parties 210; *Tom Jones* 268

Heriot, Charles 307

Hickey, William 249, 328

Hicks, David 249

Hillman, Sidney 64

Hindle Wakes (Houghton) 100

Hobson, Harold 288; on Ackland 194; Gilliatt on 284; on *Look Back* 166, 171, 231; on *Luther* 280–1; on *A Patriot for Me* 308; post-war English theatre 94–5; retirement 398; on *Slickey* 250

Hobson's Choice (Brighouse) 100–1

Hodges, Mike 368

Hoggart, Richard 236, 237

Hollander, Tom 360

Holloway, Stanley 374

Holroyd, Michael xiv, 371
Holy Living and Holy Dying (Taylor) 405, 473–4
Holyoake, George 279
homosexuality: censorship and 106, 308–10;
    Coward's percentages 135–6; criminality of
    101; the Lanes' accusations 118–20, 141; *A
    Patriot for Me* and 303–11; plays masquerading
    as straight 192; political correctness 359–60;
    Ravenhill on 190; showbiz camp 81–2, 136
Hope, Anthony: *Prisoner of Zenda* 287
Hopwood, Avery: *The Best People* (with Grey) 187
Horace, Quintus 33
The Hostage (film) 371
The Hotel in Amsterdam (Osborne) 4, 10, 313,
    339–40, 362; first production of 357–61
Houghton, Stanley: *Hindle Wakes* 100
Housman, A. E. 1
Howard, Anthony and Carol 439
Howard, Trevor 7, 430
Howarth, Donald 154, 175, 272
Hudd, Roy 418
Huddleston, Trevor 279
Hughes, Ted 467, 480
Hugo, Victor 32
Humphries, Barry 360, 452
Hurry on Down (Wain) 180
The Hurst, Clun, Shropshire 1–3; after Osborne
    6–8, 11–12; Arvon Foundation 479–80; the
    library 13–16; Osborne buys 434, 435, 437–9
Huston, John: *The Hostage* 371; *Moulin Rouge*
    371

I Have Been Here Before (Priestley) 80
Ibsen, Henrik: *Enemy of the People* 294; *Hedda
    Gabler* 343, 369, 381
Illness as Metaphor (Sontag) 54
Inadmissible Evidence (Osborne) 68, 166, 225,
    393; censorship 253; characters and summary
    of 294–7; dreamscapes of 458; Osborne
    directs 405–6; feels like self-prophecy 365–6;
    Osborne 235; parody of Wilson 237–8;
    Rattigan's praise for 193; revived by National
    Theatre 467–9; Williamson in 7, 327; writing
    of 292
Indian Mutiny (film) 371
Innes, Christopher: *Modern British Drama* 187
Ionesco, Eugène 91, 157
Isherwood, Christopher 263, 268; grand drag balls
    268–9, 304; Mary Ure and 198, 199, 209–10

Jackson, Glenda 411
Jacobi, Derek 83, 318
James, Henry 134–5
Jaspers, Karl 32
Jeffrey Bernard is Unwell (Waterhouse) 453
Jellicoe, Ann 154
Johnson, Colonel J. F. D. 307–8
Johnson, Paul 479
Johnston, Alison 455
Jones, Jack 239, 240
Joyce, James xiv, 162; "The Day of Rabblement"
    301

Jumpers (Stoppard) 362

Kael, Pauline 289
Kafka, Franz 53, 296
Kane, Sara 189
Kaufman, George S. 170
Kazan, Elia 136
Kempson, Rachel 375, 376–7, 447
Kennedy-Cox, Sir Reginald 178
Kenwright, Bill: produces *Déjàvu* 454–9
Kerr, Walter 294–5
Kierkegaard, Søren 32
The Killing of Sister George (Marcus) 308
Kilmartin, Terence 285
A Kind of Loving (film) 181
King, Philip: *See How They Run* 89
King Lear (Shakespeare) 38
Kipling, Rudyard 58
Kitchen, Michael 381
The Kitchen (Wesker) 327
Korda, Alexander 197
Kovaks, Stephan 305
Kramer, Hilton 156
Kretzmer, Herbert 326
Krost, Barry 371–4, 387, 462
Kureishi, Hanif 379
Kushner, Tony: *Angels in America* 233
Kydd, Robert 398, 399

La Plante, Lynda 464
Lady Chatterley's Lover (Lawrence) 108
Lahr, John 358
Lane, Pamela (first wife) 4, 333; affair with
    dentist 127–8; and "Alison" 114–16, 119,
    123–4, 125, 128, 130–2; course of marriage
    124–32, 133; divorce 200; later years 132,
    398; nickname 10; Osborne falls in love with
    113–15; on Osborne's sexuality 141;
    Osborne's unresolved feelings 298, 322;
    parents oppose marriage 116–20; pregnancies
    125; warns against Jill Bennett 313; wedding
    120–2
Langan, Peter 391
Larkin, Philip 166, 220
Laughter (Barnes) 217
Lawrence, D. H. 97, 100, 162; on bloodless
    drama 189; *Lady Chatterley's Lover* 108
Lawrence, T. E. 58
Lawson, Dominic 478
Leavis, F. R. 237
Lee, Elizabeth M. 401, 423
Lee-Potter, Lynda 19
Lefevre, Robin 360
Legitimacy Act (1959) 272
Leigh, Vivien 94, 210, 214, 432
Leno, Dan 220
Lessing, Doris 164, 244, 246–8, 259; on Bennett
    341; *Walking in the Shade* 247
Leveaux, David 469; directs *The Father* 442–3
Lewenstein, Oscar 169, 177, 216, 232, 289, 346;
    advice 374; three plays at once 362
Linden, Stella 104–5

Index

Lipman, Maureen 390
Littler, Emile 253–4
Littlewood, Joan 93, 182, 216
Livingstone, Fred and Florence 286
Lloyd, Marie 30
Logue, Christopher: CND and 243
London Theatre Studio 157
Loneliness of the Long Distance Runner (film) 175, 181
Lonsdale, Mab (later Ackland) 193–5
Look Back in Anger Casebook Series 187
Look Back in Anger (Osborne) 327; acceptance 38; context of writing 93–102; Creighton/Cliff 124; Desmond rejects 133; Devine accepts 110, 152, 153–6, 159–60; enduring significance of xv; English context of premiere 178–9; family and 61–2; film of 180; first Broadway production 203; Helen Dawson's prize choice 390; and later Osborne 335; Miller on 98; Moscow production 232; mother and 22; NY production 484; original manuscript 162–7; Osborne's family and 42, 46–7; O'Toole and 453; as outsider view 156; Pamela/Alison 114–16, 119, 123–4, 125, 128, 130–2; Pamela Lane in revival 298; Plater on 463–4; politics of 230–1; reception of 168–73, 176; revisted in Déjàvu 445–6; revivals 188–9, 362, 406, 450; Richardson directs 153; royalties 200; the Runnings on 74–5; school influence 67; title(s) 163–4; wedding 120; writing of 84, 132
Lorrimer, Claire (Pat Clark) 410
The Lost Summer (Osborne) 187
Lotis, Dennis 251
Lousada, Anthony 262–3
Lucky Jim (Amis) 180
Lulu (Wedekind) 309
Luther (Osborne) 17, 91, 260; censorship 253; conception and sources 278–82; critics on 280–1; Devine and 327; Finney and 175; Gilliatt reviews 285; redeems Osborne's reputation 276–7; religion and Osborne 277–8; religious ecstasy 458
Lyric Theatre 450

Macaulay, Rose 243
McCarthy, Mary 227; essay on Look Back in Anger 171–2; on A Patriot for Me 305, 306
McCrum, Robert 3, 461, 464; chapter on Bennett 443–4; Writer's Guild award ceremony 463
McCullin, Donald 194
McDonagh, Martin: The Cripple of Inishman 189
McDowell, Malcolm 406
Mace, Edward 398
McEwan, Geraldine 327
MacGowran, Jack 327
McGuinness, Sonia 167, 241, 257, 314, 338, 395; on Bennett 323, 352, 353–4; on Gilliatt 298–300, 328; Osborne's breakdown 330; sacked while pregnant 356–7; types out plays 298–9
McKellen, Ian 179, 354–5
McKenna, T. P. 455

Macmillan, Harold 178–9, 240, 244
MacMillan, Sir Kenneth 186, 251
Madgwick, Donald 105
The Magic Lantern (Bergman) 476
Man and Superman (Shaw) 233
A Man for All Seasons (Bolt) 281
The Man in the Glass Booth (Shaw) 211
Mankowitz, Wolf 232, 237
Marber, Angela 354
Marber, Patrick 354; Closer 189, 233
Marcus, Frank 376; The Killing of Sister George 308
Margaret, Princess 287
Margate 57
Marsh, Dr Kenneth 428
Martin, Kingsley 243
Martinez, Carlos (the Jackal) 373
Maschler, Tom 164
Mason, Canon Richard 402, 403, 404
Massey, Anna 398
Matheson, Eve 455
Maugham, Somerset 58, 89, 91, 174, 308
Maw, D. S. J. 43, 427–9, 441
Medwin, Michael 371
Melly, Diana 411
Melly, George 244, 411
Melville, Herman 159
Mercer, David 367
Merchant, Vivien 467
Merivale, Jack 210
Merrick, David 203, 251, 406
Middlemass, Frank 87–8, 121, 141
Middleton, Thomas: The Changeling 259
A Midsummer Night's Dream (Shakespeare) 255
Miller, Arthur: The Crucible 176, 213; Death of a Salesman 99, 233; on Look Back in Anger 98; Olivier and 213–14; politics of the soul 234; A View from the Bridge 310
Miller, Jonathan 287, 439
Miller, Max 136–7
The Miller (journal) 71–2
Milligan, Spike 291
Minette/The Great Bear (Osborne) 105–6, 124
Mirfield monastic community 279
Modern British Drama (Innes) 187–90
A Modest Proposal (Swift) 230
Monroe, Marilyn 210
Montagu, Helen 360, 374, 384, 387; Déjàvu and 452–4; on Helen Dawson 389
Montagu, Lord Edward 101, 147, 252
Montand, Yves 210
Moore, Dudley 354
Mortimer, Emily 396
Mortimer, John 18, 209, 399, 411, 484
Mortimer, Penelope 332, 390, 399, 411
Moscow Art Theatre 232
Mother Courage (Brecht) 217, 233
Moulin Rouge (film) 371
Mountbatten, Lady Pamela 249
The Mousetrap (Christie) 309
Mrs Warren's Profession (Shaw) 107
Muggeridge, Malcolm 183, 472

JOHN OSBORNE

The Mulberry Bush (Wilson) 176
Mumaim, Abdul 407–8
Murray, Alec 257
Music Hall: Billy Bennett 2; The Entertainer and
218–21; influence in theatre 216–17; influences
on Osborne 5–6, 34, 56, 382; memorial service
and 478; Osborne's mother and 22

The National Health (Nichols) 217
National Theatre: A Bond Honoured 325–6;
graveside wreath 476; Thatcher and 229
Neville, John 244
New Theatre (Albery): The Hotel in Amsterdam
362
Newman, Cardinal John Henry 1–2
Newman, Paul 310
Nicholas Nickleby (Dickens) 53
Nichols, Mike 332, 400
Nichols, Peter 89, 437–8, 439; The National
Health 217; Privates on Parade 217
Nichols, Thelma 390, 437–8, 439
Nicholson, Ben 256
Nicolson, Harold 174
Nightingale, Benedict 186, 458
1956 and All That (Rebellato) 187, 237
Norman, Barry 326
Norman, Frank 183
Nude with a Violin (Coward) 101
Nunn, Trevor 379

Oakley, Dr 428
O'Brien, Edna 411
O'Casey, Sean 100
Odets, Clifford 99
Oh! What a Lovely War (Theatre Workshop) 183,
216
Old Times (Pinter) 362
The Old Water Mill, Hellingly 286
Olivier, Laurence: affair with Plowright 210, 214;
appeals to censors 308; Beaumont and 94;
beginnings 83; and campness 81; Devine and
157, 320; The Entertainer 12, 75, 93, 213–16,
327; as father figure 69, 73; "Larry Oliver" 215;
Miller changes attitude 213–14; Nolan
unimpressed by 417; on Osborne as actor 86–7;
Osborne mother and 23; reaction to Look Back
176; social relations 7, 136, 143, 291, 398, 409,
411, 432
O'Neill, Eugene 99, 225, 296
Orton, Joe: Entertaining Mr Sloane 308
Orwell, George 32, 147; politics of 236–7
Orwell, Sonia 256
Osborne, Colin see Shaw, Colin
Osborne, Faith (sister) 24, 480–3
Osborne, John James: acting career: entrance
78–85; First Love 368; Get Carter 368; Lane
finds jobs for 125, 127; as Orlac 20; others'
comments on 86–9; The Parachute 367, 368;
production company 90, 124–5; as Redl 327;
Roc Players 113, 121, 122; appearance: acne
104; bearded 362; impresses Hare 363; later
years 397; moustache 335; tailor 4; Ure

smartens up 198; beliefs and convictions 75–6;
Anglicanism 402–4; anti-Europeanism 228–9;
causes and turns 235–8; socialism 229–33 see
also politics; character of: almost a gentleman
2; Bennett's effect on 363–5, 369–70, 380–1;
burial tokens 11; collapse of confidence 362–5,
369–1; community life 406–13; contradictions
of 5, 17–20; disappointed with Nolan 419–22;
father figures 69–70, 158–61, 317–21; fears
129–30, 206, 240, 280; first fame and success
199–206; food preferences 299; at knife-point
372–3; Krost on 372; later cut off existence
439–40; list of betrayers 455; money matters 75,
125–6; nicknames 143; possessions and 13–16;
prefers isolation 339; refuses grandchildren 416;
religion 16–17; restlessness 313–14; Rickards
on 258; self-education 147, 174, 200, 201;
suffering xiii–xiv; death of 474, 475; burial 9,
11–12; funeral 476; memorial service 477–9;
Nolan and 425; obituaries and tributes 475;
early life and family 280; atmosphere at home
53–5; at Belmont College 64–8; birthplace
23–4; Christmas 471–2; cousin's view of 49–52;
dislike of mother 21–3, 37–41, 60, 74; effect of
sister's death 480–3; friendship with Mickey
31–3; home atmosphere 28–30, 31; "outings"
33–4; reading 32; relationship with father
46–9, 55–7, 58–63; ill-health and depression:
breakdown 322–3, 328, 329–33; childhood 32,
34–5; circulatory problems 370; contemplates
suicide 365; depressions 42–5; diabetes 427–9,
441, 449–50, 464–5; drinking and pills 387–8,
440–1; duodenal ulcer 471; gout 370; internal
bleeding 380; last months 472–4; twisted
hernia 440, 441, 449; marriages: divorcing
Bennett 391–6; engagement to Renee 79–80,
82, 104; nicknames for wives 10; paternity of
Colin 267, 270–5; physical violence 353, 394;
wedding to Bennett 334–8; wedding to Dawson
391, 399, 402; wedding to Gilliatt 265;
wedding to Lane 113–32; wedding to Penelope
Gilliatt 283–6; wedding to Ure 196–201 see
also Bennett, Jill; Dawson, Helen; Gilliatt,
Penelope; Lane, Pamela; Ure, Mary; money
matters: casual Woodfall accounts 434–5; debt
in later years 433–6, 460–1, 465; divorce
settlements 393, 395; estate left 479–80; film
money 288–9, 346–7; income from plays 435;
new accountant 435, 442; spending 200–1,
289–92, 397, 407; taxes 371, 446, 450; Texas
buys manuscripts 465; sexuality: Creighton and
133–50; father's draws the facts of 56; writing
career: acting failure as fuel 89–92, 93; adapts
Strindberg 235; Angry Young Man label 164–5,
179; applauded 456; Benn Bros journalism
70–2, 80; collapse in confidence 386–8;
Coriolanus adaptation 379, 381–2; on Desert
Island Discs 404–5; early struggle 126–8; as
"ex-playwright" 1–2, 188, 392–3, 460–1; failed
film projects 371; The Father adaptation 442–3;
filmscripts 301; Hedda Gabler adaptation 381;
journalism 199, 470; last works 476–7; later

Index

ideas 405, 430–2; obituaries and tributes 14–15; Oscar for screenplay 288–9; *The Picture of Dorian Gray* adaptation 379–80, 381, 382; plays before breakthrough 103–10; post-war context 93–102; Ravenhill on 188–90; rehearsals and 468–9; review of *Noel Coward Diaries* 190; revivals of classic plays 405–6; self-education 71–3; Writer's Guild award 462–5 *see also* **titles of works** in bold

Osborne, Nellie Beatrice (née Grove, mother): acted by Atkins 38–9; attends Ure wedding 197; character of 24–6, 205; Gilliatt and 292–3; Lane and 121–2; last years and death of 39–40; letters to son 26–8, 35–7; Osborne's childhood and: germ phobia 54; holiday snapshot 33; home atmosphere 28–9, 31; husband's last days 59–61; marriage 51; nephew on xv; and Osborne's illnesses 34–5; Osborne's dislike of 23, 37–41, 60, 74, 404; portrayal by Osborne 21–3

Osborne, Nolan (daughter) xv, 258, 414–26; after parents' breakup 332, 337, 378; Bennett and 324, 370; birth of 301–2; chucked out 421–4; estranged from Osborne 17, 414–15, 424–6; Gilliatt's treatment of 401–2; grandmother and 40; life in Kent 400–2, 406; mother's death 467

Osborne, Thomas Godfrey (father): character of 24; death of 42, 54–5; desire to write 56; illness 24, 28, 45–6, 48–9, 53–4, 56–61; death of 60–3; marriage 25, 51; music and 405; personality: arguments 18; relationship with son 46–7, 55–7; as "Uncle Goff" 51–2

Osborne extended family 47–50, 66; religion and 277

Ostrovsky, A. N.: *The Storm* 248

O'Toole, Peter 175, 310, 371; *Déjàvu* and 452–4

Owen, Robert (Osborne pseudonym) 105–6

Owners (Churchill) 375

Oxford Experimental Theatre 110

Ozick, Cynthia 134

Page, Anthony 304, 310, 314, 355, 406, 469; on Bennett 343

Palmer, Tony 430, 455–6, 473; *England, My England* 476–7

The Panther's Feast (Aspey) 303

The Parachute (television) 367, 368

Parfitt, Judy 357

Parker, Anna (granddaughter) 415

Parker, Joshua (grandson) 415

Parker, Simon 415, 425

A Patriot for Me (Osborne) 14, 147, 252–3, 268–9, 327; 166; actors shy from 310–11; censorship 36, 307–8, 310; concept of 303–4; Devine and 317; drag queens 7; painting from 6; reception of 304–8; revival 279, 406, 431; Schell and 7; as self-hatred 138

Paul, Leslie 164

Peace in Our Time (Rattigan) 97

Penn, Eric 253, 337

Personal Enemy (Osborne): censorship and 106–8; Pamela's judgement 124

Peter, John 186, 234

Phoenix Theatre 277

The Picture of Dorian Gray (Wilde): Osborne's adaptation 379–80, 381, 382

The Pink Room/Absolute Hell (Ackland) 193–5

Pinter, Harold 18, 184, 211, 243, 411; as actor 90, 175; in ascendancy 362; on honours 472; memorial service 478–9; *Old Times* 362; politics 233; *A Slight Ache* 472; witches curse 467

Plater, Alan 462–3

Plath, Sylvia 467

Plays and Players (Esslin) 326

Playwrights Mafia 33

Plomley, Roy 404–5

Plowright, Joan 157, 175, 409; affair with Olivier 214; Osborne and 210–11, 431–2, 431–4; Osborne mother and 23

Plummer, Christopher 310

Poe, Edgar Allan 32

politics: anti-Europeanism 228–9; anti-royalty 215–16; Communist disillusionment 236; "Damn you, England" letter 239–42, 266–7; nuclear protest 239–46; within the theatre 177–8

Porter, Tony (cousin) 48, 49–52; on Nellie Beatrice xv

Portscatho, Cornwall 407

Powell, Rachel 198

Priestley, J. B. 58, 95, 240, 243, 286; angry 188; *I Have Been Here Before* 80

The Prince and the Showgirl (film) 213

The Prisoner of Zenda (film) 34

The Prisoner of Zenda (Hope) 287

Prisoners of War (Ackerley) 308

Private Lives (Coward) 96, 190

Privates on Parade (Nichols) 217

Procktor, Patrick 7, 312–13, 411

Purcell, Henry 147, 473, 476–7

Pygmalion (Shaw) 91

Pyjama Tops 375

The Quare Fellow (Behan) 183

Ramsay, Peggy 322–3

Ransom (Harry) Humanities Research Center 162–3, 465, 479

Ratcliffe, Michael 186

Rattigan, Terence 266; admires Osborne 192–3; Beaumont and 94; context of 97–8; and Creighton 90; Devine and 157; plays of: *The Browning Version* 192; *The Deep Blue Sea* 97, 192; *French Without Tears* 96; *Peace in Our Time* 97; *Separate Tables* 188, 309, 394; *The Sleeping Prince* 213; *Variations on a Theme* 308; Ravenhill on 190; reaction to *Look Back* 176; sacked by the critics 188; upper class roles 89

Ravenhill, Mark: on *Look Back* 188–90; *Shopping and Fucking* 188–9

Raymond, Paul 375

Read, Sir Herbert 245

The Real Thing (Stoppard) 75, 343
The Reason Why (Woodham-Smith) 347
Rebellato, Dan 97; *1956 and All That* 187, 237
Redgrave, Michael 157
Redgrave, Vanessa 73, 83, 142, 291, 327, 342–3; CND 243, 244; on Gilliatt 260; *The Seagull* 158
Regent's Park Nursing Home 330
Reisz, Karel: New Wave cinema 180–1; *Saturday Night and Sunday Morning* 175
Relative Values (Coward) 88, 101
The Reluctant Debutante (Douglas-Home) 89
repertory theatre 83–5
Resting Deep (Osborne) see **The Devil Inside**
Reynolds, Major A. J. 66–7
Rich, Frank 203
Richardson, Natasha 411, 447
Richardson, Ralph 83, 93, 94, 234, 411; *Old Times* 362
Richardson, Tony 7, 143, 266, 434; background 175; changes in theatre 176; on biography xiv; on Coward 191; death of 142, 454; as director: *Charge of the Light Brigade* 301, 340; *Cuckoo in the Nest* 87; *Inadmissible Evidence* 297; *Look Back in Anger* 153, 154, 166, 170; *Luther* 277; New Wave cinema 180–1; Osborne in rehearsal 468–9; *A Patriot for Me* 304–5; rejects *Slickey* 251; *Tom Jones* 268, 288–9; on Finney's suit 450; French holiday 262, 263; on French theatre 157; friendship with Osborne 291; as best man 197, 286; as brother figure 73; falling out 246–51, 340; Mary Ure and 209–11; Osborne's fame 199; pit-stop joke 451; reconciliation 389, 406; shares flat 3, 142; Gilliatt and 264; likes *Déjàvu* 447–8; in Moscow 232; protects Devine 266; Rickards and 256, 263
Rickards, Jocelyn 91, 274, 286, 360; affair with Osborne 256–8; on Bennett 313, 392; career 255–6; continued friendship 291; on Creighton and Osborne 140; drag costume 304; end of the affair 260–1, 262–9; illness 466; on Gilliatt 260–1; nickname 10; Osborne's affair with 210, 255, 297; Osborne's breakdown 329–30; on Osborne's end 458; attitude to Helen 466; retreat in France 241; and *The World of Paul Slickey* 251
Rickman, Alan 464
Rider Haggard, H. 58
Roberts, Rachel 382
Robeson, Paul 22, 405; *Othello* 197
Room at the Top (Braine) 180, 181
Roots (Wesker) 175
Rosenthal, Jack 390
Rosoman, Leonard 6, 7, 291, 322
Royal Court Theatre 153; class and 174–8; Devine and 266, 317, 319–20; Devine's retirement from 311–12; hard times 277; *Luther* and 281; no notice of Osborne's death 476; outing to see Ken Dodd 223–3; rejects *A Sense of Detachment* 375; rejects *Déjàvu* 448; vetoes *The Entertainer* 216 see also *A Patriot for Me;*

Inadmissible Evidence; Look Back in Anger; The Entertainer; The Hotel in Amsterdam
Royal Literary Fund 465
Running, Arnold: as father figure 70–7; on Osborne's sexuality 140–1
Running, Pamela 71, 73–5
Russell, Bertrand 243, 266

Saint-Denis, Michel 157
St James Theatre, Broadway 277
St Michael's School, Limpsfield 402, 423
Saint's Day (Whiting) 187
Salad Days (Slade) 308–9
Sallis, Peter 398
Saltzman, Harry 203, 209
Sampson, Anthony 481
Saroyan, William 361
Sartre, Jean-Paul 32
Saturday Night and Sunday Morning (film) 175, 181
Sayle, Alexei 219
Scenes from Provincial Life (Cooper) 180
Schell, Maximilian 7, 311, 314; directs *First Love* 368
Schiff, Stacy 9
Schlesinger, John 181; *Sunday, Bloody Sunday* 309
Schoenman, Ralph 243
Scofield, Paul 83, 93, 310; acts with Mary Ure 197, 199; *The Hotel in Amsterdam* 4, 358–9, 361; on romantic words 339–40; understanding Osborne 359
Scott, Zachary 210
The Seagull (Chekhov) 158
The Secret Agent (Conrad) 371
See How They Run (King) 89
Sellers, Peter 291
A Sense of Detachment (Osborne) 51, 66, 220, 374–7, 447
Separate Tables (Rattigan) 188, 309, 394
Shakespeare, William: *King Lear* 38
Shaw, Artie 166
Shaw, Colin (Osborne): birth of 267; paternity of 270–5
Shaw, Fiona 83
Shaw, George Bernard 58, 97, 100, 162; from actor's point of view 91; *Heartbreak House* 91, 384–5; *Man and Superman* 233; *Mrs Warren's Profession* 107; *Pygmalion* 91; state of the nation dramas 185; *You Never Can Tell* 128
Shaw, Glen Byam 157
Shaw, Jennifer 271, 273
Shaw, Robert: affair with Mary Ure 207, 211–12; attitude to family 271; paternity of Colin 258–9, 270–5
Shawn, William 400
Shellard, Dominic: *British Theatre Since the War* 106, 187
Sheppard, Richard 481
Sheridan, Richard Brinsley 100
Sherrin, Ned 463
Shine, Marie 320
Shippard, Renee 79–80, 82, 104, 140

Index

Shopping and Fucking (Ravenhill) 188-9
Shorter, Eric 223
Signoret, Simone 210
Sillitoe, Alan 185; CND and 244; *Saturday Night and Sunday Morning* 181
Singer, Linda 393, 394-5
Skelhorn, Sir Norman 310
Skelton, Barbara 256
Slade, Julian: *Salad Days* 308-9
Slag (Hare) 362
The Sleeping Prince (Rattigan) 213
A Slight Ache (Pinter) 472
Smith, Bessie 226
Smith, Maggie 291, 327, 342, 411, 480, 483; *A Bond Honoured* 325
Snowdon, Lord (Antony Armstrong-Jones) 249, 285, 287, 291, 411
The Soldier's Tale (Stravinsky) 318
Sonnenberg, Ben 284-5
Sons and Lovers (Lawrence) 197
Sontag, Susan: *Illness as Metaphor* 54
Soviet Union: Hungarian uprising 236; Moscow *Look Back in Anger* 232
Spark, Muriel 476
Spender, Stephen 256, 462
Spiegel, Sam 371
Spinetti, Victor 182
Sprague, Jane 262, 263, 266
Stafford-Clark, Max 448, 469
Staley, Thomas F. 465, 479
Standing, John 336, 375, 377, 455
Stanley, Robert Patrick 309
Steele, Tommy 249
Steiner, George 185, 277
Stephens, Robert 86, 175, 209, 291, 327; attends wedding 197; *A Bond Honoured* 325; campness 81; King Lear after hours 470; lunch at Sardi's 202; models role on Osborne 201; on *A Patriot for Me* 311; *The Soldier's Tale* 318
Stevenson, Robert Louis 58
Stoppard, Dr Miriam 390
Stoppard, Tom 162, 186; in ascendancy 362; *Jumpers* 362; *The Real Thing* 75, 343
Storey, David: *The Changing Room* 362-3; *This Sporting Life* 181
The Storm (Ostrovsky) 248
Stotesbury, Christine 300-1, 324, 401-2; later relationship with Nolan 416; Nolan's diary and 417; on Osborne family 301
Strachey, John St Loe: *The Theory and Practice of Socialism* 32
Strachey, Lytton xiv, 365, 371, 385
Street-Porter, Janet 411
A Streetcar Named Desire (Williams) 116
Strindberg, August: *Dance of Death* 132; Osborne adapts *The Father* 235, 442-3, 476
Styron, William: *Darkness Visible* 44
A Subject of Scandal and Concern (television) 279
Suddenly Last Summer (Williams) 106
Suez crisis 178-9
Sunday, Bloody Sunday (film) 309
Swift, Jonathan: *A Modest Proposal* 230

Tanfield, Paul 250
Tapper, Terry 80
A Taste of Honey (Delaney) 35, 175, 181-2, 308
Taw and Torridge Arts Festival 177
Taylor, A. J. P. 243
Taylor, Elizabeth 201
Taylor, Jeremy 473-4; *Holy Living and Holy Dying* 405
Tearle, Godfrey 344-5, 370
Ten Little Niggers/And Then There Were None (Christie) 89
Thatcher, Margaret 234; National Theatre and 229
theatre: the Angry decade 164-5; Aunt Edna 98, 99, 101, 177; Brechtian 217-18; changing fashions of 187-8; class and 174-7; context of *Look Back* 182-6; critics 168, 326, 398-9; Littlewood and 182-3; national anthem 178; non-British influences 157; post-war context 93-102 *see also* Music Hall; repertory theatre
Theatre Workshop 182-3
The Theory and Practice of Socialism (Strachey) 32
"They Call It Cricket" (Osborne, essay) 184-5
Thomas, Gareth 455
Thomas, Henry 398
Thomas, Norene 398, 411
Thompson, E. P. 236
Thompson, Emma 450
Thorndike, Sybil 94, 327
Thorndike Theatre, Leatherhead: *Déjàvu* 454-6
Time Present (Osborne) 234, 340, 357, 360; 362; conception of 334; drawing room 335; success for Bennett 342-4
Time Remembered (Anouilh) 197
Tolstoy, Leo 232
Tom Jones (film): Finney and 450; money from 201; Osborne's adaptation of 6; planning 268; profits from 434; success of 288-9
Took, Barry 464
Toynbee, Philip 256
Travers, Ben: *Cuckoo in the Nest* 87
Trevis, Di: revives *Inadmissible Evidence* 467-9
Trevor-Roper, Hugh 240
Trewin, J. C. 169-70
Try a Little Tenderness (Osborne, TV drama) 398
Tunbridge Wells, Kent: Handel and Osborne 429-30
Turgenev, Ivan Sergeevich: *First Love* 368
Tushingham, Rita 175
Tutin, Dorothy 83
Tynan, Kathleen 285, 291
Tynan, Kenneth 11, 137, 164, 172, 244, 288, 291, 370; on actor Osborne 86; argues with Wesker 372; de Vega adaptation 325; on Dennis 266; emphysema 400; on *The End of Me Old Cigar* 382; Gilliatt and 285; on Left identification with Osborne 231; on *Look Back in Anger* 166, 171; on *Luther* 17, 280-1; on Max Wall 221; on Osborne first fame 200-1; on *A Patriot for Me* 305-6; post-war English theatre 94-5; soirées 201

JOHN OSBORNE

Under Plain Cover (Osborne) 205, 287–8, 439
Ure, Mary (second wife) 4, 7, 111, 333; affair
  with Shaw 207, 211–12; birth of Colin 241,
  267; career of 197; character of 75, 197–9, 212,
  248; Creighton and 140; desire for children
  198, 207–8, 258; divorce 270; no nickname 10;
  Osborne's affairs and 208–11, 255; Osborne's
  campness 136; and Osborne's mother 26;
  paternity of Colin 258–9, 270–5; Plowright and
  431–2; politics of 242; in the pool 209–11;
  wedding 121, 196–7, 200

Van Druten, John 120
Van Italie, Jean-Claude 309
Variations on a Theme (Rattigan) 308
Vaughan Williams, Ralph 147, 405
Vega Carpio, Lope de 36; *A Bond Honoured*
  325–6
Ventor, Isle of Wight 57–9
Venus Observed (Fry) 214
Vera (Dawson) 9
Victim (film) 309
Vidal, Gore 476
A View from the Bridge (Miller) 310
Vile Bodies (Waugh) 250
Villa Rosario, Anacapri: house party with
  Rickards 255–69
Vosper, Margery 133

Wain, John 164; *Hurry on Down* 180
Waiting for Godot (Beckett) 183–4
Walden, Ben 221–2, 399, 471
Walden, Brian 399
Walking in the Shade (Lessing) 247
Wall, Max 6, 221, 381
Wall, Mickey 28, 31–3
Waller, Fats 405
Wardle, Irving 152, 176, 186, 311, 326
Washout Wives Club 390
Watch It Come Down (Osborne) 234–5, 369,
  371; ends run 392; Hall's production of 383–8,
  432
Waterhouse, Keith 173; *Billy Liar* 181; *Jeffrey
  Bernard is Unwell* 453; Music Hall 220; on
  Osborne's politics 232–3
Waugh, Auberon 476
Waugh, Evelyn 162, 404; *Brideshead Revisited* 180;
  Vile Bodies 250
Webber, Robert 136
Wedekind, Frank: *Lulu* 309
Weigel, Helene 217
Welles, Orson: *Citizen Kane* 163
Wells, H. G. 32
Wells, John 229
Welsh, Irvine: *Trainspotting* 189
Wesker, Arnold 154, 162, 186, 190, 292, 390,

411, 472; argues with Tynan 372; CND and
  243; *The Kitchen* 327; Osborne's memorial
  service and 478–9; politics 237; *Roots* 175
Wesker, Dusty 390
West, Mae: *The Drag* 309
West of Suez (Osborne) 235, 362–3, 418; tepid
  reception of 366–7
Whitehead, E. A.: *Alpha Beta* 362
Whitelaw, Billie 182
Whiting, John: *Saint's Day* 187
Whitman, Walt 135, 162
Who's Afraid of Virginia Woolf? (Albee) 233
Wildeblood, Peter 147
Wilde, Oscar 3, 97, 100; *The Picture of Dorian
  Gray* 379–80, 381, 382
Williams, Emlyn 96
Williams, Raymond 236, 237
Williams, Tennessee 99, 123, 162, 230, 310, 361;
  A Streetcar Named Desire 116; *Suddenly Last
  Summer* 106
Williamson, Nicol 7, 93, 314, 320, 327; buys
  Hellingly 338; as fellow actor 87; in
  Inadmissible Evidence 297; revives Maitland 406;
  uses Osborne's manner 201
Wilson, Angus 147, 185; *The Mulberry Bush* 176
Wilson, Colin 164
Wilson, Harold 229, 237–8, 308
Wilson, Lanford 309
Wilson, Sandy: *The Boyfriend* 250
Wilson, Snoo 463
Windsor, Barbara 182
Wollheim, Richard 256
Wood, Charles 82, 186, 198, 476–7
Woodcock, Patrick 330, 355–6, 427
Woodfall Films 175, 180–1, 461; accounts 434–5;
  dissolved by feud 346; owes Finney 450;
  Saltzman and 203; *Tom Jones* 288–9; from
  Woodfall Street 198
Woodham-Smith, Cecil: *The Reason Why* 347
Woolf, Henry 90
The World of Paul Slickey (Osborne) 278;
  censorship of 249–54; disaster of 249–54
Worsthorne, Peregrine 169, 237
Worstward Ho (Beckett) 159
Wright, Nicholas 225, 358
Writers' Guild Lifetime Achievement Award
  462–5

Yankee Doodle Dandy (film) 221
Yeats, William Butler 162
You Never Can Tell (Shaw) 128
Young, B. A. 377
Young Man Luther (Erikson) 280
Young Vic Company: *A Sense of Detachment* 375
You're Not Watching Me, Mummy (Osborne,
  TV drama): 398

Acknowledgements

I am deeply indebted, first, to Thomas F. Staley and his colleagues at the Harry Ransom Humanities Research Center, Austin, Texas, where the Osborne archives were essential for the preparation of this book.

My thanks also to two other institutions where I conducted research: the British Library and London Library. I am grateful to the Terence Rattigan Estate for permission to publish the Rattigan–Osborne letters, © The Charitable Trust of Sir Terence Rattigan, Copyright Agent: Alan Brodie Representation Ltd; as well as to the Tony Richardson Estate for quotations from his letters; Shelagh Delaney for quotations from A Taste of Honey; Wallace Shawn for the letter of his father, William Shawn, to Osborne; Don Bachardy for extracts from the diaries of Christopher Isherwood, including those from the forthcoming second volume; and Peter Hall for extracts from his diaries. The lines from T.S. Eliot's 'Usk' are reproduced with the permission of Faber & Faber and the T.S. Eliot Estate.

Among the individuals who provided me with their invaluable private letters, I am particularly grateful to Angela Conner for permission to publish the letters of her sister, Penelope Gilliatt, to Pamela Lane for her letters, and to Jocelyn Herbert for permission to publish her letters to Osborne as well as those of George Devine. My gratitude for the use of their private correspondence also goes to Jocelyn Rickards, Robert Fox, D.S.J. Maw, Richard Eyre, Robin Dalton, Sonia McGuinness, Peter Nichols, Eric Shorter, Barry Krost, Arnold Running, Peter O'Toole (with thanks to Bobby Zarem), and Michael Billington.

To the many people who were interviewed and are mentioned in the unfolding narrative of the book, I would like to offer my collective thanks. I am enormously grateful to all of them. A number of others helped me with the book, but their names don't appear in it. I would therefore like to thank Sean Naidoo, Griselda Grimond, Natasha Richardson, John Cornwell, Michael Holroyd, Margaret Drabble, Bill Germano, Tony Kushner, Ben Hytner Q.C., Richard Mangan, Paul Warwick, Anthony Holden, Ann Pennington, Al Davidian, Peter Foges, Charles

Spencer, David Aukin, Dr Rachel Heilpern, Dr Walter Odajnyk, Peter Eyre, Adrienne Breen, David Kernan, Freda Rumbold, Linda Gillies, Vernon Dobtcheff, Victor Spinetti, Adrian Mitchell, Sir Kenneth Bradshaw, Eric Shorter, William Fox, Julian Ashby, Sheridan Morley, Jean Stein, Valerie Newman, David Nathan, Shirley Plater, Sydney H Weinberg, Trent Duffy and Fran Kiernan.

I would also like to thank a prince among men, and, more unusually, among lawyers, George Sheanshang, for his typically generous advice, as well as Chuck Bennett of International Management Group for all his advice and free dinners. John Goodwin read the first half of the manuscript and encouraged me to write the second half when I drifted into a year-long nap. My gratitude also to Gordon Dickerson – Osborne's literary agent – for re-checking numerous stories and facts, and to the Arvon Foundation for continuing the support of Osborne's literary executor, Helen Osborne.

Lastly, my thanks to Paula Hogben at Random House for expertly transcribing all the interview tapes, and to Poppy Hampson at Chatto & Windus for help with illustrations and final checks. I am especially thankful to Christie Hickman for her singular editorial care and her knowledge of the Osborne era. To Alison Samuel, my extremely patient publisher and editor at Chatto & Windus, I will always be grateful beyond measure.